Introducing Employment Relations

Introducing Employment Relations

A critical approach

FOURTH EDITION

Steve Williams

OXFORD
UNIVERSITY PRESS

OXFORD
UNIVERSITY PRESS

Great Clarendon Street, Oxford, OX2 6DP,
United Kingdom

Oxford University Press is a department of the University of Oxford.
It furthers the University's objective of excellence in research, scholarship,
and education by publishing worldwide. Oxford is a registered trade mark of
Oxford University Press in the UK and in certain other countries

First edition 2005
Second edition 2010
Third edition 2014
Impression: 1

Published in the United States of America by Oxford University Press
198 Madison Avenue, New York, NY 10016, United States of America

British Library Cataloguing in Publication Data
Data available

Library of Congress Control Number: 2016961065

ISBN 978-0-19-877712-0

Printed in Great Britain by
Bell & Bain Ltd., Glasgow

Contents

Acknowledgements

I remain grateful to Derek Adam-Smith for his contribution to earlier editions of this book. This new edition has benefited from dialogue with my colleagues at the University of Portsmouth, particularly Peter Scott, Iona Byford, Yvonne Rueckert, and Tom Higgins. As always, undergraduate and postgraduate students at Portsmouth helped to provide a stimulating environment for thinking about, and reflecting on, employment relations matters. Writing this new edition was made easier by having early access to the contributions included in the book I edited with Peter Scott—*Employment Relations under Coalition Government: The UK Experience, 2010–15* (Routledge 2016)—particularly the chapters by Enda Hannon, Roger Welch, Simonetta Manfredi, Alex Balch, and Steve French and Andy Hodder. I am also very grateful to the colleagues who offered such positive comments on the previous edition of this book.

The following people and organizations kindly gave permission to use their material: Sarah Pass, for her article on high-commitment management; Martin Upchurch, for material from his analysis of a survey of employment relations academics; Mike Savage, for the results from the BBC's Great British Class Survey; the Joseph Rowntree Foundation, for material from its study of what low-paid workers think would improve their lives; War on Want, for material from its reports on working conditions in global clothing factories; Thomson Reuters, for the case study on annualized hours at Premier Foods; and the Trades Union Congress, for material from its 'Britain needs a Pay Rise' and 'Work your Proper Hours Day' campaigns, and from its 2014 Equality Audit.

I am particularly grateful to Kate Gilks of Oxford University Press for all her patient advice, guidance, and support when writing this new edition. I would also like to thank the reviewers who provided very useful feedback on both the initial proposal and the draft chapters. Once again, Anna has had to put up with my commitment to a big writing project. As ever, her support was valued.

Steve Williams, October 2016

Guide to the book

Introducing Employment Relations uses a number of learning features to help you check and develop your learning.

Chapter objectives
The main objectives of this chapter are to:

* examine the characteristics of work and employment relatio economies;
* develop an understanding of the nature of employment rela
* consider the perspectives applied to employment relations
* provide a critically informed assessment of approaches to e

Chapter objectives

Each chapter opens with a list of objectives, which outline the main concepts and themes that will be covered providing you with a clear idea of what you can expect to learn from the chapter. These bullet-point lists can also be used to review your learning and plan your revision.

Introductory case study: The importance

In August 2016, there was a week-long protest involving hundreds of place outside the company's London headquarters. Deliveroo—whos food to customers from restaurants like Pizza Express, which do not means of a specialist app—hires its delivery staff on a formally self-em

Case studies

Varied, real-world case studies open and close every chapter, illustrating the key concepts discussed to help you make the link between employment relations theory and practice.

Insight into practice 1.5:   The role of the Tra

Traditionally, the Trades Union Congress (TUC), which was founded i in employment relations. First, it is involved in adjudicating disputes of them should represent particular groups of workers, though this a minor importance (McIlroy and Daniels 2009). Second, it provides its education and training. Third, perhaps most importantly, the TUC rep the trade union movement in general, in relations with government f TUC's role has changed in two key respects. One of the changes conc

Insight into practice boxes

These vignettes expand on specific examples in the chapter to show how employment relations have played out in a range of real-life situations.

Employment relations reflection 1.3:   The femin
employment relations

There has been a significant growth of interest in feminist perspective Traditionally, matters like trade unions and collective bargaining were attention to gender relations—defined as relations between men and employment relations (Wacjman 2000; Holgate, Hebson, and McBri notable exceptions (e.g. Pollert 1981). The feminist critique of orthod that there is now a better appreciation of the influence on employme

Employment relations reflections boxes

These boxes prompt you to reflect on different viewpoints or a particular issue, to aid your understanding and develop your critical thinking skills.

International perspective 3.7:   The institutio
Union

There are five principal EU institutions. The European Commission, co each member state, is responsible for promoting and effecting legislat The Court of Justice of the European Union (CJEU), which encompasse (ECJ), deliberates on matters of EU law and on issues that are of EU-wid Parliament, made up of directly elected members from all EU countrie influence though it can now obstruct and amend legislation in some

International perspective boxes

International examples ensure you have a broad understanding of employment relations in a global context.

Historical perspective 1.7: Industrial democracy a

When Theresa May became UK prime minister in July 2016 she expre
arrangements that would give worker representatives a position on c
in the question of industrial democracy, an idea which has a long hist
there was an important movement towards workers' control and inde
Threats of plant closures and job cuts associated with industrial restru
'work-ins' in which workers and their unions attempted to maintain t
The most famous instance occurred following the announcement of

Historical perspective boxes

To understand where we are now, you need to know where we have come from. These boxes offer historical context to current employment relations issues.

LEGISLATION AND POLICY 2.5: The UK government's schemes

Between 2010 and 2015, the UK government's work experience sche
amount of controversy after it emerged that unemployed people had
work, including cleaning homes and offices, with the threat of having
declined to participate (Malik, Ball, and Davies 2012). Some jobseeke
unpaid stewards during the Queen's Diamond Jubilee celebrations, a
night before under one of London's bridges over the River Thames (M

Legislation and policy boxes

The key legislation and policy that build the framework of employment relations are explained and analysed in these handy boxes.

Contesting employment relations 1.1: The effort b
junior doctors' dispute in England

The dispute between the 55,000 junior doctors in England and the UK g
changes to their contracts provides a good example of the effort bargai
months of 2016, doctors represented by their trade union—the British N
undertook six separate strikes, including two 'all-out' strikes, which saw
of emergency as well as routine care. The dispute was caused by the gov
coverage, particularly at weekends, without having to invest more mon
cutting or removing additional payments for doctors working 'unsocial
exchange for an overall average increase of 13.5 per cent in their basic

Contesting employment relations boxes

Conflict underlies employment relations, and this feature takes a closer look at thought-provoking, real-life examples where employment relations are challenged, including the causes and the effects for both employees and organizations.

Section summary and further reading

- The employment relationship should be conceptualized not
  or effort bargain. This refers to the ongoing process of struggl
  employment relationships between an employer, who wishes
  productive effort, and an employee, who is concerned with i
  wages and better working conditions, from his or her labour.
- Conceptualizing it as a bargain implies that the potential for c
  the employment relationship. Not only is there is a basic anta
  employee, but work and employment relationships are also

Section summaries and further reading

These summaries allow you to check your learning progress at the end of every section. Use the suggested further reading materials to locate more information on specific aspects of employment relations and to extend your understanding of specific theories and perspectives.

Assignment and discussion questions

1. What are the main features of the employment relationship a
2. With regard to the objectives of employment relations, explai
   and 'voice'.
3. What is meant by the concept of managerial prerogative in
   main constraints on the exercise of managerial prerogative?
4. Which of the three perspectives on employment relations—ur
   fits your own view of the world of work? Why?

Assignment and discussion questions

Apply your knowledge with end-of-chapter questions that test your skills of reasoning and argument, as well as allowing you to practise for your exams.

Key terms and concepts

Agenda for Change: a national pay and grading scheme that covers employees in the National Health Service.

Annualized hours: arrangements that specify the number of hours to be worked by employees over a

**Equality barga
designed to re
interventions

**Equal opportu

Key terms and concepts

This comprehensive glossary defines the key terms and concepts used in the book.

Guide to the Online Resource Centre

This book has a dedicated Online Resource Centre, offering supporting materials for students and registered lecturers. Go to www.oxfordtextbooks.co.uk/orc/williams4e/ to find out more.

Resources for students include an online glossary, additional case studies, video links, and regular updates to help you stay up to date with the latest research and gain access to a wide selection of reliable and authoritative content. Resources for lecturers include PowerPoint slides, suggested answers for questions in the book, and figures and tables from the book to aid your teaching.

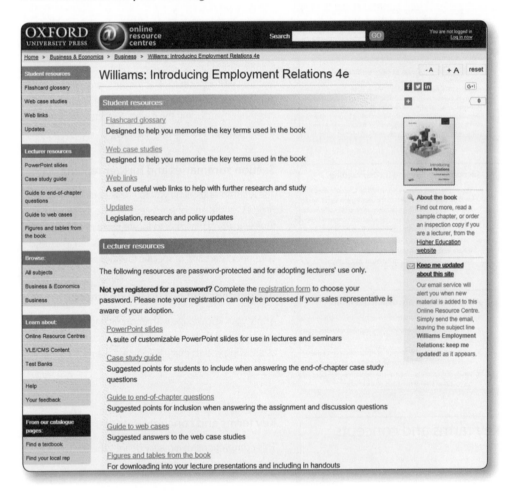

List of tables

List of figures

List of boxes

Insight into practice

Employment relations reflection

International perspective

Historical perspective

Legislation and policy

Contesting employment relations

List of abbreviations

ACAS	Advisory, Conciliation and Arbitration Service
BECTU	Broadcasting Entertainment Cinematograph and Theatre Union
BIS	(Department of) Business, Innovation and Skills
BMA	British Medical Association
BME	Black and minority ethnic
BUIRA	British Universities Industrial Relations Association
CAC	Central Arbitration Committee
CBI	Confederation of British Industry
CEEP	European Centre of Enterprises with Public Participation and of Enterprises of General Economic Interest
CEF	College Employers' Forum
CIPD	Chartered Institute of Personnel and Development
CJEU	Court of Justice of the European Union
CSA	Child Support Agency
CSO	Civil society organization
CWU	Communication Workers Union
DDA	Disability Discrimination Act
ECHR	European Court of Human Rights
ECJ	European Court of Justice
EEC	European Economic Community
EES	European Employment Strategy
EHRC	Equality and Human Rights Commission
EIF	European Industry Federation
EO	Equal opportunity
EOC	Equal Opportunities Commission
EPOS	Electronic point of sale
EPZ	Export processing zone
ET	Employment tribunal
ETI	Ethical Trading Initiative
ETUC	European Trade Union Confederation
ETUI	European Trade Union Institute
EU	European Union
EWC	European works council
FBI	Federal Bureau of Investigation
FBU	Fire Brigades Union

FDI	Foreign direct investment
FLA	Fair Labor Association
GDP	Gross Domestic Product
GFA	Global Framework Agreement
GLA	Gangmasters Licensing Authority
GLAA	Gangmasters and Labour Abuse Authority
GMB	General, Municipal and Boilermakers' Union
GSP	Generalized System of Preferences
GTR	Govia Thameslink Railway
GUF	Global Union Federation
HCA	Healthcare assistant
HMRC	Her Majesty's Revenue and Customs
HR	Human resources
HRM	Human resource management
HSE	Health and Safety Executive
ICE	Information and Consultation of Employees (Regulations)
ICO	Information Commissioner's Office
ICT	Information and communications technology
IDS	Incomes Data Services
IFA	International framework agreement
ILO	International Labour Organization
ITF	International Transport Workers' Federation
ITUC	International Trade Union Confederation
IWGB	Independent Workers Union of Great Britain
LGB	Lesbian, gay, and bisexual
LGBT	Lesbian, gay, bisexual, and transexual
LIFO	Last in, first out
LPC	Low Pay Commission
MAC	Migration Advisory Committee
MD	Managing diversity
MFGB	Miners' Federation of Great Britain
MNC	Multinational company
MoU	Memorandum of understanding
NAO	National Audit Office
NAPO	National Association of Probation Officers
NASUWT	National Association of Schoolmasters Union of Women Teachers
NCB	National Coal Board
NGO	Non-governmental organization
NHS	National Health Service

NLW	National Living Wage
NMW	National Minimum Wage
NUJ	National Union of Journalists
NUM	National Union of Mineworkers
NUT	National Union of Teachers
OECD	Organisation for Economic Co-operation and Development
OMC	Open method of coordination
ONS	Office for National Statistics
PAMSU	Pret a Manger Staff Union
PAT	Police Arbitration Tribunal
PCS	Public and Commercial Services Union
PCSO	Police community support officer
PNB	Police Negotiating Board
PRB	Pay review body
PRP	Performance-related pay
RAH	Royal Albert Hall
RCN	Royal College of Nursing
RMT	Rail, Maritime and Transport Union
SMCPC	Social Mobility and Child Poverty Commission
SNB	Special negotiating body
SNP	Scottish National Party
TGWU	Transport and General Workers' Union
TTIP	Transatlantic Trade and Investment Partnership
TUC	Trades Union Congress
UCATT	Union of Construction Allied Trades and Technicians
UCU	University and College Union
UDM	Union of Democratic Mineworkers
UEAPME	European Association of Craft, Small and Medium-Sized Enterprises
ULR	Union Learning Representative
UN	United Nations
USDAW	Union of Shop Distributive and Allied Workers
VoC	Varieties of Capitalism
VPS	Variable payment system
WERS	Workplace Employment Relations Survey/Study
WTD	Working Time Directive
WTR	Working Time Regulations

Preface: about this book

The fundamental concern of employment relations as a field of study is with investigating the nature of the relationship that exists between employers and their employees and workers—or the employment relationship, as it is generally known. Given that work and employment is such an important aspect of people's lives in advanced industrialized societies like the UK, the need to understand work and employment relationships is evidently of great importance.

Traditionally, studies of employment relations were often dominated by a concern with understanding the role of trade unions (membership bodies comprised of workers), and how their activities helped to regulate work and employment relationships. In other words, the emphasis was on how people's terms and conditions of employment—wages, hours, holidays, benefits, etc.—were influenced by the actions of trade unions who bargained collectively with employers on behalf of the workforce as a whole. Such joint regulation, as it is called, remains an important element of contemporary employment relations.

Yet, as will become evident, simply focusing on how work and employment relationships are regulated is an inadequate foundation for understanding employment relations. We also need to consider the experiences of workers themselves, and how, often collectively in trade unions, they challenge and contest aspects of their employment relationships. Moreover, the decline of the trade unions means that we also have to fashion a broader, less restrictive approach to understanding contemporary employment relations, one that builds on the traditional features of employment relations as a field of study, but which also takes into account the circumstances of the twenty-first-century environment in which it operates.

This book is distinguished by four main characteristics. First, it adopts an explicitly critical approach to employment relations. What is meant by this? Rather than understanding employment relations just as concerning the regulation of employment relationships, the subject is conceptualized as the study of the way in which work and employment relationships are regulated, experienced, and contested. Clearly, we need to understand the ways in which the rules that govern work and employment relationships are constituted; but how do workers experience these relationships, and how far, and in what ways, do they challenge, or contest, their employment situations?

This is what distinguishes the approach taken in this book from those which have an explicitly managerial or practitioner focus. The 'professional' body for human resources (HR) practitioners—the Chartered Institute of Personnel and Development (CIPD)—and its framework of 'professional standards' exercise a strong influence over the content of many employment relations courses and modules. Some people have suggested that this book should also be oriented more towards practitioners, with its contents arranged in a way that matches the CIPD's standards. The problem with this, though, is that one purpose of this book is explicitly to challenge an overly prescriptive and managerialist perspective which focuses on how to manage employment relations better. But 'better' for whom? As the content of this book repeatedly shows, what's 'better' for employers is by no means always beneficial for workers, and is often downright harmful to their interests. A distinctive feature of this book is that it tries to offer a broader, more intellectually rigorous and critical approach to understanding employment relations, one that is not limited to a narrow, managerial perspective. Far from being a weakness, the fact that its content is not aligned with the CIPD's standards is an advantage. In particular, it means that the interests of workers can be taken seriously. Managers and HR practitioners are important, to be sure; but employment relations should be for everyone. Thus this book does not seek to match CIPD standards. By reading it, though, students on CIPD programmes, including HR practitioners and managers, will acquire a better understanding of employment relations and how it really operates, than they would by restricting themselves to books that follow the CIPD's specifications.

Second, the book treats employment relations in a more thematic way than is often the case in conventional accounts. These tend to be influenced by an assumption that trade unions and collective bargaining constitute its principal subject matter. Though still important, the diminishing significance of joint regulation means that such an approach is no longer tenable. Rather than devote chapters to trade union organization and collective bargaining in their own right, instead the focus is on the broader themes of trade unions and worker representation (see Chapter 6), and developments in pay determination and working time (see Chapters 7 and 8). This more thematic approach better captures the broader conceptualization of employment relations advanced in this book.

Third, an important aim of the book is to establish the contemporary relevance of employment relations. The broader, critical approach, which focuses on the ways work and employment relationships are regulated, experienced, and contested, means that a range of current employment relations issues can be considered. A key aim is to demonstrate the continued importance of employment relations, based on the assumption that, as a field of study, its boundaries are wide-ranging and cannot be restricted just to the study of trade unions and collective bargaining. In this edition, then, particular attention is given to topics such as: self-employment (Chapter 2); work and employment in the 'gig economy' (Chapter 2); the implications of 'financialization' for the management of employment relations (Chapter 5); 'living wage' campaigns (Chapter 7); and 'zero-hours contracts' (Chapter 8).

This is not to suggest that trade unions and collective bargaining are no longer of significance. On the contrary, they are important features of contemporary employment relations, as is evident throughout the book. But employment relations cannot be restricted just to the study of joint regulation; it encompasses a much broader range of structures, processes, and activities. Much of the book, but Chapters 2, 3, and 4 in particular, are informed by the need to consider the broader dimensions of employment relations. What happens at work is influenced by, and also helps to inform, economic, political, and social change. Thus there is the need to recognize how factors constituted mainly outside the workplace, such as gender, shape employment relations patterns and activities (see Chapter 4). The contemporary focus is further informed by the inclusion of material taken from a wide range of recent and up-to-date research findings.

Fourth, while for reasons of space we concentrate largely on developments in Britain, it is important to recognize that employment relations is a topic which is of international significance. European Union (EU) policies influence employment relations in important ways (see Chapter 3). Examples taken from the experience of other countries are provided at various points in the book, where appropriate. Moreover, Chapter 11 is devoted to the implications of economic globalization for employment relations.

Before setting out the main features of this book, it is necessary to consider why it goes under the title of 'introducing employment relations' rather than 'introducing industrial relations'. As other writers have noted (e.g. Blyton and Turnbull 2004), the term 'industrial relations', although still widely used, is often associated with developments in traditional industries, like manufacturing, and with an emphasis on trade unions and joint regulation; 'employment relations', however, is more appropriate to understanding greater diversity in work and employment patterns. For this reason, it is better suited to the approach adopted here even though the terms 'industrial' and 'employment' relations can be, and often are, used interchangeably.

The book is organized in five main sections. In Part 1, comprising Chapter 1, an introduction to employment relations as a field of study is provided, presenting the main actors, processes, outcomes, and dimensions of employment relations.

In Part 2, the thematic assessment of issues, debates, and developments in employment relations commences with a focus on the dimensions of employment relations. Chapter 2, for example, considers economic and employment change, particularly in light of the 2007–8 financial crisis, the subsequent 'great recession' of the late 2000s, and its aftermath. Chapter 3 is concerned with the political dimension of employment relations. It covers relevant public policy developments, and also assesses the implications of European integration for employment relations, in light of the June 2016 narrow referendum vote in favour of the UK leaving the European Union. In Chapter 4, the concern is with the implications of social divisions for employment relations. Inequality and disadvantage are durable features of jobs and the labour market, and the chapter considers the effectiveness of interventions designed to tackle them.

The thematic approach is continued in Part 3 of the book, which is devoted to four key elements of employment relations. Chapter 5 considers the management of employment relations, including the nature and impact of sophisticated human resource management approaches to managing people at work. In Chapter 6 the focus is on how workers' interests are represented in employment relations. While traditionally trade unions were the main vehicle representing the interests of workers, their decline has stimulated interest in non-union representation arrangements. Nevertheless, unions have made efforts to revitalize themselves in ways designed to enhance their representational capacities. Chapter 7 is concerned with developments in pay determination. Due to the decline of collective pay-setting mechanisms by means of trade unions there is now greater interest in the managerial role in determining pay. Moreover, the regulation of low pay is a topical matter, as is evident from the growing interest in 'living wages'. Issues relating to working time have become important features of employment relations. Chapter 8 covers the key working time trends and patterns, examines how working time is used, and assesses the effectiveness of laws designed to regulate excessive working hours.

Part 4 of the book is concerned with conflict in employment relations. One of the principal features of work and employment relationships is that, because of their different interests, there is always the potential for conflict to arise between a worker and employer. Chapter 9 is concerned with investigating the various manifestations of labour conflict—which include, but are not restricted to, strikes. Chapter 10 is devoted to the main processes designed to prevent conflict from occurring, or to resolve it when it does occur; it also offers a critical assessment of arrangements for enforcing employment rights.

The purpose of Part 5 is to consider employment relations in broader perspective. Chapter 11 is concerned with understanding the implications of globalization for employment relations, and how employment relations operates in a more globalized world. The brief concluding Chapter 12 draws together the main themes of the book to demonstrate the importance of understanding employment relations.

Each chapter includes a number of supporting pedagogical features. Regular boxes devoted to employment relations reflections, insights into employment relations practice, international and historical perspectives, legislation and policy interventions, and exemplars of how work and employment relationships are contested, are used to illustrate the material in the main text. Each main section comes with a summary of the key points of the material covered in the preceding pages, and guidance on further reading suggestions. All the main chapters commence with a brief introductory case study, which is designed to demonstrate the relevance of the subject matter, and a longer case study at the end, with questions attached. There are also assignment and discussion questions to reinforce learning activity.

The Online Resource Centre companion website contains further relevant features, such as additional case studies and research updates. As you read this book, you will soon become aware that change is a constant feature of employment relations. There are a number of important questions which had still to be addressed as this book was completed. Following the June 2016 referendum vote, how will the UK actually leave the European Union and, when it does, what will happen to the employment rights and protections that come from Europe? What will happen to the freedom of EU citizens to work in the UK, and that of UK citizens to move to jobs in the rest of Europe? To what extent, and in what ways, will Theresa May's Conservative government, which took office in July 2016, pursue a different policy agenda to that of David Cameron's? In particular, will all the initial talk about looking after the interests of working people and eschewing austerity translate into substantive action? See the Online Resource Centre for relevant updates.

Part 1

Introducing employment relations

The nature of employment relations

Chapter objectives

The main objectives of this chapter are to:

- examine the characteristics of work and employment relationships in market economies;
- develop an understanding of the nature of employment relations;
- consider the perspectives applied to employment relations as a field of study;
- provide a critically informed assessment of approaches to employment relations; and
- introduce the main employment relations actors, processes, outcomes, and dimensions.

1.1 Introduction

Employment relations is a field of study concerned with understanding work and employment relationships, and specifically how these relationships are regulated, experienced, and contested. It affects the lives of most people in contemporary societies. In the UK, for example, over 30 million people are in employment of some kind; many of those who are not depend on the income generated from a partner's or parent's job for their subsistence. The purpose of this chapter is to consider the nature of employment relations, in three main sections. First, in Section 1.2 the focus is on the nature of work and employment relationships in market economies. Second, in Section 1.3 the main perspectives that have been applied to employment relations as a field of study are assessed. Third, Section 1.4 introduces the main actors and processes in employment relations, highlights the principal outcomes of employment relations, and says something about the dimensions of employment relations. The concluding Section 1.5 then emphasizes the value of studying employment relations.

 Introductory case study: The importance of employment relations

In August 2016, there was a week-long protest involving hundreds of Deliveroo workers which took place outside the company's London headquarters. Deliveroo—whose business involves delivering food to customers from restaurants like Pizza Express, which do not have their own delivery service, by means of a specialist app—hires its delivery staff on a formally self-employed basis. This means workers

(continued...)

lack a range of employment protections, even though, to all intents and purposes, they are treated by the company as if they are employees. The dispute was sparked by a proposed change by Deliveroo to its workers' pay arrangements in London. Instead of receiving an hourly rate of £7.00 per hour plus £1.00 for every delivery, the proposed new system would see workers paid per delivery only (at £3.75 for each delivery). Alarmed that the change would be likely to result in a significant fall in their earnings, the workers stopped work and mounted the protest. Their action was supported by the Independent Workers Union of Great Britain (IWGB). After a few days, Deliveroo's chief executive apologized for the dispute, and the company started to make some concessions. It proposed that existing workers could continue under the old pay scheme, albeit with some rather stringent conditions attached, and made a commitment to ensuring that, temporarily anyway, they would be guaranteed a minimum hourly payment. The immediate dispute only ended, however, after Deliveroo made a further concession, by withdrawing a measure which would have compelled existing workers to accept the new contractual terms on a supposedly trial basis. While the IWGB claimed victory, the extent to which the workers were successful is not altogether clear. Deliveroo is at liberty to hire new workers on the revised pay-per-delivery basis, and seems likely to want to make it more widespread.

Knowledge and understanding of employment relations are essential if we are to comprehend properly the background to, and implications of, events like the campaign by Deliveroo workers to defend their earnings. We need to understand how the relationship between employers and workers operates, and the factors that influence it, including the broader economic, political, and social circumstances. It is important to understand and explain why the relevant employment relations actors, especially managers, workers, and trade unions, behave in the ways they do. Understanding why workers take action to protest against, or change, aspects of their employment relationships, and the methods they use to do so, are also integral features of employment relations. Effective knowledge and understanding of contemporary employment relations makes important events like the campaign by Deliveroo workers, against proposed changes that would have seen their earnings slashed, more readily comprehensible.

1.2 The employment relationship and employment relations

As a field of study, employment relations is concerned with understanding work and employment relationships, and has a particular focus on the relationship between employers and their employees (BUIRA 2009; Colling and Terry 2010). Although the main emphasis is on the employment relationship, not all workers are, formally at least, directly employed by employers; they may be hired on a self-employed basis, for example, while to all intents and purposes being employees—see the introductory case study of Deliveroo (there is more coverage of 'bogus' self-employment in Chapter 2). By conceiving of employment relations as covering work and employment relationships in a broad sense, then, it enables us to accommodate such changing patterns of work, while upholding a special concern with the employment relationship. This section is concerned with the nature of the employment relationship as a 'wage–work bargain'; examining how employment relationships are regulated and identifying the sources of the rules that govern work and employment relationships, and that take the form of terms and conditions of employment like pay, benefits, and working conditions.

1.2.1 The employment relationship as a 'wage–work bargain'

To an important extent, the employment relationship is a market exchange in which an employer hires a worker to undertake a particular job for an agreed price (e.g. wages, benefits)

(Budd 2011). Work and employment relationships are thus an integral feature of capital-ist market economies, which are characterized by the central importance of contracts and the capacity of the law to enforce contractual obligations and property rights (Sisson 2010). From a market-based perspective, work is a commodity like any other; and both a worker and his or her prospective employer are equally free to choose whether or not they want to enter into a contractual relationship (Budd 2011). The employment relationship is viewed as a conventional contract, 'and the parties owe no responsibilities to one another beyond those expected of participants acting in good faith' (Sisson 2008: 11). The employment contract captures the reciprocity evident in the agreement by an employer to provide workers with wages in exchange for their willingness to engage in productive effort. Thus it is ostensibly characterized by the free and equal willingness of the parties to exchange resources.

The main advantage of using a market-based contractual framework to characterize the employment relationship is that it captures the way in which the employment relationship is an economic transaction, something that concerns the willingness of workers to offer their capacity to labour in exchange for the promise of wages (Kahn-Freund 1977). But there are three fundamental problems with viewing the employment relationship in purely market-based, contractual terms.

First, the notion of a contract assumes that both parties to it come together in a free and equal way, without any obligation or pressure on them to participate. However, the indi-vidual worker is generally in a much weaker position than the prospective employer. It is rare for workers to be in a position where they have as much freedom to choose between alternative offers of employment as employers have in selecting employees. Moreover, the consequences of refusing an offer of employment are potentially much more serious for the worker, since jobs, and the wages they attract, are for most people their primary source of income. Employers can generally simply offer the job to someone else (Fox 1974). In real-ity, therefore, work and employment relationships are generally characterized by a marked imbalance of power between a relatively powerful employer and a relatively powerless indi-vidual worker (Sisson 2008, 2010).

Second, by accepting an offer of employment, workers come under the authority of an em-ployer. A purely contractual approach, then, fails to capture the way in which work and em-ployment relationships are infused by power, characterized by the capacity of an employer to command and the obligation on the worker to obey (Kahn-Freund 1977; Sisson 2010). Thus the 'brute facts of power' (Fox 1974: 183) mean that it is inappropriate to consider the employment relationship straightforwardly as a market-based contract, in the sense of a vol-untary agreement between two equal parties (Wedderburn 1986). Indeed, a key advantage of the employment relationship for employers concerns the scope it gives them to direct the activities of employees, through what Sisson (2008: 25) calls 'residual control rights'—some-thing which should not be possible where a worker is hired as a self-employed contractor to undertake a specific one-off task.

The third reason why work and employment relationships cannot be understood in purely contractual terms is that labour is not a commodity in the conventional economic sense. Employers do not buy employees in the way that a consumer purchases a tin of baked beans from a supermarket. Rather, they secure the capacity of employees to engage in productive work—their potential labour power. Having hired an employee, the employer must then con-vert latent labour power into productive effort—through systems of control and supervision, for example, or by eliciting the employee's motivation and commitment. Labour power, then, is an 'entirely fictitious commodity' (Polanyi 1957: 72); employers buy the capacity of workers to engage in productive effort. The distinctive characteristic of labour is that it is not an inanimate commodity, but is embodied in actual human beings (Edwards 2003; Sisson 2008; Kaufman 2010a; Meardi 2014a).

A key implication of this is that the employment relationship is 'open-ended' or 'indeterminate' (Fox 1974; Marsden 1999; Sisson 2010). What this means is that when an employment contract is formed, it is impossible for the parties to specify all of the likely obligations. Neither the employer nor the employee can foresee all the eventualities that may arise during the term of the contract. 'In a commercial contract, a product or service is supplied for a price. In the labour contract, the worker sells their ability to work, which is translated into actual labour during the course of the working day. Expectations about standards of performance have to be built up during the process of production' (Edwards 2003: 14). The result is that the characteristics of the employment relationship are the outcome of both 'market' and 'managerial' relations (Flanders 1975; Sisson 2008). Market relations help to determine wages, or the price of a worker's employment, whereas managerial relations are concerned with establishing how much work is to be undertaken by the employee, of what kind, how quickly, and the sanctions for non-compliance (Edwards 2003; Colling and Terry 2010).

Rather than viewing the employment relationship as a contract, then, it is more accurate to consider it as an ongoing series of contracts, which are continually being re-negotiated between employers and their employees as changes in their circumstances alter the expectations of the parties, and thus their behaviour (Commons 1924; Colling and Terry 2010). Workplaces are best conceptualized as 'negotiated orders', marked by 'dialogue, day-to-day consensus building and "give-and-take" ' between employers and employees (Sisson 2008: 34). The employment relationship is not a one-off transaction, as the market-based perspective would suggest. Rather it has to be viewed as a dynamic process: one in which an employer, due to an efficiency-driven concern to produce goods or deliver services more cheaply, seeks greater effort from employees, who have their own, different interests (e.g. protection from unjustified dismissal or being able to influence decisions) (Budd 2004). One very important consequence of all this is that there is always the potential for conflict to arise between workers and employers. This is what has sometimes been termed the 'labour problem' (Kaufman 2004; Meardi 2014a).

 Contesting employment relations 1.1:   The effort bargain in action: the junior doctors' dispute in England

The dispute between the 55,000 junior doctors in England and the UK government over proposed changes to their contracts provides a good example of the effort bargain in action. In the first few months of 2016, doctors represented by their trade union—the British Medical Association (BMA)—undertook six separate strikes, including two 'all-out' strikes, which saw them withdrawing provision of emergency as well as routine care. The dispute was caused by the government's aim to extend NHS coverage, particularly at weekends, without having to invest more money. To achieve this, it proposed cutting or removing additional payments for doctors working 'unsocial hours' (e.g. Saturdays), in exchange for an overall average increase of 13.5 per cent in their basic pay. Overall, however, most doctors would face a substantial fall in their earnings under the government's package of reforms.

A massive proportion—98 per cent—of doctors voted to strike in protest. The dispute intensified after the government said it would impose the new contract. Talks to resolve the dispute resulted in a proposed new deal, which the BMA recommended that doctors accept. However, in July 2016 a majority of doctors (58 per cent) rejected the new terms in a ballot, despite which the government announced its intention to press ahead with imposing a new contract. While the government has largely been concerned with securing greater efficiency, the doctors have resisted its efforts to change their contracts, not only because of the adverse consequences for their pay and working conditions, but also because they believe it would jeopardize patient safety.

The employment relationship is best conceptualized as a 'wage–work bargain' or 'effort bargain' (Behrend 1957), marked by attempts by both employers and workers to influence and adjust its terms in ways that benefit their own interest (see Contesting employment relations 1.1 for an illustrative example). As already mentioned, there is always the possibility that the interests of employers and employees will come into conflict (Baldamus 1961). Underlying the employment relationship is a constant potential struggle over its terms—over what Goodrich called 'the frontier of control' (Hyman 1975). Some perspectives characterize the employment relationship as a 'stark conflict of interests' (Hyman 1975: 27) between an employer who is concerned to extract the maximum effort from employees at minimum cost, and an employee whose concern is to secure better wages and limit the amount of work he or she is expected to undertake.

But it is overly simplistic to view the employment relationship just in terms of conflict between employers and employees; cooperation is also an essential feature (Edwards 1986, 2003). Employees share an interest with their employer in maintaining the competitiveness of their firm, for example; otherwise their jobs, and hence their livelihoods, are jeopardized (Kelly 1998). The employment relationship is, then, characterized both by cooperation and the potential for conflict (Sisson 2010). The power differential in favour of the employer renders it an essentially exploitative relationship; employers use their superior power to shift the terms of the wage–work bargain in a way that benefits their interests. Employees react to this, often by organizing themselves collectively in trade unions, to combat the imbalance of power. Although cooperation is an important characteristic of the employment relationship, there remains a basic antagonism between employers and employees that generates an inherent potential for conflict (Edwards 1986, 2003).

1.2.2 Regulating work and employment relationships

Clearly, the market plays a part in influencing employment relations, particularly wages, which to varying degrees reflect the outcome of the relationship between the supply of, and demand for, labour. As has been established, however, the employment relationship is best viewed as a dynamic social and economic relationship, rather than just a straightforward market-based transaction. So where do the rules that govern work and employment relationships come from, and how do they operate, if not solely the product of markets? How are matters such as pay, working hours, holiday entitlement, and the extent to which employees are able to influence decisions that affect them at work, determined? The tensions and uncertainties evident in work and employment relationships mean that understanding how they are regulated, in the sense of devising and operating rules that govern them, is a central feature of employment relations as a field of study (BUIRA 2009; Colling and Terry 2010).

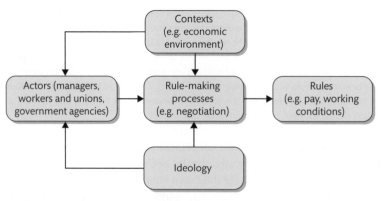

Figure 1.1 A simplified version of Dunlop's systems model

The systems-based approach to understanding employment relations, for example, is con-cerned with how the rules which govern employment relationships are established (Dunlop 1958). An employment relations system comprises four key elements (see Figure 1.1). First, there are three main groups of actors: managers, workers and trade unions, and governmen-tal agencies. Second, these actors interact within specific contexts, for example the nature of the economic environment. Third, their interaction results in the production of a body of rules ('rule-making') which govern how employment relations operates (e.g. pay, work-ing conditions). Negotiation between managers and unions is an example of a rule-making process. Fourth, an employment relations system is held together by an ideology: a 'set of ideas and beliefs commonly held by the actors that helps to bind or to integrate the system together as an entity' (Dunlop 1958: 16). An example of an ideology would be the preference for non-state intervention, or 'voluntarism', which long dominated employment relations in Britain (see Chapter 3).

The rules-based approach, concerned with the regulation of employment relationships, had a major influence on the development of employment relations as a field of study. It became defined as 'the study of the rules governing employment, together with the ways in which the rules are made and changed, interpreted and administered. Put more briefly, it is the study of job regulation' (Clegg 1979: 1). If the regulation of the employment relationship is so important to developing an understanding of employment relations, how then are the rules generated?

Five main sources of rules which govern work and employment relationships can be identi-fied (see Figure 1.2), although it is important to recognize that the influence of each source will vary according to the context. First, managers attempt to determine the terms of the employment relationship unilaterally, through the use of their prerogative. Exercising control over employees—the terms and conditions of their employment, and their behaviour—is an essential feature of management activity. The concept of managerial prerogative, or the 'right' to manage, is integral to understanding the management of employment relations. It should be understood primarily in ideological terms since it 'reflects an area of decision-making over which management believes it has (and acts as if it does have) sole and exclusive rights of determination and upon which it strenuously resists any interference' (Storey 1983: 102).

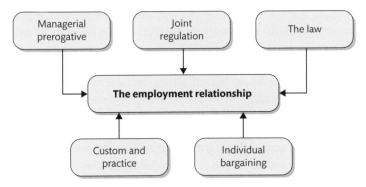

Figure 1.2 Sources of rules in employment relations

What factors influence this belief in the right of managers to exercise control over employment relations? Most obviously, managerial prerogative rests on the role of management as the legitimate agent of the employer—the organization and its shareholder owners. This is supported by statutory obligations that compel managers to undertake their function and operate in the interests of the shareholders. Managerial prerogative is also founded on the belief that managers have the right to exercise control over employment relations by virtue of their abilities, expertise, and leadership skills (Storey 1983: 103–4). The right to manage, then, is important as an ideology, or set of ideas, to which many managers, especially senior ones, subscribe. In practice, though, managerial prerogative is constrained in two important ways.

First, it is necessarily influenced by the characteristics of the organizational environment, such as the state of product and labour markets. Low unemployment levels may oblige managers to improve pay and conditions in order to attract and retain employees. Second, the efforts of workers themselves who, to a varying degree, challenge and contest managerial imperatives often limit the extent to which managers can exercise control in practice (Blyton, Heery, and Turnbull 2011). Thus the nature of the employment relationship itself, as a wage–work bargain, implies that managerial prerogative, though important as an ideology that informs managers' behaviour, is never absolute.

The second source of rules concerns the ability of some workers to influence aspects of their own terms and conditions of employment by engaging in individual bargaining with employers. Given the power differential that exists in the employment relationship, few have the ability to exercise significant influence in this way, though individuals may obtain their employer's consent to relatively minor changes in work arrangements, such as starting and finishing times. Workers who possess particular skills for which there is high demand—in certain types of professional information technology work, for example—enjoy greater power to extract more favourable terms from employers. Perhaps the most obvious example of individual bargaining in practice concerns the activities of top professional sportspeople—footballers and the like—who, because of their exceptional individual talent, can negotiate with prospective employers (i.e. their clubs) from a genuine position of strength.

Third, more commonly (though less so than used to be the case), the rules that govern work and employment relationships are determined by collective bargaining between employers and trade unions, through 'joint regulation'. The unequal balance of power between the individual employee and the employer in the employment relationship impels employees to combine in, and organize, trade unions. One of the main purposes of these collective organizations of employees is to influence, principally through negotiations with employers, the terms of the wage–work bargain. Collective agreements are the outcome of the collective bargaining process. They may be procedural, setting out rules that govern the bargaining relationship between the employer and the union, or substantive—those that deliver concrete results to employees in the form of pay rises or changes to working hours, for example.

The fourth source of rules that govern work and employment relationships emanates from the state, legislation in particular. Whereas the emphasis in Britain used to be on the desirability of joint regulation as a source of rules in employment relations (Flanders 1974), in recent years legislation has come to exercise an ever greater influence, for example to challenge discrimination (see Chapter 4) or to alleviate low pay (see Chapter 7). Rules that govern work and employment relationships therefore reflect broader societal values, and changes in those values (Sisson 2010).

Fifth, rules are also generated informally through the day-to-day experiences of, and relationships between, managers and workers. Often referred to as 'custom and practice', informal rules are tacitly understood expectations of what is, and what is not, acceptable, and are important features of employment relations (Blyton, Heery, and Turnbull 2011). Numerous workplace studies demonstrate the way in which unwritten, informal, and tacit understandings influence the terms of the wage–work bargain (e.g. Brown 1973; Scott 1994)—see Contesting employment relations 1.2 for an illustration.

 Contesting employment relations 1.2:   Custom and practice in action

In December 2004, a dispute arose between management and staff working in Post Office Counters, the retail arm of the Post Office, over Christmas opening hours. It was customary practice for staff to cease work at lunchtime on Christmas Eve, even though this had never been put in writing. Managers, however, wanted post offices to remain open until 4.00pm on 24 December, making it more like any other normal working day. They were concerned that the business would suffer if customers went elsewhere to do their last-minute Christmas shopping for stationery products and the like. This example demonstrates the importance of custom and practice rules in employment relations.

These sources of rules do not exist in isolation from each other. Plenty of research studies demonstrate, for example, that the presence of robust joint regulation enhances the effectiveness of legislation designed to protect workers. For instance, workplace health and safety legislation tends to be more rigorously enforced where trade unions are present.

Although it highlights the important role that trade unions often have in influencing managerial decision-making through joint regulation, the rules-based approach to understanding employment relations has a number of related weaknesses (Hyman 1975). First, it tends to concentrate on the formal institutions of job regulation, trade unions and collective bargaining in particular, perhaps to an unwarranted degree (Colling and Terry 2010). Second, following on from this, the rules-based approach implies an emphasis on stability and order in the employment relationship. Dunlop's model, in particular, has been criticized for being too static (Kaufman 2011). The processes by which workplace rules are challenged and changed, and the dynamic nature of the wage–work bargain, influenced as it often is by informal expectations and understandings based on custom and practice, can be neglected. Third, and perhaps most importantly, the rules-based approach overlooks the way in which the employment relationship, understood as a wage–work bargain, is marked by contention as employees attempt to exercise control over their working lives. A proper understanding of employment relations, then, not only demands an analysis of how the employment relationship is regulated, but also of how employees experience, challenge, and contest the rules.

 ### Section summary and further reading

- The employment relationship should be conceptualized not as a contract, but as a wage–work or effort bargain. This refers to the ongoing process of struggle over the terms of work and employment relationships between an employer, who wishes to convert latent labour power into productive effort, and an employee, who is concerned with increasing the return, in the form of wages and better working conditions, from his or her labour.

- Conceptualizing it as a bargain implies that the potential for conflict is an inevitable feature of the employment relationship. Not only is there is a basic antagonism between an employer and employee, but work and employment relationships are also exploitative, characterized by an imbalance of power between a powerful employer and a relatively powerless individual employee.

- In addition to the influence of the labour market, there are five sources of rules governing work and employment relationships: managerial regulation; joint regulation; individual bargaining; the law; and custom and practice expectations. While the regulation of employment relations is a key feature of employment relations as a field of study, we also need to understand how workers experience and contest the rules.

Both Edwards (2003) and Colling and Terry (2010) are excellent guides to the nature of employment relations. The contributions made by Keith Sisson (2008, 2010: Chapter 3) are also highly recommended.

1.3 Employment relations as a 'field of study'

Employment relations is not an academic discipline in its own right; it is better thought of as a 'field' or an 'area' of study (Edwards 2003; Heery et al. 2008; Sisson 2010). It is multidisciplinary in nature, drawing on concepts and debates from disciplines such as sociology, economics, political science, and law (Colling and Terry 2010; Sisson 2010; Meardi 2014a). The origins of employment relations as a field of study can be traced to the nineteenth century. This period saw the first major studies of the trade unions and collective bargaining, for example (Webb and Webb 1920a). It was also characterized by significant instances of worker unrest, the causes of which governments and official agencies were anxious to understand (Hyman 1989; Kaufman 2014).

For much of the twentieth century, this was manifest in an emphasis on how the institutions of job regulation, particularly the bargaining role of trade unions, shaped work and employment relationships (Ackers and Wilkinson 2003; Frege 2008). Indeed, the development of employment relations as a field of study 'was part and parcel of a practical and intellectual response to the rise of trade unions and collective bargaining, as central institutions of twentieth century industrial society' (Ackers 2011: 45). Perspectives in this tradition were heavily influenced by the need for a proper historical understanding of the institutions they described. They were characterized by intricately detailed historical accounts of the development of trade unions, and collective bargaining arrangements in particular (see Flanders and Clegg 1964).

1.3.1 Unitary and pluralist perspectives on employment relations

One of the leading writers on employment relations during the 1960s and 1970s, along with Flanders and Clegg, was Alan Fox. In 1966, he established a distinction between unitary and pluralist 'frames of reference' in employment relations. These frames of reference are not theories of employment relations; they are perspectives that can be applied to employment relations (Blyton and Turnbull 2004). Fox articulated them as 'ideologies of management' (Fox 1966: 10): beliefs held by managers about how employment relations should operate. They can be likened to lenses, tools which people use to 'perceive and define social phenomena'— in this case the nature of the employment relationship—and which thus influence and shape their actions (Fox 1974: 271).

The unitary perspective is characterized by an emphasis on cooperative relations at work. Since the relationship between employees and their employer is marked by a 'unity of interests' (Budd and Bhave 2008: 103), this perspective rejects the assumption that a basic antagonism exists between them; conflict is largely caused by external agitators—trade unions—whose interference disrupts the harmonious state of relations that would otherwise exist. Holders of unitary beliefs rely on the 'liberal use of team or family metaphors' (Fox 1974: 249) when conceptualizing the nature of the employment relationship. Managers, in particular, often use the team analogy to describe relations in their organizations, based on the assumption that employers and their employees share the same goals—something that renders managerial prerogative legitimate, and trade union representation unnecessary. In his evidence to the 1994 House of Commons Employment Committee investigation into the future of trade unions, for example, the then chief executive of Zurich Insurance contended that it is 'the job of the company to create an environment in which a trade union becomes irrelevant ... the very nature of the unions, sitting in there in a divisive capacity, stops the employees and managers of an organization getting together as one team' (House of Commons Employment Committee 1994: 342).

The unitary perspective on employment relations is often criticized for advancing an unrealistic view of workplace life, in particular for denying the basic antagonism that characterizes the employment relationship. Yet, as a perspective on the nature of employment relations, and, furthermore, one which is subscribed to by a large number of managers (Poole and Mansfield 1993), it must be taken seriously (Edwards 2003). For one thing, unitary thinking underpins much of the current emphasis on engaging and securing the organizational commitment of employees (Budd and Bhave 2008), as Chapter 5 demonstrates. Moreover, most managers, if asked their views about the nature of the employment relationship, would articulate a unitary perspective, stressing the importance of common goals, shared objectives, and the supposed absence of any conflict of interest between an employer and employee. These beliefs influence their behaviour, most notably the importance of upholding managerial prerogative, and of resisting what they see as trade union interference in the operation of their organizations (Head and Lucas 2004; Cullinane and Dundon 2014). In 2012, for example, the food and drink chain Pret a Manger responded to the establishment of a trade union in the company—the Pret a Manger Staff Union (PAMSU)—by workers pressing for higher wages, by dismissing a leading PAMSU activist (Myerscough 2013).

By contrast, the pluralist frame of reference is a perspective which recognizes the existence of a basic antagonism in the employment relationship, and hence the inevitable potential for conflict. The concept of pluralism is derived from political theory, where it is used to capture the way in which states and governments have to mediate between a potentially highly diverse range of competing interest groups when formulating their policies. Having to accommodate the views of a diversity—or plurality—of interests means that political power is not exercised in a straightforwardly top-down manner, but is more diffuse, linked to the respective influences of different interest groups over policy outcomes.

With regard to employment relations, pluralism recognizes that employers and employees have different interests, which need to be reconciled if the organization is to function effectively, and that each is dependent on the other (Heery 2016). The principal concern of pluralists is with ensuring that any disorder arising from these differences of interest is managed appropriately, and contained in a way that prevents it from causing too much disruption. Thus there is an emphasis on developing procedures that are designed to resolve disputes, or prevent them from occurring, in particular the establishment of bargaining relationships with trade unions, given the array, or plurality, of interests that potentially exist within the organization.

Therefore, 'management has to face the fact that there are other sources of leadership, other focuses of loyalty, within the social system it governs, and that it is with these that management must share its decision-making' (Fox 1966: 8). In other words, managers cannot assume that the organization is characterized by shared interests and common goals; in particular, employees will have divergent interests, and may want to express them through their own independent institutions, trade unions. 'At the heart of the pluralist position is a conviction that the employment relationship embraces two equally legitimate sets of interests, those of employers and those of employees' (Heery et al. 2008: 14–15). Unions, then, are not external agitators to be resisted if harmonious relations are to be upheld, but are the legitimate representatives of employees' interests. They intervene to support the interests of workers in the employment relationship, whose position is generally subordinate to that of their employer. Furthermore, from a pluralist perspective, government regulation in employment relations, in the form of laws that protect working people (e.g. minimum wages), is also justified on the grounds that, like trade union organization, it helps to rectify the inherent imbalance of power in favour of employers (Budd 2011; Heery 2016).

The pluralist frame of reference was enormously influential in the development of employment relations as an academic field of study (Ackers and Wilkinson 2003; Frege 2008; Heery 2016). The emphasis on employment relations as the 'study of the institutions of job regulation' (Flanders 1975) was informed by a belief in the legitimacy of trade unions, and accorded a special role to collective bargaining as the means by which they secured their goals, something that became the 'dominant paradigm' (Ackers and Wilkinson 2003: 7; Kaufman 2014).

During the 1960s and 1970s, the pluralist orthodoxy developed in the context of the emergence of employment relations as an important public policy issue (Hyman 1989; Ackers and Wilkinson 2003). Governments were concerned that the growth of workplace bargaining between union representatives and managers generated unnecessary levels of disruptive labour conflict and inflationary wage increases. From a pluralist perspective, the solution was not, as the holders of unitary views would argue, to resist the encroachment of the unions as a means of reasserting managerial authority; rather, stronger bargaining relationships between employers and unions should be encouraged, given the advantages of developing robust and effective procedures for containing, or institutionalizing, conflict through joint regulation (Heery 2016). According to one leading pluralist, the 'paradox, whose truth managements have found it so difficult to accept, is that they can only regain control by sharing it' (Flanders 1975: 172). Until the 1980s, then, the pluralist perspective exercised an important influence over both public policy and even management attitudes towards employment relations, though not at the expense of the latter's fundamentally unitary beliefs.

1.3.2 Challenges to pluralist orthodoxy

The main challenge to the pluralist employment relations orthodoxy of the 1960s and 1970s initially came from the development of radical perspectives on employment relations. These share with pluralism a belief in the essentially antagonistic nature of the employment relationship. However, they do not accept its assumption that conflict can be contained by the development of procedures, or even that it is desirable to attempt to do so. Radical approaches reject the assumption that conflict in employment relations can be accommodated in a straightforward fashion. Rather, the employment relationship is marked by a 'structured antagonism' arising out of the different interests of employers and employees. This means that not only is there always the potential for conflict to arise, but also that efforts to contain it will always be partial and incomplete (Edwards 1986). Moreover, radical approaches put a pronounced emphasis on the persistence of unequal power relations in the employment relationship, the reality of managerial control and domination over employees, and the role played by wider social forces in creating and maintaining inequalities and exploitative relations at work (Budd and Bhave 2008).

One of the most prominent perspectives coming under the radical label is that of Marxism. Kaufman (2011: 17) observes that the 'essence of the employer–employee relationship under capitalism, from a Marxist perspective, is domination, control and exploitation of labour in order to provide profit so firms can further accumulate capital'. The principal feature of Marxism, which distinguishes it from the radical approach in general, is the emphasis it places on how the exploitation of workers in the employment relationship generates class conflict between the working class, who produce goods and services, and the owners of capital— something that results in deepening class consciousness and the development of a socialist political project (see Gall 2003).

What criticisms, then, do radical perspectives such as Marxism make of the pluralist perspective? First, they contend that pluralism fails to address the issue of power seriously enough, assuming that, in an environment where bargaining relationships have been established, a balance of power exists between employers and unions (Fox 1974), although this has been challenged by pluralist writers (Clegg 1975). Employers, by virtue of their ownership of, and control over, the production of goods or delivery of services, enjoy far greater power than even the most well-organized union (Fox 1974).

Second, radical writers argue that pluralism is an essentially conservative ideology, concerned with upholding the existing order in society rather than challenging it (Fox 1974; Goldthorpe 1977). Thus, while pluralism ostensibly appears to advance the interests of employees, by recognizing the desirability of union organization and collective bargaining, in fact the development of procedures ensures they are kept within narrow limits, and do not challenge the economic power of employers. Joint regulation contains conflict, resolves it, and thus ameliorates its potential for disruption in a way that helps the interests of capital rather than those of labour.

Following on from this, the third main criticism of the pluralist approach is that by focusing on procedural reform, it neglects the important substantive outcomes for employees (Hyman 1989). In other words, pluralism is more concerned with the system of joint regulation than whether or not it produces anything worthwhile for employees.

Some have suggested that the radical approach places an unwarranted emphasis on conflict and disorder in employment relations (Ackers and Wilkinson 2003). However, the main value of taking a radical, critical perspective is that it draws our attention to the inadequacy of institutions of job regulation, such as collective bargaining, when it comes to challenging prevailing systems of managerial control and domination. It also highlights the large extent to which developments in employment relations reflect broader, deep-rooted economic and social structures.

A number of important sociological studies of workplace employment relations were strongly influenced by a radical perspective. Huw Beynon's study of Ford's Halewood car manufacturing plant is a particularly notable example of the genre (Beynon 1973). Since the 1980s, though, the influence of radical perspectives has waned (Ackers and Wilkinson 2005), partly because of a changed political environment and partly because of the pronounced decline in the level of trade union membership and organization, decreasing strike levels, and the dwindling extent of collective bargaining activity. The main challenges to pluralist orthodoxy in employment relations increasingly come from elsewhere: from other critical perspectives such as feminism (see Employment relations reflection 1.3), and in particular both from the resurgence of unitary thinking associated with the rise of human resource management (HRM) and the dominance of neo-liberal ideology.

Employment relations reflection 1.3: The feminist critique of employment relations

There has been a significant growth of interest in feminist perspectives on employment relations. Traditionally, matters like trade unions and collective bargaining were studied without paying much attention to gender relations—defined as relations between men and women—and how they affect employment relations (Wacjman 2000; Holgate, Hebson, and McBride 2006), though there were some notable exceptions (e.g. Pollert 1981). The feminist critique of orthodox employment relations means that there is now a better appreciation of the influence on employment relations of factors that are constituted outside of workplaces, particularly gender (Greene 2003). The development of feminist perspectives has contributed to a welcome broadening of the employment relations field (Heery et al. 2008); the challenges of reconciling paid work with family responsibilities, like childcare for example, have received more attention as a result.

Taking HRM first of all, as Chapter 5 demonstrates, there has been growing interest in how organizations can develop more sophisticated managerial approaches to engage and enhance the commitment of their staff as a means of realizing improvements in business performance. Contemporary 'human resource management follows the unitarist belief that effective management policies can align the interests of employees and employers and thereby remove conflicts of interest' (Budd 2004: 6). Growing interest in the 'neo-unitary' (Farnham and Pimlott 1995) character of HRM demonstrates the extent to which perspectives drawn from the discipline of psychology, in particular those concerning human relations at work, such as the relationship between work, commitment, and performance, influence the study of employment relations (Godard 2014). From this perspective, employment relations is fundamentally aligned with a managerial perspective, and is concerned with finding ways of building employee engagement and maintaining positive working relationships (Emmott 2005, 2015).

The rise to prominence of HRM, accompanied by a pronounced resurgence of unitary thinking in employment relations, occurred at the same time as, and cannot be seen in isolation from, the increasing dominance of neo-liberal ideology in the political sphere. Neo-liberalism is marked by the belief that economic growth and competitiveness are best achieved by allowing businesses as much freedom to operate as possible. In employment relations, the influence of neo-liberalism has been manifest in efforts by governments to weaken the alleged regulatory burdens—legal employment protections, collective bargaining with trade unions—which supposedly impede employers' flexibility (see Chapter 3). External regulation imposes extra unnecessary costs on employers, and undermines their capacity to manage employment relations efficiently, hindering competitiveness and diminishing employment prospects. Unions use their collective muscle to raise the price of labour, making employers uncompetitive and putting jobs at risk. To those who argue that workers need legal or collectively bargained protections to prevent employers from exploiting them, neo-liberals might reply that the most important 'right' enjoyed by workers is the right to have a job, something that regulation, by raising the cost of labour, jeopardizes. Neo-liberals might also point to other adverse consequences of regulation, such as its tendency to privilege 'insiders' (protecting those already in jobs) at the expense of 'outsiders' (people looking for a job, but unable to get one because employers are reluctant to bear the supposed risk of hiring new staff) (Heery et al. 2008: 18–19).

The profound influence of neo-liberal ideology is evident when it comes to government policy towards employment relations and the preference for deregulation and weak trade unions (see Chapter 3). One of the most obvious ways in which the neo-liberal ascendancy has affected employment relations concerns the flexibility enjoyed by companies like Deliveroo to avoid the costs of complying with legal employment rights and protections by hiring workers on supposedly self-employed contracts (see the introductory case study). As Chapter 2 shows, the growth of bogus self-employment arrangements is part of a broader trend of workers increasingly being treated as a commodity, viewed by employers as cheap and disposable resources towards whom they have few obligations or responsibilities.

1.3.3 **The relevance of employment relations**

Some have expressed a concern that as a result of these developments employment relations struggles to demonstrate its relevance (Ackers and Wilkinson 2003). As a field of study it was long characterized by a concern with the importance of trade unionism and collective bargaining, and underpinned by a dominant pluralist perspective (Ackers and Wilkinson 2005;

Heery et al. 2008). The rise of HRM and the neo-liberal ascendancy imply that employment relations has become a more marginal concern, perhaps only of interest to those working and managing in parts of the economy—like the public sector—where joint regulation remains commonplace.

But as this book shows, employment relations is about much more than just trade unions and collective bargaining, important as they are. Moreover, neither the rise of HRM nor the dominance of neo-liberalism have made employment relations any less important as a field of study—far from it. As we see in Chapter 5, there are a number of major problems with both HRM and the unitary assumptions that underpin it. Managing employment relations is a challenging task, requiring managers to navigate a difficult path between having to control workers, which involves coercing them into providing effort, and gaining their consent—made all the more harder in an environment where pressures for short-term performance improvements are paramount.

Neo-liberalism might be in the ascendancy as a political ideology, but studying employment relations not only shows that there are limits to employment deregulation and labour commodification, but also points to the important countervailing pressures that exist. The problem with the neo-liberal perspective is that when applied to employment relations it is too simplistic. Neo-liberalism focuses just on the regulation of work and employment relationships, with the assumptions that labour can be treated as a commodity and regulation operates largely on a unilateral, managerial basis. But, of course, labour is not a commodity. Work and employment relationships are characterized by an effort bargain, in which workers have their own interests, which differ from their employers', in a way that can generate contention (Meardi 2014*a*). Neo-liberalism is important to understand as a political ideology, one that has exercised an important influence on the policies of governments; but it does little to help us appreciate how employment relations actually operates.

Key elements of what makes employment relations distinctive as a field of study—the focus on work and employment relationships and how they are regulated, experienced, and contested, and a concern with recognizing and promoting the interests of working people—mean that it remains a vital topic of contemporary enquiry (Ackers and Wilkinson 2005). Studying employment relations means that one has to recognize the importance of topics such as power and justice, and that employers and employees may have competing interests, things that are largely absent from HRM texts (BUIRA 2009). In addition, issues relating to work and employment relations are integral to the way in which many emerging economies such as China have developed (e.g. Friedman 2014).

The relevance of pluralist and Marxist perspectives endures. Heery (2016: 18), for example, shows how pluralism in employment relations has evolved in response to labour market issues like low pay and insecure employment, as well as the 'irresponsible exercise' of unilateral managerial prerogative. Whereas in the past pluralism was concerned with the problems created *by* labour, with joint regulation embraced as a means of mitigating disorder, nowadays it is much more focused on understanding, and alleviating, problems *for* labour. As a consequence there is a much greater emphasis given to the part that effective legal regulation of work and employment relationships can play in helping to promote order (Heery 2016: 7, 18). Work in the Marxist tradition continues to offer important insights into many areas of employment relations, especially when it comes to understanding structures of managerial control (see Chapter 5) and the dynamics of labour conflict, particularly the major contribution made by mobilization theory (Kelly 1998)—see Chapter 9. As a field of study, then, employment relations has become more 'complex and diverse' (Meardi 2014a: 603); but it has by no means been made redundant by the rise of HRM and the neo-liberal ascendancy—in fact it is more important than ever.

 Section summary and further reading

- The unitary perspective, which denies the basic antagonism in the employment relationship, can be criticized for being unrealistic, though its tenets influence the attitudes and behaviour of managers.

- Traditional pluralism recognizes the potential for conflict, but tends to focus on how it can be contained by the development of procedures, particularly collective bargaining arrangements.

- Radical approaches, which developed out of a critique of pluralism, reject the assumption that conflict in employment relations can be accommodated in a straightforward fashion. Not only is the potential for conflict to arise ever-present, but also efforts to contain it will always be partial and incomplete.

- As a field of study, employment relations was traditionally concerned with understanding the rules that govern employment relationships, in particular joint regulation and collective bargaining between trade unions and employers. This is too narrow an approach; it has been rendered untenable, moreover, by declining unionization and falling levels of collective bargaining. However, key elements of what makes employment relations distinctive as a field of study, notably a concern with the interests of workers, make it a valuable topic of contemporary enquiry.

Budd and Bhave (2008) are good on 'frames of reference' in employment relations. See Heery et al. (2008) for an assessment of pluralist orthodoxy in employment relations and the principal challenges to it. Hyman (1975) is the standard Marxist introduction to employment relations. For the nature of employment relations as a field of study, see Ackers and Wilkinson (2003). See Meardi (2014a) for the relevance of employment relations. Heery (2016) has written an insightful essay on pluralism in employment relations.

1.4 Employment relations: actors, processes, outcomes, and dimensions

Having outlined the nature of the employment relationship and considered the main perspectives on employment relations as a field of study, the purpose of this section is to introduce the main actors, processes, and outcomes of employment relations, and illustrate its key dimensions.

1.4.1 Employment relations actors

Clearly there are two fundamental actors in employment relations—workers and employers—without whom work and employment relationships could not exist. For the most part, though, employers vest day-to-day control of employment relations matters in the hands of appointed managers. Furthermore, employers may combine in associations to handle employment relations matters. While the experiences of workers are integral to the approach taken in this book to employment relations as a field of study, they frequently organize in trade unions—collective bodies of workers that act to support and protect their interests. We have already established that legislation plays an increasing role in regulating work and employment relationships. Thus, as well as examining the role of employers, managers, employers' associations, and unions in employment relations, the nature of state intervention is also worthy of scrutiny. In this section, then, we offer a brief introduction to the roles of the three main employment relations actors—employers and management, trade unions, and the state. However, researchers have begun to note the increasing array of other actors who play an important role in contemporary employment relations (see Employment relations reflection 1.4).

Employers and management

Except in very small firms, employing organizations entrust day-to-day control to salaried managers who are responsible, among other things, for managing employment relations. As has already been seen (see Section 1.2.2), a belief in managerial prerogative, or the 'right' to manage employment relationships unilaterally, without interference from third parties like trade unions, underpins managers' behaviour in employment relations. Yet managerial efforts to secure employee compliance will always be frustrated and thus incomplete. The nature of the employment relationship as a wage–work bargain invariably limits the scope of managerial prerogative, and also provides workers with opportunities to challenge managerial control. Therefore, in understanding how the employment relationship is managed, it is important not to oversimplify by concentrating solely on managerial attempts to secure control (Storey 1985; Hyman 1987). To realize the efficient production or delivery of goods and services, managers must secure a degree of legitimacy, or consent, among those they manage (Legge 2005).

Employment relations reflection 1.4: New and emerging actors in employment relations

Most studies of employment relations understandably focus on the activities of key actors like employers, workers, and trade unions. However, there is a growing amount of scholarly interest in the role of other actors who are involved with employment relations matters in some way, like community groups and non-governmental organizations (NGOs). This is consistent with a shift towards the articulation of a broader understanding of employment relations in contemporary societies, one that expands its 'terrain to explore the links between employment and other spheres of social and economic life, and research new and previously neglected actors' (Heery and Frege 2006: 603). Williams, Abbott, and Heery (2011a), for example, focus their attention on the employment relations role and activities of 'civil society' organizations (CSOs), a label that encompasses living wage campaign groups, faith bodies, public interest legal organizations, charities, pressure groups, social movement organizations, and community groups. The campaigning organization Stonewall, for example, lobbies on behalf of lesbian, gay, and bisexual people, and works with employers to improve the way they manage sexual orientation issues. Vulnerable workers, particularly those who are based in parts of the economy where trade unions are weak, often rely on agencies like the network of Citizens Advice Bureaux for help and support with employment-related matters (Abbott 2004). The increasing attention being given to these new and emerging employment relations actors illustrates how the boundaries of employment relations as a field of study have been widened, and that it is not just restricted to unions and joint regulation.

Historically, employers sought to uphold managerial prerogative in the workplace by externalizing collective bargaining with trade unions through employers' associations. By bargaining with unions away from the workplace, on a multi-employer basis, employers aimed to 'neutralize' union power in the workplace. In matters that went unregulated by collective agreements, particularly those pertaining to the organization and pace of work, the assumption was that management prerogative would predominate (Sisson 1987). Although employers' associations sometimes engaged in crude anti-union activities such as undermining strikes, their role in the joint regulation of employment relations, particularly through multi-employer collective bargaining and procedures for resolving disputes, became an important means of maintaining managerial control, and thus upholding employers' interests (McIvor 1996). Since the 1960s, however, the role of employers' associations has declined in significance, linked to the erosion of multi-employer bargaining. Increasing numbers of firms, especially larger ones, chose to develop organization-specific procedures for handling employment relations matters (Gospel 1992)—see Chapter 7.

One of the most striking features of contemporary employment relations concerns the growing extent to which employers have sought to regain control over their own arrangements, and manage employment relations directly. At first, this took the form of a pluralist concern with responding to, and managing the consequences of, trade unionism. Since the 1980s, though, the managerial employment relations agenda has taken on a more unitary ethos, linked to the decline of joint regulation. The rise of a sophisticated HRM approach to managing people at work, based on the use of techniques designed to raise organizational commitment and boost business performance, is emblematic of a more assertive managerial agenda in employment relations (see Chapter 5). Much more interest has been directed at the role of employers and management as a result (Kaufman 2011). One indication that employers are taking the management of employment relations more seriously concerns the growing proportion of workplaces with access to specialist employment relations managers, who have specific responsibility for managing human resources in organizations (Kersley et al. 2006). That said, however, much of the day-to-day work involved in dealing with workplace employment relations issues—handling employee grievances, for example, or disciplining workers (see Chapter 10)—is undertaken by non-specialist front-line managers.

Trade unions

As has already been established, there is an imbalance of power in the employment relationship in favour of the employer. The main way in which workers attempt to challenge this power differential is to combine in collective organizations, trade unions, so that they can influence the terms of their employment relationships from a position of greater strength. This was precisely the role played by the Independent Workers Union of Great Britain (IWGB) in the 2016 dispute over Deliveroo's pay arrangements (see the introductory case study). One of the earliest and most well-known definitions of a trade union, dating from the end of the nineteenth century, refers to it as 'a continuous association of wage earners for the purpose of maintaining or improving the conditions of their working lives' (Webb and Webb 1920*b*: 1).

Table 1.1 Major trade unions in the UK

Trade union	Membership
Unite	1,405,838
Unison	1,270,248
General Municipal and Boilermakers union (GMB)	625,243
Union of Shop, Distributive and Allied Workers (USDAW)	434,622
Royal College of Nursing (RCN)	429,414
National Union of Teachers (NUT)	376,208
National Association of Schoolmasters Union of Women Teachers (NASUWT)	330,485
Public and Commercial Services Union (PCS)	231,323
Communication Workers Union (CWU)	197,462
Association of Teachers and Lecturers (ATL)	189,479
British Medical Association (BMA)	154,603
Prospect	115,258
University and College Union (UCU)	105,447

Source: Certification Officer (2016)

For our purposes, however, a trade union can be defined as a body comprised mainly of workers that, by means of collective organization and mobilization, represents and advances their interests both in the workplace and in society at large. It does so by providing workers with protection from the arbitrary exercise of managerial prerogative, bargaining with management over the terms and conditions of their employment, giving them influence over decisions that affect them at work, and by providing them with a means of bringing about political changes that are favourable to their interests. Trade unions are ostensibly democratic bodies: organizations which comprise, and work on behalf of, their members. Trade union members pay a subscription—usually between £10 and £25 per month—to benefit from the services of their union, including the right to influence its policies.

See Table 1.1 for a list of the major trade unions in Britain (those with more than 100,000 members). The largest unions tend to be so-called 'general' unions, which recruit members from a wide range of industry sectors and occupations. A good example is Unite, which was formed in 2007 following the merger of the Transport and General Workers Union (TGWU) and Amicus. The list in Table 1.1 also includes some notable unions which organize largely on the basis of a single industry, like the Union of Shop, Distributive and Allied Workers (USDAW) in retail. Some unions operate on a narrower occupational basis, though because they tend to be rather small, they are largely absent from the list in the table. However, two organizations which do appear in the table—the Royal College of Nursing (RCN), a union of nurses, and the British Medical Association (BMA), which represents doctors—do possess a strong occupational identity.

Another feature of Table 1.1 worth noting concerns the relatively large number of major trade unions which operate in the public sector—education unions like the National Union of Teachers (NUT) and the University and College Union (UCU), for example. During the nineteenth and twentieth centuries, the development of trade unions was concentrated among primary and manufacturing industries. However, since the 1970s employment in these areas has fallen substantially. At the same time, workers in the public sector have become increasingly unionized. The growing proportion of trade union members who work in the public sector, many of whom are women employed in professional occupations like teaching, has had a marked effect on the changing character of trade unionism.

 Insight into practice 1.5: The role of the Trades Union Congress

Traditionally, the Trades Union Congress (TUC), which was founded in 1868, fulfils three broad roles in employment relations. First, it is involved in adjudicating disputes between unions over which of them should represent particular groups of workers, though this activity is now only of relatively minor importance (McIlroy and Daniels 2009). Second, it provides its union affiliates with services like education and training. Third, perhaps most importantly, the TUC represents, and acts on behalf of, the trade union movement in general, in relations with government for example. In recent years the TUC's role has changed in two key respects. One of the changes concerns the development of a more explicit campaigning role on matters such as low pay, zero-hours contracts, and workplace equality. Linked to this, the second change has involved the TUC developing a role as the organization which speaks on behalf of working people as a whole, rather than just as the voice of the trade union interest (Heery 1998b, 1998c). However, union mergers and amalgamations have threatened the TUC's role. The trend towards so-called 'super-unions' like Unite, for example, which was formed from the merger of the Transport and General Workers Union and Amicus, has perhaps eroded the authority of the TUC (McIlroy and Daniels 2009).

Finally, in this introduction to the role of the trade unions, it is important to mention the role and activities of the Trades Union Congress (TUC)—see Insight into practice 1.5. The TUC is a confederation of fifty-one unions, and acts as the voice of the trade union movement in Britain. Very few major unions are not affiliated to the TUC; of those that appear in Table 1.1, only the RCN and BMA are outside it.

The state

Although management and unions are the principal parties in employment relations, it is also important to emphasize the important influence exercised by the state (Kelly 1998; Meardi, Donaghey, and Dean 2016). It is conventional to understand the effects of state activity on employment relations in four ways. First, employment in the state, or public, sector is a major element of contemporary employment relations, and at various points in this book we consider some of its distinctive features, such as pay determination (see Chapter 7). Second, states enact legislation in the area of employment relations, such as that designed to regulate trade union behaviour (see Chapter 3) or establish minimum wages (see Chapter 7). Third, states operate arrangements to help employers and unions resolve disputes, notably arbitration and conciliation machinery (see Chapter 10). Fourth, the economic and political policies pursued by the governments of national states also have important implications for employment relations.

There is often an emphasis on the coercive, repressive role of the state, and the way it operates to suppress trade unions and the interests of working people (Kelly 1998)—see

International perspective 1.6 for example. Yet state policy is not characterized just by the repression of the labour interest. States need to win the consent of their populations in order to maintain a stable order suitable for businesses. This points to the importance of having a sophisticated understanding of the influence of the state on employment relations; its approach is characterized by a mixture of coercion and consent (Kelly 1998). Government policy-makers and officials do not just respond to demands from employers; they also have to be responsive to the concerns of working people (Edwards 1986). Moreover, state intervention, in the form of legislation, provides workers with potential opportunities to organize and mobilize in pursuit of their interests (Meardi, Donaghey, and Dean 2016), particularly when it comes to exerting pressure for more effective enforcement arrangements (see Chapter 10).

 International perspective 1.6: Union repression around the world

State repression of trade unions and workers' rights is a distinct feature of contemporary employment relations in many countries. The International Trade Union Confederation (ITUC) publishes regular reports documenting violations of workers' rights and instances of union repression around the world. Whereas many countries restrict the ability of trade unions to organize workers in some way, or limit opportunities for collective bargaining, the ITUC's reports demonstrate the violence exhibited towards independent trade unionism in some places. By far the most dangerous place for trade unionists is Colombia in South America, one of the ten 'worst' countries in the world to be a worker, according to the ITUC. While the number of assassinations of union activists declined during the 2000s, there were still forty-nine such murders in 2010, and twenty in 2015. The Colombian government has claimed that the violence is a consequence of many years of civil war and the activities of numerous powerful armed groups of guerrillas who controlled much of its territory for long periods of time. But there is evidence that the Colombian state encouraged the killings.

Sources: ITUC (2012, 2015a); Blackburn and Puerto (2013)

1.4.2 Employment relations processes

As highlighted earlier (see Section 1.2.2), the regulation of employment relationships is of central importance to employment relations as a field of study. The traditionally dominant pluralist perspective on employment relations is marked by a concern with understanding joint regulatory processes, especially collective bargaining. In its narrow sense, collective bargaining is simply a means of determining pay and conditions of employment involving unions, who negotiate or bargain with employers. Beatrice and Sidney Webb, the first serious students of collective bargaining, suggested that it is largely an economic process, the collective equivalent of individual bargaining (Webb and Webb 1920a).

By acting collectively through trade unions, workers can secure more for themselves from the employment relationship than would be possible just from their own individual efforts. This is because it gives them more bargaining power, particularly where they are prepared to use forms of industrial action like strikes—temporary stoppages of work—as a lever to enforce their demands. Disputes which arise from conflicts of interest over the terms and conditions of employment relationships often cannot be settled internally by employers and employees, or by unions. Therefore, to mitigate any disruptive effects, states generally operate third-party arrangements for resolving them. In the UK, for example, the Advisory, Conciliation and Arbitration Service (ACAS) not only helps to settle collective disputes between unions and employers, but also intervenes in the case of individual disputes, when a worker wants to litigate against an employer—see Chapter 10 for further details.

Collective bargaining is more than just a means of determining employment terms. It also fulfils a broader, political function. Flanders (1975) stressed that collective bargaining is a rule-making process. Not only does it set the terms and conditions on which labour is hired, but it also gives workers, through their unions, rights to challenge and influence managerial decisions over such things as the organization of work. Thus collective bargaining, as a process of 'job regulation', is an important means of giving workers voice over, and enabling them to participate in, matters that affect them in their working lives. This was a particularly strong theme of the 1960s Donovan Royal Commission which, heavily imbued with the dominant pluralist thinking of the time, stated that where it was properly undertaken 'collective bargaining is the most effective means of giving workers the right to representation in decisions affecting their working lives, a right which is or should be the prerogative of every worker in a democratic society' (Royal Commission 1968: 54). Yet, as a form of worker participation, collective bargaining on its own only goes so far; in theory, more direct forms of worker control give workers greater influence over how their organizations are run by making them more democratic (see Historical perspective 1.7).

Historical perspective 1.7: Industrial democracy at work

When Theresa May became UK prime minister in July 2016 she expressed a concern with establishing arrangements that would give worker representatives a position on company boards, reviving interest in the question of industrial democracy, an idea which has a long history. During the 1960s and 1970s, there was an important movement towards workers' control and industrial democracy (Poole 1986). Threats of plant closures and job cuts associated with industrial restructuring stimulated a number of 'work-ins' in which workers and their unions attempted to maintain the operation of plants themselves. The most famous instance occurred following the announcement of the closure of the Upper Clyde Shipbuilders yard near Glasgow. Workers and shop stewards occupied the yard for a period of time to prevent its closure (Foster and Woolfson 1986). There was also much interest in how workers' interests could be represented on company boards of directors (Brannen 1983). In the 1970s, a government committee of inquiry recommended that union representatives should have parity with shareholders on the boards of large companies, with an 'intermediary' group of ostensibly independent directors, appointed by mutual consent, maintaining a balance between the two sides. But employer opposition and the hostility of influential union leaders, who were concerned about the threat to the primacy of collective bargaining, ensured that the proposals came to nothing.

However, there has been renewed interest in the benefits of greater industrial democracy. Some in the trade union movement argue that the UK would do well to follow the example of Germany, with its successful economy, where union representatives sit on the supervisory boards of major companies (TUC 2012a). In October 2013, the TUC published a report calling for the UK's system of corporate governance to be improved, including by having worker representatives sit on company boards (TUC 2013). The experience of other European companies demonstrates that effective worker representation on company boards is associated with better economic and social outcomes. Having worker representatives on boards improves the quality of decision-making, and can help to cultivate a longer term approach to business success. Workers enjoy a better quality of working life, which has positive effects on productivity. There are some potential difficulties, however. Worker representatives on boards might become too closely associated with unpopular management decisions, undermining their legitimacy.

For the pluralists, collective bargaining not only gives workers a voice over matters that affect them at work, but is also an important means by which the inherent conflict in the employment relationship can be accommodated—or, as it is often put, institutionalized. In other words, the presence of collective bargaining enables managers to contain conflict, to keep it within acceptable limits, and it is therefore an effective means of managing employment relations and extending managerial control (Flanders 1975). The principal radical critique of collective bargaining is that it contains workers' militancy within boundaries that are acceptable to employers. By institutionalizing conflict, it runs counter to the real interests of workers. Moreover, by becoming enmeshed in the process of bargaining with management, unions come to adopt a fundamentally conservative ethos, concerned with the procedural details of negotiations and agreements rather than with advancing the substantive interests of their members. Whereas workers want to improve their terms and conditions of employment, and to secure greater influence over workplace decisions, in the bargaining process union leaders may prefer to focus on establishing and maintaining stable relationships with employers, thus sustaining the institutional security of the union, rather than challenging them (Hyman 1989). In practice, however, one cannot readily distinguish between union leaders' concern with stable and secure bargaining relationships and the desire of their members for improved pay and conditions. Workers have a concern with the security and survival of their union because without it they have no means of winning better employment terms. And the position of union leaders becomes problematic if, in the bargaining process, they are not seen to be delivering benefits for their members (Smith 2001).

Workers also collectively influence their employment relationships and express their voice through the process of joint consultation. Whereas collective bargaining involves employers having to negotiate with a union over the terms and conditions of employment relationships—something that may require them to make concessions in order to secure an agreement—consultation is less threatening to managerial prerogative. For this reason, it is often preferred by managers, in as much as they can find out employees' views without being bound by them (Hall and Purcell 2012). With consultation, workers 'influence but in no way determine managerial policy and practice' (Poole 1986: 71). Consultation is often seen as an appropriate process for handling matters where there is a supposed greater propensity for cooperation and a commonality of interests between management and workers, such as health, safety, and welfare issues, as opposed to the more explicitly conflictual collective bargaining relationship (Clegg 1979; Marchington 1989). However, it is often difficult to maintain a rigid distinction between consultation and collective bargaining, not least because union representatives often try to use consultation machinery as a bargaining forum. Moreover, bargaining itself is increasingly becoming more akin to consultation in the way it operates (see Chapter 7).

There is a great diversity of consultation arrangements evident in practice (Marchington 1994; Hall and Purcell 2012). They are now used more expressly as managerial, rather than joint regulatory, processes (see Chapter 6 for further details). This is consistent with the broader decline of trade unions and collective bargaining, and the rise to prominence of a more unitary employment relations ethos. As a result, there is now a much greater concern with the role played by managerial processes in employment relations (Sisson 2010). These include HRM interventions such as performance management and absence management tools, which are used by employers to control the behaviour of employees in a more rigorous manner. Managerial processes for handling the grievances of employees and improving their behaviour and conduct—their 'discipline'—have become a more central feature of employment relations (see Chapter 10).

Perhaps the most notable example of this greater emphasis on the role played by managerial processes in regulating employment relationships concerns the question of worker voice. As we have seen, in a pluralist employment relations environment, workers have a say, and can gain some influence over decisions that affect them at work, through the process of collective bargaining by trade unions, supplemented by joint consultation. However, a prominent feature of the more unitary employment relations climate concerns the greater use of managerially driven and controlled techniques for communicating with, and involving, employees. The term 'employee involvement' can be applied to managerial initiatives that are designed to further the flow of communication at work as a means of enhancing the organizational commitment of employees (Hyman and Mason 1995). This encompasses measures such as 'team briefings'—arrangements that enable managers to convey information about the organization and the workplace to employees on a regular basis (see Chapter 5).

Trade unions and collective bargaining remain important features of employment relations, particularly in public sector organizations and among many large private sector companies. However, as a field of study which is concerned with the regulation of employment relationships, as well as how they are experienced and contested, employment relations is also concerned with developing a critical understanding of relevant managerial regulatory processes (Sisson 2010). Furthermore, it encompasses the process of legal enactment, something which has become more important given the greatly increased extent to which employment relationships have come to be governed by statutory regulation (Colling and Terry 2010). Examples include laws prohibiting discrimination against certain defined categories of workers (see Chapter 4) and laws enacting minimum wage protection (see Chapter 7). Nor must we overlook the important extent to which informal expectations and custom and practice understandings play a prominent part in influencing the wage–work bargain (Colling and Terry 2010). As a field of study, then, employment relations is not just concerned with collective bargaining, important though that still is; it has a broader, more inclusive dimension, being concerned with all of the processes that are used to regulate work and employment relationships.

1.4.3 The outcomes of employment relations

Clearly, the production of rules that govern work and employment relationships is the most obvious outcome of employment relations. The traditional focus in employment relations concerned how collective bargaining, involving the joint regulation of work and employment relationships, produces rules in the form of negotiated collective agreements between employers and trade unions. There are two types of collective agreement. Procedural agreements set out the details of how collective bargaining operates, specifying the topics that come within the scope of bargaining activity for example. Substantive agreements concern the actual outcomes of the bargaining process: any changes to pay, hours, holidays, etc.—the substance of employment relationships—that result from a bargaining exercise.

Managerial regulation also generates procedural rules in the form of arrangements for handling performance and absence issues, dealing with grievance and disciplinary cases, and for informing and consulting with employees. Where no unions are involved, managers not only enjoy more scope to determine rules governing these matters unilaterally, but can also exercise more control over the determination of pay and employment conditions. When it comes to substantive outcomes, managerial goals in employment relations tend to focus on matters such as work effort and productivity rates, and levels of attendance and engagement. There has been growing interest in how employment relations can be managed to engage and win the organizational commitment of staff, with the goal of improving business performance (see Chapter 5). This development is associated with the neo-unitary challenge to pluralist orthodoxy mentioned in Section 1.3.2.

However, a key feature of employment relations as a field of study, and one that distinguishes it from HRM, is a concern with the outcomes for employees, not just with regard to tangible benefits like wages and benefits, but also more intangible effects such as job satisfaction, justice, and dignity at work (Ackers and Wilkinson 2005; Heery et al. 2008). Moreover, the dynamic nature of the employment relationship as a wage–work bargain means that there is always the potential for employees to challenge the rules under which they operate. When it comes to employment relations, then, efforts by workers to contest employment relations, either collectively (through strikes, protests, and other forms of labour conflict) or on a more individual basis (e.g. employee grievances and litigation against employers, or more informal means like withholding effort), should also be considered as notable elements.

Clearly, much of the interest in employment relations outcomes is concerned with workplace and organizational matters such as pay, working conditions, and productivity. However, employment relations operates at multiple levels, influencing matters beyond the boundaries of the organization itself (BUIRA 2009; Sisson 2009). In much of the public sector, like local government for example, employers and unions conclude collective agreements over pay and some employment conditions at industry sector level. Even in the absence of multi-employer bargaining, there is evidence that firms in the same industry sector operate similar pay arrangements (Arrowsmith and Sisson 1999). Employment relations also produces outcomes which are of broader significance for economic and social life more generally, illustrating its multilevel nature. For example, there has always been a strong interest in the social and economic implications of collective bargaining arrangements for matters such as wage inequality and inflation (Heery et al. 2008). Keith Sisson (2009, 2010: chapter 3), moreover, examines how the nature and structure of employment relationships influence a wide range of indicators, including business performance, economic growth, health, living standards, family lives, and personal development. This further demonstrates the importance of understanding employment relations as a field of study.

1.4.4 **The dimensions of employment relations**

Work and employment relations are also marked by particular economic, political and legal, and social dimensions; these are not just contextual influences, but are integral to how employment relations operates. First of all, there is an economic dimension to employment relations. Clearly, work and employment relationships are influenced by, and interact with, the nature of the economic environment. The implications of the 2008–9 economic recession and its aftermath, particularly the period of sluggish economic growth, are considered in more detail in Chapter 2. One of the most pronounced effects of the economic situation has been stagnant wages, and as a consequence many people have seen their incomes and living standards tightly squeezed. This has stimulated growing interest in ways of tackling low pay effectively, through interventions like 'living wages', which in turn help to shape the economic and employment environment—see Chapter 7.

A large part of Chapter 11 is devoted to examining the relationship between economic globalization and employment relations. Globalization has affected employment relations, to be sure, but new ways of regulating work and employment relationships through arrangements like labour codes of conduct point to the centrality of employment relations to the way that globalization has developed and functions. Changes in the labour market and the composition of employment, like the use of more flexible employment arrangements such as part-time and temporary work, and the growing proportion of female employment, are also integral features of employment relations (see Chapters 2 and 4). One of the most important developments has been the rapid growth in the use of contractual arrangements that do not guarantee workers a fixed number of hours—so-called 'zero-hours contracts' (see Chapter 8). Again, these are changes that not only affect employment relations, but are also integral to how it operates.

There is a marked political and legal dimension to employment relations. The law is a notable source of the rules that govern employment relationships; and, of course, the nature of the political system determines the kinds of laws that are enacted. During the 1980s and 1990s, for example, one of the key political aims of the Conservative governments under Margaret Thatcher and John Major was to weaken the role of the trade unions. This resulted in a number of pieces of legislation that heavily restricted how trade unions operate (see Chapter 3). Political change, in the form of the Labour governments of Tony Blair and Gordon Brown between 1997 and 2010, produced a change in emphasis. While Labour did little to reverse the anti-union measures of their Conservative predecessors in government, it did not add to them. Labour was also more ready to enact legislation providing individual employment protections, through interventions like the National Minimum Wage, and by signing up to European Union (EU) laws designed to be supportive of workers' interests. Under the 2010–15 Conservative–Liberal Democrat coalition government, however, there was a substantial change in emphasis. Believing that people have too many rights at work, it took a series of measures aimed at easing the supposed burden of employment regulation on employers, including new restrictions on the ability of aggrieved workers to claim legal redress for breaches of employment rights (see Chapters 3 and 10). These examples demonstrate that employment relations is a highly politicized field of study, with politics integral to how it operates.

Employment relations is also marked by an important social dimension. For one thing, the underpinning values and beliefs that influence people's attitudes and behaviour affect employment relations in important ways. There is evidence that since the 1980s Britain has become a more tolerant society. For example, the annual British Social Attitudes Survey demonstrates that prejudice against homosexuality has declined considerably. Changes in social attitudes of this kind influence employment relations, for example by encouraging greater awareness and acceptance of equality and diversity measures. However, as Chapter 4 shows, discrimination has by no means become less important. Class-based disadvantage is rife. While the level of racial prejudice fell substantially during the 1990s, it appeared to edge up again during the 2000s, perhaps because of the negative way in which the media report immigration issues (Creegan and Robinson 2008). Concerns over immigration influenced people's attitudes towards the European Union (EU), contributing to greater unease, and even hostility, towards the project of European integration. In 1992, for example, 40 per cent of people in the UK supported leaving the EU, or staying in an EU with its powers reduced; by 2015 this had risen to 65 per cent (Curtice 2016). In the aftermath of the June 2016 referendum vote in favour of leaving the EU there was a notable upsurge in racism and racist hate crime (EHRC 2016a). These examples highlight the important extent to which social values, and changes in the social context, are integral to how employment relations operates.

 ### Section summary and further reading

- The main employment relations actors are employers and managers, workers and trade unions, and the state. However, the role of 'new actors' like community-based organizations and other civil society organizations has received increasing scrutiny.

- The key employment relations processes include collective bargaining and consultation arrangements. Managerial processes used to regulate employment relationships, such as communication techniques, are also important; nor should the importance of informal expectations and understandings in employment relations be overlooked.

- In terms of outcomes, traditionally the emphasis was on how collective bargaining and other processes generated procedural and substantive rules that govern employment relationships. Employment relations is not just concerned with improvements in organizational efficiency; it is also marked by a focus on the implications for workers, notably the extent to which they experience fair and equitable treatment at work and the degree to which they can influence decision-making in organizations. As a multilevel field of study, it is also responsible for a range of broader social and economic outcomes.

- Employment relations operates in a number of dimensions. The economic, employment, political, legal, and social dimensions not only influence work and employment relationships, but are also integral to how they function.

See Heery et al. (2008) for further insights about the main employment relations actors, processes, and outcomes. Sisson (2009, 2010: chapter 3) is very good on examining the broader social and economic outcomes of how work and employment relationships are organized.

1.5 Conclusion: the value of employment relations

The main purpose of this chapter has been to introduce the nature of work and employment relationships, to consider employment relations as a field of study, and to introduce the main actors, processes, and outcomes of employment relations, also with reference to the key dimensions of employment relations. The subject matter of employment relations is sometimes thought to be restricted to trade unions and collective bargaining; and because of their diminished significance, it is therefore no longer very important as a field of study (Emmott 2005). However, while unions and collective bargaining still play a major role, employment relations is about much more than just these things (Sisson 2009, 2010). It views work and employment relationships as more than just market transactions, expressing a concern with how they are regulated—in the form of rules that govern work and employment relationships, and that comprise people's terms and conditions of employment. Given that the 'employment relationship is something that the great majority of us are involved in for much of our lives' (Sisson 2008: 6), this is clearly something which is highly relevant. Moreover, it is not enough just to take into account the regulation of work and employment relationships; how workers experience these relationships, and the circumstances under which they come to contest them, and mobilize against their employers, are also important matters. From this perspective, the continued value and relevance of employment relations as a field of study is evident from the example of Deliveroo discussed in the introductory case study.

Employment relations reflection 1.8:   The value of employment relations

In 2009, Martin Upchurch undertook a survey of academics about the teaching of employment relations in British universities (Upchurch 2009). He asked respondents why they thought the teaching of employment relations was still important. Among the comments he received in response were:

Business still operates within the bounds of rules, regulations and limited resources. [Employment relations] offers a conceptual way to explain the politics and relations of power in the world of work . . . [and] also draws the attention of students as it brings a more critical perspective to their understanding of management and work.

[The study of employment relations] is a valuable way of exposing students to new ways of thinking and challenging their pre-conceptions . . . By studying the inherent tensions in the employment relationship (through the use of hugely relevant current affairs examples) students can start to develop the all important skills of critical thought.

[Employment relations] recognises the issues of power and conflict in the workplace and how these dynamics are managed . . . We help students to challenge their misconceptions over how the employment relationship is really managed and we help produce future managers with a greater insight into the ways of the workplace.

[Employment relations is] probably one of the few subjects on a business degree that really requires any wider political engagement from students . . . and particularly also the recognition that there are alternative perspectives to viewing the world than 'managerialist' ones.

[Employment relations is] a vital part of the employment landscape and in the context of a globalising world is a very important subject of relevance to working people everywhere.

The subject matter of employment relations is thus concerned with the 'totality' of work and employment relationships (Kaufman 2010a: 102). In addition to a concern with the role of employers, unions, and collective bargaining, the study of employment relations incorporates the activities of a wide range of new and emerging actors such as civil society organizations, recognizes the manifold processes involved in the regulation of employment relationships, and pays heed to a broad range of outcomes at multiple levels. As a consequence, employment relations as a field of study is 'uniquely placed' to develop a more effective understanding of how business and management operates (Colling and Terry 2010: 4), not least because it recognizes the importance of the broader economic, social, and political dimensions which affect, and in turn are influenced by, work and employment in organizations. As a field of study which is concerned with managing people at work effectively, HRM is 'narrow and impoverished' by comparison (Colling and Terry 2010: 4). It is generally too managerialist, concerned with how managers can manipulate the attitudes, behaviour, and performance of employees in pursuit of organizational goals (BUIRA 2009). Employment relations, though, is characterized by an important critical dimension. It exposes managerial objectives and activities to rigorous scrutiny, not taking them at face value; recognizes that workers also have independent interests which they pursue; and attests to the tensions, uncertainties, and potential for conflict that underpin work and employment relationships (see Employment relations reflection 1.8).

Given that, directly and indirectly, employment affects the majority of people in countries like the UK, it should be evident that a good level of knowledge and understanding of employment relations is essential if one is going to appreciate properly the nature of contemporary business and management, and their relationship with society. While if conceived narrowly as the study of trade unions and collective bargaining, employment relations may have become marginalized, the broader perspective adopted here views it as a field of study that continues to be highly relevant. It concerns work and employment relationships, and all of the various features of, and influences over, these relationships—something that is of vital interest to individual workers, organizations, and societies.

 ## Assignment and discussion questions

1. What are the main features of the employment relationship as a 'wage–work bargain'?
2. With regard to the objectives of employment relations, explain what is meant by 'efficiency', 'equity', and 'voice'.
3. What is meant by the concept of managerial prerogative in employment relations? What are the main constraints on the exercise of managerial prerogative?
4. Which of the three perspectives on employment relations—unitary, pluralist, or radical—most closely fits your own view of the world of work? Why?
5. Why is 'power' such an important concept in understanding employment relations?

 Visit the Online Resource Centre that accompanies this book to develop your understanding of this chapter and keep up to date with the latest developments in this area.
www.oxfordtextbooks.co.uk/orc/williams4e/

 ## Chapter case study: Employment relations at Amazon

Online retailer Amazon has become one of the most well-known firms in the world. First entering the UK market as a bookseller in 1998, the US company has subsequently greatly expanded the range of products it sells, which now includes household goods, music downloads, and electronics among other things. In 2016, Amazon announced plans to create 3,500 new jobs, linked to the development of new products and services—such as an expansion into delivering fresh food—taking its UK workforce to over 15,000. However, along with other leading multinationals, such as Google, Vodafone, and Starbucks, Amazon has been condemned for the way it structures its tax affairs. In 2014–15, for example, despite UK sales of some £5.3 billion, Amazon paid just £11.9 million in tax. It was able to do this because the ownership of its UK business had been transferred to a subsidiary based in Luxembourg, an arrangement that enables it to reduce its UK tax liability.

(continued...)

But tax is not the only aspect of Amazon's business which has come in for criticism. The company's approach to work and employment relations matters has often been a source of concern for many. Professional, technical, and managerial staff based in the US have drawn attention to the highly competitive working environment propagated by Amazon and the presence of intensive and punishing work regimes. Women employees seem to be particularly disadvantaged by an excessively strict and punitive system of performance management and discipline—one was given a 'performance improvement plan' after having had breast cancer—and the company has been the subject of numerous complaints about unfair treatment and discrimination.

In the UK and Europe, though, it is the state of working conditions in its mammoth warehouses—or 'fulfilment centres'—that has generated the most controversy. Trade unions like the GMB claim that many of Amazon's workers have low pay and poor conditions, with wages often at, or just above, the statutory National Minimum Wage. Work in its warehouses is often highly insecure, with many staff taken on through temporary employment agencies rather than hired by the firm directly, meaning that they can be disposed of more readily when they are not needed. Amazon chooses the locations of its centres very carefully. They are often situated in parts of the UK which are quite deprived economically, and where there are few alternative sources of employment—such as in Yorkshire, South Wales, and Staffordshire. Not only does this enable Amazon to access government grants and loans for creating jobs, but also ensures that it can take advantage of a vulnerable workforce, who are particularly dependent on the company for their livelihoods. Working conditions in the warehouses themselves are highly oppressive. Workers are required to use electronic handsets which specify the precise time needed to select a product. They have complained about the intense pressure involved in processing orders, with their movements constantly tracked throughout the warehouse to make sure they are keeping up to speed, and disciplinary action taken against those whose performance is not deemed to be up to scratch. Workers have described how they feel they are treated as 'machines'. It seems inevitable that such intense and highly stressful working conditions will damage their physical and psychological health and well-being.

The organization Amazon Anonymous was founded in 2013 specifically to campaign against the company's taxation and working practices. It has called for consumers to boycott Amazon and use other retailers for their purchases. Workers and unions have also taken action to highlight the problems in Amazon, and to try and improve pay and working conditions in the company. In February 2013, for example, the GMB union organized protests outside nine of Amazon's warehouses, including Doncaster, Swansea, and Milton Keynes. It says its aim was to draw attention to the low pay offered by Amazon, and to get the company to agree to pay its entire staff a 'living wage'—enough for workers to actually live on. Amazon itself, however, rejects the claims that it is a bad employer, saying that it provides its staff with 'a safe and positive working environment, which includes on-the-job training and opportunities for career progression'. The company also says that its permanent workforce enjoys benefits such as healthcare and pension plans.

Like many US companies, Amazon opposes trade union representation for its staff. When it was becoming established in the UK, it was able to prevent a union presence by using a combination of targeted rewards, the establishment of a staff consultative forum, and threats against employees with strong union sympathies. The assistant secretary of the Scottish Trades Union Congress has claimed that Amazon is a 'predatory, anti-union' employer, which offers jobs with weak employment standards. Since 2013, Amazon workers organized by the Verdi union in Germany have made efforts to improve pay in the company, bringing it into line with the collectively bargained industry rate, something that has included a series of strikes. All this shows that while Amazon clearly makes strenuous efforts to regulate work and employment relationships unilaterally, the experiences of its workers, along with the support from unions and campaigners, have generated a significant degree of contention.

Sources: Kelly and Badigannavar (2004); Boyd (2012); BBC News (2013*a*); BBC Panorama (2013*a*); O' Connor (2013); Bowers (2015); Kantor and Streitfeld (2015); Butler (2016*a*)

Questions

To what extent do you agree with trade unionists who claim that companies like Amazon are bad employers?

What, if anything, should be done to improve employment standards in such companies?

Part 2

The dimensions of employment relations

2 Employment relations in the contemporary economy

Chapter objectives

The main objectives of this chapter are to:

- examine the implications of changes in the economy and labour market for work and employment relations;
- explore the implications of the economic recession and its aftermath for employment relations;
- explain and interpret the rise in self-employment;
- characterize and assess the nature of employment flexibility; and
- explore the nature of occupational change.

2.1 Introduction

This chapter examines the implications for work and employment relations of developments in the contemporary economy, particularly the labour market. Economic and labour market change, by altering the power held by the different parties, exercises a profound influence over work and employment relations. There is a view that there has been a shift towards greater cooperation between employers and workers, reflecting the growth of employment flexibility and the rise of a more knowledge-based economy. However, the economic recession, and the nature of the labour market recovery in its aftermath, highlights just how tenuous this 'new economy' thesis really is when it comes to interpreting changes in work and employment relations.

Section 2.2 provides an overview of the impact of the recession on the economy and the labour market, indicating how increased competitive pressures have encouraged firms to use workers more efficiently. In Section 2.3 the focus is on self-employment and how the rise in the number of self-employed people can be explained and interpreted. While some of the growth in self-employment is the product of enterprising individuals keen to escape the confines of coercive employment relationships and secure greater autonomy for themselves, much of it can be attributed to the lack of alternative employment opportunities and is of rather low quality. Section 2.4 is devoted to flexible employment—covering the topics of temporary and agency work, working time flexibility, and wages. Rather than being an expression of greater mutuality, flexibility has been used by employers to cheapen labour, leaving workers more insecure and vulnerable. Whereas there is undoubtedly a trend towards greater 'knowledge work', Section 2.5 shows that the nature of occupational change is in fact rather complex, with much work and employment continuing to be of an insecure, 'precarious' kind. Overall, the chapter points to the notable extent to which changes in the economy and labour market have contributed to the increased 'commodification' of labour, characterized by the attempts of employers to secure productive effort from workers at the lowest possible cost, and render them more disposable.

 Introductory case study: Migrant worker exploitation and forced labour in the UK food industry

As Chapter 1 shows, an integral feature of work and employment relationships in capitalist market economies in the UK is that individual workers are supposedly at liberty to determine not only whether or not they want to take up an offer of employment from an employer, but also to leave that employment if they wish. Given the dependent status of the worker, however, it is questionable how much freedom or liberty workers really enjoy, especially in relation to an employer. Work and employment relationships generally, then, have a fundamentally coercive character. The concept of 'forced labour', though, tends to be 'associated with slavery-like conditions in poor countries and with the actions of authoritarian states' (Geddes et al. 2013: 3), or with incidents of human trafficking that involve the cross-border transport of undocumented migrants by criminal gangs.

Yet there is a growing appreciation of the extent to which the integral dimensions of forced labour—marked by excessive coercion—are prevalent in some parts of the UK economy. In low-paying sectors which are characterized by high levels of migrant labour—such as food production and processing—employers' demands for flexibility, in the form of a cheap, disposable, and easily substitutable workforce, are so intense as to induce a degree of exploitation and vulnerability that effectively constitutes forced labour (Geddes et al. 2013; Balch 2016).

Despite a high-profile attempt by the UK government to deal with the issue of 'modern slavery' (see Chapter 3), its desire to be 'business-friendly', by privileging employers' flexibility and promoting the virtues of a deregulated labour market, has prevented it from taking sufficiently robust action. Unscrupulous employers enjoy considerable freedom to benefit from a supply of cheap, disposable migrant labour. Not only can this generate extreme levels of exploitation, but it also contributes to an environment in which forced labour flourishes (Balch 2015).

2.2 Work and employment relations: the 'new economy' or 'commodification'?

One of the most important influences on work and employment relations concerns developments in the economy, especially those relating to the changes in the composition of employment and the labour market. There are long-term changes evident, notably the process of de-industrialization and the shift in employment from manufacturing to services. The latter half of the twentieth century saw the decline of staple industries such as coal mining, iron and steel making, and shipbuilding, and also the erosion of the country's manufacturing capacity. There has been a pronounced shift in employment in favour of the service sector—banking, finance, retailing, leisure, and hospitality, for example. See Table 2.1 for details of how

Table 2.1 The proportion of UK jobs in manufacturing and service industries, selected years 1979–2016

Year	Proportion of jobs in manufacturing (%)	Proportion of jobs in services (%)
1979	26.0	61.4
1984	20.5	67.5
1989	18.4	70.0
1994	15.8	74.2
1999	15.0	76.0
2004	11.6	80.0
2008	9.9	80.1
2012	8.1	83.0
2016*	7.8	83.2

* March 2016

Source: Office for National Statistics (http://www.statistics.gov.uk); licensed under the Open Government licence v.3.0

the proportions of manufacturing and services jobs in the economy have changed since the 1980s. Whereas by 2016 only around 8 per cent of the workforce worked in manufacturing (some 2.5 million people), over 80 per cent were based in the service sector. This change in the composition of employment has had some notable consequences for employment relations. For example, trade unions and collective bargaining have less of a presence in private services; therefore the fall in manufacturing employment has been one factor behind their decline (see Chapters 6 and 7).

Any analysis of the economic context, however, also has to encompass developments in the shorter term, most evidently the impact of the 2007–8 global financial crisis, and the subsequent period of economic recession and weak growth. From 2008, many advanced economies experienced a pronounced economic downturn, which was instigated by the collapse in 2007 of the sub-prime mortgage market in the United States, followed by the failure of a number of major banks and investment firms (Mason 2009; Stiglitz 2010; Krugman 2012; Wolf 2014). As a consequence, the UK economy went into a steep decline, resulting in a recession which was the 'longest and deepest since the 1930s' (Lansley 2012: 5). In one calendar year alone—2009—gross domestic product (GDP) fell by 4.2 per cent.

The then Labour government, under the premiership of Gordon Brown, took a series of measures to counteract the recession, which were successful in restoring economic growth in 2010. Its successor, the Conservative–Liberal Democrat coalition government, which took office in May 2010, instituted a strict deficit-reduction plan—mainly involving cuts in public expenditure (a so-called 'austerity' programme)—to tackle the substantial deficit that had arisen in the government's accounts and thus regain the confidence of the international financial markets (Williams and Scott 2016a). However, it soon became evident that the coalition's emphasis on austerity, far from stimulating an economic recovery, in fact delayed it for a period of two years. The result was much lost growth. Another recession was only narrowly avoided, before the government changed direction and eased off on austerity from 2012 onwards (Hannon 2016).

Table 2.2 UK unemployment, selected years 1979–2016

Year	Total unemployed	Unemployment rate (%)
1979	1,432,000	5.4
1984	3,241,000	11.8
1989	2,082,000	7.2
1994	2,675,000	9.5
1999	1,728,000	6.0
2004	1,465,000	4.8
2008	1,777,000	5.7
2012	2,555,000	8.0
2016*	1,630,000	4.9

* May–July 2016

Source: Office for National Statistics (http://www.statistics.gov.uk); licensed under the Open Government licence v.3.0

Economic recessions have pronounced adverse consequences for jobs. The recession of the early 1980s, for example, which hit the strongly unionized manufacturing sector particularly hard, generated a high level of unemployment. Between 1979 and 1984, the number of recorded unemployed rose from under 1.5 million (5.4 per cent of the workforce) to over 3 million (11.8 per cent). During the late 1990s and early 2000s, though, unemployment fell markedly, to less than 5 per cent of the workforce in 2004 (see Table 2.2). However, between 2008 and 2012 unemployment grew again by nearly 800,000, to 2.5 million—from 5.7 per cent to 8.0 per cent of the workforce (see Table 2.2). Young workers were particularly badly hit (Lansley 2012). Unemployment among 18–24 year olds increased by 53 per cent between 2008 and 2012; by the end of 2012 around a fifth of workers in this age group (over 800,000 young people) were unemployed.

From 2013 onwards, there was evidence of an economic recovery in the UK. In 2014 the economy grew by 2.8 per cent, an impressive figure relative to other countries. The positive news on growth seemed to be reflected in the labour market (Blanchflower 2015). There was a marked decline in unemployment between 2012 and 2016, with the unemployment rate falling to just 4.9 per cent, the lowest for over a decade (see Table 2.2). In the period between 2010 and 2014, some 1.4 million new private sector jobs were created. Not only were a record number of people in employment—some 31 million in 2015—but the rate of employment (the proportion of people aged between 16 and 64 who are in employment) also rose to a record high—reaching 73 per cent (Hannon 2016).

However, such seemingly positive news on the economy and jobs perhaps masks some more profound underlying economic and labour market weaknesses. Concerns have been raised about the fragility of the UK's economic recovery: that it is too dependent on consumer spending and an inflating housing market, with manufacturing remaining weak (Hannon 2016; Williams, Scott, and Welch 2016). Moreover, by 2015, and especially the early part of 2016, there were signs that the rate of economic growth was falling. The economic implications of so-called 'Brexit', following the June 2016 referendum vote which narrowly went in favour of the UK leaving the European Union (EU), remain to be seen, although many experts predict lower growth in the medium to long term.

The labour market, though, appeared to remain buoyant, reflected in the falling rate of unemployment. Yet a closer look at the kind of jobs that have been created since the recession not only raises some important doubts about the nature of the supposed jobs recovery, but also points to some underlying weaknesses in the labour market. Although the headline figure of unemployment may have fallen markedly, there are over 3 million workers who are 'underemployed'—that is, unable to work as many hours as they want (see Section 2.4.2). Much recent employment growth has been on a supposedly self-employed basis, and some strong concerns have been expressed about the poor quality of such work (see Section 2.3). And many workers without jobs are part of the 'hidden' unemployed. For example, around 40 per cent of the 2.5 million people receiving incapacity benefits could be in a position to re-enter the workforce, but they are often based in areas of the country, like parts of the North of England and South Wales, where there are few jobs available (Lansley 2011).

Before the recession of the late 2000s, there were claims that profound changes in work and employment relations were occurring, part of a shift to a so-called 'new economy' marked by a greater degree of cooperation between workers and employers. Three developments appeared to stand out. First, the employment relationship itself seemed to be diminishing in importance, given the increasing number of people who apparently work without one, in particular as supposedly autonomous and independent self-employed freelance contractors. Second, a dramatic shift towards more flexible forms of employment was held to be occurring, exemplifying a supposed greater mutuality of interests at work. Flexibility not only enables employers to manage labour more efficiently, but also gives workers more choice over their working arrangements. Third, changes in employment, most notably in the occupational structure, seemed to be transforming the nature of work itself, leading to a 'knowledge economy', characterized by an increase in the proportion of people engaged in 'knowledge work'.

These developments supposedly portend a shift away from emphasizing the inherent conflict of interest that exists between workers and employers to a more unitary concern with shared interests and consensus. However, the economic downturn and its effects highlight how this 'new economy' thesis is really quite tenuous when it comes to interpreting changes in work and employment relations. As the remainder of this chapter demonstrates, the principal trend has rather been towards the greater 'commodification' of labour (Grimshaw 2015), something which not only challenges the assumption that employment relations is now characterized by a greater degree of cooperation between workers and employers, but actually implies greater scope for conflict.

What is meant by the term 'commodification'? As Chapter 1 shows, labour itself is not a conventional commodity; when employing workers employers purchase their capacity to engage in productive effort, which involves 'managerial' as well as 'market' relations (Flanders 1975). In the contemporary economy, however, efficiency imperatives mean that employers increasingly look to reduce the cost of employing labour, exposing workers to market forces, making them disposable, and rendering them more insecure and vulnerable. This process of commodification is manifest in efforts by employers to cheapen labour—through attempts to secure increases in workers' effort at the least possible cost—eschewing any obligations to their workforces and undermining their rights, for the purpose of increasing efficiency. The success of firms such as Sports Direct (see the end-of-chapter case study) is to a large extent predicated on commodifying labour.

 Section summary and further reading

- Long-term economic trends, such as the shift in employment from manufacturing to services, have important implications for work and employment relations.

- The financial crisis of 2007–8 and the subsequent economic recession had a profound impact on employment relations. Although the economy has begun to recover since 2013, and employment has grown, the recovery is nonetheless fragile and masks some underlying weaknesses in the labour market.

- Prior to the recession there were claims made about the development of a 'new' economy, marked by greater levels of self-employment, flexibility, and 'knowledge' work, all of which imply a more cooperative climate of work and employment relations. However, in the light of the recession and its aftermath, and in the context of a weak labour market, there has been a notable process of labour commodification, which highlights the important potential for conflict inherent in work and employment relationships.

For an overview of key economic and labour market trends and developments in the aftermath of the 2007–8 financial crisis and subsequent recession, see Blanchflower (2015) and Hannon (2016).

2.3 Self-employment: a harbinger of the 'new economy'?

One of the most striking recent labour market trends concerns the pronounced increase in the number of self-employed workers in the UK, particularly since the 2007–8 global financial crisis and subsequent economic recession. To a large extent, employment growth since the recession has been driven by increasing self-employment (Hatfield 2015; Hannon 2016; ONS 2016c). According to one study, over two-fifths (44 per cent) of new jobs created between 2010 and 2015 were organized on a self-employed basis (TUC 2015a). Of the 118,000 new full-time jobs created between March and May 2016, 104,000 (88 per cent) were self-employed positions (Farrell 2016).

On the one hand, the rise in self-employment can be viewed in positive terms. It reflects the shift towards a new economy which is marked by the growing propensity of individual workers to be entrepreneurial, preferring to work for themselves, rather than coming under the authority of a single employer. Moreover, the development of new digital platforms make it easier for workers to operate on a freelance, self-employed basis, giving them greater scope to create, and benefit from, opportunities to market and sell their labour power to customers.

On the other hand, though, there is plentiful evidence to suggest that for the most part the recent substantial growth in self-employment has been a function of the lack of alternative job opportunities in a weak labour market, accentuated by the way many employers have looked to reduce their costs by insisting that workers are hired on a cheaper, ostensibly

Table 2.3 Self-employment in the UK, 1984–2016

Year	No. of self-employed (000s)	Self-employed as a proportion of all those in employment (%)
1984	2,695	11.1
1988	3,216	12.3
1992	3,447	13.5
1996	3,506	13.5
2000	3,256	11.8
2004	3,618	12.7
2008	3,826	13.0
2012	4,194	14.2
2016*	4,756	15.0

* May–July

Source: Office for National Statistics (http://www.statistics.gov.uk); licensed under the Open Government licence v.3.0

self-employed basis, rather than directly as employees. Attention has also been drawn to the poor quality of many self-employed jobs, particularly in terms of endemic low pay and high levels of insecurity. From this perspective, increasing self-employment is more a manifestation of the greater commodification of labour, and not the rise of a new, more enterprise-based economy.

2.3.1 The rise of self-employment

One of the most prominent features of debates about the development of the 'new economy' concerns the supposedly greater significance of work undertaken by self-employed freelance contractors who are—in theory anyway—liberated from the constraints associated with being in a relationship with, and thus under the control of, a single employer (Handy 1994; Leadbeater 1999). As can be seen from Table 2.3, between the mid-1980s and mid-1990s the number of self-employed people in the UK grew by nearly a million. Self-employment was supported by successive Conservative governments, who viewed its growth, and also that of small businesses in general, as the mark of a dynamic and competitive economy in which enterprise thrived (Goss 1991). It became a particularly prominent feature of some industries, such as the media and IT sectors (Platman 2004; Tremblay and Genin 2010).

Despite the claimed benefits of self-employment and freelance working arrangements, the number of self-employed scarcely grew between the early 1990s and mid-2000s, fluctuating at a level close to the 3.5 million mark (see Table 2.3). The table also shows that the proportion of self-employed actually fell during the late 1990s, to under 12 per cent of the workforce, before gradually rising again in the 2000s, to 13 per cent in 2008. There was little appetite on the part of most workers to go freelance and become self-employed contractors (McGovern et al. 2007), particularly during a period of economic growth when jobs were relatively abundant.

From around 2008, however, a significant change was evident, with a marked, rapid increase in the number of self-employed. Table 2.3 shows that between 2008 and 2016 there was an increase in the number of self-employed to over 4.7 million, with the proportion of the workforce in self-employment increasing to 15 per cent. Some have claimed that this rise in self-employment can, at least in part, be attributed to greater demands from workers for flexibility, autonomy, and independence (Hatfield 2015). There is evidence that most self-employed workers enjoy working for themselves, not least because it seems to offer increased scope to engage in meaningful, more creative work (Dellot and Reed 2015). Undoubtedly, many workers make a deliberate and positive choice in favour of becoming self-employed; the freedom and flexibility that self-employment offers is viewed as highly desirable (Barley and Kunda 2004; Kirkpatrick and Hoque 2006; Citizens Advice 2015; Hatfield 2015), including the supposed ability to turn down offers of work. In the media industry, for example, many freelance workers welcome the autonomy they believe comes from being self-employed (Platman 2004).

However, the degree of control enjoyed by self-employed contractors varies according to factors such as their market situation. For example, self-employed translators with a wide client base have a rather high degree of autonomy, since they are not dependent on a small number of companies for work. Freelance editors and proofreaders, though, generally work for just one or two publishing clients and are dependent on them for commissions (Stanworth and Stanworth 1995; Fraser and Gold 2001). Moreover, it is important not to exaggerate the benefits of self-employment, since it can be associated with inferior employment conditions, like the absence of paid holidays, and may also be a source of considerable insecurity (Kirkpatrick and Hoque 2006; D'Arcy and Gardiner 2014).

The rapid growth in self-employment since 2008 by no means heralds a shift to a new economy in the manner anticipated by those who view freelance contracting as a reflection of positive choices by workers keen to secure greater autonomy. For one thing, changes in the structure of the labour market appear to be one of the factors that have driven self-employed numbers upwards. These include the fact that the workforce is ageing, as older workers increasingly opt to remain in the labour market as an alternative to, or as part of a phased, retirement—but just not as employees. In addition, fewer people seem to be leaving self-employment (D'Arcy and Gardiner 2014; Hatfield 2015; ONS 2014a). There is also a strong body of evidence which suggests that the growth in self-employment has been fuelled by the weak state of the labour market and the absence of directly employed job opportunities caused by the economic recession and the subsequent period of low growth (CIPD 2012; TUC 2015a). Concerns have been raised about the poor quality of many self-employed jobs, with workers often operating as so-called 'odd-jobbers', 'picking up whatever bits and pieces of work are available', such as selling goods online, in the absence of good quality and secure positions as employees (CIPD 2012: 2; TUC 2015a; Hannon 2016).

In addition, while genuine self-employment is commonplace in some parts of the economy, particularly in sectors like media, publishing, and IT, in others it is often a function of organizations' decisions to divest themselves of responsibility for operating services on an in-house basis rather than a reflection of an increased entrepreneurial desire on the part of workers to become self-employed. For companies such as City Link (see Insight into practice 2.1) there are advantages in hiring workers on an ostensibly self-employed basis, rather than directly as employees. Perhaps most importantly, it can reduce labour costs. Firms do not have to pay workers' National Insurance contributions, for example, or meet the cost of providing a range of statutory employment rights, such as paid annual leave.

More profoundly, in operating such arrangements firms ensure that workers themselves have to bear more of the risks of employment. This is particularly evident when it comes to cases of 'bogus' self-employment (see Section 2.3.2), which exemplify the important extent to which rising levels of self-employment have driven the commodification of labour—some firms have taken advantage of the recession and weak labour market to operate with cheaper and more flexible sources of labour in order to reduce their costs. In general, the self-employed tend to exhibit higher levels of insecurity and vulnerability than employees (D'Arcy and Gardiner 2014).

Their income is often lower too. Studies demonstrate that not only do self-employed workers earn on average substantially less than employees, but also there was a considerable decline—of some 22 per cent—in the average earnings of the self-employed in the period between 2008–9 and 2014 (D'Arcy and Gardiner 2014; ONS 2014a; TUC 2015a). This would seem to confirm that a large proportion of new self-employed positions created during the recession and its aftermath were of the low-paid, 'odd-jobber' type (Blanchflower 2015). Moreover, diminished average earnings for the self-employed seem to have made a notable contribution to the overall falling living standards in the recession and post-recessionary period (Hannon 2016)—see Section 2.4.3. For the TUC (2014a), the growth in self-employment came 'at the expense of more secure employee jobs. Many newly self-employed workers do the same work as employees but with less job security, poorer working conditions and often less take-home pay'. This is exemplified by the use of 'bogus' self-employment arrangements that contribute to the commodification of labour.

2.3.2 **Bogus self-employment**

The concept of 'bogus' self-employment refers to the way in which much work that is supposedly arranged on a self-employed basis is in reality simply disguised employment—at a lower cost to the employer. Bogus self-employment is a long-standing feature of some parts of the economy. In the construction industry, for example, firms often hire staff as supposedly self-employed contractors when in fact the workers are managed, and operate, as if they are directly employed (Behling and Harvey 2015; Seely 2015). The construction union UCATT estimates that around half of all workers in the construction industry are falsely self-employed (UCATT no date). In the hairdressing sector, workers are often expected to hire what are supposedly their own chairs on the premises of salons.

Pushing workers into bogus self-employment enables firms to realize cost savings. Yet this often leaves workers manifestly more exposed and vulnerable. They are obliged to take on more of the risks and costs of employment, given the unwillingness of companies to enter into a long-term and direct relationship with them. As supposedly self-employed contractors, workers are not entitled to a wide range of employment rights, including access to holiday pay, sick pay, redundancy pay, and the right to be paid the National Minimum Wage. And although workers are often dependent on client companies for work, these companies have no reciprocal obligations to them beyond the terms of the immediate contract.

There are a range of tests which can be used to determine whether or not someone is genuinely self-employed. Can they decide what work they undertake, when, and how? Can they turn down work tasks? Can they hire somebody else to do the work instead of them? Do they work for more than one client? If the answer to questions like these is 'yes' then the person concerned is likely to be truly self-employed, in the sense of working for him or herself. Yet workers are often given no choice by an employer as to their employment status, simply being instructed to work on a self-employed basis, even when applying the relevant tests would see them classified very clearly as employees (Citizens Advice 2015). The collapse of the delivery company City Link in December 2014 highlights some of the adverse consequences of bogus self-employment for workers—see Insight into practice 2.1.

 Insight into practice 2.1: The collapse of City Link

Founded in 1969, and operating from over fifty depots across the UK, on Christmas Eve 2014 the delivery company City Link went into administration, with most of its workers finding out about the firm's collapse the following day. The business had racked up substantial losses over previous years, before being bought by a private equity firm in 2013. The leader of the RMT union called the decision to enter administration the 'bitterest blow any group of workers could receive on Christmas Day'. A week later, on New Year's Eve 2014, it was announced that the overwhelming majority of City Link's staff—some 2,300 employees—were to be made redundant. However, the firm also used around 1,000 'service delivery partners', mainly delivery drivers, hired on a self-employed basis, who, because they were not classified as employees, were not entitled to any redundancy payments. Moreover, some of these supposedly self-employed workers lost thousands of pounds in unpaid earnings from work they had undertaken before the firm went into administration. Not only were they unaware that City Link was in trouble—indeed they appear to have been conned into thinking it was trading healthily—but they had also been asked to work additional hours, and thus take on extra costs, in the busy pre-Christmas period.

The collapse of City Link casts light on the dubious practice of bogus self-employment in the delivery sector. It is an expanding area of the economy; but fierce competition between delivery firms has resulted in strong pressures to cut costs, with bogus self-employment becoming a popular arrangement as a consequence. It is claimed that self-employed status motivates delivery workers to work hard for themselves and thus increase their earnings, by more than if they were employed on a regular salary. However, such workers are also exposed to much greater risk. In the case of City Link, they were required to lease a van, pay for a company uniform, and operate to a delivery schedule that rarely provided them with anything like the advertised headline earnings. If self-employed drivers were unable to work for any reason, then they would receive no income, and risked falling into debt.

Sources: BBC News (2014*a*); House of Commons (2015); O'Connor and Barrett (2015); Rankin and Butler (2015)

The recessionary economic climate prompted a growing incidence of bogus self-employment, as unscrupulous employers looked to take advantage of the weak labour market to push more of the costs of employment onto workers and avoid having to respect their employment rights (TUC 2015*a*). One estimate suggests that close to half a million workers are falsely self-employed (Citizens Advice 2015). The practice of bogus self-employment appears to have spread to parts of the economy where it was previously little known, such as the food-processing sector (Leighton and Wynn 2011). There have been substantial increases in self-employment in both the care and cleaning sectors—areas which traditionally used very few self-employed workers—as 'rogue' and 'unscrupulous' employers have made use of the legal ambiguities around determining people's employment status to exploit workers (Citizens Advice 2015).

One of the UK's leading courier companies—CitySprint—hires workers as self-employed contractors; as such they are not entitled to be paid the National Minimum Wage. Yet to all intents and purposes they are managed as employees: workers wear the company uniform, have to register for work each day, have a regular series of jobs which are scheduled by CitySprint, and have their performance monitored. Such falsely self-employed workers have freedom all right—the 'freedom to be controlled and abused' (Chakrabortty 2016a). Employers use bogus self-employment arrangements to deny workers their legitimate employment rights, to underpay them, and dispose of them as required, while at the same time still expecting them to comply with managerial instructions as if they were employees. This exemplifies efforts by employers to treat workers as if they are little more than commodities, deemed as disposable, and to whom they owe few, if any, obligations.

Bogus self-employment not only has some highly adverse consequences for workers, but it also creates some broader economic problems. In construction, for example, false self-employment has been linked to a shortage of skills, in as much as it constitutes a barrier to training and development activities. Firms claiming not to employ workers are unlikely to be interested in supporting them when it comes to acquiring new skills. In this way, then, the practice of bogus self-employment, based on cheapening and commodifying labour, militates against innovation and hinders progress towards improving long-term economic competitiveness (Behling and Harvey 2015). Furthermore, firms which 'aim to do the right thing and want to employ their staff legitimately, face a competitive disadvantage' (Citizens Advice 2015: 3). This is because they face the prospect of being undercut by employers who can provide a cheaper service by avoiding the costs of employing staff directly.

2.3.3 Self-employment in the 'gig economy'

To what extent does the rise of digital labour platforms enable workers to benefit from selling their labour power to clients on a self-employed basis? New digital, mobile technologies have the potential to affect work and employment relations in some profound ways. In particular, it is claimed that they give workers manifold opportunities to offer their skills, talent, and expertise to clients directly, in return for an agreed payment, without the need for this relationship to be mediated by an employing organization. The so-called 'gig economy', in which workers and clients contract with one another in one-off market transactions, would seem to embody a shift towards greater mutuality, in that the self-employed worker has the ultimate choice over whether or not he or she wants to undertake a work assignment, and is not subject to the confines of a coercive employment relationship (Degryse 2016).

The most well-known digital labour platform is the transport service Uber, which only started in 2009, and yet by 2016 operated in more than 400 cities across seventy-two countries (*The Economist* 2016). Uber claims its role is to 'connect drivers with riders'. To do this it operates a mobile app which allows registered users to request a trip using their smartphones. An algorithm routes the request to the nearest available driver and calculates a price for the trip, based on current levels of local supply and demand, out of which Uber takes a sizeable cut. The most important detail, for our purposes, is that Uber claims not to directly employ any of its drivers; instead they are 'independent contractors' or 'driver-partners', working for themselves, who offer 'ride-shares'. Other digital labour platforms, such as UpWork, Handy, and TaskRabbit, which match clients needing services or tasks performed with workers potentially willing to undertake them, also disclaim any role as an employer (Degryse 2016). Firms like Uber and UpWork claim to operate simply as platforms, offering a frictionless marketplace within which workers and clients can transact with one another. The self-employed basis of the assignments is claimed to be liberating for workers. On its website Uber asserts that:

> When you drive with Uber, you decide when and how long to work. So you'll never have to choose between earning a living and living life. It's easy to make money helping people get around. How much is completely up to you. With so many riders in every city, there's op-portunity at every turn.

There is little doubt about the popularity of online labour platforms. One estimate suggests that some 5 million people in the UK are in some way involved in the gig economy. The most popular kind of work undertaken involves online work that can be undertaken at home, often so-called 'click work', such as tagging pictures. But offline work activities (e.g. cleaning and driving tasks) are also commonly organized through digital labour platforms (Huws and Joyce 2016). However, there have been cautions against some of the 'exaggerated claims being made by some about the impact of the gig economy' (Brinkley 2016: 12). Perhaps only around one in twenty workers regularly secure work through online platforms, although this figure could rise as the gig economy expands.

Enthusiasts for the gig economy emphasize the potential of digital labour platforms to transform work and employment relations in a highly positive way. They point to a future where, with the widespread diffusion of mobile digital devices such as smartphones, work-ers no longer need to be confined to a coercive employment relationship; rather they have greater opportunities to work for themselves, as empowered freelance contractors, able to freely choose what work they want to undertake, who to undertake work for, and when it is undertaken. The take-away food service Deliveroo, for example, promises its self-employed delivery workers 'flexible shifts and competitive pay' and the freedom to 'work to your own schedule'.

There is some evidence that workers value the freedom and flexibility provided by plat-forms like Uber (Knight 2016). However, there is a growing appreciation that, far from trans-forming work for the better, digital labour platforms simply accentuate some of the most undesirable features of work and employment relationships in ways that increase the com-modification of labour. For one thing, digital platforms operate as marketplaces in ways that are distinctly unfavourable to workers—a function of a highly asymmetrical power relation-ship. They do this by encouraging workers to bid for work, and thus undercut one another, reducing the potential for earnings and eroding labour standards (Labour Research 2016). Income from jobs in the gig economy is generally rather modest (Huws and Joyce 2016). De-spite the promise of 'competitive' pay rates, generally those working for Deliveroo only barely make the minimum wage (Stern 2015).

A further difficulty concerns the claim that workers hired through digital platforms are, as supposedly self-employed contractors, free from the confines of a coercive employment re-lationship. Yet firms such as Uber operate highly sophisticated feedback systems, which allow clients to rate the performance of workers, and these then influence how many more 'gigs', and of what kind, they get in future (Knight 2016). Uber drivers whose ratings are considered too low run the risk of being 'deactivated', and thus barred from receiving further work. Many claim that with so many regulations governing their activities Uber treats them as if they were directly employed by the company (*The Economist* 2015). This is further evidence of an asymmetrical power relationship which operates to the disadvantage of workers.

Moreover, like self-employed workers in general, workers operating as supposed freelancers in the 'gig economy' do not benefit from the legal rights that accrue to employees, such as the right to be paid the minimum wage, the right not to be unfairly dismissed, and the right to paid holidays. Part of the reason that firms like Uber have enjoyed huge commercial success so quickly is because they refuse to acknowledge that they have any kind of responsibility towards their workers, such as an obligation to respect their statutory employment rights (Degryse 2016). The digital economy offers workers new opportunities, to be sure; but this comes at the expense of greater risk, insecurity, and vulnerability.

Contesting employment relations 2.2:   Challenging Uber

The rise of Uber, the controversial transport company, which in many ways exemplifies the rise of the digital platform economy, has not gone unchallenged. Regulatory authorities have prohibited Uber from operating in some parts of Europe, such as in France, the Netherlands, and Germany, generally because the way its mobile app operates is held to breach strict legislation governing taxi services. Both in the UK and elsewhere, Uber's business model has been challenged by workers and unions who claim that the company's insistence that its drivers work for themselves as independent self-employed contractors is bogus. Uber in fact exercises strict control over the drivers that use its service, to the extent that it 'deactivates' those whose ratings fall too low or who reject too many jobs. Supported by the GMB union, Uber drivers in the UK have filed legal claims for paid holidays and minimum wage protection. Some have also protested against an increase in the fees charged to drivers by Uber. Even in California, Uber's home state, the company has faced mounting legal challenges, including a lawsuit from a group of Uber drivers claiming that they should be classified as employees, and thus be entitled to the appropriate rights and benefits, rather than self-employed contractors. In some instances opponents of Uber have opted for more direct action. In February 2015, for example, London black cab taxi drivers blocked streets with their cars as part of a protest against what they perceive as unfair competition from Uber—Uber drivers are not subject to anything like the same kind of regulatory requirements, in terms of matters like background checks and insurance for example, as licensed taxi drivers. The biggest protests have occurred in France. In January 2016, for example, thousands of taxi drivers demonstrated against Uber as part of a broader, national one-day strike in opposition to the French government's economic policies.

Sources: The Economist (2015); Harris (2015); Helier (2015); Chrisafis (2016); Hook (2016); Labour Research (2016)

There has been some speculation that digital labour platforms operate in ways that are akin to the 'sharing economy', whereby online mechanisms enable individuals and communities with shared interests to connect and collaborate with each other and forge stronger social ties, to the benefit of all (*The Economist* 2015). But this appears to be highly misplaced. There is nothing 'sharing' about the way that companies like Uber, Deliveroo, and so on exploit the labour power of workers. Like any conventional employer, they make use of workers to extract value and secure a return, in the form of revenue. What is distinctive about the digital labour platforms, however, is the extreme degree to which they reject any idea that they might have a responsibility to the workers without whom, when all is said and done, they would not have a business at all. Left unchecked, the spread of the gig economy has the potential to markedly increase the extent to which labour is commodified. No wonder the activities of companies like Uber have proved to be so controversial—see Contesting employment relations 2.2.

Section summary and further reading

- Self-employment is often thought to exemplify the development of a 'new economy', marked by a growing spirit of enterprise on the part of individual workers who prefer to work for themselves, rather than operate within the confines of a conventional employment relationship. However, it is often more a function of the absence of alternative employment opportunities, particularly in a weak, post-recession labour market.

- The number of self-employed workers in the UK has risen significantly in the period since the recession of the late 2000s. However, much new self-employment appears to be of a rather low quality, and there has been a substantial decline in the average income of the self-employed.

- Much new self-employment would appear to be bogus, in the sense that it is used by unscrupulous employers to disguise a standard employment relationship, in order to reduce the costs associated with providing employment rights and paying tax and welfare contributions.

- The rise of digital labour platforms has been hailed by some as providing an opportunity for supposedly self-employed workers to benefit from the gig economy by allowing them to sell their labour power directly to clients. However, platforms like Uber are marked by a pronounced asymmetrical power relationship, which renders workers insecure, vulnerable, and ultimately highly disposable.

D'Arcy and Gardiner (2014) offer the best analysis of the post-recessionary rise of self-employment in the UK. For the phenomenon of bogus self-employment, see studies undertaken by the TUC (2015*a*) and Citizens Advice (2015). There is little available so far on the implications of the rise of digital labour platforms for work and employment relations. The best coverage of the relevant issues is provided by Degryse (2016).

2.4 Flexibility in work and employment relations

The growing prevalence of 'flexible' employment arrangements, particularly temporary and part-time working schedules, might appear to symbolize the increasingly cooperative basis of work and employment relations in the 'new economy' of the twenty-first century. For employers, flexible employment offers scope for efficiency savings, allowing them to pay staff only when work is needed, in a way that is responsive to fluctuations in demand (van Wanrooy et al. 2013*b*). Moreover, one of the most powerful arguments in favour of flexible employment arrangements is that, in addition to providing benefits for employers, they allow people to exercise greater choice over their working lives—for example by enabling workers to reconcile caring responsibilities with paid employment (Warren, Pascall, and Fox 2010).

In challenging the assumption that flexible forms of employment necessarily embody greater mutuality in work and employment relations, more critical interpretations view flexibility as less about operating innovative employment arrangements that satisfy the interests of both workers and employers, and more about the search for a cheaper and more disposable workforce, which is expected to work more intensively (e.g. Beynon et al. 2002). From this perspective, the greater use of flexible employment arrangements, particularly when they are operated for managerial purposes, often contributes to the commodification of labour. This is a trend which is particularly apparent when we look at how employers have attempted to secure flexibility and improve their competitiveness by instituting wage freezes, pay cuts, and, in some cases, not paying workers for their efforts at all—a particularly egregious way of cheapening labour.

2.4.1 Numerical flexibility: temporary employment and agency labour

When it comes to temporary employment arrangements, one way in which employers can try to gain flexibility is by using directly employed staff, but hiring them on fixed-term contracts. This numerical flexibility allows managers to take on new staff to fill a vacancy, or to meet an unanticipated short-term rise in demand, without committing them to a long-term relationship. Yet the use of this type of flexibility is rather modest, and there is no evidence of any notable increase in temporary employment arrangements. While the share of temporary employment rose during the early 1990s, to 7.1 per cent of the workforce in 1994, it fell back to just 5.5 per cent by 2008, before gradually increasing again up to 2012 in the context of the economic downturn and then stabilizing at just over 6 per cent of the workforce—some 1.6 million workers (see Table 2.4). In 2004 just over one-fifth (22 per cent) of workplaces contained some employees on fixed-term and temporary contracts; seven years later, in 2011, the proportion was largely the same (23 per cent) (van Wanrooy et al. 2013a). However, the use of fixed-term contracts is particularly common in the public services, especially health and education, where funding uncertainties and budgetary constraints often conspire to make it difficult for employers to offer staff a permanent contract (Beynon et al. 2002). Fixed-term or temporary contracts are used in over a half of public sector workplaces (51 per cent), but just a fifth (21 per cent) of workplaces in the private sector make use of them (van Wanrooy et al. 2013b).

What accounts for the lack of any significant increase in the use of directly-employed, temporary staff? One reason is that European Union (EU) legislation, which obliges employers to treat temporary staff no less favourably than their permanent equivalents when it comes

Table 2.4 The proportion of temporary employees and part-time workers in the UK, selected years 1984–2016

Year	Temporary employees (%)	Part-time workers (%)
1984	5.5	21.0
1989	5.5	22.3
1994	7.1	24.5
1999	7.1	25.1
2004	6.1	25.9
2008	5.5	25.3
2012	6.4	27.3
2016*	6.2	26.4

* May–July

Source: Office for National Statistics (http://www.statistics.gov.uk); licensed under the Open Government licence v.3.0

to matters like pay, means that some of the cost benefits associated with using this form of flexible employment have diminished. A further explanation is that because of the economic climate many employers, particularly in the public sector, have opted to save money instead by not filling vacant positions; as employees' fixed-term contracts expire, they are less likely to be replaced than was previously the case.

As Table 2.4 shows, there is some evidence that the prevalence of temporary working rose in the aftermath of the recession. Some of this was of an involuntary nature as workers took up short-term casual positions when faced with the paucity of permanent jobs (Gregg and Gardiner 2015; TUC 2015a; Hannon 2016). There are also claims that temporary working is actually rather more common than official statistics show. This is because much temporary agency working goes unreported (TUC 2015a). Employers can look to secure numerical flexibility not just by hiring temporary labour themselves, but also by making use of external employment agencies.

Agency temps are a common feature of some parts of the economy—in the construction industry, for example (Purcell, Purcell, and Tailby 2004; Forde, MacKenzie, and Robinson 2008), and in other sectors where migrant workers comprise a large proportion of the workforce, such as hotels, food processing, cleaning, social care, and agriculture (James and Lloyd 2008; McDowell, Batnitzky, and Dyer 2008; Knox 2010; McKay and Markova 2010; Hopkins 2014; Potter and Hamilton 2014). The agency employs the workers, or may hire them as ostensibly self-employed contractors, thus sparing the organization the costs, such as holiday pay, and duties that come with being an employer. According to official estimates there are some 300,000 temporary agency workers in the UK, around 1 per cent of the workforce (Forde and Slater 2014). However, this figure is widely reckoned to be a substantial underestimate, with the true number likely to be in excess of a million—over 3 per cent of the workforce (TUC 2015a).

Using temporary agency labour benefits employers in a number of ways, most importantly in relation to cost savings and greater flexibility. Such workers often have lower pay, worse employment conditions, and fewer employment rights than their directly employed counterparts. Hiring agency labour can also be a relatively efficient way of accommodating short-term fluctuations in demand, or even, in some cases, of filling vacancies (McKay and Markova 2010; TUC 2015a). In the food-processing industry, for example, pressures from powerful supermarket chains for reductions in costs, combined with highly unpredictable, short-term variations in demand, require agency workers who can be hired on a temporary—sometimes daily—basis (Hopkins 2014).

In theory, workers can choose whether or not they want to take on an assignment, thus enabling them to work in a flexible manner of their own choice. In reality, however, the mutuality embodied in this vision of the temporary assignment is rarely evident. Studies of temporary agency working highlight how agencies reward people whom they perceive to be good performers with regular assignments. Workers who refuse assignments, however, are less likely to be offered future work (Forde 2001; Sporton 2013).

One of the most distinctive features of temporary agency labour is that it is marked by a 'triangular' relationship, involving not just the employer and the worker, but also a third-party intermediary in the form of the agency (Forde and Slater 2014; Strauss and Fudge 2014). By hiring staff through agencies, employers secure flexibility by disclaiming any obligations towards the workers engaged in this way, who have fewer rights and protections, and rendering them highly disposable (Theodore and Peck 2014). Daily hiring is often the norm. One study showed how agencies 'telephoned workers the day or the evening before work to tell them when, and where, they would be working the following day' (Sporton 2013: 451). Agency workers are often preferred because they are viewed as being more disposable. See Contesting employment relations 2.3 for how one company, in this case BMW, responded to the difficulties arising from the recession by dismissing its agency workforce. They were, in the words of one of those who were sacked, treated as 'second-class' workers.

 Contesting employment relations 2.3: Agency workers and employment flexibility at BMW

Faced with rapidly declining car sales as a result of the economic recession, in February 2009 BMW ended weekend working at its Cowley plant near Oxford, which makes the Mini. Some 850 agency workers were sacked with just one hour's warning. Because they were not employed directly by BMW, the agency staff enjoyed few employment rights, and were not entitled to any redundancy pay. They were simply paid one week's wages to cover the notice period. Yet many members of the supposedly 'temporary' workforce had worked in the plant for several years. One agency worker said he had been treated like a 'second-class' employee: 'I've worked here for three and a half years and now I'm being sacked for no reason. I've been used.' Angry workers reportedly booed and threw fruit at BMW managers on hearing that they were to lose their jobs. While there is now European Union legislation which gives agency workers more rights (see Chapter 3), it did not come into force until 2011, and would not have given the workers affected by BMW's shift closure much additional protection anyway. This case shows that the benefits of employment flexibility, which in this case amounted to the freedom enjoyed by BMW to dismiss workers as easily as possible, are often one-sided in favour of employers.

Sources: BBC News (2009*b*, 2009*c*); Macalister and Pidd (2009).

There are numerous well-documented reports regarding the highly exploitative treatment experienced by agency workers, especially migrant workers (e.g. TUC 2007; Wilkinson 2012; Sporton 2013; Gentleman 2014; Potter and Hamilton 2014). They demonstrate the important extent to which employment flexibility is often synonymous with low pay, poor working conditions, extreme work pressures, and a high level of job insecurity (James and Lloyd 2008; McKay and Markova 2010). In the agriculture and food-processing sectors, fierce competitive pressures and highly unpredictable and variable patterns of demand have created the conditions under which migrant agency workers are often used as a source of cheap and disposable labour (MAC 2014; Strauss 2014). Hiring staff through agencies enables the agriculture and food companies to avoid any responsibility towards the migrant workers they use to carry out their business activities (Gentleman 2014).

Because of their ambiguous legal status, undocumented migrant workers are particularly susceptible to ill treatment by agencies. See the introductory case study for details of concerns relating to the alleged use of forced labour in some parts of the UK economy. A recent study of the Northern Ireland mushroom industry identified a pervasive 'climate of fear' prevalent among the largely migrant agency workforce (Potter and Hamilton 2014: 397), which was stoked by the often duplicitous behaviour of the agencies themselves, which failed to respect workers' statutory employment rights. As one female worker observed:

> There's no overtime pay, holiday pay, sick pay, maternity pay, or unsocial hours pay

(Potter and Hamilton 2014: 401).

Clearly some workers benefit from being able to undertake temporary work, particularly those who are relatively privileged and have the skills and expertise that enable them to take advantage of the flexibility offered by short-term assignments (Strauss 2014). However, for many others, especially migrant workers, temporary working is associated with greater exploitation, particularly when it is undertaken through intermediary agencies (MAC 2014). The treatment of such workers, and especially the extent to which employers use migrant agency labour to divest themselves of any obligations or responsibilities towards their workforces, exemplifies the extent to which labour has become increasingly commodified.

2.4.2 Temporal flexibility: flexible work time arrangements

Another way in which employers can gain flexibility in employment relations concerns changes to working time arrangements—so-called 'temporal flexibility', which is considered more fully in Chapter 8. The most obvious type of temporal flexibility is part-time working. Table 2.4 indicates the growth in the proportion of part-time workers (those working in jobs for fewer than 30 hours per week) in the economy during the 1980s and 1990s. In 1984 just over a fifth (21 per cent) of workers were employed on a part-time basis; by 1999 this had risen to a quarter (25.1 per cent). However, there was no further growth over the subsequent decade. Yet there was then a notable surge in part-time employment between 2008 and 2012. During this period, the number of people in part-time employment rose by around 621,000, to over 27 per cent of the workforce; over the same period there was a corresponding decline in full-time employment. After 2012, however, the proportion of part-time workers ebbed a bit, falling to just over 26 per cent of those in employment in 2016. Nevertheless, over 8 million workers in the UK are employed on a part-time basis.

The provision of more flexible working time arrangements is often viewed as an unambiguously positive development in as much as it benefits employers, who are able to organize work schedules in a way that matches variations in demand for their products and services, and workers, who choose part-time working in order to reconcile employment with their family or other responsibilities. However, the emphasis on 'choice' pays insufficient heed to constraints such as childcare responsibilities (Felstead and Jewson 1999). There is plenty of evidence that, as a result, women workers in particular are trapped in low-paid part-time jobs, which generally offer few opportunities for advancement compared to full-time positions (Bradley et al. 2000).

One of the curious features of the economic recession of the late 2000s was the relatively low peak in the level of unemployment (see Section 2.2)—bearing in mind, of course, that the headline number of unemployed does not capture the full scale of joblessness in the economy. Moreover, unemployment fell quite rapidly after 2012. For some, this was evidence of a sustained economic recovery accompanied by robust employment growth and a strengthening labour market. However, the headline employment and unemployment figures masked a significant increase in the level of underemployment, encompassing people who are not able to get as many work hours as they want (Clark 2014; TUC 2015*a*). Much of the increase in part-time employment between 2008 and 2012 was of an involuntary nature, in the sense that workers only went into part-time jobs because the weak state of the labour market meant that full-time positions were unavailable. Nearly a fifth of part-time workers reported that they would prefer to have a full-time job (Cam 2012; Lansley 2012). Intriguingly, such involuntary part-time employment grew even as the economy recovered, and the level of unemployment fell, something that one leading labour market expert described as 'unprecedented' (Blanchflower 2015: 78).

Between 3 and 3.5 million workers in the UK (some 10 per cent of the workforce) are thought to be underemployed, a rise of around a million since 2008 (ONS 2014*b*; TUC 2015*a*). In addition to involuntary part-time employment, the growth in the level of underemployment was fuelled by one of the key ways in which employers responded to the recession—cutting costs through reduced working hours. Opportunities for paid overtime were curtailed in around a fifth (19 per cent) of workplaces; and reductions in basic working hours were instituted in some one in seven (14 per cent) workplaces (van Wanrooy et al. 2013*b*).

Chapter 8 shows the large extent to which employers have sought to find efficiencies through the use of highly flexible working time schedules, which are often not only irregular, but also somewhat unpredictable. Contracts of employment that do not offer workers any guaranteed hours—so-called 'zero-hours contracts'—have become increasingly commonplace. The irregularity and unpredictability of many people's working hours has contributed to an increasing climate of employment insecurity, with workers often having very little choice over their working time arrangements (O'Hara 2014; TUC 2015*a*). One consequence of all this has been the rise of a 'culture of commodified labour' (Clark 2014: 87), with workers treated as if they were cheap and disposable resources towards whom employers need have few, if any, responsibilities or obligations.

2.4.3 **Flexibility, wages, and living standards**

Flexibility is not just of a numerical or temporal nature. It can also involve efforts by employers to improve competitiveness through reforms to pay systems and structures that affect the wages and living standards of workers. Chapter 7, for example, covers attempts to reform pay and bargaining arrangements in public sector organizations to make them more flexible and efficient. A key driver is the aim to reduce wage costs, as a means of driving improved competitiveness. One common way of doing this is to 'outsource' some activities to firms that then take on responsibility for providing services such as cleaning, catering, and security. This enables organizations to divest themselves of any obligations towards these staff since it is the outsourcing company, as the contractor, that becomes the employer. Although the law is supposed to protect the wages and conditions of staff who change employer as a result of an outsourcing exercise, there is often a fear that, in pursuit of higher returns, contractors will find ways of lowering their labour costs. For this reason, in 2015 the National Gallery in London was affected by around 100 days of strikes as its workers protested against plans to privatize visitor and security services.

One of the main ways in which employers responded to the recession was by attempting to secure greater flexibility with regard to the wages and conditions of their workers.

This most commonly involved freezing or cutting wages to allow organizations to cut costs or regain competitiveness. Around two-fifths (41 per cent) of managers in general, and approaching two-thirds (64 per cent) of managers in the public sector, reported that wage levels had been frozen or cut in their workplaces as a result of the recession (van Wanrooy et al. 2013b). In some cases, such as in the motor industry, measures were agreed with recognized trade unions as the price to be paid for maintaining the viability of the business and protecting jobs. Elsewhere, however, decisions to cut wages were highly contentious, particularly in local government where some councils instituted pay cuts in order to save money. In 2011, for example, Shropshire Council dismissed its workforce of 6,500, before re-hiring them on new contracts, mostly at lower rates of pay. Evidently, the efficiency savings offered by such flexibility over pay and conditions enabled many employers to withstand the effects of the recession and protect jobs, one of the reasons why the overall level of unemployment did not rise as high as had been anticipated (CIPD 2013a).

The recession evidently had an immediate impact on pay. After 2008 average real wages (after controlling for inflation) collapsed, exacerbating a trend that was evident even before the start of the recession (Lansley 2012; Clark 2014). The longest sustained period on record of falling real wages in the UK saw average real wages fall by 10.4 per cent between 2007 and 2015 (TUC 2016a). The 'unparalleled collapse in real wages' in Britain (Plunkett, Hurrell, and Whittaker 2014: 23) was larger than in any other major economy (Monaghan and Nardelli 2014; TUC 2016a). Even as the economy began to grow again, in 2013 and 2014, there was little evidence that wage levels were recovering (McKnight 2015). In line with its policy of austerity, the 2010–15 coalition government imposed a public sector pay freeze for the first three years of its period in office, followed by two successive years when annual pay rises were capped at 1 per cent (Hannon 2016). Most workers in the UK were still worse off in 2014 than they had been before the recession (CBI 2014). Although the rate of unemployment fell sharply after 2012, accompanied by a surge in employment levels, the 'flipside of the employment numbers has been the astonishing, and virtually unprecedented, fall in real wages' (Blanchflower 2015: F77).

Flexibility over wages seems to have helped employers to retain staff, enabling them to cut costs and realize efficiency savings without necessarily having to resort to job losses (or instituting fewer job losses than would otherwise have been the case). However, the overall diminution in people's living standards, caused by an unprecedented squeeze on wages, was profound (Lansley 2011; Plunkett, Hurrell, and Whittaker 2014; Corlett, Finch, and Whittaker 2016: 12). One authoritative study showed the extent to which living standards had 'fallen dramatically since the recession, as income growth has failed to keep pace with the rate of inflation', and estimated that in 2013–14, six years after the financial crisis, average household income was still some 6 per cent lower than it had been beforehand. This decline in average incomes was mainly the result of falling real earnings (Adams, Hood, and Levell 2014: 126).

 Contesting employment relations 2.4:   The TUC's 'Britain Needs a Pay Rise' campaign

Since 2013 the Trades Union Congress (TUC) has campaigned vigorously for sustained pay increases, particularly for low-paid workers, using the slogan 'Britain Needs a Pay Rise'. This included a national demonstration in London in October 2014. The TUC highlights the unprecedented squeeze on wages and income in the aftermath of the recession and its adverse impact on people's living standards. Its figures show that in 2016 the median annual pay of workers was £2,270 less in real terms than it was in 2008, a gap of £44 per week. The TUC points to some of the consequences of the squeeze on incomes, including rising levels of household debt as families struggle to make ends meet. There are sound economic reasons, the TUC asserts, for prioritizing wage increases, especially for the low paid. Not only is 'getting money back into people's pockets . . . essential to securing a strong recovery', but it would also help to foster sustainable, long-term growth, as well as being fairer.

To a certain extent the collapse in earnings and declining living standards were a function of changes in the structure of the labour market. As mentioned in Section 2.4, much of the post-recessionary growth in employment masked a notable increase in the level of 'underemployment', marked by involuntary part-time employment, for example, or workers on zero-hours contracts who would prefer more hours. A large proportion of the employment growth evident in the aftermath of the recession has been of an irregular, casual kind, and generally low paid (TUC 2015a). The economic recovery has also been marked by an increase in self-employment, albeit much of it of a 'bogus' kind. As mentioned in Section 2.3, many new self-employed positions attract a low income (Citizens Advice 2015). Between 2008 and 2014 average income from self-employment fell by more than a fifth (22 per cent). Not only are many new self-employed positions characterized by low earnings, but also the increase in self-employment has been partly responsible for diminishing income levels and living standards (ONS 2014a; Blanchflower 2015). The overall fall in earnings and the squeeze on living standards have had a profound impact. Many workers have become more dependent on welfare benefits to supplement their incomes; some have been pushed into poverty (O'Hara 2014; Lansley and Mack 2015). Trade unions responded to the crisis in living standards by vigorously campaigning for wage increases. The Britain Needs a Pay Rise initiative, organized by the Trades Union Congress (TUC) (see Contesting employment relations 2.4), was a particularly prominent example (Hannon 2016).

Perhaps the most contentious way in which some employers have tried to secure greater flexibility in work and employment relationships, and to take advantage of the weak post-recessionary labour market, is by instituting measures to completely avoid paying workers for the jobs that they do. In some areas of work, particularly in the media industry, it has become increasingly commonplace to find menial, entry-level tasks being undertaken by a cadre of young unpaid 'volunteer' staff—often known as 'interns'—who undertake work experience for no wages, or for expenses only, in exchange for training, work experience, and the opportunity to develop contacts, perhaps with the chance of securing a glamorous, well-paid job on a newspaper or in television as a result. Internships and unpaid work experience placements can be viewed as beneficial for workers, given the opportunity they provide to gain a foothold in otherwise hard to access careers.

However, there are concerns that interns are used by employers as a source of cheap, or even free, labour (Perlin 2011; Bach 2012). While much of their work involves running errands or procuring refreshments, it can also encompass tasks that workers would normally expect to be paid for, such as handling reception duties. In the media industry there are concerns that some employers, particularly those running online news sites, attract students and interns to undertake unpaid labour—including writing or broadcasting content—with the promise of further paid opportunities in the future, which frequently do not material-ize. Research by the National Union of Journalists (NUJ) revealed that a substantial majority of student journalists who had had content published or broadcast by media outlets while they were on internships or work experience schemes received no payment. It notes that 'in recent years work experience has grown from a short placement as part of a recognized course, in which you did not expect payment, to months of unpaid or poorly-paid work where you are doing work that should be paid for' (NUJ 2015: 2). In 2015, one major pub-lisher of local and regional newspapers—Newsquest—was reportedly charging students a fee of £120 to have their work published. In the same year it made profits of nearly £60 mil-lion and cut its paid workforce by over 200. As Chapter 4 shows, the growing use of unpaid internships and work placements in some industries is a major career obstacle for people from low-income families, who cannot afford to work for free. There is also a concern that some unscrupulous employers use internships as a ruse to avoid having to pay staff the National Minimum Wage (see Chapter 7).

LEGISLATION AND POLICY 2.5: The UK government's work experience schemes

Between 2010 and 2015, the UK government's work experience schemes generated a considerable amount of controversy after it emerged that unemployed people had been compelled to take unpaid work, including cleaning homes and offices, with the threat of having their benefits withdrawn if they declined to participate (Malik, Ball, and Davies 2012). Some jobseekers on a scheme were used as unpaid stewards during the Queen's Diamond Jubilee celebrations, and obliged to sleep outside the night before under one of London's bridges over the River Thames (Malik 2012). Some employers took advantage of government schemes to replace proper workers—who would have to be paid at least the National Minimum Wage—with unemployed people on unpaid work experience.

In February 2013 Cait Reilly, an unemployed geology graduate, won her court case against the government after she claimed that requiring her to undertake unpaid work for retail firm Poundland, or else lose her unemployment benefit, was unlawful. The Court of Appeal ruled that people like Reilly had been given insufficient information about their rights and the likely sanctions if they failed to participate in the government's work experience schemes. According to Reilly, who had to give up her voluntary work for a local museum to do the work, the two weeks she spent at Poundland

were a complete waste of my time, as the experience did not help me get a job . . . I was not given any training and I was left with no time to do my voluntary work or search for other jobs. The only beneficiary was Poundland, a multimillion-pound company. Later I found out that I should never have been told the placement was compulsory. I don't think I am above working in shops like Poundland. I now work part-time in a supermarket. It is just that I expect to get paid for working.

(BBC News 2013b)

The government had to enact hasty retrospective legislation to avoid potentially costly claims for compensation from others who had been pushed into unpaid work experience schemes. Some major retailers, including the bookseller Waterstones, discontinued their involvement in the schemes because of controversies like this, and also the campaigning efforts of unions and activists. In November 2015, the Conservative government announced plans to wind up some of its more controversial work experience schemes.

Rather controversially, government schemes designed to provide unemployed people with work experience, and thus ostensibly help them to find genuine jobs, have also encouraged employers to use workers as cheap, or even free, labour (see Legislation and policy 2.5). Such schemes did little to help the labour market prospects of those compelled to participate; instead, they largely served to exacerbate casualization and sustain the market for cheap labour (Grimshaw 2015; O'Hara 2014). Despite their seemingly laudable purpose—to reduce expenditure on welfare benefits by getting unemployed people into jobs—government welfare-to-work programmes often operate in ways that promote the greater commodification of labour. By compelling people to take up employment—any kind of employment—they support the development of a low-wage, casualized labour market to the benefit of employers wanting cheap labour (Berry 2014; Williams and Scott 2016*b*).

There is a growing awareness that the kind of economic 'recovery' seen in the UK, based on a surfeit of low-paid, casualized jobs, which are often filled by underemployed workers, is not just disadvantageous for workers themselves, but also has some distinctly adverse consequences for the economy at large. In particular, increasing concerns have been raised about the productivity implications of the kind of labour market recovery evident in the UK (e.g. TUC 2015*c*). The concept of 'productivity' refers to the amount of output produced for each unit of input—say an hour of an individual's work. While many countries have seen a decline in levels of productivity, in the UK the 'productivity problem' is particularly acute, and was accentuated during the recession and its aftermath (Blanchflower 2015; Hannon 2016). Although the number in employment has reached a record high, and the rate of unemployment has fallen to below its pre-crisis level, all the evidence suggests that employers are not using the increase in potential labour power very efficiently. Without a sustained improvement in productivity the long-term prospects for sustained economic growth are weak (Weldon 2016).

The conventional understanding is that low wages reflect poor productivity. In this interpretation, the problems evident in the labour market, notably a surfeit of irregular, casualized, low-paid work, are largely caused by weak productivity levels. These are therefore best tackled through measures such as greater capital investment and increased skills training—making workers more productive, and raising the value of their labour power. Being able to work harder, or smarter, will allow businesses to become more productive and share the proceeds of the ensuing extra growth with workers in the form of higher wages and better conditions. The difficulty with this argument is that the recent experience of the UK indicates that a large part of the 'productivity problem' is not caused by the presence of obstacles that prevent workers from supplying more effort, but rather by structural weaknesses in the economic and labour market recovery which have lowered the demand for higher quality jobs (TUC 2015*c*).

From this perspective, it is not that low wages reflect poor productivity; rather the other way around—that the UK's productivity difficulties are caused by the nature of the labour market, and particularly the nature of the labour market recovery which has occurred since the recession. There is too high a proportion of low-paid, casualized jobs being created—think of the bogusly self-employed delivery worker, or the online 'click worker' tagging pictures referred to in Section 2.3—that are either simply not very productive, or difficult to make more productive. Indeed, employers often prefer to hire cheap labour—through agencies, for instance (see Section 2.4.1), on zero-hours contracts (see Section 2.4.2), or as 'interns'—rather than invest in skills training or new equipment, because it makes rational sense for them to do so (P. Mason 2016). See the example of Sports Direct in the end-of-chapter case study. To a large extent the company's success rests on the exploitation of a relatively cheap, easily disposable, and hard-working—but not especially productive—workforce in its highly labour-intensive warehouses.

During 2015 there was growing confidence expressed that, after seven years in which wages lagged behind price rises, the tide was beginning to turn (Blanchflower 2015; Corlett and Gardiner 2015). Pay growth picked up—in the first three months of 2015 real wages increased by 2.7 per cent, the fastest since the financial crisis of 2007–8. With inflation remaining at a low level, rising wages seemed to portend that a recovery in incomes and living standards was in progress. However, this optimism may have been misplaced. By the first half of 2016, the increases evident the previous year seemed to have dissipated, in a way that will lengthen the time taken for living standards to recover fully from the crisis. This suggests that there are some underlying factors that are responsible for making wage growth 'sluggish' (Corlett, Finch, and Whittaker 2016: 12). A continued pay squeeze in the public sector is partly responsible. But there are also other reasons, most notably the increasing proportion of casualized jobs in the economy marked by irregular hours and earnings and the afore-mentioned productivity problems.

In this section the emphasis has been on the characteristic forms of employment flexibility manifest in contemporary work and employment relations, particularly in the period since the crisis that began in 2007–8. The increasing prevalence of irregular, insecure, and low-paid employment is a function of employers' demands for flexibility in a weak and lightly regulated labour market. That the economic recovery proved to be so lethargic is hardly surprising, given the poor quality of so many new jobs. Moreover, many of these jobs are not all that productive, and often do not pay very much, holding back sustained improvements in living standards.

 ## Section summary and further reading

- Flexibility is sometimes thought to express mutuality in work and employment relations, based on the belief that both employers and workers have a shared interest in developing flexible employment arrangements. However, employers' demands for flexibility have promoted greater labour commodification.

- Numerical flexibility involves adjusting the numbers working for an employer, by using workers employed on temporary contracts and agency-supplied labour. There has been no significant increase in the use of such arrangements, but workers are often treated as if they are highly disposable, particularly in parts of the labour force where migrants predominate.

- Temporal flexibility is concerned with adjustments in working time. There has been a significant increase in irregular and unpredictable patterns of working time which, while beneficial for employers in terms of generating efficiencies, have adverse consequences for workers. While the level of unemployment has fallen rapidly since 2012, a substantial number of workers are underemployed.

- Employers have also been able to secure flexibility in work and employment relations by squeezing pay, and sometimes by not paying workers at all. Real average earnings fell for seven years—between 2008 and 2015—with adverse consequences for incomes and living standards. The increasing number of low-paid, casualized jobs have contributed to the fragility of the UK's economic recovery, in particular by holding back productivity.

Enda Hannon (2016) provides a very good overview of labour market and employment trends. The TUC's (2015a) publication *The Decent Jobs Deficit* is a good source of information about the development of an increasingly casualized and commodified workforce. The Resolution Foundation is a very useful source of information about wages and living standards.

2.5 Occupational change: the rise of the knowledge worker?

A further feature of debates about the changing nature of work in the 'new economy' concerns the implications of occupational change for work and employment relations, in particular the supposed rise in the number of knowledge-based jobs undertaken by managers and professionals. The assumption is that the growth of knowledge work in the economy has helped to encourage a more cooperative employment relations environment. While it is certainly the case that the proportion of managerial and professional jobs has increased, this does not necessarily imply that knowledge work has become more prevalent. Moreover, one of the characteristic features of occupational change concerns the growing number of poor-quality, or 'bad', jobs in the economy, that are often precarious in nature. The commodified basis of much precarious employment points to the continued potential for conflict in work and employment relations.

2.5.1 Towards a knowledge economy?

This is an area of long-standing interest. During the 1960s, for example, the concept of 'post-industrialism' was developed by the American writer Daniel Bell as a means of analysing how technological change was generating an increase in professional, managerial, and technical occupations, in which jobs were more highly skilled and inherently more satisfying for those who undertook them, relative to declining manual labour (Kumar 1986; Oesch 2013). While evidence of such a change was decidedly lacking, the broad idea that technological change and innovation increasingly generate jobs that demand higher levels of knowledge on the part of those who undertake them has proven to be remarkably durable (e.g. Castells 2001). The UK government, for example, has often emphasized the importance of the emerging knowledge economy as a source of future growth and prosperity (Warhurst 2008).

One way we can assess the nature of changes in jobs is by classifying them into particular occupational categories. See Table 2.5 for details of occupational change in the UK between 1984 and 2014. The data presented here would seem to indicate a pronounced shift towards a more knowledge-based economy, as signified by a growing proportion of managerial and

Table 2.5 Occupational change in the UK, 1984–2014 (% all in employment)

	Managers & senior officials	Professional occupations	Associate professional & technical occupations	Administ-rative & secretarial	Skilled trades	Personal services	Sales & customer service	Process, plant & machine operatives	Elementary occupations
1984	12.1	8.4	10.1	15.0	16.4	4.1	6.1	11.8	16.1
2004	15.3	11.8	14.3	12.6	11.4	7.5	8.0	7.9	11.3
2014	15.9	14.5	15.4	11.8	7.7	9.5	7.8	6.2	12.2

Sources: Anderson (2009); Office for National Statistics (http://www.statistics.gov.uk); licensed under the Open Government licence v.3.0

professional positions in the economy, which are generally associated with high-skill, non-routine, well-paid jobs. Between 1984 and 2014, the proportion of managerial and professional jobs in the economy rose from 12.1 per cent to 15.9 per cent, and from 8.4 per cent to 14.5 per cent, respectively. Over three decades, the share of professional and managerial positions has risen from around a fifth of the workforce to approaching a third. At the same time, the proportion of jobs in 'elementary occupations', such as unskilled labouring work, has declined—from 16.1 per cent to 12.2 per cent.

The increasing proportion of managerial and professional jobs in the economy is not just limited to the UK; what Oesch (2013: 31) calls 'occupational upgrading', namely the large-scale shift away from lower-skilled towards higher-skilled positions, is also evident internationally. The rise of so-called 'good jobs' has largely been caused by a combination of technological change—especially the development and widespread diffusion of information and communication technologies—and the changes in the global economy associated with the process of 'globalization' (see Chapter 11) (Kalleberg 2016). It is claimed that competitiveness in a more globalized economy increasingly depends on knowledge and information, something that demands a more highly skilled workforce, who have the intellectual and technical abilities to enable their employers to take the advantage (Wilson et al. 2014: 61). For some, technological change, in particular, has driven occupational upgrading, increasing the demand for managerial, professional, and technical staff who have the appropriate high-level skills and intellectual capacity. At the same time, middle-level positions, particularly those of a routine, administrative nature, have diminished in number. In Europe there has thus been 'a gradual decrease in the number of workers bending over assembly lines, cutting machine tools, typing documents, or answering telephones. In parallel, job opportunities have improved for employees drafting documents and analysing data, counselling clients and negotiating contracts, teaching students, and caring for patients' (Oesch 2013: 146).

Occupational change of this kind is thought to have some major implications for work and employment relations. In particular, it is sometimes assumed that the rise of the information-based, knowledge economy, in which jobs will increasingly be of a managerial, professional, and technical kind, reduces the need for traditional management approaches, and erodes the potential for conflict in the employment relationship. Not only is extensive management control redundant in the new knowledge economy, but also greater cooperation between employers and their employees is inevitable given the harmony of interests that arises between them (Nolan and Slater 2003).

However, there are some major problems with this way of thinking about the nature of occupational change and its implications for work and employment relations. For one thing, the 'knowledge work' concept is a very crude and unsatisfactory tool for analysing the nature of occupational change (Thompson and Warhurst 1998). Much so-called 'knowledge work' consists of rather basic, routine, and mundane data-processing activities that are founded on the manual labour of workers, rather than what they contain in their heads (Poynter 2000). All jobs require workers to use knowledge, but the concept of 'knowledge work' implies the use of complex analytical and decision-making skills and a substantial amount of discretion and autonomy. Too often, though, 'simply using or applying knowledge in a job is enough for some to be regarded as a knowledge worker' (Warhurst and Thompson 2006: 792). Call centre workers and software developers both use sophisticated information and communications technologies as an integral feature of their jobs. Their work and employment relations arrangements, however, differ markedly. Software developers enjoy a far greater degree of discretion at work, and control over their own employment arrangements, than call centre workers (Baldry et al. 2007).

Even jobs in many so-called 'professional' occupations involve routine customer service work or information-processing activities, 'with low levels of discretion and analytical skill' (Fleming, Harley, and Sewell 2004: 735). In some cases, such as in HM Revenue and Customs (HMRC) in the UK, work restructuring and the reorganization of work processes meant that ostensibly 'knowledge workers' saw their levels of discretion and autonomy being significantly diminished (Carter et al. 2011). When we examine the nature of occupations more closely, then, and in particular the content of the jobs that comprise them, we are presented with a rather different picture than that which has been advanced by advocates of the knowledge economy thesis. Far from necessarily promoting greater knowledge work, the introduction of new technology often reduces autonomy and intensifies workloads.

Another problem with the view that the development of a 'knowledge economy', marked by a growing proportion of managerial and professional jobs, has created a more cooperative and consensual climate of employment relations is that it neglects the important extent to which any kind of wage labour has the potential to produce conflict, irrespective of the employment situation of the workers concerned. As private firms face ever greater competitive pressures, and with public sector organizations increasingly being constrained by austerity-driven budget cuts, efforts by employers to secure more work from their employees for less reward remain an enduring feature of work and employment relations. The behaviour of managers towards workers is often strongly influenced by pressure to comply with exacting short-term financial targets in a way that is inimical to the development of long-term, stable, and secure employment relationships (Beynon et al. 2002; Thompson 2011)—see Chapter 5. Even seemingly genuine 'knowledge' workers, such as the staff employed in the Irish subsidiary of the US multinational studied by Cushen and Thompson (2012), can be highly discontented in their jobs if they feel that the wage–work bargain is being manipulated too much in favour of their employer. There is nothing intrinsic to 'knowledge work' that makes the workers involved inherently more cooperative. This was evident in 2016 when junior doctors in England undertook strike action over changes to their contracts—see Chapter 1.

2.5.2 Occupational change and polarization

A further problem with the proposition that there is a growing knowledge economy which has encouraged a more cooperative employment relations climate concerns the assumption that the labour market is increasingly being dominated by a rapidly growing proportion of people working in professional, managerial, and technical occupations. For one thing, much of the expansion of professional occupations has occurred as a result of restructuring in the public sector, changes to the delivery of education and health services for example, not as part of a supposed shift to a knowledge economy. Assertions about the greater predominance of highly skilled, professional jobs in the economy should therefore be treated with a considerable degree of caution (Nolan and Wood 2003). Most of the evidence indicates that the labour market 'is not being flooded by armies of mobile, high powered knowledge workers whose ownership of their own assets has companies at their mercy' (Thompson 2013: 480).

Instead, something of a consensus has developed around the view that, rather than a straightforward occupational upgrading occurring, the occupational structure is becoming increasingly polarized. The number of highly skilled, well-paid, non-routine jobs at the top of the labour market—software engineers, financial analysts, management consultants, and the like—which require high levels of specialized intellectual knowledge and aptitude, and are generally well remunerated, has been increasing. But so too have poorly paid, routine jobs at the bottom (e.g. Goos and Manning 2007; Warhurst 2008; Kalleberg 2011; Lansley 2011; Holmes and Mayhew 2012). Thus 'while management, professional and technical jobs are expanding, so too are routine services jobs, particularly in personal services and retail and hospitality' (Warhurst and Thompson 2006: 793).

For this reason, then, the occupational structure is increasingly thought to resemble an 'hourglass' structure, 'with a widening bulge of employment at both the top and the bottom, but a narrowing of opportunity in the middle' (Clark 2014: 69). As the proportion of 'good' jobs higher up the occupational structure and 'bad' jobs at the bottom both increase, there has been a diminution in the number of middle-ranked jobs such as those involving semi-skilled manufacturing work or linked to clerical and administrative positions (Kalleberg 2011; Holmes and Mayhew 2012). This 'hollowing out' of middle-level, intermediate positions, especially those concerned with the kind of routine, administrative functions that once proliferated, has been largely a product of technological change (McIntosh 2013; Wilson et al. 2014). Instead of asking a typist or secretary to draft correspondence, as would generally have been the case before the 1990s, managers now do it themselves on their desktop or mobile devices. New technology has eradicated much of the routine, but often secure and relatively well-paid employment in manufacturing environments (McIntosh 2013; Clark 2014).

According to one authoritative report, over the period 2010–20 the number of middle-ranking jobs in sales and customer services is forecast to decline slightly, while the diminution of administrative and secretarial positions is predicted to quicken, accelerating the process of 'hollowing out' (Wilson et al. 2014). That said, however, the continued importance of intermediate occupations—think about salespeople for example—should not be overlooked (McIntosh 2013). Even by 2022 there are still expected to be some 3 million administrative and clerical positions in the UK (Wilson et al. 2014).

⊙ Insight into practice 2.6:   The obstacles to progression in low-paid work

Studies of low-paid work suggest that while some employers have made an effort to encourage career progression, workers at the bottom of the labour market face considerable obstacles to advancement, not least a lack of available opportunities. In low-paying sectors of the economy, such as hotels and retail, a further difficulty is that there is little use for high-level skills and qualifications, making employers reluctant to invest in training. This makes it more difficult for staff to progress (Lloyd and Mayhew 2010). Research undertaken in the UK café sector shows that, in order to motivate staff, the branded chains have put in place arrangements which ostensibly facilitate advancement, including 'highly structured systems of training and development, alongside clear pathways to progression' (Lloyd and Payne 2011: 43). However, promotion to junior management positions is not necessarily all that attractive in terms of pay because such roles do not attract wages that are all that much higher than those of shop-floor workers. To move out of low pay is a gradual, lengthy process with little prospect of real short-term reward. Moreover, advancement often requires staff to be more flexible in respect to both their place and times of work, which is a particular obstacle for workers with caring responsibilities.

Despite acknowledging the importance of polarization, especially in the UK, some claim that the growth in both the number and proportion of highly skilled, knowledge-oriented jobs at the top of the occupational structure outstrips that of routine, low-paid positions (Oesch 2013). Others, however, reject 'optimistic predictions' concerning the supposed growth in high-quality jobs, and contend that, consistent with the broader trend of polarization, 'employment growth is weighted towards the bottom' (Thompson 2013: 480). From this perspective, the economy is generating a substantial number of 'bad' jobs, especially in parts of the expanding service sector such as cleaning, catering, and caring occupations, where employment is often irregular, insecure, and low-paid (Kalleberg 2011, 2016). These 'bad jobs' are not necessarily low-skilled (McIntosh 2013); for example, caring roles generally require workers to exhibit an extensive array of often highly complex and tacit skills and attributes, particularly when it comes to building relationships with clients. However, such jobs do tend to be low-paid, are often quite insecure, and generally provide workers with little in the way of autonomy and discretion. Moreover, there are rarely opportunities for progression up the job ladder, leaving many workers stuck in poorly remunerated positions which offer precious little scope for advancement (see Insight into practice 2.6).

2.5.3 Precarious employment

Clearly the increasing number of 'bad' jobs in the economy—those that are routine, insecure, low-paid, and generally offer few opportunities for advancement—highlights a major problem with the assumption that a knowledge economy marked by more consensual employment relations arrangements has come to predominate. The kind of flexibility often pursued by employers, including the use of 'bogus' self-employment (see Section 2.3.2) and agency labour (Section 2.4.1), the growing problem of 'underemployment' (Section 2.4.2), and the rise of 'free labour' (Section 2.4.3), has contributed to making the jobs of an increasing number of workers more vulnerable (Kalleberg 2009, 2011; Pollert and Charlwood 2009).

This has prompted a concern with characterizing 'precarious employment', explaining why it has become more commonplace, and establishing its extent. For Hewison (2016: 428) the concept of precarious employment refers to 'work that exhibits uncertainty, instability, vulnerability and insecurity where workers are required to bear the risks of work'. The growth in precarious employment is a function of the increased commodification of labour, to the extent that it is a consequence of employers' efforts to promote more 'market-mediated' work and employment relationships (Kalleberg 2011).

Employment relations reflection 2.7: The experiences and perceptions of low-paid workers

Research by the Joseph Rowntree Foundation, which draws on the experiences and perceptions of low-paid workers in three sectors of the economy—retail, hospitality, and care—provides insights about the nature of their jobs and what could be done to improve them. In general, the workers were profoundly aware of their position at the bottom of the organizational hierarchy, the extremely limited extent to which they were able to influence decision-making processes, and the obstacles which prevented them

(continued...)

from advancing. A fatalistic attitude to work was evident. It was the convenience of their jobs that most satisfied the workers. However, an overarching 'feeling of powerlessness' was identified. Opportunities for promotion were sometimes shunned. This was because any (rather small) pay rise would be insufficient to compensate for the perceived stress associated with taking on extra responsibilities, as well as impeding their flexibility. In general, despite 'valuing the flexibility and convenience of their work, and seeing few other options available, employees across the three sectors generally described working in a low-paid job as stressful, insecure and precarious'. What would improve their jobs? Higher pay would give people more security. But it was also believed that employers could treat them in a fairer manner, perhaps by offering help with childcare, and doing more to make them feel part of the organization.

Source: Hay (2015)

Some commentators think that precarious employment has become the 'dominant feature of social relations between employers and workers in the contemporary world' (Kalleberg 2009: 17), with adverse consequences for the economic well-being both of individual workers and the communities they live in. For example, migrant workers are often concentrated in jobs such as those arranged through agencies, which are of a precarious and vulnerable nature (McKay and Markova 2010; McDowell, Batvitzky, and Dyer 2012; Hopkins 2014; Potter and Hamilton 2014). Studies of work and employment relations in sectors such as contract cleaning and social care highlight the extensive low pay, the often irregular working hours, and the lack of opportunities for workers to progress and ascend the job ladder (EHRC 2014; Kingsmill 2014). See Employment relations reflection 2.7 for the experiences and perceptions of low-paid workers in the retail, hospitality, and care sectors.

For some, precarious employment arrangements have become so pervasive that they have helped to foment a new social grouping—the so-called 'precariat'. In two major books, Guy Standing (2011, 2014) has written about the growing prominence of this precariat—a new class of people, often young workers, who are employed in insecure, low-paid, 'dead end' jobs which offer few, if any, opportunities for career progression. Members of the precariat operate as a largely casual and disposable source of labour, a function of employers' demands for greater flexibility. Standing (2011) emphasizes that the emergent precariat is a global phenomenon. In the UK, it is reckoned that around 15 per cent of people are members of the precariat. Their lives tend to revolve around short-term and poor-quality jobs. Being regularly in and out of work, members of the precariat tend to be among the poorest and most disadvantaged in society, and are particularly badly affected by government welfare cuts (Mike Savage 2015). Whereas traditionally stable, long-term jobs enabled members of the established working class to develop durable occupational or career identities linked to their employment position, the irregular, fragmented, and unstable character of any work the precariat are able to find leaves them unable to do this. As a result they find themselves cut off from, or lacking any connection with, established industrial and political institutions, such as the trade union movement. For Standing (2011), this is one of the things that makes the emergent precariat a 'dangerous class'. Members of the precariat may often be isolated and divided from one another, but they do have some common interests—most notably the desirability of doing something about the short-term, insecure, and disposable character of their employment situations—which could form the basis of a radical challenge to the existing social and economic order (Standing 2011, 2014).

Accounts of the rise of 'precarious employment' can be insufficiently rigorous, lack a broader perspective on the background to, and nature of, the 'precarious' concept, and present a rather exaggerated view of change in work and employment. Critics like Doogan (2009), for example, question just how much more insecure and precarious jobs in general have actually become. The concept of the 'precariat' has come in for particular critical scrutiny. Guy Standing's claims are often based on a weak and sometimes dubious evidence base (Conley 2012a). Moreover, the extent to which members of the precariat have common interests, and thus can be conceived of as a distinct social class grouping, has also been questioned (Breman 2013). Nevertheless, with its focus on the experience of disadvantaged young workers, its appreciation of their fragmented and unstable employment arrangements, and its understanding of what this means for their working lives, the concept of the precariat has generally been welcomed (Conley 2012a; Kalleberg 2012; Thompson 2013). In particular, it symbolizes an important and profoundly damaging consequence of employers' demands for greater flexibility and competitiveness—namely the greater commodification of labour, manifest in the rise of 'low-paid, poor-quality, precarious or zero-hours contracted work' (Mike Savage 2015: 354; Hewison 2016).

Clearly the economic recession and its aftermath saw an increase in the prevalence of precarious employment, as evidenced by the rise of bogus self-employment and the greater use of irregular and casualized employment arrangements. Far from improving the prospects for cooperation in work and employment relations, occupational change, in the form of a growing proportion of 'bad jobs' (Kalleberg 2016), has done the very opposite. It has increased the degree to which workers are exposed to market forces, and rendered them more disposable. To the extent that it furthers labour commodification, the increasing prevalence of precarious employment arrangements highlights the profound latent conflict of interest that lies at the heart of work and employment relationships.

 ## Section summary and further reading

- There are a number of problems with the view that the growth of a 'knowledge economy', marked by a growing proportion of managerial and professional jobs, has created a more cooperative and consensual climate of employment relations. One of these concerns the difficulties inherent in defining 'knowledge work'.

- Another is that occupational change involves not only the expansion of jobs at the top end of the labour market, but also of those at the bottom, where precarious low-skilled, poorly paid, routine work undertaken by vulnerable workers is commonplace. The process of occupational polarization has seen the decline of middle-level jobs in areas such as administrative and clerical work.

- The rise of precarious employment has stimulated interest in the concept of the 'precariat'—a term used to describe the expanding category of workers engaged in low-paid, irregular, and casualized employment. Despite having attracted some criticism, the precariat concept nonetheless highlights the extent to which labour has been commodified and some of its consequences.

See Warhurst (2008) for a critical assessment of the 'knowledge economy'. Kalleberg (2009, 2011, 2016) has written about 'good jobs' and 'bad jobs'. The book chapter by Hewison (2016) provides a good overview of precarious employment. See Standing (2011, 2014) for the concept of the precariat.

2.6 Conclusion

Perhaps the most notable theme to emerge from this assessment of the implications of economic change for employment relations is the extent to which the competitive pressures characteristic of a capitalist market economy have encouraged employers to find ever cheaper, more efficient ways of managing labour, resulting in downward pressure on employment conditions. This has been particularly evident in the period since the 2007–8 crisis. Although employment growth has been healthy, there are concerns about the poor quality of the new jobs that have been created, as illustrated by the growth of 'bogus' self-employment and the nature of employment in the 'gig economy'.

The material covered in this chapter demonstrates the important extent to which employers are increasingly trying to secure flexibility and enhance their competitiveness through efforts to operate with cheaper and more disposable workforces, towards whom they show few responsibilities and obligations. The economic recession and its aftermath, in particular the weak state of the labour market, have given employers greater scope to impose flexibility, manifest in cuts to wages for example. Flexibility in work and employment relations is not necessarily marked by a mutuality of interest between workers and employers. It may provide the latter with short-term improvements in competitiveness, but this comes at the expense of a more casualized workforce.

Moreover, there is little support for the view that, by generating a greater amount of 'knowledge work', changes in the occupational structure have promoted a more cooperative employment relations climate. For one thing, there is nothing inherently cooperative about work and employment relationships in sectors that are characterized by a greater use of knowledge. More importantly, occupational change involves not only the expansion of jobs at the top end of the labour market, but also those at the bottom, where poorly paid, routine work undertaken by vulnerable workers is commonplace. This is clear from the growing prevalence of precarious employment arrangements, to the extent that some have claimed it has engendered a new and distinctive social class—the 'precariat'.

Taken together, all these developments highlight the important extent to which changes in the economy and the labour market have resulted in a more 'commodified' labour force. This is marked by the greater efforts of employers to secure productive effort from workers at the least possible cost, which can involve attempts to divest themselves of the responsibilities and obligations that go with employing people—such as providing employment rights and protections—thus rendering workers more disposable. Far from inducing a more cooperative climate of employment relations, economic and labour market changes, by inducing commodification, have made the potential for conflict in work and employment relationships more conspicuous.

 ### Assignment and discussion questions

1. Why has the number of self-employed jobs risen so sharply since the financial and economic crisis? To what extent can the growth in self-employment be attributed to a greater belief among workers in the virtues of working for themselves?

2. Critically assess the main implications of the 'gig economy' and the rise of digital labour platforms for work and employment relations.

3. Critically assess the proposition that flexible employment arrangements are equally advantageous for employers and workers.

4. What is meant by the concept of the 'precariat'? How far do you agree with the view that the precariat has become a distinct social group?

5. What is meant by the concept of 'labour commodification'? To what extent do you agree with the view that labour has become more 'commodified'?

 Visit the Online Resource Centre that accompanies this book to develop your understanding of this chapter and keep up to date with the latest developments in this area.
www.oxfordtextbooks.co.uk/orc/williams4e/

 Chapter case study: Commodifying labour at Sports Direct

Sports Direct is one of the most successful retailers in the UK. With over 670 stores worldwide, in 2015 it made a profit of £241 million on revenues of some £2.8 billion. Its founder, Mike Ashley, who retains a controlling interest in the firm, is reported to be worth some £3.5 billion. One of the major reasons why Sports Direct has been so successful is because of the highly efficient way in which it uses labour in its warehouses, particularly its Shirebrook site in Derbyshire, England. Eschewing advanced technology, Sports Direct relies very heavily on a workforce comprised mainly of staff hired through agencies to undertake the extremely labour-intensive work. The agency workers are guaranteed very few hours of work, and thus pay. But the relationship is highly asymmetric. The agencies make it clear that they are not obliged to offer hours of work in excess of the rather low guaranteed minimum; however, they specify that the workers 'must' accept 'any suitable assignments'. The lack of regular, guaranteed hours, and the agency-based system, which allows Sports Direct to divest responsibility for employing staff, are both major sources of insecurity for workers.

Exacerbating their insecurity, workers are constantly in fear of dismissal in what is a highly regimented, strictly monitored, and rigidly disciplined environment. Those alleged to have committed six misdemeanours over a six-month period—which include 'excessive chatting', too many toilet breaks, and even being absent from work because of illness—risk being dismissed under a 'six strikes and you're out' policy. The practice of mandatory end-of-shift searches, which take place outside of paid working time, mean that workers often do not receive the statutory minimum wage. They could even have fifteen minutes' wages docked for being just one minute late for starting work. During the first half of 2016 there was a Parliamentary inquiry by the House of Commons Business, Innovation, and Skills Committee, which was established to investigate abusive working practices in Sports Direct. According to the inquiry this policy is 'used as a punitive measure, which denigrates the workers at Sports Direct and gives the management unreasonable and excessive powers to discipline or dismiss at will' (House of Commons Business, Innovation, and Skills Committee 2016: 9). Unsurprisingly, some workers report being too frightened to take sick leave. The working environment itself is poor, with extensive breaches of health and safety evident. Ambulances and paramedics have to attend Shirebrook to deal with incidents on a regular basis; one woman even gave birth in a warehouse toilet.

For nearly six months, Ashley declined to appear and give evidence to the Committee, despite repeated invitations to do so. Eventually, in June 2016 he relented. During his appearance he professed his ignorance of, and even claimed to be 'shocked' by, the working practices in his company. The success of Sports Direct in large part stems from the great extent to which it uses labour as a commodity; not just because it is so keen to get the most effort from the workforce at the least cost,

(continued...)

but because of its reluctance to accept that it has any responsibilities or obligations to workers whom it looks to treat essentially as disposable commodities. Ashley promised to review working practices in Sports Direct. The company has vowed to make improvements, including the suspension of the 'six strikes and you're out' policy and ending the system of pay deductions. Pressure from trade unions, however, prompted the company's shareholders to insist that a fully independent review is put in place.

Sources: Channel Four (2015a); Goodley and Ashby (2015a); Goodley and Ashby (2015b); Unite (2015); Gayle and Butler (2016); House of Commons Business, Innovation, and Skills Committee (2016)

Questions

Why have the working practices in Sports Direct warehouses attracted so much controversy? Sports Direct is a very successful company—why did it wait until the Parliamentary inquiry, and the associated critical media coverage, before promising to make improvements?

3 The politics of employment relations

Chapter objectives

The main objectives of this chapter are to:

- demonstrate the influence of the political dimension of employment relations;
- examine how employment relations policy developed in historical perspective;
- interpret public policy developments in employment relations under the 1997–2010 Labour governments;
- examine the employment relations policies pursued by the coalition and Conservative majority governments since 2010; and
- consider the implications of European Union policy and the broader process of European integration for employment relations.

3.1 Introduction

In this chapter the concern is with the political dimension of employment relations. One of the most distinctive features of employment relations as a field of study is that it is highly politicized; in other words, employment relations arrangements, institutions, and processes are infused by, and cannot be understood without reference to, the political environment. This chapter considers the implications of public policy developments and explores the implications for employment relations of European integration, including the influence of the European Union's (EU) 'social dimension'. Section 3.2 starts by providing some historical context, outlining the main developments in public policy prior to 1997, when Tony Blair's Labour government was elected to office. This provides the background for the material in Section 3.3, which covers the main employment relations policy developments under Labour between 1997 and 2010. Section 3.4 focuses on the changes enacted by the Conservative–Liberal Democrat coalition government, which was in office between 2010 and 2015, and the subsequent Conservative majority administration. In Section 3.5 the emphasis is on the implications of European integration for employment relations, encompassing the waning impact of EU social and employment legislation under the 'social dimension', set against the context of economic recession, the privileging of deficit reduction as an economic policy tool, and the propagation of extreme austerity measures. Moreover, the June 2016 referendum vote to take the UK out of the EU needs to be viewed in the context of concerns about deteriorating labour standards and the adverse consequences of EU immigration.

Introductory case study: The European Union's Agency Workers Directive

In June 2008, European Union (EU) employment ministers agreed to enact legislation, in the form of a directive, which would give workers employed through temporary agencies entitlement to the same basic pay and conditions as workers directly employed to do the same job. The agreement came six years after the legislation was first proposed. The lengthy delay was in large part due to the then Labour government's opposition to the proposed directive. It agreed with employers' bodies that such legislation would impede the UK's labour market flexibility and hinder competitiveness. Following pressure from the trade unions, which supported the legislation, the UK government convened talks between the Confederation of British Industry (CBI), on behalf of employers, and the Trades Union Congress (TUC). In May 2008 they agreed a compromise whereby agency workers would have to serve a qualifying period of twelve weeks before they were entitled to equivalent pay and conditions. With this deal in place, the UK government dropped its opposition to the Directive, facilitating the following month's agreement between EU employment ministers.

The Directive passed into UK law in January 2010 in the form of the Agency Workers Regulations 2010, and was due to take effect the following year. In August 2010, though, the prime minister in the new coalition government, the Conservative David Cameron, emphasized his opposition to the new legislation. He said that with regard to the rights of agency workers, 'I think we have to look at this very carefully. Sometimes you find if you pile on extra rights and obligations, you just end up with fewer people in jobs.' Nevertheless, in October 2010 the then Liberal Democrat employment relations minister Ed Davey confirmed that the government would not be reviewing the Agency Workers Regulations, and they eventually came into effect in October 2011.

The lengthy, tortuous progress of this piece of EU employment legislation is instructive for what it tells us about the politics of employment relations in a number of respects. First, it demonstrates the increasing influence of EU legislation on employment relations, particularly after Labour under Tony Blair signed up to the Social Chapter in 1997. Second, the case demonstrates how EU legislation designed to guarantee minimum employment standards has conflicted with successive governments' desire to respect employers' demands for flexibility, rather than improve protections for workers. Third, the case is also instructive for what it reveals about the right-wing Conservatives' preferred approach to employment relations. Generally, they view employment regulation with a pronounced disdain, something which has had a marked influence on developments in employment relations policy since 2010 when the Conservatives returned to government, initially in coalition with the more centrist Liberal Democrats.

3.2 Public policy and employment relations

In order to understand contemporary developments in employment relations policy properly, key elements of the historical background need to be covered. The starting point is to explain the concept of 'voluntarism' and the important influence it has exercised historically over employment relations policy. The growth of state intervention in employment relations during the middle part of the twentieth century is considered, before the main features of Conservative policy towards employment relations under the governments of Margaret Thatcher and John Major between 1979 and 1997 come under scrutiny.

3.2.1 **Voluntarism and employment relations in Britain**

An appreciation of the importance of voluntarism is crucial to understanding the nature of employment relations in Britain. In essence, it refers to the preference for the terms of the employment relationship to be determined voluntarily by employers and trade unions, with state interference only as a last resort (Dickens and Hall 2010). The roots of the voluntaristic tradition can be traced as far back as the seventeenth and eighteenth centuries. During this period, the development of capitalism was informed by the complementary ideologies of economic laissez-faire and market individualism in which the recognition of private property interests predominated (Hyman 1975; Fox 1985a). Nascent capitalist entrepreneurs were resistant to state intervention in their affairs and preferred, wherever possible, to handle their own affairs.

The dominance of market individualism and laissez-faire ideologies provided the foundation for the development of 'collective laissez-faire' as the dominant state approach to employment relations—a preference that employers should deal with employment relations matters, and with unions, themselves, without direct intervention by the state (Davies and Freedland 1993). Employers could deal with union activities in ways that did not threaten their interests too severely, thus obviating the need for more explicitly repressive measures. Trade unions also favoured voluntarism because it allowed them to bargain freely with employers without interference from a pro-employer judiciary (Flanders 1974). The absence of state intervention in relationships between workers, unions, and employers is generally thought to have had a pronounced and long-standing influence on employment relations during the twentieth century (Kahn-Freund 1964). While some legislation was considered desirable, in the area of health and safety for example, unlike many other countries the regulation of the employment relationship in Britain came to be determined largely by a combination of collective bargaining and managerial prerogative, without the development of a comprehensive system of statutory employment rights (Fox 1985a; Hyman 2001).

Howell (2005), though, contends that the state exercised a more profound influence over the development of employment relations than has hitherto been acknowledged, not so much through legislation, but rather by establishing and maintaining the conditions under which collective bargaining thrived. Moreover, during periods of sustained industrial unrest governments often intervened quickly to repress trade union activity (Geary 1985). Judicial hostility to organized labour—laws were interpreted in ways that benefited employers, for example (Fox 1985a)—undermined unions' legitimacy. This demonstrates that the state's role in employment relations is far from that of a neutral, disinterested observer. Rather, it is largely concerned with providing an environment which privileges the interests of employers, something that has, for the reasons outlined above, generally implied limited direct state intervention in employment relations, but does not rule out a more coercive approach if that is dictated by circumstances (Hyman 1975).

3.2.2 **Growing state intervention and employment relations**

During the mid-twentieth century there was a marked increase in the extent of state intervention in employment relations. For one thing, the 1960s and 1970s saw a growth in the statutory regulation of work and employment relationships in areas such as redundancy payments, the dismissal of employees, equal pay, and sex and race discrimination. Hitherto, the prevailing assumption was that, apart from some exceptions like health and safety at work, employment rights were more effectively promoted through collective bargaining. For a number of reasons, including economic efficiency, social change, and pressure from workers for improved rights, this period saw a substantial growth (which continues in the present period) in the 'juridification'—that is the regulation of social and economic activity by the law—of work and employment relationships (Davies and Freedland 1993).

Perhaps the most notable manifestation of greater state intervention in employment relations, however, related to government efforts to manage the economy. The policy priority of full employment, achieved through stimulating demand, caused upward pressure on wages with potentially inflationary consequences. Governments therefore intervened to try and win trade union agreement to restrain their wage-bargaining behaviour through a series of largely voluntary 'incomes policies' (Kessler 1994). Prompted by growing discontent in their membership, over time the unions became increasingly hostile to incomes policies, which impeded the ability of governments to incorporate and integrate the unions in processes of state economic management (Hyman 1975).

Historical perspective 3.1: The 'winter of discontent' 1978–9

Whenever there is an increase in the level of strike activity in Britain, politicians and media commentators invariably speculate about the parallels with the industrial unrest of 1978–9, which became popularly known as the 'winter of discontent', a phrase of Shakespearean origin. So what was the 'winter of discontent'? The term is used to refer to the series of strikes which affected road haulage, transport, and public services during the winter of 1978–9. The industrial unrest of this period is often presented as the result of excessive union militancy, a sign that the trade unions had become too powerful. In reality, however, it expressed the profound discontent experienced by many workers, particularly in the public services, who were unhappy at the relative decline in their standard of living as a result of wage restraint policies. Nevertheless, the strikes, and particularly the way they were presented by the largely anti-union media, undermined the popularity and legitimacy of the Labour government led by James Callaghan, helping to usher in a Conservative administration under the leadership of Margaret Thatcher in May 1979.

Alongside the development of incomes policies, during the 1960s and 1970s the development and evolution of tripartite arrangements for economic and industrial policy formulation was further evidence not only of greater state involvement in economic planning and management, but also of government efforts to incorporate business representatives, union leaderships, and the TUC into state policy-making processes (Davies and Freedland 1993). 'Tripartism' refers to the participation of unions, employers, and government representatives in operating state institutions. It is important to acknowledge the repressive basis of this attempt to incorporate the union interest. Incomes policies and tripartite arrangements reflected government efforts to accommodate trade union power, and to try to shape and control it, in order to sustain economic growth and the long-term viability of the capitalist market economy (Hyman 1989). However, pressure from workers, who became increasingly hostile to wage restraint because of the adverse consequences for their living standards, restricted the extent to which unions were able to cooperate with governments in managing the economy (Hyman 1989). In particular, wage restraint policies provoked a wave of industrial action during 1978–9, a period which became popularly known as the 'winter of discontent' (see Historical perspective 3.1).

3.2.3 Public policy under the Conservatives: towards neo-liberalism?

There was a marked policy shift during the 1980s and 1990s under Conservative governments led by Margaret Thatcher and John Major. On entering office in 1979, the Conservative government's economic policy was dominated by a concern to reduce inflation through tight control of the money supply and an explicit abandonment of the objective of full employment. It placed a greater emphasis on the free play of market forces as a source of enhanced economic competitiveness, rejecting demand management as a tool of economic policy. Moreover, the Conservatives had little regard for tripartite methods of economic policy formulation, and over time abolished most of the state institutions that exemplified tripartism (Crouch 1995). Thus there was a 'distancing of unions from the corridors of power' (Davies and Freedland 1993: 427).

The trend towards increasing juridification of employment relations did, however, continue under the Conservatives, albeit with a markedly different emphasis, as they oversaw a large-scale programme of employment relations reform by means of six major Acts of Parliament between 1980 and 1993, largely designed to weaken the trade unions (Crouch 1996; Dickens and Hall 2010). Excessive union power was perceived to be a major constraint on economic competitiveness; thus the reform of employment relations was central to attempts to boost the economy.

What, then, were the Conservatives' principal aims in reforming the legislation governing unions and employment relations? First, they wished to reduce the power of trade unions in the economy (Davies and Freedland 1993). Legislation was passed that severely restricted the ability of unions to undertake lawful industrial action, in particular by mandating that unions must win the support of a majority of members in a properly constituted postal ballot before action could be taken—see Chapter 9 for further details. The operation of closed shop arrangements (see Chapter 5) was also outlawed.

Second, Conservative governments were eager to diminish the scope for legitimate political activity by trade unions, something that involved attempts to challenge the links between the unions and the Labour Party (Davies and Freedland 1993). Many unions, even those that are not affiliated to Labour, maintain political funds and use them for general campaigning purposes. The 1984 Trade Union Act obliged trade unions operating political funds to win the support of their members for such arrangements in a ballot at least once every ten years.

A third aim of the Conservatives' legislative programme was to promote greater internal democracy in trade unions, to restore membership control of union policies and leaderships, and thus, it was anticipated, instil greater moderation in union behaviour (Martin et al. 1995). For example, the Trade Union Act 1984 mandated that union general secretaries and executive bodies be subject to periodic election in a ballot. It was reinforced by the 1988 Employment Act, which made postal ballots mandatory in union elections.

The policy of 'giving unions back to their members' was based on an assumption that the moderate mass of trade union members was being coerced by militant union leaderships into taking unnecessary industrial action, and thus their voice needed to be heard, principally through a greater role for ballots (McIlroy 1991). However, the Conservatives' real aim seems to have been to use the rhetoric of individual members' rights as a way of undermining collective union power, thus reducing the effectiveness of trade unionism (Martin et al. 1995).

Historical perspective 3.2:   The defeat of the 1984–5 miners' strike

Conservative governments of the 1980s and 1990s did not rely solely on the reform of employment law to suppress trade unionism, as the experience of the 1984–5 miners' strike demonstrates. In March 1984, the leadership of the National Union of Mineworkers (NUM), under Arthur Scargill, called a national strike aiming to defeat the National Coal Board's (NCB) plan, backed by the government, to close twenty pits with the loss of over 100,000 mining jobs. Miners in Yorkshire walked out and were followed by those in other regions, including Scotland and South Wales. The strike was to last for a year. Controversially, the NUM's leadership did not authorize a ballot—largely on the basis that the strike was underway anyway—and many miners in areas where the pits were not under immediate threat of closure, Nottinghamshire for example, only participated reluctantly.

Throughout the course of the dispute, the extensive powers of the state were deployed to ensure that the miners were defeated. In the years preceding the strike, the government had made arrangements for alternative energy supplies, and had built up coal stocks in preparation for a lengthy struggle. A special cabinet sub-committee was instituted, chaired by the prime minister, Margaret Thatcher, to oversee the state's response once the strike had started. Figures associated with the Conservative Party, like businessman David Hart, helped to arrange support for miners who wished to return to work, and assisted the formation of a breakaway union, the Union of Democratic Mineworkers (UDM) in Nottinghamshire. They also backed legal actions by NUM members against their union for allegedly breaching its own rules by not holding a ballot. Eventually, in October 1984 the union had its assets seized, or 'sequestrated', by the courts.

The resources of the Security Service, MI5, were used to undermine the strike's effectiveness; it had an agent placed within the NUM's leadership. Extensive military-style policing tactics, including the use of roadblocks on motorways, were deployed to prevent NUM pickets from travelling around the country blocking the supply of coal to electricity-generating plants and obstructing efforts to return to work. Nearly 9,000 miners were arrested in 1984 as a result. In March 1985, after holding out for a year, the NUM called off the strike and organized a return to work, having failed in its attempt to use industrial action to prevent the pit closure programme.

Sources: Beynon (1985); Milne (2004)

The scale of the Conservative governments' legislative reform of employment relations during the 1980s and 1990s is suggestive of a marked shift towards the repression of union activity by the state, which also extended to the use of its powers to combat industrial disputes (see Historical perspective 3.2). What accounts for such a 'sustained assault' (Howell 2005: 133) on trade unionism in Britain? One approach puts the onus on the ideological character of the Conservatives' programme (Wedderburn 1989). From this perspective, the Conservatives' legislative programme was underpinned by a coherent set of values and principles associated with the 'new right'. The reform of employment relations was strongly informed by a neo-liberal belief that economic prosperity is best secured through deregulated markets, including labour markets, employment rights and protections, and weak trade unions (Davies and Freedland 2007; Dickens 2014).

An alternative approach emphasizes the pragmatic and opportunistic aspects of Conservative policy-making (Auerbach 1990). Rather than reflecting a coherent neo-liberal ideology, anti-union laws tended to be passed in response to particular events or were influenced by prevailing circumstances. For example, the measures designed to restrict 'unofficial' industrial action that were included in the 1990 Employment Act resulted from a series of industrial disputes in transport the previous year.

A reasonable conclusion is that the Conservatives' legislative programme was founded on a combination of neo-liberal ideology and political opportunism (Davies and Freedland 1993; Howell 2005). Some measures, though, such as the abolition of the closed shop for example, do seem to have been driven more by ideology than others (Davies and Freedland 1993). Yet the opportunistic character of much of the Conservatives' later legislative interventions demonstrates that, while the policy regime had become much more repressive, union resistance compelled the state to respond to particular challenges to its authority as and when they arose (Davies and Freedland 1993).

What were the effects of the Conservatives' legislative programme? To what extent did their reforms weaken union power? We should not ignore the possibility that Conservative governments were only able to enact such restrictive policies because of the degree to which the unions had already been weakened by economic developments, such as job losses in manufacturing and increasing levels of unemployment (Dunn and Metcalf 1996). Nevertheless, the sheer scale of state repression of the unions during this period, of which the legislation was only one part, significantly undermined the economic power of trade unionism.

However, the Conservatives were rather less successful in realizing their aim of challenging the political basis of trade union activity, by mandating political fund ballots for example. Trade union members support and value the political campaigning activities of their unions. Not only have they voted strongly in favour of retaining political funds, but also in some cases have supported establishing new funds (Leopold 1997, 2006).

Efforts to reform the internal government of the trade unions by encouraging greater 'democracy' as a source of union moderation were similarly largely unsuccessful. Given the complexity of its demands, legislation stimulated greater centralization of authority in the unions, enhancing the authority of union leaders, but reducing members' participation in union affairs (Undy et al. 1996). There is no evidence that the balloting provisions encouraged moderation—in fact rather the opposite. In general, the obligation that union leaders be elected by postal ballot at least once every five years seems to have favoured radical challenges to more moderate general secretaries. In thinking that more effective balloting arrangements would induce greater union moderation, Conservative politicians were, then, profoundly mistaken. If anything, union leaders tend to exert a moderating influence on a generally more combative membership.

Overall, then, the Conservatives' programme of employment relations reform contributed to the diminution of trade union power, largely because of the severe constraints legislation imposed on strikes and other forms of industrial action. However, the Conservatives' other aims—the depoliticization of the unions and the encouragement of greater union democracy and moderation—do not appear to have been so successful. Moreover, as shown in Section 3.5, the Conservatives' deregulatory agenda came under challenge from the growing amount of European Union legislation during the 1980s and 1990s (Dickens and Hall 2010).

Section summary and further reading

- For many years, the principle of voluntarism, or collective laissez-faire, in which the government abstained from directly intervening in relations between employers, employees, and trade unions, characterized the role of the state in Britain.

- During the 1960s and 1970s, there was a marked increase in the degree of state intervention in employment relations. The use of incomes policies, the development of tripartite arrangements, and the growing statutory regulation of the employment relationship all eroded, but did not significantly undermine, the voluntarist ethos.

- During the 1980s and 1990s, Conservative governments used the machinery of the state, most conspicuously by enacting repressive legislation, to undermine the power and legitimacy of the trade unions.

For voluntarism in Britain, see Flanders (1974) and Hyman (2001). Davies and Freedland (1993) offer the best account of the growth of state intervention in employment relations during the 1960s and 1970s. For a critical overview of the Conservatives' anti-union legislation, see McIlroy (1991). There is an overview of the policy background in Dickens and Hall (2010: 298–301).

3.3 Labour and employment relations in Britain, 1997–2010

The extent to which the employment relations policies of the Labour governments under Tony Blair and Gordon Brown between 1997 and 2010 broke with the deregulatory, employer-friendly approach pursued by Thatcher and Major's Conservative administrations during the 1980s and 1990s has been much debated. Because of its historic close links with the trade unions, it might have been expected that Labour would have looked to reverse some of the Conservatives' neo-liberal policies. Indeed, at the beginning of the twentieth century it was the leading trade unions of the time, along with a group of prominent socialists, who played a key role in establishing the Labour Party—in order to give working people a more effective political voice in Parliament. Since the 1980s, though, and especially under the leadership of Tony Blair between 1994 and 2007, the Labour leadership has distanced the Party from the unions.

3.3.1 Labour's employment relations policies

Having originally opposed the Conservatives' legislative changes, during the early 1990s the Labour Party revised its employment relations policies following a string of election defeats, and came to favour retaining most of the changes. This formed part of a broader shift in Labour policy towards the endorsement, and indeed the celebration, of a dynamic free market economy (Coates 2000). In particular, Labour elaborated a notably enthusiastic acceptance of the desirability of a deregulated labour market as a source of economic competitiveness (e.g. DTI 2006), signalling a marked convergence with the neo-liberal policies that had been followed by previous Conservative governments. Labour's retention of the bulk of the anti-union legislation it inherited from its Conservative predecessors 'marked a shift in the political consensus of the most significant kind' (Davies and Freedland 2007: 111).

Although the unions enjoyed greater involvement in policy deliberations, over the level of the National Minimum Wage for example, this did not constitute a major revival of tripartism by any means (Davies and Freedland 2007). Set against this, though, Labour extended the scope of the juridification of employment relations (see Dickens and Hall 2009, 2010), instigating a major expansion in the scope of employment rights—something that did distinguish its approach from that of its Conservative predecessors. Labour's policy interventions in employment relations between 1997 and 2010 can be categorized under five main themes (see Legislation and policy 3.3 for an overview of the relevant legislation).

LEGISLATION AND POLICY 3.3: The main elements of Labour's legislative programme

- Minimum Wage Act (1998): established the National Minimum Wage, and a procedure for determining its level and scope.

- Employment Relations Act (1999): provided for a new statutory procedure whereby employers would be obliged to recognize a trade union for collective bargaining purposes where there is support from a majority of the workforce.

- Employment Act (2002): extended rights to paid maternity leave; introduced two weeks' paid paternity leave; gave parents of young children the 'right' to request flexible working arrangements.

- Work and Families Act (2006): extended the 'right' to request flexible working arrangements to workers who care for adults; provided for the extension of paid maternity leave to a year, with the opportunity for some of it to be shared with fathers.

- Employment Act (2008): provided for measures to improve the enforcement of the National Minimum Wage; established new arrangements to encourage internal resolution of individual employment disputes.

- First, Labour was keen to encourage greater partnership between employers and trade unions (Brown 2000, 2011), which informed the development of proposals incorporated into the 1999 Employment Relations Act, and discussed in Chapter 5, obliging employers to recognize a union for collective bargaining where there is support from a majority of the workforce. Labour's agenda, however, was marked by an explicitly unitary perspective on social partnership, one that envisages employment relations as being concerned with developing a 'harmony of interests' (Howell 2004); a trade union presence was viewed as legitimate only in so far as it helps to enhance business competitiveness, dependent on the goodwill of employers (Smith and Morton 2006).

- Second, Labour also articulated the need for greater 'fairness' in employment relations, particularly through the establishment of minimum employment standards that prevent workers from being overly exploited (Dickens and Hall 2009, 2010; McKnight 2015). One can point to important policy initiatives like the National Minimum Wage (NMW) as evidence of Labour's commitment to creating a more extensive system of individual employment rights (see Chapter 7). At the same time, though, in emphasizing the benefits of Britain's 'flexible' labour market, Labour was wary of the supposed threat to economic competitiveness of extending employment protection beyond a minimum floor of rights (DTI 2006).

- A third feature of Labour's employment relations programme was the increased emphasis accorded to developing 'family-friendly' policies, designed to improve the balance between home and paid work responsibilities (Nash 2006; McKnight 2015). It introduced a 'right' to request flexible working, for example (see Chapter 8), extended the period of paid maternity leave, and enacted legislation providing for paid paternity leave and unpaid parental leave (see Chapter 4). Yet the extent to which Labour was genuinely committed to securing change in this area, given its reluctance to legislate effectively against excessive working hours (see Chapter 8), is perhaps questionable.

- Fourth, Labour extended both the breadth and depth of equality and anti-discrimination legislation (McKnight 2015), a topic which is considered in more detail in Chapter 4. Yet while over time equality issues became an increasingly important priority for Labour, its reluctance to antagonize employers caused it to resist enacting measures like the Agency Workers Directive, which would have helped to reduce employment discrimination and disadvantage (Bewley 2006).

- The fifth aspect of Labour's approach to employment relations policy concerned its efforts to encourage people to move off welfare benefits and into paid employment— the so-called 'welfare-to-work' agenda (Davies and Freedland 2007). A policy emphasis on 'making work pay', based on strengthening and widening the system of in-work benefits, including tax credits, distinguished Labour's approach, and was a key part of its commitment to reducing poverty (Waldfogel 2010; McKnight 2015). Moreover, measures like the minimum wage helped to improve the attractiveness of work and encourage people to leave welfare as a result. The centrepiece of Labour's welfare-to-work policy were the various New Deal programmes, offering skills training and employment advice to people who experience labour market disadvantage, particularly young workers (Harari 2010). However, critics argue that Labour put too much emphasis on forcing people into work, by using threats to withdraw benefits, and gave insufficient attention to altering the perceptions of employers, who are often prejudiced against people with little, or uneven, work experience (Dwyer 2008; Berry 2014).

Some parts of Labour's employment relations programme were influenced by the need to comply with EU legislation. It is important to acknowledge the more supportive approach taken by Labour to the regulation of employment relations by the EU than was the case under its Conservative predecessor in government, the most evident feature of which was the government's signing of the 'Social Chapter' after entering office in 1997 (see Section 3.5). The result was to increase markedly the scope of juridification in employment relations with EU-derived legislation on such matters as parental leave, equality and discrimination in employment, information and consultation rights for employees, and new rights for part-time and fixed-term contract workers (Dickens and Hall 2009, 2010).

Yet Labour often enacted—'transposed'—EU legislation reluctantly and, where possible, with opt-outs from key provisions, as with the Working Time Directive (see Chapter 8). The argument about the Agency Workers Directive, highlighted in the introduction to this chapter, demonstrates how Labour strived to ensure that when the requisite legislation was enacted it was done in a way that privileged employers' flexibility. This 'minimalist' approach to transposing EU directives accords with the emphasis Labour placed on the appropriateness of a flexible, deregulated labour market, both as a means of sustaining economic competitiveness and maintaining the goodwill of employers (Howell 2005; Davies and Freedland 2007). Moreover, notwithstanding the increase in rights and protections at work under Labour, the machinery for enforcing them remained weak and fragmented (Dickens 2012*a*).

3.3.2 Interpreting Labour's approach to employment relations

How, then, can Labour's approach to employment relations between 1997 and 2010 be interpreted? Clearly, Labour's legislative programme marked a change in emphasis from the approach taken by the Conservatives (Dickens and Hall 2010). Labour took some notable steps to 're-regulate' (Dickens 2014: 243) employment relations, using legislative provisions to expand the scope of employment protections, establish minimum employment standards, and guarantee 'universal' rights such as the statutory minimum wage (Howell and Kolins Givan 2011; Grimshaw 2015; McKnight 2015). There was an emphasis on protecting vulnerable workers, and important measures were taken to extend the scope and degree of equality provisions and to promote work–life balance (McKnight 2015).

Yet Labour's approach to employment relations was also marked by a striking degree of continuity with that taken by its Conservative predecessors in government. This was evident with regard to the importance Labour attached to the desirability of maintaining a flexible, competitive market economy in which business can thrive, and thus generate jobs, unfettered by the activities of trade unions (DTI 2006; Davies and Freedland 2007). Labour retained just about all of the Conservatives' anti-union legislation, meaning that the law continued to impose substantial restrictions on trade union activities (Smith and Morton 2006). From this perspective, employment relations policy under Labour was informed by an underlying neo-liberal belief in the virtues of employment flexibility and deregulation, and ensuring that the activities of the unions remain tightly controlled (Smith and Morton 2006; Daniels and McIlroy 2009; Smith and Morton 2009). Unsurprisingly, then, Labour's relationship with the unions came under an increasing amount of strain—see Employment relations reflection 3.4.

Employment relations reflection 3.4: The relationship between trade unions and the Labour Party

In 2016 there were fourteen trade unions affiliated to, and thus formally part of, the Labour Party. Traditionally union members could pay a 'political levy' which went to Labour. The link with the Labour Party was viewed as an essential way in which workers, collectively through their unions, can influence public policy. During the 2000s there was a growing rift between the Labour Party and its affiliated trade unions as the latter became increasingly disenchanted with the Labour government's policy programme. Two unions—the National Union of Rail, Maritime and Transport workers (RMT) and the Fire Brigades Union (FBU)—disaffiliated from the Labour Party, although the latter has now re-affiliated following the 2015 election of veteran left-winger Jeremy Corbyn as Labour leader. Other trade union affiliates threatened to withdraw their financial support and made some symbolic cuts. Yet most union leaderships strenuously resisted efforts to break with the Labour Party, fearing that such an outcome would prejudice their political influence and thus lose the unions any voice in government (Leopold 2006). The relationship between Labour and the unions prevailed, but it came under increasing strain.

(continued...)

At the same time, though, the Party became increasingly reliant on its affiliated unions for financial support, particularly as donations from wealthy individuals dried up amidst controversies over political funding (McIlroy 2009). In 2014, Labour received £26m in donations, with most of this money coming from large trade union affiliates such as Unison, Unite, and the GMB.

However, Labour's union funding base has come under challenge from two directions. The first of these concerns internal Labour Party reforms. In the aftermath of allegations that the Unite trade union had recruited some of its members to the Labour Party without their knowledge or consent, Labour changed its constitution. Members of affiliated unions can now either join Labour directly, or must actively consent to becoming an 'affiliated supporter', rather than being affiliated by their union. This change may mean that Labour's income from affiliation fees falls (French and Hodder 2016). However, the creation of the new 'affiliated supporter' status was designed to generate a larger, more active and engaged cadre of Labour backers. An influx of new members and affiliated supporters helped to secure Corbyn's initial leadership victory and subsequent re-election in September 2016.

The second challenge to Labour's union funding base has come from government proposals for reform. The 2015 Conservative government originally proposed that each of the 4 million members of union affiliates who pay the political levy must actively 'opt in' to paying it at least once every five years, rather than choosing to 'opt out' as at present. Labour was predicted to lose as much as £8 million in income each year as a consequence. However, the government was forced into making a number of concessions before it could win parliamentary approval for its proposals—see Section 3.4.3. One of these was that the requirement to 'opt in' to paying the political levy will only apply to new union members, not existing members.

While accepting that neo-liberalism exercised an increasingly marked influence over Labour's approach to employment relations between 1997 and 2010, it is necessary to offer a more nuanced assessment of its policy interventions than simply ascribing them to neo-liberal ideology. Three points are relevant in this respect. First, bear in mind that Labour was keener to progress change in some areas than it was in others. For example, it seemed more at ease promoting work–life balance policies, given the greater scope for securing support from employers, than it was with extending trade union rights (Dickens and Hall 2010).

Second, following on from this, the overall coherence of Labour's approach in government should not be overstated. It is partly to be understood as an 'amalgam of competing values' (Dickens and Hall 2009: 340). Yes, there was a strong degree of continuity with the approach taken by the Conservatives in the 1980s and 1990s; but there were also important differences. While neo-liberal ideology was undoubtedly an important influence on policy interventions, it sometimes conflicted with pressures coming from both inside and outside government (e.g. trade unions, campaign groups) for greater regulation of employment relations. A good example of this was the response to the tragic deaths of twenty-three Chinese cocklepickers who drowned while working in Morecambe Bay in 2004. Following pressure from unions, and also some of its own supporters in Parliament, the Labour government established the Gangmasters Licensing Authority (GLA), whose job is to regulate labour providers in employment sectors with large numbers of migrant workers (such as agriculture)—see Chapter 10.

The example of the GLA points to the third distinctive feature of Labour's approach—a predilection for establishing institutions as a means of dealing with controversial areas of employment relations policy, and of reconciling the different interests of employers' bodies and trade unions in a way that promotes partnership and cooperation (Brown 2011). The Low

Pay Commission, which was established in 1998 to make recommendations about the level of the minimum wage, is perhaps the most obvious example of this—see Chapter 7.

Overall, then, how can Labour's approach to employment relations be assessed? Perhaps the main outcome was that voluntarism, which had already been undermined by the policies of previous governments, such as the Conservative anti-union legislation of the 1980s and 1990s, increasingly departed the scene. Under Labour there was a marked increase in the juridification of the employment relationship, the result of which is that employment protection 'relies increasingly on legal rights not collective organization' through trade unions (Dickens and Hall 2010: 317; Howell and Kolins Givan 2011).

Labour articulated a distinctive approach to employment relations policy which held that the main purpose of government regulation is not to help correct the imbalance of power between workers and employers but to support and enhance economic competitiveness (Howell 2005; Davies and Freedland 2007). In this way, aspirations towards fairness and better employment standards can be reconciled with, but are clearly subordinate to, the need to maintain labour market flexibility as a source of improved business performance. This explains the Labour government's opposition to EU measures like the Agency Workers Directive, designed to improve workers' rights (see the introductory case study). Labour market regulation was pursued only in so far as it did not challenge the prevailing neo-liberal assumption that deregulation is the most effective means of generating improvements in economic competitiveness.

 ### Section summary and further reading

- Between 1997 and 2010 the Labour governments of Tony Blair and Gordon Brown instituted some important changes in employment relations policy, notably the development of new statutory protections in the area of individual employment rights.

- Labour did, however, retain the overwhelming bulk of the anti-union legislation it inherited from the Conservatives, and its employment relations policy interventions were designed not to upset employers. This reflected a largely uncritical acceptance of neo-liberal ideology: that economic competitiveness is contingent on deregulated and flexible labour markets, making the strengthening of union and workers' rights undesirable.

For insightful analyses of Labour's approach to employment relations, see the work of Dickens and Hall (2006, 2010) and Brown (2011). For a robust critique of Labour's neo-liberalism, see the work of Smith and Morton (2006, 2009).

3.4 Employment relations under coalition and Conservative governments since 2010

Although Labour lost a substantial number of seats at the May 2010 general election, no party was able to command a parliamentary majority. Following five days of extensive bargaining, the Conservatives—the party with the largest number of MPs—concluded an agreement with the third largest party, the Liberal Democrats, to govern in a coalition. This section commences by providing an overview of the coalition's broad economic and political agenda, before examining the 'reasserted neo-liberalism' (Grimshaw and Rubery 2012) evident in employment relations. It then covers the main employment relations policies pursued by the majority Conservative administration elected in 2015 during its first year in office.

3.4.1 The UK coalition government's economic and political agenda

The outcome of the inconclusive May 2010 general election was the formation of a coalition government between the Conservative Party and the Liberal Democrats, with David Cameron as prime minister. When they were in office during the 1980s and 1990s the Conservatives pursued a robust anti-union and deregulatory policy agenda which was informed by neo-liberal ideology. Under David Cameron, who became its leader in 2005, the Conservative Party had initially tried to 'modernize' itself, in the sense of formulating policies that would appeal to a broader range of voters and thus win electoral support, including an apparent abandonment of the neo-liberal emphasis on the importance of markets and deregulation that had previously dominated its approach. However, in the aftermath of the 2007–8 financial and economic crisis its modernizing efforts were increasingly eclipsed by the growing predominance of a more conventional deregulatory agenda in the area of employment relations policy, manifest in concerns about how the perceived burden of 'red tape' associated with employment protections inhibited employers' flexibility (Williams and Scott 2010, 2011).

Moreover, the leadership of the Liberal Democrats—the Conservatives' coalition partners—also increasingly came to favour neo-liberalism. In the past, the Liberal Democrat policy agenda was dominated by a social liberalism approach. This views state intervention, including employment regulation, as a necessary and desirable means of promoting liberal principles such as greater social justice and reduced inequality. From the mid-2000s onwards, however, the influence of social liberalism diminished, especially under the leadership of Nick Clegg, sidelined by the revival of the classical tradition of market liberalism, which emphasizes the virtues of the small state and the desirability of free markets (Marshall and Laws 2004; Gray 2010; Grayson 2010).

In the aftermath of the 2010 general election the decision to form a coalition between the Conservatives and the Liberal Democrats was to a large extent predicated on the belief that a stable government, capable of lasting five years, was necessary to tackle the consequences of the financial and economic crisis. The Liberal Democrats acquiesced to the view, vigorously propagated by the Conservatives, that the overriding economic priority was to reduce the size of the budget deficit (the gap between current government revenues and expenditure) (Williams and Scott 2016a). Fears of a Greek-style sovereign debt crisis were exaggerated to win over the Liberal Democrats and to get them to support the Conservatives' economic programme, with the eradication of the budget deficit as its centrepiece (Gamble 2015; Whiteley et al. 2015).

Prioritizing the tackling of the budget deficit was designed to restore the UK's economic stability and provide the conditions to secure renewed sustained, long-term economic growth. The emphasis on speedily eliminating the budget deficit also had the political advantage of allowing the coalition parties to blame the preceding Labour government for the country's economic difficulties (Gamble 2015; Williams and Scott 2016a). The coalition's economic agenda—to eliminate the budget deficit over a single, five-year parliamentary term—was dominated by major planned reductions in public expenditure—so-called 'austerity'—rather than securing revenue gains through tax rises (HM Government 2010).

The theoretical rationale for what became known as 'expansionary fiscal contraction' was that rapid action to combat the budget deficit, largely through austerity measures (i.e. spending cuts), would quickly help to restore the confidence of the financial markets, help to attract investment, restore competitiveness, and thus stimulate economic growth (Lee 2015; Williams and Scott 2016a). However, the coalition's approach, particularly the emphasis on austerity, stopped the nascent economic recovery in its tracks. For the first two years of the coalition's period in government—between 2010 and 2012—the UK economy failed to grow; another recession was only narrowly avoided (Wren-Lewis 2015). Contrary to the expectations of those who advocated expansionary fiscal contraction, its actual effects on the economy were highly damaging. As a result, in 2012 the government changed its approach and reduced the speed at which it planned to reduce the budget deficit (Hannon 2016), with the consequence that by 2015–16 the deficit had fallen by slightly more than half of its size five years previously; but by no means was it even close to being eradicated.

While the coalition's economic policy agenda was ultimately something of a failure, it nonetheless bound the Conservatives and Liberal Democrats together. But the coalition was also predicated on a shared neo-liberal belief in the virtues of free markets and deregulation. The notable degree of ideological affinity between the respective party leaderships was an important precondition for coalition (Lee 2011; Beech 2015). The coalition government's emphasis on reducing the budget deficit, largely through reductions in public expenditure, was based on the neo-liberal belief that a significant reduction in the size of the state was an essential precondition for economic growth (Williams, Scott, and Welch 2016). Prioritizing deficit reduction and the emphasis on austerity were fundamentally political choices, not economic necessities, and were informed by a strong belief in the desirability of reducing the size of the state and the role of government (Beech 2015; Gamble 2015; Williams and Scott 2016a). However, the impact of the austerity measures hit the poorest and most vulnerable members of society particularly hard (Clark 2014; Grimshaw 2015), and one of the consequences was a substantial increase in people's dependency on emergency food aid (Loopstra et al. 2015).

3.4.2 The coalition government's 'reasserted neo-liberalism' in employment relations

To what extent, and in what ways, did the Conservative–Liberal Democrat coalition's approach to employment relations between 2010 and 2015 diverge from that taken by Labour? The framework of employment rights and protections established by Labour between 1997 and 2010 was left largely intact (Williams, Scott, and Welch 2016). This was exemplified by the cross-party consensus in support of the National Minimum Wage. Continuity was also evident when it came to the coalition's advocacy of improved rights to parental leave and flexible working (see Chapter 4), extending a policy agenda that Labour had originated when it was in power during the 2000s. The lack of enthusiasm on the part of the Liberal Democrats also meant that little change was evident in the field of collective labour law—covering matters such as trade unions and strikes—to the occasional frustration of the Conservatives, who favoured a more robust anti-union approach (French and Hodder 2016). Moreover, political considerations—the Liberal Democrats strongly supported the UK's membership of the European Union—prevented the Conservatives from making any progress in rescinding EU social and employment rights (Lynch 2015)—see Section 3.5.2.

That said, however, there is a strong degree of support for the view, expressed by Grimshaw and Rubery (2012), that the coalition's period in office saw a 'reasserted neo-liberalism' come to prominence, distinguishing its period in office from that of its Labour predecessor. Unlike Labour, which had focused on institution-building in employment relations, the coalition was more concerned with dismantling and undermining these institutions (Williams, Scott, and Welch 2016). Whereas Labour had established new employment rights and protections with too much of an eye on privileging employers' flexibility, or as an aid to improving competitiveness, the coalition's onus was, where possible, on eroding them (Welch 2016).

This was predicated on the belief that the UK was over-regulated, and that employers needed greater flexibility in order to improve competitiveness. The coalition government believed that an excessive amount of employment regulation had made employers fearful of taking on new staff. Making it easier to fire workers, it was presumed, would encourage employers to hire them in the first place and thus help to promote growth (BIS 2012a)—an archetypal neo-liberal claim, despite the lack of any supporting evidence (e.g. BIS 2012b). Central to the coalition's approach was an assumption that, beyond operating an unspecified 'core of fundamental employment protections', the government should abstain from intervening to regulate employment relationships. The coalition propounded a rather idealistic and abstentionist 'vision for the labour market in which both employers and workers are informed and empowered, able to negotiate their relationship within a framework of fundamental protections, with minimal intervention by the Government' (BIS 2011: 6).

The coalition's deregulatory agenda was evident in a number of areas of work and employment relations policy, including the weakening of equality legislation (see Chapter 4) and workplace health and safety, where it took steps to reduce the number of proactive inspections (James, Tombs, and Whyte 2013; James 2016). There was a particular concern with reforming the arrangements for resolving employment disputes, particularly the system of employment tribunals, including the introduction of tribunal fees (Welch 2016)—see Chapter 10. The coalition also increased the qualifying period before which an employee is entitled to claim unfair dismissal, from one year in a job to two years. Overall, the coalition presided over a shift towards a system of employment relations within which workers not only have fewer rights and protections, but also increasingly lack a means of enforcing them (Welch 2016).

LEGISLATION AND POLICY 3.5: The Modern Slavery Act 2015

As shown in Chapter 2, increasing concerns have been raised about extreme levels of exploitation of migrant workers, including claims that forced labour has become commonplace in some parts of the economy. During the coalition's period in office between 2010 and 2015, the Labour opposition kept raising the issue of how migrant workers were treated, in a way that put pressure on the government to act. It did so by enacting the Modern Slavery Act 2015. The legislation consolidates existing laws prohibiting slavery and human trafficking, and increases the maximum penalty for those convicted of human trafficking from fourteen years to life imprisonment. The Act also imposes a new obligation on businesses to disclose the action they are taking to ensure that their supply chains are free from enslaved workers. Why was the coalition government so keen to progress this measure? One reason was that it provided a tactical political advantage, namely enabling the coalition to 'spike Labour's guns on migrant exploitation without conceding the need for greater levels of regulation in the labour market' (Balch 2016: 157). Politically, the Modern Slavery Act was useful for another reason, in that it

(continued...)

helped establish the moral credentials of the coalition in general, and the Conservatives in particular, especially as the 2015 general election neared (Balch 2016). Yet the practical consequences of the Act are unclear. Moreover, critics have attacked the government's refusal to include measures that would protect foreign domestic workers who enter the UK on visas that tie them to their employers (Kalaayan 2015).

This was particularly apparent from the marked extent to which, under the coalition, labour become more 'commodified', as a consequence of neo-liberal austerity measures and the drive towards a 'market society' (Grimshaw 2015). The coalition government's welfare policies, in particular, were designed to ensure a supply of cheap, flexible, and disposable labour for employers (Williams and Scott 2016*b*)—see Chapter 2. An important consequence of greater commodification was that, notwithstanding the existence of formal employment rights and protections, workers were increasingly unable to access or enforce them because of the irregular or casualized nature of their work (Welch 2016). At the same time, though, such developments also contributed to pressure for greater 're-regulation' in employment relations. The development of legislation concerned with tackling the problem of 'modern slavery' can be viewed in this light—see Legislation and policy 3.5. The Liberal Democrat side of the coalition, in particular, was sensitive to concerns that the balance of power in the labour market had swung too far in favour of employers (Williams, Scott, and Welch 2016). As a result, it advanced some relatively modest reforms to the law regulating zero-hours contracts (see Chapter 8).

3.4.3 The 2015 Conservative majority government's employment relations agenda

At the May 2015 UK general election, the Conservatives won a small but almost entirely unexpected parliamentary majority, allowing David Cameron to continue as prime minister without the need to involve the Liberal Democrats—who won just eight seats, down from fifty-seven in 2010—in government. Labour was badly affected by the surge of support for the Scottish National Party (SNP), losing all but one of its seats in Scotland. Under the leadership of Ed Miliband, Labour had developed policies designed to tackle some of the more egregious problems evident in the increasingly casualized labour market, including tighter regulation of zero-hours contracts and action to mitigate low pay through a greater emphasis on promoting the so-called 'living wage' (Williams, Scott, and Welch 2016).

Given the Conservative election victory, this was all largely academic. Nevertheless, the Conservatives, rather cleverly, adopted some of Labour's policies as part of a strategy designed to foster their long-term political aspirations, and maintain their electability, by demonstrating that they are the party best positioned to look after the interests of working people (Spours 2015). In the field of employment relations, this emphasis on consensus is most apparent with regard to the new 'National Living Wage' (NLW) policy which took effect in April 2016. As Chapter 7 shows, the initial NLW rate—£7.20 per hour for workers aged 25 and over—was rather less than that considered to be a living wage by experts. Effectively, it is a rise in the National Minimum Wage for older workers. Importantly, moreover, the NLW will not necessarily leave many working people better off, since cuts to in-work welfare benefits mean that the income of lots of low-paid workers will nonetheless diminish. What it does do, though, is to convey a message that the Conservatives are supportive of working people, and wish to do more to improve their lives, with the added political benefit that it helps to marginalize Labour.

As Spours (2015) contends, however, the Conservatives have not only sought to advance their agenda, and secure a long-term electoral advantage, through efforts to align themselves with the political consensus, over matters such as low pay. They have also tried to maintain their domination over the English (and hence the UK) political landscape through more coercive measures. This was exemplified by the enactment of the Trade Union Act, which became law in May 2016. Liberated from the constraints of governing in coalition with the Liberal Democrats, one of the first major initiatives of the newly elected majority Conservative administration was to propose legislation that imposes severe new restrictions on the trade unions. This included mandating tighter restrictions in industrial action ballots (Darlington and Dobson 2015; Smith 2015)—see Chapter 9. It is noteworthy that after eighteen years in opposition or coalition, one of the first major steps by the Conservatives, once they had secured a majority, was to resurrect the kind of anti-union agenda that dominated their approach to employment relations during the 1980s and 1990s (Williams, Scott, and Welch 2016). Weakening the power of the unions, as the Act aims to do, will help to shift the balance of power in employment relations further in favour of employers and contribute to increased labour market insecurity (Darlington and Dobson 2015).

LEGISLATION AND POLICY 3.6: The implications of devolution for employment relations

During the late 1990s Tony Blair's first Labour government established devolved governments in Scotland and Wales for the first time. Northern Ireland was also given its own elected government again, twenty-five years after the British government imposed direct rule on the province. Devolved government poses a potentially significant obstacle to the UK Conservative government's employment relations aspirations. During the period of coalition government between 2010 and 2015 in particular, both the SNP government in Scotland and the Labour administration in Wales pursued social and employment policies that rejected neo-liberal austerity and were more supportive of engaging positively with trade unions, in contrast to the approach which predominated at UK level. The Scottish government opposed the introduction of employment tribunal fees, claiming that they undermined efforts by aggrieved workers to secure justice for problems at work. In Wales, the Welsh government mounted a successful legal challenge against the UK government when it argued for continued special arrangements for regulating wages in the low-paid agriculture sector.

With the arrival of a majority Conservative government at Westminster, pressures for divergence have increased. The Scottish government, for example, opposed the Conservatives' trade union legislation, and made efforts to try and prevent it applying in Scotland. In England the UK government became involved in an antagonistic industrial dispute with junior doctors over the imposition of new employment contracts; whereas the Scottish and Welsh governments avoided confrontation by choosing not to pursue contractual changes.

Sources: Williams and Scott (2016c); Williams, Scott, and Welch (2016)

Part of the rationale for imposing further restrictions on the unions is that this can help to maintain Conservative domination by reducing the prospect that its controversial policies will be successfully challenged. Nevertheless, during 2015–16 parliamentary opposition, particularly in the upper House of Lords, where the Conservatives do not have a majority, stymied proposed welfare cuts, reductions in police budgets, and efforts to liberalize Sunday trading (see Chapter 8 for the latter). Vigorous lobbying against the new trade union legislation, both inside and outside Parliament, forced the Conservatives to drop some of the measures originally proposed for the Trade Union Act, including proposals to regulate unions' use of social media, to require all union members to 'opt in' to paying political levies, and to stop the automatic deduction of membership fees from salaries. Devolution in the UK also poses a challenge to the Conservative government's employment relations aspirations—see Legislation and policy 3.6.

While Labour's electoral prospects under the leadership of left-winger Jeremy Corbyn, who became leader in September 2015, might seem poor, his election (and 2016 re-election) as party leader signals a break with the prevailing neo-liberal consensus that privileges employers' flexibility. Labour now puts a greater emphasis on the desirability of improving workers' rights and restoring trade union freedoms (Williams, Scott, and Welch 2016). There are also signs of a potential change of approach from the Conservative government, under David Cameron's successor as prime minister, Theresa May, who replaced him following the June 2016 EU referendum vote. As well as intimating that a softening of austerity might be in prospect, and that a less punitive benefits system would be desirable, May's new administration has evinced a concern with the interests of workers, including a suggestion of involving worker representatives on company boards (see Chapter 1).

 ### Section summary and further reading

- The formation of the coalition government between the Conservatives and Liberal Democrats in May 2010 was predicated on the claim that a stable government was needed in order to tackle the effects of the financial and economic crisis. However, the coalition's deficit-reduction plan, based mainly on austerity, was largely unsuccessful.

- The leaderships of the coalition parties expressed a shared neo-liberal ideological belief in the desirability of giving employers greater flexibility, exemplified by the pronounced emphasis given to deregulating employment relations in a way that helped to facilitate labour commodification.

- Before David Cameron's departure as prime minister, the majority Conservative government had attempted to extend and reinforce its political domination through measures designed to reflect consensus (e.g. around the desirability of tacking low pay) and through a more coercive strategy towards trade unions.

For further information about the coalition government's policies on employment relations, see the chapters contained in Williams and Scott (2016d). Williams, Scott, and Welch (2016) cover the prospects for employment relations under the Conservative majority government elected in 2015, albeit in a chapter written before Theresa May's appointment as prime minister in July 2016.

3.5 Employment relations and the politics of European (dis)integration

Between 1957, when it was established as the European Economic Community (EEC), and 2016, the European Union (EU) expanded in size—from six to twenty-eight countries. The development of the EU was also characterized by a process of greater integration, involving a general deepening of relationships between its member states. Fundamentally, this project of European integration was economic in nature. It was centred on advancing 'four freedoms'— the free movement of capital, goods, services, and workers—throughout the EU. However, the outcome of the June 2016 referendum vote, when 52 per cent of UK voters voted in favour of leaving the EU, perhaps signals that the era of greater integration has come to an end, and that from now on it might be more appropriate to refer to a process of disintegration occurring. That said, though, the UK has often taken a rather detached position, having excluded itself from a number of notable EU measures—the Schengen border-free zone, for example, and the euro single currency. As this section shows, moreover, UK governments have frequently been ambivalent, at best, and downright hostile at worst, towards EU social and employment legislation. It also demonstrates the large extent to which employment issues—anxieties about deteriorating labour standards and concerns about the impact of EU migration—influenced the outcome of the referendum vote.

Before proceeding any further, there are three things that need to be acknowledged. First, the respective roles enjoyed by the different EU bodies need to be understood. See International perspective 3.7 for details of the relevant institutions. Second, you should also be aware that the EU is based on a series of treaties which establish its powers, or 'competences', relative to those of its member states (Hepple 2005). One of the biggest sources of political conflict in the EU has been the resistance of the UK government to reforms that are perceived to weaken its national powers, and this includes powers to effect employment laws.

 International perspective 3.7: The institutions of the European Union

There are five principal EU institutions. The European Commission, comprising representatives from each member state, is responsible for promoting and effecting legislation, and monitoring its progress. The Court of Justice of the European Union (CJEU), which encompasses the European Court of Justice (ECJ), deliberates on matters of EU law and on issues that are of EU-wide significance. The European Parliament, made up of directly elected members from all EU countries, has traditionally lacked much influence though it can now obstruct and amend legislation in some areas. The European Council involves regular meetings of EU leaders. It sets the EU's overall direction and priorities. Most power, however, rests with the Council of the European Union. Comprising ministers from member states, it represents the interests of member state governments, and is the principal decision-making body of the EU.

In respect of employment relations, though, the role of the 'social partners', bodies representing the interests of employers and unions at EU level, must also be acknowledged. There are three main employers' organizations. Founded in 1958, Business Europe represents the interests of private sector

(continued...)

employers. The Confederation of British Industry (CBI) is one of its forty affiliates from thirty-four different countries. The European Association of Craft, Small and Medium-Sized Enterprises (UEAPME) represents the interests of small and medium-sized employers. The European Centre of Enterprises with Public Participation and of Enterprises of General Economic Interest (CEEP) acts on behalf of public sector employers in around twenty countries. The European Trade Union Confederation (ETUC) is the social partner that represents the interests of the trade unions. Founded in 1973, it encompasses eighty-nine national trade union confederations, including the British TUC, from thirty-nine different countries. The ETUC supports the activities of ten European industry federations (EIFs), bodies that represent the interests of trade unions in specific industrial sectors, including IndustriAll—the European Federation for Industry and Manufacturing Workers.

Third, alongside an emphasis on market integration the EU also possesses a 'social dimension', which encompasses employment relations matters. It comprises four main elements: (1) legislation, largely in the form of directives which the governments of individual member states are required to implement in their own territories; (2) social programmes, including assistance and support to help unemployed people into work for example (outside the scope of this book); (3) 'social dialogue', discussions between employers' bodies and trade union organizations; and (4) something called the 'open method of coordination' (OMC), which encompasses voluntary, non-binding measures to realize employment-related goals (see Vaughan-Whitehead 2015: 3–12). (See 3.5.2 for more on the OMC.)

3.5.1 The EU 'social dimension'

The EU was instituted as the European Economic Community (EEC), or the 'Common Market' as it became popularly known, in 1957 when France, Italy, West Germany (as it then was), and the Benelux countries (Belgium, the Netherlands, and Luxembourg) acceded to the Treaty of Rome. Britain joined the EEC sixteen years later. As its name suggests, the EEC was designed as a vehicle for greater economic cooperation across Western Europe: a means of promoting market integration. This meant that, initially at least, there was little concern with promoting any kind of social dimension, except in so far as it enhanced economic cooperation (Bridgford and Stirling 1994; Teague 1999; Hyman 2010). As a result, matters relating to 'labour law and social protection were seen as almost exclusively national functions' (Hepple 2005: 199).

Although the 1970s saw some progress in giving the EEC a more active social and employment dimension, these efforts accelerated in following decade, in the context of the progress towards the anticipated conclusion of the Single European Market, which took effect in 1993 (Hyman 2010). The social dimension was developed to facilitate the 'upward' or 'positive' harmonization of employment rules and regulations throughout the EU. Instituting a cross-Europe floor of labour standards would protect the interests of workers and help to maintain the existence of a 'European Social Model'—comprising strong welfare states, robust employment regulations, healthy trade unions, and effective collective bargaining arrangements—moderating the impact of market forces on the lives of workers (Meardi 2012).

Nevertheless, a central motivating force underpinning the increased emphasis given to social and employment policy during this period was the need to secure support for, and the legitimacy of, further economic integration in Europe (Bridgford and Stirling 1994; Grahl 2015). Moreover, without the development of minimum labour standards, the ability of multinational corporations to redirect investment, and therefore jobs, to locations where labour costs are lower—'social dumping' as this became known—would otherwise go unchecked (Adnett and Hardy 2005).

UK Conservative governments, under Margaret Thatcher and John Major, profoundly opposed the expansion of the European Community's competence in the area of social and employment policy (Davies and Freedland 1993). The 1993 Treaty of European Union, agreed in 1991 in the Dutch town of Maastricht, in fact comprised two separate documents. One included a new 'Social Chapter' that gave the EU more scope to legislate on a range of social and employment matters, including information and consultation rights for workers, and was signed by all the member states except the UK. The other, which the UK Conservative government signed, left this chapter out.

It was only after Labour took office in 1997 that this situation changed, as it brought the UK under the aegis of the Social Chapter, which was formally instituted by that year's Treaty of Amsterdam. As a result, EU directives relating to matters such as parental leave rights and information and consultation rights for workers had to be implemented. Sex discrimination in employment had come within the purview of the EU since the Social Action Programme of the 1970s. Importantly, however, the Treaty of Amsterdam also extended the scope of the EU's competence in employment-related matters to cover matters relating to other aspects of discrimination, on the grounds of race and ethnicity, sexual orientation, religion or belief, and age (Davies and Freedland 2007). This resulted in two new directives being agreed in 2000: a framework directive covering equal treatment in employment and occupations, and a directive dealing with racial discrimination. See Legislation and policy 3.8 for details of the major EU directives in the area of employment policy enacted after 1993.

LEGISLATION AND POLICY 3.8: Major European Union directives in the area of employment relations since 1993

- The Directive on the Adaptation of Working Time (1993): provides for the regulation of working hours, rest breaks, and holiday periods (see Chapter 8).

- The European Works Council Directive (1994): provides for the establishment of transnational information and consultation arrangements in multinational companies operating in Europe. A revised directive was agreed in 2009 (see Chapter 6).

- The Posting of Workers Directive (1996): gives workers who are posted abroad to another EU member state for a limited period of time the right to the same core pay and conditions enjoyed by local workers (see Section 3.5.3).

- The Parental Leave Directive (1996): provides for minimum standards of parental leave provision within the EU; a revised directive was agreed in 2009.

(continued...)

- The Directive on Equal Rights and Treatment for Part-Time Workers (1997): prohibits employers from giving part-time workers less favourable pay and conditions than equivalent full-time staff.
- The Fixed-Term Contract Workers Directive (1999): prohibits employers from giving workers on fixed-term contracts less favourable pay and conditions than equivalent permanent staff.
- The Race Directive (2000): establishes minimum standards of Europe-wide legal protection for individuals on the grounds of racial or ethnic origins.
- The Framework for Equal Treatment in Employment and Occupations Directive (2000): prohibits direct or indirect discrimination on grounds of religion or belief, disability, age, or sexual orientation.
- The National Information and Consultation of Employees Directive (2002): provides for information and consultation arrangements among firms employing fifty workers or more (see Chapter 6).
- The Agency Workers Directive: first proposed in 2002 and eventually agreed in 2008, this directive provides for agency-supplied temporary workers to get pay and conditions that are comparable with those enjoyed by permanent employees—subject to certain conditions (see the introductory case study).

The 1993 Maastricht Treaty also gave a major boost to another aspect of the developing social dimension—the process of 'social dialogue'. Between the 1960s and 1980s, the European Commission supported various initiatives designed to facilitate discussion between trade union bodies and employers' organizations on matters of mutual interest (Hall 1994; Waddington and Hoffman 2003). Moreover, the 1987 Single European Act obliged the Commission to encourage the development of social dialogue between the social partners at European level (Carley 1993; Bridgford and Stirling 1994). It was thought that legislative proposals in the field of social and employment policy would stand more chance of success if they already had the support of the trade unions and employers' organizations (Hall 1994).

The Maastricht Treaty provided for the conclusion of 'framework agreements' between the social partners. In areas where directives had been proposed, trade unions and employers' organizations at EU level were given an opportunity to reach an agreement themselves, which could then be taken forward and adopted as legislation. The Maastricht Treaty also established the basis for 'framework agreements' between the social partners that could be implemented voluntarily across the EU member states without the need for legislative action (Keller and Sörries 1999). See Insight into practice 3.9 for details of how social dialogue has progressed.

 Insight into practice 3.9:The outcomes of social dialogue

Social dialogue operates in three broad ways. First, at EU level the social partners (employers' organizations and trade union bodies) can reach their own negotiated 'framework agreement' on a proposal, which is then taken forward and enacted as EU legislation in the form of an appropriate directive. Directives regulating parental leave and the rights of part-time and fixed-term contract workers were all put into effect following agreement between the social partners (Keller and Sörries 1999). However, Business Europe only participated reluctantly. Since the 1990s this element of social

(continued...)

dialogue has produced rather little at EU level. In specific industry sectors, however, some progress has been evident (Degryse 2015). In 2012, for example, a framework agreement was concluded on health and safety in the hairdressing sector. However, opposition from some member state governments led to its implementation being postponed (Bandasz 2014).

Second, social dialogue at EU level can also lead to voluntary framework agreements between the social partners, which do not have legislative effect. Four such agreements have been concluded: on telework (2002), workplace stress (2004) (see Prosser 2011), harassment and violence at work (2007), and 'inclusive labour markets' (2010). A major problem with the voluntary approach is the difficulty of guaranteeing compliance across EU member states (Keller 2003). In addition, employers' bodies can be reluctant to engage in meaningful dialogue because they are wary of encouraging cross-border bargaining with unions.

Third, social dialogue also operates at industry level between sector-specific employers' organizations and union federations. The European Commission has invested a great deal of effort into encouraging dialogue between the social partners at industry sector level. While there has been a modest increase in the coverage of sectoral social dialogue during the 2000s, measurable progress, in terms of actual outcomes, has been rather modest (Keller and Weber 2011).

How can the EU's social dimension be interpreted? Business groups are often highly critical of the additional regulation created by EU legislation, citing the increased costs it supposedly generates. The Working Time Directive, which limits working hours (see Chapter 8), is viewed as particularly harmful, despite the flexibility offered by 'opt-outs'. Consistent with the neo-liberal, deregulatory ethos which increasingly informed its approach to employment relations policy in general, during the 2000s Labour took a decidedly employer-friendly approach to the implementation of EU labour law, evident in its long-standing opposition to the Agency Workers Directive.

Unsurprisingly, given the primacy of its neo-liberal ideological belief in the virtues of deregulation, the 2010–15 coalition government, particularly the increasingly 'Eurosceptic' Conservative element, was instinctively hostile to social and employment laws emanating from Europe. The Conservatives, in fact, held a long-standing belief in the desirability of regaining national-level control over EU social and employment law, as part of their broader aim to repatriate EU powers back to the UK. To do so, however, required treaty change, and thus the agreement of all twenty-seven other member states. Given this practical difficulty, perhaps it is not surprising that the Conservatives dropped their aspiration to repatriate EU social and employment law back to the UK when it came to negotiating the 2010 coalition agreement with the pro-EU Liberal Democrats (Williams and Scott 2011; Lynch 2015). However, this did not prevent the coalition, especially the Conservatives, from engaging with the issue of EU social and employment law, and how it could be relaxed, given the assumption—based largely on complaints from employers—that it hinders business flexibility and undermines competitiveness (Williams and Scott 2016c).

A particular challenge for the Conservative leadership, moreover, was the need to find a response to the challenges posed by the increasingly popular United Kingdom Independence Party (UKIP), which advocated the UK leaving the EU (Lynch 2015), and also the vocal Eurosceptic element evident within the Conservative Party at large. As a consequence, in 2013 prime minister David Cameron announced that a future Conservative government would attempt to re-negotiate the terms of the UK's membership of the EU before holding a referendum. The largely unexpected 2015 Conservative general election victory meant that, liberated from having to govern in coalition with the pro-EU Liberal Democrats, Cameron was obliged to uphold his pledge to hold such a vote. The referendum, which took place in June 2016, saw the UK electorate narrowly vote in favour of leaving the EU.

Although some Conservative ministers dissented, and campaigned for the leave side, the government's official position was to support the campaign to remain. This was on the basis that Cameron's negotiations with other EU leaders during the winter of 2015–16 had given the UK sufficient concessions to enable him to recommend a vote in favour of staying in the EU. Intriguingly, however, a demand to repatriate EU social and employment law back to the UK was not one of the government's formal negotiating objectives. This omission appears very odd indeed given the hostility expressed by the Conservatives towards EU-derived employment rights and protection over many years.

Why were these not up for review during the process of re-negotiating the UK's membership of the EU? The reason relates to practical politics. There is no doubt that Cameron and his ministers would like to have excluded the UK from the coverage of EU social and employment law; but winning the agreement of all the other member states, as he needed to do, was never going to be remotely possible. Moreover, winning the referendum and remaining in the EU, as Cameron and most leading government ministers wanted, necessitated attracting votes from Labour supporters and trade unionists who value the employment rights and protections offered by Europe (Williams, Scott, and Welch 2016). Most trade unions, and the Trades Union Congress (TUC), officially supported the campaign to keep the UK in the EU. They saw EU directives as providing workers with important rights and protections—a counterweight to the more neo-liberal policy approach often favoured by successive UK governments. What happens to European social and employment legislation once the UK actually leaves the EU is one of the many issues that needs to be determined, although the government's initial preference seemed to be for keeping the existing rules in place.

3.5.2 **The demise of 'Social Europe'**

However, not all unions favoured the UK remaining in the EU. There is a critical perspective which suggests that the social dimension has not been a very effective means of enhancing workers' rights (Wedderburn 1995). Key aspects of employment relations policy, such as collective bargaining and the right of workers to associate in trade unions, still largely come within the prerogative of individual member states. The EU is primarily a vehicle for promoting market integration (Martin and Ross 1999), largely benefiting the interests of multinational companies, with social and employment measures having a markedly subordinate status. Moreover, during the 2000s the social dimension of the EU has been decidedly weakened, in favour of a more pronounced neo-liberal emphasis on promoting economic competitiveness and business flexibility (Crespy and Menz 2015). In the 2016 referendum campaign, the organization Trade Unions Against the EU, for example, called for a 'Europe that guarantees the rights of workers and does not put the interests of big business above that of working people', something that it reckoned was impossible within an EU which pursues a predominantly neo-liberal policy agenda. For this reason, the Rail, Maritime, and Transport Union (RMT) was one of the unions which supported a vote to leave the EU.

There has been some progress made towards strengthening the EU social dimension. Perhaps the main advance came in 2009, when the new Lisbon Treaty of European Union came into effect, which included a number of measures relating to social matters, most notably the inclusion of the Charter of Fundamental Rights of the European Union as an appendix (Pochet and Degryse 2010).

First published in 2000, the Charter contains fifty-four articles arranged in seven chapters. One of the chapters deals with the theme of 'solidarity', encompassing rights to fair and just working conditions, collective bargaining, and taking strike action.

That aside, though, during the 2000s the overall level of EU interest in social and employment policy initiatives diminished considerably. New legislative initiatives were few and far between; where changes to employment law did arise they were largely concerned with revising existing directives (e.g. Parental Leave Directive, European Works Council Directive) rather than instituting anything new (Hyman 2010; Pochet and Degryse 2010). Moreover, EU policy-makers increasingly eschewed measures to enhance labour standards, instead looking more to policies designed to improve economic competitiveness through increased labour market flexibility and employment deregulation (Hyman 2010; Crespy and Menz 2015). There was a greater emphasis on 'negative harmonization' (Adnett and Hardy 2005; Hepple 2005), encompassing policies designed to reduce the barriers to job creation, and enacting measures that support business flexibility and improve competitiveness (Crespy and Menz 2015). From this perspective, labour standards hinder economic prosperity, and so should be weakened. Negative harmonization involves the freeing up of markets, including labour markets, on a Europe-wide basis, minimizing the effects of employment regulation to give employers more flexibility (Hyman 2011; Meardi 2012). See Table 3.1 for the main differences between positive and negative harmonization.

This neo-liberal emphasis on competitiveness and business flexibility was symbolized by the so-called 'Lisbon agenda' which dominated EU thinking during the 2000s. At the Lisbon summit of 2000, EU governments established the strategic aim that by 2010 Europe would 'become the most competitive and dynamic knowledge-based economy in the world, capable of sustainable economic growth with more and better jobs and greater social cohesion' (Adnett and Hardy 2005: 86–7). The Lisbon agenda portended a more neo-liberal emphasis on markets, competition, and flexibility, something which became more evident as the 2000s went on (Pochet and Degryse 2010; Hyman 2011; Meardi 2014b).

Table 3.1 Positive and negative harmonization of labour standards

Positive harmonization	Negative harmonization
Preference for legal measures to promote employment protection ('hard regulation')	Preference for non-legal measures to improve the quantity and quality of jobs ('soft regulation')
Minimum employment standards	Improving labour flexibility
Active role for the social partners in advancing employment regulation	Reduced role for social partners, limited to social dialogue
Reducing social dumping	Promoting competitiveness
'Social Europe'	'Market Europe'

The development of the European Employment Strategy (EES), for example, signalled a shift in the EU's priorities away from legislating to establish minimum labour standards, towards a greater emphasis on using labour market measures to improve economic competitiveness and create jobs of meaningful quantity and quality (Hepple 2005; Hyman 2005). The scope of the EES includes guidelines which among other things encompass: measures to encourage job creation; efforts to improve the standard of vocational training; anti-poverty initiatives; and the promotion of gender equality. Under the EES, the key mechanism for promoting change is not employment legislation in the form of directives, but rather the 'open method of coordination' (OMC). This is an approach to realizing employment objectives which relies on targets and other non-legislative interventions, based on coordinating activities across EU member states. Individual countries draw up 'national action plans' which indicate what they are doing to achieve EES objectives. The aim is that individual governments can share and learn from each other's experiences (Vaughan-Whitehead 2015). The importance attached to the EES suggests that social protection, including measures to combat discrimination for example, remains a major EU priority. That said, though, its overall results have been disappointing (Bieling 2012; Meardi 2012). Moreover, the onus is generally on diluting labour standards and facilitating employment deregulation, at the expense of measures that support working people (Meardi 2012; Grahl 2015).

Although trade unions and sympathetic politicians successfully opposed some of the more extreme deregulatory proposals, the neo-liberal emphasis in EU policy-making became increasingly apparent as the 2000s progressed (Crespy and Menz 2015). Nowhere was this more evident than in the European Commission's Europe 2020 strategy. Launched in 2010, and replacing the Lisbon agenda set in train a decade earlier, the Europe 2020 initiative is a ten-year programme designed to help steer European countries out of economic recession by promoting smart, sustainable, and inclusive growth (European Commission 2013).

A careful analysis of the Europe 2020 strategy reveals the large extent to which it both continues and intensifies the neo-liberal EU policy agenda evident during the 2000s. There is a strong emphasis given to the importance of completing the Single European Market, tackling barriers that hinder cross-border economic activity. Major imperatives are to promote greater labour market flexibility and pursue further deregulation, with little attention given to advocating interventionist social policies that would improve people's working lives (Bieling 2012). Growth and efficiency are prioritized, at the expense of social rights. The role of government is to help people cope with more insecure environments, for example by encouraging a greater focus on skills development, not to moderate the sources of insecurity (Daly 2012). For Hyman (2011: 15), then, the Europe 2020 strategy exemplifies the 'neoliberal character, once at least partially contained, of European integration'. It also 'demonstrates how, within current EU governance, social policy has been reduced to a subsidiary component of economic policy' (Hyman 2011: 19).

The way in which the EU responded to the eurozone crisis stemming from the global financial crash and subsequent economic downturn showed just how deeply committed EU policy-makers are to advancing neo-liberal policies and negative harmonization. As previously mentioned, the Europe 2020 strategy makes provision for new economic governance arrangements, which some see as adding further momentum to the neo-liberal imperative for reduced social protection, weakened employment rights, and efforts to secure wage moderation (Hyman 2011). In response to the crisis, though, member states agreed a number of measures designed to increase EU control over national budgets (the UK largely excepted), further entrenching negative harmonization. This 'new European interventionism' (Leschke, Theodoropoulou, and Watt 2015) obliges governments to balance their budgets, effectively creating a permanent austerity regime across Europe (Hyman 2011; Barnard 2012). In order to promote greater budgetary discipline, the EU has been increasingly prepared to intervene in national-level employment relations arrangements, for the purpose of encouraging greater bargaining flexibility and wage moderation (Leschke, Theodoropoulou, and Watt 2015; Schulten and Müller 2015).

The main EU policy response to the crisis was to encourage, and in some cases compel, member states to take concerted action to pursue neo-liberal policies, including promoting greater labour market flexibility and deregulation, on the basis that regaining the confidence of international financial markets was essential for a sustained economic recovery across the eurozone (Meardi 2014b; Lehndorff 2015). This was manifest in the weakening of employment protection legislation (Heyes and Lewis 2015), and efforts to secure greater wage moderation by undermining established collective bargaining arrangements and reducing the power of the unions (Hermann 2014). Those countries that were particularly badly affected by the crisis and needed bailouts in order to restore their finances, such as Greece and Portugal, were required to institute wide-ranging labour market reforms designed to give employers greater flexibility and control over wages. These would, it was claimed, boost competitiveness and thus restore economic growth. However, there is little evidence that these neo-liberal policies were very effective (Vaughan-Whitehead 2015; Williams and Scott 2016c: 233–4).

Any economic recovery that did transpire arose 'by virtue of impoverishment' (Lehndorff 2015: 234). As Barnard (2012: 98) observes, people suffered greatly because of the economic crisis and its 'devastating effect on jobs'; yet it was the response of the EU, and its emphasis on the desirability of employment deregulation, which presented the 'more pernicious threat to workers'. Nowhere were the combined effects of austerity and deregulation quite so devastating as in Greece, where the reform measures worsened the country's economic situation, leading to a massive rise in unemployment, widespread poverty, and manifold social problems—see the end-of-chapter case study.

During the 2000s the idea of 'social Europe' was already in retreat as EU policy-makers increasingly favoured prioritizing market reforms to boost competitiveness over action to protect and advance the interests of workers and unions (Meardi 2012, 2014b). If 'social Europe' was ailing before the crisis, the EU's response, which was to aggressively insist on neo-liberal austerity and deregulation, has been pretty much to finish it off, doing immense damage to the traditional elements of the European 'social model' in the process (Lehndorff 2015; Vaughan-Whitehead 2015). Evidently, the EU can no longer be relied on very much for measures that protect working people. Moreover, it has become the main protagonist of a race to the bottom in labour standards across Europe (Barnard 2012). It is easy to understand why support for the EU has fallen across Europe, not just in the UK.

3.5.3 European Union enlargement and employment relations

EU enlargement and the pressures for negative harmonization which it has generated have also contributed to the demise of the social dimension of European integration. Since 1957, when the Treaty of Rome was agreed, the European Union has expanded from the six

Table 3.2 Accession dates of EU countries

Countries	Date
Belgium, France, Italy, Luxembourg, Netherlands, West Germany	1957
Denmark, Ireland, UK	1973
Greece	1981
Portugal, Spain	1986
Austria, Finland, Sweden	1994
Cyprus, Czech Republic, Estonia, Hungary, Latvia, Lithuania, Malta, Poland, Slovakia, Slovenia	2004
Bulgaria, Romania	2007
Croatia	2013

countries that originally comprised the EEC (West Germany, France, Italy, and the 'Benelux' countries—Belgium, the Netherlands, and Luxembourg) to twenty-eight by 2016. The UK, for example, joined in 1973. During the 1980s and 1990s there was further expansion, with the accession of countries such as Greece, Spain, Austria, and Sweden. In 2004, ten countries joined the EU, including Poland, Hungary, and the Czech Republic, which until the 1990s had been part of the Soviet Bloc. Romania and Bulgaria acceded three years later, and Croatia became the twenty-eighth member state in 2013 (see Table 3.2).

One of the effects of enlargement in the 2000s was to weaken political support for a rigorous social dimension that encompasses legislative interventions designed to enhance labour standards in the EU as a whole. While it is important not to over-generalize, many of the new accession states tend to be sympathetic to neo-liberal, deregulatory policies in the area of employment relations. This is particularly the case with the Baltic states—Latvia, Lithuania, and Estonia (Woolfson and Sommers 2016).

Yet perhaps the most obvious impact of EU enlargement has been the increase in labour migration it has generated; people from the so-called A8 Eastern European countries have more scope to travel to Western Europe in search of work. One of the key principles of the EU is free movement of workers between countries—in other words, the removal of barriers that prevent citizens of one member state from working in another. The number of EU immigrants living in the UK has risen substantially. In 1995 there were just 900,000 citizens of other EU countries living in the UK; twenty years later, in 2015, the number had increased to 3.3 million—6.5 per cent of the working age population. Nearly a million (29 per cent of the total number of EU immigrants) were born in Poland (Wadsworth et al. 2016). Although there was a temporary fall in the inflow of EU immigrants to the UK between 2008 and 2012 because of the recession, the pace of immigration from the EU increased sharply again from 2013 onwards (Portes 2016). For many people, immigration and its consequences, particularly the effects of the influx of workers from Eastern Europe, was the paramount reason for supporting the UK's departure from the EU (Portes 2016; Rolfe and Hudson-Sharp 2016), and thus had a marked influence on the June 2016 referendum result.

There is a widely held belief that migrant workers take jobs that would otherwise have gone to UK-born workers, and undercut their wages. However, 'the view of the tabloid press that migrants "take our jobs" and "cut our pay" is misplaced' (Reed and Latorre 2009: 34).

There is little or no evidence that immigration from other EU countries has either damaged the employment prospects of UK-born workers or driven down wages. If anything, the influx of generally young migrant workers has helped the economy to grow faster than it would otherwise have done. Their labour market participation stimulates demand for goods and services—creating new businesses, and helping existing businesses to grow—which increases demand for labour and raises productivity levels, with positive consequences for jobs and wages (Sumption and Somerville 2010; Portes 2016; Wadsworth et al. 2016).

That said, though, it is clear that the increased level of EU migration has created difficulties. Business leaders in the UK tend to support the free movement of labour. They contend that labour migration improves the supply of labour, allowing businesses greater flexibility and adaptability, thus producing a more dynamic and competitive economy (Balch 2016). Employers value migrant workers, not because they have an antipathy towards indigenous, UK-born workers, but because their availability helps to ensure that vacancies are filled, facilitating business growth (Rolfe and Hudson-Sharp 2016). Increased levels of migration from the A8 countries of Eastern Europe may not have had a direct adverse effect on the quantity of jobs and wage levels in general; however, the flexibility they provide to employers does often imply a deterioration of labour standards in practice. Many of the jobs taken by migrant workers from Eastern Europe are of a poor quality. Migrants themselves are treated as a useful source of disposable labour, something which can aid business competitiveness, but with adverse consequences for employment conditions (Rolfe and Hudson-Sharp 2016). While the claim that migrant workers have a superior work ethic—being more reliable, harder-working, and more disciplined than UK-born workers—is not entirely supported by the evidence, what does very much appeal to employers is the flexibility they provide (MAC 2014; Rolfe and Hudson-Sharp 2016). They are viewed by employers as 'good' workers, in the sense of being compliant with managerial directives, such as working more hours at short notice (Thompson, Newsome, and Commander 2013). In sectors such as food processing the supply of migrant labour has allowed employers to develop highly flexible employment arrangements—using temporary and zero-hours contracts for example—which, by rendering workers more disposable (see Chapter 2), has driven improvements in business competitiveness (Rolfe and Hudson-Sharp 2016).

Yet there is no automatic link between migration and the dilution of labour standards. The onus is on governments to enforce existing employment protections, or to extend them, so that migrant workers are not used by employers as a cheap and easily disposable workforce in a way that contributes to the deterioration of labour standards. The application of existing enforcement arrangements in areas of the economy where large numbers of migrants are employed is recognized as being inadequate (MAC 2014); moreover, migrant workers themselves are often reluctant to act on labour rights abuses, either because they are unaware of their entitlements, or because their vulnerability makes them reluctant to complain (Barnard, Ludlow, and Fraser Butlin 2016).

A stronger system of employment rights and protections, allied to a tougher enforcement regime, might have ensured that increased levels of EU immigration were accommodated without some of the adverse consequences for labour standards which arose, and which fuelled the vote in favour of leaving the EU. There is clearly an expectation that the UK's departure from the EU will see it establish more restrictive immigration arrangements—perhaps a system of work permits for EU citizens?—ending the free movement of labour (to and from the UK at least).

While much attention has been directed towards the impact of migration from Eastern Europe on employment relations, EU enlargement has also helped to facilitate the deterioration of labour standards in another important respect. The expansion of the single market, involving the dismantling of economic barriers within the EU, has enhanced the capacity of multinational companies to engage in social dumping; it has become easier for them to move production to Eastern European countries, where wages are lower and labour standards generally weaker. Relocation, or often merely the threat of relocation, means that workers in Western Europe come under pressure to moderate their wage demands, for example, or to accept worse employment conditions (Anderson 2011; Meardi 2012).

EU enlargement, then, has brought into sharper focus the contrast between 'positive' and 'negative' harmonization as competing visions of how labour regulation across Europe should operate (Hepple 2005; Meardi 2012). On the one hand, positive harmonization portends an interventionist role for the EU in setting or encouraging minimum employment standards to ensure that workers throughout Europe are adequately protected. On the other hand, however, the emphasis of negative harmonization is on creating a level playing field of employment standards through deregulation, allowing employers greater scope to benefit from an integrated and open market.

For those, like the trade unions for example, who want to maintain and improve on existing employment standards, the increased mobility of businesses and workers in an enlarged EU poses a major challenge. This has been evident in some high-profile industrial disputes which concern the use of cheap foreign labour to undermine employment rights and protections (e.g. Donaghey and Teague 2006). In early 2009, for example, there were walk-outs in the UK in support of workers at the Lindsey oil refinery, who were striking in protest at the use of cheaper foreign construction labour (Gall 2012b). For Barnard (2009: 277), the dispute symbolized how the principle of market integration came 'face to face with angry protestors fearful about their jobs at a time of deep recession'.

CJEU rulings also pose a major threat to the future of the social dimension in an enlarged EU. In the 2007 Laval and Viking cases, for example, it held that industrial action by trade unions which hindered the free movement rights of employers in a single market was unlawful, even if the action in question complied with the national law of the country where it occurred (e.g. Woolfson, Thörnqvist, and Sommers 2010; Freedland and Prassl 2015). The following year, the CJEU ruled in the Rüffert and Luxembourg cases that only in certain narrowly defined circumstances could governments and other public authorities mandate labour standards which had the effect of preventing employers in other countries from offering services (Hyman 2010).

There are a number of implications of this 'Laval quartet' of decisions. Although the CJEU recognizes the rights of workers and trade unions to engage in collective bargaining and to undertake industrial action, the scope of these rights is highly circumscribed—and they are clearly subordinate to the rights of employers to benefit from social dumping. In general the rulings make it very much harder for unions in Western Europe 'to protect, through collective bargaining, established worker rights from undercutting by Central Eastern European providers' (Meardi 2012: 14). They highlight the threat posed by EU enlargement, in combination with a neo-liberal emphasis on free markets, to employment standards across Europe.

The CJEU, in trying to strike a balance between the principle of upholding labour standards on the one hand, and the principle of supporting market integration on the other, has come down on the side of the latter (Hyman 2010; Lindstrom 2010; ETUC 2015; Ségol 2015). EU law, based on the primacy of advancing the single market, takes precedence over, and may even negate, national-level efforts to enhance labour standards, jeopardizing the ability of governments to regulate employment relations within their own territories (Dølvik and Visser 2009; Cremers 2010).

The CJEU's rulings also highlight the weakness of the Posting of Workers Directive (1996), which was designed to give workers who are posted abroad to another EU member state for a limited period of time the right to the same core pay and conditions enjoyed by local workers. In theory, this should have helped to combat social dumping, by preventing employers from bringing in workers from abroad to do jobs on lower rates of pay and with worse conditions than indigenous workers. In practice, though, the Posting of Workers Directive has done little to prevent social dumping, suggesting that more needs to be done to make it an effective employment relations policy instrument (Cremers, Dølvik, and Bosch 2007).

Overall, then, EU enlargement has accentuated the potential for social dumping by exacerbating a 'race to the bottom' in labour standards, further contributing to the demise of 'social Europe' (Donaghey and Teague 2006; Meardi 2012). EU legislation in the area of social and employment policy has done little to counter the increased scope for multinational companies to benefit from the removal of economic and political barriers, including using social dumping as a way of reducing costs. Despite much rhetoric about the EU's social dimension, the material covered here demonstrates the large extent to which it has been subordinate to powerful pressures of market integration. Perhaps a stronger and more effective social dimension might have made some UK voters, concerned about the erosion of their employment rights and protections, more favourable to the EU, to the extent of increasing support for the 'remain' side in the June 2016 referendum.

The tottering EU social dimension is unlikely to be revived through judicial interventions. Rather, the actions of trade unions and EU citizens themselves offer the best chance of shifting the process of European integration in a more socially desirable direction. The mobilizing efforts of the ETUC and other union bodies have done much to ensure that workers' interests are heard at EU level (Lindstrom 2010). Moreover, the democratically elected European Parliament sometimes acts as a bulwark against neo-liberal policies that would otherwise weaken the social dimension still further.

Section summary and further reading

- During the 1980s and 1990s, the development of the 'social dimension', encompassing legislation in areas such as working time, and information and consultation rights for workers, became an increasingly important aspect of the process of European integration. Nevertheless, it remained subordinate to the process of market integration and was progressed largely in so far as it helped to legitimize greater economic union.

- The importance of the social dimension diminished during the 2000s, linked to the growing neo-liberal emphasis on free markets inspired by the Lisbon agenda and evident in the Europe 2020 strategy.

- If 'social Europe' was ailing before the 2007–8 financial and economic crisis, the EU's response, which was to aggressively insist on neo-liberal austerity and deregulatory measures, has effectively destroyed it, doing immense damage to the traditional European 'social model' in the process.

● By exacerbating a 'race to the bottom' in labour standards, EU enlargement has also contributed to the demise of 'social Europe'. Major legal rulings exemplify the threat that EU enlargement, in combination with a neo-liberal emphasis on free markets, poses to employment standards across Europe.

The best short overview of the employment relations implications of European integration is Hyman (2010). Both Adnett and Hardy (2005) and Hepple (2005: chapters 8 and 9) are also highly recommended. See Williams and Scott (2016c) for UK government policy and the EU. Both Lehndorff (2015) and Vaughan-Whitehead (2015) offer critical perspectives on the EU's response to the financial and economic crisis.

3.6 Conclusion

This chapter has examined the highly politicized nature of work and employment relations. One thing that will be evident is the large extent to which both UK governments and the EU have been concerned with developing and enacting policies that provide businesses with a supportive environment in which they can pursue growth more readily. The Conservatives' legislative reforms of the 1980s and 1990s, for example, were impelled by a belief that excessive union power was an obstacle to economic competitiveness, and that greater labour market deregulation was a necessary, and indeed desirable, component of wealth creation. Between 1997 and 2010 Labour made some notable policy interventions ostensibly designed to favour workers and trade unions; yet in general they were enacted in ways that ensure they do not conflict with the primacy of a neo-liberal belief that deregulated labour markets and weak trade unions are necessary components of a competitive economy. Between 2010 and 2015, moreover, the 'reasserted neoliberalism' (Grimshaw and Rubery 2012) of the Conservative–Liberal Democrat coalition government's approach to employment relations was evident from its wide-ranging programme of employment deregulation. The majority Conservative government, which was elected in 2015, prioritized measures designed to impose further restrictions on trade unions, particularly their capacity to organize strikes and industrial action and their ability to engage in campaigning activities. Looking beyond the UK, the impetus of the EU's 'social dimension' has dwindled considerably, reflecting its subordination to the process of market integration, something that the process of EU enlargement has brought into particularly sharp focus. The nature of the future relationship between the UK and the EU, following the outcome of the June 2016 referendum vote in favour of leaving the EU, will have some profound implications for employment relations.

 ### Assignment and discussion questions

1. What is voluntarism in employment relations? Why has its significance declined?

2. Assess the extent to which Labour's employment relations policies between 1997 and 2010 were marked by continuity with the approach taken by its Conservative predecessors in government.

3. To what extent were the employment relations policies of the 2010–15 UK coalition government marked by a 'reasserted neo-liberalism'?

4. What is meant by the 'social dimension' of the EU? How successful has the EU been in achieving its social objectives?

5. What have been the main effects of EU enlargement on employment relations? To what extent does the UK's decision to leave the EU reflect popular concerns about the impact of enlargement?

Visit the Online Resource Centre that accompanies this book to develop your understanding of this chapter and keep up to date with the latest developments in this area.
www.oxfordtextbooks.co.uk/orc/williams4e/

Chapter case study: The EU and employment relations reform in Greece

Nowhere has the demise of 'social Europe' been more evident than in Greece, where the response to the financial and economic crisis has emasculated social and employment standards. As a result of the crisis, Greece's debt levels became unsustainable, and it was obliged to seek financial support to make repayments to its creditors. Because it is a member of the eurozone single currency area, Greece was unable to respond to its economic problems by devaluing its currency, or by inflating the money supply. Instead, the so-called 'troika', comprising the European Commission, the European Central Bank, and the International Monetary Fund, agreed to release funds to Greece so that it could make appropriate repayments to its creditors, on condition that it implemented severe austerity measures designed to reduce its budget deficit and improve the competitiveness of its economy by reducing labour costs—so-called 'internal devaluation'.

The measures required of Greece were set out in three successive 'memoranda of understandings' (MoUs), the first of which took effect in 2010. For Karamessini (2015: 108), these MoUs were used to promote neo-liberal 'shock therapy' in Greece. The austerity measures included some highly regressive tax rises and substantial cuts to pensions. Greece was also required to progress 'internal devaluation' through liberalizing employment relations reforms designed to improve competitiveness by increasing labour market flexibility, weakening employment protections, and reducing labour costs (Koukiadaki and Kretsos 2012; Yannakourou and Tsimpoukis 2014)—all part of a 'massive attack on employees' rights' (Karamessini 2015: 116). Specific measures included a large reduction in the minimum wage, among other things. However, the most far-reaching changes related to collective bargaining. The established system of centralized, national-level pay bargaining was abandoned; the prevalence of industry-level bargaining between employers and unions also diminished markedly. These changes were predicated on the basis that giving individual employers greater flexibility over pay bargaining would weaken the power of the unions, lead to reductions in wage costs, and thus improve economic competitiveness (Karamessini 2015; Koukiadaki and Kretsos 2012). Between 2009 and 2013 average per capita real wages fell by a quarter.

However, there is little evidence that the neo-liberal austerity and deregulation of the kind imposed by the troika on Greece has been successful in any way. They sapped the Greek economy of much-needed demand, leading to widespread factory closures and business collapses. Between 2008 and 2016, the Greek economy shrank by a quarter. The unemployment rate—which was 9.5 per cent in 2009—rose to over 27 per cent in 2013, and was still 24 per cent in early 2016. The labour market situation of young workers was even worse, with around a half those aged 25 or under not able to find work. To be sure, the financial and economic crisis had adverse effects for the Greek economy. However, it was the neo-liberal reforms imposed by the troika, and its unwillingness to ease the burden of debt, which inflicted by far the most damage, and not just on the economy, which contracted hugely as a result, but on the lives of working people (Karamessini 2015). The combination of mass unemployment, enormous reductions in wages, tax rises, and pension cuts severely impoverished many Greek families (ETUC 2014).

Despite the evident failure of the troika's policies, and the distress they caused, during 2015 and 2016 it was still exhorting Greece to implement further neo-liberal austerity measures, backed by the implicit threat of forcing the country's complete economic collapse if the Greek government failed to comply. The EU played an integral part in the process of impoverishing Greece, not just through the European Commission's role in the troika, but also more importantly in its role promoting 'market fundamentalism' in general (Yannakourou and Tsimpoukis 2014: 368). The extent to which employment rights and protections have been diminished in Greece, and the large degree to which the unions and collective bargaining have become marginalized, must surely extinguish any faint hopes that the EU is in any way concerned with promoting 'social Europe'.

Question

To what extent do you agree with the view that the experience of Greece shows that the idea of a 'social Europe' is now effectively defunct?

4 Social divisions and employment relations

 Chapter objectives

The main objectives of this chapter are to:

- explain the nature of employment disadvantage based on social divisions, and to consider its implications for employment relations;
- assess the main developments relating to anti-discrimination and equality legislation and policy in employment relations;
- consider the extent, nature, and implications of employer-led initiatives designed to reduce disadvantage, including equal opportunities policies and diversity management initiatives; and
- examine the efforts made by trade unions to represent the interests of workers from disadvantaged social groups and to promote equality.

4.1 Introduction

Following on from Chapters 2 and 3, which focused on employment relations in the contemporary economy and the politics of employment relations respectively, this chapter, the third of those that aim to analyse employment relations developments in a broader dimension, focuses on the influence of social divisions. By this we mean aspects of disadvantage and inequality that are socially constituted, reflecting people's shared social characteristics, like gender for example. The aim of this chapter is to provide you with a good knowledge of the nature, and principal features, of inequality and disadvantage in employment relations, and to enable you to develop a critical understanding of the main ways in which they have been addressed. The starting point—in Section 4.2—is a brief assessment of the dimensions of inequality and disadvantage at work, including a discussion of divisions based on social class. Following on from this, in Section 4.3 the focus is on the evolving legal and policy framework governing equality and diversity issues, including family-friendly and work–life balance measures. Section 4.4 is concerned with understanding and interpreting employers' interventions, particularly equal opportunities and diversity management policies; it also examines the role played by the trade unions in promoting equality.

 Introductory case study: The 2010–15 UK coalition government and disabled workers

Since 1995 UK law has offered disabled workers some protection from discrimination. Moreover, the Equality Act (2010) aims to ensure that workers with disabilities are protected from discrimination, harassment, or victimization arising from their disability. The law obliges employers to make

(continued...)

'reasonable adjustments'—changes or adaptations to the working environment—designed to remove or minimize the impact of any conditions, so that workers with disabilities can be accommodated without being disadvantaged. Under the 2010–15 Conservative–Liberal Democrat coalition government, however, ill treatment of disabled workers actually became more prevalent. Austerity-based funding cuts made public sector employers more reluctant to contemplate making appropriate reasonable adjustments. And disabled workers report greater levels of harassment and unlawful discrimination. The way that benefit recipients were stigmatized as welfare scroungers by the government and sections of the media was responsible for a notable increase in negative attitudes towards disabled workers. Coalition benefit cuts were designed to push disabled people into jobs, with little heed paid to the barriers (e.g. employers' negative attitudes) that hinder their participation in employment. Disabled workers reported greater levels of poor treatment by employers, including the presence of an increasingly punitive approach over matters like performance standards, which sometimes translate into perceived bullying and harassment. The coalition government's portrayal of equality protections as bureaucratic 'red tape', which unnecessarily hinders employers from managing staff in ways that serve business needs and promote competitiveness, contributed to a climate in which disabled workers' rights were increasingly compromised.

Sources: Foster and Scott (2015); Harwood (2015); Manfredi (2016)

4.2 Discrimination, disadvantage, and inequality in work and employment relations

Workers often experience discrimination, disadvantage, and inequality in employment relations on the grounds of their social characteristics. For many years, the principal focus of studies of workplace inequality concerned the so-called status divide between manual and non-manual workers. In this section, the extent to which class-based disadvantage still affects work and employment relations—often expressed in concerns about supposedly stalled social mobility—is examined. The focus of attention then switches to the importance of other manifestations of inequality and disadvantage in work and employment relations, based on shared social characteristics such as gender.

4.2.1 Social class, the status divide, and employment disadvantage

Traditionally, the most fundamental divisions in society are those that are seen to arise from social class. The concept of class refers to hierarchical divisions in society which reflect differences in people's access to material resources. Social inequality and disadvantage are the consequences of differences in people's life chances, including access to education and employment opportunities, which reflect their class position. Historically, class differences in society both reflected, and in turn exercised an important influence over, work and employment relationships. While the concept of social class has long been the subject of much debate and controversy, one thing that is clear is that someone's economic situation, in particular their occupation, is a major determinant of their class position. You need only think about how strongly the term 'working class' is associated with routine, manual labour in factory settings. Thus the concept of social class captures the way in which people shared a sense of collective identity based on their work situation.

Traditionally in employment relations, class divisions were manifest in the status divide that existed between manual, blue-collar workers and their non-manual, white-collar 'staff' counterparts for much of the twentieth century. In manufacturing industry, for example, manual workers enjoyed less favourable terms and conditions of employment, including a longer working week, shorter holidays, and fewer fringe benefits (Wedderburn and Craig 1974). Non-manual work, largely undertaken in office environments, was associated with higher status, better terms and conditions of employment, and greater job security. White-collar employees were more likely to benefit from sick pay arrangements, and enjoy longer holidays, a shorter working week, greater opportunities for promotion, and more autonomy at work (Price 1989). One of the most influential efforts to understand social class, based on the position of individuals in employment relations, distinguished between a professional, managerial 'service' class, an 'intermediate' class comprised of those working in junior managerial, technical, and clerical occupations, and a 'working' class, consisting of manual workers (Goldthorpe 1980).

But in the twenty-first century does the concept of social class, with all that it entails for employment relations, still have any relevance? Politicians often refer to the UK as a 'classless society', implying that the importance of social class as a source of disadvantage has diminished, and that it no longer acts as a barrier to individual self-advancement. It is often held that the salience of class has declined (e.g. Pakulski and Waters 1996), and that other sources of social identity, like gender or ethnicity for example, have become more important sources of disadvantage. Alternatively, inequality arises not so much from differences in people's collective class position, but rather reflects variations in the talent and ability of individual workers, and thus their capacity to improve their livelihoods and advance their careers (see McGovern et al. 2007: 81–3).

Organizational restructuring, in particular the demand for greater workplace flexibility, is held to have undermined traditional occupational patterns, and thus eroded the established distinction between manual and non-manual employees (Bradley et al. 2000). In some areas, such as in local government, unions and employers have concluded 'single status' agreements in order to promote harmonization, though progress towards implementation has been protracted (Wright 2011). Yet, while undoubtedly an important aspect of contemporary employment relations, harmonization has been of limited overall significance. Although occupational change has rendered the distinction between manual and non-manual employment less important than it once was, not least because of the growth of non-manual jobs in the economy, the status divide remains a durable feature of employment relations, and thus a source of workplace inequality. Access to a variety of benefits, including occupational pension schemes, paid holiday entitlement, and sick pay, is still strongly linked to one's position in the occupational—and by implication the class—hierarchy (McGovern et al. 2007).

In the context of growing income inequality, there has been a resurgence of interest in the concept of social class, and the implications of class divisions (Savage et al. 2013; Mike Savage 2015). The salience of class is evident in the work of Owen Jones. In his book *Chavs* he highlights the extent to which members of the working class have been belittled and demonized by those in power, as a means of avoiding having to do anything to tackle the causes and effects of rampant inequality. Precarious jobs, low pay, and limited opportunities for progression are portrayed as being the fault of young working class people themselves, not a consequence of powerful structural barriers in society that prevent them from improving their life chances (Jones 2012).

A particularly prominent example of the growing interest in class divisions came in 2013 with the publication of the results of the BBC's 'Great British Class Survey'. The academics behind the survey hold that it is inappropriate to conceive of class largely in relation to occupation and employment relationships. Rather, people's class position is the outcome of the interplay between 'economic capital' (wealth and income), 'cultural capital' (tastes, interests, and activities), and 'social capital' (social networks, friendships, and associations). As a result, the traditional distinction between the upper, middle, and working classes is no longer valid. Instead, seven new social classes can be identified (Savage et al. 2013; Mike Savage 2015)— see Employment relations reflection 4.1. The new model 'separates out three main groups: a small elite at the top, massively better off than the others, a somewhat larger 'precariat' at the bottom, who score lower than others in relation to all three kinds of capital, and then five other classes in the middle, who have a much more hybrid mix of sorts of capital and can't be put in a simple hierarchy' (Savage 2015: 172).

Employment relations reflection 4.1: The BBC's Great British Class Survey

The results of the BBC's Great British Class Survey, based on data supplied by 161,400 people and an additional representative survey of over 1,000 people, were published in 2013. Seven new social classes were identified.

- The 'elite'—people with high levels of economic, social, and cultural capital which sets them apart; e.g. top executives (6 per cent of the population).
- The 'established middle class'—with relatively high levels of economic, social, and cultural capital, although not as high as the 'elite'; e.g. police officers, engineers (25 per cent).
- The 'technical middle class'—a new, rather small class with high economic capital but rather low levels of social and cultural capital; e.g. pharmacists (6 per cent).
- The 'new affluent workers'—made up largely of young people with only medium levels of economic capital, but higher levels of cultural and social capital; e.g. electricians, plumbers (15 per cent).
- The 'emergent service workers'—often young people living in major towns and cities, they tend to have rather low economic capital but very high amounts of cultural and social capital; e.g. bar staff (19 per cent).
- The 'traditional working class'—tend to be older, and have lower than average scores on all three capitals; e.g. care workers, van drivers (14 per cent).
- The 'precariat'—with low levels of economic, social, and cultural capital, they lead very insecure lives (see Chapter 2), e.g. care workers (15 per cent).

The BBC also published a 'class calculator' test which people can use to see where they fit in.

Sources: BBC Online (2013); Savage et al. (2013); Mike Savage (2015)

The contribution of the BBC's Great British Class Survey to rekindling interest in social class, and how class shapes and influences people's lives, including at work, is highly welcome. Yet there are some problems with the seven-class model derived from the results of the survey. One criticism is that it fails to conceive of class in relational terms, but rather treats it as a cluster of attributes which can be used to categorize people. The problem with this approach is that it neglects the important extent to which classes influence, and interact with, each other. There is also something of an over-reliance placed on people's cultural activities, at the expense of their occupation and the nature of their work and employment relationships. Moreover, for an approach which seemingly plays down the relevance of occupations, most of the seven categories, especially those in the 'middle', reflect broad occupational types. Yet people from the same occupation (e.g. care workers) are present in more than one class. As a result the model lacks coherence (Bradley 2014).

Class-based disadvantage is thought to be related to the claimed diminution of social mobility: that fewer people from modest circumstances are able to progress up the occupational hierarchy and secure better-paid managerial and professional jobs. A lack of social mobility is held to be responsible for the persistence of inequality, for example by limiting access to top jobs and reducing opportunities for people from low-income backgrounds to progress up the career ladder. The UK government's Social Mobility and Child Poverty Commission (SMCPC) asserts that although 'people can, and do, move up and down the class and income scale ... being born to a less privileged family is still far too likely to mean disadvantage as an adult' (SMCPC 2015a: 7).

Studies of professions, like law and accountancy, demonstrate the large extent to which entry to elite firms and access to top positions are dominated by people from privileged backgrounds, especially the privately educated (Ashley 2010; Milburn 2012; Macmillan, Tyler, and Vignoles 2015; Ashley and Empson 2016). Just 7 per cent of children attend private, fee-paying schools. Yet top jobs in business and the professions are disproportionately filled by people educated outside the state system—74 per cent of judges, for example, and 48 per cent of senior civil servants (Kirby 2016).

Research carried out by the SMCPC points to the reasons why people with less privileged backgrounds struggle to enter top professions. For one thing, firms focus their recruitment activities on a small number of supposedly 'elite' universities, which are dominated by students from well-off and privately educated backgrounds. Their approach to what constitutes 'talent', moreover, is imbued with class-based values and assumptions, such as the degree of ease with foreign travel, that favour privileged candidates (SMCPC 2015a, 2015b). Concern has been expressed about the growing expectation in some occupations, such as journalism and the media, that young people undertake a period of unpaid work experience or an internship before securing paid employment. This often disadvantages those from low-income families, who cannot afford to work for free, and therefore acts as a barrier to social mobility (Milburn 2012). Not only is class-based inequality objectionable on the grounds of social justice—shouldn't people from low-income backgrounds have similar opportunities to those with richer parents?—but it also inhibits economic efficiency by restricting the pool of talent open to business (Independent Commission on Social Mobility 2009).

What can be done to improve social mobility? Leading sociological experts have raised questions about the government's strategy for enhancing social mobility, particularly its emphasis on improving diversity at the top through the provision of better educational opportunities, including widening access to higher education. They contend that, rather than declining, in recent decades social mobility has in fact been largely stable. This followed a marked increase in absolute social mobility between the 1940s and 1970s, which was the product of a major expansion in the number of jobs in managerial and professional occupations during this period (e.g. Goldthorpe and Jackson 2007). But this expansion has now ceased. Genuine upward social mobility—i.e. an increase in the proportion of young people from less privileged backgrounds going into managerial and professional occupations—would thus need to be complemented by a corresponding level of downward mobility—i.e. fewer children from relatively well-off families going into good jobs—something which few politicians, let alone wealthy parents, would find palatable. Providing better educational opportunities, or operating schemes designed to encourage a more socially diverse workforce in top professions (e.g. Ashley 2010; Ashley and Empson 2016), have done little to change this. If politicians genuinely want to improve social mobility they should prioritize policies designed to create more 'top end' jobs (Goldthorpe 2016). As it is, though, by international standards the UK is characterized by a relatively high proportion of low-paid jobs—see Chapter 2— which offer limited opportunities for career progression (SMCPC 2015a).

Clearly, society remains 'riven' by social divisions centred on class (Erickson et al. 2009: 202). Not only are they still evident in employment, but work itself is an important source of the social class divide given the large extent to which one's occupation influences one's overall life chances (e.g. health, access to education). Moreover, in the absence of any trend towards greater upward social mobility, the class position of one's parents, derived from their occupations, and the way in which this affects the life chances of their children, continue to exercise a profound influence over work and employment relations.

4.2.2 Disadvantage at work: towards a broader agenda

Though important, on its own the persistence of class inequality is not sufficient to account for the employment disadvantage found in contemporary workplaces. Other sources of social identity, like gender for example, are also responsible for creating divisions in work and employment relations. Indeed, social class often intersects with them to compound inequality and disadvantage (Moore 2011). Low-paid women workers, for example, may encounter disadvantage on the basis of their class position and their gender.

Historically, women were channelled by employers, often with the support of male-dominated trade unions, into poorly paid, low-skilled jobs that offered few opportunities for promotion (Bradley 1989), or were excluded from the workforce entirely. There is evidence of progress towards greater gender equality. Over half (51 per cent) of employees are now women (van Wanrooy et al. 2013a). Growing numbers of women have secured entry to professional and managerial jobs, in areas such as education, health, and the law (Crompton and Sanderson 1990; Walby 1997; EHRC 2010). By 2013 a half of workers in professional occupations, and a third of managers, were female (ONS 2013). There are even some encouraging signs of an increase in the number of women on company boards, albeit from a very low base (Davies 2015).

Yet the progress towards greater gender equality at work should not be overstated. For one thing, although its extent has been eroded, the segregation of jobs and occupations based on gender remains a marked feature of contemporary employment relations. Women continue to be significantly under-represented in executive and managerial roles at the top of organizations. There are important structural constraints that inhibit women from advancing in organizations, in particular efforts by relatively powerful men attempting to exercise power over, and exclude, them (Bradley 1999).

Segregation is also manifest in respect of the over-representation of women in particular occupations, such as that of supermarket cashier for example, or nursing, and their under-representation in others (Bradley et al. 2000; Bradley and Healy 2008). Although female participation in the labour force has grown, much women's employment is concentrated in poorly remunerated, part-time jobs in the service sector, where opportunities for career progression are very limited (Women and Work Commission 2006), and which are often depicted as being less important than full-time jobs. Women are often disadvantaged by the widespread prevalence of pregnancy discrimination; see the end-of-chapter case study for details.

The persistence of gender segregation at work is perhaps one of the main reasons why the gender pay gap has proved to be so resilient. This is the difference between the average earnings of men and those of women, and is a major aspect of gender-based disadvantage. Over the years this gap has narrowed; in 2015 women in full-time employment on average earned 9.4 per cent less per hour than male full-timers, down from nearly 40 per cent in the early 1970s. However, the gap is wider when all employees, not just those employed on a full-time basis, are taken into account: it then stands at 19.2 per cent (ONS 2015). The reason the gender pay gap is wider when comparing the average hourly earnings of all male and female employees, not just full-timers, is because a disproportionately high number of women are concentrated in occupations marked by a predominance of low-paid, part-time jobs.

Although so far this discussion has largely been concerned with inequality based on gender, this should not imply that other sources of disadvantage are somehow less important. In spite of changing social attitudes and growing tolerance about people's sexual orientation, reports of homophobic bullying and discrimination against lesbian, gay, and bisexual (LGB) people persist (e.g. EHRC 2010; Colgan and Wright 2011; Einarsdóttir, Hoel, and Lewis 2015). Prejudice against people on grounds of their age also appears to be widespread (Sweiry and Willitts 2012).

When it comes to religion or belief, people belonging to some social groups are clearly disadvantaged. Muslims, in particular, are grossly under-represented in professional and managerial positions, experience substantially higher than average rates of unemployment and economic activity, and are more likely than others to be in low-paid jobs (Demos 2015; House of Commons Women and Equalities Select Committee 2016a). Muslim women are 71 per cent more likely to be unemployed than white Christian women, even after controlling for factors such as educational background and language competence (Dugan 2015).

There is also a long history of discrimination against disabled people in employment, who are especially prone to unemployment or segregation in poorly paid and low-skilled jobs as a result (Barnes 1992). The experience of disabled workers in organizations is often marked by incidents of bullying, harassment, and other examples of discriminatory behaviour (Foster 2011). The introductory case study showed how, under the 2010–15 coalition government, the position of disabled workers worsened as a result of the government's emphasis on austerity and its deregulatory policies (Harwood 2015; Manfredi 2016).

Disadvantage on grounds of 'race' and ethnicity is also a feature of employment; generally, black and minority ethnic workers are more likely to be unemployed, or work in low-paid jobs with few career prospects, than their white counterparts, and are considerably less evident in managerial roles (Bradley and Healy 2008; TUC 2016b). Nearly a third (30 per cent) of black and minority ethnic workers have witnessed or experienced racial harassment or bullying from managers, colleagues, or customers (BITC 2015). Migrant workers frequently encounter discrimination and disadvantage in employment, often being concentrated in jobs that are of a precarious nature (McDowell, Batvitzky, and Dyer 2012). Many lack knowledge or awareness of their rights at work, which makes them vulnerable, and they are liable to be treated unjustly by employers as a consequence (Clark 2011).

Different dimensions of social divisions often intersect with one another, creating the potential for multiple disadvantages. Although large numbers of women have entered managerial and professional occupations, many others lack access to such positions and work in low-paid jobs with few opportunities for career progression, not just on account of their gender, but also because of their class position. Women from ethnic minorities may experience inequality on the grounds of their gender and their ethnicity (e.g. Kamenou, Netto, and Fearfull 2013). It is often women of Pakistani and Bangladeshi origin who suffer from the most pronounced disadvantage (Bradley and Healy 2008).

 ### Section summary and further reading

- Inequality at work has long been manifested in the status divide, reflecting divisions based on social class, which harmonization initiatives have done relatively little to eradicate. The persistence of class-based disadvantage is evident from the concerns that have been expressed over how to improve social mobility.

- Notwithstanding the importance of social class, a broader conceptualization of social divisions at work is desirable, one that considers the implications for work and employment relations of disadvantage arising from other shared social characteristics, such as age, sexual orientation, disability, race and ethnicity, and gender, which often intersect.

See Mike Savage (2015) for a lively and engaging overview of social class, based on the results of the BBC's Great British Class Survey. See Erickson et al. (2009: Chapter 8) for an overview of the relevance of social class and other aspects of inequality. Details of the work of the Social Mobility and Child Poverty Commission (now just the Social Mobility Commission) can be accessed from its website (https://www.gov.uk/government/organisations/social-mobility-commission).

4.3 Public policy, anti-discrimination legislation, and equality at work

This section is concerned with examining the implications of the principal legislative interventions designed to challenge inequality and disadvantage at work, and the public policy assumptions that underpin them. Following an analysis of how the legislation evolved between the 1970s and the 1990s, we consider the manifold changes enacted by Labour governments during the 2000s, including the extension of protection from discrimination and the provision of rights to 'family-friendly' working arrangements. The legal framework relating to equality at work is then interpreted and assessed, after which there follows a critique of the 2010–15 Conservative–Liberal Democrat coalition government's approach to equality and anti-discrimination issues.

4.3.1 The development of equality and anti-discrimination legislation

The development of anti-discrimination and equality legislation has been a notable feature of employment relations since the 1970s. Initially, governments were concerned with discrimination on grounds of sex and race; though by the 1990s the need to challenge discriminatory treatment with regard to people with disabilities was also recognized. See Legislation and policy 4.2 for details of the main pieces of anti-discrimination and equality legislation enacted between the 1970s and 1990s.

LEGISLATION AND POLICY 4.2: The main equality and anti-discrimination legislation of the 1970s to 1990s

- *Equal Pay Act (1970)*: provided for equal pay between men and women when engaged in 'like work'.
- *Sex Discrimination Act (1975)*: prohibited direct and indirect discrimination in employment in relation to gender.
- *Race Relations Act (1976)*: prohibited direct and indirect discrimination in employment in relation to race and ethnicity.
- *Equal Pay (Equal Pay for Work of Equal Value) Regulations (1983)*: provided for equal pay between men and women when engaged in work of equal value.
- *Disability Discrimination Act (1995)*: obliged employers to make 'reasonable adjustments' to ensure that a disabled employee, or potential employee, was not substantially disadvantaged; small firms were exempted.

During the 1970s, legislation designed to promote equality at work helped to erode the voluntarist basis of employment relations in Britain. The 1970 Equal Pay Act, which came into effect fully in 1975, provided for equal pay between men and women when engaged in 'like work'. Also in 1975, the principle that pregnant women be entitled to a period of paid maternity absence was established, alongside protection against discrimination on the grounds of pregnancy.

The 1975 Sex Discrimination Act made direct and indirect discrimination against women in employment unlawful. Direct discrimination refers to circumstances where, for example, a man or woman is not considered for employment, or for promotion, or a pay rise, among other things, purely because of their sex. The concept of indirect discrimination, however, concerns the situation where a condition of employment is applied 'to both sexes of a kind such that the proportion of one sex who can comply with it is considerably smaller. An example might be when a police force specifies that all candidates for the post of police officer must be two metres tall' (Cockburn 1991: 28–9). Similarly, the 1976 Race Relations Act prohibited direct and indirect discrimination in employment on the grounds of race. See Table 4.1 for key concepts related to the area of discrimination.

Pressure from campaigning groups and trade union activists was an important impetus for the enactment of legislation covering equal pay and sex discrimination in particular (Cockburn 1991). Yet the development of anti-discrimination legislation was, and to a large extent continues to be, marked by a 'liberal' approach to securing greater equality (Dickens 2000*a*). This involves trying to ensure that people are accorded equal treatment regardless of their social characteristics (Jewson and Mason 1986). Progress towards equality is best achieved by using formal procedures, covering recruitment, selection, and promotion decisions for example, that encourage managers to treat people as if they are the same, reducing the salience of social differences (Liff and Wacjman 1996).

Table 4.1 Discrimination—key concepts

Concept	Definition
Direct discrimination	Unfair discrimination that arises where someone is treated less favourably in employment on account of their sex, race, etc.
Indirect discrimination	Unfair discrimination that arises where a condition of employment is applied which results in a worker being treated less favourably on account of their sex, race, etc.
Positive action	Measures designed to correct the under-representation of certain groups of workers through interventions which help their employment prospects (e.g. training and development)
Positive discrimination	Measures designed to correct the under-representation of certain groups of workers by giving them preferential treatment (e.g. quotas)—unlawful in the UK

With the 'radical' approach to securing greater equality, however, a greater emphasis is given to the importance of influencing outcomes directly, rather than on ensuring that processes are in place to treat people the same, regardless of their social characteristics. Radical measures encompass, for example, 'positive action' to deal with, say, the under-representation of particular categories of workers, such as women or black and minority ethnic workers. This might take the form of dedicated training interventions designed to increase their participation. While the law traditionally has not encouraged positive action, unlike 'positive discrimination' it is not unlawful. Positive discrimination involves giving members of disadvantaged social groups preferential treatment in the jobs market or in promotion decisions. For example, Norway has instituted a controversial system of gender quotas for company boards (see International perspective 4.3).

 International perspective 4.3: Gender quotas on company boards

One form of positive discrimination which has attracted growing interest concerns efforts to tackle the under-representation of women on company boards through some kind of quota system. Women comprise only around one in seven board members of major companies in Europe. Some European countries have already enacted measures to tackle this under-representation. Norway was a particularly notable pioneer. In 2003 it enacted controversial legislation requiring company boards to have at least 40 per cent representation of each sex by 2008. The law had a marked positive impact in respect of improving female board-level representation (Seierstad 2011; Wang and Kelan 2013). Much of the benefit, though, seems to have been gained by a relatively small number of female directors, who each sit on more boards. Concerns have also been expressed that any improvements have largely been cosmetic, with few advantages accruing to women in general. That said, though, a key consequence of the legal change was to counteract the 'idea that a career in business is for "men only"' (Teigen 2012: 88). The Norwegian model has attracted the interest of EU policy-makers. In 2012, the European Commission proposed the introduction of a new Gender Balance Directive, which would set an objective of at least 40 per cent of non-executive positions on the boards of major companies being held by women by 2020 (European Commission 2012). Progress has been slow, however, not least because of opposition from some member states, including the UK, which prefers a voluntary, business-led approach (see Section 4.3.4). As a result, there is little likelihood that the 2020 target date will be achieved.

Conservative governments of the 1980s and 1990s largely eschewed legislative interventions as a means of effecting change, in favour of voluntary employer- and market-led efforts (Dickens 1997; Webb 1997; Dex and Forth 2009). They promoted 'a privatized route to equality, with an emphasis on individual organizations deciding what is in their interests' (Dickens 1999: 11). The principal exception was the 1995 Disability Discrimination Act, which obliged large employers to make 'reasonable adjustments' to ensure that people with disabilities, encompassing both physical and mental impairments, were not substantially disadvantaged in employment, and did not experience less favourable treatment, without adequate justification—the result of many years of campaigning by pressure groups and disability activists. Conservative efforts at avoiding further legal intervention in the area of equality were stymied by the obligations that went with membership of the European Economic Community (EEC) (Davies and Freedland 1993; Dickens 1997).

4.3.2 Equality and anti-discrimination policy under Labour 1997–2010

The extension of anti-discrimination legislation and the support given to 'family-friendly' working were two key elements of Labour's employment relations policy programme between 1997 and 2010. See Legislation and policy 4.4 for details of the main legislative provisions. It is also important to recognize that other policies enacted by Labour also helped to alleviate employment disadvantage. The 1999 introduction of the National Minimum Wage (NMW), for example, particularly benefited low-paid women workers (see Chapter 7).

LEGISLATION AND POLICY 4.4: Equality and anti-discrimination legislation under Labour 1997–2010

- *Maternity and Parental Leave Regulations 1999*: enacted in order to comply with the EU's 1996 Parental Leave Directive. Established the right of parents to take up to thirteen weeks of unpaid parental leave, offered parents the right to unpaid time off work to attend to family emergencies, and increased the minimum period of maternity leave to eighteen weeks.

- *Race Relations Amendment Act 2000*: obliged public sector employers to promote positive race relations.

- *Part-time Workers (Prevention of Less Favourable Treatment) Regulations 2000*: prohibited employers from treating part-time workers less favourably than a full-time equivalent. Enacted in order to comply with the EU's 1997 Directive on Equal Rights and Treatment for Part-time Workers.

- *Fixed-term Employees Regulations 2002*: prohibited employers from treating employees on fixed-term contracts less favourably than an equivalent permanent employee. Enacted in order to comply with the EU's 1999 Fixed-term Contracts Directive.

- *Employment Act 2002*: extended the minimum period of paid maternity leave to twenty-six weeks, introduced two weeks' paid paternity leave, and established a new right for parents to request flexible working arrangements.

- *Employment Equality (Sexual Orientation) Regulations 2003*: gave workers protection against discrimination on the grounds of sexual orientation. This legislation was enacted in order to comply with the EU's 2000 Equal Treatment Directive.

(continued...)

- *Employment Equality (Religion or Belief) Regulations 2003*: gave workers protection against discrimination on the grounds of religion or belief. This legislation was enacted in order to comply with the EU's 2000 Equal Treatment Directive.
- *Disability Discrimination Act 1995 (Amendment) Regulations 2003*: among other things, this did away with the exemption for small employers, placed an obligation on public sector employers to promote disability equality, and, in order to comply with the EU's 2000 Equal Treatment Directive, reduced the scope for employers to avoid making reasonable adjustments.
- *The Employment Equality (Age) Regulations 2006*: prohibited age discrimination in respect of employment and vocational training, and introduced a new 'default' retirement age of 65, which was later rescinded; enacted in order to comply with the EU's 2000 Equal Treatment Directive.
- *Work and Families Act 2006*: extended the right to request flexible working to carers of adults, provided for the extension of paid maternity leave to a minimum of thirty-nine weeks along with the expectation that it would subsequently be increased to a year, and provided for the introduction of additional paternity leave, some of which could be paid.
- *Equality Act 2006*: provided for the establishment of the Equality and Human Rights Commission; imposed a new duty on public bodies to promote gender equality.
- *Equality Act 2010*: consolidated all existing equality and anti-discrimination legislation in one piece of overarching legislation; provided for greater consistency of treatment across the various 'protected characteristics'; imposed a 'general equality duty' on public authorities; and provided for some degree of positive action in selection and promotion decisions.

The scope of anti-discrimination law was extensively widened under Labour (Dex and Forth 2009). In 2004, for example, disability discrimination legislation was extended to cover all employers. Most of the impetus for reform was stimulated by EU legislation (Dickens 2007), in particular a 2000 framework equality directive that prohibits discrimination in employment on the grounds of age, sexual orientation, and religion or belief. EU legislation also influenced the equality agenda in other respects. For example, directives establishing that part-time workers and employees on fixed-term contracts should not be less favourably treated than their full-time and permanent counterparts were enacted, and subsequently implemented in the early 2000s, because of a concern to promote gender equality. The over-representation of women in part-time and temporary jobs meant that where employers treated people undertaking them less favourably than others then this could amount to discriminatory treatment on the grounds of gender. However, workers who believe they are disadvantaged as a result of their part-time status must identify appropriate full-time workers as comparators. Extensive job segregation, though, means that part-time workers generally do not undertake the same jobs as full-timers. This makes such comparisons problematic, and as a result few part-time workers are in a position to benefit from the legislation (McColgan 2000; McKay 2001).

The strengthening of equality legislation was a further aspect of change in the public policy framework during the 2000s, unrelated to Britain's membership of the EU. The introduction of positive duties to promote race, gender, and disability equality in the public sector—a form of positive action—was a significant development (Dex and Forth 2009). This signified a move, albeit limited, away from a liberal conception of achieving equality, based on treating everyone in the same way, to a situation where it is recognized that in order to alleviate inequality at work, employers need to do more to assist people from disadvantaged groups (Conley

2011; Kirton and Greene 2015). In the public sector, at least, Labour pursued a 'stronger *and* broader' approach to equality and diversity issues: broader, through efforts to 'integrate equality and diversity in the public service workforce with the delivery of public services sensitive to diverse communities', and stronger, as exemplified by the shift to a more radical orientation, marked by the use of positive action, monitoring arrangements, and targets (Bach and Kessler 2012: 89).

Perhaps the most important piece of equality legislation enacted by Labour—the 2010 Equality Act—came right at the end of its period in office. The Act's main purpose was to modernize the legal framework relating to equality and diversity matters, making it more straightforward and ensuring greater consistency of approach (Conley 2011; Burton 2014; Kirton and Greene 2015). The Equality Act consolidated all of the existing equality and anti-discrimination laws, incorporating them into one single piece of overarching legislation, and in some areas—gender reassignment for example—extended the coverage of legal protection. Discrimination is prohibited on the grounds of nine 'protected characteristics': age, disability, gender reassignment, marriage or civil partnership, pregnancy and maternity, race, religion or belief, sex, and sexual orientation. In some areas, the Equality Act extended the obligation on employers not to discriminate against workers with certain protected characteristics; it prohibited indirect discrimination on the grounds of disability, for example; it also made employers liable if their staff are harassed by a third party, such as a customer or client, because of a protected characteristic, if they have not taken sufficient steps to prevent it.

The Equality Act additionally placed a 'general equality duty' on public authorities to eliminate unlawful discrimination and promote equality and 'good relations' across all of the protected characteristics except for marriage and civil partnership (the Public Sector Equality Duty—PSED). It also sought to encourage positive action by permitting an employer to take a protected characteristic into account when choosing between otherwise similarly qualified candidates for a vacancy or a promotion. This was a relatively minor, but potentially highly symbolic, departure from the hitherto dominant liberal approach to promoting equality and diversity, which aspires to treat people as if they are all the same (Conley 2011; Kirton and Greene 2015).

During the 2000s Labour also took steps to promote more 'family-friendly' employment policies and a better 'work–life balance'. The 'family-friendly' label is used to describe a wide variety of different practices that may help parents and carers reconcile their work with their domestic responsibilities, including, among other things, provisions for maternity, paternity, and parental leave (see Table 4.2), childcare facilities, job-sharing measures, and other forms of flexible working arrangements. The term 'work–life balance' has increasingly been preferred to 'family-friendly', not least because it implies a focus on workers in general, not just those with family responsibilities. However, the main problem with the work–life balance concept concerns the assumption that a distinction can easily be made between people's 'work' and their 'lives' (Scholarios and Marks 2004). In reality, of course, they overlap and interact with each other in subtle, complex, and dynamic ways (Warhurst, Eikhof, and Haunschild 2008).

To some degree, Labour's approach was predicated on the obligation to enact EU legislation under the 'Social Chapter' (see Chapter 3), particularly the Parental Leave Directive, which gives parents the right to take a period of unpaid leave—now up to eighteen weeks—before a child's fifth birthday and an entitlement to unpaid time off work in order to manage

Table 4.2 Parental leave—key concepts

Concept	Definition
Maternity leave	Leave taken by the mother before, during, and after the birth of a child
Paternity leave	Leave taken by the father during and after the birth or adoption of a child
Parental leave	Leave that can be taken by either parent in the first few years after the birth or adoption of a child

family crises, such as a child's sickness. But Labour also went beyond what was strictly required to comply with EU legislation, introducing the right of fathers to take up to two weeks' paternity leave, for example, and extending the period of paid maternity leave for mothers. It also legislated to give parents and carers of adults the right to have their requests for flexible working arrangements (e.g. part-time working) taken seriously by employers—see Chapter 8.

Labour's policy agenda was informed by the belief that providing as many people as possible, especially women and lone parents, the opportunity to reconcile their family responsibilities with undertaking paid employment is advantageous to employers because of the supposed business benefits, like improved staff morale, reduced absenteeism, and easier recruitment, that arise (HM Treasury and DTI 2003). Its efforts were thus focused on encouraging employers to improve their family-friendly and work–life balance practices voluntarily. There is some evidence that employers accept such a business case rationale. In the hospitality industry, recruitment and retention difficulties have encouraged some major employers to invest in flexible working time arrangements in order to hold on to female staff with young children (Doherty 2004). The presence of work–life balance arrangements is associated with lower turnover of staff and reduced levels of employee absence (Beauregard and Henry 2009). Overall, however, there are rather mixed findings when it comes to the relationship between flexible working time arrangements and performance outcomes, suggesting that there is no 'unequivocal' business case for work–life balance in organizations (de Menezes and Kelliher 2011).

4.3.3 Evaluating Labour's legal and policy framework

In assessing developments in the legal and policy framework governing discrimination and equality at work, it is important to recognize that Labour's interventions contained a number of positive and progressive features. The scope of anti-discrimination legislation was considerably widened; it became unlawful for an employer to discriminate against a worker on the grounds of his or her sexual orientation, for example. The increased emphasis placed on promoting parental leave was aimed at encouraging greater involvement of fathers in child-raising activities, rather than assuming that this is a role for mothers. However, concerns were expressed that the 'family-friendly' measures enacted by Labour may have accentuated, rather than diminished, gender disadvantage at work, by not doing enough to challenge the presumption that it is largely the responsibility of mothers to adapt their employment arrangements, not fathers (Dickens 2007; EHRC 2009). Most requests for flexible working come from women, reflecting the gendered assumptions that govern the respective roles of mothers and fathers. Yet part-time working arrangements and other forms of flexible employment, which are dominated by women, often provide limited opportunities for career development or progression. Women who undertake flexible working, especially part-time employment, may be perceived by male managers as lacking the commitment to the job and the organization necessary for promotion (Lewis 1997).

Three other problems with Labour's approach can be identified. First, efforts to tackle discrimination and promote equality at work were tempered by a desire to avoid overly disturbing business interests (Dean and Liff 2010; Kirton and Greene 2015). For example, Labour resisted extending the equality duties to private sector employers, limiting their overall impact (Dean and Liff 2010). The prevailing assumption behind the approach taken by policy-makers was that voluntary interventions by employers are a more effective way of improving equality outcomes than legislative measures, and that equality action has to be 'justified in terms of promoting efficiency and competitiveness' (Dickens 2007: 468), rather than for reasons of social justice (Dex and Forth 2009). Pursuing equality was desirable, but only in so far as it accorded with the interests of employers—an 'inadequate basis for the pursuit of equality' (Dickens 2007: 474).

 Insight into practice 4.5: The individualized basis of responses to disability discrimination legislation

The Disability Discrimination Act (DDA) 1995 obliges employers to make 'reasonable adjustments' to accommodate disabled workers so that they are not put at a substantial disadvantage in employment, or when looking for employment. Based on interviews with disabled workers in the public sector, Foster (2007) demonstrated that the adjustment process is often damaging to the workers concerned, some of whom experience stress or ill health as a result. Even when the process of adjustment produced a satisfactory outcome for the worker, delays in implementation could cause difficulties. The most significant finding, however, concerned the informal, individualized basis of the adjustment process: much depended on the disabled employee's relationship with their line manager. The problem with such a highly individualized approach, though, is that it lacks transparency, contributing 'nothing to the development of broader policy-making and practice' (Foster 2007: 81). Moreover, a worker's disability comes to be perceived as a problem for the individual, to be resolved through negotiation with his or her line manager, rather than a structural issue for the organization as a whole.

A second problem concerns the liberal, equal treatment approach that tended to underpin Labour's approach, something which left the structural causes of inequality at work largely unchallenged. Disadvantage came to be presented as a problem for the individual worker, rather than as something that stemmed from the way organizations operate (see Insight into practice 4.5). Perhaps the biggest obstacle to the take-up of family-friendly and work–life balance practices, for example, is that they often come under the control of line managers who can be reluctant to allow employees to make use of them, in spite of what organizational policies might say (Hyman and Summers 2004; Gatrell 2005).

In some parts of the economy, such as in call centres and the retail sector, there is often a conflict between the flexibility needed by employers (in particular the expectation that staff will work additional hours at short notice to cope with an unanticipated rise in calls) and demands from workers for predictable working time arrangements so that they can plan their family responsibilities effectively (Hyman and Marks 2008; O'Brien-Smith and Rigby 2010).

More generally, increasing work demands (see Chapter 8) often militate against efforts to promote better work–life balance. Nearly a third (31 per cent) of full-time employees report that their jobs interfere with their lives outside work (van Wanrooy et al. 2013a).

Although the 2000s saw the introduction of some limited duties to promote equality, in the public sector at least, for the most part any kind of positive action designed to achieve greater equality was eschewed by policy-makers. Yet the emphasis on establishing a level playing field, on which, in theory, people compete on the same terms, fails to appreciate the extent to which the rules of the game conform to the experiences of relatively privileged sections of the workforce, like men (Dickens 1992). For all its good intentions, the Equality Act 2010 contained nothing to tackle underlying sources of inequality and disadvantage, such as the pattern of occupational segregation, that cause discrimination (Burton 2014).

A third problem with the legal framework relating to equality and discrimination at work concerns the rather weak arrangements for enforcing rights. Two types of enforcement mechanism exist: administrative measures and legal arrangements (Dickens 2007). With regard to the former, in 2007 a new Equality and Human Rights Commission (EHRC) was established to replace three pre-existing organizations concerned with promoting gender, race, and disability respectively. The rationale for creating an all-encompassing equality body was that with the introduction of new discrimination laws covering age, sexual orientation, and religion or belief, it made sense to establish a single agency, which would be a more effective guardian of equality than a number of smaller, issue-specific bodies (Dean and Liff 2010). In theory, a single equality body should be able to articulate a more integrated and systematic approach to tackling discrimination and promoting equality. However, the EHRC's achievements have been disappointing, not least because of the damage inflicted on it by the coalition government between 2010 and 2015 (as explained in Section 4.3.4).

The second type of enforcement mechanism concerns attempts by workers who have experienced unlawful discrimination to gain legal redress by submitting a claim to an employment tribunal (ET), which can award financial compensation to successful claimants. The weaknesses of ETs as vehicles for enforcing workers' rights are considered in more detail in Chapter 10. Here, though, the focus is on their limitations as arrangements for challenging unlawful discriminatory practices. One problem is that the onus is on an individual worker to take the appropriate action, by raising a complaint, when they might either lack knowledge about how to make a discrimination claim, or may be anxious about the consequences of submitting one (Dickens 2007; Burton 2014; Kirton and Greene 2015).

One way of resolving this would be to allow individual claimants to come together as a group to submit so-called 'class actions', since discrimination rarely affects just one individual worker, but is generally a collective experience (Bradley and Healy 2008). Because such 'class actions' are prohibited in the UK, ETs often have to handle multiple individual claims together. After submitting a claim, having to go through a tribunal hearing can be an unpleasant experience for the workers involved (Aston, Hill, and Tackey 2006). Even in the minority of cases where a discrimination claim is upheld, the remedy is usually in the form of financial compensation, generally less than £10,000. Employers are under no obligation to eradicate the discriminatory practice that prompted the claim in the first place (Dickens 1997; Burton 2014). The Equality Act 2010 did include a provision enabling ETs to make wider recommendations relating to the workforce in general in successful discrimination cases, such as introducing diversity training. However, in line with the 2010–15 coalition government's aim of reducing the amount of employment 'red tape' which supposedly impedes employers' flexibility (see Chapter 3), it was abolished by the Deregulation Act 2015.

During the 2000s, Labour largely favoured employer-led moves to promote equality at work, with legislative action treated as an undesirable last resort when voluntary efforts failed (Roper, Cunningham, and James 2003). However, little was done to oblige employers to eradicate discriminatory practices at work. The idea was that equality action is best fostered by a relatively light touch legislative regime within which employers are encouraged, because it is in their own interests, to take voluntary initiatives to promote equality (Dickens 2007).

4.3.4 Equality under the 2010–15 coalition government: deregulation and austerity

When it came to office in 2010, the Conservative–Liberal Democrat coalition government claimed that it had a strong commitment to promoting equality, part of its ambition to build a 'fairer Britain', and would take a similar approach to that pursued by its Labour predecessor (Manfredi 2016). Under the leadership of David Cameron, in opposition the Conservative Party had emphasized the importance of promoting greater gender equality and improving people's work–life balance, part of a policy agenda calculated to appeal particularly to women voters (Williams and Scott 2010).

Yet it was the Liberal Democrat side of the coalition that provided a lead in developing work–life balance policy, manifest in the 'Modern Workplaces' initiative. This encompassed two strands. One of these was the ambition to increase the involvement of fathers in child-raising activities by means of a new system of shared, flexible parental leave, which came into effect in 2015. Assuming they qualify (at least one parent must have twenty-six weeks of continuous service with their employer, for example), then both partners can share up to fifty weeks of parental leave (thirty-seven weeks of which can be paid) during the first year following the birth or adoption of a child. But few fathers are expected to make use of the opportunity to have an extended period of parental leave. Many will not be eligible because their partners are not in work, while the level of weekly statutory paternity pay (£139.58 in 2016) may also act as a disincentive. The second strand, which took effect in 2014, concerned the extension of the right to request flexible working to cover all employees. At the same time, however, the statutory procedure which had governed the process of requesting flexible working was replaced by a rather less onerous obligation on employers simply to deal with requests in a 'reasonable manner' (Manfredi 2016).

More generally, though, the coalition government's policies acted to compromise equality—in two notable respects. The first concerned the coalition's deregulatory agenda (see Chapter 3). The coalition explicitly characterized equality provisions as 'red tape', burdens on business that hinder employers and restrict competitiveness and growth (Dickens 2014; Conley and Page 2016; Manfredi 2016). This was exemplified by its abandonment of several key measures contained in the Equality Act 2010, but which had yet to become law when the coalition entered office, and the repeal of some that had. Plans to implement compulsory equal pay audits for large and medium-sized employers and a proposed new duty on public bodies to tackle inequalities based on social class—the first instance of the law being proposed to tackle class-based disadvantage—were among the discarded measures (Conley 2014). Although the general duty on public sector employers to promote equality—the PSED—was retained, its effectiveness was diminished, particularly by the removal of any obligation to conduct equality impact assessments (Conley 2011; Kirton and Greene 2015; Manfredi 2016). As already mentioned, the coalition's Deregulation Act 2015 removed the power of employment tribunals to make recommendations for changes in employers' practices in successful discrimination claims.

These changes were predicated on the belief that employers were hamstrung by excessive regulation, and needed greater flexibility if business was to be competitive (Burton 2014). The coalition government preferred to promote voluntary, business-led efforts to promoting equality, especially when it came to the issue of the gender pay gap. Its 'Think, Act, Report' initiative focused on promoting greater transparency, and urged employers to sign up to demonstrate their commitment to tackling gender pay inequality in their organizations: identifying any issues around gender equality ('think'); taking action to fix those issues ('act'); and detailing how they ensure gender equality ('report'). But the results were deeply unimpressive. Although some 200 employers signed up to the campaign, only a handful actually published any meaningful data about the extent of their gender pay gaps, rendering the whole exercise somewhat pointless (Kirton and Greene 2015; Manfredi 2016). It was only because of the tenacity of Labour MP Sarah Champion, who was successful in pushing the relevant legislation through Parliament in 2014–15, that private sector employers with 250 or more employees became required to publish information about their gender pay gaps (Manfredi 2016).

Elsewhere, the coalition government's overall preference for a voluntary approach, with employers encouraged to take action on the self-interested basis that improvements in equality are good for business, was evident in the matter of female representation on company boards. The UK government opposed EU moves to legislate for board-level equality (see Section 4.3.1). Instead it supported a voluntary, business-led initiative, which was successful in achieving its objective of increasing the proportion of women board members of major UK-based companies from a paltry 12.5 per cent in 2010 to at least 25 per cent by 2015 (it actually reached 26.1 per cent). Davies (2015: 9) reflected on how this was achieved:

> We worked up the business case for change and spoke language business understands. The value-add of diverse perspectives, the economic arguments on talent management and the modernizing of British business. We spoke of global credibility, impact to reputation, the longer-term stability of our economy and the UK's competitive position on the global stage.

This success points to something very important about the coalition's approach to equality, namely its preference for interventions that largely benefit professional and managerial women. The position of others, however, notably worsened, largely because of the impact of austerity measures (Manfredi 2016). Austerity severely compromised equality, particularly in respect of gender. The impact of cuts to jobs, wages, and pensions in the public sector was felt disproportionately highly by women; they were also more likely to be disadvantaged by the withdrawal of public services, and often had to bear the burden of tasks left undone by the retreat of state provision (Fawcett Society 2012; Manfredi 2016). The introductory case study demonstrates the adverse impact of austerity, and the coalition's other priorities, including its preference for employment deregulation, on workers with disabilities.

Austerity measures also meant that the EHRC's capacity to promote equality and combat discrimination, particularly in the area of race, was severely compromised—in some people's view deliberately so, because otherwise it might have mobilized opinion against coalition policies (Conley 2012b; Holloway 2012). The 2010–15 coalition government instigated major cuts to the organization's budget, severely diminishing its capacity to challenge discriminatory practices and promote equality (Kirton and Greene 2015). In 2009–10 the EHRC had an annual budget of £62 million and employed some 450 staff; by 2015–16 its budget had fallen to just £22 million with only around 200 staff.

Despite advances in some areas—the new system of shared parental leave for example, and the growth in the proportion of women on the boards of major companies—anti-discrimination and equality measures were less of a priority for the coalition government than had been the case under Labour during the 2000s. Moreover, the primacy attached by the coalition government to austerity, and its view of equality measures as undesirable regulation which, in order to boost business competitiveness, needed to be diluted, meant that between 2010 and 2015 a much more antagonistic approach towards equality was evident. There is little evidence, so far, that the Conservative majority administration which took office in May 2015 will take a different path, as illustrated by the end-of-chapter case study on pregnancy discrimination.

 ## Section summary and further reading

- Legislation prohibiting discrimination in work and employment on the grounds of sex and race developed during the 1970s. It was informed by a liberal conception of equality which holds that disadvantage is best alleviated by establishing measures which ensure that people are treated the same, irrespective of their gender or ethnicity.

- During the 2000s, Labour governments made some notable changes to the legal framework, including extending the scope of anti-discrimination legislation, and establishing a range of policies designed to promote more family-friendly working arrangements.

- The policy and legal framework relating to equality and discrimination matters has a number of major weaknesses, including a reluctance to challenge the interests of employers, the predominance of a liberal, equal treatment ethos which fails to address the structural causes of employment disadvantage, and the presence of a weak enforcement regime which puts too much responsibility for tackling discrimination onto individual workers and not enough of an onus on employers.

- Despite some positive policy interventions, including the introduction of a new system of shared parental leave, overall the 2010–15 coalition government's record on equality was poor. Its austerity and deregulatory policies compromised equality in some important respects.

For further information about the legislative and policy framework governing equality, including the Equality Act 2010, see Kirton and Greene (2015: chapter 6) and Dean and Liff (2010: 429–33). Manfredi (2016) tackles the coalition's record. The work of Linda Dickens on equality and anti-discrimination legislation is highly recommended (e.g. Dickens 2007). See Jewson and Mason (1986) for further details of the liberal and radical approaches to equality. See the Equality and Human Rights Commission's website for details of its work.

4.4 Equality and diversity at work

In this section the concern is with organizational initiatives designed to challenge inequality and disadvantage at work. Equal opportunities (EO) policies are the main tool used by employers to promote equality in the workplace. There has been an increasing amount of interest in the concept of managing diversity (MD) as a means of challenging disadvantage at work. Many organizations have also established policies dealing with work–life balance and family-friendly working issues. However, trade unions play a key part in promoting effective action in this area.

4.4.1 Understanding equal opportunities policies

During the 1980s and 1990s, many large employers in the public and private sectors increasingly committed themselves to the pursuit of equal opportunities, in particular by styling themselves as 'equal opportunity employers' and enacting formal EO policies (Dex and Forth 2009). This trend continued during the 2000s. In 2004, 66 per cent of workplaces with five or more employees were covered by a formal policy; by 2011, this had risen to 77 per cent (van Wanrooy et al. 2013b). Much of the increase reflects the growing prevalence of EO policies in smaller, private sector workplaces, even if they are more commonly found in larger workplaces (Walsh 2007; Dex and Forth 2009; van Wanrooy et al. 2013a). Whereas in the past EO policies were generally restricted to the areas of sex and race, there is evidence that, under the influence of legislation, their scope has widened to cover disability, and also age, religion, and sexual orientation (Walsh 2007).

Under the influence of the legislative framework, organizational EO policies are typically marked by a 'liberal' orientation when it comes to tackling inequality at work (Jewson and Mason 1986; Bach and Kessler 2012). There is therefore an overwhelming emphasis on the development of a 'level playing field' (Webb 1997), so that all workers are treated in the same way. As applied to the recruitment and selection of staff, for instance, the emphasis is on ensuring that procedures exist which enable employers to choose staff on the basis of their suitability for the job, irrespective of their social characteristics (Kirton and Greene 2015).

Why, though, have EO policies become so commonplace in organizations? Compliance with the law is the most significant influence on organizational practice; EO policies are designed to ensure that the organization is less liable to litigation on the grounds of sex, race, and, more recently, disability, religious belief, age, and sexual orientation discrimination. Bradley and Healy (2008: 81) acknowledge that concerns about the weakness of the legislation protecting workers from discrimination are well justified. Nevertheless, they maintain that legislative provisions 'may act as an incentive for good practice' in organizations. Employers have been encouraged to develop EO policies in order to avoid discrimination cases that could potentially damage their reputation.

The pursuit of EO in organizations has also been informed by a belief that inequality and unfair discrimination at work are inherently undesirable and, in the interests of social justice, should be eradicated (Davies and Thomas 2000). However, the social justice rationale for equality action has been eclipsed by the one that stresses the advantages to businesses of reducing inequality and disadvantage in the employment relationship (Dickens 1997; Glover and Kirton 2006; Kirton and Greene 2015; Conley and Page 2016).

There is no one business 'case' for equality action. Rather, it is proposed that the promotion of equality will, to varying degrees, generate certain business advantages (Dickens 1994; Liff 2003). These include being able to draw on a wider pool of talent when recruiting employees, retain important staff, benefit from the contribution of groups whose skills and potential input might otherwise have been neglected, match the characteristics of customers, and sustain a positive corporate reputation (Dickens 2000a; Liff 2003). Since the desirability of equality action is bound up with its potential contribution to enhancing organizational performance, business arguments may be more effective in stimulating improvements, in particular by securing the commitment of managers, than a social justice rationale (Dickens 1994; Liff 2003).

The growing adoption of organizational EO policies would seem to reflect 'a progressive increase in employers' commitment over time' (Dex and Forth 2009: 253). They have made a positive difference to the position of some groups of workers, particularly relatively well-off women who are better able to gain access to managerial and professional jobs (Webb 1997). This was evident in the case of the airline company studied by Rutherford (1999). Over a long period of time it had developed a range of sophisticated EO practices, such as job-sharing arrangements, designed to increase the number of women in management roles. Yet the proportion of women in senior management roles remained stubbornly low—largely, it seems, because of an assumption that such jobs required excessive working hours, something that was difficult to reconcile with women's family responsibilities.

4.4.2 Equal opportunities policies: a critical assessment

There are four main problems with EO policies as tools for challenging discrimination and disadvantage at work. The first is that they are often merely rhetorical statements of intent that help to conceal the presence of discriminatory workplace practices (Kirton and Greene 2015). In other words, the presence of a formal policy need not have much of an effect at all on employment relations processes and arrangements. Just because there is an equal opportunities policy in place should not be taken as a sign that unfair discrimination is absent (Aitkenhead and Liff 1991; Bradley and Healy 2008). The experiences of the black trade union activists studied by Healy, Bradley, and Mukherjee (2004) were marked by incidents of racial discrimination, even in companies that were noted for their supposedly eager pursuit of equal opportunities. See Insight into practice 4.6 for evidence of the persistence of racist and sexist attitudes and behaviours in organizations.

 Insight into practice 4.6: Racial disadvantage at work—the experiences of black and minority ethnic women trade unionists

Despite the growing use of equal opportunities policies, Bradley and Healy's (2008) study of the experiences of black and minority ethnic (BME) women trade union activists demonstrates that discrimination on grounds of race and ethnicity remains a prevalent feature of organizational life. Four aspects of discriminatory practice seem particularly noteworthy. First, the organizations in which the women worked were highly segregated on the basis of both gender and race. Black women managers were rare. Second, racism was reportedly commonplace, albeit in a less explicit fashion than in the past. Bradley and Healy (2008: 146) point to the persistence of what they call 'everyday racism', meaning the 'remarks, actions and behaviours which, in a small way but persistently, emphasise difference from the majority'. Examples include the use of phrases such as 'you people' or 'you lot' when referring to BME staff. Third, racial stereotyping seemed to be a common feature of organizational life. The women were often made to feel as if they were inferior on the grounds that they were black. According to one woman, 'managers make us feel like as if we don't have brains, even if you do cleaning they say you are not doing it properly ... This is the way they treat us ...' (Bradley and Healy 2008: 148–9). Fourth, sometimes managers were accused of failing to take complaints of racial harassment seriously. The experiences of these women indicate that we should take care not to assume that the expansion of equal opportunities policies in organizations has necessarily eradicated racist and sexist attitudes and behaviours.

In practice, EO policies are often just 'empty shells'. This means that in many workplaces covered by a formal EO policy there are either few practices to support it, or if there are, practices such as the ability to undertake job-sharing, for example, are restricted to certain groups of workers (Hoque and Noon 2004). Rigorous arrangements for evaluating the operation of EO policies tend to be rather rare (Dex and Forth 2009). For example, fewer than a quarter (23 per cent) of workplaces are covered by formal arrangements for monitoring recruitment and selection (van Wanrooy et al. 2013b). Overall, then, while formal EO policies have become more prevalent in organizations, inadequate arrangements for monitoring and evaluating how they operate limit the extent to which they can be used as effective tools for mitigating discrimination and disadvantage.

A second problem with organizational EO policies is that their focus is often rather narrow, concerned with assisting women managers to break the 'glass ceiling' and secure more senior positions, for example. Employers are often uninterested in developing interventions that would benefit the many more female workers who are employed in jobs characterized by low pay and poor working conditions, and whose prospects are obstructed more by the presence of a 'sticky floor' rather than a glass ceiling (Cockburn 1991; Dickens 1997). For example the National Health Service (NHS) has pursued a gender equality agenda that prioritizes increasing the proportion of women in professional and managerial jobs. Such an approach, however, has 'little relevance to women in clerical and administrative grades, much less ancillary workers such as cleaners, catering staff and health-care assistants' (Richards 2001: 27).

The third obstacle to the progress of employer-led equality initiatives concerns the attitudes and behaviour of line managers, who are generally responsible for implementing them in practice. But many such managers lack appropriate knowledge or understanding of how to manage equality issues effectively (Kirton and Greene 2015). Equality initiatives are often treated as unimportant, or even resisted, by managers who see them as an infringement on their prerogative, especially during periods of organizational change. This was apparent in a civil service agency that, among other things, gave line managers more discretion over equal opportunities. Although a minority of managers did take the opportunity to progress these issues, most had only a 'hazy perception of the role they were expected to play in maintaining and developing' equal opportunities (Cunningham, Lord, and Delaney 1999: 70), and some expressed downright hostility.

Linked to this, the fourth weakness of EO policies as devices designed to reduce unfair discrimination at work is that they generally fail to challenge those features of the cultures and structures of organizations that privilege men. This was evident in the case of a high-street bank. The company had a long-standing formal commitment to equal opportunities. In practice, however, major barriers to women's progress existed. Managers were expected to undertake excessive working hours—something of a problem for women with family responsibilities. Moreover, it was assumed that once they had children, women would lack the appropriate level of organizational commitment necessary for promotion. If a woman expressed an interest in flexible working, so as to combine work and family responsibilities more easily, this was taken as a sign that she was not interested in pursuing a career. Thus management in the organization, especially senior roles, was dominated by men. 'Formal equality statements expressed concern about this situation but there were far more powerful informal practices which reinforced it' (Liff and Ward 2001: 30).

It is important not to underplay the significance of EO initiatives. In some areas they have fostered a 'climate of equality', enabling women to challenge long-established structures of job segregation (Bradley 1999). By itself, though, employer-led equality action is a rather weak means of challenging such discrimination in employment (Dickens 2000a). A major source of this weakness is that it is underpinned by an assumption that equality is best promoted on the basis that it delivers important business benefits. Yet there are a number of problems with this approach. For one thing, employers may focus their efforts on improvements in areas where it is easier to secure change, or where the business benefits are more easily identifiable (Dickens 1999). This explains the popularity of initiatives designed to erode the glass ceiling and increase the proportion of female managers in senior positions. Challenging long-established patterns of job segregation and low pay, which operate to the disadvantage of women workers in particular, is a much more complicated and difficult area and will not be in the interests of employers who secure important cost advantages by maintaining a pool of cheap, low-paid female labour (Dickens 1994). In such cases 'a business case can be articulated against [equal opportunities] action' (Dickens 1999: 10).

The supposed business benefits of equality action may be difficult to identify at an organizational level (Colling and Dickens 1998). Equality initiatives, moreover, can be perceived by employers as business costs, rather than as investments that can help to enhance organizational performance, and are liable to be withdrawn if no advantage is apparent (Dickens 2000a). While it seems that in general there are no additional major costs to employers of operating formal equality policies and practices, nor are there any real benefits (Riley, Metcalf, and Forth 2013). Efforts to challenge inequality and disadvantage at work based on business case arguments are therefore bound to be 'partial' and 'selective' (Dickens 1997). Furthermore, making equality action contingent on identifying business benefits means that deep-rooted and structural causes of disadvantage are often neglected (Kirton and Greene 2015).

4.4.3 **Towards managing diversity?**

In contrast to the emphasis on equal treatment and fair procedures that characterizes the liberal model of equal opportunities, interventions designed to produce equal outcomes are at the heart of the radical model. 'It seeks to intervene directly in workplace practices in order to achieve a fair distribution of rewards among employees, as measured by some criterion of moral value and worth' (Jewson and Mason 1986: 315). The radical model recognizes that structural factors particular to certain socially disadvantaged groups inhibit their participation in employment—for example women's greater share of domestic responsibilities (Webb and Liff 1988). Thus equality 'of access is an illusion while the white, male, full-time worker with few domestic responsibilities is seen as the norm' (Kirton and Greene 2015: 122). Positive discrimination, then, such as setting employment quotas, may be necessary if equality at work is to be achieved.

The main problem with the radical approach is that it invites the complaint that certain groups of workers are the unworthy beneficiaries of 'special treatment', which may erode support for equality initiatives. Nor does it 'promise any improvement *in the nature of the organisation itself*' (Cockburn 1989: 217, original italics). Instead, Cockburn (1989) proposes that it is more useful to distinguish between 'short' and 'long' equality agendas. Whereas the short agenda is concerned with rather superficial managerial interventions designed to

Table 4.3 The key characteristics of equal opportunities and diversity management approaches

Equal opportunities	Diversity management
A 'liberal' approach (sameness)	Recognizing and celebrating difference
Emphasis on the 'level playing field'	Attractive to managers
Equal treatment (group-based)	A more individualistic approach
The use of formal procedures (e.g. selection)	Emphasis on culture change

improve equality of opportunity, at its longest the equal opportunities agenda should be a transformative programme, dedicated to challenging the power of privileged groups of white, male employees (Liff 2003).

One of the claims made for the managing diversity (MD) approach is that it holds out the promise of transformative organizational change as a means of eroding disadvantage in employment (Blakemore and Drake 1996; Kirton and Greene 2015). It offers the prospect of 'a more radical challenge to the problem of disadvantage and discrimination by requiring organizations to adapt to individuals and groups rather than vice versa' (Dean and Liff 2010: 428). The MD approach has become increasingly influential, particularly in the United States, as a means of challenging discrimination and disadvantage in the employment relationship (Glover and Kirton 2006; Greene and Kirton 2009; Oswick and Noon 2014; Kirton and Greene 2015). What, then, are the main assumptions that underpin the MD model, and what are its principal characteristics?

Whereas the liberal equal opportunities approach emphasizes the importance of equal treatment and sameness as the best way of reducing disadvantage, the MD model contends that disadvantage is more effectively tackled by acknowledging and lauding differences between employees (Kandola and Fullerton 1994; Greene and Kirton 2009; Healy, Kirton, and Noon 2010). See Table 4.3 for the key characteristics of the EO and MD approaches. In the MD approach, the emphasis on recognizing individual differences stands in marked contrast to the primacy of tackling group-based disadvantage that is central to liberal EO programmes (Liff 1997, 2003). Thus there is 'a move away from the idea that different groups should be assimilated to meet an organizational norm' (Kirton and Greene 2015: 127)—one which is often, of course, based on the experiences of those who are relatively privileged in the labour market, such as white males (Liff and Wacjman 1996).

A further aspect of the MD approach which distinguishes it from an equal opportunities approach is that it is supposedly more attractive to managers (Liff 1997; Noon 2007; Kirton and Greene 2015). The emphasis on managing individual employees, and of realizing their potential in a way that benefits the business, is something that line managers, who might otherwise be sceptical of the value of equal opportunity initiatives, can more easily appreciate (Greene and Kirton 2009). In contrast to the EO approach, which is often perceived as an external imposition, particularly through government regulation, MD is said to be more easily aligned with, and supportive of, the needs of the business (Ross and Schneider 1992; Glover and Kirton 2006; Healy, Kirton, and Noon 2010; Oswick and Noon 2014). For example, the use of employee networks, or 'affinity groups' as they are sometimes called, is a feature of diversity management in the United States, which has now spread to the UK.

Some argue that because they operate under the aegis of employers these networks rarely enjoy the power to challenge undesirable discriminatory practices in organizations (e.g. Healy and Oikelome 2007). However, in places they seem to have become an increasingly prominent diversity management tool, helping to shape and influence the organizational diversity agenda. Colgan and McKearney's (2012: 373) study of lesbian, gay, bisexual, and transexual (LGBT) networks suggests that they provide workers with a 'mechanism for visibility, community, and voice'.

The most profound claim for the MD approach, though, is that if organizations are to acknowledge and manage individual differences effectively, and thus realize the full potential of their employees, they should review the way they operate. Underpinning the MD approach, therefore, is the assumption that an organization must 'recognize that *it* has to change to adapt to employee differences rather than simply expecting employees to fit in with its pre-existing practices' (Liff 1999: 68).

There is some evidence that where organizations take diversity seriously, and alter their practices accordingly, it can benefit employees. This is apparent from a study of the experiences of lesbian, gay, and bisexual (LGB) workers in sixteen 'good practice' case study organizations which had committed themselves to operating in ways that supported and enhanced diversity, for example by developing LGB networks. Even though LGB staff were aware that the employers had not done all they could to recognize and promote the benefits of diversity, they felt that their experience of employment had been enhanced by the adoption of an MD approach (Colgan et al. 2007).

Managing diversity, then, appears to hold out the potential for a transformation in employer attitudes towards equality, consistent with the 'long' approach discussed earlier in this section. In many cases, the diversity agenda has given equality practitioners in organizations more influence and authority, particularly because of the greater scope it gives them to integrate their goals with the overall needs of the business (Kirton and Greene 2009).

Generally, however, the MD approach promises significantly more than it actually delivers. There are three major problems. First, in practice it is often difficult to distinguish between an EO and an MD approach. Line managers prefer to deal with individual differences in a standardized way, more akin to a conventional equal opportunities mode of action (Greene and Kirton 2009: 163). MD may involve little more than a simple re-labelling of conventional equal opportunities initiatives (Kirton and Greene 2015), perhaps to make them more palatable to managers.

Second, the MD approach has been criticized for offering a 'sanitized' and 'unthreatening' perspective on workplace differences (Webb 1997: 163). It is a model that is designed to be comfortable for managers, not to challenge their assumptions or prejudices (Noon 2007). Workers themselves rarely have any input into how diversity management operates, with the result that the policies and practices associated with it often lack credibility (Greene and Kirton 2009). The emphasis on individuals, moreover, means that pressure to change potentially discriminatory organizational practices is often absent; they do not have the collective power to effect reforms enjoyed by socially disadvantaged groups (Webb 1997). As a result, understandings of 'differences', and of whether and how they should be valued, generally come within the prerogative of managers, who may support diversity only as long as it delivers explicit organizational benefits, or does not cost them anything (Webb 1997; Glover and Kirton 2006).

Third, although in theory the MD approach holds out the promise of transformative organizational change in order to enable individual differences to be recognized and valued, in practice it generally leaves established beliefs and practices unchanged (Dickens 2000*a*). Its focus on individual difference fails to recognize that disadvantage is a collective, social phenomenon which is group-based, and thus it is rarely used to challenge those long-standing features of organizations that systematically privilege, say, men (Liff 1997; Dean and Liff 2010). Often diversity 'may have more to do with corporate image-building than with the kind of interventions designed to facilitate more egalitarian work organization and increased inclusion of women' (Webb 1997: 166).

Ashley's (2010) study of diversity initiatives among City of London law firms exemplifies the limits of the MD approach. Efforts to diversify the class base of the legal profession, by acknowledging and rewarding individual difference based on social class—for example, opening up positions to more working-class candidates—were largely unsuccessful. Although good for the corporate reputation, they did very little to challenge the perception among senior lawyers that a more diverse class base would damage the image of their profession—an attitude which is 'deeply entrenched' in institutional structures and practices. Indeed, the presence of diversity initiatives notwithstanding, the expectation that 'non-traditional candidates should assimilate to existing organizational norms ... remains unchanged' (Ashley 2010: 723).

Like conventional equal opportunities approaches, to which they often bear a marked resemblance, MD policies are, given their status as employer-led methods of generating change, somewhat weak interventions for challenging inequality and disadvantage in employment (Greene and Kirton 2009). As Noon (2007) observes, the rationale for the MD approach is based on similar business case arguments to those that inform the development of equal opportunities initiatives more generally, and suffers from the same kind of problems. These include a tendency to focus solely on short-term performance improvements, which might not immediately be apparent, and a realization that there are often considerable benefits for employers of not taking action to deal with workplace disadvantage. Greene and Kirton's (2011) research in a government department demonstrates that the diversity management approach is more robust and durable when it is grounded in more than just narrow business case arguments. Despite a major restructuring exercise and associated job losses, diversity management in this public sector organization was sustained through the involvement of trade unions and employee representatives, and by the requirement to comply with its statutory obligation to promote equality.

4.4.4 Trade unions, collective bargaining, and workplace equality

Clearly managerial interventions are of limited effectiveness in challenging discrimination and disadvantage in employment. In this section the contribution of trade unions and collective bargaining is examined. The emphasis is largely on gender equality, which is where most union activity has been concentrated. Such efforts present major challenges for the unions, which have traditionally been reluctant to accept the belief that workers in the same industry, occupation, or organization might have different interests based on aspects of their social identity, like gender or ethnicity (Kirton and Greene 2015: 183).

Historically, trade union practices and collective bargaining activity have often operated to the detriment of women and black and minority ethnic workers. With regard to gender, for example, unions often colluded with employers to exclude women from skilled, and therefore more highly paid, jobs, helping to reinforce patterns of occupational segregation and a sexual division of labour that privileged the work of men over that of women (Bradley 1989). Union collective bargaining priorities, moreover, reflected dominant male assumptions concerning the inferior value of women's labour (Charles 1986). It is important to recognize, therefore, that historically the trade unions were largely uninterested in promoting gender equality at work. Indeed, their activities helped to support 'those very mechanisms in the organization of work which make patterns of gender segregation so difficult to break down' (Rees 1992: 85). Unions tended to operate in ways that privileged the interests of men, and had an overly masculine culture in which women, and their interests, were marginalized (Cunnison and Stageman 1993).

Since the 1980s, though, the unions have, albeit rather slowly and unevenly, sought to represent the interests of an increasingly diverse workforce more effectively, those of women in particular. They have done so for three related reasons. First, economic change has eroded the traditional heartlands of trade unionism in male-dominated manufacturing industries. Employment growth has been concentrated largely in the service sector, which is characterized by high levels of female employment.

Second, with the decline of male-dominated manual industries, trade unionism is increasingly concentrated in areas such as health and education, disproportionately populated by female employees. During the 2000s, the proportion of women employees who are trade union members overtook that of male employees; in 2015 nearly 27.7 per cent of women were trade unionists compared to just 21.7 per cent of men (BIS 2016b).

Third, influenced by feminism, women themselves have challenged the male-dominated structures and decision-making processes of trade unions (Cunnison and Stageman 1993; Colgan and Ledwith 2002). For these reasons, then, unions have made equality and diversity issues more of a priority (Moore 2011; Kirton and Greene 2015). This extends beyond gender equality; for example, the trade union movement has made greater efforts to challenge discrimination and disadvantage in employment on the grounds of race and ethnicity (Sullivan 2011). Moreover, trade union 'disability champions' play an important part in representing the interests of disabled workers, including by encouraging employers to improve their policy and practice (Bacon and Hoque 2015).

One of the key levers used by unions is to ensure that equality issues are covered in collective bargaining with employers. The concept of equality bargaining refers to initiatives undertaken by trade unions that are designed to reduce the employment disadvantage of particular groups, such as women workers, through interventions directed at employers (Colling and Dickens 1989, 2001). In the past, union bargaining priorities and activities discriminated against women at work by systematically undervaluing the contribution of their labour. Moreover, unions often supported pay structures that disadvantaged women—for example, those that accord high value to length of service.

However, while collective bargaining has done much to sustain workplace inequality, it also has the potential to erode it (Cockburn 1991). Unions may be more capable of securing equality action on the basis of social justice, rather than for narrow, insecure, and partial business reasons (Colling and Dickens 1998). Through trade union action, collective bargaining may give women workers greater influence over their pay and employment conditions. It 'provides a way of giving women a voice; an ability to define their needs and concerns and to set their own priorities for action' (Dickens 2000b: 197).

There is a good deal of evidence that a union presence has a positive influence on the organizational equality agenda, not least by inducing employers to improve their practices (Heery 2006; Hoque and Bacon 2014; Kirton and Greene 2015). Unions have increasingly been active in promoting and articulating equality issues as priorities for collective bargaining, including demands for pay equality between men and women, and greater access to family-friendly working arrangements (Bewley and Fernie 2003). The shop workers' union USDAW, for example, has used legislative changes and drawn on business case arguments in bargaining for improvements in work–life balance provision among major retail firms (O'Brien-Smith and Rigby 2010; Rigby and O'Brien-Smith 2010).

There are also a growing number of trade union equality representatives, whose activities seem to have contributed to the improved treatment of equality and diversity matters in those employing organizations where they are based. Their presence enables unions to represent the interests of a diverse workforce more effectively (Moore 2011; Bacon and Hoque 2012). Equality practices are more evident, and equality outcomes are generally better, in unionized workplaces compared to non-unionized workplaces (Dex and Forth 2009; Dean and Liff 2010; Hoque and Bacon 2014; Kirton and Greene 2015).

However, equality bargaining has become increasingly difficult to sustain. For one thing, the adverse economic climate seems to have created a 'tougher climate' for union negotiators attempting to advance equality issues, with employers becoming more difficult to engage (TUC 2012b: 6). The political context has also become less conducive to equality bargaining. Whereas Labour encouraged initiatives like equality representatives, the 2010–15 coalition government was far less supportive of trade union action to promote equality. Moreover, its policy of austerity, involving reductions in government spending, meant that retrenchment dominated the agenda of major public sector employers, marginalizing equality issues in general, and equality bargaining in particular (Briskin 2014; Milner and Gregory 2014; Oliver, Stuart, and Tomlinson 2014).

One of the areas where trade union equality action has been most prominent is that of equal pay between men and women. Groups of largely female workers, such as speech therapists for example, have benefited from pay rises generated by successful union equal value campaigns (Bradley 1999). Trade unions have sometimes been able to use legislative measures, and the threat of potential equal pay claims on a mass scale, to induce employers to act (Colling and Dickens 1998). Unions such as Unison and the GMB have strongly supported, and helped to coordinate, equal pay claims by female health and local government workers who were, or had been, employed in jobs which attracted lower pay rates and fewer benefits than equivalent workers in largely male-dominated areas.

Yet efforts to harmonize pay and conditions, for example the implementation of 'single status' arrangements in local government, have caused some difficulties for equality bargaining. On the one hand, unions have been successful in winning compensation for female council workers—cleaners, cooks, and care assistants—who had historically been underpaid, as in the case of Birmingham City Council. On the other hand, in some cases unions have been the target of legal action themselves, by women workers encouraged by an aggressive breed of 'no-win, no-fee' lawyers who contend that trade union efforts to resolve equal pay claims through collective agreements with employers have been negligent (Dean and Liff 2010). This is on the basis that a union which negotiates a settlement which, while improving the pay of women workers, does not fully reimburse them for any lost earnings arising out of the operation of discriminatory pay systems in the past, is not effectively representing its members' interests. Yet the activities of no-win, no-fee lawyers undermine union efforts to secure a fair deal for all workers through collective bargaining, and may jeopardize public services and jobs as employers struggle to find the money to fund compensation payments. Unions consider collective bargaining to be a fairer and more sustainable means of promoting gender pay equality in public sector organizations (Oliver, Stuart, and Tomlinson 2014). But the problem is that equal pay litigation has the potential to reduce the appeal of equality bargaining (Conley 2014).

The extent to which unions have been successful in promoting effective equality action is related to the degree of internal pressure for change (Heery 2006). More attention has been given to recruiting, organizing, and facilitating activism amongst groups of workers whose interests have hitherto been under-represented by unions (see Insight into practice 4.7). Unions have also taken steps to alter their representative structures, and the way their decision-making processes operate, to accommodate the interests of a diverse membership and ensure their interests are represented (see Kirton and Greene 2015: 190–3).

 Insight into practice 4.7: Auditing union progress in promoting equality and diversity

In 2014, the Trades Union Congress published an 'equality audit' which examined the actions trade unions have taken to improve the representation of under-represented groups of workers and to facilitate their activism (TUC 2014*b*). The audit highlighted some important union successes:

- The Prospect union had made successful efforts to raise the profile of professional women working in the STEM (science, technology, engineering, and mathematics) field. The campaign was underpinned by a belief in the desirability of inspiring more women to develop successful careers in a traditionally male-dominated area, and improving women's union representation.

- The National Association of Probation Officers (NAPO) had developed a National Black Network for BME members to share their experiences, and as a means of attracting new members and developing more union activists.

- The Public and Commercial Services Union (PCS), which organizes civil servants, operates a self-organized LGBT group—PCS Proud. It undertook a successful, high-profile social media campaign to attract more members.

- As part of its efforts to organize young workers, the Unite trade union has been targeting apprentices for recruitment, including through the use of various social media interventions.

However, union efforts to improve the representation and participation of under-represented groups of workers have faced a number of obstacles, including increasingly less supportive employers, especially in the public sector, and the adverse consequences of austerity-related funding cuts.

In assessing the extent and nature of these changes, it is useful to employ, in modified form, the distinction between liberal and radical approaches discussed in Section 4.3.1. The liberal approach is concerned with reducing the barriers that prevent people from disadvantaged groups participating in unions or benefiting from their services; by seeking to remove discriminatory practices it aims to establish a 'level playing field' (Kirton and Greene 2002). Certain measures, including the appointment of equality or women's officers and ensuring

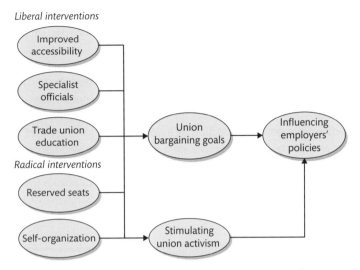

Figure 4.1 Liberal and radical interventions used by trade unions to promote equality

that union meetings are made more accessible by offering childcare facilities, for example, have been taken to help promote equality of access (Colgan and Ledwith 2002).

Most trade unions have generally adopted a liberal approach to the way they promote internal equality, particularly with regard to gender. The main weakness of this approach, however, is its failure to challenge male-dominated union power structures, which often operate in ways that disadvantage women (Kirton 1999; Bradley and Healy 2008). Liberal measures are viewed by some as an ineffective means of securing the effective participation of under-represented groups, such as black and women members, in trade unions, and that more radical interventions may be necessary (Healy and Kirton 2000). The radical approach implies that positive action is required in order to enable union members from disadvantaged social groups to participate in trade unions and thus have their interests represented more effectively (Kirton and Greene 2002; Dean and Liff 2010). See Figure 4.1 for an illustration of how unions use both liberal and radical interventions.

There are two principal measures that come under the 'radical' label. The first concerns the provision of special, or 'reserved', places for representatives from particular social groups, such as women workers, on union decision-making bodies. This has become a more common feature of trade union practice, though it is still limited to a minority of unions, such as the public services union Unison (McBride 2001). However, trade unionists, including many women, often dislike the potential divisiveness generated by having reserved seats (Bradley 1999). Women who take them up are often made to feel inferior; they can be treated as second-class union representatives whose contributions should be limited to issues that specifically concern women members, and thus can be easily marginalized (Kirton and Healy 1999; Colgan and Ledwith 2002). Perhaps the most fundamental criticism of reserved seats, though, is that although their presence advances the representation of individual women in trade unions, they are less effective in promoting the interests of women as a disadvantaged social group. In other words, tinkering with policy-making structures in a way that enables more women to participate as individuals does little to challenge the embedded, and collectively generated, male-dominated norms and assumptions that determine union action (McBride 2000, 2001).

The second 'radical' measure used by some unions to promote internal equality and diversity concerns the establishment of internal structures that enable members from disadvantaged groups to organize and represent themselves through what is known as 'self-organization' (Virdee and Grint 1994). This refers to arrangements that provide a separate space for collective organization and action by union members and activists, on the basis of their shared social characteristics. To secure more effective representation, self-organization offers a means by which members from disadvantaged social groups can work together, separately from established union decision-making structures, to pursue their collective interests. Of all unions, Unison has the most sophisticated set of arrangements: black, disabled, lesbian and gay, and women members all have the opportunity to self-organize (Terry 1996; McBride 2000).

Whereas reserved seats focus on improving representative democracy in unions, self-organization is designed to enhance the participation of members from disadvantaged groups. It enables them to work together, to construct 'a sense of identity, political consciousness, confidence and solidarity and to develop and practice activist skills' (Colgan and Ledwith 2002: 178). Self-organization, therefore, explicitly challenges the notion that workers are a homogeneous group with a single set of common interests that can be articulated and represented by a trade union in an unproblematic manner. It recognizes that, by virtue of belonging to particular social groups, workers may have diverse interests, and that traditional assumptions about participation in trade unions, which assumed a commonality of interest, are therefore inappropriate. One particularly prominent instance of self-organization was promoted by the GMB union, which established a dedicated branch for Polish migrant workers (Fitzgerald and Hardy 2010).

Studies of self-organization in practice show that, while not all that common, it nonetheless gives members and activists a forum that they can use to develop participation, and to bring issues that specifically concern them onto the union agenda (Colgan and Ledwith 2000; Parker 2002). Women-only groups in trade unions help to provide female trade union officers with an effective base of support (Kirton and Healy 2013). Moreover, black members' networks are not only an effective way of stimulating involvement and participation, but also serve to encourage greater discussion of race equality issues in a trade union context (Bradley, Healy, and Mukherjee 2002). Self-organization arrangements may also serve to generate union activism, giving members a sense that they are able to effect changes that benefit their working lives (Colgan 1999; Bradley and Healy 2008).

The positive effects of self-organization may, however, sometimes be limited in practice. For one thing, it relies on the willingness of members to participate in union affairs, something that cannot be assumed. Moreover, apart from in Unison, separate organizing is generally limited to women (Kirton and Greene 2002). Where the links with established policy-making bodies are tenuous, self-organization can also lead to the interests of disadvantaged social groups becoming marginalized. Autonomy, then, may foster exclusion (Colgan and Ledwith 2002), particularly if powerful union interests feel challenged. In Unison, for example, the policy issues discussed in the women's self-organized groups have rarely made it onto the agenda of the powerful mainstream decision-making bodies (McBride 2000, 2001).

Although the relationship between the self-organized groups and established decision-making structures may improve over time (Colgan 1999), self-organization may in fact reinforce rather than ameliorate the under-representation of disadvantaged groups in trade unions. That said, however, there is no doubting that the self-organizing approach has fostered greater trade union involvement among workers who belong to groups that often experience exclusion, like black and minority ethnic women for example. Their enthusiasm for the self-organization approach indicates that despite the problems we have identified, it can be a valuable means of revitalizing union organization and of enabling trade unions to represent diversity more effectively (Bradley and Healy 2008).

 ### Section summary and further reading

- There has been an increase in the extent and coverage of equal opportunities policies among public and private sector organizations. EO policies are characterized by a liberal approach to challenging disadvantage in employment, in which the importance of using formal procedures to ensure equality of treatment is emphasized.

- The managing diversity approach is concerned with how organizations can manage and take advantage of individual differences. In practice there is often some overlap with traditional equal opportunities approaches. Moreover, the MD model does not do much to challenge those aspects of organizational structure and culture that continue to privilege white males.

- Trade unions play an important part in advancing greater equality at work. Through their bargaining and other efforts unions are able to promote a higher incidence of equality practices and better equality outcomes, based on a social justice rationale. They have also taken steps to improve the representation of members from disadvantaged social groups, though such initiatives have largely been of a liberal nature.

For an overview of the issues pertaining to managing equal opportunities and diversity in organizations, see Kirton and Greene (2015: chapter 5) and Dean and Liff (2010). Bradley and Healy's (2008) interviews with black and minority ethnic women trade unionists highlight some negative features of organizational practice. For an in-depth analysis of MD in practice, see Kirton and Greene (2009). For an overview of trade unions and equality, see Kirton and Greene (2015: chapter 7) and Dean and Liff (2010: 433–6).

4.5 Conclusion

Inequality and disadvantage, linked to social divisions, are important features of work and employment relations. Like Chapters 2 and 3, the material in this chapter demonstrates that relationships between employers and employees at work cannot be understood just in the context of the workplace, but are also informed by wider economic, political, and social influences that transcend particular employment situations. For example, although the practice of trade unionism is clearly founded on collective values and the need for unity to combat hostile employers, historically it was also often concerned with excluding groups of workers, such as women for example, in order to advantage a privileged male minority. Nevertheless, unions have come under pressure to operate more inclusively, not least because their traditional constituencies, male-dominated industries based on manual labour, have dwindled in significance. They have taken up the interests of women workers and other socially disadvantaged groups more readily, and have altered their structures to enable them to be more effectively represented.

Union activity in these areas, while not without its difficulties, is an important catalyst for greater equality in work and employment relations. Employer-led efforts, based on a rather narrow and insecure conception of the business advantages of equality action, can be of limited effectiveness. Equal opportunities policies, which emphasize the need to treat everybody the same regardless of their social characteristics, are strong on rhetoric, but often short on action. The managing diversity model, despite its ostensibly more transformative approach, does little to challenge socially generated disadvantage and inequality at work, and in practice is often little different from a more conventional equal opportunities agenda. A trade union presence, though, can exert pressure on employers to deliver a more effective set of equality policies, such as better work–life balance arrangements.

Nevertheless, the 'initiative in addressing equality issues now rests substantially with employers, prompted and shaped to some extent by the law' (Dean and Liff 2010: 436). Equality and diversity action in organizations increasingly occurs within, and is informed by, a legal framework which is the product of growing state intervention in this area of work and employment relations (Dex and Forth 2009). While anti-discrimination and equality laws have been in place since the 1970s, in general they lack effectiveness; the liberal, equal treatment values that underpin the legislation discourage positive action, and employers are rarely obliged to undertake initiatives that promote equality, even if they are found to be operating discriminatory practices. During the 2000s, Labour extended the scope of anti-discrimination legislation and encouraged organizations to adopt family-friendly policies and work–life balance arrangements for their staff, although it was extremely reluctant to compel businesses to improve their practices. Despite its concern with the issue of social mobility, the emphasis placed by the 2010–15 Conservative-Liberal Democrat coalition government on austerity measures and employment deregulation severely compromised equality.

 ## Assignment and discussion questions

1. Why have governments prioritized improvements in social mobility? What, if anything, should be done to improve social mobility?

2. Critically assess the main strengths and weaknesses of the legal framework relating to discrimination and equality at work.

3. To what extent do organizational equal opportunities policies help to combat disadvantage and inequality in work and employment relations?

4. Why might employers be more sympathetic to the managing diversity agenda than to the liberal equal opportunities approach?

5. Critically assess the main ways in which the trade unions have responded to the particular problems of disadvantaged groups in work and employment relations.

 Visit the Online Resource Centre that accompanies this book to develop your understanding of this chapter and keep up to date with the latest developments in this area.
www.oxfordtextbooks.co.uk/orc/williams4e/

Chapter case study: Pregnancy discrimination at work

Under the Equality Act 2010 pregnancy and maternity are 'protected characteristics', which means that employers who subject workers to disadvantage or detriment on these grounds are behaving unlawfully. Yet research shows that discrimination against women who are pregnant, on maternity leave, or have just returned from maternity leave, is widespread. Trade unions and campaigning organizations have pressed for firmer action to be taken to root out the scandalous and unacceptable level of pregnancy discrimination. In 2013 Maternity Action, which convenes the Alliance Against Pregnancy Discrimination in the Workplace, published a report which included examples of agency workers being 'quietly let go' when they became pregnant, workers not being given their jobs back when returning from maternity leave, and bullying and harassment of pregnant workers. Maternity Action's report found that 'pregnancy and maternity discrimination is both widespread and deeply entrenched, with a significant minority of employers holding outdated and wholly inappropriate attitudes. This is bad for women and their families, bad for gender equality, and bad for the economy'. It called on the government to start 'pulling employers into line when they have acted unlawfully'.

In 2013, the UK government and the Equality and Human Rights Commission (EHRC) responded to the growing calls for something to be done to tackle the issue of pregnancy discrimination by launching a large-scale research project. The full findings were published in 2016, based on interviews with 3,254 mothers. Over three-quarters (77 per cent) reported having experienced a negative or potentially discriminatory experience during their pregnancy, while they were on maternity leave, or on their return from maternity leave. Half (50 per cent) claimed that pregnancy had adversely affected their opportunities, status, or security in employment (e.g. not being offered opportunities for promotion). Two-fifths of mothers (41 per cent) reported that there had been a risk to, or impact on, their health and welfare; a fifth (20 per cent) had experienced harassment or negative comments; and over one in ten (11 per cent) felt forced to leave their jobs because of their pregnancy— amounting to 54,000 mothers each year.

What can be done to tackle the scandal of pregnancy discrimination? One of the EHRC's key recommendations arising from the research is that stronger leadership is needed from both government and business to ensure that employers better appreciate the business benefits of attracting and retaining talented female staff, and of treating workers fairly. More could be done to raise awareness of pregnant workers' rights. Most employers who participated in the research (84 per cent) felt it was in their interests to support pregnant workers; and over three-quarters of mothers thought their employer had been supportive. However, pregnancy discrimination often arises because line managers have insufficient knowledge and understanding of workers' rights and entitlements.

What about enforcing the law more effectively? Surely this would help to mitigate unlawful pregnancy discrimination? Maternity Action reckons that few women take action against discriminatory employers, either because they are unaware of their rights, are harassed if they do try and assert their rights, or lack the time, energy, and resources to pursue an employment tribunal (ET) claim. The reluctance of women to assert their rights has been exacerbated by the introduction of ET fees (see Chapter 10). The EHRC has recommended that more needs to be done to reduce the barriers that prevent workers who have experienced pregnancy discrimination from accessing justice, including a review of the system of ET fees. The Conservative government, however, rejected this. It played down the problem of pregnancy discrimination, claiming that it was limited to just a 'small minority' of employers. Moreover, nothing should be done that might 'alienate' employers 'who are doing the right thing'. From this perspective, voluntary business case arguments, based on the desirability of attracting and retaining talented staff, are the most effective means of combating pregnancy discrimination. The problem with this approach, though, is that it gives employers who remain unaware of the business case arguments, or are unconvinced by them, free rein to carry on behaving unlawfully. If you believe that pregnancy discrimination should be prohibited by law, why would you oppose action to enforce it properly?

Sources: Maternity Action website; James (2011); Maternity Action (2013); BIS (2016*a*); EHRC (2016*b*); HM Government/EHRC (2016); House of Commons Women and Equalities Select Committee (2016*b*)

Question

To what extent do you support the UK government's view that unlawful pregnancy discrimination is best tackled through increased efforts to communicate the business benefits of attracting and retaining talented female staff to employers?

Part 3

Key elements of employment relations

5 Managing employment relations

Chapter objectives

The main objectives of this chapter are to:

- examine how the management role in employment relations developed in a context of growing unionization;
- examine how employers have challenged the role and influence of trade unions;
- consider the implications of the statutory procedure for union recognition;
- explore the extent to which the rise of sophisticated human resource management has transformed the management of employment relations; and
- consider the inherent challenges and tensions evident in the management of employment relations.

5.1 Introduction

This chapter is concerned with developments in the management of employment relations. The decline of the unions means that there is now a much greater interest in managerial approaches. Rather than having to react to, and accommodate the demands of, trade unions, managers supposedly have more opportunities to shape and influence employment relations. The chapter starts by tracing the historical development of employment relations management, and the important concern with managing with trade unions that dominated the managerial agenda prior to the 1980s. Section 5.3 focuses on the nature, scope, and dimensions of the managerial challenge to trade unionism that has dominated employment relations since the 1980s, before considering the implications of legislation that compels employers to recognize a union where this is wanted by a majority of the workforce. Union decline has provided employers with an opportunity to innovate when it comes to employment relations. Section 5.4 critically examines the main features of a sophisticated human resource management (HRM) approach to managing employment relations, based on attempts to drive performance improvements through higher levels of organizational commitment and engagement on the part of employees. However, as the material in Section 5.5 shows, there are some inherent major challenges and tensions when it comes to managing work and employment relationships, which impede managerial efforts to promote consistent approaches.

Introductory case study: Financialization and employment relations—the case of Boots

One of the main features of this chapter concerns the important degree to which financial imperatives—notably ever-increasing demands that businesses improve their short-term financial performance—influence the day-to-day management of employment relations in organizations. The case of the pharmacy chain Boots demonstrates some of the issues and problems caused by the process of 'financialization'. Founded in the 1850s, during the twentieth century the company's stores became a staple of British high streets. Boots was well known for its paternalistic approach to managing employment relations—securing employee loyalty in return for long-term job security. In 2007, however, backed by a private equity fund, the Monaco-based businessman Stefano Pessina bought Boots for £11 billion, £9 billion of which was borrowed, and took the company—which became Alliance Boots, with its headquarters in Switzerland, allegedly for tax reasons—off the stock market. The debt used to finance the deal was loaded onto Alliance Boots' balance sheet, obliging the company's management to prioritize extracting short-term value from the business in order to service the debt— which included pronounced efforts to squeeze labour costs. 'Medicine Use Reviews' for the NHS became a lucrative source of income for Boots. Pharmacists reported coming under increasing pressure to hit weekly targets for these Reviews, even if patients did not require them. Stringent performance management arrangements eroded the pharmacists' knowledge and status as professionals. Boots made strenuous efforts to avoid having to recognize an independent trade union, using a tame, employer-friendly internal staff association as a device to subvert unionization. Cost-cutting pressures resulted in job losses and increased work pressures for remaining pharmacists, leading to claims that overwork potentially compromised patient safety. Job losses also resulted in store-based pharmacists being left on their own for long periods of time, so they were unable to rely on the assistance of colleagues to make sure that the right drugs were dispensed in the correct doses, increasing the likelihood of mistakes. The case of Boots—which in 2014 merged with the US drug store company Walgreens—illustrates the issues and challenges that arise for managing employment relations in an environment where financialization means that the agenda is dominated by securing short-term efficiency savings.

Sources: Seymour (2013); Chakrabortty (2016*b*)

5.2 Managing with trade unions

As Chapter 1 showed, a belief in managerial prerogative, or the right to manage, underpins management behaviour in employment relations. Historically, although managements vigorously attempted to exclude trade unions from their workplaces, in practice the strength of union organization in many areas of the economy obliged them to try to sustain their prerogative by accommodating workers' demands. During the twentieth century, employers often recognized unions for collective bargaining so as to mitigate disruption, and foster order and stability (Hyman 1975). This was, however, in large part a reaction to the pressure coming from workers themselves to organize unions (Clegg, Fox, and Thompson 1964). Attempts to exclude unions caused too much disruption, given the collective power that workers were able to wield. Thus employers took a pragmatic approach, recognizing unions, but doing so in a way that disturbed managerial prerogatives as little as possible (Gospel 1992).

During the 1960s and 1970s, in a context of growing union power, companies that had hitherto not recognized a union often found it advantageous to do so in order to quell workplace militancy. For example, management in the biscuit works studied by Scott (1994) were aware of a growing union presence in the factory and chose to accommodate it by means of a centralized negotiating relationship with full-time union officers, from which workplace union activists were distanced. The company embraced collective bargaining with a recognized union, but did so in a way that upheld managerial rights and secured workplace order. Although, for pragmatic reasons, employers may have chosen to recognize unions, this certainly doesn't mean that they accepted their legitimacy, and indeed they made every effort to restrict union influence over employment relations in the workplace. For much of the twentieth century, many employers chose to try to exclude unions from their workplaces by dealing with them through employers' associations. However, the growth of workplace bargaining prompted employers to look for more sophisticated ways of managing employment relations in unionized environments.

5.2.1 Managerial innovation in employment relations: the pluralist agenda

Attempts to bargain with unions by means of employers' associations contributed to the widespread neglect of employment relations management in many firms—or what Hyman (2003) refers to as the 'tradition of unscientific management'. The historical weakness of the personnel management function in Britain has long been acknowledged (e.g. Flanders 1975). Writers point to the history of unsophisticated managerial control systems, the lack of complex managerial hierarchies in firms, and the slow, and indeed relatively late, diffusion of scientific management techniques (Tolliday and Zeitlin 1991; Gospel 1992). Employers exhibited a preference for ad hoc, informal, and unsophisticated ways of managing their workforces, such as a reliance on simple payment by results techniques.

Employers found it increasingly hard to maintain managerial prerogatives in the workplace. During the 1940s and 1950s, there was a marked growth in the incidence of workplace bargaining in Britain, particularly in the engineering sector (Gospel 1992). Not only did this reflect the increasing difficulty employers had in upholding managerial rights in the workplace, but the weakness of agreements reached by means of multi-employer bargaining and a tight labour market created by full employment—which enhanced workers' bargaining power—were also contributory factors (Terry 1983). The reluctance of senior managers to take control over their own employment relations during this period in a resolute and strategic way, and to come to terms with, and accommodate the growth of, workplace unionism, rather than see it as a threat to be nullified, was seen by the pluralists as a major error, contributing to industrial disputes and workplace disorder (Flanders 1964, 1975).

Managers were encouraged to take greater control over employment relations in the workplace by formally recognizing the legitimacy of shop-floor unionism rather than by trying to extinguish it, something that would only cause greater disruption. Such a prescription characterized the findings and recommendations of the 1965–8 Royal Commission on Trade Unions and Employers' Associations, established under the chairmanship of Lord Donovan. It was set up to examine the system of employment relations and to make proposals for its reform, given the detrimental effect aspects of the system were claimed to have on economic performance (in particular 'wage drift'—inflationary increases in earnings caused by workplace bargaining—and associated high levels of labour conflict). Influenced by prominent pluralist writers such as Allan Flanders, Donovan identified managerial weakness as a prime source of

Britain's employment relations problems and strongly recommended that, in order to rectify them, managers should secure greater control over workplace employment relations (Royal Commission 1968).

During the 1960s and 1970s, in a context of growing union militancy, managers adopted a notably more interventionist approach in respect of workplace employment relations anyway, in order to contain and accommodate trade union power and thus exercise greater control. Employers were increasingly the 'main instigators in reshaping the system of industrial relations in Britain' (Gospel 1992: 140). Perhaps the most significant managerial intervention during this period was the rise of 'productivity bargaining', heralded as a major managerial initiative in the reform of employment relations. The theory and practice of productivity bargaining were popularized by Allan Flanders's celebrated study of the negotiation of a path-breaking collective agreement, known as the 'Blue Book', at Esso's Fawley oil refinery near Southampton during the early 1960s (Flanders 1964). The productivity agreement struck at Fawley saw management 'buy out' overtime and other inefficient practices in return for higher basic earnings and a fixed working week. It was envisaged that this approach would encourage order and stability as well as generating productivity improvements (Flanders 1964).

Over and above the features of the agreement itself, the deal struck at Fawley was held to be significant in two important respects. First, it was an example of managerial innovation in employment relations, standing out from the hitherto ad hoc, unsophisticated, and reactive approach to employment relations exhibited in most British firms (Flanders 1964). Second, the agreement appeared to possess a 'higher order function', being the 'very embodiment of pluralist industrial relations' (Ahlstrand 1990: 61, 60). It represented an attempt by management to secure control of the workplace through cooperative means, by explicitly recognizing the legitimacy of the unions as the representatives of the workforce, rather than trying to marginalize or exclude them (Flanders 1964).

The Fawley experiment, then, appeared not only to be beneficial for the employer, in that it led to improved economic performance, but it also seemed to secure, and legitimize, the interests of employees through the establishment of a cooperative relationship with the unions. Ensuing productivity gains were limited, though, and largely the result of staffing cuts rather than the more efficient utilization of labour, and overtime working remained commonplace. Managers, moreover, never eschewed their unitary beliefs; indeed, they used productivity agreements to undermine union power in the workplace, part of a long-term strategy to manage without unions altogether (Ahlstrand 1990).

During the late 1960s and early 1970s, there was a marked increase in the popularity of productivity agreements, though they varied considerably in their scope, detail, and outcomes. Perhaps their most important function, however, was to signal the growth of a more resolute and sophisticated approach to the management of employment relations in British firms (Clegg 1979), contributing to the declining incidence of multi-employer bargaining through employers' associations. Furthermore, workplace trade unionism, particularly the role of shop stewards (see Chapter 6), became increasingly formalized as managers encouraged, or 'sponsored', them in an attempt to accommodate union power (Terry 1983). In the Cadbury's confectionery plant at Bourneville, for example, managers acceded to the operation of a closed shop arrangement (see Historical perspective 5.1) as part of an attempt to contain and accommodate the growing influence of the shop stewards, and to steer it in a 'responsible and realistic' direction (Smith, Child, and Rowlinson 1990: 195).

Historical perspective 5.1: Managing with the closed shop

Union membership agreements, or 'closed shops' as they are more popularly known, were a major feature of British employment relations for many years. Under closed shop arrangements, union membership was a condition of employment. The 'pre-entry' closed shop restricted particular jobs to members of a specific union. The more commonplace 'post-entry' closed shop made union membership mandatory when a worker commenced employment. While union pressure was an important factor stimulating the growth of closed shop arrangements (McCarthy 1964), it was largely due to management acquiescence that they became increasingly widespread in British industry during the 1970s (Dunn and Gennard 1984; Marchington and Parker 1990; Gospel 1992). This was part of the broader concern of managers to accommodate and contain workplace trade unionism, so as to push it in a moderate and cooperative direction.

By 1980, some 5 million workers may have been covered by closed shop arrangements, mostly of the post-entry type (Millward et al. 1992). Margaret Thatcher's Conservative governments, however, made reform of the closed shop a key feature of their legislative assault on the trade unions until, with the enactment of the 1990 Employment Act, the operation of a closed shop was effectively made unlawful altogether. Perhaps a more influential factor contributing to the decline of the closed shop—by 1990 only about half a million workers were still covered by such an arrangement (Millward et al. 1992)—was the decline of employment in those industries, such as printing for example, where it was prominent.

From this overview of how employment relations was managed before the 1980s, it should be clear that while employers accepted trade unionism, this reflected a pragmatic response to circumstances—notably union power—rather than a genuine belief in the virtues of a pluralist approach. If managers had to deal with trade unions, they tried to do so in such a way that it contained workplace militancy. Managers may have been obliged to respond constructively to the implications of growing union power, but their fundamentally unitary values generally remained constant.

 ## Section summary and further reading

- Employers have long played a leading role in employment relations by initiating union recognition, albeit under pressure from workers for union representation. In forming employers' associations and instituting multi-employer bargaining arrangements, employers sought to maintain managerial prerogative in the workplace by externalizing their relationship with trade unions.

- The growth of workplace bargaining and its effects encouraged firms to develop a more sophisticated approach to managing employment relations in the workplace, accommodating trade union power rather than attempting to repulse it.

- The reform of employment relations in the 1960s and 1970s—the conclusion of productivity agreements for example—while predominantly management-led, was encouraged by the need to accommodate growing union power. There was no general shift in managerial philosophy away from unitary values, rather a pragmatic acceptance of pluralist approaches as the most effective means of ensuring stability in employment relations.

Gospel (1992) is the most authoritative study of the historical development of the management of employment relations. Allan Flanders's classic 1964 account of the Fawley experiment, *The Fawley Productivity Agreements* (Flanders 1964), is seminal. It should be read in conjunction with Ahlstrand (1990).

5.3 Challenging unions

Since the 1980s, the changes in the economic and political environment discussed in Chapters 2 and 3 have made it easier for employers to challenge the influence of trade unions, compounding the fundamentally unitary preferences of managers and the frequently held view that a union presence is undesirable because it would restrict managerial prerogative, raise labour costs, and hinder organizational flexibility (Poole and Mansfield 1993; Cullinane and Dundon 2014). Managers no longer find it necessary to reach pragmatic accommodations with the unions in order to contain their power. Even where they had hitherto encouraged a union presence, such as in the Cadbury's Bourneville plant, managers attempted to undermine, and even extinguish, a formal union presence (Smith, Child, and Rowlinson 1990). In this part of the chapter the concern is with the ways in which employers have sought to challenge trade unionism, and with the implications of the statutory union recognition procedure introduced in 2000.

5.3.1 Union exclusion

Perhaps the most obvious measure of union exclusion in Britain was the substantial fall in the incidence of union recognition which occurred during the 1980s and 1990s, particularly in the private sector (Blanchflower and Bryson 2009; Simms and Charlwood 2010)—see Table 5.1. Although the level of union recognition held up rather well in the public sector, by 1998 unions were recognized in only around a quarter of private sector workplaces.

The main reason for the decline in the level of union recognition was that private sector employers increasingly turned 'their back on trade unions' (Blanchflower and Bryson 2009: 56). For most of the twentieth century, an employer's decision to recognize a union, or not to recognize one, was a voluntary matter—influenced, of course, by the organizing efforts of workers and unions. In general, employers were never legally obliged to deal with a union—in theory, they could withdraw recognition from, or 'derecognize', trade unions as they saw fit. This was certainly one reason for the decline in the level of union recognition which commenced during the 1980s.

During the 1990s, the trend of union derecognition accelerated, and was even extended to the Fawley oil refinery, which thirty years previously had been celebrated as the epitome of pluralist employment relations (Smith and Morton 1994; Claydon 1996). Yet complete derecognition has been relatively rare; where it does happen it is largely an opportunistic

Table 5.1 Percentage of workplaces with a recognized union, 1980–98

	All workplaces	Private manufacturing	Private services	Public sector
1980	64	65	41	94
1984	66	56	44	99
1990	53	44	36	87
1998	41	29	23	87

Workplaces with twenty-five or more employees
Sources: Millward, Bryson, and Forth (2000: 96); Kersley et al. (2006: 120)

response by managers to declining union membership and organization. In 2012, for example, Virgin Media cited the purported lack of support for trade union representation among its employees to justify derecognition, on rather dubious grounds, prompting union claims that the company was 'stealing' union recognition. By itself, union derecognition does not account sufficiently for the overall decline in union recognition in Britain during the 1980s and 1990s. Of rather more importance was the reduced likelihood that employers in new workplaces would recognize unions in the first place (Machin 2000; Blanchflower and Bryson 2009).

While not as prominent as the headline fall in union recognition, even where unions do retain a formal workplace presence employers have become keener to challenge their role. In some circumstances this involves nakedly aggressive attempts to suppress trade unions, by victimizing union representatives for example (Gall 2010c). Employers have also tried to restrict the influence of unions over the regulation of employment relationships by reducing the scope of union recognition, limiting the number of matters it covers (Blanchflower and Bryson 2009).

New methods of direct communications between management and employees, such as team briefings for example, which are designed to encourage greater organizational loyalty and commitment and to foster among the workforce a sense of identification with their employer, have also been used to exclude trade unions and reduce their influence (see Section 5.4.2). Moreover, as Chapter 6 shows, so-called 'partnership agreements' between employers and unions exemplify the way in which employers may uphold union recognition for pragmatic reasons, but seek to shape the relationship in a manner that better suits their interests.

5.3.2 Statutory union recognition in Britain

Except for the 1970s, when statutory procedures existed for a time (see Beaumont 1981), until 2000 employers were never under a legal obligation to recognize a union. The third statutory recognition procedure was enacted by the 1999 Employment Relations Act, and came into effect in June 2000. It was the outcome of the 1997 Labour government's commitment to introducing a measure that would oblige employers to recognize a union where the majority of the workforce wanted it (DTI 1998). The Trades Union Congress (TUC) anticipated that the new statutory recognition procedure could produce as many as a million new trade union members. For further details of how the procedure operates see Figure 5.1 and Legislation and policy 5.2.

LEGISLATION AND POLICY 5.2: The statutory union recognition procedure in Britain

Under the procedure, if a union has a recognition claim for a particular group of workers dismissed by the employer it can make an application to a state body, the Central Arbitration Committee (CAC), which decides if the claim is a valid one for the purposes of the statutory procedure. It does not apply in workplaces where fewer than twenty-one workers are employed. CAC must also determine whether there is sufficient support for unionization among the workforce: at least 10 per cent must be union members, with the likelihood that a majority of the workforce would vote in favour of union recognition in a ballot. If these tests are met, and no other union is recognized for the group of workers in question, then CAC can mandate union recognition if 50 per cent or more of the relevant workers

(continued...)

are members of the union, or it can order a ballot of the workforce. To secure recognition, a union must win approval from a simple majority of those voting, as long as this constitutes a threshold of 40 per cent of the relevant workforce. For example, in a workforce of 100 people, if thirty-nine people vote in favour of union recognition, even though none vote against, then recognition would not be awarded because the 40 per cent threshold would not have been met. See Figure 5.1 for a diagrammatic representation. A code of practice (DTI 2005) governs matters like union access to the workforce in the run-up to a recognition ballot. The Employment Relations Act (2004) made some changes to how the statutory union recognition procedure operates. In particular, employers and unions are prohibited from engaging in 'unfair practices', namely the use of incentives, threats, or any other kind of 'undue influence' to sway workers' votes.

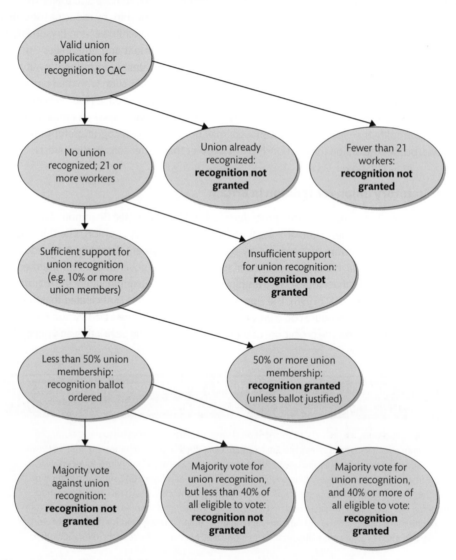

Figure 5.1   A simplified model of the statutory union recognition procedure

The introduction of the new statutory recognition procedure would, at first glance, appear to be a distinctly union-friendly act; the principle underlying the policy is that union recognition should be granted where the majority of the workforce votes in favour of it. However, the procedure was enacted in a way that was in fact largely favourable to employers (Wood and Goddard 1999; Gall 2012a; Moore, McKay, and Veale 2013). For example, it does not apply where there are fewer than twenty-one employees. Even if an employer is obliged to recognize a union by means of the statutory route, the scope of bargaining is limited to pay, hours, and holidays. Moreover, there are no guaranteed outcomes since the right to recognition is limited to simply the 'right to invoke a procedure' (Brown et al. 2001: 183; Gall 2012a). Some have criticized the limited scope of the statutory recognition procedure, particularly its rather narrow conception of what constitutes legitimate union representation, based on demonstrating majority support in a workplace ballot (e.g. Bogg 2012; Moore, McKay, and Veale 2013).

As mentioned in Legislation and policy 5.2, the principle of majority support for union recognition is qualified by the need for a union to win the support of at least 40 per cent of the relevant workforce, including non-voters. The government's aim was that the existence of the statutory procedure would encourage employers and unions to reach their own voluntary recognition agreements (Oxenbridge et al. 2003; Gall 2010b; Brodtkorb 2012). The statutory procedure should prevail only if they were unable to reach a deal themselves. Gall (2012a: 412) characterizes this approach as 'legally induced voluntarism' in the sense that the 'explicit intention of its creators was to use the law to thereby allow unions to *try* to effect change in behaviour of employers in the voluntary arena'.

What, then, have been the effects of the statutory union recognition procedure since it came into existence in 2000? The first thing to appreciate is that the upsurge of new union recognition agreements dates from the mid-1990s, before the statutory procedure took effect (Gall 2012a). Knowing that legislation could soon compel them to recognize a union, some employers struck voluntary deals with trade unions beforehand. The number of new recognition agreements peaked during the early 2000s, soon after the statutory procedure came into effect, before subsequently declining. By April 2016, it had directly resulted in 281 new agreements, 137 of them without a ballot, from a total of 955 applications by unions (CAC 2016). Among the companies obliged to recognize trade unions as a direct result of the procedure are: Kwik Fit, the car repairer; Honda, the car manufacturer; and Fyffes, a company which imports and distributes fresh produce, especially bananas.

Yet during the period 2000–10 alone, there were nearly 3,000 new recognition agreements reported overall, covering more than three-quarters of a million workers (Gall 2012a). The overwhelming majority of new recognition deals, then, have been of a voluntary kind. Clearly, a major effect of the statutory procedure has been to stimulate voluntary union recognition by employers (Wood, Moore, and Ewing 2003; Moore, McKay, and Veale 2013), as its designers intended. The preference for voluntary agreements demonstrates that in some cases unions have been successful in putting pressure on employers to concede recognition without needing to invoke the statutory procedure, though its existence is clearly an influence. As the 2000s went on, the number of new recognition agreements in general, and the number of applications submitted to CAC in particular, dwindled (Gall 2012a; Moore, McKay, and Veale 2013). However, although just twenty-eight union applications for recognition were submitted to CAC in 2010–11, since 2014 the number has picked up again (CAC 2016).

Table 5.2 Percentage of workplaces with a recognized union, 2004–11

	All workplaces	Private manufacturing	Private services	Public sector
2004	22	13	13	90
2011	22	9	12	92

Workplaces with five or more employees
Source: van Wanrooy et al. (2013*b*: 59)

Perhaps the main reason for the declining number of new recognition agreements is that, following the introduction of the statutory procedure, unions focused on firms which they knew would be relatively easy targets for recognition claims—those with strong union support among the workforce. As the years went on, though, these firms were picked off, meaning that the unions increasingly had to operate on 'harder terrain' (Gall 2007). They have found it difficult to make contact with workers in non-union workplaces in the private services sector, where employers are often hostile to unionization (Gall 2010*b*). In addition, the economic recession seemed to contribute to the diminishing trend of new recognition agreements; cost pressures made employers more reluctant to contemplate recognizing a union (Brodtkorb 2012).

Recognition successes for unions have largely come about in sectors of the economy where they are already strong, particularly in manufacturing (Blanden, Machin, and Van Reenan 2006). There is little sign that unions have been able to expand their influence by securing recognition agreements in key parts of the 'new economy', like the telecommunications and retail sectors (Gall 2007). That said, though, during the 2000s the overall level of union recognition seemed to stabilize as the decline which had been evident in the 1980s and 1990s bottomed out. Table 5.2 shows that unions are recognized in around a fifth (22 per cent) of all workplaces with five or more employees. Union recognition has held up relatively well in larger workplaces, perhaps reflecting union organizing efforts—see Chapter 6. Nearly half of all employees (47 per cent) are in workplaces where there is a recognized union (van Wanrooy et al. 2013*b*).

5.3.3 Employers' responses to union recognition claims

The large extent to which some employers will go to resist unionization has impeded attempts by unions to secure new recognition agreements (Heery and Simms 2011). Employer opposition to union recognition seems to have contributed to the declining number of new recognition agreements evident during the 2000s (Gall 2007, 2012*a*). Companies like the road haulage firm Eddie Stobart have actively tried to avoid having to recognize a trade union. While it is difficult to detect a common, dominant pattern (Heery and Simms 2010), there are three broad ways in which employers try to resist union recognition. First, some have followed an aggressive strategy of 'union suppression', involving the use of anti-union consultants, the victimization of union activists, and other intimidatory tactics designed to forestall a union presence (e.g. Heery and Simms 2010; Moore 2011). In 2007 Kettle Chips, which makes upmarket snacks and crisps at its factory in Norwich, hired a prominent US union-busting firm to dissuade workers from supporting union recognition.

There are cases where employers have attempted to influence the outcome of a recognition ballot by threatening that unionization could damage the interests of the business, perhaps by putting future investment plans in jeopardy, and thus pose a risk to jobs (Moore, McKay, and Veale 2013: 121). Although it is unlawful to dismiss workers for activities relating to union recognition, some employers have tried to resist unionization by firing union activists, illustrating their preparedness to 'invest whatever is necessary to defeat unions' (Moore 2004: 16). Employers in the United States often pursue a blatantly aggressive anti-union policy in order to protect managerial prerogative (see International perspective 5.3).

 International perspective 5.3: Anti-unionism in the United States

Visceral hostility towards trade unionism and collective bargaining has been a long-standing feature of employment relations in the United States. Attempts by unions to gain recognition for collective bargaining purposes have generally been met by robust employer opposition, something that seems to have increased since the 1970s (Moody 2013). Companies wanting to remain union-free frequently employ specialist anti-union consultants to advise on ways of resisting unionization efforts (Logan 2006). In his book on work and employment relations in the US, *The Big Squeeze*, Steven Greenhouse recounts similar stories of workers across a range of firms being fired, in violation of federal law, for supporting unionization efforts. For example, following years of struggle to resist union recognition, numerous legal challenges, and the use of specialist anti-union consultants, the EnerSys company eventually frustrated the stated wish of the majority of the workforce in its South Carolina battery factory for union recognition by closing it down (Greenhouse 2008).

Second, more commonly employers make use of a 'substitutionist' approach to forestall unionization: providing employees with alternative, in-house methods of representation such as a company council, or using rewards, like pay rises, to demonstrate that union recognition is unnecessary (Gall and McKay 2001). One of the problems with the statutory union recognition procedure is that a trade union is prevented from making an application for recognition where the employer already recognizes another union, even if that union is not independent of management, as in the case of Boots—see the introductory case study (Moore, McKay, and Veale 2013). Moreover, companies like The Body Shop and Pizza Express have developed employee involvement and communications arrangements in an attempt to demonstrate to their staff that they do not need union representation. While this may be a more sophisticated way of resisting recognition than the union suppression approach, it should not in any way be portrayed as the 'benign face of anti-unionism'; rather, substitution is 'simply one tactic among others that employers use to remain union free' (Heery and Simms 2010: 10). As part of their efforts to avoid union recognition, managers at the Royal Albert Hall have proposed introducing a new 'staff forum'—see Contesting employment relations 5.4.

 Contesting employment relations 5.4: Resisting union recognition at the Royal Albert Hall

The Royal Albert Hall (RAH) is one of London's most prestigious concert and entertainment venues. In December 2014, representatives of the broadcasting and entertainment union BECTU approached the RAH management inviting it to engage in discussions with BECTU about securing a voluntary recognition agreement. This would enable the union to represent staff and negotiate over matters relating to pay, hours, and holidays. RAH management, however, turned down the request, on the basis that it detected no demand for union recognition from its employees. Responding to a BECTU campaign for recognition, RAH management conceded that it would grant the union recognition if it could demonstrate that this was supported by a majority of the workforce. In an independently supervised ballot of the workforce, which was conducted in the summer of 2015, 117 employees voted in favour of union recognition, and 109 against, on a turnout of 72 per cent. BECTU assumed that RAH management would, in line with its previously stated position, accede to union recognition because of the majority vote in favour. However, the RAH chief executive claimed that because only 38 per cent of all staff (including those who did not vote) voted in favour, the organization would continue its policy of not recognizing BECTU. To do otherwise, he asserted, would amount to 'imposing' union recognition on all staff, when most did not appear to want it. Instead, the RAH proposed to introduce a new 'staff forum', the purpose of which would be to motivate and engage staff, and keep them better informed. BECTU's general secretary, Gerry Morrissey, lambasted the decision by RAH management to 'change the rules' in the aftermath of the ballot outcome, which could only be explained by the fact that 'they didn't get the result they wanted'.

Sources: BECTU (2015*a*, 2015*b*); Birkwood (2015); Hemley (2015)

The third way in which employers try to resist unionization is by refusing to engage meaningfully with the union even after recognition has been granted. This was the case in a marketing company's call centre. In the two years following the recognition agreement, the employer refused to bargain seriously with the trade union. As a result the workforce began to question the effectiveness of union representation, and support for it dwindled (Kelly and Badigannavar 2004).

Any overall assessment of the effectiveness of the statutory recognition procedure and its contribution to extending unionization must acknowledge the large amount of employer resistance it has generated. Given such opposition to trade unionism, and the way the relevant legislation was designed not to antagonize employers (Moore, McKay, and Veale 2013), the direct impact of the statutory union recognition procedure on its own has been relatively limited. Nevertheless, indirectly it stimulated a substantial upsurge in voluntary recognition activity during the 2000s (Gall 2012*a*). As a result, some consider the procedure to have been a modest success, a 'work in progress' which can be built on to encourage a stronger union presence in the economy (Brodtkorb 2012: 86).

Others, though, offer a more pessimistic prognosis, seeing the declining number of new recognition agreements in general, and CAC applications in particular, as evidence of the much diminished relevance of the statutory recognition procedure. As one commentator puts it, the 'statutory recognition procedure is dying—not with a bang, but with a whimper' (Bogg 2012: 410) as the number of new agreements falls away, with little prospect of any reversal (Gall 2012*a*). A major challenge for the unions, and one that militates against any easy turnaround in their fortunes, concerns the growing proportion of non-union workplaces in the economy, linked to changes in the composition of employment. Although the decline in the level of trade union recognition seems to have ceased, unions are recognized in little more than one in ten private sector workplaces (van Wanrooy et al. 2013*a*). By itself, the statutory recognition procedure holds out little prospect of reversing the process of union exclusion, given the opposition of employers and the weaknesses evident in the procedure itself (Gall 2012*a*; Moore, McKay, and Veale 2013).

 Section summary and further reading

- The process of union exclusion is best illustrated by the decline in the level of union recognition by employers. Although some employers have derecognized trade unions, the fall in the prevalence of union recognition mainly reflects the growth of non-union workplaces, with newly established sites operating in growing sectors of the economy being unlikely to recognize unions in the first place.

- A statutory union recognition procedure was introduced in 2000. An employer is obliged to recognize a union for collective bargaining purposes if the majority of the workforce wants it. The procedure, however, was implemented so as not to antagonize employers, and its direct impact has therefore been limited.

- There was a marked increase in union recognition activity during the early 2000s, most of it on a voluntary basis, as anticipated by the designers of the statutory procedure. As the decade progressed, however, there was a notable fall in the number of new recognition agreements, with employer resistance being a major impediment. Moreover, the growing proportion of new non-union workplaces means that the overall level of union recognition in the private sector has continued to decline.

For data on union recognition trends up to the 2000s, see Blanchflower and Bryson (2009). The most detailed and in-depth analysis of the statutory union recognition procedure and its effects is provided by Moore, McKay, and Veale (2013). The CAC website contains more details of its work.

5.4 Sophisticated human resource management and employment relations

Given the diminished extent of union recognition, to what extent have managements been able to develop new, more sophisticated techniques for managing employment relations? The terms 'personnel management' and 'personnel manager' have come to be replaced by 'human resource management' (HRM) and 'human resource manager' in organizational vocabularies. There is an assumption that the rise of a sophisticated HRM approach is associated with a change in the focus of managing employment relations: away from a concern with securing employee compliance with organizational rules and accommodating the potential for conflict in the employment relationship, towards a much greater emphasis on promoting employees' engagement, cooperation, and commitment to the organization. This section considers the nature of sophisticated HRM as a managerial approach, accounts for its growing importance, and critically assesses whether or not it has transformed the management of employment relations.

5.4.1 Sophisticated HRM and the management of employment relations

An initial obstacle to be overcome when discussing the concept of HRM is that it tends to be used in different ways. On the one hand, 'HRM' is sometimes used as an umbrella label for managing people in organizations, being interchangeable with the term 'personnel management'.

On the other hand, a second way of interpreting HRM is to view it as a particular approach to managing the workforce, based on a unitary concern with engaging and involving employees, winning their commitment to the organization, and thus driving improvements in business performance. The term 'sophisticated HRM' is used here to refer to this second, narrower conceptualization, distinguishing it from the broader approach. Whereas in the past the job of managing employment relations was dominated by the issues that arose from having to deal with unions, the focus now is said to be on developing and sustaining a climate in which individual employees feel valued and engaged, in a way that promotes trust and enhances organizational performance (Emmott 2005, 2015).

There are a number of features of sophisticated HRM that supposedly make it distinctive. It puts a greater emphasis on the fit between employment policies and the overall business objectives of the organization. Linked to this, there is a concern with managing people in a way that helps to enhance business performance, through interventions designed to involve employees and enable them to express voice over, and thus influence, organizational and workplace decisions (Wood 2013). In contrast to a traditional personnel management approach, which relies on bureaucratic methods such as the provision of regular pay increments to maintain control in the workplace, under a sophisticated HRM regime there is a greater emphasis on techniques for managing organizational culture (Bolton 2004; Legge 2005). This is done through the manipulation of symbols, values, and beliefs in the workplace, sometimes including efforts to encourage employees to identify with their employer's brand, and behave accordingly (Cushen and Thompson 2012).

Perhaps most importantly, a sophisticated HRM approach to managing employment relations is associated with a preference for weak or non-existent trade unions. It is marked by a unitary ethos, threatening unions by seeking to bind individual employees to the organization and reducing the potential for conflict of interest. The onus is on the cooperative and harmonious nature of relations between managers and workers. Any conflict is either frictional, caused by short-term, easily resolved problems, like personality differences for example, or the product of external agitators, such as trade union activists. Sophisticated HRM, then, is not presented as an anti-union approach to managing employment relations, in the sense of seeking to drive unions out or actively resisting them. Rather, it can be conceived of as a 'substitute' for trade union organization (McLoughlin and Gourlay 1994).

The management style of DeliveryCo, the multinational courier company studied by Dundon and Rollinson (2004), would seem to embody such an approach. Characterized by an emphasis on developing a strong organizational culture, it was supported by the use of a range of sophisticated HRM interventions, including an extensive system of direct communication methods. The company's approach to managing its staff was perceived to be a crucial component of its business strategy, by helping to enhance customer service for example. DeliveryCo did not recognize a trade union. But the company claimed that this was not because it was against unions; rather its 'pro-individual' stance, which meant that employees were treated well, made a union presence irrelevant. This seems to have been acknowledged by some of its staff. According to one of DeliveryCo's call centre agents: 'I don't think we need a union, you can always go to somebody. If you are not happy with your manager's decision then you can go to the big boss, and they don't mind you doing that' (Dundon and Rollinson 2004: 145). The result is a more engaged workforce, whose high morale and organizational commitment drives improvements in business performance.

In practice, however, the rhetoric of sophisticated HRM is often used to mask a more coercive reality, marked by the treatment of employees as costs which have to be minimized (Gratton et al. 1999; Legge 2005). Sophisticated HRM practices sit easily alongside, and may even help to uphold, more traditional management approaches based on securing employee compliance (Bacon 1999). The promotion of workplace fun in some call centres, for example, is in part designed to obviate efforts by workers to contest aspects of their otherwise mundane and intensive jobs (Baldry et al. 2007). Claims that the sophisticated HRM approach makes unions redundant, and that it is not anti-union, generally fail to stand up to scrutiny. It has a political agenda, marked by the desirability of weakening the power of the unions and enhancing managerial prerogatives in the workplace. Its unitary ethos reflects the dominant political climate, one in which the trade unions, given the decline in their power and the hostile public policy environment, have largely been on the retreat (Legge 2005). Employers' claims to be 'non-union' rather than 'anti-union' should be treated with caution. Sophisticated HRM often operates as a benign façade obscuring the more authoritarian reality (Bacon 1999). The reluctance of employees to embrace trade unionism in such circumstances is often not a reflection of progressive management policies, but more the result of either an inability to see what value union membership could offer them or, in some cases, an aversion to trade unions (McLoughlin and Gourlay 1994; Dundon and Rollinson 2004).

 Insight into practice **5.5:**   Managing employment relations in Ryanair

The successful airline Ryanair takes an approach to managing employment relations that is consistent with, and indeed exemplifies, the low-cost model on which it has based its business growth. It demonstrates not only that the sophisticated HRM approach is by no means universal, but also that there are alternative methods of managing human resources which may be as effective, if not more so, in business terms. Cabin crew staff are employed on short-term contracts through agencies, not the airline itself, with pay and other benefits, such as holiday entitlement, that are low by industry standards. Workers enjoy few opportunities to be involved in, or to influence, decision-making processes. Rather, the degree of involvement is minimal. The airline takes a 'low-road' approach to managing employment relations based on its low-cost, efficiency-driven business model (O'Sullivan and Gunnigle 2009). Ryanair has become well known for its prominent anti-trade union stance. Where its workers have asked for union representation, the company has vigorously opposed it. In 2015 Ryanair closed its base in Denmark because of its aversion to negotiating with unions there over staff pay and conditions (Crouch 2015b).

The supposed rise of a sophisticated HRM approach should not divert attention from the way in which organizations commonly make use of more coercive, efficiency-driven approaches to managing employment relations, often involving tighter control over performance standards—see Insight into practice 5.5 for the example of Ryanair. Employers try to derive performance improvements, not from developing a more committed and engaged workforce, but through efforts to exert tighter control over the activities of their workers. The growing use of arrangements to monitor and manage employee performance (Sisson and Purcell 2010) testifies to the 'harder', more coercive basis of HRM in practice (Taylor 2013).

Between 2004 and 2011, the proportion of workplaces with formal arrangements in place for managing the performance of some non-managerial staff rose from 43 per cent to 70 per cent (van Wanrooy et al. 2013*b*).

Studies undertaken in a range of sectors and organizations, including the Civil Service, supermarket suppliers, financial services, telecommunications, and further education colleges, point to the development of more stringent arrangements for controlling, monitoring, and evaluating the performance of workers (Carter et al. 2011; Newsome, Thompson, and Commander 2013; Taylor 2013; Mather and Seifert 2014). In colleges, for example, employers rely on a combination of methods, including target setting, electronic registers, audits and inspections, and classroom observations, to monitor and control staff, with the aim of driving improvements in performance standards (Mather and Seifert 2014).

For Taylor (2013), performance management arrangements in organizations constitute a 'new workplace tyranny', to the extent that they enable managers to exercise stricter control over, and monitor, the activities of workers in a highly coercive manner. As the experience of supermarket supply chains shows, this has arisen because of pressures to remain competitive in challenging market conditions (Newsome, Thompson, and Commander 2013). The economic recession and its aftermath seem to have played a part in further marginalizing commitment-based HRM (Taylor 2013). Roche and Teague's (2012) extensive study of Irish firms, for example, shows that while efforts had been made to motivate and secure increased organizational commitment from staff, the priority attached to 'getting the business back in shape' meant a move to a much more robust approach with regard to matters of employee discipline and performance. More generally, pressures arising from greater 'financialization' (see Section 5.5.1), in large part the result of a greater emphasis on enhancing short-term shareholder value, have also prompted organizations to take a more stringent approach to managing employee performance as a means of gaining efficiencies (Thompson 2013).

Based on such evidence, then, it would be unwise to claim that the development of sophisticated HRM has transformed employment relations for the better. As shown in Section 5.5, competitive pressures and the need to enhance short-term financial performance preclude many organizations from investing in the kind of sophisticated, progressive management techniques necessary to foster greater organizational involvement and commitment. This is not to say that there has been no change in the way employment relations is managed, however. Perhaps the most notable development concerns the greater degree of control enjoyed by managers over elements of the employment relationship as a result of the decline of the trade unions and joint regulation (Brown and Marsden 2011); approaches to managing employment relations are often still dominated by the desirability of preserving managerial prerogative (Cullinane and Dundon 2014), not least through the kind of coercive measures associated with the development of more stringent performance management techniques and the greater discipline they impose on staff.

5.4.2 Managing employee voice

The question of employee voice is central to debates around sophisticated HRM and the desirability of managing employment relations in a way that stimulates greater organizational commitment and engagement from employees (Marchington 2008; Budd, Gollan, and Wilkinson 2010). Voice mechanisms are designed to provide employees with a say over workplace and organizational decisions (Wilkinson and Fay 2011; Wilkinson, Dundon, and Marchington 2013; Wilkinson et al. 2014a). Voice has traditionally been associated with trade union representation; it was expressed through the medium of collective bargaining, based on a pluralist understanding that employees and employers have different interests which need to be reconciled. Much of the growing interest in managing employee voice, however, reflects the more dominant unitary paradigm, under which it operates as a central feature of efforts by employers to effect high-commitment management and raise levels of employee engagement (Wilkinson and Dundon 2010; Barry and Wilkinson 2016). In this context, then, voice can be seen to involve the 'transmission of ideas to managers in order to improve organizational performance' (Dundon et al. 2005: 312), in the absence of, or as a substitute for, trade unions.

There are three main types of arrangement for articulating employee voice present in organizations, two of which—direct communications and direct participation—are considered here; the third—indirect voice mechanisms, using some kind of representative structure, such as a staff consultation forum—features in the section on non-union systems of employee representation in Chapter 6. Taking direct communication arrangements to start with, it is very evident that since the 1980s there has been a substantial increase in the use of techniques for communicating information between managers and staff (Kersley et al. 2006; McGovern et al. 2007; Willman, Gomez, and Bryson 2009; van Wanrooy et al. 2013b). The 'cascading' of information downwards through the management hierarchy has become a commonplace feature of workplace life. Moreover, regular workforce meetings, newsletters, and team briefings have become increasingly popular methods for communicating information to employees. Formal workforce meetings of some kind are present in 90 per cent of workplaces (van Wanrooy et al. 2013b: 64–5).

What about arrangements that enable staff to communicate their views 'upwards' to managers? Such upward forms of communication encompass surveys of staff attitudes, the use of electronic mail to convey views and information to managers, and suggestion schemes, which enable employees to propose ways of improving organizational practice. While such practices seem to be linked to a more positive workplace climate, increasing employees' job satisfaction and trust in management (Willman, Gomez, and Bryson 2009), there is not much evidence that it improves their organizational commitment or work performance (Marchington 2001). In the past, opportunities for employees to communicate their ideas, concerns, and suggestions upwards to managers were rather limited (Scott 1994; Gratton et al. 1999); the flow of information was generally one-way, from managers to workers, with the latter accorded few opportunities to express their voice.

There are some indications that employers have invested in methods that enable workers to express their views to management; staff surveys are regularly conducted in 38 per cent of workplaces, for example. A similar proportion of workplaces (40 per cent) operate two-way team briefing arrangements, where at least a quarter of the time is set aside for the input of employees (van Wanrooy et al. 2013b). Yet there remains a managerial preference for restricting voice to providing information to staff, rather than receiving, and actively responding to, their views. There is an emphasis on conveying information to employees, with the aim of influencing their behaviour, rather than allowing employees opportunities to exercise genuine voice (Danford et al. 2005). While more workplaces seem to be making use of workforce meetings of one kind or another, there is no evidence that more time is being

Table 5.3 Percentage of all workplaces with direct communication arrangements between managers and employees, 2004 and 2011

	2004	2011
Meetings between senior managers and all employees, with at least 25 per cent time for questions	46	46
Team briefings, with at least 25 per cent time for questions	37	40
Any face-to-face meetings, with at least 25 per cent time for questions	57	58
Regular use of email to all employees	35	49
Suggestion scheme	25	25
Employee survey in last two years	35	38
Problem-solving groups	18	14

Workplaces with five or more employees
Source: van Wanrooy et al. (2013*b*)

devoted to allowing workers to express their views (van Wanrooy et al. 2013*b*). See Table 5.3 for details of changes in the prevalence of direct communication arrangements between 2004 and 2011.

The second type of voice arrangement considered here concerns mechanisms that enable employees to participate directly in matters relating to the organization of their work and job tasks—in problem-solving or work improvement groups for example, or through teamworking arrangements (Proctor and Benders 2014). It is often thought that giving employees greater influence and voice over the organization of their work and changes in work processes is essential if companies are to secure the levels of commitment necessary for the production of high-quality goods and services, and thus thrive in increasingly competitive global markets (Boxall and Purcell 2011). Work improvement groups and teamworking arrangements, for example, have been depicted as forms of 'intelligent' workplace flexibility, to the extent that they enable workers to contribute to, and even exercise a degree of control over, aspects of production or service delivery (White et al. 2004: 46).

On the positive side, it is evident that during the 1990s there was a substantial increase in the prevalence of 'intelligent flexibility', evidenced by the growing incidence of problem-solving groups and teamworking arrangements for example (White et al. 2004). On a more pessimistic note, though, this growth appears to have stalled during the 2000s; for example, the prevalence of problem-solving groups appears to have diminished (van Wanrooy et al. 2013*b*). The use of 'intelligent flexibility' is still only evident in a minority of workplaces, contributing to a widespread perception among workers that they should have more influence over issues that affect them at work (McGovern et al. 2007). Moreover, managers can use forms of 'intelligent flexibility', such as teamworking initiatives, to enhance their control over employees, by undermining their influence and increasing effort levels (Danford 1998).

5.4.3 **Managing employee engagement**

Employee voice is often thought to be a key dimension of efforts to promote greater employee engagement, a topic which has attracted growing interest, especially since the publication of the government-backed MacLeod Report in 2009 (MacLeod and Clarke 2009). The question of how employers can secure a more engaged workforce—and thus derive the benefits which supposedly arise from it, including claims about improvements in business performance—has become an increasingly prominent feature in debates about managing employment relations (Truss et al. 2014). Even the fast-food chain McDonalds, often considered to be a company which is characterized by low levels of pay and employee discretion, has emphasized its commitment to improving the engagement of its workforce, not least because this is presumed to result in better customer service (Fairhurst 2008).

What, then, is meant by 'employee engagement'? There are a large number of psychological studies devoted to the concept of 'work engagement', relating to people's cognitive, emotional, and physical attachment to work (Bailey et al. 2015). With 'employee engagement' there is often a more managerial focus evident, manifest in a concern with employee behaviours. Engagement can thus be defined as: 'being positively present during the performance of work by willingly contributing intellectual effort, experiencing positive emotions and meaningful connections to others' (CIPD 2010: 5). Workers can be engaged: intellectually, by thinking hard about their jobs and how they can be done better; affectively, by feeling positive about doing a good job; and socially, by actively taking opportunities to discuss work-related improvements with others at work (CIPD 2010).

In theory, greater engagement benefits both employers—through enhanced business performance and innovation—and employees—by creating a more positive and stimulating working environment (MacLeod and Clarke 2009). It is claimed that greater levels of employee engagement are the product of: the provision of meaningful work; jobs where workers have autonomy, and access to the resources needed to do them effectively; opportunities for constructive feedback on job performance; the commitment of senior management in the organization, and the presence of 'positive' and 'authentic' leadership styles; the support of front-line managers; and the presence of opportunities for workers to express voice over workplace and organizational decisions (CIPD 2010; Bailey et al. 2015).

All of this sounds highly unobjectionable; who could possibly be against efforts to promote an engaged workforce? Moreover, surely employees themselves must welcome the attention that is being paid to how they can be engaged (Guest 2014)? There are some problems, however. For one thing, employee engagement has a strong unitary dimension, in the sense that it captures how 'employees should understand, identify with, and commit themselves to the objectives of the organization they work for' (Emmott 2015: 663). It is therefore a highly managerialist concept; but one that has also, moreover, been criticized for its crudeness. For Purcell (2014: 244), the purpose of employee engagement is to 'get better workers and indoctrinate them on organizational goals and their role in achieving them … taking us back to a dangerously simplistic view of work relations'. While obviously important to understand as a managerial ideology, it is not all that clear whether employee engagement has much relevance to the day-to-day management of employment relations in workplaces.

Another problem with the prominence accorded to employee engagement concerns the panic that has been stoked about the magnitude of the supposed 'engagement deficit' in the UK, the scale of which, according to one report, is 'staggering' (Rayton, Dodge, and D'Analeze 2012: 6). Regular surveys conducted by the Chartered Institute of Personnel and Development demonstrate that only a minority of employees are actually 'engaged' (e.g. CIPD 2014). For Coats (2010: 42), low levels of employee engagement are an indictment of the inadequacy and ineffectiveness of attempts by employers to develop sophisticated management techniques and voice arrangements, something he describes as a 'failure of enlightened HRM'.

But some have questioned whether there is really a problem with employee engagement, or rather the supposed lack of it. The survey methods used to measure engagement are often not very effective, and cannot be relied on. More importantly, what is so wrong with employees being disengaged anyway? From a unitary perspective clearly there is a problem with this, given the belief that workers share the same interests as their employer, and that work and employment relationships are fundamentally cooperative in nature (see Chapter 1). But how realistic are these assumptions considering that all work and employment relationships have the potential for conflict, because workers and employers have different interests? What the surveys show is not necessarily a lack of employee engagement—although they may well do— but rather that the simplistic, unitary beliefs which underpin it are misplaced (Purcell 2014).

Engagement, then, is important to understand as a managerial ideology, but otherwise its relevance to contemporary employment relations is somewhat limited. For Guest (2014), it is not at all clear what organizations are supposed to do to improve engagement levels. Where practical lessons have been attested, their overall relevance is questionable. In the NHS, for example, much of the basis for improved employee engagement was predicated on the voice, involvement, and participation of staff, which included the input of their trade unions (Dromey 2014). Elsewhere, though, a major obstacle to increased engagement concerns the prevalence of low-trust relations, based largely on the widespread belief evident among employees that senior organizational managers are too distant, lack interest in staff issues, and are not sufficiently concerned with giving them effective voice (Purcell 2012; Sanders 2012). Moreover, low levels of job discretion and the lack of genuine opportunities to exercise voice experienced by many employees also militate against progress towards better engagement. Perhaps most importantly, though, the nature of the financial and economic climate in general means that employers increasingly have to treat employees as costs to be minimized, rather than as assets to be valued, and are thus simply unable to deliver the kind of environment in which high levels of engagement are possible (Thompson 2011, 2013).

5.4.4 Managing employment relations and performance

As mentioned in Section 5.4.1, one of the most distinctive aspects of a sophisticated HRM approach is the emphasis on managing employees in a way that enhances business performance. This contrasts with the traditional pluralist approach in which the priority was to manage with, and accommodate the effects of, trade unionism and collective bargaining. Since the 1990s there has been a notable interest in how the presence of sophisticated HRM practices—variously called 'high commitment', 'high involvement', or 'high performance' practices—can positively affect organizational performance (Godard 2004; Purcell and Kinnie 2007; Proctor 2008; Paauwe, Wright, and Guest 2013; Harley 2015). The increasing attention being devoted to engaging staff is largely predicated on the belief that there is a business case for tackling the 'engagement deficit' (Rayton, Dodge, and D'Analeze 2012).

What kinds of management interventions are encompassed by the high commitment approach? Writers like Pfeffer (1998) have produced a list of practices which are assumed to be universally applicable when it comes to generating performance improvements. There are four types of practice deemed to be particularly powerful when it comes to generating commitment (White et al. 2004; Kersley et al. 2006):

- The presence of formal teamworking arrangements, particularly those which allow team members some responsibility for deciding how work should be done and who should do it.

- The existence of a functionally flexible workforce, who are well trained and have the necessary skills to undertake a variety of jobs in their workplace.

- The operation of employee voice and involvement practices. Where staff are able to exercise some influence over managerial decision-making, by participating in problem-solving groups for example, this can be taken as evidence of a high commitment approach.

- The use of sophisticated reward mechanisms which offer incentives to workers for demonstrating commitment and performing well.

High commitment practices are claimed to improve business performance by producing a better quality workforce who are more committed to, and engaged with, business goals because they enjoy more fulfilling working lives. To the extent that they develop a greater sense of identification with the organization and are more involved in decisions that affect them in the workplace, employees will, it is assumed, perform better and be more productive (Wood and de Menezes 1998). The high commitment management approach increases 'discretionary work effort' (Huselid 1995); people who are managed well at work and feel engaged will contribute more (see Figure 5.2). The positive impact of so-called high commitment or high performance management practices is, it is argued, more pronounced when they are used not in an idiosyncratic, ad hoc way, but in a mutually supportive fashion, or in 'bundles' (Huselid 1995; MacDuffie 1995). Teamworking arrangements, for example, should produce better results where they are operated in combination with appropriate recruitment and selection and reward practices.

There is no consensus about the implications of sophisticated HRM for organizational performance. Some have suggested that while there is a link between the use of high commitment practices and greater productivity, this relationship does not extend to a positive effect on financial performance (Wood and Bryson 2009). Others, though, point to the positive association that exists in general between the use of high commitment HRM and firm

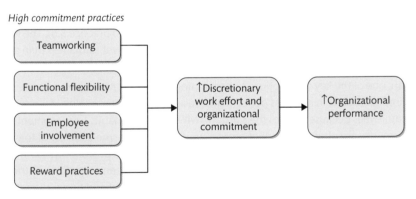

Figure 5.2 The high commitment model

performance (Paauwe, Wright, and Guest 2013). A major study of a number of large public and private sector organizations, including the Nationwide Building Society and Jaguar Cars, demonstrates that there is a connection between the use of sophisticated HRM practices, organizational commitment, and business performance. However, the behaviour of front-line managers seems to be of crucial importance (Purcell et al. 2003); a large part of the effectiveness of the high commitment approach depends on how practices are actually operated by line managers in particular workplaces (e.g. Purcell et al. 2009; Alfes et al. 2013).

How valid are the suppositions that, first, the use of high commitment management practices has become more commonplace and, second, that their presence generates improved business performance? There are a number of difficulties in assuming that the high commitment paradigm has come to dominate the way employment relations is managed (Legge 2005). Six major problems can be identified.

- First, the prevalence of high commitment practices remains rather low; relatively few workplaces make use of a substantial number of them as a coherent package. The high commitment approach to managing people at work is present in only a minority of workplaces, and does not appear to have become more widespread (Wood and Bryson 2009). In the US many employers prefer to operate a more conventional 'command and control' approach to managing employment relations, based on extensive rules and little employee involvement (Kaufman 2010b). Moreover, as Section 5.4.1 shows, a coercive approach to managing employees, based on establishing and enforcing tighter performance standards, remains commonplace.

- Second, a further problem concerns the proposition that there is a link between high commitment HRM and business performance. Research studies in this area tend to exaggerate the extent of any association. Closer analysis of the relevant data reveals that the relationship between high commitment practices and business performance is often less clear-cut than is sometimes claimed (Godard 2004; Wall and Wood 2005).

- Third, there is no consensus on what practices should comprise the high commitment management approach (Purcell and Kinnie 2007; Paauwe, Wright, and Guest 2013), although the importance of techniques that foster employee voice and involvement has been emphasized by some (e.g. Wood 2013). This means that we have to exercise a great deal of care when considering the relationship between sophisticated HRM and business performance. There is also some evidence that traditional personnel management techniques, which recognize and reward employees' contributions for example, may have a more profound effect on performance (see Insight into practice 5.6). The high commitment approach promises a lot, but in reality may deliver rather less than simply conventional good personnel management practice (Godard 2004).

- Fourth, one of the key assumptions underpinning the high commitment approach—that improvements in business performance result from a better quality of working life for employees because it raises their productivity—is questionable. Improvements in performance are often the result of heavier workloads, and come with few of the benefits for workers that are supposed to be associated with new ways of working (Kaufman 2010b). As mentioned in Section 5.4.1, efficiency gains are often a function of stricter performance management techniques, not the contribution of additional 'discretionary work effort' by more highly committed employees (Thompson 2013).

- Fifth, in the high commitment approach there is often a tendency to treat human resource practices as formal managerial interventions, readily identifiable and thus, when presented as variables, making the effects of their presence supposedly easy to measure. But the management of the employment relationship is a process; it possesses a dynamic, and should not be reduced to a set of formal practices. How these function in workplaces, where, for example, managers and workers may contest their operation or interpret them in different ways from those intended, is a much more complex and less easily measurable matter. Studies of the relationship between high commitment management practices and business performance increasingly recognize the important role played by front-line managers in influencing the extent to which practices are actually put into effect (Purcell and Hutchinson 2007), as well as the responses of employees. When considering the effects of high commitment practices, a distinction should be made between 'intended' practices (those that the organization aims to enact), 'actual' practices (those that line managers actually do enact), and 'perceived' practices (those that are experienced by the workforce) (Purcell and Kinnie 2007; Purcell et al. 2009).

- Sixth, and finally, the research methodology that underpins studies of the relationship between sophisticated HRM and performance raises doubts about the appropriateness of the high commitment paradigm and its contribution. One leading commentator accuses much of the extant research of being 'riddled with error both with respect to data on HRM and on outcomes' (Guest 2011: 10). We have already seen that there is no consensus on what practices constitute a high commitment approach, but the specification and measurement of business performance are also often somewhat rudimentary too (Purcell and Kinnie 2007). Research studies rely for their data on responses from managers who, unsurprisingly, offer a biased and partial perspective, and may know little of how the practices they identify are interpreted in the workplace. While there may be an association between sophisticated HRM and performance, it is not necessarily a causal one (Paauwe, Wright, and Guest 2013). Workers who contribute more effort may be more committed and engaged as a result, not the other way around. Firms that are performing well may be in a better position to afford to implement expensive HRM interventions. Thus it can be difficult to disentangle cause and effect when it comes to measuring the impact of sophisticated HRM (Wall and Wood 2005). Taken together, these methodological criticisms mean that we have relatively little knowledge of 'which practices or combinations of HR practices have the most impact, nor when, why or for whom they matter' (Guest 2011: 10–11).

 Insight into practice 5.6: High commitment working—the view from below

Undertaken over a period of four years, Sarah Pass's (2005) study of four manufacturing departments in a major healthcare company demonstrates some of the problems with the assumption that high commitment management practices bring about performance improvements. As well as the interviews she undertook with workers, one of the strengths of her investigation is that she actually worked in a

(continued...)

production capacity in the firm herself, and so is particularly well placed to comment on its activities. Pass discovered that performance improvements came from the exercise of close managerial control over the workforce and heavy work pressures, not the kind of sophisticated HRM interventions that are supposed to engender greater organizational commitment. Increases in performance were also seen to result from the use of traditional personnel management practices which offered recognition and respect, and thus generated good relationships. When workers felt their contribution was recognized, were treated by managers with respect, and were able to form robust and supportive relationships, they responded more positively to managerial interventions.

It is increasingly being recognized that in order to understand the relationship between sophisticated HRM and performance properly, the impact of management practices on workers, and how workers respond to them, needs to be considered (Purcell and Kinnie 2007; Purcell et al. 2009; Guest 2011). Too much of the interest in high commitment HRM has been concerned with managerial objectives in the employment relationship and how they can be realized, whereas the implications for workers tend to be rather neglected (Kaufman 2010b; Harley 2015). Studies that draw on the experiences of workers tend to reveal that performance improvements are driven by more intensive managerial control and greater work pressures, rather than the presence of a more committed workforce.

However, it is not just workers' experiences that we need to consider, but also their interests. If we view the employment relationship as a wage–work bargain, marked by the potential for a conflict of interests, then it helps us to understand why the high commitment management approach—indeed any managerial interventions—will ultimately prove unsatisfying to managers. This is because workers have different interests to those of their employers, and will thus experience, and react to, management practices in ways that do not conform to managerial expectations. Teamworking arrangements, for example, may upset existing social relationships in an organization and thus damage morale, commitment, and ultimately performance (Jenkins and Delbridge 2007). Writers on human resource management often criticize the assumption of those like Pfeffer (1998) who propagate a set of universal best practice techniques for managing people at work in a way that enhances business performance, preferring to take a contingency perspective instead. This asserts that firms would do better to operate practices that best fit in with their overall business strategy (Boxall and Purcell 2011). An employment relations perspective, though, highlights another, perhaps more important, dimension of the 'best fit' concept—that in order to improve the effectiveness of their practices, managers must make an effort to ensure that they conform to the expectations of employees.

The importance of this is evident from Cushen and Thompson's (2012) study of Avatar, the Irish-based subsidiary of a US multinational company, which employed highly skilled workers in a knowledge-intensive environment. The high-performing firm operated an extensive range of best practice management techniques designed to promote the organizational commitment and engagement of staff. You might think, then, that the use of high commitment practices was linked to the financial success of the firm, by increasing discretionary work effort in the manner assumed by the proponents of sophisticated HRM. This assumption would be wrong though. The workforce regarded efforts by the company to promote commitment and engagement with something close to contempt, viewing them as patronizing and insulting. They were particularly aware of the marked contradiction between the positive messages espoused by managers about how wonderful everything was, and that they should take pride from identifying with the company's values, and the reality of the strict controls over pay and growing job insecurity that were engendered by the need to conform with tight financial constraints. The workforce was high-performing, not because they were committed to the organization and its values, but out of an intrinsic interest in their knowledge-intensive and challenging jobs, over which they could exercise control.

Even in situations where managers have been able to develop and sustain a sophisticated HRM approach, this does not necessarily mean that they are effective in influencing and shaping employees' attitudes and behaviour. In the case of the multinational courier company mentioned in Section 5.4.1, despite the use of a high commitment approach, many staff remained unhappy about the lack of influence they had over decisions that affected them at work (Dundon and Rollinson 2004). The different interests of employees mean that the effectiveness of managerial interventions of any kind is always going to be partial and incomplete.

 ## Section summary and further reading

- Whereas traditional approaches to managing employment relations were dominated by a concern to manage the consequences of trade unionism, it is claimed that contemporary organizations are taking a more sophisticated HRM approach to managing employees. Rather than accommodating the potential for conflict, the prime focus of managerial endeavour in employment relations is concerned with building employee engagement, winning organizational commitment, and improving business performance.

- Yet the extent of change has been somewhat limited, and falls well short of being a genuine transformation. While elements of a 'soft' approach to HRM are increasingly evident, the management of employment relations is dominated by a concern to control employees and enhance managerial prerogative, rather than use innovative new practices to encourage employees' voice, commitment, and engagement.

- There is much interest in how the presence of sophisticated HRM, and so-called high commitment or high performance practices in particular, contributes to improvements in business performance. However, there are some major problems with the high commitment approach, not least a tendency to overlook the experiences and attitudes of employees.

While over ten years old now, Legge (2005) remains the best critical assessment of the HRM phenomenon. For the management of employment relations in non-union firms, see Dundon and Rollinson (2004). Wilkinson, Dundon, and Marchington (2013) provide an overview of developments in employee voice. For high commitment management and performance, see Purcell and Kinnie (2007) and Paauwe, Wright, and Guest (2013). See Purcell (2014) for a critical perspective on employee engagement.

5.5 Understanding the management of employment relations

The growing influence of management as an employment relations actor has generated an increasing amount of interest in how its role should be understood. Care needs to be taken, however, not to exaggerate the degree of consistency evident in managerial approaches.

Two features of work and employment relationships hinder the capacity of managers to develop consistent approaches to the management of labour: the tensions arising from the dual function of labour in a capitalist market economy and the nature of the employment relationship as a wage–work bargain.

5.5.1 Managing employment relations in a financialized market economy

The first key factor that hinders managerial consistency in employment relations concerns the tensions arising from the dual function of labour in a capitalist market economy—workers are both a source of value to organizations, and represent a cost (Sisson and Storey 2000). The case of HP, a firm which espoused a sophisticated HRM approach, is instructive. Intense competitive pressures compelled the firm to reduce its workforce, resulting in increased pressure and lower morale among those who remained. Inevitably, such feelings influenced the perceptions and behaviour of employees, thus ensuring that its HRM techniques were rendered less effective as a result (Truss 2001).

One of the distinctive features of business in Anglo-Saxon economies like the UK is the long-established predominance of short-term pressures on companies to improve their performance, judged according to strict financial criteria (Ackroyd and Proctor 1998). This has often imposed constraints on the ability of employers to develop long-term, systematic approaches to managing employees in a manner designed to secure their organizational commitment and engagement. In recent years, however, the extent to which financial imperatives influence the management of employment relations, and the nature of this influence, have attracted growing attention. There has been a particular concern with understanding the implications of an increasingly 'financialized' economy, not least because of the degree to which it induces employers to treat workers more as commodities, the cost of which needs to be minimized to maintain and improve business competitiveness.

The concept of 'financialization' captures the increasing extent to which the activities of governments and employers are not just influenced by, but are also subordinated to, the interests of finance capital (Lapavitsas 2011). In Europe, for example, many countries have come under severe pressure to weaken employment rights and protections, and thus reduce the costs to business of employing workers. The idea is that this provides an environment which is highly attractive to investors wanting to realize short-term gains, thereby maintaining the confidence of international financial markets (Prosser 2014).

At company level, moreover, short-term financial pressures on firms to maximize returns to their shareholder investors also have profound implications for the management of employment relations. In order to satisfy demands from investors for rapid gains in value, employers have to be more attentive to managing staff in a way that quickly delivers efficiency savings and lowers the cost of employment. Reductions in employment, and increased workloads for remaining staff, are thus important consequences of greater financialization, given the greater onus on firms to produce short-term shareholder value (Thompson 2011). In addition, it is important to recognize the growing extent to which the value of firms is contingent on their status as financial assets, to be traded in the financial markets, rather than on the goods they produce or the services they provide to customers (Applebaum and Batt 2014). In an increasingly financialized market economy, dominated by pressure from investors for short-term returns, profits come more from 'financial channels and financial engineering rather than production and product markets' (Thompson 2013: 475). This is exemplified by the rise of private equity; see Employment relations reflection 5.7 for details of how this has affected employment relations.

Employment relations reflection 5.7: Private equity and employment relations

The trend towards greater 'financialization' is particularly manifest in the rise of the private equity model of business ownership (Clark 2009). During the 2000s, the growth of private equity funds attracted a considerable amount of attention. Private equity funds borrow large sums of money from institutional investors, used in combination with small amounts of their own to take over companies, removing their shares from the stock market. The debt becomes the responsibility of the acquired business, which becomes highly leveraged as a result (Applebaum and Batt 2014). The idea is that through rigorous control over costs, and away from the public eye, the fortunes of the business are improved. This helps to service the repayments on the debt incurred and leads to handsome rewards for the members of the private equity fund when the business is subsequently put up for sale. Among the companies that were taken under the control of private equity funds, before being sold on, are Alliance Boots, Birds Eye, and the car park firm NCP.

The impact of private equity ownership on employment relations has prompted a lively debate. Some argue that its effects have been positive. While private equity takeover sometimes results in job losses, in general it helps to stabilize and even raise employment levels. This is because previously under-performing companies are made more secure, thus supporting jobs (Bacon et al. 2010; Bacon and Wright 2008). However, critics contend that pressure to reduce costs has adverse consequences for staff employed in firms taken over by private equity. Not only do private equity funds look for efficiency savings through job cuts, but they also try to lower costs by eroding terms and conditions of employment and making remaining employees work harder. Legislation that exists to protect employees' pay and conditions when their business is sold does not apply to private equity takeovers (Clark 2008).

The onus placed on squeezing value from acquired businesses—to service debt repayments and make them attractive to potential purchasers—can adversely affect union representation (Applebaum and Batt 2014). In 2004, for example, the private equity funds CVC Capital Partners and Permira took joint control of the car rescue firm the AA in a deal worth £1.75 billion. A year later the AA derecognized the GMB union, replacing it with a body which purported to act as an independent trade union, when in reality it was a management-controlled staff association. The AA's private equity owners—between 2007 and 2014 it was joined with Saga and owned by the Charterhouse private equity fund—sought to extract greater value from its workforce by cutting jobs, eroding working conditions, and disposing of union recognition. Around a half of the AA's patrol workers were pushed out of the company. Those who remained saw a significant rise in their workloads and were subject to increasingly stringent performance management arrangements. Although the AA is no longer owned by private equity, it remains a highly financialized business which is burdened with debt (I. Clark 2010, 2016).

Financialization, centred on short-term demands for improved profitability and returns to shareholders, militates against efforts to build consistent, long-term approaches to managing employment relations designed to build trust, and deliver improved levels of commitment and engagement (Sisson and Purcell 2010). The result is a kind of 'disconnected capitalism', marked by the inability of employers to provide environments which permit the development of long-term, high-trust systems of managing employment relations (Thompson 2003, 2011). Employers demand more commitment and engagement from their staff; but short-term financial imperatives mean that they are increasingly unable to invest in the kind of practices—assurances of job security, robust and durable voice arrangements, and extensive training and development—most likely to deliver high-trust employment relations (Thompson 2013).

This highlights the relevance of what Thompson (2011) calls a 'political economy' perspective on work and employment relationships, one that points to the influence of the structural constraints imposed by financial markets on firms, and how they shape the management of employment relations within them. The case of Avatar, the Irish-based subsidiary of a major US multinational mentioned in Section 5.4.4, illustrates this well. The firm put a strong emphasis on using an extensive range of best practice approaches to managing employment relations, designed to elicit greater employee commitment. However, Avatar's obligations to the financial markets, particularly its pledge to increase returns to shareholders, meant that it was obsessed by cutting costs, including through voluntary redundancies and outsourcing business activities. As a result, not only was it unable to deliver on its commitment-based promises, but also its employees were enraged by the hypocrisy evident in its stance, given their high levels of insecurity (Cushen and Thompson 2012).

Increasing financialization not only hinders employers from operating sophisticated HRM regimes, but it also has some profoundly adverse consequences for workers. Demands for short-term extraction of value and reductions in labour costs generate pressure to weaken employment rights and protections (Heyes, Lewis, and Clark 2014; Prosser 2014). They are also a major reason why we have seen a tightening of performance standards and the development of a more coercive approach to managing performance. Moreover, workers are required to bear more of the risks and costs of employment (Thompson 2013). Efforts to commodify labour (see Chapter 2)—through the use of bogus self-employment arrangements, zero-hours contracts, and increasingly precarious forms of employment—are in large part a product of financialization, and the imperative to drive down labour costs in a way that profoundly disadvantages workers.

After a decade of private equity ownership, the highly financialized AA is so burdened by debt (see Employment relations reflection 5.7) that it may have to switch to using patrol staff on cheaper, ostensibly self-employed contracts, rather than employing them directly (Clark 2016). In some cases, cutting costs through reductions in staff numbers can pose a serious risk of harm. The introductory case study of Boots, for example, includes claims that the highly financialized company has pursued efficiency savings to such an extent that its overworked pharmacists pose a risk to patient safety. In order to make financial savings, some major betting shop chains, such as Ladbrokes, have instituted 'single staffing' policies, with the result that shop staff often have to work alone in the evenings, at considerable risk to their safety (Lamont 2016). All this points to the marked divergence that exists between the message conveyed by the sophisticated HRM approach, with its emphasis on securing performance improvements through a more committed and engaged workforce, and the rather more unpleasant reality for many workers, particularly those employed in highly financialized businesses.

5.5.2 **Managing the wage-work bargain**

The second key factor that hinders managerial consistency in employment relations concerns the nature of work and employment relationships as a wage–work bargain (see Chapter 1). What this means is that managing employment relations is not just about exercising control over workers through the use of coercion, but also involves gaining their cooperation and consent. To be sure, as the previous section makes clear, increasing financialization, and the demands for efficiency savings arising from it, mean that employers have taken a more obviously coercive approach to managing employment relations (e.g. more exacting performance management arrangements). There is also the important extent to which employers have tried to extend their control over workers by commodifying labour. But as Chapter 1 shows, labour is not a commodity in the conventional sense. Employers can attempt to commodify labour; and labour has, indeed, become more commodified. This is a major feature of contemporary employment relations (see Chapter 2). But because labour is embodied in actual human beings, who have their own agency and interests, commodification always has limits. This can be seen in the case of the AA. Despite all their negative experiences, many of the company's workers retain their membership of a union which continues to strive to regain recognition from the employer (Clark 2016).

That said, though, the methods by which managements exercise control over workers have been a long-standing feature of workplace studies. For example, a distinction has been made between two types of managerial control strategy: 'direct control', in which managers closely regulate and supervise the activities of workers; and 'responsible autonomy', where control is exercised by deliberately ceding to workers some degree of discretion over how they carry out their work tasks (Friedman 1977). In order to sustain management prerogative, organizations have been compelled to design ever more sophisticated techniques; the growth of formal personnel policies and procedures can be seen as an attempt to secure 'bureaucratic control' (Edwards 1979). Given the extent to which it is concerned with securing organizational culture change, the rise of sophisticated HRM is, in some interpretations, a more robust and—in so far as it is concerned with manipulating the meaning employees attach to their work—a more insidious way of securing managerial control (Willmott 1993).

In service industries, where the relationship between the employee and the customer is a key source of competitive advantage, managers have been obliged to develop novel techniques in an attempt to exercise control (see Insight into practice 5.8). This may, for example, involve using customers themselves (Korczynski 2002). Some companies use fake, or 'mock', customers. Their job is to establish that employees are fulfilling their role in the prescribed manner by pretending to be consumers (Fuller and Smith 1991). In some sectors, most famously the airline industry but also elsewhere, such as in call centres, companies have attempted to control the operation of the service encounter through the manipulation of workers' feelings or emotions (Hochschild 1983; Taylor 1998). Delta Airlines, for example, used wide-ranging and sophisticated training methods to ensure that its cabin crew acted appropriately, in particular by smiling, in all of their interactions with customers. Thus, 'the emotional style of offering the service is part of the service itself' (Hochschild 1983: 5).

Insight into practice 5.8:   Tipping as a source of management control?

In some parts of the economy, restaurants for example, customer tips, as part of the 'total reward system' for front-line customer service staff, are viewed as an important component of workers' remuneration since they offset low rates of basic pay (Mars and Mitchell 1976). The practice of tipping, moreover, particularly where it has been 'institutionalized'—that is, become a standard and accepted feature of workplace life—can serve to enhance managerial control of customer service workers, such as waiting staff. In a study of the Central Restaurant Group, Ogbonna and Harris (2002: 730–1) noted that the use of tipping was an 'integral part of reward', and had 'a long history in the organization', a reflection of its founder's belief that 'the best way to generate enthusiasm, loyalty and the required customer service behaviour from front-line staff was in encouraging them to keep their own tips'.

Three main reasons underpinned the institutionalization of tipping in Central Restaurant Group. First, as a motivational tool it helped to improve employees' performance. Second, it allowed the company to pay a low basic wage, helping to keep labour costs down. Third, it enabled management to maintain control, albeit indirectly, over employees' behaviour during the customer service encounter.

The institutionalization of tipping in Central Restaurant Group served to reinforce managerial control over employees' behaviour in three ways. First, competition for tips encouraged self-interest among the workforce and thus impeded the development of a collective ethos which might challenge managerial standards. Second, by keeping basic pay low, managers fostered among the waiting staff a sense of dependency on the tips. Third, the company used a number of means, including communications processes, to promote its approach to tipping.

Since tips comprised a substantial proportion of their earnings, workers were understandably supportive of the Central Restaurant Group's approach. Nevertheless, there was some dissatisfaction among workers over the behaviours it was felt necessary to produce in order to receive tips. Managers sometimes encouraged flirting, a form of potentially exploitative sexual labour, as a means of keeping customers happy. Ogbonna and Harris (2002: 742) suggest that such activity is a 'degrading and debasing' feature of front-line customer service work, and that workers may feel obliged to 'prostitute' themselves in exchange for the possibility of additional tipped income. They conclude, however, that despite the high level of management manipulation inherent in the institutionalization of tipping and its potentially exploitative implications, workers nonetheless used the system for their own ends. They were not the passive dupes of managers, but rational and calculative actors aware of what they needed to do to maximize their earnings.

The importance of control notwithstanding, as mentioned earlier managers also need to secure the cooperation and consent of their staff. Thus 'management strategy is always a blend of consent and coercion, though the nature of that blend varies between companies and between the various levels within each company hierarchy' (Fox 1985b: 66). Consent was traditionally secured by means of accommodations with trade unions (Hyman 2003), consistent with a pluralist approach to managing employment relations. Yet, even in non-union environments, managers must operate in such a way as to gain the cooperation of, and thus secure legitimacy among, those they manage (Dundon and Rollinson 2004).

It is sometimes assumed that small firms offer environments where employers enjoy untrammelled prerogative. It is certainly rare to find a union presence, and small firm employers often express a marked hostility towards trade unions, regarding them as a potential obstacle to their ability to run the business as they like (Rainnie 1989). One of the owner-managers interviewed in a study of manufacturing businesses in the East Midlands told the researcher:

'I'll never be told what to do by a bloody trade unionist; this is my business' (Marlow 2002: 33). Yet the absence of unions from small firms does not mean that we should assume the presence of a harmonious employment relations climate—the accepted wisdom for many years (Rainnie 1989). Nor does management autocracy go unconstrained. Efforts have been made to understand the diversity of employment relations arrangements in small firms, based on the influence of product and labour market factors (e.g. Rainnie 1989; Goss 1991). For example, in sectors of the economy like the clothing trade the emphasis is on treating workers as a cost, to be hired and fired according to the vagaries of the market, with little need for stability, and employing vulnerable, often female workers from ethnic minorities, who are highly dependent on the employer for paid work (Goss 1991: 84).

Yet market forces do not operate in isolation; they shape the activities and behaviour of employers and workers (Ram and Edwards 2003). This demands a more sensitive and dynamic interpretation of employment relations in small firms. There are three related dimensions of this. First of all, the importance of managerial choices needs to be acknowledged; the management of employment relations in small firms, just like elsewhere, is not determined solely by markets, but also to a degree reflects the choices made by managers themselves, albeit within specific contexts (Ram and Edwards 2010).

The second dimension concerns the need to recognize the 'embeddedness' of small firms in wider familial, ethnic, and community networks, as well as their market presence (Ram and Edwards 2003, 2010; Edwards et al. 2006). For example, many Asian-owned firms in the clothing and restaurant sectors operate with low pay and highly exploitative working conditions; yet the presence of common ethnic bonds means that generally workers are more tolerant of their circumstances (Jones and Ram 2010; Ram and Edwards 2010). Importantly, there seems to be nothing inherent about the greater level of job satisfaction evident among workers in small firms; rather, it constitutes a tactical, 'pragmatic' response to their specific situations. Even relatively well-paid workers in small professional service firms would contemplate changing jobs if going elsewhere meant getting higher pay and better benefits (Tsai, Sengupta, and Edwards 2007: 1802).

Third, a dynamic approach also captures the 'complex, contested and conflictual nature of employment relations in small firms' (Ram and Edwards 2010: 238). Although 'bound by market constraints', employment relationships in small firms are nonetheless 'socially negotiated' (Marlow 2002: 39), and thus constitute a wage–work bargain, just as in larger organizations. For example, in their examination of WaterCo, a company that supplies water facilities to offices and other locations, Dundon and Rollinson (2004: 91) found that even in the absence of a trade union, 'workers were not passive recipients of the conditions they experienced. Rather, they exerted influence in return and, in so doing, partially shaped how management regulated the employment relationship'. Even where informality seems to prevail, with the absence of formal arrangements and procedures for dealing with human resource matters, it is based 'mainly on unwritten customs and the tacit understandings that arise out of the interactions of the parties at work' (Ram et al. 2001: 846), rather than the unconstrained use of managerial prerogative by employers in the absence of unions. The increasing amount of individual employment protection legislation seems to have prompted small and medium-sized firms to formalize their approach to employment relations, through the greater use of written procedures covering matters like the recruitment, selection, and dismissal of employees. How these formal procedures operate, though, is very much influenced by informal day-to-day negotiation between managers and staff (Atkinson, Mallet, and Wapshott 2016).

Even in small low-wage firms, where it would be anticipated that workers would be extremely vulnerable to the vagaries of the market, they do exercise some influence over the nature of their employment relationships, not least because employers often need to elicit their cooperation (Edwards and Ram 2006). This is evident from a study of employment relations in small Asian-owned firms in the West Midlands clothing industry. Monder Ram's (1994) *Managing to Survive* focuses on the dynamic nature of the employment relationship, as a 'negotiated order'. He discovered that to portray employment relations in these firms as autocratic was far too simplistic an approach. Rather, managerial authority was bounded by the need to construct and reconstruct bargains with workers over the pace of work tasks, and the wages payable for undertaking them. Space for 'informal accommodations' was created by the workers' intricate knowledge of the production process, given the imperative for a steady flow of output. Thus 'workers were not passive in the face of authoritarian managements; they would endeavour to alter the terms of the effort bargain if they felt that they were not "fairly" rewarded' (Ram 1994: 122).

Familial, ethnic, and community ties—no matter how much they may cause workers to identify with their employers—do not necessarily eradicate the potential for conflict in the small firm employment relationship, or the importance of 'negotiated consent' as the basis for managing employment relations, even in parts of the informal economy where the flouting of labour laws is commonplace (Ram, Edwards, and Jones 2007; Jones and Ram 2010). The absence of unions from small firms does not imply a harmonious employment relations environment; nor does it necessarily mean that an autocratic managerial approach prevails. Rather, managing the employment relationship, as a wage–work bargain, in these circumstances involves a complex and dynamic process of tacit and informal negotiation with workers who have interests of their own.

This section has demonstrated that the management of employment relations in market economies is marked by two contradictory tendencies: first, the desirability of treating employees as assets to be valued, while at the same time being obliged to consider them as commodities that can be discarded if necessary; and second, that managing employment relations is more than just about exercising control over workers, and upholding coercion, but also involves the need to secure their consent and cooperation. These tensions pose significant challenges to organizations which are keen to manage employment relations in a long-term, purposive, or 'strategic' way. For Hyman (1987: 30), 'there is no "one best way" of managing these contradictions, only different routes to partial failure'. In other words, management can never enjoy complete control over employment relations, and the results of their interventions may differ substantially from the intended outcomes.

Section summary and further reading

- The nature of employment relations makes it difficult for managers to pursue effective long-term and strategic approaches. On the one hand, managers view their employees as valued assets whose cooperation and consent is deemed essential to achieving organizational objectives. On the other hand, however, the pressures associated with increasing financialization mean that there is more of an onus on managers to exercise control over workers, and to treat them more as disposable commodities.

- A further factor that makes it difficult for managers to develop long-term, consistent methods of managing employment relations concerns the nature of the employment relationship as a wage–work bargain. Evidence from small firms demonstrates that managing the employment relationship, as a wage–work bargain, involves a complex and dynamic process of tacit and informal negotiation with workers who have interests of their own.

Sisson and Purcell (2010) offer a very useful overview of the main issues and challenges relating to the management of employment relations. For employment relations in small firms, see the chapter by Ram and Edwards (2010). See Thompson (2011) for the value of a 'political economy' approach to managing employment relations and the concept of 'disconnected capitalism'. For a classic thought-provoking and sophisticated conceptualization of the management of employment relations, see Hyman (1987).

5.6 Conclusion

What, then, are the salient aspects of the way contemporary employment relations is managed? Clearly, pressures to sustain and expand the scope of managerial prerogative and accommodate the influence of trade unions are long-standing features of the management of employment relations. Employers have taken advantage of the economic and political climate to challenge the influence of trade unions. Among newly established workplaces, union recognition is rare; where unions do retain a formal presence, managers have attempted to erode their influence through the use of sophisticated HRM techniques. The way in which some employers have responded to the introduction of the statutory union recognition procedure demonstrates that anti-union values are still commonplace.

The development of sophisticated HRM, the use of high commitment management practices, and the emphasis being accorded to 'employee engagement' supposedly portend a transformation in the management of employment relations. Whereas in the past the managerial agenda was dominated by the need to accommodate the trade unions, the key emphasis now, it is claimed, is concerned with engaging employees and building their organizational commitment as a key source of improved business performance. However, the extent to which the fundamental basis of managing employment relations has changed is questionable. There is little sign that the high commitment approach has become widespread, or that employees have become more engaged. One of the problems is that there is an important contradiction lying at the heart of managing employment relations. Employees are supposed to be treated as a valued asset; but at the same time they are a cost to the business. The increasingly financialized environment, marked by an onus on driving short-term improvements in business performance and profitability, has contributed to a process of commodification, in which workers are often treated as disposable commodities, to be used and discarded as necessary, rather than as a long-term source of value.

Yet the chapter also points to the limits of commodification, based on an appreciation of the employment relationship as a wage–work bargain. Although attempts to expand the scope of managerial prerogative are a defining feature of the way employment relations is managed, not least because of the emphasis placed on realizing efficiency gains, the very nature of the employment relationship, as a 'negotiated order', means that this prerogative is inevitably limited in practice. In order to realize the efficient production of goods and services, managers must not only seek to exercise control over their employees, but are also compelled to win their consent and cooperation. Thus the scope for commodification, even in highly financialized environments, is inherently limited by the nature of the employment relationship as a wage–work bargain. All this renders consistency in managerial approaches, such as the pursuit of sophisticated HRM, difficult to achieve in practice.

 ## Assignment and discussion questions

1. Why and how do managers seek to retain their prerogative in employment relations?

2. Critically assess the effectiveness of the statutory trade union recognition procedure as a means of extending the presence of unions in the economy.

3. In theory, why might a sophisticated HRM approach to managing employment relations, based on the operation of 'high commitment practices', lead to improved business performance? What are the main obstacles in practice?

4. What is meant by the concept of 'employee engagement'? How important is it for employees to be 'engaged' at work? What, if anything, could employers do to improve engagement levels in their organizations?

5. To what extent, and in what ways, has greater 'financialization' influenced the management of employment relations?

 Visit the Online Resource Centre that accompanies this book to develop your understanding of this chapter and keep up to date with the latest developments in this area.
www.oxfordtextbooks.co.uk/orc/williams4e/

 ## Chapter case study: Blacklisting trade unionists in the construction industry

Employers are sometimes prepared to take extreme measures to undermine the legitimate role and activities of trade unions. Blacklisting, for example, has a long history. It involves operating covert lists of the names, personal details, and employment history of trade unionists, which are shared among employers, in order to deny them employment, or to dismiss them. The GMB union calls blacklisting 'illegal corporate bullying', claiming that it is a deep-rooted feature of the construction sector. During the twentieth century a business association called the Economic League maintained a list of trade union activists and others thought to be undesirable subversives, which it made available to sympathetic employers (Druker 2016).

However, blacklisting hit the news during 2009 following a raid by the Information Commissioner's Office (ICO) on the premises of The Consulting Association, a firm run by Ian Kerr apparently on behalf of the construction company Sir Robert McAlpine (BBC Panorama 2013b). It operated a database which contained the names and details of over 3,000 workers. Major construction companies, such as Balfour Beatty, Carillion, and Wimpey paid The Consulting Association an annual fee, and an additional amount each time they wanted the name of an individual worker to be checked against The Consulting Association's records. The database contained details of individuals' personal lives (including car registration numbers) along with unfavourable comments on their supposed conduct. Workers were labelled as 'militants', 'bad news', or 'extreme troublemakers'. Electrician Steve Acheson, for example, campaigned to improve health and safety standards on construction sites. As a result his name, address, and mobile telephone number found their way onto The Consulting

Association's database. His work activities were monitored; and he often found himself dismissed, or refused work (Ewing 2011). Kerr was convicted and fined £5,000 for data protection offences. But the case drew attention to the scandalous treatment experienced by some workers, who had been sacked or denied employment because of legitimate trade union activities, or for raising health and safety concerns. Professor Keith Ewing, a prominent human rights expert, has called blacklisting 'a nasty, secretive and unaccountable practice that causes untold misery for individuals who are entrapped unwittingly by its covert nature, incapable of challenging what is being said and used against them, and unable to understand why their lives are being blighted by the failure to secure work' (Ewing 2009: 2).

Successive governments have failed to tackle the problem of blacklisting effectively. Only in 2010, in the aftermath of The Consulting Association scandal, did Labour take action. It put into effect powers to prohibit the operation of blacklists and to make it unlawful for employers to deny a worker employment, or to dismiss or demote them, because of a blacklist entry. However, there is concern that the legislation is inadequate. Blacklisting has not been made a criminal offence. Moreover, workers do not have a specific right not to be blacklisted (Ewing 2010). Victims of blacklisting and trade unions in the construction industry have taken civil action to secure compensation for their losses. In 2016, several major companies, including Balfour Beatty and Sir Robert McAlpine, formally apologized for having engaged in the practice of blacklisting and agreed to compensate victims in an out-of-court settlement that could reach £75 million (Macalister 2016).

You can read the full story of the blacklisting scandal in the book by Dave Smith (himself a victim of blacklisting) and Phil Chamberlain—*Blacklisted: The Secret War between Big Business and Union Activists* (Smith and Chamberlain 2015). There are claims that blacklisting still occurs on major construction sites, such as London's Crossrail project (Ewing 2011; Milne 2012; BBC Panorama 2013b). Druker (2016), however, reckons that formal blacklisting arrangements, of the kind that historically characterized the construction industry, are rare now—although this does not preclude the possibility of blacklisting operating informally. For one thing, employers are sensitive to the reputational damage arising from being found to have colluded in blacklisting. And, perhaps more importantly, employers have plenty of other—less obviously egregious—ways of avoiding a union presence now.

Questions

Why has blacklisting been such a particularly prominent feature of the construction industry? What insights does the blacklisting scandal provide about the employment relations approach taken by major construction companies?

6 Trade unions and worker representation

Chapter objectives

The main objectives of this chapter are to:

- explore the ways in which trade unions represent the interests of workers;
- examine the extent and causes of the decline in union membership;
- examine how unions have responded to decline and tried to revitalize themselves; and
- assess non-union arrangements for representing workers' interests.

6.1 Introduction

In this chapter, the concern is with how the interests of workers are represented, something that has traditionally been done through the 'single channel' of trade unionism. Therefore Section 6.2 begins by considering how unions represent workers' interests. However, declining unionization levels have reduced the extent to which workers enjoy effective representation of their interests. The onus, then, is on how unions have responded to decline, and tried to revitalize themselves, in ways that improve their representational capacities. Four major approaches are assessed in Section 6.3. First, unions can best demonstrate their relevance, and improve their prospects, by focusing on delivering services to their members ('servicing unionism'). The second approach holds that union revival is contingent on engaging with employers in a cooperative fashion, best illustrated by the attention devoted to 'partnership' in employment relations. Third, the 'organizing unionism' approach, however, holds that union revitalization is best achieved by organizing and mobilizing new members in the workplace, in opposition to employers. The distinctive feature of the fourth approach—'community unionism'—is that union renewal is contingent on mobilizing working people outside of workplaces, in place-based communities, in collaboration with community and social movement organizations. However, to understand developments in the representation of workers, there is a need to consider both how unions have sought to respond to the decline in membership, and alternative forms of worker representation. In Section 6.4 the focus is on non-union systems of employee representation, including an assessment of the implications of European Union (EU) legislation concerning information and consultation rights for workers.

Introductory case study: Unite community membership

One of the topics covered in this chapter concerns the efforts of some unions to revitalize themselves by operating more widely away from particular workplaces in place-based communities. Since 2012, the largest union in the UK—Unite—has developed a community membership scheme. For just 50 pence per week, people not in work (students, carers, the unemployed, and the retired) can join Unite and, in return, gain access to union services, such as a legal helpline. For Unite, though, the community membership scheme is not just about providing services. It is also viewed as a key mechanism for building stronger communities and giving the people in them greater power over their lives. Unite community branches have actively campaigned to protect local NHS services, for example, and against cuts to welfare benefits that would further impoverish communities. The initiative has also prompted the establishment of a number of local Unite community centres. For Steve Turner from Unite, the development of the community scheme came from a desire to 'instil in our communities trade union principles of justice, fairness, dignity, solidarity, and to extend our political and social reach back into our communities'. There is some evidence that community mobilization can help workers involved in industrial disputes. In Liverpool, for example, members of the local community branch supported workers employed at a Tesco depot who were protesting against redundancies, adding to the pressure on the employer.

Sources: Milmo (2012*a*); Holgate (2015*b*); Unite website

6.2 Trade unions, worker representation, and the 'representation gap'

The main functions of the trade unions were covered in Chapter 1. This section examines the principal ways in which trade unions represent the interests of workers, set against an outline of how the unions developed, before focusing on the decline in union membership that commenced in the 1980s, and assessing the factors that caused it.

6.2.1 Trade unions and the representation of workers' interests

There are four main ways in which trade unions represent the interests of workers. First, unions insure workers against difficulties and problems that arise during the course of their working lives. The provision of friendly benefits was a major function of the early unions of skilled workers (Webb and Webb 1920*a*). During the twentieth century, the importance of friendly benefits as a union function declined markedly, not just because collective bargaining became the principal way in which unions sought to regulate the employment relationship, but also because the state's role in providing welfare benefits such as unemployment assistance expanded considerably. Nevertheless, one of the defining features of union organization is that it reflects the wishes of workers collectively to insure, or protect, themselves against problems at work. And while union membership may be predicated on workers' demands for insurance against individual problems at work, it is something that is achievable only through robust collective organization (Williams 1997).

The second way in which unions represent the interests of workers is by bargaining on their behalf with managers over pay and other terms and conditions of employment. Importantly, collective bargaining is not just an economic process, concerned with setting the terms on which workers are hired; it is also a political activity since it enables workers, through their union representatives, to influence, and thus regulate jointly with managers, workplace decision-making (Flanders 1975). Contemporary trends in collective bargaining activity are discussed in Chapter 7.

The third way in which unions represent the interests of workers concerns the activities of stewards, unpaid union representatives based in the workplace. These lay representatives are generally the first point of contact for union members, and act to advocate their interests to managers, supporting and standing up for them in the workplace (Coates and Topham 1980), sometimes as a safeguard against hard-line employers. Workplace union representatives have long played a key role in representing the collective interests of workers (Terry 2010). However, one problem is that stewards and lay representatives are essentially concerned with representing the (sometimes narrow and sectional) interests of their own members, which hinders union efforts to expand their membership base. Moreover, the way stewards represent their members' interests is often shaped by their assumptions about the kinds of issues that are legitimate for union action. Munro's (1999) study of shop steward organization among ancillary staff in the health service demonstrates the influence of a relatively narrow 'trade union agenda' dominated by the concerns of male workers. This affects stewards' behaviour in that they may ignore issues of particular importance to women workers, such as childcare provision.

Fourth, unions do not just represent the interests of their members in the workplace, but also in the broader political arena. Indeed, by seeking to advance the interests of workers in general, and not just those of their members, unions act as a 'sword of justice' (Flanders 1975)—campaigning for effective laws governing employment rights, for example. In Chapter 3, the influence of unions in the Labour Party was highlighted. The introduction of the National Minimum Wage in 1999 (see Chapter 7), the culmination of a successful campaign run within the Party by some trade unions to secure a manifesto commitment to introduce it, demonstrates how unions can use political channels to advance workers' interests. Unions have increasingly looked to alternative, broader ways of representing workers' interests politically, other than through the Labour Party. For example, the union movement has increasingly campaigned to improve the rights and employment conditions of mostly non-unionized 'vulnerable' workers, such as migrants (TUC 2008).

6.2.2 Declining unionization and the 'representation gap'

One of the most prominent features of employment relations during the twentieth century was the growth of trade union membership, as workers organized collectively to ensure that their interests were represented effectively. Table 6.1 shows that overall trade union membership numbers and union density (the proportion of employees who are union members) rose in two distinct phases. First, the period between 1880 and 1920 saw a major expansion of trade unionism. The development of 'general' unions, in industries such as the docks, transport, and gas (in two waves, first during the 1880s, and then during the 1910s), demonstrates how, under the influence of prominent leaders, many of whom were imbued with a socialist outlook, increasing numbers of semi-skilled and unskilled workers became organized (see Hyman 2001). Unlike their skilled craft counterparts, most of the workers who unionized in this period looked to secure improvements in their pay and conditions through widespread collective organization and a readiness to use strikes and engage in political activity. By 1910, trade union membership had reached over 2.5 million, albeit concentrated in certain areas such as coal mining—the Miners' Federation of Great Britain (MFGB) was the largest union in the country—engineering, railways, and cotton production.

Although trade union membership had already started to edge upwards again during the late 1930s, after falling back to under 5 million during the economic depression, the second main period of growth occurred between the 1940s and 1970s. Economic recovery after the Second World War was predicated on the growth of manufacturing industry: the mass production of electrical goods and other standardized products such as motor vehicles. Full employment encouraged greater shop-floor bargaining activity, creating the conditions that enabled trade unionism to flourish at workplace level (Terry 1983). Moreover, the rather monotonous nature of the assembly-line work in large-scale factory environments, allied with the more vigorous exercise of managerial prerogative, generated increasingly adversarial and 'low-trust' relations between managers and workers (Fox 1974).

Although the shop steward position originated in the first two decades of the twentieth century (Hinton 1973), the growth of workplace bargaining saw a massive rise in their numbers, particularly in engineering and parts of manufacturing industry, thus generating a 'shift in authority' in the trade unions away from the salaried cadre of full-time professional officials (Royal Commission 1968; Terry 1983). Shop steward organization spread to the public sector, and their numbers reached 335,000 by the early 1980s (Charlwood and Forth 2009). Legislation of the 1970s, which obliges employers to give shop stewards of recognized unions a reasonable amount of paid time off work to undertake union activities, reflected the prevailing pluralist policy assumption that by accepting and integrating workplace unionism, rather than challenging it, managers could effectively contain labour conflict.

By the 1970s, perhaps the most striking feature of employment relations in the UK was the strength of trade unionism. Trade union membership peaked at over 13 million in the late 1970s, with some 55 per cent of employees being unionized (see Table 6.1). Much of the rapid acceleration in union membership during the 1960s and 1970s reflected the increased unionization of 'white-collar' workers in office-based occupations in sectors such as central and local government administration. By 'the end of the 1970s nearly 40 per cent of all trade unionists were in white-collar jobs' (Price 1983: 155).

Trade unionism traditionally constituted the 'single channel' by which workers had their interests represented in the UK (Terry 2010). However, the long-term decline in the level of union membership means that many people no longer enjoy effective representation at work. Although the fall in the number of union members has attracted most attention, it has to be seen in the context of the broader diminution of joint regulation as a means of regulating employment relationships. Chapter 5 considered the falling incidence of union recognition since the 1980s. The decline in the level of collective bargaining coverage is discussed in Chapter 7. Union workplace organization has also been rendered less effective by the increased preference of managers for bypassing shop stewards, and communicating with workers directly (Marchington and Parker 1990). In 1980, lay trade union representatives were present in 53 per cent of workplaces, whereas in 2004 they were present in just 38 per cent of workplaces (Kersley et al. 2006); over the same period the number of union representatives fell by two-thirds (Charlwood and Forth 2009). Since 2004, however, this decline appears to have stabilized (van Wanrooy et al. 2013b), and new union representative roles have been established—see Employment relations reflection 6.1.

Table 6.1   Trade union membership, 1892–1979

Year	Union membership	Union density (%)
1892	1,576,000	10.6
1900	2,022,000	12.7
1910	2,565,000	14.6
1917	5,499,000	30.2
1920	8,348,000	45.2
1926	5,219,000	28.3
1933	4,392,000	22.6
1938	6,053,000	30.5
1945	7,875,000	38.6
1950	9,829,000	44.1
1955	9,741,000	44.5
1960	9,835,000	44.2
1965	10,325,000	44.2
1970	11,187,000	48.5
1975	12,026,000	51.0
1979	13,447,000	55.4

Source: Bain and Price (1983)

Employment relations reflection 6.1:   The impact of union learning representatives

Employers who recognize a trade union are obliged to give union representatives—such as shop stewards—a reasonable amount of time away from their work to undertake their union duties. A recognized union is also entitled to appoint safety representatives, whose activities include investigating health and safety issues and making representations to managers. The 2002 Employment Act provided for the establishment of union learning representatives (ULRs), also allowing them time off work to undertake their role. ULRs work to promote learning, training, and development activities, by raising awareness of the opportunities that are available to workers for example, or by encouraging employers to improve their provision. According to the Trades Union Congress (TUC), by 2010 it had trained some 23,000 ULRs (Moore 2011). They make an effective contribution to widening participation in learning activities at work. Not all employers, however, support the objective of enhancing opportunities for workplace learning. Some have failed to engage constructively with ULRs, and managers are markedly less convinced that they have a positive impact on training than ULRs themselves (Wallis, Stuart, and Greenwood 2005; Cassell and Lee 2009; Hoque and Bacon 2011). There have been criticisms of the ULR initiative, claiming that it is designed to weaken unions by encouraging them to take too cooperative a stance towards employers. Others, however, contend that the presence of ULRs not only makes a positive difference to training and learning activities but also helps to revitalize unions by raising their profiles, mobilizing members, and generating activism (Moore 2011; Saundry, Antcliff, and Hollinrake 2016). The ULR model has been taken forward as a useful way of achieving progress in other areas of employment relations too, such as the development of union equality representatives (see Chapter 4).

Table 6.2 Trade union membership and density (employees), 1980–2015

	Union membership*	Density (%)§
1980	12,239,000	54.5
1985	10,282,000	49.0
1990	8,577,000	37.8
1995	7,113,000	32.4
2000	7,119,000	29.8
2005	7,083,000	28.6
2010	6,589,000	26.6
2015	6,493,000	24.7

* Great Britain (1980–90), UK (1995–2015); § proportion of employees who are union members
Sources: Waddington (2003); BIS (2016*b*)

Nevertheless, membership decline is perhaps the starkest indication of the collapse of the union movement's fortunes. Table 6.2 shows that in 1980 there were over 12 million union members in Britain, some 54 per cent of the workforce. During the 1980s union membership fell by a third. Membership decline continued during the 1990s, although at a more gradual pace; by 2000 fewer than three in ten employees (29.8 per cent) were union members. Union membership continued to fall during the twenty-first century. As shown in Table 6.2, by 2015 there were around 6.5 million union members in the UK. In the three-and-a-half decades between 1980 and 2015 the overall level of trade union membership fell by some 6 million; by 2015 fewer than a quarter of employees (24.7 per cent) were union members, compared to over a half (54.5 per cent) in 1980.

What explains such a dramatic reversal of fortunes for the unions? Trade union decline can be attributed to the interaction of a complex range of relevant factors (Simms and Charlwood 2010). Economic changes, for instance, have had some influence. For one thing, workers do not have the same incentive as they once did to organize in unions. The extent of the union wage premium (the extra amount typically earned by unionized workers through collective bargaining compared to non-unionized workers) has narrowed considerably (Metcalf 2005; Blanchflower and Bryson 2009). Nevertheless, on average unionized workers still earn 14.1 per cent more than non-unionized workers; for young workers, aged between 16 and 24, the difference is 42.7 per cent (BIS 2016*a*).

Moreover, economic globalization enables companies to become more internationally mobile, something which has reduced the bargaining power of workers and unions (Anner et al. 2006)—see Chapter 11. Periods of economic recession can also have an adverse effect on union membership levels. During the recession of the early 1980s, for example, factory closures and job losses were concentrated in what were then strongly unionized parts of the economy such as manufacturing. Union membership decline continued, however, albeit at a slower rate, even during periods of economic growth when employment levels rose (Fernie 2005), such as during the mid-1990s and in the first half of the 2000s. This suggests that declining unionization is influenced by long-term changes in the economy, particularly changes in the composition of employment.

The compositional approach asserts that, since the 1980s, employment has been contracting in areas where unions are strong and increasing in areas where they are weak. Thus the number of full-time, male-dominated jobs in large manufacturing enterprises, where unionization tends to be commonplace, has dwindled considerably. Most employment growth has been in the private services sector, where jobs are often held by women on a part-time basis, and where unions are relatively weak. Much of the decline in the level of unionization can therefore be attributed to the failure of unions to organize in new workplaces, and thus gain recognition from employers in expanding areas of the economy (Machin 2000).

Some argue that changes in the structure of employment have eroded the kind of collective experiences and values that used to bind working people together, and which underpinned unionization (Simms and Charlwood 2010). In the past, workers in large-scale manufacturing enterprises, for example, developed a sense of collective endeavour, based on a strong sense of shared interests. Workers today, however, tend to be located in relatively small office environments or industrial units, often isolated from others engaged in similar jobs. They are no longer so exposed to unions, and as a consequence are less likely to see their relevance. However, compositional change seems to have been responsible for only around a third of the fall in union membership (Blanchflower and Bryson 2009).

Economic restructuring and changes in the composition of employment have had adverse consequences for trade union membership levels across many advanced economies. However, the decline has been more marked in the UK than it has elsewhere (Simms and Charlwood 2010), suggesting that there are other factors which have had an effect. For Blanchflower and Bryson (2009: 56), union membership decline has largely been caused by 'employers turning their back on trade unions', manifest in a greater unwillingness to contemplate union recognition, and efforts to weaken their influence by using techniques associated with a sophisticated human resource management approach (see Chapter 5). In those parts of the economy where the fall in trade union membership has been particularly pronounced—such as in financial services—managers seem to be less supportive of a union presence (van Wanrooy et al. 2013b). Moreover, efforts by employers to avoid unions have been aided by important developments in the political and legal spheres. As Chapter 3 delineates, during the 1980s and 1990s Conservative governments led by Margaret Thatcher and John Major passed laws which strictly regulate the activities of the unions (Simms and Charlwood 2010), just about all of which were subsequently retained by Labour. Employers have thus been able to challenge and restrict the influence of unions with a greater degree of confidence.

In terms of an overall assessment, it would seem that the dramatic fall in union membership during the first half of the 1980s was the product of compositional change and the massive job losses linked to the recession of that period. By the 1990s, the consequences of the Conservatives' legislative changes were beginning to take effect, fostering a climate in which the exercise of managerial prerogative was strengthened and union confidence undermined. In addition, the decline in the wage premium associated with union membership meant that workers had less of an incentive to join unions, while ongoing compositional change continued to erode membership levels.

During the late 1990s and early 2000s, the decline in the overall level of trade union membership largely stabilized. This was partly because of employment growth in the strongly unionized public sector up to 2010. Bear in mind that union density varies greatly by sector and industry—see Table 6.3. In the public sector 54.8 per cent of employees are trade unionists, compared with just 13.9 per cent of employees in the private sector. Over a half (51.8 per cent)

Table 6.3 Union density by sector and industry, UK 2015 (selected industries)

	Union density (%)*
All	24.7
Private sector	13.9
Public sector	54.8
Education	51.8
Public administration and defence	45.7
Electricity and gas	42.3
Health and social work	40.6
Transport and storage	37.5
Manufacturing	16.8
Financial services	14.0
Construction	13.1
Wholesale, retail, and motor trade	12.7
Hotels and restaurants	3.5

* proportion of employees who are union members

Source: BIS (2016*b*); licensed under the Open Government Licence v.3.0

of employees in education are trade union members, compared with fewer than one in twenty-five (3.5 per cent) employees in hotels and restaurants. Moreover, Labour provided the unions with a less hostile public policy climate than its Conservative predecessors, even if, as was shown in Chapter 3, it was far from being pro-union; it encouraged employers and unions to work more in partnership (see Section 6.3.2). The unions also started to devote more resources to recruiting and organizing new members (see Section 6.3.3).

However, such efforts did little to counteract the effect of ongoing compositional changes which continued to nibble away at union density, especially in the private sector. While the overall level of union membership may have largely stabilized, increasing employment levels mean that the proportion of employees who are union members has continued to fall (BIS 2016*b*). Even in the public sector, which is perhaps now the last major stronghold of trade unionism in the UK, there are signs that the prevalence of union membership has diminished (Scott and Williams 2016). Yet by no means have all unions equally experienced membership decline. Some trade unions, particularly those representing professional employees mainly in the public sector, such as teachers and nurses, have increased their membership (Simms and Charlwood 2010). Trade unions are becoming increasingly feminized, as the proportion of female union members (27.7 per cent in 2015) outstrips that of males (21.7 per cent).

Some unions which are prepared to challenge employers by threatening and engaging in strikes and other forms of industrial action, like the Rail, Maritime, and Transport (RMT) union, have benefited from membership growth during the 2000s. Nevertheless, the overall diminution of trade union membership, allied with declining levels of union recognition (see Chapter 5), has given rise to a 'representation gap', in the sense that growing numbers of workers have little or no opportunity to have their interests represented at work (Towers 1997; Heery 2009*a*). Some might say that unions are not really needed any more given the growth in statutory employment rights, such as the National Minimum Wage, enacted by Labour between 1997 and 2010. Yet the legal framework of employment rights and protections is a far from effective substitute for trade union representation—not least because when they have problems aggrieved workers are expected to find redress themselves, when they may not have the knowledge or resources to do so effectively (see Chapter 10). Without a union presence, statutory employment rights and protections are much more difficult to enforce (Terry 2010).

 Section summary and further reading

- Trade unions represent the interests of workers by providing them with protection, or insurance, against problems that affect them at work, bargaining collectively with employers on their behalf, acting as a workplace advocate, and in the broader, political arena.

- For much of the twentieth century union membership increased; it became a particularly prominent feature of some industrial sectors, such as manufacturing. By the 1960s and 1970s union membership had become commonplace among white-collar workers.

- There has been a marked fall in the overall level of trade union membership since the 1980s. This was caused by a combination of factors, including changes in the composition of employment, employer policies of union exclusion, and the hostile anti-union policy climate propagated by Conservative governments during the 1980s and 1990s.

- While the fall in overall union membership is perhaps the starkest dimension of union decline, it is just one aspect of the broader diminution of union power, something that also includes falling levels of union recognition and dwindling numbers of workplace union representatives. The result has been a growing 'representation gap', with workers increasingly unable to have their interests represented effectively at work.

For an overview of union membership trends and the factors that influence them, see Simms and Charlwood (2010). The Department for Business, Innovation, and Skills (BIS) produces an annual analysis of trade union membership data (e.g. BIS 2016b).

6.3 Trade union revitalization

If workers are to have their interests represented effectively, much depends on the extent to which trade unions can revitalize themselves. The purpose of this section is to assess the four main ways in which unions have tried to assert their relevance in contemporary employment relations: by focusing on delivering services to members, engaging in 'partnership' with employers, seeking to organize and mobilize new members in the workplace, and developing a more community-oriented focus.

6.3.1 Servicing unionism and union mergers

Providing services to their members is an integral feature of trade unions. As mentioned in Section 6.2.1, a major function of the early trade unions was to provide their skilled craft-worker members with 'friendly benefits' such as unemployment and sick pay (Webb and Webb 1920b). During the twentieth century the rise of the welfare state, and the system of state benefits, meant that provision of individual benefits became less important as a union activity. Nevertheless, in some countries, particularly in the US and also to some extent the UK, the provision of collective bargaining was explicitly articulated as a membership service.

To this extent, unions functioned as market actors, using their collective bargaining power to secure increased material rewards for their members (Hyman 2001). One of the ways in which unions have responded to membership decline has been by focusing on extending the range of services they provide. How far, then, can a so-called 'servicing unionism' approach, based on attracting new members and, more importantly, retaining existing members, through the provision of attractive services, help the process of union revitalization?

One area where unions have expanded their service provision quite substantially concerns financial benefits—discounted insurance packages, credit card deals, and the like. These do not tend to be viewed as very important, however (Waddington and Whitston 1997; Ackers 2015). Education and learning services, though, are often well patronized and highly regarded by union members. The public service union Unison, for example, supports adult education through its Return to Learn programme. Although such services are aimed at, and designed to benefit, individual members, by giving them more confidence they can also help to increase union participation and collective organization (Munro and Rainbird 2000). For workers who are in receipt of, and involved in, learning services they can provide a 'route to union activism' and help strengthen unions (Moore 2011: 94).

This collective dimension of ostensibly individual union services is also evident when it comes to the provision of representational services to members. While collective bargaining is no longer as important as it once was, especially in the private sector (see Chapter 7), the provision of representational services has become a much more important function. Unions play an increasingly important part in supporting individual members in grievance and disciplinary cases, and representing them in legal cases against employers where relevant. Growth in the coverage of individual employment protections—e.g. the right not to be unfairly dismissed, the right not to be discriminated against on unlawful grounds, and the right to be paid the National Minimum Wage—mean that unions spend much more time and money now on undertaking casework on behalf of individual union members. For many members, this is a highly valued union function (e.g. Danford et al. 2014), particularly in a climate where performance pressures, among other things, have contributed to an employment relations environment where workers have more problems. Importantly, however, while union representational services are generally targeted at, and used by, individual members, their effectiveness often depends on the strength of collective organization in the workplace concerned (Williams 1997). Effective representation, moreover, can also help to organize and mobilize workers on a collective basis.

Unions have restructured how they operate in order to enhance their service provision. This includes internal changes designed to ensure that groups of workers who often experience employment disadvantage (e.g. black and minority ethnic workers) benefit from union membership (see Chapter 4). Furthermore, one of the main ways in which the trade unions have responded to membership decline, and the imperative to deliver attractive services to their remaining members, has been through engaging in merger activity. In 1980, there were over 500 different independent UK unions in existence; by 2015 there were just 149, with much of the decline being the result of mergers. The largest union in the UK—Unite, with some 1.4 million members—was formed in 2007 following the amalgamation of Amicus and the Transport and General Workers' Union. Amicus itself had grown out of a series of mergers during the early 2000s, involving unions in engineering, the printing industry, and finance (Simms and Charlwood 2010).

Rationalization has occurred for a number of reasons, with some unions, such as the GMB general union, encouraging mergers with smaller unions as part of an expansionary growth strategy. But mergers have proved attractive because they raise the prospect of being able to deliver union services, especially collective bargaining, more efficiently. That said, though, mergers rarely deliver the anticipated efficiency gains (Undy 2008). Moreover, by diluting union identity, mergers potentially undermine workers' commitment to their union (Ackers 2015). Perhaps more fundamentally, even if merger activity benefits the specific unions concerned, it has not done very much to revitalize the trade union movement as a whole. On their own, mergers do nothing to generate new members for unions. They increase individual unions' share of the existing 'market' for members, without actually growing it (Willman 1989).

6.3.2 Partnership

A second major way in which trade unions have responded to declining membership and attempted to demonstrate their relevance is by trying to work in 'partnership' with employers, on the basis that a trade union presence can help to enhance business performance and enable the successful management of change in a way that upholds union influence and protects jobs (Simms and Charlwood 2010; Terry 2010). The assumption is that a revival of trade unionism is best achieved by eschewing adversarial relations with employers and instead concentrating on promoting greater cooperation (Wilkinson et al. 2014b; Johnstone 2015).

There is nothing new about cooperative employment relations arrangements. During the 1980s, for example, there was much interest in so-called 'new style' collective agreements, which were actively promoted by some moderate trade unions. Under these agreements, employers guaranteed recognition to a single union in exchange for the union accepting greater flexibility and a commitment to act responsibly, refraining from strikes and industrial action (Bassett 1987; Garrahan and Stewart 1992). Since the late 1990s, though, there has been a renewed interest in cooperative relationships between employers and unions, manifest in the form of 'partnership agreements', which have become a major feature of employment relations (Stuart and Martinez Lucio 2005; Bacon and Samuel 2009; Johnstone 2016).

A total of 248 new partnership agreements were recorded over the period from 1998 to 2007, with 10 per cent of employees working in organizations covered by them (Bacon and Samuel 2009). Among the well-known companies which have signed partnership agreements with trade unions are Barclays Bank, Legal & General, and Tesco. Most agreements, though, seem to be situated in the public sector, for instance in health organizations (Bacon and Samuel 2009).

One of the problems in assessing partnership agreements concerns the rather ambiguous concept of partnership itself, which can be open to differing interpretations (Stuart and Martinez Lucio 2005; Johnstone 2015). Nevertheless, partnership agreements can be defined as: 'formal collective agreements to enhance cooperation between employers and independent trade unions or staff associations', based on a 'mutual recognition of competing and shared interests' (Bacon and Samuel 2009: 232). They are generally rooted in a series of core principles: sets of 'shared values and beliefs that establish the behaviours, attitudes, and expectations required for cooperative industrial relations' (Samuel and Bacon 2010: 432).

In addition to the broad principles of partnership agreements, we also need to be concerned with their specific provisions. The content of partnership agreements tends to be dominated by matters relating to employee voice, especially arrangements providing for consultation and representative participation, enabling unions in particular to exercise greater influence over organizational decision-making (Johnstone, Ackers, and Wilkinson 2009; Johnstone, Wilkinson, and Ackers 2010; Johnstone and Wilkinson 2016). Yet, reflecting their modest aims, partnership agreements generally lack much substance. They tend to be marked by a concern with process issues—arrangements for operating voice through recognized unions, for example—rather than specific goals (Samuel and Bacon 2010).

Why has partnership become a prominent feature of employment relations? Partnership agreements were given considerable encouragement by the Labour administrations of 1997–2010, based on the belief that cooperative relationships at work are a central feature of a 'modernized' system of employment relations (Stuart and Martinez Lucio 2005; Bacon and Samuel 2009; Johnstone, Ackers, and Wilkinson 2009; Wilkinson et al. 2014b; Johnstone 2015, 2016). The benefits of partnership were strongly promoted by the TUC (1997). For the unions, partnership is viewed as attractive in so far as it enables them to maintain an organizational presence, and may even give them more influence over decisions (Guest and Peccei 2001). In an otherwise hostile environment, partnership appears to guarantee the unions a presence, a degree of institutional security, and some (however limited) influence over organizational decision-making (Wills 2004; Donaghey 2016).

Yet the impetus for partnership has largely come from employers (Oxenbridge and Brown 2005). Partnership agreements are attractive to firms operating in increasingly competitive market conditions since they offer the prospect of both a harmonious employment relations environment and a more flexible, committed workforce—matters that are seen as crucial to improvements in business performance (Badigannavar and Kelly 2011). Managers in the banking sector, for example, viewed partnership as a key means of breaking away from traditionally adversarial relationships with trade unions and disruptive strikes (Johnstone, Wilkinson, and Ackers 2010; Geary and Trif 2011). In the public sector, where most partnership agreements are in place, partnership has contributed to the reform of public services by securing union cooperation with change initiatives (Bacon and Samuel 2009; Bach and Kessler 2012). Partnership agreements also assist managerial efforts to secure, and gain support for, organizational change (Oxenbridge and Brown 2005; Samuel 2007; Johnstone, Ackers, and Wilkinson 2009).

Advocates of partnership contend that it not only benefits employers, but also that workers enjoy greater job security, are better informed about decisions, and retain union representation (Samuel and Bacon 2010; Johnstone 2015). There is some evidence to support a 'mutual gains' (Kochan and Osterman 1994) perspective on partnership, with benefits accruing to the employer, the workforce, and the recognized trade union (e.g. Kochan et al. 2009; Glover, Tregaskis, and Butler 2014). In NatBank, for example, partnership meant that the union enjoyed a stronger influence over decision-making, employees felt more informed and involved when it came to decisions that affected them, and managers profited from having better quality information and feedback (Johnstone, Wilkinson, and Ackers 2010). There is evidence that partnership working can strengthen trade unionism. In the financial services firm Legal & General, for example, the partnership agreement meant that while the union lost influence over pay determination, it gained more involvement in a wider range of issues, such as staff training and development. The union gained members, and also benefited from the development of a stronger cadre of activists, as a result of partnership (Samuel 2005).

An alternative assessment of partnership is that rather than promoting 'mutual gains' it is characterized more by 'constrained mutuality' (Geary and Trif 2011). This view holds that workers and unions do benefit from partnership agreements, but employer interests dominate (e.g. Guest et al. 2008). While partnership gives unions 'institutional security', helping to secure them a formal presence at an organizational level, it nonetheless shifts the balance of power firmly in favour of management. One of the main dangers of partnership for the trade unions concerns the distance that is potentially opened up between those union representatives who are party to managerial decision-making, and use their position to influence it, and the members, who may become disillusioned about the extent to which, as they view it, the union is really representing their interests in opposition to management (see Oxenbridge and Brown 2004; Danford et al. 2014). In the case of Barclays, for example, partnership meant that the union was not considered to be fighting on behalf of its members' interests as strongly as it ought to have done; it appeared to have developed a relationship with the bank that was too cosy and cooperative (Wills 2004).

In addition to the 'mutual gains' and 'constrained mutuality' approaches to understanding partnership, there is also a third—'pessimistic'—perspective (Geary and Trif 2011). This sees partnership as having been advanced primarily as part of an employers' agenda to circumscribe the influence of recognized trade unions and enhance managerial prerogative, with few if any genuine benefits accruing to workers. Partnership, then, is inimical to robust trade unionism and the effective representation of workers' interests. Partnership agreements are used as instruments for reinforcing managerial prerogative, with the aim of weakening trade union influence (Taylor and Ramsay 1998; Evans, Harvey, and Turnbull 2012; Danford and Richardson 2016). The 'pessimistic' perspective on partnership recognizes that management almost always drives the partnership, often with the threat of union derecognition, or of major workforce reductions, hanging in the background if the unions do not concur (Marks et al. 1998; Kelly 2005a). There is little evidence that partnership arrangements provide workers with genuine employment security (Oxenbridge and Brown 2002; Evans, Harvey, and Turnbull 2012)—see Insight into practice 6.2. Studies which compare workers in partnership organizations with those in similar non-partnership organizations indicate that for the most part it is the latter who have the more positive experiences (e.g. Badigannavar and Kelly 2004).

 Insight into practice 6.2: Partnership at Borg Warner

Studies of partnership agreements that consider how far they benefit employees are rare. Suff and Williams (2004), though, asked employees at Borg Warner in South Wales, a manufacturer of specialist components and systems for vehicles that has developed a celebrated partnership approach with the Amicus trade union, about whether or not they had benefited from it. The partnership agreement, known as the 'Margam Way', after the location of the plant, comprises a ten-point plan that, among other things, emphasizes the importance of transparency and good communications. Managers and union representatives cited the positive impact of partnership, in particular the way in which the development of cooperative relations enabled the business to grow.

What were employees' views though? How did they experience partnership in practice? Most of those surveyed (57 per cent) thought it had improved their working lives, and had enabled the union to participate more effectively in organizational decision-making. Thus there was general backing for the partnership approach. Nevertheless, despite the emphasis on communications many staff felt that they had limited influence over decisions that affected them at work. While partnership had increased their job security, on the whole people considered themselves to be insecure in their jobs, a reflection of the competitive market environment and the history of job losses at the plant. Job satisfaction was high, but generally employees did not see this as a product of the partnership agreement. Although partnership had to some extent helped to improve the reputation of Borg Warner as a 'good' employer, employees still exhibited a low level of trust in management.

In this case, a partnership agreement did produce some benefits for employees, and the plant had remained open, ensuring that some jobs were secured. However, it did not prevent extensive job losses from occurring during the 2000s, which generated an increased sense of insecurity among the workforce (Evans, Harvey, and Turnbull 2012). Moreover, the level of cooperation between management and employees was strictly bounded, and fell well short of that proposed by the 'mutual gains' model. The partnership agreement was dominated by management. Ensuring the competitiveness of the plant was used as a device for securing cooperation from shop stewards, resulting in reduced support for the union from a workforce who considered it to be ineffective at representing their interests (Evans, Harvey, and Turnbull 2012).

Efforts to capture the complexity of partnership in practice focus on how partnership agreements sometimes exhibit elements of all three perspectives. This was the case in the bank studied by Geary and Trif (2011). Some maintain that partnership needs to be understood as a complex and evolutionary process, a work in progress if you like, meaning that its effectiveness cannot just be reduced to a concern with the specific features of partnership agreements and their outcomes (Johnstone, Ackers, and Wilkinson 2009). Yet the overall assessment must be a negative one. Since they are arrangements that are designed to alter existing management–union relations, partnership agreements do little for the millions of workers without access to union representation (Badigannavar and Kelly 2004). Generally, the partnership agenda is firmly under the control of managements, and has for the most part been elaborated under conditions of union weakness (Terry 2004; Kelly 2005a; Danford and Richardson 2016).

Advocates of partnership point to its resilience at workplace level, and its capacity to deliver mutual gains in some circumstances, things that make it a highly relevant feature of contemporary employment relations (Johnstone 2015). Yet there is now a much less supportive political climate for partnership. The 2010–15 coalition government evinced little interest in advocating partnership in employment relations, being more concerned with promoting greater deregulation; and one of the first major acts of the 2015 majority Conservative administration was to enact legislation attacking trade unions—the Trade Union Act 2016 (see Chapter 3). Moreover, neither the nature of the labour market, which is increasingly marked by efforts to commodify labour (see Chapter 2), nor the financialization pressures associated with the development of a more 'disconnected' capitalism (see Chapter 5), provide much in the way of support for facilitating deep and long-lasting management–union collaborations. Increasingly short-term competitive pressures mean that partnership, however desirable, simply cannot be sustained in practice (Dobbins and Dundon 2015a; Simms 2015).

As the limits of the partnership approach became increasingly evident, it is notable that support for it dwindled among a new generation of trade union leaders who are more sceptical about the benefits of cooperating with employers. Some unions, the Rail, Maritime, and Transport (RMT) union for example, have been successful and grown in membership by explicitly challenging employers, and securing improvements in pay and conditions through being prepared to mobilize and engage in strikes and other forms of collective industrial action (Darlington 2009). Research undertaken in the Public and Commercial Services Union (PCS), another union that has eschewed partnership in favour of a more adversarial approach to advancing the interests of its members, demonstrates that strike action is associated with increases in union membership (Hodder et al. 2016).

6.3.3 Organizing unionism

In 1899, the Workers' Union's first full-time district organizer, Will Buchan, initiated a recruitment drive at Sir Thomas Lipton's City Road warehouses in London. The 1,300 workers were badly paid, and experienced poor working conditions. As Hyman (1971: 19) reports: 'Girls worked a 10-hour day with only one half-hour break, carrying heavy loads in unhealthy conditions; often they fainted, and the time lost was deducted from their wages'. Perhaps unsurprisingly, Buchan's attempts to organize these workers met with considerable success at first, and a new branch of the Workers' Union was established. As the union became more powerful, however, Lipton took measures to undermine its position, and dismissed many of the leading union activists among the workforce. By early 1900, union organization in the warehouses had collapsed (Hyman 1971). The Workers' Union was to go on to become one of the most important general unions in Britain during the first two decades of the twentieth century, eventually to become a part of the Transport and General Workers' Union (TGWU), which is now Unite. Nevertheless, its failure to secure a presence because of intense employer hostility at Lipton's warehouses in 1899 demonstrates that the process of organizing workers into unions can be a daunting task.

As this case shows, there is a long history of efforts to organize workers into unions in the UK (Simms, Holgate, and Heery 2013), although by the late twentieth century, union organizing activity had dwindled markedly (Beaumont and Harris 1990). In recent years, however, there has been an increased emphasis on how unions themselves can rebuild their strength and expand their membership through intensive and focused activity to expand their territories, by organizing new workers. The 'organizing unionism' approach, based on mobilizing workers collectively and challenging the interests of employers, serves as a model for union renewal (Byford 2011; Heery and Simms 2011; Heery 2015; Simms 2015). The increased focus on organizing activity has been called 'probably the most significant development in British trade unionism of recent years' (Simms, Holgate, and Heery 2013: 1).

The so-called 'organizing model' of trade unionism is marked by four key characteristics. First, 'organizing' is distinguished from straightforward 'recruitment' of new members because of its emphasis on 'union building': changing the culture of unions by fostering greater participation and activism among union members themselves (Bronfenbrenner and Juravich 1998; Simms and Holgate 2010a; Simms, Holgate, and Heery 2013; Heery 2015).

Second, organizing unionism is characterized by an emphasis on building unionization among groups of workers that the unions have largely neglected in the past, and who frequently suffer from labour market disadvantage (Simms, Holgate, and Heery 2013; Heery 2015). For example, the TUC has emphasized improvements in the representation of part-time and young workers (Heery 1998*b*; TUC 1997)—see Employment relations reflection 6.3 for prospects for unionization among young workers. In the United States, the organization of immigrant workers, particularly those from Latin America, is seen as crucial to the revival of the trade unions, notwithstanding the poor historical record of American unions in this area (Milkman 2000). There is also an associated concern with broadening the reach of trade unionism, manifest in efforts to extend union representation into non-union parts of the economy (Simms and Holgate 2010*a*).

Employment relations reflection 6.3:   Prospects for unionization among young workers

Unionization rates among young workers are low. Just 9 per cent of 16 to 24 year olds are union members, compared with 24.7 per cent of all employees (BIS 2016*b*). However, despite having largely neglected them in the past, trade unions are increasingly recognizing the importance of organizing young workers, by establishing dedicated youth sections for example (Hodder 2015). Research shows that this low union density does not reflect a more hostile attitude to trade unions on the part of young workers. In fact, they tend to be rather well disposed towards unions, but they often work in parts of the economy where union organization is either weak or absent entirely, like hotels and restaurants (e.g. Waddington and Kerr 2002; Freeman and Diamond 2003; Byford 2009).

Tailby and Pollert (2011) conducted a survey of around 500 young workers aged between 16 and 29. Despite workers having manifold problems and grievances, such as experiencing bullying or not receiving holiday pay to which they were entitled, their efforts to resolve issues at work on an individual basis were largely unsuccessful. Asked why they had not joined a union, the most common responses from workers were that there was no union present in their workplace, or that they had not been asked. There was 'almost no evidence of hostility to unions' (Tailby and Pollert 2011: 515). While the youngest group of workers—16 to 21 year olds—tended to be 'uninformed' and 'have no opinions' about unions, those aged between 22 and 29 were knowledgeable about unions, and expressed a 'relatively pro-union' stance (Tailby and Pollert 2011: 518).

Third, perhaps the most distinctive feature of organizing unionism is the use of a specialized cadre of skilled, professional organizers, whose role is to build union organization (Simms, Holgate, and Heery 2013). After examining developments in Australia and the United States, in the late 1990s the TUC established a dedicated 'Organizing Academy', whose purpose was to develop a 'cadre of specialist organizers' (Simms and Holgate 2010*a*). Union-sponsored trainees undertook a year-long training programme, combining classroom-based learning and real-life organizing activity with their union sponsors (Heery et al. 2000*b*; Simms and Holgate 2010*b*). The intention was that, on completing their training, participants should be well placed to become dedicated union organizers who are able to use their skills to expand union organization in Britain.

The fourth characteristic of organizing unionism concerns the use of innovative organizing tactics. These include 'mapping' the workforce in particular establishments, identifying those workers who are more susceptible to trade unionism, person-to-person recruitment techniques, and the choice of particular 'levers' or grievances that union organizers can use to build support (Heery et al. 2000*a*; Heery and Simms 2011; Simms, Heery, and Holgate 2013). An emphasis on the importance of collective mobilization, as a means of challenging employers' interests, is generally a prominent feature of organizing campaigns. Research shows that union organizers have used a 'set of arguments that stressed the value of collectivism and which were oppositional in their stance to the employer' (Heery and Simms 2011: 33).

Notwithstanding these features, there is some doubt about the extent to which a distinctive 'organizing model' operates in practice (Gall and Fiorito 2011). Some of the leading unions, the GMB general union for example, have not been involved in the Organizing Academy, sometimes preferring to establish their own initiatives (Heery and Simms 2008; Daniels 2009). Different unions use the organizing approach for different purposes (Simms and Holgate 2010b). This is evident when we look at the experiences of two unions that have successfully increased their membership—the Public and Commercial Services Union (PCS) and the Rail, Maritime, and Transport (RMT) union. Their approach to union organizing emphasizes 'collective workplace mobilization through industrial action' (Gall and Fiorito 2011: 238). Greater union effectiveness comes from a preparedness to threaten and engage in strikes and industrial action, based on the mobilization efforts of lay union activists against employers (Simms and Holgate 2010b). In the case of the RMT, for example, collective mobilization and strikes have manifestly helped to strengthen union organization in the London Underground (Darlington 2012).

There is some evidence that unions have used the organizing model effectively to secure recognition from employers. The Communication Workers Union (CWU), for example, was recognized by 'Typetalk', a not-for-profit call centre service operated as a joint venture between a charity and the telecommunications firm BT, following an intense organizing campaign. The language used to frame the campaign was carefully fashioned. A contrast was drawn between the progressive policies the organization pursued with regard to its client base and its opposition to unionization. Union organizers developed a 'language of "dignity", "fairness" and "respect", stressing union membership as a human right and emphasising that the rights of employees were ... equally important as the rights of clients' (Simms 2007: 125). They identified a series of specific grievances, such as health and safety problems, which they could use to mobilize support from the workforce for union recognition. The recognition campaign also involved the establishment of an organizing committee, comprising union activists, who took the leading role in recruiting new members and raising awareness of the union's activities. A key objective was to 'encourage activists to be independent of officials and to address their own problems' (Simms 2007: 127). As a result, the organizing campaign was rather successful, in the sense of securing the objective of union recognition, despite managerial opposition to unionization. That said, however, the emphasis in the Typetalk campaign of organizing in the workplace means that union activists there are not effectively integrated in the structures of the wider union (Simms 2007).

Elsewhere, though, the effectiveness of organizing unionism has often been hindered by a number of major constraints (see Heery and Simms 2008). The most important external obstacle has been employer opposition to union organizing initiatives (Heery and Simms 2011). Employer hostility to unionization in the charity Scope, for example, was a major reason why the organizing campaign there did not result in union recognition (Simms 2007).

Opposition from employers is not the only obstacle impeding the effectiveness of the organizing model, by any means. There are also some notable internal constraints within unions themselves. One is that organizing unionism demands considerable investment on the part of the unions involved (Simms 2003; Heery 2015; Simms 2015), something which is generally

lacking as resources are limited (Heery and Simms 2011). Moreover, internal union opposition to the development of an organizing approach is also relatively widespread (Heery and
Simms 2008). Servicing existing members is often viewed as more of a priority than organizing activity, the effectiveness of which is constrained as a result (Simms and Holgate 2010a;
Byford 2011). Where organizing activity does take place, there is a tendency for unions to
concentrate on consolidating their existing membership bases in sectors like manufacturing,
rather than attempt to take the resource-intensive step of seeking to organize workers in
areas of the economy where their presence is weak (Daniels 2009; Heery and Simms 2011).
A good example of such 'infill' activity (Simms, Holgate, and Heery 2013) concerns the efforts
of a union in the higher education sector to organize contract research workers in universities
(Badigannavar and Kelly 2005).

Two major difficulties with the organizing unionism approach can be identified. First, the
underlying assumption that workers are relatively easily organized, especially where they
have demonstrable grievances, is often mistaken (Heery and Simms 2008). As Badigannavar
and Kelly (2005) show in their study of contract university researchers, a number of factors,
including the extent to which workers blame their employers for their grievances, and the
degree to which they expect a union to remedy them, help to explain why some organizing
campaigns succeed whereas others fail. Organizing campaigns may also stall because the
workers concerned do not identify with the union. There are 'instances of women, members
of ethnic minorities and younger workers proving difficult to recruit because unions were not
perceived as "their" institutions' (Heery and Simms 2008: 35).

A second difficulty with the organizing unionism approach is the contradiction that exists
between, on the one hand, the need for union officials to exercise some degree of control
and, on the other hand, the emphasis on encouraging workers themselves to organize and
pursue unionization. Although without some degree of coordination from above it is difficult to see how unions can mobilize effectively to improve people's working lives, initiatives
designed by union leaderships to boost workplace unionism may be of limited effectiveness since they are perceived to be bureaucratic interventions and thus lack support on the
ground (Carter 2000). Perhaps the best way of characterizing organizing campaigns is to see
them as involving a degree of 'managed activism' (Heery et al. 2000c). To be effective they require coordination from above and management by union officials; but they also depend on
the participation and activism of the workers concerned for their success (e.g. Simms 2007).

The organizing unionism model has an explicitly outward-looking focus, given that a leading objective is to extend union organization into areas where it has hitherto been weak, and
thus offer representation to workers who would previously have lacked it. Yet it has faced
criticism on two fronts. One focuses on the reluctance of unions to embrace organizing unionism wholeheartedly, preferring to concentrate on building membership in areas of existing strength (Heery et al. 2003; Daniels 2009). From this perspective, organizing unionism,
while welcome, has not been sufficiently effective when it comes to reversing union decline.
It has 'at best stabilized union membership rather than generated renewal' (Heery and Simms
2011: 43).

A second, more profound criticism rejects organizing unionism as a route to union revitalization entirely. For Ackers (2015: 119), stronger workplace union organization is best achieved
by trying to work constructively and engage with employers, particularly through partnership, not by challenging them. Support for organizing unionism is based on the 'delusion' that

by engaging in 'militant conflict' unions can build support and thrive in the long term. Yet a key challenge for the unions is how they can expand their representative capacity to cover the millions of workers who would benefit from, but do not currently enjoy, independent and effective representation at work. A focus on organizing means that at least unions seek legitimacy by appealing to, and looking to advance the interests of, workers; this contrasts with the partnership approach, where unions are often more concerned with maintaining cooperative relationships with employers (Simms 2015).

6.3.4 Community unionism

There is also a further problem with the organizing approach to union renewal, which is that it is largely restricted to workplaces. The 'community unionism' approach, however, holds that trade union revitalization is contingent on unions being more outward looking, reaching out to extend their capacities beyond the workplace, in broader place-based communities, and thus being better positioned to advance the interests of working people. There is a growing recognition that in order to organize workers who suffer from labour market disadvantage more effectively, and to improve their livelihoods, the focus of union activity needs to extend beyond the workplace to encompass the wider communities in which workers live (McBride and Greenwood 2009; Holgate 2015b).

What has stimulated the growing interest in community unionism as a model for union revitalization? One reason concerns the difficulties faced by unions trying to organize in the workplace, particularly in a context of increased hostility from employers, and their consequent diminished power (Holgate 2015b). Moreover, a greater focus on organizing in place-based communities, rather than employer-controlled workplaces, could help unions to increase their membership. It 'may provide greater opportunities to engage with different groups of workers who might otherwise remain outside of the reach of the unions' (Holgate 2015a: 460-1). Community unionism offers better prospects for organizing and mobilizing low-paid and precariously employed workers, especially migrant workers and other groups of vulnerable workers, who have been particularly disadvantaged by the changes in employment and the labour market documented in Chapter 2 (Tapia and Turner 2013; Heery 2015; Alberti 2016b).

Three broad types of community unionism can be identified. The first concerns organizations that support and campaign on behalf of workers who experience labour market disadvantage. It is particularly evident in the United States. Perhaps the best known examples of this type of community unionism are the immigrant worker centres, organizations that work to improve the prospects of poorly paid, vulnerable, and disadvantaged workers (Fine 2006).

The second type of community unionism relates to how established trade unions themselves have tried to 'reposition themselves as community organizations' (Heery 2015: 442). This has involved unions attempting to develop more of a community-based dimension to their activities and engage more directly with the communities where people live and work, something that includes organizing and mobilizing efforts. However, there is a considerable degree of variation evident, with 'no single model or approach' prevalent, and unions often take very different approaches (Holgate 2015b: 449). The largest union in the UK—Unite—has developed a 'community membership' and 'community branch' scheme, for example, alongside its other more conventional activities (see the introductory case study).

The third type of community unionism has perhaps attracted the most interest from those concerned with union revitalization. This is the prospect for coalitions between unions and community organizations, and the extent to which they can help to advance the interests of workers by facilitating greater mobilization and increasing the bargaining power of unions (Wills and Simms 2004; Tattersall 2009, 2010; Holgate 2015*b*). Working in partnership with community organizations can 'add to the organizing and mobilizing capacity of unions, providing additional organizers and leaders and drawing upon their own networks to build support for organizing campaigns' (Heery 2015: 551). Perhaps the best example of this type of community unionism concerns the joint coalition working undertaken by the grass-roots community organization London Citizens and unions such as Unison, over the campaign for a living wage (Holgate 2009, 2015*b*). Engaging with community organizations in this way can enhance the mobilizing capacity of unions, giving them more power to achieve their objectives, in a way that advances the interests of workers (Tattersall 2009; Moore 2011).

Community unionism of this kind also implies that unions operate as part of broader social movements (Tapia and Turner 2013). The concept of social movement unionism sees trade unions as operating within, and contributing to, movements dedicated to promoting social and economic justice, including combating inequality. This encompasses global action designed to tackle labour rights abuses for example (see Chapter 11).

The rise of community unionism raises the prospect of trade union revitalization, based on unions' ability to engage with, and potentially represent, a more diverse workforce, thus helping to promote social and economic justice and tackling labour market inequality and disadvantage. Where unions can operate effectively in communities, beyond the confines of the workplace, it renders them less dependent on employers. There are some problems, however. The strength of the unions traditionally rests on their workplace organization. Too much of a focus on operating beyond the workplace, in wider communities, can raise its own difficulties. Workers can find themselves marginalized, for example, with reduced capacity to mobilize against their employer (Alberti 2016*a*; James and Karmowaska 2016). Community unionism is no panacea; nor should it be pursued at the expense of unions' traditional strengths. For one critic of community and social movement unionism, to 'remove unions from their workplace base and transform them into general leftist campaigning organizations is another recipe for marginalization and decline' (Ackers 2015: 120).

A second problem with community unionism concerns the way in which it has operated in practice. Unions have been reluctant to engage in coalitions with community organizations in anything other than a gradual, hesitant, and intermittent way (Fitzgerald 2009; Alberti 2016*a*). Holgate (2015*a*: 478) claims that 'deep' coalition building has been absent, with union involvement in community coalitions largely being dominated by just a narrow concern with boosting union membership.

Third, perhaps a more profound difficulty affecting coalition working between unions and community organizations concerns the pronounced cultural and structural differences that exist between them. The case of London Citizens shows the importance of 'relational power' to successful mobilization by community organizations, based on strengthening members' involvement and their leadership capacity. They have a culture which privileges the development of relationships, with successful mobilizing predicated on 'high levels of trust and loyalty towards other members and the organization'. Union activity, however, remains dominated by a 'service-driven culture', based on providing services to individual members—reflecting what union members want from their membership—in a way that can undermine the effectiveness of joint working (Tapia 2013: 671, 681; Holgate 2015a, 2015b). There has been some trade union opposition to working with community organizations on ideological grounds. Faith-based organizations are sometimes viewed as being prejudiced against gay people, for example (Holgate 2009). Collaboration has also been hindered by the belief that community organizations are not vigorous enough when it comes to challenging employers (Holgate 2015b).

 ### Section summary and further reading

- One way in which unions have sought to respond to decline has been to focus on extending and improving the services they offer to members, facilitated by the rationalization that has been prompted by extensive union merger activity. On its own, a 'servicing unionism' approach is unlikely to promote union revitalization. However, the effectiveness of servicing also has to be considered to the extent that it can stimulate collective mobilization.

- Partnership agreements offer unions the opportunity to consolidate their workplace presence by engaging and cooperating with employers. The concept of mutual gains which underlies partnership implies that employers, unions, and workers all benefit from partnership working. Generally, however, partnership agreements reflect union weakness and largely serve the interests of employers.

- There has been a marked revival of interest among unions in organizing workers, associated with the concept of 'organizing unionism'. Attempts to initiate novel organizing campaigns have come up against both external constraints, like employer opposition, and internal obstacles, such as a lack of resources.

- The 'community unionism' approach holds that building external solidarities, especially with place-based community organizations, is vital to union revitalization. Unions are better positioned to advance the interests of working people in a more precarious and unstable labour market. However, differences between unions and community organizations, and the lack of a direct connection with people's workplaces, can cause problems.

Simms and Charlwood (2010) provide a sound guide to the fortunes of the unions and union responses to decline. For overviews of the partnership phenomenon see Terry (2010: 291–3) and Johnstone (2015). The most substantial overview of the organizing approach is offered in the book *Union Voices* (Simms, Holgate, and Heery 2013); see also Simms (2015). For community unionism, see Holgate (2015b).

6.4 Non-union forms of employee representation

The decline in the 'single channel' of union representation has prompted an increased amount of interest in alternative methods of promoting worker voice—non-union systems of employee representation, like information and consultation arrangements for example. Would works councils, as found in many European countries, be an effective alternative? The German 'dual system' of employee representation (see International perspective 6.4), based on the formal separation of collective bargaining from participation rights, has received a considerable amount of attention (e.g. Towers 1997). This section is devoted to assessing the phenomenon of non-union systems of employee representation, explaining why this has become such an important employment relations topic.

International perspective 6.4: The system of works councils in Germany

Collective bargaining in Germany is largely conducted at multi-employer level between trade unions and employers' associations. Works councils (which can be established in any private sector company with five or more employees and which enjoy specific rights to information, consultation, and co-determination), however, are technically independent from the unions. Co-determination, which in effect allows the works council the right to reject management proposals, applies to 'social' issues, including payment methods, overtime arrangements, and the allocation of working hours. Works councils have information and consultation rights over matters pertaining to, among other things, the working environment, job design, and new technology, as well as information rights on financial issues. Nevertheless, their formal separation notwithstanding, the respective roles of unions and works councils generally overlap to a large degree (Gumbrell-McCormick and Hyman 2010). Works councillors are elected by the entire workforce, for a term of office of four years, and are obliged by law to cooperate with management 'in a spirit of mutual trust' for the benefit of employees and the establishment. However, the legacy of German unification, competitive pressures, and increasing demands from employers for greater flexibility, particularly over the determination of pay and conditions, may have weakened the system of works councils in Germany (Gumbrell-McCormick and Hyman 2010). Employers seem increasingly keen on finding ways to avoid having to deal with works councils (Gold and Artus 2015).

6.4.1 The development of non-union systems of employee representation

There is nothing new about non-union systems of employee representation; indeed, information-sharing and consultation arrangements can exist in unionized and non-unionized firms alike. Historically, though, consultation was viewed by trade unions as inferior to, and less desirable than, collective bargaining as a method of articulating workers' interests (Marchington 1994; Hall and Purcell 2012). This is because with consultation managers retain the right to make the final decision, whereas bargaining means managers may have to compromise and moderate their objectives to produce a negotiated, and thus jointly agreed, settlement to a problem or dispute.

The decline of union representation has prompted a growing level of interest in the role of non-union systems of employee representation as a means of promoting greater worker voice (Gollan 2007, 2010; Kaufman and Taras 2010; Gollan and Lewin 2013; Dobbins and Dundon 2014; Gollan et al. 2015). Generally, non-union employee representation arrangements are established by employers to enable managers to inform and consult with staff indirectly, often by means of elected or appointed employee representatives. They can be described as 'employer-sponsored bodies of formally organized employee voice' (Donaghey et al. 2012: 164). Companies like Pizza Express, B&Q, and Standard Life, which do not recognize unions and view maintaining their non-union status as desirable, have developed in-house arrangements for informing and consulting staff in the form of 'employee forums' or 'company councils'.

What has prompted employers to consider non-union systems of employee representation, in the form of arrangements that enable managers to inform and consult with employee representatives for example? One common motive stems from the concern to avoid union recognition (Dobbins and Dundon 2014). In other words, non-union employee representation arrangements serve to act as a substitute for union representation, helping to preclude an 'active union presence' (Gollan 2007: 104). Also, some of the enthusiasm for non-union systems of employee representation is linked to the introduction of the statutory union recognition procedure discussed in Chapter 5, and is best understood as an attempt to subvert unionization (e.g. Heery and Simms 2010).

However, there is a growing recognition that union avoidance is not the only motivation for establishing non-union systems of employee representation. They have also been developed as part of a sophisticated HRM approach to managing employment relations, one of which is designed to enhance business performance by giving workers more opportunity to express their voice at work (Dobbins and Dundon 2014; Gollan et al. 2015). Non-union systems of employee representation can be used to facilitate improved communications with staff, as a way of facilitating organizational change, or to improve levels of engagement (Gollan 2007; Hall and Purcell 2012; Gollan et al. 2015). The important extent to which non-union systems of employee representation are designed as managerial tools to promote the importance of cooperative employment relations and shared interests, in a distinctly unitary fashion, must be recognized (Butler 2009; Donaghey et al. 2012; Dobbins and Dundon 2014). However, the outcome of employee representation arrangements that stem mainly from the managerial aim of improving organizational performance is a highly restricted form of employee voice, one over which management enjoys significant control (Hall and Terry 2004).

Another important reason for the growing interest in non-union systems of employee representation relates to the introduction of European Union (EU) legislation concerning information and consultation rights for workers in areas such as redundancy and health and safety (Terry 2010; Hall and Purcell 2012). In public policy terms these developments were rather significant. For one thing, under certain circumstances employers became obliged to establish formal information and consultation arrangements, involving elected employee representatives—a marked shift in emphasis away from the previously voluntarist approach (Hall and Edwards 1999). Moreover, EU legislation has eroded the hitherto dominant single-channel system of employee representation. Perhaps its main effect, though, has been to articulate an increasingly pronounced framework of legal rights underpinning employee representation (Terry 2010). This is particularly evident when we consider two substantial pieces of EU legislation, brought in under the 'Social Chapter', which are specifically concerned with information and consultation arrangements: the Information and Consultation Directive (see Section 6.4.3) and the European Works Council Directive (Section 6.4.4).

Employment relations reflection 6.5:   Representing workers' interests beyond the workplace

Much of the interest in non-union forms of employee representation has justifiably been concerned with workplace-based arrangements such as systems for informing and consulting with staff. However, bodies which operate outside the workplace, in society at large, may also act in ways that help to protect and support the interests of workers. Civil society organizations (CSOs) include charities, pressure groups, and other non-governmental organizations. Some provide workers with advice, support, and legal representation. The gay rights organization Stonewall, for example, sometimes sponsors legal cases by workers who have been discriminated against at work on the grounds of their sexuality. CSOs lobby governments for legislative and policy changes that benefit workers, including better family-friendly working rights. They often work with employers to improve conditions for workers who frequently suffer from employment disadvantage, such as migrant workers. CSOs also sometimes campaign alongside trade unions to improve the pay and employment conditions of specific groups of workers, such as homeworkers (Williams, Abbott, and Heery 2011b).

Changes in the law, and the encouragement given to non-union arrangements, mean that the pattern of employee representation has become increasingly complex and fragmented (Gospel and Willman 2003). See Employment relations reflection 6.5 for details of how the activities of civil society organizations provide workers with voice. While the single channel of union representation remains important in some areas—in the public sector, for example, and among large private employers—its significance has decidedly waned. Moreover, there is growing interest in the use of 'hybrid' or 'dual channel' employee representation arrangements (Charlwood and Terry 2007; Terry 2010; Dobbins and Dundon 2014). In these situations some employees in the same workplace have access to union representation, and others non-union arrangements, or no representation at all. Essex County Council, for instance, operates an employee forum alongside trade union recognition for collective bargaining (IDS 2011a).

In some cases, employers have pursued a strategy of 'double-breasting' when it comes to employee representation. This refers to instances where unions are recognized in some workplaces, but with non-union arrangements established in others (Dundon et al. 2015). Cullinane et al.'s (2012) case study of a British multinational and its Irish subsidiary provides a good example of 'double-breasted' employee representation in practice. The company pursued a determinedly non-union approach in its Irish operations, despite operating with union recognition in its home country base.

Yet despite the erosion of the single channel of union representation, even in unionized organizations, and the increasing evidence of 'hybrid' and 'double-breasted' approaches, union-based arrangements have not been driven out by non-union systems of employee representation (Dobbins and Dundon 2014). The most notable consequence of the diminishing significance of the 'single channel' of employee representation through collective bargaining by trade unions is that many employees—around a half—have no access to any representation at all (van Wanrooy et al. 2013b; Dobbins and Dundon 2014). Despite the supposed benefits for employers of having non-union systems of employee representation, their actual presence is rather uncommon.

6.4.2 Non-union systems of employee representation in practice

Studies of non-union systems of employee representation demonstrate how diverse they are in practice (Kaufman and Taras 2010; Gollan et al. 2015). In some cases, like that of Delta Airlines for example, they are used as part of a long-term sophisticated HRM strategy which is designed to encourage employee participation (Kaufman 2013). There are examples where non-union systems of employee representation operate in ways that genuinely benefit the workforce. This was evident in the case of the telephone and online bank studied by Tuckman and Snook (2014). Here, employee representatives were able to use the employee forum, which had been initiated by human resources (HR), to engage in a form of bargaining with managers in a way that helped to protect the interests of the workforce. Generally, however, non-union systems of employee representation are inadequate substitutes for trade unions when it comes to articulating the interests of employees, and lack legitimacy as a result.

Non-union systems of employee representation, precisely because they are management tools, rarely have sufficient power to influence managerial decision-making, and are thus viewed by employees as ineffective arrangements for protecting and supporting their interests at work (e.g. Terry 1999; Lloyd 2001; Donaghey, Cullinane, and Dundon 2015). They are used as negotiating forums only very infrequently; workers may get some additional voice, but without the 'muscle' to enforce it (Kaufman and Taras 2010: 268). In a study of non-union employee representation at the Eurotunnel call centre, Gollan (2003) discovered that managers largely saw the company council as a vehicle for communicating information to staff rather than giving them voice. Most employees surveyed 'stated that the company council was not effective in representing general employee interests' (Gollan 2003: 537).

Kaufman and Taras (2010) maintain that non-union systems of employee representation can produce some positive benefits for employees, because it is in the employer's interest for them to do so. Their very existence means that workers will expect to be able to express their voice or have their interests represented; if this not does happen, they will lack legitimacy and fall into disrepute as a result, with adverse consequences for morale and the increased prospect of unionization. The case of 'Web Bank' highlights the importance of ensuring that non-union systems of employee representation provide workers with genuine opportunities to influence managerial decision-making if they are to endure (Johnstone and Wilkinson 2015). Sustaining them, however, and ensuring that they operate in ways that match employees' expectations, present major challenges (Kaufman and Taras 2010; Donaghey et al. 2012; Dobbins and Dundon 2014).

Some of the challenges inherent in operating non-union systems of employee representation are evident from Butler's (2009) case study research in a bank and a company making refrigeration products. In the latter, financial difficulties, and the priority placed by the firm on the need for speedy decision-making, meant that consultation became less important, and the non-union employee representation system was marginalized as a result. The initially 'proactive approach to consultation was frustrated by financial imperatives and ultimately both sets of workers viewed consultation as a marginal, remote and peripheral exercise' (Butler 2009: 210). The highly competitive environment in which the bank operated meant that it had to take decisions, for instance over branch closures, quickly. Employees were critical of the quality of the consultation process and felt that the non-union system of employee representation operating in the company lacked sufficient influence over managerial decision-making processes.

For these reasons, then, non-union systems of employee representation are generally perceived by workers to be ineffective substitutes for a union presence, often because they become restricted to straightforward information-sharing (Gollan 2007; Donaghey et al. 2012). In both Eurotunnel and South West Water, for example, attempts to replace unionized systems of employee representation with non-union arrangements proved to be unsuccessful, as unions regained recognition rights (Bonner and Gollan 2005; Gollan 2007). Although they can sometimes produce initial benefits for employees, the effectiveness of non-union systems of employee representation often diminishes over time because of an unsupportive climate, a lack of employee influence, and insufficient independence from management (Donaghey et al. 2012; Gollan and Kalfa 2015).

6.4.3 The Information and Consultation of Employees Regulations

One key piece of EU legislation dealing with information and consultation matters is the Information and Consultation Directive, which was agreed in 2002 and implemented in the UK by means of the Information and Consultation of Employees (ICE) Regulations 2004. This legislation was highly significant, in theory at least: for the first time most employees in the UK became covered by a comprehensive statutory framework governing rights to information and consultation (Hall et al. 2013; Butler et al. 2015; Hall, Purcell, and Adam 2015). The purpose of the Directive was to ensure that employers have arrangements in place for informing and consulting with their staff. The legislation establishes the circumstances under which employers may be obliged to inform and consult with employee representatives over certain matters, including likely employment changes, and to ensure that staff are kept informed about matters like business performance. Consultation is defined as 'the exchange of views and the establishment of dialogue' (Hall and Purcell 2012: 55–63).

Lobbying from employers meant that one of the Labour government's main objectives when designing the ICE Regulations was to ensure that firms were given a considerable amount of flexibility over their information and consultation arrangements (Hall 2006; Hall and Purcell 2012; Hall, Purcell, and Adam 2015). The 'way the regulations are drawn up in the UK gives considerable freedom to choose the form and frequency of consultation' (Purcell and Hall 2012: 7). An additional feature of the government's approach to implementing the Information and Consultation Directive was to stress the positive contribution that employee involvement can make to business performance (Gollan and Wilkinson 2007). In other words, arrangements for informing and consulting staff should be viewed primarily as managerial tools, designed to help employers realize their business goals, not to enhance the representation of workers' interests in the employment relationship (Hall and Purcell 2012).

The implementation of the ICE Regulations was staged. Initially in April 2005 they applied to employers with 150 or more employees; coverage was extended to all employers with fifty or more employees in 2008. The main features of the Regulations include the following:

- There is no automatic obligation on employers to establish arrangements for informing and consulting with employees or their representatives; at least 10 per cent of the workforce must submit a written request, either to the employer or to a state body—the Central Arbitration Committee (CAC).

- In the event of a valid request, arrangements must be put in place to enable appropriate employee representatives to be elected or appointed.

- The employer and employee representatives then have six months to reach a negotiated agreement governing the operation of information and consultation arrangements.

- In some circumstances an employer is entitled to claim that employees are already covered by appropriate information and consultation arrangements. So-called 'pre-existing arrangements' must satisfy certain conditions (e.g. they have to be in writing and cover all employees).

- Where there is a pre-existing arrangement in place, any request to change it must be supported by a majority of employees in a ballot, and by at least 40 per cent of all those eligible to vote (including abstainers).

- Where a valid request is made, but is ignored by an employer, or where negotiations do not produce an agreement within the six-month time period, then a default statutory model procedure for information and consultation, as prescribed by the Regulations, applies.

The UK government's 'minimalist' approach to implementing the legislation in a way that prioritizes business flexibility means that it is unlikely to enhance the representation of workers' interests through stronger provisions for information and consultation (Hall and Purcell 2012: 82). For one thing, there is no automatic 'right' of employees to be informed and consulted; employers need not do anything unless the 10 per cent 'trigger' is pulled—a rather unlikely prospect for the most part (Hall and Purcell 2012; Dobbins and Dundon 2015b; Hall, Purcell, and Adam 2015). Employers enjoy plenty of latitude to avoid having to institute information and consultation arrangements even where there is substantial demand from employees (Cullinane et al. 2015). Moreover, there is no formal role envisaged for trade unions (Terry 2010; Hall and Purcell 2012).

The ICE Regulations also permit employers to obtain their employees' agreement to 'direct' forms of information and consultation—that is, directly between managers and staff, without the need for employees to have representatives to act on their behalf (Dobbins and Dundon 2015b). This is consistent with the government's view that informing and consulting with employees should primarily be seen as a means of involving staff, improving their commitment to organizational goals, and thus enhancing business performance, and not as a means of enabling them to have their interests represented more effectively. With the exception of the default model, there is nothing in the Regulations governing the structure and content of information and consultation, whether they are pre-existing arrangements or those negotiated under the Regulations (Hall and Purcell 2012). The ICE Regulations, therefore, 'give substantial latitude to employers, either to do nothing, or to design a consultative arrangement in whatever way they want' (Purcell and Hall 2012: 13). Perhaps unsurprisingly, then, research into the impact of the ICE Regulations shows that at best they have only had a 'very limited' effect in stimulating new consultation arrangements (van Wanrooy et al. 2013b: 61).

Where firms do operate information and consultation arrangements, it is generally for internal managerial reasons, such as avoiding trade unions (Hall et al. 2013). There are signs of 'considerable voluntary activity in terms of reviewing, modifying, and introducing information and consultation arrangements but this has largely been employer-led', not a direct result of the legislation (Hall and Purcell 2012: 112). This is consistent with a 'risk assessment' rather than 'compliance' approach (Hall 2006). In other words, employers have been concerned with reviewing, altering, and strengthening their existing information and consultation practices in the light of the new legislation, rather than with having to take action to ensure that their arrangements comply with it. This was the case with the retail chain B&Q, which revised its 'Grass Roots' system of employee consultation partly as a consequence of the ICE Regulations (Hall 2005). While some employers have taken purposive action to improve their information and consultation arrangements, including allowing employees and their representatives to exercise an influence over the results, this has been driven by 'internal organizational dynamics' and not the legislation, the effect of which has been 'largely periph-eral' (Hall et al. 2013; Hall et al. 2015).

Although the ICE Regulations provide unionized employers with an opportunity to chal-lenge existing union-based representation arrangements centred on collective bargaining, there is not much sign that this has actually happened in practice (Hall et al. 2015). Alter-natively, the legislation may provide unions with an opportunity to secure a foothold in non-union firms by organizing a request for information and consultation arrangements, for example, or by using information and consultation machinery as a platform for union representatives. Yet research on the impact of the ICE Regulations has found little evidence that unions have taken advantage of the legislation to develop and expand their presence in non-union workplaces (Hall et al. 2015).

There is little to suggest, then, that the ICE Regulations will do much to advance the rep-resentation of workers' interests in employment relations; information and consultation ar-rangements are generally tightly controlled by employers. On paper, employees would seem to have much stronger rights to be informed and consulted by their employers than in the past. However, in reality, these supposed rights are highly circumscribed, given the extensive control over information and consultation arrangements enjoyed by employers and manag-ers, the 'continued managerial indifference to employee representation and ... preference for unilateral managerial action', the lack of effective enforcement arrangements, and the continued weakness of trade unions (Terry 2010: 294).

6.4.4 European works councils

European works councils (EWCs) are transnational arrangements for informing and consulting with employee representatives on a Europe-wide basis. In 1994 the EU agreed legislation—the European Works Council Directive—which provides for the establishment of transnational information and consultation machinery in 'community-scale undertakings'—multinational companies that employ at least 1,000 employees in the European Economic Area (EU member states plus Iceland, Norway, and Liechtenstein), including at least 150 in each of two or more of these countries. The purpose of the EWC Directive was to promote more effective information and consultation arrangements in multinational firms operating in Europe (Waddington 2011a).

The completion of the Single European Market, and the process of internationalization it encouraged, meant that there was greater pressure to institute arrangements that would allow employees to influence corporate decisions increasingly being made at a European level (Hall and Marginson 2005). The EWC Directive aimed to ensure that worker repre-sentatives are informed and consulted about matters with a transnational bearing including, among other things, the economic and financial situation of the firm, likely employment trends, the implications of investment decisions, and substantial changes to working meth-ods and production processes.

Strong importance was attached to allowing firms to operate arrangements that suited their particular circumstances. Thus Article 13 of the EWC Directive gave multinational com-panies operating in Europe scope to develop their own machinery for informing and con-sulting with worker representatives (Timming and Whittall 2015). Until 1996, they were able to establish arrangements which could be 'tailored to the circumstances of the enterprise'

(Carley and Hall 2000: 105). Over 400 'Article 13' agreements, as they became known, were eventually concluded, in firms such as Deutsche Bank and Unilever. Because the EWC Directive was enacted under the 'Social Chapter' (see Chapter 3), the UK did not come under its aegis until 2000, after the Labour government under Tony Blair reversed the 'opt-out' secured by John Major, his Conservative predecessor as prime minister. Nevertheless, a number of UK firms which had a substantial presence in other European countries, and were thus obliged to set up transnational information and consultation machinery for staff there (United Biscuits, for example), extended the coverage of their EWCs to the UK voluntarily.

After 1996, firms could no longer take advantage of 'Article 13' agreements; that route was closed. Instead, the mechanism for establishing EWCs is specified in Article 6 of the Directive, and involves the establishment of something called a 'special negotiating body' (SNB). Firms that meet the definition of a 'community-scale undertaking' are obliged to institute an SNB on receiving a written request from 100 or more employees, or their representatives, in at least two EU member states; or they can set one up voluntarily themselves. The purpose of the SNB is to determine the constitution and procedure of the EWC, including its coverage (what areas of the firm and which employees will it cover?), its scope (what issues will it handle?), its composition (e.g. the balance between managerial and employee representatives, and the process for choosing employee representatives), and how it is intended to operate (e.g. the timing and format of EWC meetings), subject to certain minimum specifications set out in the Directive. If the SNB process fails to reach agreement on how the EWC should operate, or where an employer ignores a valid request to establish an SNB, the EWC Directive lays down a default model, in the form of a set of 'subsidiary requirements' which have to be applied, such as a minimum of one meeting each year. While there are no reported cases of the EWC's subsidiary requirements being put into effect, the content of so-called Article 6 agreements often resembles them in important respects (Hall and Marginson 2005: 206), suggesting that SNBs use them as a model when negotiating their own firm-specific arrangements. See Insight into practice 6.6 for the details of an EWC agreement at UK-based multinational Diageo.

 Insight into practice 6.6:   The EWC agreement at Diageo

Diageo is a UK-based multinational drinks company whose brands include Baileys, Guinness, and Johnnie Walker. In 1998 it negotiated an EWC agreement with employee representatives, establishing the Diageo Europe Forum. The agreement was revised in 2002, following further negotiations between the company and employee representatives. The Forum, which meets once a year, comprises two senior management representatives and thirty-five employee representatives, drawn from across the company's European operations, though nearly half come from the UK (with ten representatives) and Ireland (seven). Half of the UK's representatives are trade union representatives, mainly from Diageo's Scottish operations, and half are non-union representatives, mainly from London. The Forum is designed to act as a vehicle by which Diageo can inform and consult with employee representatives on matters relating to, among other things, business performance, company strategy, the employment situation, organizational change, and the introduction of new working methods and production processes. While the approach to consultation is restricted to that laid down by the original EWC Directive, namely the 'exchange of views and establishment of dialogue', the Diageo agreement also specifies that the views of employee representatives must be heard, and that managers should respond to them in a timely fashion.

Sources: EIRO (2002); European Works Council database

Consultation was limited by the Directive to 'the exchange of views and establishment of dialogue' between management and employee representatives (Carley and Hall 2000: 105), and few companies went beyond this when instituting Article 13 EWCs (Marginson et al. 1998: 25). Panasonic, for example, emphasized that the scope of its EWC was strictly limited to 'consultation' as defined in the Directive (Kalman 1999). Trade union bodies criticized this element of the EWC Directive, contending that consultation obligations should be strengthened, something that has informed their approach to the revision of the EWC Directive (described later in the section). In particular, they argued that there should be a greater onus on firms to respond to proposals put forward by employee representatives in EWC meetings.

In May 2016, the European Trade Union Institute's (ETUI) EWC database recorded 1,093 active councils, across 1,026 multinational companies (MNCs) (some firms are covered by more than one body). Just under two-fifths of eligible multinationals have an EWC in place (remember that there is no obligation on companies to establish an EWC without a valid request being made that triggers the SNB process). However, the growth in the number of new EWCs has slowed, as smaller MNCs seem less inclined to accommodate requests (Jagodzinski 2011).

Studies of EWCs show that they are marked by a high degree of variation, especially over the degree to which employee representatives are informed or consulted (Timming and Whittall 2015). There are a number of competing influences on the way EWCs operate in practice. As shown later in this section, a firm's product market strategy can exercise an important effect. EWCs tend to be more active in companies which have highly integrated, internationalized operations, relative to those whose product lines are more diverse and nationally oriented. The influence of the multinational's home country is also important; EWCs in UK-based companies, for example, tend to be less active than those whose headquarters are in France or Germany (Hall and Marginson 2005).

There are three major reasons why EWCs, as provided for by the original EWC Directive, have been inadequate arrangements for improving the representation of workers' interests at a transnational level. First, they lack the power to influence managerial decisions effectively. This was evident in the case of the Swedish multinational companies studied by Huzzard and Docherty (2005), for example. Waddington (2006) surveyed EWC worker representatives in the engineering sector. In general, they did not consider that their respective EWCs had much of an influence over managerial decisions.

Second, linked to this, the absence of a formal role for trade union representatives can contribute to the ineffectiveness of EWCs. One of the main weaknesses of the original EWC Directive was that it did not provide for a formal trade union presence. Not only did this lead to a perception that EWCs were insufficiently powerful relative to management (Waddington 2006), but it may also have helped to legitimize union-avoidance tactics. Panasonic, for example, needed to establish arrangements to select employee representatives to its EWC from its non-unionized sales company. Instead of extending union recognition, it chose to establish a new non-union consultative committee from which the EWC delegates could be nominated (Kalman 1999).

Third, studies of how EWCs operate indicate that in general they are seen by employers as a means of helping them realize their business objectives, rather than as arrangements that help to ensure that, through a process of genuine consultation with their representatives, workers have their interests protected. EWCs tend to be used by senior managers as vehicles for communicating with staff, helping to disseminate information and legitimize managerial decision-making (Redfern 2007; Waddington 2011*a*; Timming and Whittall 2015). The security firm G4S, for example, claims its EWC is a 'really useful communications channel', although employee representatives have noticed a greater willingness by management to listen to their views (IDS 2011*a*). The EWC representatives surveyed by Waddington (2011*b*) rated the quality of consultation by managers as poor, with the councils used largely as vehicles for information-sharing. Interviews with worker representatives in a UK-based manufacturing company pointed to 'a concerted effort on the part of central management to use the EWC as a means by which to communicate the need for restructuring, to build company culture and to co-ordinate a Europe-wide strategic HRM policy' (Timming 2007: 255).

Article 13 agreements, in particular, tend to be used as managerially-led devices to stimulate improved business performance through better communication with employees. In the case of the fast-food chain McDonald's, for example, the EWC was used by the company as 'just another institution to be captured for management; another method of "getting the message across"' (Royle 2000: 193). In such cases, EWCs are primarily used as one of a range of techniques designed to improve the management of human resources in multinationals, rather than as arrangements for strengthening worker representation at a transnational level. There are further factors, moreover, that limit the representational capacity of EWCs. Generally, there are few formalized arrangements that enable EWC representatives to forge effective relationships with national-level systems of information and consultation (Waddington 2006). The activity of worker representatives is often overly influenced by a national frame of reference, reflecting conditions in their home countries, rather than a genuinely transnational mode of understanding—though this may be changing as representatives develop a more 'European' outlook (Waddington 2006).

It would be wrong, though, to imply that EWCs have made no contribution to enhancing the representation of workers' interests at transnational level. Although the original EWC Directive did not provide the unions with a formal role, the presence of union representatives on many EWCs gives these bodies some degree of independence from managerial control (Waddington 2011*a*). Furthermore, in some cases union representatives have used EWCs as mechanisms for building networks of international cooperation and information-sharing (Huzzard and Docherty 2005; Waddington 2011*a*; Timming and Whittall 2015). Yet some notable difficulties exist in practice. This was clear in the case of a multinational manufacturing and merchanting company. Genuine consultation was rare; managers came to EWC meetings to report on decisions that had already been made. Delegates had no opportunity to challenge managerial decision-making or to influence decisions. A frustrated British representative claimed: 'We should be able to challenge things. What happens now is we are just told things. The unions put forward an alternative plan and the company ignores it. That surely isn't right?' (quoted in Wills 2000: 94).

It is important to recognize that the effectiveness of EWCs varies according to the presence of specific factors, particularly the extent to which production and other operations are integrated transnationally (Hall and Marginson 2005). In his study of six UK-based multinationals, for example, Redfern (2007) found that EWCs were more active, in terms of networking and information-sharing between representatives, in unionized companies with a single product line and a Europe-wide management structure. In the highly internationalized and integrated vehicle manufacturing sector, the trade unions have used EWCs as the building blocks of a stronger, more transnational union movement (Greer and Hauptmeier 2008). The quality of information-sharing and consultation is better where senior union representatives are involved with the EWC (Waddington 2011*a*).

Undoubtedly, EWCs 'have become an established feature of the international employment relations landscape' (Hall and Purcell 2012: 53). However, the extent to which they are able to operate in ways that advance the interests of workers at transnational level largely depends on the capacity of trade unions to cooperate across national borders and use them as vehicles for enhancing international labour solidarity. The revised ('recast') EWC Directive, which took effect in 2011, helps in this respect. Among other things, it provides for a greater trade union role and establishes stronger, clearer, and more detailed obligations on multinationals when it comes to the process of information-sharing and consultation (Waddington 2011*a*: chapter 7). Employee representatives have greater scope to express their views, and to have them taken into account by the employer before organizational decisions are made, rather than just over how they are implemented (Jagodzinski 2011: 210–12; Hall and Purcell 2012: 63–4).

 ## Section summary and further reading

- The decline in the 'single channel' of union representation has prompted an increased interest in alternative methods of promoting worker voice—non-union systems of employee representation, like information and consultation arrangements for example.

- Union avoidance has typically been an important reason for the development of non-union systems of employee representation. However, there is growing evidence that their use is predicated on a sophisticated HRM approach to managing employment relations, designed to enhance business performance by giving workers more opportunity to express their voice at work. Nevertheless, non-union systems of employee representation are generally used to enhance managerial prerogative, not to give workers adequate independent representation of their interests.

- The Information and Consultation of Employees (ICE) Regulations implement an EU directive which is designed to ensure that staff have access to information and consultation arrangements. However, the government transposed the directive in a way that minimizes its impact, not least the requirement that at least 10 per cent of employees make a written request for information and consultation arrangements before an employer is required to do anything.

- While there are signs that in some cases EWCs have developed their own distinctive agenda, and can operate in ways that support the transnational representation of workers' interests, overall the experience of EWCs in this respect has generally been rather disappointing. Indeed, they are often used more as additional channels which multinational companies can use to communicate with staff.

Hall and Purcell (2012) provide an extensive study of consultation in employment relations. The most extensive study of non-union systems of employee representation is Gollan (2007). But also see Dobbins and Dundon (2014) and Kaufman and Taras (2010) for good overviews. See Dobbins and Dundon (2015*b*) for an overview of the ICE Regulations. For EWCs, Timming and Whittall's (2015) overview is recommended.

6.5 Conclusion

For many years trade unions have been responsible for representing workers' interests. By virtue of their collective organization, unions can provide individuals with protection, or insurance, against problems at work. They also bargain with management on behalf of their members, seeking to alter the terms of the wage–work bargain in favour of their members. Unions operate in the workplace itself, where the lay union representative, or shop steward, not only negotiates with management, but also advises, supports, and represents his or her members. Finally, unions represent the interests of workers in the wider political arena, for example by influencing the legislative process. Nevertheless, the complex nature of workers' interests poses considerable challenges for unions as they attempt to carry out their representative functions. Workers generally want protection for themselves as individuals, but this requires collective action to be effective. Unions must therefore demonstrate their relevance to individuals, while at the same time operating as a collective agency on behalf of what may be a considerably diverse membership.

Perhaps the most important implication of this overview of employee representation in the workplace is that it is not representation mechanisms, by themselves, that give workers influence over the decisions which affect their working lives, but those that are effective (Kelly 1998). Non-union systems of employee representation are generally used as management tools to improve communications, or to avoid a union presence. They lack the power and legitimacy of agencies that are independent of the employer, like trade unions, and thus do not help to offer workers adequate representation of their interests. And although a trade union presence is a necessary condition of effective representation, it is not a guarantee.

What are the prospects for union revitalization? Clearly, providing members with services, including representational and bargaining services, is an essential function of any trade union. However, the unfavourable climate in which trade unions operate, marked by greater employer hostility (see Chapter 5), means that the servicing approach, on its own, is unlikely to improve unions' prospects. Unions often have to engage with employers in a cooperative fashion, if only to secure a presence. The concept of 'partnership' has become popular among union leaderships specifically because, in a hostile environment, cooperation with employers is seen as the most effective way of guaranteeing 'institutional security'. Clearly a union presence, however constrained, is important. Without it, workers would have little protection against threats to their pay and employment conditions. However, given the large extent to which they are driven by employers, partnership agreements do not seem to be very effective mechanisms for advancing workers' interests and promoting union revitalization beyond their existing strongholds.

Under the organizing unionism approach the prospects for union revitalization are brighter. This is because, unlike the servicing and partnership models, which are essentially about consolidation, organizing is explicitly concerned with growing trade unionism, by recruiting and mobilizing new members. That said, though, the impact of organizing unionism has been rather limited, not least because of the difficulties caused by employers. Understandably, then, the community unionism approach, which involves unions engaging in mobilizing working people and advancing their interests beyond the workplace, and thus outside the control of employers, has proved to be an attractive means of attempted revitalization. While the development of a community-based focus has the advantage of widening the appeal of trade unionism, there is a potential danger that unions become too neglectful of workers' interests in the workplace.

Assignment and discussion questions

1. Critically assess the proposition that: 'workers no longer need to be represented at work by a trade union or other body since, in the twenty-first century, management fully take account of the needs and views of workers when making decisions that affect them'.

2. Critically evaluate the main reasons for the overall decline in union membership between the 1980s and 2000s.

3. Why have some unions promoted partnership? What do workers and unions gain from partnership agreements? What are the main drawbacks of partnership agreements when it comes to advancing the representation of workers' interests?

4. You have been asked to advise a trade union on how it might go about recruiting younger workers into membership. In small groups, or by talking to friends, identify what younger people want from employment, and explain what unions could do to meet these needs.

5. What are the main strengths and weaknesses of non-union arrangements for promoting employee representation at work?

 Visit the Online Resource Centre that accompanies this book to develop your understanding of this chapter and keep up to date with the latest developments in this area.
www.oxfordtextbooks.co.uk/orc/williams4e/

 Chapter case study: Community unionism in action—the '3 Cosas' campaign at the University of London

The campaign for better pay and conditions and union recognition among outsourced contract workers—cleaners, security staff, and maintenance workers—at the University of London points to the positive impact that a purposeful community focus can have on ensuring that low-paid and vulnerable workers are able to advance their interests. The 3 Cosas ('things' in Spanish) campaign commenced in 2011 when a group of largely Latin American workers, working at the University of London's administrative headquarters but actually employed by external contractors, initiated a drive for improved sick pay, holiday pay, and pension entitlements, in line with those received by workers directly employed by the University. During 2013–14 the campaign developed, involving a mixture of workplace and community-based activities. There were three instances of conventional strike action, for example, focused at the level of the workplace, and involving cleaners, porters, and maintenance staff. But there was also an important 'community' dimension to the workers' action. This involved the 'development of a campus-based coalition including a range of political and community allies', such as the students union, academic staff, and organizations of migrant workers. Allied to this, the campaign also included a notable 'social movement' element, in that it involved the extensive use of social media to mobilize support among the public, both within the University and beyond (Alberti 2016b: 92). Demonstrations were used as an effective means of raising wider awareness of the dispute, and of putting pressure on the university and its contractors to meet the workers' demands.

As a result of the campaign the workers did win better sick pay, longer holidays, and access to improved pension arrangements, albeit not the same level of entitlements as for directly employed staff. It is clear that the university found the adversarial campaigning approach pursued by the workers troublesome, as did the workers' union, Unison, which withheld its support from the campaign, and, in conjunction with university management, sought to portray the gains secured by

(continued...)

the workers as a victory for moderation and its ability to negotiate an effective deal. Yet without the strikes and demonstrations, it is unlikely that the university and its contractors would have made any concessions. Unison's lack of support for the 3 Cosas campaign resulted in around seventy workers leaving to form a new union—the Independent Workers Union of Great Britain (IWGB). By 2016 the IWGB had grown to over 600 members across the UK, mainly in London, with around 200 members in its University of London branch. The IWGB branch remains committed to the objective of winning for contract staff the same sick pay, holiday, and pension entitlements received by those who are directly employed. As an officially certified union it provides members with advice, representation, and support, including in grievance and disciplinary cases, and fights employment tribunal cases on behalf of members whose employment rights have been breached. The IWGB branch also pursues a fourth 'cosa', demanding that it be formally recognized for the purpose of collective bargaining. Not only would this help to protect the gains already secured by the union, but it would also better enable the IWGB to push for further improvements. One of the main lessons from the case is that successful union revitalization is contingent on a 'combination of workplace and community tactics', because of the way in which this helps to facilitate effective mobilization and collective solidarity (Alberti 2016*b*: 100).

Sources: Stopes (2013); Chakrabortty (2014); Alberti (2016*b*). The 3 Cosas campaign is on Facebook.

Question

To what extent, and in what ways, can a greater community focus assist trade union revitalization?

7 Pay determination and employment relations

Chapter objectives

The main objectives of this chapter are to:

- provide an overview of the development and contraction of collective bargaining;
- explore the reasons for the resilience of collective bargaining in the public sector;
- assess the ways in which employers have used their greater freedom to manage arrangements for pay determination; and
- examine efforts to tackle low pay, particularly the statutory National Minimum Wage and voluntary 'living wage' campaigns.

7.1 Introduction

Pay is at the heart of employment relations as a field of study: the 'receipt of a wage in return for an employee's labour under guidance of an employer's authority is the conventional definition of an employment relationship' (Grimshaw and Rubery 2010: 350). The purpose of this chapter is to look more closely at key developments in pay determination. In Section 7.2 the initial focus is on the joint regulation of pay through collective bargaining with trade unions. It covers the evolution, development, and decline of collective bargaining as a means of setting pay, set against an appreciation of the important degree to which collective bargaining has proved to be resilient in the public sector. Section 7.3 is concerned with one of the key implications of the diminution of collective bargaining, which is the increased level of unilateral managerial control over pay determination, particularly in private firms. The last major part of the chapter (Section 7.4) is devoted mainly to understanding efforts to mitigate low pay, with a particular emphasis on the background to, and the operation and consequences of, the National Minimum Wage, and also a concern with understanding voluntary 'living wage' campaigns.

Introductory case study: The National Living Wage dispute at HMRC

One of the major features of this chapter concerns government efforts to tackle low pay through statutory minimum wages. In April 2016, the UK Conservative government introduced a new 'National Living Wage' (NLW) of £7.20 per hour, giving workers aged 25 and over employed on the minimum wage a pay rise of 50 pence per hour. In theory, then, they should be better off as a result. However, this has not always been the case as employers try to offset the cost of the increased wages by cutting hours of work. This was the case on Merseyside in the north-west of England where cleaners working in the offices of Her Majesty's Revenue and Customs (HMRC), but employed by a contractor, the Danish headquartered multinational ISS, were told that their hourly pay would rise to the level of the NLW. However, because the company, which made a profit of £250 million in 2015, claimed it could not afford the increase in its wage costs, it chose to reduce workers' hours, leaving them no better off than before. In fact, some were worse off after the change because the loss of hours resulted in them losing tax credit and benefit payments. The irony is that HMRC is the government agency responsible for enforcing compliance with the NLW. However, HMRC washed its hands of all responsibility for the dispute, claiming that the cleaners' pay and conditions were a matter for their employer—ISS. Following a two-day strike, and further threatened strike action, in September 2016 ISS backed down, and agreed to reinstate the cleaners' hours.

Sources: Lawrence (2016a, 2016b, 2016c)

7.2 Collective bargaining and pay determination

Historically, most employees had their pay set through collective bargaining between employers, or employers' associations, and trade unions. One of the most notable recent developments in employment relations has been the diminished importance of collective bargaining as a pay-setting tool, particularly in the private sector. Nevertheless, collective bargaining, including multi-employer arrangements, has proven to be more resilient in public sector organizations, albeit mitigated by pressures for greater flexibility and occupational re-structuring. While the importance of collective bargaining as a means of determining pay has declined, it continues to influence earnings for millions of workers throughout the economy.

7.2.1 The evolution and development of collective bargaining

At the beginning of the 1980s, collective bargaining was the predominant method of pay determination in Britain (Marginson 2012), with over 70 per cent of employees covered by collective agreements (Daniel and Millward 1983). It found favour among employers, as well as among union leaders, because it enabled conflict to become 'institutionalized'—accommodated and contained within the bargaining relationship. The alternative was continuing instability and disorder as unions struggled to secure a presence. Thus the decision to recognize and bargain with unions reflected an acceptance on the part of employers that a union presence was inevitable—as the 'lesser of two evils' (Blyton and Turnbull 2004: 228). For much of the twentieth century, formally at least, collective bargaining commonly operated on a multi-employer, industry-wide basis. Moreover, national bargaining arrangements also became established across the public sector (Carter and Fairbrother 1999).

The main advantage of multi-employer arrangements for employers was that they could be used to exclude union influence from the workplace. However, the inadequacies of industry-level collective agreements enabled more localized bargaining to flourish in the private sector (Royal Commission 1968; Hyman 1975). During the 1950s and 1960s, in a climate of full employment, shop stewards in the engineering industry were able to negotiate with managers over bonuses, overtime arrangements, and incentive payments, and reach local settlements that were outside of, and in addition to, the industry agreements (Sisson and Brown 1983; Brown 2010).

The influence of multi-employer bargaining was inevitably eroded, and concerns about the consequences arose. The increasing gap between the rates agreed by means of industry-level bargaining and the actual earnings of workers, augmented by locally negotiated supplements—or 'wage drift' as it became known (Royal Commission 1968; Brown 1973)—was perceived to have inflationary consequences. In addition, informal workplace bargaining tended to 'sap management control over work' (Brown, Marginson, and Walsh 2003: 200), and generated a multitude of small-scale, often short industrial disputes which, taken together, were deemed by policy-makers to be detrimental to economic performance.

Although dominated by the experience of the engineering sector, the Donovan Royal Commission (1965–8) found that much of the blame for these problems could be laid at the door of management who, it was asserted, should take a greater degree of responsibility for shaping their own employment relations arrangements (Royal Commission 1968). While the extent of Donovan's influence is questionable—single-employer bargaining was rising in popularity anyway as employers sought to develop organization-specific arrangements—the 1970s saw a decline in the incidence of multi-employer bargaining (Brown 1981, 2010; Brown, Bryson, and Forth 2009).

7.2.2 The contraction of collective bargaining

Since the 1980s, there has been a marked diminution in the pay-setting role played by collective bargaining (Brown, Bryson, and Forth 2009; Marginson 2012, 2015). This contraction of collective bargaining has been expressed in three main ways: the substantial decline in the coverage of collective bargaining; the decentralization of bargaining where it does exist, manifest in the almost complete disappearance of multi-employer bargaining from the private sector; and a narrowing of the scope of collective bargaining.

First, with regard to the diminution of collective bargaining coverage, whereas in 1984 collective bargaining covered some two-thirds (66 per cent) of workplaces with twenty-five or more employees, by 2004 this had fallen to under a third (32 per cent). Moreover, over the same twenty-year period the proportion of employees covered by collective bargaining declined from 70 per cent to 39 per cent—see Table 7.1 for further details. While much of the decline occurred during the 1980s and 1990s, the contraction of collective bargaining coverage continued during the early 2000s (Brown and Nash 2008; Brown 2010). By 2011, collective bargaining was present in just 13 per cent of all workplaces with five or more employees, and just 7 per cent of private sector workplaces (van Wanrooy et al. 2013a). Only one in six (16 per cent) employees in the private sector was covered by collective bargaining—see Table 7.2. That said, though, the coverage of collective bargaining seemed to stabilize during the latter half of the 2000s; between 2004 and 2011 there was no further decline in

Table 7.1 The contraction of collective bargaining coverage, 1984–2004

	1984	1990	1998	2004
Workplaces with any collective bargaining (%)				
All workplaces	66	52	40	32
Private sector	47	38	24	16
Public sector	99	86	84	82
Employees in workplaces with any collective bargaining (%)				
All workplaces	70	54	42	39
Private sector	52	41	32	25
Public sector	95	78	67	79

Workplaces with 25 or more employees
Source: Brown, Bryson, and Forth (2009)

the proportion of private sector workplaces with collective bargaining, or that of employees covered by collective bargaining arrangements (van Wanrooy et al. 2013*b*). Table 7.2 shows that the proportion of all employees covered by collective bargaining declined between 2004 and 2011, from 28 per cent to 23 per cent, largely because of an apparently substantial fall in collective bargaining coverage in the public sector. Nevertheless, there remains a marked differentiation between collective bargaining coverage in the public sector, where it is still commonplace, and the private sector, where it has become much rarer. Collective bargaining and pay determination arrangements in public sector organizations are examined in Section 7.2.3.

There is a pronounced association between workplace size and collective bargaining coverage. Collective bargaining is rarer in smaller workplaces than in larger workplaces. Table 7.3 shows that whereas just 16 per cent of employees in workplaces with fewer than fifty employees are covered by collective bargaining, this proportion rises to 38.7 per cent of employees in larger workplaces, those with fifty or more employees. Collective bargaining coverage also varies extensively by industry sector. The most obvious variation is that between the private

Table 7.2 Changes in collective bargaining coverage, 2004–11

	2004	2011
Workplaces with any collective bargaining (%)		
All workplaces	15	13
Private sector	7	7
Public sector	70	57
Employees in workplaces with any collective bargaining (%)		
All workplaces	28	23
Private sector	16	16
Public sector	68	44

Workplaces with 5 or more employees
Source: van Wanrooy et al. (2013*a*), licensed under Open Government Licence v. 3.0

Table 7.3 Collective bargaining coverage by workplace size and industry sector, 2015

	Employees' pay covered by collective bargaining (%)
All	27.9
Workplaces with fewer than 50 employees	16.0
Workplaces with 50 or more employees	38.7
Public administration	61.3
Education	52.1
Electricity and gas	50.3
Transport and storage	46.2
Health and social work	37.3
Financial services	23.2
Manufacturing	21.2
Construction	15.2
Wholesale, retail, and motor trade	15.6
Hotels and restaurants	5.4

Selected industries

Source: BIS (2016*b*), licensed under Open Government Licence v. 3.0

and public sectors, as mentioned already. However, there are further variations in collective bargaining coverage which are worth noting. In some industries the presence of collective bargaining is rare indeed. Only around 5 per cent of hotel and restaurant employees, for example, are covered by collective bargaining, compared to around a half of workers in the electricity and gas and transport and storage sectors. These variations show that, while its coverage has clearly diminished substantially, collective bargaining continues to be present in many areas of the economy. In some parts of the private sector, such as in electricity, railways, and chemicals, collective bargaining has maintained an important influence, whereas in others, such as construction and food manufacturing, it has declined markedly (Brown 2010: 259).

What, then, accounts for the large-scale 'retreat' (Brown, Bryson, and Forth 2009: 31) of collective bargaining, particularly in the private sector? There are a number of factors which could plausibly explain the decline of collective bargaining, including the presence of a hostile legal and public policy environment during the 1980s and 1990s. Conservative governments of that period discouraged collective bargaining, a reflection of their espoused belief in individualism. It was portrayed as an archaic process that, by restricting managerial flexibility, undermined business performance. There may also have been a compositional effect. The changing composition of the workforce, in particular the increasing proportion of employees working in the private services sector, where collective bargaining had never been widespread outside a few sectors such as food retailing, may have contributed to the diminution of collective bargaining. Collective bargaining is also much rarer in newer workplaces—those established since the 1980s—than it is in older workplaces.

However, Brown, Bryson, and Forth (2009: 22) contend that the influence of such public policy and compositional effects on the 'collapse' of collective pay determination was limited. Collective bargaining coverage continued to decline even during the 2000s under Labour governments that offered it an ostensibly more favourable climate (Brown 2010). Moreover, just 10 per cent of the decline in collective bargaining coverage in the private sector is estimated to be attributable to compositional change. Instead, collective bargaining has diminished largely because of the rise of more competitive market conditions, including greater international competition, which have encouraged employers to pursue greater control and flexibility over pay determination (Brown 2010). Whereas for much of the twentieth century relatively slack product markets gave employers a certain degree of latitude when it came to pay, making them receptive to demands from trade unions for collective bargaining arrangements, since the 1980s increasingly tough market conditions and greater competition have forced 'employers to tighten their control over employment, of which reducing the leeway for unions and reducing their influence over the conduct of work is a part' (Brown, Bryson, and Forth 2009: 22).

While robustly expressed, this explanation for the decline of collective bargaining—based on the primacy of product markets, and intensified competition within them—is by no means entirely convincing. What about the role of actors like employers and unions, the choices they make, and the nature of the political-legal environment that shapes these choices (Marginson 2012)? These questions help to direct our attention to the diminution of union power in the private sector. Not only have unions been increasingly unable to secure bargaining arrangements in new workplaces, but employers have also attempted, often successfully, to exclude them from existing workplaces, in an effort to forge more direct relations with their staff. Thus the decline in collective bargaining coverage reflects the determination of managers to extend their prerogative to the area of pay determination, something that both was enabled by, and further contributed to, the frailty of the trade union movement.

The second major collective bargaining trend since the 1980s concerns the decentralization of pay bargaining activity. During the 1980s and 1990s, multi-employer bargaining in the private sector almost disappeared, except for a few industries like electrical contracting (Gospel and Druker 1998). Multi-employer bargaining now exists in only a very small proportion—just 2 per cent—of private sector workplaces (van Wanrooy et al. 2013b). Where collective bargaining prevails in the private sector, it is now almost always undertaken at single-employer level (Brown, Bryson, and Forth 2009; Marginson 2015). Although the importance of multi-employer bargaining had been dwindling well before the 1980s, that decade saw the termination of national agreements across a range of sectors, including retail banking, engineering, and food retailing (Brown and Walsh 1991; Brown, Marginson, and Walsh 1995). This trend continued into the next decade in such a way that multi-employer bargaining, 'which had greatly diminished in importance in the 1980s, became even more of a rarity in the 1990s' (Cully et al. 1999: 228). The principal reason for the decline of multi-employer bargaining concerned the ambition of firms to align pay more closely with business performance, and to exert greater control over pay outcomes in a more competitive environment. Without control over their own bargaining arrangements, firms found it difficult to secure increasingly necessary flexibility over pay (Brown and Walsh 1991; Brown, Marginson, and Walsh 2003; Marginson 2015).

The third key collective bargaining trend concerns its narrowing scope. Collective bargaining has become less about hard negotiation, and is more likely to take the form of managers sharing information with union representatives, or consulting with them, rather than actually negotiating. Particularly in the private sector, collective bargaining is marked by 'a lack of confrontation and by a more consultative style over a relatively wide range of issues'

(Brown and Nash 2008: 102). While the role of collective bargaining is most evident when it comes to pay-setting, it is also important to remember that the scope of bargaining can cover a potentially wide range of other employment issues, like holiday entitlement, for example, or grievance and disciplinary procedures. In the private sector, the scope of collective bargaining has narrowed markedly—the range of issues on which employers are willing to negotiate with trade unions fell substantially during the 2000s (van Wanrooy et al. 2013b; Marginson 2015). Evidently, it is not just the coverage of collective bargaining that has declined, 'but also its influence where it is still to be found' (Brown 2010: 262).

7.2.3 Collective bargaining in public sector organizations

While the extent of unilateral regulation of pay by managements has undoubtedly risen, this by no means implies that collective bargaining has become extinct. We have already seen that there is a widespread variation in the incidence of collective bargaining arrangements throughout the economy. In the public sector, collective bargaining, often of the multi-employer type, continues to exert a powerful influence over the determination of pay. In 2011, collective bargaining covered 57 per cent of public sector workplaces—see Table 7.2. However, this table also shows a marked decline in the coverage of collective bargaining in the public sector during the 2000s. Whereas 68 per cent of employees in public sector workplaces were covered by collective bargaining in 2004, by 2011 this had fallen to 44 per cent. This decline seems to be partly related to the greater role played by pay review bodies (PRBs) in determining pay and conditions in the public sector, especially in health (van Wanrooy et al. 2013b)—though some see the PRB process as a form of collective bargaining, rather than as supplanting it (see later in this section).

 Insight into practice 7.1: The erosion of national bargaining in the further education sector

National bargaining has been significantly eroded in the further education (FE) sector in England and Wales. FE colleges used to come under the control of their respective local authorities, who were the employers of college staff. Pay rates were negotiated nationally between representatives of the local authorities and the appropriate trade unions. Conditions of service were also determined by multi-employer bargaining at national level. The 'Silver Book' agreement—as it was called because of the colour of its cover—among other things set upper limits on the number of teaching hours that lecturers could work on a weekly and annual basis.

In 1993, the colleges were taken out of local authority control and, in a process called 'incorporation', became employers of college staff in their own right. It was anticipated that the newly established College Employers' Forum (CEF), an employers' association which took on the job of representing the colleges' employment relations interests, would continue to negotiate agreements with the unions, which would then apply throughout the sector. The CEF's leadership, however, developed an ambitious reform agenda. Since college budgets were to be squeezed, it proposed replacing the Silver Book with a 'flexible' contract that placed no specific limitations on college lecturers' workload. This provoked a lengthy and bitter industrial dispute as the main lecturers' union tried to resist the imposition of the new contracts. While some colleges were able to impose the CEF's contract, many introduced,

(continued...)

either unilaterally or after negotiations with local union representatives, a version of their own which included some workload limits. By the end of the 1990s, then, a large variety of different contractual arrangements existed in the sector.

Pay remained formally subject to national bargaining, although the inability or reluctance of many colleges to implement annual recommended awards in full—or at all in some cases—because of purported financial difficulties led to an increasingly disparate set of pay rates across the sector, as well as a number of industrial disputes. During the 2000s, attempts were made by both the employers and the unions to reinforce the authority of national agreements linked to the availability of more funds for the sector. Reinstating their influence, though, proved difficult, given the diversity of employment arrangements present in the college sector.

Source: Williams (2004)

During the 1980s and 1990s, Conservative governments encouraged the reform of pay determination arrangements in the public sector, in particular by promoting the desirability of greater local managerial flexibility. Decentralized bargaining was seen as complementing the devolution of operational decision-making to local managers, hence making employment relations more 'responsive to the needs of managerial efficiency and labour market conditions, and more sensitive to employee performance' (Winchester and Bach 1999: 45). During this period, however, national bargaining in the public sector proved to be rather resilient (Corby 2000). The main exception was the Civil Service, where responsibility for pay determination was devolved to individual executive agencies, such as the Benefits Agency. Change in the Civil Service was more profound largely because of the government's direct influence over employment relations arrangements—although even here decentralization was moderated by the desirability of exercising close control over pay settlements (Bach 2010; Bach and Kessler 2012). Elsewhere, except for further education colleges, where there were a specific set of factors that led to the erosion of national bargaining (see Insight into practice 7.1), the extent of decentralization was limited. In the health service, for example, efforts to promote local pay deals were undermined by a combination of management ambivalence and union opposition (Thornley 1998; Carr 1999; Bach and Kessler 2012).

During the 2000s, Labour governments focused their efforts on 'modernizing' pay arrangements in the public sector. In this context, 'modernization' involved tackling problems of gender inequality, putting more of an emphasis on linking pay with performance, and enabling greater local managerial flexibility over employee reward—all to be achieved through partnership working with relevant public sector trade unions (Bach and Kessler 2012). This was manifest in the development of national frameworks applying to broad pay and conditions matters; but they contained space to give managers sufficient flexibility at local level when implementing them. The best known example came in the health service. The ambitious 2004 'Agenda for Change' agreement established a highly centralized national pay and grading system, designed to be operationalized by managers in individual health service trusts (Bach 2010). These efforts to build in space for local flexibility notwithstanding, overall the Labour government's efforts during the 2000s to 'develop more integrated and coherent systems of pay determination' represented a shift towards greater centralized control over pay determination arrangements (Bach, Kolins Givan, and Forth 2009: 323).

Nevertheless, there was one further aspect of the modernization agenda in public sector employment relations which encouraged localization, namely the greater use of 'assistant' roles, such as teaching assistants in schools, healthcare assistants (HCAs), and police community support officers (PCSOs) (Bach 2011). Faced with pressures to improve service delivery, make cost savings, and improve efficiency, public sector managers attempted to secure greater local flexibility by altering the composition of their workforce. One popular way of re-profiling the workforce was to use greater proportions of auxiliary staff, whose pay and conditions, unlike those of established occupations, are generally not subject to determination at national level. Although HCAs now come under the national Agenda for Change pay and grading system, workforce re-profiling initiatives have been a commonplace way of promoting employment flexibility and realizing efficiency savings. Increasing numbers of teaching assistants and police community support officers testify to the attractiveness of this approach for employers (Bach, Kessler, and Heron 2006; Loveday, Williams, and Scott 2008).

Perhaps the foremost reason for the durability of centralized, national-level arrangements for determining public sector pay concerns the role of the system of pay review bodies (PRBs). These are formally independent institutions, whose members are appointed by the government, which, after evaluating appropriate data and submissions from interested parties such as trade unions, make non-binding recommendations to the government on pay increases and any other relevant matters within their remit. PRBs were originally created for specific groups of public sector employees, such as doctors and dentists and senior civil servants, and also members of the armed forces. However, their remit subsequently widened to encompass nursing staff and 'professions allied to medicine' (including midwives and health visitors), and schoolteachers, in 1983 and 1991 respectively. In 2001, prison officers were also given a pay review body. Linked to the Agenda for Change agreement, during the 2000s the scope of the pay review body for nursing staff and professions allied to medicine was widened to encompass all NHS staff, with the exception of doctors and senior managers, and renamed the NHS Pay Review Body. The most recently established pay review bodies are those covering the police and officers of the National Crime Agency. The pay of around 2.5 million public sector workers now comes under the auspices of various PRBs (see Table 7.4).

Governments came to prefer PRBs over traditional collective bargaining arrangements because they were thought to reduce the prospect of labour conflict in key public sector occupations. The PRB process, with its ostensibly rational, ordered, and consensual approach to determining pay outcomes, seemed less likely to cause disputes than traditional collective bargaining, with its more adversarial dynamic, and was also thought likely to help reduce the power of the public sector unions (White 2000). It also conveys an impression that the government is an indifferent bystander, allowing it to avoid being drawn into potentially messy employment relations issues while still being able to exercise a strong influence over pay issues (Bach, Kolins Givan, and Forth 2009; Bach and Kessler 2012). Moreover, compared to 'traditional forms of national pay bargaining, the review body process has encouraged a more systematic analysis of a wider range of issues relating to affordability, recruitment and retention, morale, workload and job roles' (Bach 2010: 162).

During the 1990s and 2000s the presence of PRBs in certain parts of the public sector undoubtedly hindered the development of local bargaining arrangements since recommendations generally apply nationally, restricting the ability of managers to secure local pay flexibility. But how should the PRB process itself be understood? In one interpretation, PRB

Table 7.4 The system of pay review bodies

	Year established	Coverage
Senior Salaries Review Body	1971	Judges, senior civil servants, senior officers of the armed forces
Armed Forces Pay Review Body	1971	Members of the navy, military, and air force
Review Body on Doctors' and Dentists' Remuneration	1971	Doctors and dentists with any part in the National Health Service
National Health Service Pay Review Body	1983	Originally covered nurses and 'professions allied to medicine' (e.g. radiographers); in 2003 its remit was extended to all health professions, and extended again in 2007 to include all non-clinical support staff
School Teachers' Review Body	1991	Schoolteachers in England and Wales
Prison Service Pay Review Body	2001	Prison officers, prison governors, and operational and support staff in England, Wales, and Northern Ireland
National Crime Agency Remuneration Review Body	2013	National Crime Agency officers with operational roles
Police Remuneration Review Body	2014	Police officers at or below the rank of Chief Superintendent in England, Wales, and Northern Ireland

Source: Office for Manpower Economics, https://www.gov.uk/government/organisations/office-of-manpower-economics

arrangements should be viewed as a 'particular type of collective bargaining' (Brown and Nash 2008: 95), perhaps akin to bargaining at 'arm's length' (Winchester and Bach 1995). Rather than being a 'substitute' for the collective bargaining process, pay review bodies, as a kind of third-party intervention, are in fact 'part of it' (Burchill 2000: 155). In other words, the review bodies mediate between the claims of the unions, representing the collective interests of their members, and the counter-claims of the employer representatives (Burchill 2000). On this basis, then, studies which purport to show a dramatic decline in collective bargaining coverage in the public sector during the 2000s (e.g. van Wanrooy et al. 2013a, 2013b) should perhaps be treated with a degree of caution. Much of this supposed decline simply reflects the expansion of the PRB system in the health sector.

However, more vigorous efforts by the government to influence PRBs and control their outcomes, through the guidance it provides, and the decisions it makes about whether or not to implement their recommendations, means that it has become less easy to view the PRB process as akin to a form of collective bargaining (e.g. van Wanrooy et al. 2013b). Both Labour, up to 2010, and the 2010–15 coalition government used PRBs explicitly as tools to moderate public sector pay rises (Bach 2010; Scott and Williams 2016). For this reason, they lost a lot of their effectiveness as devices for preventing disputes. In 2014, for example, the UK government took the decision to deny a large number of NHS staff in England—all those not already at the top of their incremental pay scale—the PRB recommended pay award, something which caused the first NHS strike over pay in over thirty years.

Governments have also sought to use the PRB process as a means for pursuing certain policy goals, particularly efforts to link pay outcomes more closely with measures of performance (Bach, Kolins Givan, and Forth 2009; Scott and Williams 2016). This has been one of the contributory factors—along with pension changes and concerns about the impact of funding cuts—leading to a series of teachers' strikes in England and Wales. It is evident how the PRB process provides governments with a greater degree of control over public sector pay arrangements—one reason why it was seen as a suitable model for the police (see Contesting employment relations 7.2). To this extent, then, the PRB process increasingly operates as a 'form of unilateral government pay determination that is far removed from collective bargaining' (Bach 2016: 145).

 Contesting employment relations 7.2: Reforming pay and conditions in the police

Police pay and conditions have prompted a growing degree of contention. Traditionally, these matters were determined by negotiation through a Police Negotiating Board (PNB), which comprised representatives of the police staff associations (e.g. the Police Federation, which represents rank-and-file officers—the police are not allowed to join trade unions) and employers, and made recommendations to the government, in the form of the home secretary. Where negotiation failed to produce an agreement over a particular matter, it could be referred to an independent Police Arbitration Tribunal (PAT), although the government had the final say. In 2008, the Labour government's decision not to implement a PAT recommended award in full provoked a major dispute. Forbidden by law from striking, instead many thousands of police officers protested by marching through London.

Relations between the 2010–15 coalition government and the police were particularly strained, partly because of the scale of austerity-related budget cuts. But the most controversial feature of the coalition's approach concerned the commissioning of a major two-part review of police pay and conditions under Tom Winsor, which reported in 2011 (part one) and 2012 (part two). Among the Winsor Review's recommendations were that the system of annual pay progression should be replaced by arrangements that put a greater emphasis on individual skills and contribution. Winsor also wanted the starting salary for police constables to be cut by some £4,000 to around £19,000 per annum. Perhaps the most notable feature of the Winsor Review concerned the extent to which its proposals for reform were predicated on a belief that the system of national pay bargaining in the police needed to be replaced by arrangements that would put more power in the hands of the government and senior managers. All this created further contention. In 2012, the Police Federation organized another London protest. There were even demands from rank-and-file officers for police officers to be given the right to strike. Winsor also called for the PNB system to be replaced by an independent pay review body. As a result, in 2014 a new Police Remuneration Review Body was established for the purpose of advising the government on police pay and conditions in England, Wales, and Northern Ireland, replacing the traditional system of bargaining. The new system benefits the government by giving it greater control over the costs of police pay, and senior police managers, who have more power.

Sources: Winsor (2011, 2012); Mather and Seifert (2016)

The imperative for greater government control over public sector pay-setting under the 2010–15 Conservative–Liberal Democrat coalition was one of the main reasons why initial pressure for the decentralization of pay determination fizzled out. The coalition was clearly instinctively hostile to national collective bargaining and seemed to favour more localized public sector pay arrangements. Soon after taking office it abolished a national negotiating body covering school support staff which had only just been established under Labour. Much of the impetus for reform was driven by right-wing lobbyists and pressure groups calling for greater localization of public sector pay determination (e.g. Wolf 2010; Holmes and Oakley 2012). It was claimed that public sector pay levels, being nationally determined, are insensitive to local labour market conditions, and make it difficult for private sector employers to compete for workers in relatively low-wage areas of the country. The main problem with this argument is that comparisons of pay levels which show that on average public sector pay is higher than in the private sector do not take into account marked differences in occupational structures between the sectors. They are not comparing 'like with like' (IDS 2012: 57). The public sector contains a larger proportion of people in professional and associate professional jobs, such as teachers and healthcare workers.

By 2013, much of the impetus for local pay determination in the public sector seemed to have dissipated. Union opposition and the generally unsupportive stance of most public sector employers were two significant obstacles. However, the most important reason for the government's failure to pursue greater decentralization and localization of pay-setting arrangements was its increasing determination to exercise central control over public expenditure in general, and public sector pay in particular, under the regime of austerity (see Chapter 3). The imposition of public sector pay freezes, an increasing propensity to influence the supposedly independent recommendations of PRBs, and the failure sometimes to implement PRB recommendations in full all contributed to greater centralized government control over pay, to an extent that it amounted to the effective 'nationalization' of public sector pay-setting under the coalition between 2010 and 2015 (Bach 2016; Scott and Williams 2016: 194).

That said, though, there are two main countervailing pressures to the efforts of the UK government to exercise greater control over public sector pay. One of these concerns the powers enjoyed by the UK devolved governments in certain areas. In the health service, for example, the Scottish National Party administration in Scotland and Labour in Wales implemented the 2014–15 and 2015–16 PRB recommended pay rises in full, without excluding staff who were not at the top of their respective pay scales, as was the case in England. This highlights the important extent to which devolution has contributed to the growing differentiation of public sector pay arrangements across the UK (Scott and Williams 2016).

The second countervailing pressure concerns the greater opening up of public services to alternative, non-state providers, something which potentially undermines national pay and conditions of service agreements (Bach 2012). In education, for example, the operators of new types of school, such as academies and 'free schools', are in principle not obliged to comply with national-level pay arrangements, and thus able to set their own terms and conditions of employment for schoolteachers. Although any existing employees of a school which becomes an academy have their pay and conditions protected at first, over time there is clearly greater scope for employers to secure greater local flexibility if they so wish. While national, multi-employer arrangements for determining public sector pay and conditions have proved to be remarkably resilient, changes in the organization and delivery of public services have the potential to produce greater localization and differentiation in future (Scott and Williams 2016).

Section summary and further reading

- For much of the twentieth century, collective bargaining, often in the form of multi-employer arrangements, was the principal pay-setting method in employment relations.

- Multi-employer bargaining in the private sector has become rare indeed. In order to secure greater flexibility over their own employment relations, employers increasingly prefer to bargain with trade unions themselves. Moreover, there has been a general contraction of collective bargaining coverage in the private sector, linked to changes in competitive conditions and the decline of union power relative to employers.

- In the public sector, collective bargaining, often manifest in multi-employer arrangements, has been somewhat resilient. The operation of pay review bodies for key groups of workers, a form of 'arm's-length bargaining', has contributed to the durability of national pay-setting arrangements. UK governments have increased their control over public sector pay, stifling moves to promote greater local flexibility.

Collective bargaining trends are amply covered by Brown, Bryson, and Forth (2009), Brown (2010), and Marginson (2015). See Bach (2010), Bach and Kessler (2012), and Scott and Williams (2016: 193–6) for overviews of developments in public sector pay determination.

7.3 Unilateral managerial regulation of pay

What, then, are the implications of the contraction of collective bargaining? How do employees have their pay determined, if not through the process of collective bargaining? In the private sector the most notable development concerns the large extent to which pay is now regulated unilaterally by management (Brown and Nash 2008; Druker and White 2009; Grimshaw and Rubery 2010; Marginson 2015). The purpose of this section is to examine the nature and extent of managerial innovation in pay-setting arrangements. How well have employers used the greater freedom they would seem to enjoy when it comes to managing pay issues? And what are the implications of systems for determining pay based on some kind of assessment of an employee's performance?

7.3.1 Managerial innovation in pay-setting arrangements: variable pay systems

There has been growing interest in how pay can be used as part of a sophisticated human resource management (HRM) approach (see Chapter 5) to managing employees. The term 'reward', rather than pay, is often used to refer to broader and more innovative methods of remunerating employees that assist in the achievement of organizational goals. The decline of collective bargaining, with its common rate for the job, supposedly gives managers greater scope to implement more variable arrangements for determining pay, enhancing their flexibility when it comes to rewarding individual staff (Druker and White 2009). Rather than basing pay on relatively unsophisticated criteria, such as the number of hours employees spend at work each week, for example, their grade, or their length of service, reward schemes may offer employees greater flexibility over their methods of remuneration, or align wages with performance, at the level of the worker, the work-group, or the organization. This is seen to embody a more strategic approach to the management of pay issues. For Druker and White (2009: 11), the management of reward 'is one of the key levers to be deployed in pursuit of effective HRM. If pay is to "deliver the goods" in terms of HR strategy, then it must be structured, it is argued, in order to meet HR objectives'.

It is increasingly thought that management of reward issues should not only be aligned with, and supportive of, broader HRM objectives, but also integrated with the overall strategic goals of the organization (Trevor and Brown 2014). The so-called 'new pay' approach is marked by a greater emphasis on aligning reward levels with the contribution and achievements of workers as individuals, rather than as part of a collective (Corby, Palmer, and Lindop 2009). One of the main advantages of the greater flexibility offered by the 'new pay' approach for managers concerns the way in which pay outcomes are more closely linked to individual or organizational performance, passing on more of the risks of a lack of business success to the workforce (Arrowsmith and Marginson 2010).

Arrangements for determining pay whereby pay levels may vary according to, or be contingent on, levels of output, performance, or profitability are a key source of managerial flexibility. So-called 'variable' or 'contingent' pay systems have become a more common feature of employment relations (Pendleton, Whitfield, and Bryson 2009; Brown and Marsden 2011). However, there is nothing new about variable pay systems (VPS). Incentive-based payment systems, which link an element of workers' pay to a measure of their output, have a long history in work and employment relations. Managers are often attracted to such schemes because they offer a relatively straightforward way of motivating and securing more effort from workers without the need for close supervision (Brown and Walsh 1994; Grimshaw and Rubery 2010). In practice, though, such arrangements rarely operate as effectively as managers anticipate. For example, workers may restrict their output, in order to maximize the earnings of them all as a group, and not go flat out in pursuit of a higher individual wage. Moreover, the effect of incentive payments on motivation is rarely unambiguous (Brown, Marginson, and Walsh 2003); the demotivation resulting from a failure to be awarded an expected wage bonus, for example, can outweigh any motivational advantages.

Such incentive payment schemes, where pay or bonuses are linked to output in some way—'payment by results'—are one type of VPS. The 'new pay' agenda, though, is more commonly linked with two other types of VPS: organizational-level arrangements that link reward to the success of the organization, perhaps its profitability for example, or through opportunities to purchase company shares; and performance-related pay (PRP) arrangements, whereby some or all of an employee's pay is linked to a managerial assessment of their performance, either as part of a team, or more commonly on an individual basis (Arrowsmith and Marginson 2011). There are two main reasons why variable pay arrangements are attractive to employers. First, variable pay arrangements are consistent with a 'new pay' approach in which there is an emphasis on managing reward in a way that supports overall business objectives, with more of an onus on securing greater organizational flexibility and improvements in business performance. The use of VPS 'signifies a HR management strategy that responds to the more rapidly changing business environment, and often the decentralization of business and HR responsibilities to local managers' (Arrowsmith et al. 2010: 273). Second, they are consistent with efforts to promote a more individualized approach to managing employment relations, and would appear to make collective bargaining through trade unions, with its emphasis on standardized pay rates, unnecessary (Marginson 2009; Grimshaw and Rubery 2010).

Table 7.5 Use of variable payment schemes, 2004–11, percentage of workplaces

	2004	2011
Any payment by results	31	28
Any system of pay based on an assessment of merit/performance	15	20
Any payment by results or based on merit/performance	40	40
Any profit-related pay	30	29
Any share schemes	17	9
At least one variable payment scheme	54	54

Source: van Wanrooy et al. (2013*a*: 25), licensed under Open Government Licence v. 3.0

Given the lack of progress made towards sophisticated HRM in general (see Chapter 5), perhaps it should come as no surprise that management-inspired innovations in respect of pay arrangements have been somewhat limited. The presence of VPS is far from widespread (Corby, Palmer, and Lindop 2009), though there are signs that they have come to be present in a broader range of workplaces (Pendleton, Whitfield, and Bryson 2009). While there was a marked increase in the proportion of workplaces using VPS in the 1980s and 1990s, this growth did not continue during the 2000s (Brown and Marsden 2011; van Wanrooy et al. 2013*b*). Table 7.5 shows that between 2004 and 2011 there was little change in the proportion of workplaces operating VPS overall.

Managers are often reluctant to change systems for determining pay. They prefer to tread carefully, restricting their efforts to instituting incremental, minor adjustments (Kessler 2000). Overall, managers have 'not taken advantage of the demise of collective bargaining to implement new integrated systems of individualised employee relations and pay determination' (Charlwood 2007: 43). Generally, the decline of collective pay-setting arrangements has produced 'procedural individualization' rather than 'substantive individualization' when it comes to determining pay. In other words, while the decline of collective bargaining means that procedures for determining pay have become increasingly de-collectivized, in the sense that the influence of trade unions has diminished, managers still prefer to operate standardized arrangements for rewarding staff (Charlwood 2007).

Why has change been so limited when it comes to the reform of pay systems? One important reason concerns external pressures for conformity. Decisions over pay settlements are influenced by the need to offer rises that are in line both with inflation, and with what comparable groups of workers in other organizations have been awarded (Druker and White 2009). Moreover, when it comes to designing pay systems there can be a tendency for firms to imitate each other, leading to a standardization of pay practice. Firms might aspire to manage pay in a more strategic fashion, integrated with and supportive of their competitive strategy, but the reality is often rather different (Trevor and Brown 2014). A second reason why efforts to manage pay and reward in a more strategic fashion are often unsuccessful is the reluctance of managers to bear the risks of innovation. Attempts to reform pay arrangements can disrupt employment relations, by undermining established norms of fairness and the legitimacy they offer. Managers are wary about making changes to existing payment systems. The 'tried and tested nature of arrangements, it seems, invests them with a high degree of legitimacy in the eyes of managers and employees' (Arrowsmith and Sisson 1999: 66). This is a profound obstacle to efforts by organizations to manage pay more strategically. Front-line managers, in particular, have to be sensitive to what is accept-able to their staff, to avoid stoking discontent. This can result in them amending, or even failing to implement, corporate pay policies deemed unsuitable in their workplaces (Trevor and Brown 2014).

7.3.2 The implications of performance-related pay

Perhaps the most prominent type of VPS involves attempts to link some element of an em-ployee's reward to an assessment by their manager of their merit or performance. Through a focus on the rationale for performance-related pay (PRP) and how it operates, we are better placed to understand some of the difficulties and challenges that apply when trying to in-novate in respect of pay-setting arrangements. The term PRP is conventionally associated with arrangements for determining pay that link an element of a worker's wages to some assessment of their worth, or merit. Under PRP, or individual PRP as it is sometimes called, an element of an employee's remuneration is based, over a given period of time, on an often subjective assessment of the quantity and quality of his or her work, normally by an imme-diate manager, measured against a series of targets. Its use in white-collar jobs in particular represents a shift away from pay based on job grade or length of service 'towards relating pay more directly to individual characteristics' (Kessler and Purcell 1995: 350), particularly in some parts of the public sector, where PRP schemes have been introduced in occupations such as schoolteaching (Perkins and White 2010; Bach and Kessler 2012); however, they are much more commonly found in the private sector, especially in sectors like financial services (van Wanrooy et al. 2013b).

What is the purpose of PRP? Kessler and Purcell (1995) suggest that three sets of managerial goals provide the rationale for PRP arrangements. First, managers use PRP as a way of stimu-lating pay flexibility. It ostensibly gives them greater latitude to restructure pay systems so that they support organizational objectives, though this is rarely done in a strategic way. The second set of goals relates to the desirability of enhancing employee motivation, commit-ment, and loyalty. If pay is made more contingent on their performance, then it is presumed that employees will identify with, and become more attached to, managerially determined organizational goals.

In his study of PRP in four local authorities, Heery (1998a) identified a contradictory ra-tionale underpinning the decision to adopt PRP. On the one hand, managers sought to use it to gain greater employee compliance; PRP could help to reduce shirking and augment management control. On the other hand, the implementation of PRP was also seen as a way of generating culture change, towards a climate in which an ethos of flexibility and commit-ment predominated. Perhaps this should not be surprising given that the management of the employment relationship is driven by the need to secure the compliance of employees, as well as elicit their commitment, as Chapter 5 shows.

The third set of managerial goals concerns the use of PRP as a way of challenging collec-tive bargaining arrangements and marginalizing the influence of trade unions. PRP is often seen as inimical to collective bargaining for a number of reasons, not least because it is often marked by an emphasis on rewarding individuals, and also because it threatens the role of unions as the bargaining agents of the workforce, perhaps as a prelude to, or a consequence of, derecognition (Gunnigle, Turner, and D'Art 1998; Heery 2009b).

Yet the existence of PRP is not incompatible with a trade union presence and collective bargaining (Grimshaw and Rubery 2010). While a desire to reduce the influence of trade unions and collective bargaining is a major rationale for the adoption of PRP schemes, a union presence can help to regulate how they are implemented, and shape the details (Heery 1997). Trade unions can work to improve how they function, perhaps by limiting the amount of an employee's reward that is contingent on performance, or by insisting on constraints when it comes to the scope for managerial discretion (Heery 2009b). In the banking sector, for example, unions have been rather successful in ensuring that PRP is subject to joint regulation through collective bargaining, rather than just being subject to unilateral control by management (Arrowsmith and Marginson 2011). There is evidence that 'unions have proven able to redraw the lines of collective negotiation around the size of the available pay pot and its distribution. Combined with their ability to secure greater transparency and consistency in the functioning of schemes, unions in banking have obtained a degree of standardisation of outcomes' (Marginson 2009: 115).

Moreover, the effectiveness of PRP, as with any other kind of managerial intervention in employment relations, to a large degree rests on how far it is viewed as legitimate by the workforce, particularly the extent to which it corresponds with their sense of fairness (Arrowsmith et al. 2010). When operating PRP schemes, managers have to take into account the expectations and reactions of employees. In his study of local government, Heery (1998a: 85) considers that 'PRP has been the subject of a tacit exchange between managers and employees, in which managers have refrained from an exacting application of formal procedures for fear of alienating employees'. This helps to explain, for example, the reluctance of managers to give employees low performance ratings. The experience of PRP schemes suggests that the need to win the consent of employees places important constraints on managerial discretion over how pay is determined. Like any management initiative in employment relations, then, the implementation of PRP is conditioned by the need to elicit employees' cooperation as well as their compliance.

To what extent, though, is PRP effective, in managerial terms, as a way of increasing employees' motivation, and thus their levels of performance? Key features of PRP schemes, such as the manipulation of performance targets, the subjective evaluation of performance by managers, and the fact that the performance element of pay is generally a very small proportion of overall earnings, conspire to reduce their effectiveness (Kessler 2000). Given its potential to produce variations in earnings between employees, individual PRP can lead to increased jealousies and erode staff morale. See Insight into practice 7.3 for the case of schoolteachers.

 Insight into practice 7.3: Performance-related pay for schoolteachers

The most ambitious system of PRP in the whole of the public sector to be introduced during the 2000s was brought in for schoolteachers in England and Wales by Labour. The government claimed that enhancing the pay of effective classroom teachers would lead to improved pupil performance, and thus generate improvements in educational standards. Once teachers have reached the top of the main pay scale, they can apply to cross a 'performance threshold', which involves having their performance

(continued...)

assessed against certain criteria, including pupil attainment for example, by their headteacher. If successful, they can move to an upper pay scale, receiving an immediate £2,000 pay rise (Bach and Kessler 2012: 62). Teachers overwhelmingly opposed the PRP scheme; most felt that it would not lead to improvements in teaching or better pupil performance (Farrell and Morris 2004). Furthermore, expectations that PRP would raise the performance of teachers, and thus improve pupil performance, do not seem to have been realized (Farrell and Morris 2009). Four main factors account for the failure of the PRP scheme to have had the desired effects. First, individual PRP is considered to be inappropriate in school environments. Improvements in pupils' performance are generally seen by teachers as the result of their collective effort, and are sometimes attributable to factors beyond their control, such as parental support. Second, teachers consider PRP to be unsuited to the complicated task of improving children's education. Third, teachers dislike the potential for favouritism in the way that the PRP scheme operates, particularly the subjective judgement of headteachers as to whether staff meet the threshold or not. Fourth, teachers sometimes view PRP as a divisive mechanism, with negative consequences for their morale (Farrell and Morris 2004).

Despite their hostility to PRP, teachers complied with the new arrangements on the basis that, since the additional pay was available, they might as well take it (Farrell and Morris 2004). However, a further effect of the PRP scheme has been to increase record-keeping requirements and other forms of bureaucracy. Perhaps the most significant long-term consequence of the introduction of PRP in schools is its contribution to the erosion of teachers' professional autonomy, and increasing managerial control (Farrell and Morris 2004). In 2014 the Conservative–Liberal Democrat coalition government implemented a more extensive system of PRP in schools, whereby a teacher's annual pay progression up the main scale is linked to an assessment of their performance. The introduction of the new system of PRP was one of the main factors behind a series of strikes by teachers in England and Wales between 2014 and 2016.

There is plentiful evidence that, rather than increasing workers' motivation, in practice PRP schemes have a greater demotivating effect (Marsden 2009). This can be seen from the experiences of two government agencies, the Inland Revenue and the Employment Service (Marsden and French 1998). Although most employees supported the principle of PRP, in general they were highly critical of the way the respective schemes operated in practice. In the Employment Service, for example, the individual performance targets were a source of discontent since it was difficult for employees, given that they had insufficient control over their workloads, to attain them. It was widely felt, moreover, that managers manipulated the performance review process to give higher ratings to favoured employees. In both organizations, PRP appears to have led to a significant decline in morale, caused jealousies, and reduced the level of cooperation between managers and employees.

While the principle of PRP is generally seen as fair, in practice it is often implemented in a way that disrupts established pay arrangements and, in doing so, upsets existing norms of fairness and the sense of legitimacy that they create, something which forms the basis of workplace order. Any alterations to pay-setting arrangements, particularly those that link an element of pay to performance in some way, unless handled very carefully and with due sensitivity, seem likely to have a demotivating effect (Brown and Nolan 1988; Brown, Marginson, and Walsh 2003). That said, however, PRP schemes in the public sector, while not motivating employees into supplying greater work effort, do seem to be associated with improvements in organizational performance. How is this apparent paradox to be explained? The contribution of Marsden (2009) is important here. He explains that PRP arrangements, as part of broader systems of performance management in organizations, enable workers and managers to clarify objectives and work priorities, and provide workers with a means of influencing, and indeed negotiating over, the process of goal-setting. Therefore the effectiveness of PRP schemes, and indeed variable pay systems in general, seems to depend 'less on their effect on motivation than on their direct association with a radical change in performance norms and renegotiation of job design and work rules' (Grimshaw and Rubery 2010: 361). This is consistent with viewing the workplace as a 'negotiated order' (see Chapter 1), marked by an ongoing process of negotiation and re-negotiation over the terms of the wage–work bargain (Sisson 2010).

 ## Section summary and further reading

- The contraction of collective bargaining coverage in general in the private sector means that the majority of employees in Britain have their pay determined unilaterally by management.

- The growth in the use of 'variable' or 'contingent' pay schemes seen in the 1980s and 1990s did not continue into the 2000s, and employers often prefer to operate standardized arrangements for determining pay even in the absence of trade unions and collective bargaining.

- Managers find arrangements that associate pay with performance attractive, since they offer more flexibility and help to secure the commitment of employees to business goals. While sometimes designed to undermine collectivism, PRP is not inimical to joint regulation and trade unionism. Nevertheless, despite the apparently greater freedom they enjoy to reform pay systems and influence pay settlements, managers have been reluctant to upset existing 'tried and tested' arrangements.

There is some good material on managerial approaches to pay determination in Grimshaw and Rubery (2010). Druker and White (2009), Heery (2009b), and Marginson (2009) are useful when it comes to understanding trends and developments in pay determination. Charlwood (2007) demonstrates the continuing relevance of standardized pay-setting processes. Trevor and Brown's (2014) case studies highlight the obstacles to the strategic management of pay in organizations.

7.4 Regulating low pay

One of the main implications of the diminution of collective bargaining as a pay-setting mechanism and the consequent increase in unilateral managerial regulation has been growing pay inequality. The gap between high earners and those lower down the wage hierarchy has grown markedly since the 1980s, alongside the declining reach of joint regulation. As a consequence, the question of how best to protect low-paid workers has become more of an issue. The main purpose of this section is to examine the regulation of low pay, looking at the rationale for, and impact of, statutory regulation in the form of the National Minimum Wage (NMW), which was introduced in 1999. As will become evident, although the NMW is generally reckoned to be an example of a highly successful government policy intervention, it has done rather little to reduce the problem of low pay in the economy. As a result, among campaigners on behalf of the low-paid there is growing interest in other ways of tackling poverty pay, particularly through the promotion of the voluntary living wage approach.

7.4.1 Regulating low pay through minimum wages

The first major task concerns specifying what is meant by low pay. It is generally conceived of in relative terms, not as an absolute measure (e.g. Rubery and Edwards 2003). In other words, determining the level of pay beneath which workers are classified as low-paid should be done in relation to the general level of earnings characteristic of a particular society, something which varies across regions and countries, and which changes over time. The conventional definition of low pay is pay that falls below a level of two-thirds of overall hourly median earnings. In 2015 some 5.5 million people in Britain—21 per cent of employees—were, by this definition, low-paid—earning below £7.67 per hour, or an annual salary of around £14,000 based on a thirty-five-hour week (Corlett and Gardiner 2015). Women are more likely than men to be engaged in low-paid work, and low pay is also a more common feature of jobs held by young workers (Corlett and Gardiner 2015). It is concentrated in particular occupations (e.g. cleaners, sales assistants, catering workers, bar staff), and in certain sectors of the economy—especially hospitality, social care, retail, clothing and textile manufacturing, and hairdressing (LPC 2016).

Broadly speaking, there are two main ways in which low pay is regulated in modern economies: either by collective agreements, or by means of a statutory minimum wage (Rubery and Grimshaw 2003). In the case of the first of these arrangements, a floor of wages is sometimes set by collective bargaining on an industry-by-industry basis, which for a long time has been the case in Germany for example, with governments sometimes having the power to extend the settlement to all employers in the sector, even those that are not directly party to the agreement. Centralized systems of collective bargaining can often be quite effective ways of regulating low pay, and of impeding the growth of wage inequality, especially for full-time employees. This is because they act to compress wage differentials in the sectors where they have coverage (Hayter and Weinberg 2011).

 International perspective 7.4: Minimum wage campaigns in the United States

The United States operates a federal minimum wage—currently $7.25 (£5.51 in September 2016) per hour—which sets a pay floor across the country, although many individual states also have their own higher rates. In early 2013, the newly re-elected President Obama proposed raising the federal minimum wage to $9.00 (£6.84 in September 2016) per hour, much to the consternation of political opponents and business leaders, who contended—erroneously given the findings of most research—that it would damage economic competitiveness and lead to job losses. Efforts by the Obama administration to increase the federal minimum wage were consistently blocked by the Republican-controlled Congress. Instead, there has been a focus on efforts to boost minimum wages at local and state level. In 2016, for example, the Democrat-controlled states of California and New York passed laws phasing in a $15 minimum wage. US trade unions have also campaigned vociferously for minimum wage increases. The 'Fight for $15' campaign is concentrated largely in the fast-food industry, and calls for companies like McDonalds to guarantee their workers at least $15 per hour. In April 2016, tens of thousands of workers across some 300 US cities engaged in a day of strikes, protests, and demonstrations in pursuit of the $15 target. This highlights the important extent to which efforts to regulate work and employment relationships, and secure employment protections, are the product of campaigns by workers and unions.

The second type of arrangement, a statutory minimum wage, exists in countries such as France, Spain, Portugal, and, since 1999, in the UK too. Minimum wages are often a topic of political interest and controversy around the world—see International perspective 7.4 for the case of the United States. Traditionally, Germany was one of the few advanced econo-mies not to have a statutory minimum wage; instead, multi-employer collective bargaining sets a floor of wages on an industry sector basis. However, this approach meant that workers in sectors where collective bargaining coverage is weak—often women, the low-skilled, and migrants—are disadvantaged. During the 2000s there was growing pressure in Germany for the introduction of an economy-wide minimum wage to tackle the problem of low pay. It was eventually introduced in January 2015, at a rate of €8.50 per hour.

What reasons lay behind the 1999 establishment of the NMW in the UK? Three factors were particularly important. One was concern about the need to tackle extreme levels of low pay in some sectors of the economy (LPC 2016). Second was the growing concern about ris-ing wage inequality and its adverse social and economic consequences. There is a powerful body of evidence which demonstrates that the size of the gap between high and low earners matters in some very important ways. In their book *The Spirit Level*, for example, Wilkinson and Pickett (2009) show that countries with relatively high levels of inequality (e.g. US, UK) suffer from greater social problems, higher crime rates, and poorer health outcomes, than those which are more equal. Obesity, for example, is more prevalent in the UK than it is in countries with less inequality, like Sweden.

There was a marked growth in wage inequality during the 1980s, which continued into the 1990s, albeit at a slower rate (Machin 2011). The gap between high earners and low earn-ers widened considerably, 'reaching the highest levels experienced in the twentieth century' (Machin 1999: 185). Rising inequality was fuelled by the trend for pay rises of high and rela-tively high earners to far outstrip increases for people on more modest earnings. In part it was also driven by technological change and the employment consequences of economic globalization, which reduced demand for semi-skilled and low-skilled workers (Resolution Foundation 2012). However, during the 1980s and 1990s the then Conservative govern-ment's deregulatory policies—manifest in the abolition of all bar one of the remaining wages councils, which had operated pay floors in some low-paying sectors, the diminution of trade union power, the fall in collective bargaining coverage, and greater unilateral regulation of pay by management—all helped to generate increased inequality (Brown, Marginson, and Walsh 2003; Coats 2007; Turnbull and Wass 2011; Butcher 2012; Lindley and Machin 2013).

But a third factor was also important in the establishment of the NMW; this concerned the 'political momentum' for minimum wage regulation given by Tony Blair's Labour govern-ment, elected in 1997 (Butcher 2012: R26). Labour's eventual commitment to establishing an NMW was the outcome of protracted debates and struggle as supporters of the policy, partic-ularly in some trade unions, tried to overcome the traditional ambivalence towards statutory wage-fixing that had characterized attitudes in much of the labour movement (Coats 2007; Arrowsmith 2009). Following its victory at the 1997 general election, the Labour government set up a Low Pay Commission (LPC), comprising employer and union representatives, as well as academic experts. The LPC's initial role was to make recommendations to government over such matters as the coverage of the minimum wage (i.e. to whom would it apply?), the elements of pay that could be counted towards the minimum wage (e.g. what should hap-pen to tips?), and the minimum wage rates themselves. After the NMW came into effect,

Table 7.6 National Minimum Wage rates, 1999–2015

	Workers aged 21 and over*	Uprating	Workers aged 18–20**	Workers aged 16–17	Apprentices
April 1999	£3.60		£3.00		
June 2000	£3.60		£3.20		
October 2000	£3.70	2.8%	£3.20		
October 2001	£4.10	10.8%	£3.50		
October 2002	£4.20	2.4%	£3.60		
October 2003	£4.50	7.1%	£3.80		
October 2004	£4.85	7.8%	£4.10	£3.00	
October 2005	£5.05	4.1%	£4.25	£3.00	
October 2006	£5.35	5.9%	£4.45	£3.30	
October 2007	£5.52	3.2%	£4.60	£3.40	
October 2008	£5.73	3.8%	£4.77	£3.53	
October 2009	£5.80	1.2%	£4.83	£3.57	
October 2010	£5.93	2.2%	£4.92	£3.64	£2.50
October 2011	£6.08	2.5%	£4.98	£3.68	£2.60
October 2012	£6.19	1.8%	£4.98	£3.68	£2.65
October 2013	£6.31	1.9%	£5.03	£3.72	£2.65
October 2014	£6.50	3.0%	£5.13	£3.79	£2.73
October 2015	£6.70	3.1%	£5.30	£3.87	£3.30

* 22 and over before 2010; **18–21 before 2010

the LPC remained in existence, with its role largely devoted to investigating the effects of the minimum wage, and making recommendations to the government over changes to the minimum wage rates (or 'upratings') and other relevant matters in a series of annual reports (e.g. LPC 2016).

Since their introduction in 1999, the NMW rates have been uprated several times, as can be seen from Table 7.6. A lower 'development' rate applies to workers aged between 18 and 20 (21 prior to 2010). It was introduced largely because of a concern that if young workers were to be covered by the main NMW rate it would make them too expensive for employers to hire, thus significantly damaging their labour market prospects (Metcalf 1999; Coats 2007; Sargeant 2010). Initially, the use of the lower rate for young workers was far from commonplace; employers were reluctant to operate it (e.g. Heyes and Gray 2001; Langlois and Lucas 2005). There are difficulties recruiting, motivating, and retaining younger workers at rates of pay that are below the main 'adult' NMW level; many managers view it as unfair to discriminate against them on the grounds of age (Williams, Adam-Smith, and Norris 2004), even though it is lawful, being exempt from age discrimination legislation (Sargeant 2010). Some companies, like Tesco, turned away from pay structures related to age; however, they remained common in sectors like fast-food restaurants and pubs, which employ lots of young people (IDS 2011b). As the main NMW rate increased, though, some employers reintroduced age-based differentials as a way of managing the extra costs of compliance. The use of the young workers' rate seems to have become more usual (LPC 2012). Between 2007 and 2015 the proportion of 18–20 year olds paid the lower rate more than doubled. The April 2016

Table 7.7 National Minimum Wage and National Living Wage rates, 2016

	Workers aged 25 and over (NLW)	Workers aged 21–24	Workers aged 18–20	Workers aged 16–17	Apprentices
April 2016	£7.20	£6.70	£5.30	£3.87	£3.30
October 2016	£7.20	£6.95	£5.55	£4.00	£3.40

introduction of a National Living Wage—initially at £7.20 per hour for workers aged 25 and over—seems likely to accentuate age-based differentials (LPC 2016).

Originally, the NMW did not cover workers aged below 18. The LPC and the government did not want to discourage teenagers from leaving full-time education (Sargeant 2010). However, in October 2004 the government introduced a new, lower rate of £3.00 per hour that applied to 16 and 17 year olds. This was done because of concerns raised by trade unions that some young workers were being exploited by unscrupulous employers who were paying them very low rates of pay, less than £2.00 an hour in some cases (LPC 2004). In 2010, the full 'adult' rate was extended to cover workers aged 21 and over; the same year saw the introduction of an 'apprentice' rate, payable to apprentices aged below 19 or, if older, who are in the first year of their training (LPC 2010; Butcher 2012). The most recent change concerns the April 2016 introduction of a 'National Living Wage' (NLW), initially set at £7.20 per hour—effectively a rise in the NMW for workers aged 25 and over. The NLW policy is discussed further in section 7.4.3. Table 7.7 provides details of the 2016 NMW and NLW rates.

The operation of the LPC, in particular the high level of consensus that informs its recommendations, has been praised. It has also been lauded for bringing employer and union representatives together in a spirit of 'social partnership', maintaining its independence from the government, and for its pragmatism, and the importance it attaches to basing its recommendations on rigorous evidence and analysis (Brown 2009; Butcher 2012). Yet, while no one could doubt the effective role played by the LPC in helping to make the NMW such a durable feature of the employment relations environment, it has been overly cautious, particularly when it comes to its recommended minimum wage rates—too willing to be oversensitive to claims from employers about the undesirable consequences of raising them too far (Grimshaw and Rubery 2010), especially in the period following the 2008 financial crisis and subsequent economic recession (LPC 2013).

One of the LPC's most important concerns has been to avoid any adverse economic consequences of implementing NMW rates that are too high, or that increase too quickly (Brown 2009). The fear is that employers in low-paying sectors of the economy could react to any increase in labour costs by reducing jobs. Therefore, the key challenge for the LPC has been striking a balance between 'a desire to have a high minimum, to benefit low-paid workers, against the concern that job losses might arise if that minimum were to be set too high' (Manning 2012: 3).

During the first half of the 2000s, the value of the main NMW rate grew quite substantially, exceeding both inflation and rises in average earnings. Table 7.6 shows that in some years—notably in 2001, 2003, and 2004—there was a pronounced annual uprating: nearly 11 per cent in the first of those years, and over 7 per cent in the others. Although the NMW rate was initially set at a low level, reflecting the cautious approach taken by the LPC (Coats

2007), it was subsequently raised by a relatively large amount until 2006 (Stewart 2011; Butcher 2012). Whereas in 1999 the main NMW rate amounted to a rather meagre 46 per cent of median adult hourly earnings, by 2006 it had reached 51 per cent (Butcher 2012). In the late 2000s, though, particularly in the context of the economic crisis, the LPC reverted to a more conservative approach. Between 2009 and 2013 the average annual rise in the main NMW rate was just 1.9 per cent. Some attribute this to pressure from employers (Grimshaw and Rubery 2010); but the economic downturn also seems to have prompted a greater degree of caution from the LPC, which did not want to undermine any economic recovery by raising the minimum wage rates too far (LPC 2012, 2013).

Supporters of the LPC's approach recognize that it became more cautious after 2007, but nonetheless stress that over the entire period since 1999 the value of the NMW has grown relative to average earnings (Butcher 2012). Between 1999 and 2015 the value of the main NMW rate increased by 86 per cent, outstripping both inflation and average earnings growth (LPC 2016). Since 2014, moreover, the LPC appears to have adopted a more expansive approach. The main NMW rate rose by 3.0 per cent in 2014 and 3.1 per cent in 2015, taking it to 54.5 per cent of median earnings (LPC 2016). The introduction of the NLW in April 2016 meant that the effective minimum wage for workers aged 25 and over increased by 7.5 per cent, from £6.70 to £7.20 per hour. As Section 7.4.3 shows, though, some employers took measures to mitigate the impact of the NLW and deny workers the pay rises to which they were entitled. In October 2016 the NMW rate for 21–24 year olds rose by 3.7 per cent. These rises have to be viewed in the context of the growing concerns that have been expressed about the adverse impact of stagnant wages for people's incomes and living standards, and the negative consequences for productivity and economic performance (LPC 2016)—see Chapter 2.

7.4.2 The impact of the National Minimum Wage

In considering the impact of the NMW we first need to ascertain who has benefited from it. Around 5 per cent of the workforce—some 1.2 million workers—gained directly from the 1999 introduction of the NMW (Metcalf 2008; Butcher 2012). In 2015, workers in some 1.6 million jobs (6.4 per cent of the total) were covered by that year's increase in the value of the main NMW rate (LPC 2016). Yet because the incidence of low pay is concentrated among certain sectors and occupations, increases in the NMW have had much more of an effect in some types of jobs than in others. Most of the beneficiaries, some two-thirds, are women workers, especially those employed in part-time jobs. Workers in low-paying sectors of the economy—particularly hairdressing, hospitality, retail, and social care—and those employed by small businesses have benefited disproportionately from the presence of the NMW.

Initially, though, the NMW by no means commanded universal support. During the 1990s, the Conservative Party and many business organizations opposed the minimum wage policy, claiming that it would push up inflation and have a massively adverse impact on employment; some speculated that introducing a minimum wage would put up to 2 million jobs at risk (Manning 2011, 2012). The simple economic reasoning behind these claims is that any rise in the price of labour—wages that is—without a corresponding increase in productivity, will reduce employers' demand for it. Alternatively, firms will pass on the higher costs of adapting to the minimum wage to customers in the form of higher prices. Such problems would be exacerbated if, as critics of the minimum wage expected, other groups of workers were to secure corresponding increases in their wages in order to preserve their relative position in the pay hierarchy or, in other words, restore their existing pay 'differentials'. Some US labour economists emphasize that minimum wages are associated with reductions in employment levels (e.g. Neumark and Wascher 2008).

Yet, contrary to these expectations, the introduction of the NMW appears to have had little adverse effect on the British economy; it arrived with a 'whimper rather than a bang' (Dickens and Manning 2003: 202). The low level at which the NMW was initially set meant that most firms, even in low-paying sectors of the economy, were not affected directly by its introduction; and many of those that were affected found the necessary increases in wage rates easily affordable. Overall, neither the introduction of the NMW, nor its subsequent up-ratings, seem to have had a detrimental impact on employment levels, with the possible exception of the residential care sector (Metcalf 2008; Manning 2012; De Linde Leonard, Stanley, and Doucouliagos 2014; LPC 2016). Indeed, employment in low-paying sectors of the economy, where the NMW will have had a more powerful effect, has grown more quickly than employment throughout the economy in general, even during the recession (Butcher 2012; LPC 2016). The Conservatives dropped their opposition in the early 2000s; and the 2010–15 coalition government affirmed its support for the NMW, recognizing the protection it gives low-paid workers and the incentive to work that it provides.

What explains the absence of a negative impact on employment levels? Some economists specify that minimum wages can have a positive effect because they provide people outside the labour market with an incentive to take up a job (Manning 2012). No doubt the prevailing economic context also helped. Until 2008 the UK economy grew, meaning that any increased costs to employers arising from the NMW were easily absorbed, and indeed were relatively minor compared to the revenue arising from expanding product markets (Brown 2009). Metcalf (2008) posits five plausible reasons why the NMW has had no discernible adverse employment effects:

- Employers have coped with the increased costs of the NMW by raising productivity, rather than reducing employment.
- Some of the increase in costs has been passed on to consumers in the form of higher prices.
- Firms have coped by taking a smaller share of profits.
- Employers have reduced hours of work rather than cut jobs.
- Employers have a degree of market power and thus some flexibility when determining wages; this means that they did not necessarily react to the NMW by cutting jobs.

This last point is important for understanding why the NMW has not created a 'labour market shock' and reduced employment levels, in the manner expected by some (e.g. Brown and Crossman 2000). The NMW has been relatively easily absorbed by firms in low-paying sectors of the economy, who have a variety of options open to them when it comes to offsetting the resultant higher wage costs: increasing productivity; reducing working hours; adjusting bonus payments and shift premiums; taking fewer profits; or increasing prices (Butcher 2012; LPC 2016). Far from being a shock to firms in low-paying sectors of the economy, the NMW is simply a further influence among the many that shape employment relationships within them (Adam-Smith, Norris, and Williams 2003). It is unlikely that a consistent pattern of responses to the NMW will be identified, particularly with it being set at such a low level. Rather, affected firms will react in idiosyncratic and diverse ways, influenced by the characteristics of their particular product and labour market environments (Arrowsmith 2009). Indeed, many employers have adapted to the increased costs of the NMW rises simply by 'muddling through' (Metcalf 2008).

Of course, another way in which employers in low-paying sectors of the economy can avoid the consequences of the NMW legislation is by failing to comply with it. Sports Direct, for example, has been criticized for its failure to ensure staff receive the minimum wage; at times it expected some of its shopworkers to work on an unpaid basis (House of Commons Business, Innovation, and Skills Committee 2016). While the extent of non-compliance is very difficult to measure, overall it seems to be quite rare (Manning 2012; LPC 2016). Nevertheless, concerns have been expressed that the level of non-compliance in the informal economy, where pay is arranged on a cash-in-hand basis, particularly among migrant workers, may be an issue (Croucher and White 2007; MAC 2014).

Employment relations reflection 7.5: Unpaid internships—avoiding the minimum wage?

Chapter 2 highlighted the use of unpaid internships by employers as a means of gaining cheaper labour. Some trade unions claim that employers use unpaid work experience as a way of reducing costs, and of avoiding having to pay the minimum wage, with little benefit for the workers involved. The media and broadcasting union BECTU claims that any training element in these internships is largely absent, and that the use of volunteer labour in this way 'amounts to the exploitation of young people desperate to gain a foothold in the film/TV sector' (TUC 2008: 121). The Low Pay Commission is very concerned that some employers classify unpaid positions as 'internships' to avoid complying with the NMW, when in fact the people filling them are undertaking real jobs, and that this practice is becoming more widespread (LPC 2012, 2013, 2016). The government has published guidance which specifies that unless they are genuine volunteers, or students undertaking placements of less than a year's duration, then workers directly engaged in work activities—having a role that extends beyond simply observing others—are entitled to receive at least the NMW (BIS 2013). Simply designating unpaid interns as 'volunteers' does not release an employer from their obligation to offer the minimum wage. However, there is evidence that unpaid internship positions remain commonplace. In 2016, for example, the National Trust was criticized for advertising administrative roles on an unpaid basis (Page 2014; Johnston 2016).

There are opportunities for unscrupulous employers to evade their obligation to pay workers the minimum wage. The practice of providing opportunities for unpaid work experience as a means of avoiding the NMW has proved controversial (see Employment relations reflection 7.5). The use of bogus self-employment arrangements (see Chapter 2) also enables employers to evade having to pay the NMW. In 2016, for example, it was reported that delivery workers used by the major courier company Hermes were being paid less than the NMW (Booth, Evans, and Osborne 2016). There are reports of shop and café workers being expected to 'clock off', and thus not be paid, during periods when there are no customers in their establishments (TUC 2015d). One particular scam involves classifying staff as apprentices, who are entitled only to a lower NMW rate, while failing to provide them with the requisite skills training. The high-street retail chain Next, for example, is alleged to have used this approach to reducing wage costs. Unaware they had been classified as 'apprentices', agency workers employed in an ASOS warehouse reported they had received no additional training other than that provided during their induction (Channel Four 2015a, 2015b).

The LPC claims that non-compliance is a particular problem in some areas, especially in the social care sector (LPC 2016). Funding cuts, and the nature of commissioning arrangements, have put care providers under pressure to reduce costs. As a result, workers are often only paid for the time when they are actually attending to users, not for the time spent travelling between different clients. Moreover, reductions in the time supposed to be devoted to particular clients mean that if workers are to carry out their duties properly, they can only do so on an effectively unpaid basis (BBC Panorama 2011; Ramesh 2013). One study suggests that as a result some 160,000 jobs in the care sector (11 per cent of the total) do not attract the NMW (Gardiner 2015).

There are two methods of enforcing the NMW. First, workers themselves are entitled to pursue their right to be paid the minimum wage by litigating against employers. There are a few hundred complaints about non-payment of the NMW made to employment tribunals each year. However, there are a number of problems with this method of enforcement. For one thing, workers may lack the appropriate knowledge of their rights under the NMW legislation, and so may not be aware that they have a justified complaint (TUC 2008). Even if they do have adequate knowledge, workers can be reluctant to complain about underpayment of the minimum wage—with good reason, since there is some evidence that employers victimize workers who make their voices heard, putting their jobs in jeopardy (Croucher and White 2007). Moreover, as Chapter 10 shows, the 2013 introduction of fees constitutes another obstacle preventing workers from submitting a tribunal claim. Concerns have been expressed that government reforms of the employment tribunal system have the potential to compromise NMW compliance efforts (LPC 2016).

The second method of ensuring compliance with the NMW concerns proactive enforcement by HM Revenue and Customs (HMRC). Between 1999 and 2015 HMRC enforcement activity resulted in the identification of £68 million worth of underpayment, affecting over 300,000 workers (NAO 2016). However, HMRC's approach was initially viewed as being a rather inadequate method of promoting compliance (Croucher and White 2007). During the 2000s it was reckoned that, on average, an employer could expect a visit from an enforcement officer once every 320 years—leading Metcalf (2008: 499) to observe that perhaps the really remarkable thing is 'that so many employers do comply with the NMW'. Prompted by pressure from trade unions, campaigners for the low-paid, and also the views of the LPC itself, during the latter half of the 2000s the then Labour government took steps to improve the enforcement of the NMW legislation. These included increased resources and better targeted enforcement activity by HMRC officers, and focusing on industries like clothing and textiles where there were known problems of non-compliance (LPC 2010; Patel 2011; BIS/HRMC 2013). In addition, the Employment Act 2008 established a new penalty regime under which an employer can be fined up to £5,000 per worker for a failure to pay the NMW, and improved the process by which workers could claim any wage arrears.

When the Conservative–Liberal Democrat coalition government took office in 2010 there was a worry that coalition budget cuts could damage enforcement efforts, particularly by compromising attempts to publicize the NMW (LPC 2011). Over time, however, the coalition government and its 2015 Conservative successor have strengthened NMW enforcement arrangements in a number of respects. The financial sanctions imposed on employers found to have broken the law have been increased. In 2014, for example, the maximum penalty for underpayment of the NMW was raised to £20,000 per underpaid worker. The coalition government also introduced a new policy designed to act as a deterrent against employers contemplating non-compliance with the NMW. This involves periodically publishing the names of companies found to have breached the law, together with details of the number of workers involved and the amount of underpayment. Under this policy, between 2013 and 2016 a total of 687 employers were 'named and shamed' for breaking the NMW law, amounting to £3.5 million in unpaid wages (NAO 2016). In 2015, for example, the leading fashion retailer Monsoon was identified as having failed to comply with the law since 1,400 of its staff had not been paid the NMW—because of a requirement to purchase discounted Monsoon clothing to wear on duty.

The government has also increased the resources given to HMRC for the purpose of enforcing the NMW. Between 2014–15 and 2016–17 its enforcement budget rose from £9.2 million to £20 million per year, allowing it to double the number of dedicated inspectors (NAO 2016). Concern has been expressed, however, that HMRC has been insufficiently committed to instituting criminal proceedings against employers (LPC 2012). Between 1999 and 2016 there were just nine prosecutions of employers for breaches of the NMW law (NAO 2016). The Trades Union Congress (TUC) has welcomed the increased efforts being put into enforcing the NMW. However, it argues that there is much more that could be done to ensure compliance, including greater use of prosecutions, more targeted enforcement activity, and a greater role for unions in the workplace, on the basis that collective bargaining can be a particularly effective means of tackling the problem of low pay (TUC 2015d).

7.4.3 From the minimum wage to the living wage

The NMW seems to have had some effect in moderating wage inequality, in particular by augmenting the income of the poorest working households (see Coats 2007: 57; Metcalf 2008). During the 2000s, rises in the level of the minimum wage helped to narrow the ratio between the average earnings of the lowest-paid and median pay—so-called 'lower-tail inequality' (Manning 2012; Lindley and Machin 2013). Between 1999 and 2015, workers at the lower end of the earnings scale benefited from higher wage increases than those at the middle, helping to reduce inequality (LPC 2016). That said, however, 'upper-tail inequality'— the gap between the median and top earners—continued to grow, at least until the 2007–8 crisis and subsequent economic recession, since when it seems to have moderated (Machin 2011; Lindley and Machin 2013; Belfield et al. 2016). Between 1990 and 2014–15 the share of income received by the top 1 per cent of earners rose from 5.7 to 7.9 per cent. The incomes of a small minority of people at the very top of the earnings hierarchy rose sharply relative to other groups (Resolution Foundation 2013), 'racing away' from those of people further down the scale (Brewer et al. 2008; Belfield et al. 2016). Very high earners, those at the very peak of the income distribution scale, like boardroom directors for example, have been able to secure ever higher levels of remuneration relative to others; this has prompted a debate about the desirability of regulating executive pay (see Employment relations reflection 7.6).

Employment relations reflection 7.6: Executive pay and the growth of pay inequality

One of the factors which have contributed to pay inequality in Britain has been the ever-increasing level of remuneration enjoyed by the directors of public limited companies, relative to average wages. In the 1980s the chief executive of a FTSE 100 company typically earned around twenty times the amount received by an average worker. By 2014 this had risen to 183 times the level of average earnings. Top executives continue to benefit from high annual pay increases, even as most employees have seen their earnings and living standards squeezed. In 2015, the average annual salary of a FTSE 100 chief executive was £5.5 million, up from £4.1 million in 2010 (High Pay Centre 2014, 2016). And excessive rewards at the top are not just restricted to private companies. Between 2010 and 2015 the average pay of university heads rose by 14 per cent, outstripping that of their staff, which increased by just 5 per cent (UCU 2016). Top pay often bears little relationship to how well the company has performed. It increases when the company has been successful, but tends not to diminish when performance slips (BIS 2012c: 9). Business groups such as the Institute of Directors claim that companies are operating in a global market for talent, and thus need to offer high basic salaries, and also the prospect of share options and generous bonuses, in order to attract key executives. Nevertheless, since the size of a director's remuneration package signals their importance relative to others, status, rather than the market, would appear to be the foremost influence on boardroom pay.

Excessive remuneration contributes to a range of social and economic problems, including greater wage inequality, lower levels of trust and social cohesion, and demotivated staff (Machin 2011; High Pay Centre 2014; CIPD 2015b). Some argue, therefore, that more effective regulation of executive pay would be in the wider public interest (High Pay Centre 2014). Successive governments have been reluctant to legislate to regulate boardroom pay, believing that responsibility for directors' remuneration should rest in the hands of a company's shareholders. In the early 2000s Labour introduced legislation which gave shareholders the opportunity to vote on directors' remuneration arrangements at company annual general meetings. Such votes, though, were merely voluntary, and companies could ignore them if they wished. However, widely reported corporate excesses prompted the Conservative–Liberal Democrat coalition government to introduce further regulation in 2013, including a requirement that executive pay arrangements win the approval of at least 50 per cent of a company's shareholders every three years. The 2016 announcement that BP chief executive Bob Dudley was to receive a pay increase of 20 per cent—taking his remuneration package to £14 million per year—despite the firm's falling profits, generated huge controversy. Although most of BP's shareholders (59 per cent) voted against the increase, since the vote was non-binding (BP did not have to give shareholders a binding vote until 2017), the company ignored the result. While increasing the influence of shareholders over executive remuneration arrangements is welcome, it seems unlikely, on its own, to do much to check excessive rises in top pay.

Although the NMW has made a positive contribution to reducing wage inequality at the bottom end of the income distribution scale, and in tackling extreme levels of low pay (Corlett and Gardiner 2015), it has been rather less effective when it comes to tackling the problem of low pay in general. There is a tendency for the NMW to be used 'not as a floor to pay rates but as the going rate for many occupations' in low-paying sectors of the economy (Grimshaw and Rubery 2010: 357). While the minimum wage has been highly beneficial in protecting workers who are in extremely badly paid jobs, some 5.5 million people, most of whom receive at least the minimum wage, are still classified as being 'low-paid' (Corlett and Gardiner 2015). The incidence of low pay in the UK is particularly high by international standards (Ray, Foley, and Hughes 2014). One of the reasons for this is that workers in low-paying sectors of the economy are generally excluded from the influence of collective bargaining arrangements, something which helps poverty wages to endure (Grimshaw and Rubery 2010). Although government action to strengthen NMW enforcement arrangements is welcome, more needs to be done to tackle the structural causes of low pay—such as the high prevalence of flexible working arrangements, low skills, weak productivity, and the absence of trade unions in low-paying sectors of the economy (Ray, Foley, and Hughes 2014; TUC 2015d). Some 6 million people, nearly a quarter (23 per cent) of the workforce—people working in bars, restaurants, hotels, care homes, and shops for example—do not earn enough to live on (KPMG 2015).

While the concept of the 'living wage' is not new (Bennett and Lister 2010), during the 2000s the focus of many campaigners against low pay shifted away from minimum wage provision towards greater advocacy of a 'living wage', particularly in the United States (Luce 2004). In 2001, the London Living Wage campaign was launched; it subsequently grew substantially under the auspices of networks of community organizations like Citizens UK, with grass-roots fair pay and living wage campaigns spreading around the country. The living wage concept is based on the notion that workers should be entitled to a minimum level of pay which is sufficient to enable them to maintain an adequate standard of living for themselves and their families, based on the cost of food, housing, and other essentials, keeping them out of poverty. This is not something which is part of the LPC's remit when it comes to determining the statutory NMW rates. Moreover, paying the living wage is voluntary for employers (Bennett and Lister 2010; Manning 2012; D'Arcy and Finch 2016). There are separate living wage rates for London (where living costs are higher) and the rest of the UK, calculated by the Greater London Authority's Living Wage Unit and Loughborough University's Centre for Research in Social Policy respectively. In 2015–16, the living wage rates were £9.40 per hour in London and £8.25 elsewhere.

Sometimes working in collaboration with trade unions, during the 2000s living wage campaigners linked to grass-roots community organizations like Citizens UK made strenuous efforts to promote the living wage among employers. Protests and demonstrations were organized to raise awareness of low pay in leading companies like Barclays and KPMG, especially among their contract cleaning, catering, and security staff, leveraging change by exposing them to negative publicity and the threat of reputational damage. 'The various living wage campaigns have been the most successful examples of grassroots community organizing in recent years' (Manning 2012: 21). In 2011, Citizens UK established a Living Wage Foundation, whose role is primarily concerned with encouraging and supporting the voluntary efforts of employers to ensure that workers receive a living wage. The case for paying a living wage is increasingly grounded in 'appeals to ethical business best practice and anecdotal evidence of the potential benefits to business of paying low-paid workers a higher wage' (Pennycook 2012: 5). There are advantages for employers in adopting a living wage, including reduced levels of turnover and absenteeism, greater employee loyalty, and higher productivity, which more than offset the financial costs of paying higher wages (Coulson and Bonner 2014). The cosmetics chain Lush, for example, has introduced the living wage for its workforce in London. The company claims that as a result it has benefited from having more loyal and less tired workers, because they do not have to take additional jobs to supplement their incomes (BBC News 2012a). By the middle of 2016, the Living Wage Foundation had accredited over 2,600 living wage employers, including major banks such as Barclays, Lloyds, and HSBC.

LEGISLATION AND POLICY 7.7: The National Living Wage

In July 2015, the newly elected majority Conservative government announced the introduction of a new 'National Living Wage' (NLW) for workers aged 25 and over. It came into effect in April 2016, at a rate of £7.20 per hour, and is anticipated to increase to at least £9.00 per hour by 2020. The NLW policy reflects an emergent consensus around the need to tackle low pay, and its adverse consequences, such as high levels of in-work poverty and poor productivity (D'Arcy and Davies 2016). As Chapter 3 shows, though, there was also clearly a political imperative present, with the Conservatives eager to demonstrate their concern with the interests of workers. Yet if the government is so keen to improve the pay prospects of workers, why does it have such an aversion to them organizing collectively to secure pay rises through trade unions? Why is the government setting wage rates seen as a good thing, but not trade unions? Legislation such as the Trade Union Act 2016 (see Chapter 9) weakens unions' mobilizing capacity, and thus their ability to extend their organization in a way that could benefit low-paid workers who currently work in sectors of the economy where a union presence is scarce. The government's motivation for establishing the NLW seems to have come from a desire to offset planned tax and benefit changes that would have left many low-income households substantially worse off (Williams, Scott, and Welch 2016). It is important to emphasize that the NLW is not a genuine 'living wage'. Effectively it amounts to an increase in the NMW for workers aged 25 and over; and the NLW rate is 'not set with any consideration of what is needed to meet an acceptable standard of living' (D'Arcy and Finch 2016: 15).

While some employers were supportive of the NLW policy, others, particularly those operating in low-paying sectors of the economy, such as retail and social care, expressed concern about its affordability given the increase in their wage bills (D'Arcy and Davies 2016; LPC 2016). The introduction of the £7.20 rate in April 2016—an increase of 50 pence on the NMW rate for workers aged 25 and over—resulted in some employers, such as the major retailer B&Q, taking action to recover their increased wage costs, including the withdrawal or reduction of paid breaks, overtime pay, and Sunday pay (Butler 2016b). In the medium to long term, increased productivity offers the best prospect of accommodating the NLW in low-paying sectors of the economy, something the government has been urged to prioritize (D'Arcy and Davies 2016).

The concept of a living wage seems to have a lot going for it; it is attractive to members of the public, and also for employers wanting to demonstrate their ethical credentials (Bennett and Lister 2010). Leading politicians from all the major political parties have given it their public backing. The UK Conservative government has used the language of the 'living wage' to package its policy of increasing the NMW rate for workers aged 25 and over (see Legislation and policy 7.7). Yet living wage campaigners have struggled to make progress for contract cleaners and other workers in government departments in the face of employer opposition to pay increases. Moreover, there are a number of problems with the living wage approach, which cast some doubt on its efficacy as a means of tackling the issue of low pay. Since the needs of households and families vary so widely, it is not possible to specify a rate of pay which encompasses them all (Coats 2007). There are a range of factors other than pay which influence household living standards, such as how many earners there are in the household (Manning 2012). A further problem relates to the rather low number of workers that have benefited from the living wage movement; between 2005 and 2011 only around 10,000 workers received a pay rise as a result of organizations agreeing to become living wage employers (Pennycook 2012). While workers who are paid a living wage seem to be happier, and feel more valued, it does not necessarily translate into higher earnings, not least because sometimes employers respond by reducing employees' hours (Linneker and Wills 2015).

The roster of living wage employers is dominated by large public sector organizations, many of whose workers have their pay influenced by collective bargaining, and private companies such as financial and legal firms who have relatively few low-paid workers among their direct and contractor staff. For them, the costs of agreeing to pay a living wage are minor, but the reputational gains of being viewed as a living wage employer are potentially very large indeed. Yet for firms that employ large numbers of low-paid workers, such as major retailers, any supposed business benefits could well be outweighed by the adverse impact of the increase in labour costs that would arise from paying a living wage (Pennycook 2012). It was only in September 2015 that the first major supermarket chain—Lidl—announced that it would adopt the living wage.

 ## Section summary and further reading

- While many countries operate statutory minimum wages, the first National Minimum Wage (NMW) in the UK was introduced by Labour in 1999. The establishment of the NMW was in large part a response to concerns about rising wage inequality, and its adverse social and economic effects; it was designed to reduce the level of extreme low pay by setting a legal floor for wages.

- The Low Pay Commission (LPC) is charged with overseeing the operation of the NMW, including making recommendations on minimum wage rates to the government. It has tended to take a rather cautious approach, concerned that if the NMW was introduced at too high a level, or was increased too precipitously, it would jeopardize jobs in low-paying sectors of the economy.

- In general, there have been no adverse effects of the NMW on employment. It has been accommodated by firms in low-paying sectors of the economy with relative ease. Nevertheless, there are growing concerns about non-compliance in some parts of the economy, and that unscrupulous employers can exploit loopholes to avoid paying the NMW.

- The NMW has been praised as a highly successful government policy intervention. It has played some part in reducing inequality at the lower end of the earnings scale. However, the NMW does not appear to have been a very effective tool when it comes to reducing the extent of low-paid work in the economy. There is growing interest in how far this is likely to be addressed through voluntary efforts by employers to commit to paying staff a living wage.

Grimshaw and Rubery (2010) provide a good overview of matters relating to low pay and the NMW. See the Resolution Foundation's website for details of research and analysis about low pay and related topics. There is an extensive overview of how the NMW developed in Butcher (2012). For more information about the voluntary living wage approach, see Pennycook (2012), Manning (2012), and Coulson and Bonner (2014). You can find out more about the work of the Living Wage Foundation from its website.

7.5 Conclusion

One of the most important changes in work and employment relations concerns the declining importance of collective bargaining as a means of determining pay, particularly in the private sector. Nevertheless, collective bargaining remains commonplace in the public sector, especially if the pay review body system is considered as a form of 'arm's length' bargaining.

What have been the main implications of the contraction of collective bargaining coverage? This chapter considered three particularly noteworthy developments. First, the increased extent of unilateral regulation of pay issues by management was identified. However, managers do not appear to have used their apparent new-found freedom to innovate very much in pay arrangements. Rather, they prefer to rely on established, tried and tested, and standardized approaches to pay determination. In attempting to pursue changes in employment relations, managers are constrained by the need to secure their legitimacy among the workforce. This is very important since it demonstrates that, even though the power of the trade unions has declined substantially, the wage–work bargain remains relevant as a way of conceptualizing the employment relationship, and that there are important limits to the exercise of managerial prerogative. Second, although other factors have played a part, the decline of collective bargaining as a means of determining pay has contributed to the growth of pay inequality. Moreover, as was mentioned in Chapter 1, collective bargaining is not just a pay-setting mechanism; its presence also allows workers a say, or voice, over decisions that affect them at work. The diminution of trade union power has enabled employers to secure changes to the wage–work bargain in ways that are advantageous to them, something that has helped to promote inequality. Third, the implementation of the NMW has been a significant development, given that it creates a statutory floor for wages. Such regulation of work and employment relationships through the law, however, is a weak substitute for collective bargaining. The NMW was initially set at a deliberately low, or cautious, level that was designed to alleviate the most extreme cases of low pay in a way that would not be disruptive to employers.

While it has played a part in reducing wage inequality in the lower half of the income scale, the NMW has done little to diminish the incidence of low pay, which is still extensive in some parts of the economy. Thus statutory regulation of the employment relationship is, by itself, not an adequate replacement for joint regulation as a means of securing improved pay and conditions for workers. The living wage approach is a potentially highly effective approach for improving the earnings of low-paid workers. However, the voluntary basis of the living wage, and its reliance on ethical, business case arguments, seem likely to limit its impact, particularly among employers that use large numbers of low-paid staff.

 ## Assignment and discussion questions

1. Identify the main reasons for the decline in collective bargaining coverage between the 1980s and 2000s.

2. What are the main issues and challenges of operating performance-related pay schemes for employers?

3. In your view, are the current NMW and NLW rates set too high, too low, or about right? Or would you get rid of the NMW and NLW entirely? Justify your answer.

4. Critically assess the contribution made by the NMW to tackling the problem of low pay in the UK.

5. What are 'living wage' campaigns? To what extent do you support the idea of a 'living wage', and why?

 Visit the Online Resource Centre that accompanies this book to develop your understanding of this chapter and keep up to date with the latest developments in this area.
www.oxfordtextbooks.co.uk/orc/williams4e/

Chapter case study: Campaigning for fair pay in supermarkets

Campaigns for fairer pay for workers employed in supermarkets have become increasingly vocal and well organized. In 2012 the Fair Pay Network published a report on low pay in four major national supermarket chains—Asda, Morrisons, Sainsbury's, and Tesco—called *Face the Difference*, based on interviews with 100 employees. Between them these firms employ around 900,000 staff, and they have been expanding rapidly, and are highly profitable. Their respective chief executives enjoy pay and benefits packages of between £3 million and £6 million each year. Yet many of the workers employed by these supermarket chains are paid wages so low that they are kept in poverty. The firms are not doing anything which is unlawful; they pay all their staff hourly rates which comply with both the NMW and, now, the NLW. However, the Fair Pay Network believes that the major supermarket chains could easily afford to give all of their workers a higher rate of pay which is sufficient to keep them out of poverty. The report shows that many low-paid supermarket workers face major financial problems, including increasing levels of unsecured personal debt, and that most (52 per cent) had cut their spending on food items over the twelve months prior to the research. The Fair Pay Network states that 'it cannot be acceptable to employers, employees, government or public that the gigantic employer block formed by Tesco, ASDA, Sainsbury's and Morrisons, enjoying quite colossal profits and vast executive pay packages at the top, will not commit to paying all of its employees a wage rate that keeps them out of poverty' (Fair Pay Network 2012: 8). Among other things, the Fair Pay Network recommends that the major supermarket chains should commit to paying all their workers at least a living wage (in 2015–16 this was £9.40 per hour in London, £8.25 elsewhere), and to ensuring that low-paid staff have sufficient opportunities for career progression. The report also calls on the trade unions to make more vigorous efforts to organize supermarket workers and boost union membership, so that they have more protection.

Other campaigns have focused on changing the employment practices of major supermarket chains. Sainsbury's, for example, has been specifically targeted by the 'Pay Up' campaign, which highlights the extensive profits made by the supermarket chain and the massive increases in remuneration enjoyed by its directors. Yet between 2004 and 2012 its lowest-paid workers actually saw their pay cut in real terms (after inflation), and many have to rely on credit cards or payday loans to get through the month. In May 2012, supporters of the Pay Up campaign, some of whom are linked to the activist organization UK Uncut, held a protest outside the London headquarters of Sainsbury's. A Pay Up spokesperson claimed that the supermarket chain

> has seen rising profits and booming CEO pay, but real-terms pay cuts for workers on basic rates. We want the workforce to take home a greater slice of the Sainsbury's pie. Workers at Sainsbury's have been demanding a living wage for over a year, and Pay Up is echoing that demand.

For its part, Sainsbury's claimed to treat its staff fairly, and that its pay rates were generous for the retail industry. Its arch-rival, Tesco, did not escape the attention of low pay activist campaigns either. In February 2012, one of its Express stores in Central London was forced to close for an hour because of a protest over claims that the supermarket chain had offered unpaid 'work experience' positions as part of the coalition government's controversial Work Programme to get unemployed people back into employment. Campaigners have criticized the large extent to which low-paid staff employed by the major supermarket chains have to depend on tax credits and other welfare benefits in order to maintain a basic standard of living. As a result, taxpayers are effectively subsidizing the supermarkets, because of their failure to pay a living wage, to the tune of around £1 billion per year.

These campaigns and protests demonstrate very clearly that employment relations is not just about the regulation of employment relationships, but also concerns the experiences and differential interests of workers and how the dominant interests of employers are often challenged as a result. The protests and mobilization efforts evident in these cases show how new networks of activists and campaigning coalitions are finding innovative ways of putting traditional employment relations concerns—pay and employment conditions—onto the agenda of policy-makers, unions, and employers. Some supermarket chains seem to be taking the question of low pay more seriously. The leading discounters Aldi and Lidl, in particular, have voluntarily raised the pay levels of their staff to at least the rate of the living wage, attracting a high level of positive publicity in the process. Their competitors, Tesco and Sainsbury's, acknowledge that they operate with lower basic rates of pay, but contend that these have to be seen in the context of their broad remuneration arrangements, which include paid breaks, pension contributions, and other benefits.

Sources: Fair Pay Network (2012); Felsted (2015); Meadway (2015); Taylor (2012); Pay Up website

Questions

What is the purpose of campaigns for fairer pay in supermarkets? To what extent do you think they are necessary?

8 Working time and employment relations

Chapter objectives

The main objectives of this chapter are to:

- demonstrate the importance of working time as an employment relations issue;
- identify and account for the main working time trends;
- examine how working time is used by employers, and the reasons for, and consequences of, high levels of work intensity; and
- explain how working time matters are subject to legal regulation, in particular the scope of the Working Time Regulations.

8.1 Introduction

Working time—its length, its pattern, and its use—is a central concern of employment relations. As was discussed in the introductory chapter of this book, the principal feature of the employment relationship is the exchange of wages for latent labour power—an employee's capacity to work. When a job is started it is not the worker's labour that an employer is buying, but, in effect, his or her time. It is then the task of the employer to ensure that this time is used productively (Arrowsmith and Sisson 2000). Moreover, working time has long been an issue on which trade unions have campaigned, for a shorter working week in particular.

For a number of reasons the topic of working time has attracted a greater amount of attention in recent years. Concerns have arisen about the harmful effects of excessive working hours, linked to the rise of what has become popularly known as the 'long hours culture'. Working time is now affected by a greater degree of legal regulation; in particular, the European Union's (EU) Working Time Directive has attracted rather a lot of controversy. Employers are interested in how working time can be arranged in ways that improve organizational efficiency and generate performance improvements. Moreover, policy-makers have taken measures to encourage more flexible working time arrangements, not least because of the potential they have to improve gender equality (Grimshaw and Rubery 2010; Eurofound 2012).

The chapter commences in Section 8.2 with an overview of the importance of working time as an employment relations issue and how it can be understood, before some key trends relating to the duration of working time are discussed in Section 8.3. In Section 8.4 the focus switches to flexible working time arrangements, including a critical assessment of the rise of employment contracts that do not offer any guaranteed minimum hours of work: so-called 'zero-hours contracts'. The focus of Section 8.5 is on how working time is used, with a particular emphasis on explaining prevailing high levels of work intensity. As already mentioned, the EU Working Time Directive, and the Working Time Regulations (WTR) in the UK, mean that some working time matters have become more strictly regulated by law. We look at this legislation, explain why it has been controversial, and consider its implications in Section 8.6.

 Introductory case study: Overtime bans on the railways

Working time, and how it is organized, managed, and remunerated, is an integral feature of employment relations. Some industries rely heavily on the use of overtime arrangements—getting workers to undertake more work over and above their normal working hours, often in return for a premium payment. But an over-reliance on paid overtime working can, when handled badly, create difficulties, particularly in those parts of the economy where unions are well organized and thus try to exercise a degree of control over working time arrangements. This is evident on the railways, where unions have used restrictions on overtime as a bargaining lever in disputes with employers. In December 2005, Central Trains, one of the UK's passenger rail operators, cancelled all of its services on the Sunday before Christmas because too few train drivers had reported for work. Sunday working was undertaken on the basis of voluntary overtime, in return for a premium payment. Most of the time this meant that Central Trains had sufficient drivers to maintain its Sunday timetable. In this instance, though, the failure of enough drivers to report for work caused significant disruption. Since then, train companies have experienced similar problems on a regular basis. In November 2009, for example, First Capital Connect was forced to cancel hundreds of Sunday services after its drivers declined to undertake voluntary overtime; and in December 2015 the train drivers' union ASLEF instituted a ban on non-contractual overtime working as part of its pay dispute with the company Arriva Trains Wales. The extensive disruption to rail services provided by the train operator Southern in 2016 was in part caused by the alleged withdrawal of overtime arrangements by the company (see Chapter 9).

8.2 Working time and employment relations

As mentioned in Section 8.1, the question of working time is integral to the wage–work bargain that characterizes the employment relationship.

> Under the traditional or standard employment relationship it is labour time that is sold, primarily in continuous daily blocks under open-ended contracts, and it is up to the employer to extract the anticipated labour power through the management of work organization and employee effort and performance.

(Grimshaw and Rubery 2010: 362)

Managing working time effectively is a crucial way in which employers can secure improvements in productive efficiency. Like any other aspect of the employment relationship, though, attempts by employers to control working time have always been challenged by workers. One way in which they can contest working time is by absenting themselves (Ackroyd and Thompson 1999)—see Chapter 9.

Working time has long been a key source of contestation between unions and employers, and campaigns to reduce its length were 'fundamental to the organization of the working class and the development of labour solidarity' (Arrowsmith 2002: 114). This can be seen in the long-running attempts by workers, collectively through trade unions, to shorten the length of both the working day and the working week. Although nineteenth-century campaigns by prominent liberal philanthropists helped to secure reduced working hours for women and child workers, it is important to recognize that legislation was largely the outcome of working-class pressure for reform (Arrowsmith 2002).

The reduction of working time has been a central aim of organized labour ever since, and working time issues, such as the length of the working week, have long been important matters for collective bargaining between employers and trade unions (Grimshaw and Rubery 2010; Eurofound 2012). During the 1980s and 1990s, for example, engineering unions in Germany and Britain successfully used industrial action to reduce the length of the working week. However, this often came at a price, as employers conceded fewer hours in return for greater flexibility over the utilization of working time (McKinlay and McNulty 1992; Hyman 2001). In recent years, the Trades Union Congress (TUC) has made the excessive working hours experienced by some groups of workers a campaign priority (Blyton 2011).

Perhaps the most notable recent example of how working time issues are often central to the collective bargaining agenda between employers and unions relates to the introduction of short-time working arrangements as an attempt to mitigate the effects of the economic recession. Such agreements, which were particularly evident in Germany and Italy, involve unions consenting to reduced working hours on a temporary basis in order to lessen costs and thus preserve jobs (Eurofound 2010; Lang, Clauwert, and Schömann 2013). There have also been instances in the UK. In November 2015, for example, over 2,000 members of the GMB union working for the agriculture and construction machinery firm JCB voted to reduce their weekly hours of work, helping to avert proposed job losses arising from a fall in demand for the company's products.

 Contesting employment relations 8.1: The struggle over Sunday working

Efforts by European governments to liberalize Sunday shopping hours have been challenged by unions representing retail workers. In England and Wales, large shops are only able to open for six consecutive hours on Sundays, between 10.00 and 18.00. In early 2016, the Conservative government had planned to give local authorities the power to extend Sunday shopping hours in their areas. According to the then government minister, Anna Soubry, 'extending Sunday shopping hours has the potential to help businesses and high streets better compete as our shopping habits change'. The government's plans were welcomed by big retailers; though small shops, Christian groups—keen to keep Sunday 'special'—and the shopworkers' union USDAW opposed them. The Conservatives insisted that shopworkers objecting to working Sundays would be offered more scope to 'opt out'. However, the general secretary of USDAW, John Hannett, claimed that the existing situation satisfied retailers, customers, and shopworkers, and that the government's plans were a 'betrayal of shopworkers and all those who regard Sunday as a special day'. Parliamentary opposition meant that in March 2016 the Conservative government's proposed changes were defeated. Nevertheless, governments across Europe—including in France, Greece, and Poland—have been looking at ways of deregulating Sunday shopping hours as a means of helping to promote economic growth. Although their efforts often generate strong opposition from unions, employees themselves are often more pragmatic, welcoming the opportunity to work more hours on a Sunday as long as they are paid at a premium rate.

Sources: BBC News (2016); BIS (2016c); Cabrita (2015a); R. Mason (2016)

However, the decline of the trade unions and the diminishing scope and importance of collective bargaining mean that in general joint regulation plays a less powerful part than it once did, with employers enjoying greater freedom to manage working time issues unilaterally (Grimshaw and Rubery 2010; Blyton 2011). Moreover, in some areas, such as the care sector, managing working time effectively is integral to exercising control over workers and securing efficiency (Rubery et al. 2015). That is not to say, however, that working time matters go uncontested, as is evident from both the example of the railways discussed in the introductory case study and the challenges arising from efforts to liberalize Sunday shopping hours (see Contesting employment relations 8.1).

The increased degree of managerial regulation over working time produces its own problems, tensions, and conflicts, since workers often challenge and contest efforts by employers to exercise control over this area of employment relations. Workers can use and adapt working time for their own purposes, in ways that do not necessarily conform with managerial expectations. In call centres, for example, where the pressure of customer service roles is often fairly intense, there is evidence that front-line managers may take a more lenient approach to employee absences from work in situations where the staff have developed a strong collective identity, which expresses itself in an ability to influence custom and practice expectations of how working time should be used (Deery, Iverson, and Walsh 2010). The whole question of working time, then, demonstrates very clearly the nature of the employment relationship as a 'contested terrain', and the potential for conflict that exists between employers and employees as a result, in spite of the greater degree—formally at least—of unilateral managerial control—or perhaps even because of it (Grimshaw and Rubery 2010; Blyton 2011).

Section summary and further reading

- Working time is a key feature of employment relations, being central to the wage–work bargain that underpins the employment relationship.

- Working time has long been a prime source of contestation between employers and unions; working time issues are often a key feature of the collective bargaining agenda.

- Although the decline of the unions means that organizations enjoy greater scope to exercise managerial control over working time issues, it is nonetheless an area of employment relations which is marked by a pronounced potential for conflict between employers and employees.

The best overviews of working time and employment relations are provided by Blyton (2011) and Grimshaw and Rubery (2010). For a historical perspective on the role of working time in employment relations, see Arrowsmith (2002).

8.3 Working time duration: patterns and trends

Having considered the importance of working time in employment relations, and the way trade union efforts have been directed at reducing it, what, then, have been the main trends when it comes to the duration of working time? The focus of this section is on assessing the pattern of overall working hours, with particular attention to the extent and nature of excessive working hours, or the 'long hours culture' as it is popularly known.

8.3.1 **Overall working hours**

Historically, the overall trend, at least until the 1990s, was towards the reduction in the average number of weekly working hours for full-time employees. During the 1990s, however, this trend came to an end, resulting in British full-time employees achieving the dubious distinction of having the longest average working week in the EU. This raised significant concerns about the rise of what became known as the 'long hours culture' (Arrowsmith 2002; Grimshaw and Rubery 2010; BIS 2014).

There are a number of reasons why the average weekly working hours of full-time employees rose at this time. For one thing, greater competitive pressures encouraged many businesses to find ways of increasing output while freezing, or even reducing, staff numbers. Thus employees, particularly those in white-collar jobs like professionals and managers, were obliged to work more hours, usually unpaid, to take up the slack (Beynon et al. 2002). In addition, unlike other EU countries, where specific statutory limits on working time are usual (see International perspective 8.2 for the example of France), before the advent of the Working Time Regulations in 1998 (see Section 8.6.1) in the UK working time matters were generally left outside the scope of legal regulation (Grimshaw and Rubery 2010). An additional factor was the decline in the power of the trade unions who, through their collective bargaining endeavours, had hitherto been a major influence on the shortening of the working week.

 International perspective 8.2: The thirty-five-hour working week in France

The regulation and control of working time has long been a central concern of trade unions in France, and a prime source of contestation in employment relations. For much of the twentieth century, reductions in working hours, either through legislation or employer concessions, were the outcome of intense periods of mobilization and struggle by organized labour (Jefferys 2000). A 1982 law fixed the maximum working week, before overtime payments applied, at thirty-nine hours.

Realization of the thirty-five-hour limit had to await the 1997 election of a socialist government under the premiership of Lionel Jospin. The first 'Aubry' law of 1998, named after its ministerial sponsor, offered incentives for employers who negotiated thirty-five-hour agreements that created more jobs. The second 'Aubry' law of 2000 made the maximum thirty-five-hour week mandatory for all those working in firms with more than twenty employees. The ostensible aim of the legislation was to create job opportunities, and thus reduce the level of unemployment. But the legislation was also driven by another imperative: to encourage firms to negotiate workplace agreements with local union representatives over the more flexible use of working time (Jefferys 2003). This, it was hoped, would not only stimulate workplace bargaining, and thus challenge the authority of the unions and their national power bases, but also enhance productivity through the more intensive use of working time.

Understandably, therefore, many manual workers, who bore the brunt of such flexibility initiatives, were rather restrained in their support for the thirty-five-hour week. However, the main challenge came from the right-wing presidency of Nicolas Sarkozy, who was elected in 2007 on a platform which included a pledge to loosen the thirty-five-hour law. Reforms introduced in 2008 allowed employers to reach agreements with unions and employees which provide for greater flexibility over working hours. The Socialists, who returned to power in 2012, initially overturned this policy. However, under

(continued...)

the premiership of Manuel Valls, who took office in 2014, the Socialist government changed direction, part of a broader shift towards the acceptance of a neo-liberal agenda which privileges greater labour market flexibility. Reforms proposed in 2016 would ensure that while the thirty-five-hour working week would remain in principle, French employers would enjoy greater flexibility over working hours, thus diminishing its effectiveness.

Since the late 1990s, though, the problem of so-called 'long hours' working appears to have diminished in significance, as measured by the proportion of employees working more than forty-five hours a week. Table 8.1 shows that while this figure rose in the first half of the 1990s, it subsequently declined. In 1996, 23.5 per cent of employees usually worked for more than forty-five hours a week; by 2012, this had declined to 18.0 per cent. However, there was later a slight increase—to 18.3 per cent—evident between 2012 and 2016, indicating that the prevalence of excessive working hours rose in the aftermath of the recession. An analysis of working hours data undertaken by the TUC shows that in the five years between 2010 and 2015 there was a 15 per cent rise in the number of employees working more than forty-eight hours a week (TUC 2015b).

The long-term diminution of 'long hours' working has been largely concentrated among men. Whereas 37.0 per cent of male employees usually worked for more than forty-five hours per week in 1996, the proportion fell to 25.9 per cent in 2016 (see Table 8.2). Among women, though, this period saw a slight increase in 'long hours' working (BIS 2014).

The long-term decline in the proportion of employees working 'long hours', as well as a fall in the average number of hours usually worked each week, are trends which are evident across Europe (Messenger 2011; Eurofound 2012). While the number of weekly working hours for full-time employees in the UK is still relatively high by European standards (Grimshaw and Rubery 2010), contrary to popular perception it is not the highest in the EU (see Table 8.3).

Indeed, taken as a whole, the average length of the working week in the UK is unremarkable compared to other EU countries. The relatively high number of part-time jobs means that there is a wide spread of working hours in the economy; some work for many hours in an average week, whereas others may only work for a relatively small number of hours (Grimshaw and Rubery 2010; ONS 2011).

Table 8.1 Usual weekly hours of work in main job by percentage share of employees, 1992–2012

	1992	1996	2000	2004	2008	2012
Fewer than 6 hours	1.6	1.8	1.4	1.2	1.1	1.2
6–15 hours	8.4	8.3	7.7	7.4	6.5	6.6
16–30 hours	13.6	15.2	16.1	17.6	18.0	19.9
31–45 hours	55.3	51.3	52.3	54.3	55.5	54.3
Over 45 hours	21.1	23.5	22.5	19.6	18.8	18.0

Source: Office for National Statistics (http://www.statistics.gov.uk); licensed under the Open Government licence v.3.0

Table 8.2 Usual weekly hours of work in main job by percentage share of employees, 2016*

	All employees (%)	Men (%)	Women (%)
Fewer than 6 hours	1.1	0.8	1.5
6–15 hours	6.1	3.3	9.1
16–30 hours	19.6	8.6	30.8
31–45 hours	54.9	61.5	48.1
Over 45 hours	18.3	25.9	10.5

*May–July

Source: Office for National Statistics (http://www.statistics.gov.uk); licensed under the Open Government licence v.3.0

Table 8.3 Average number of weekly hours usually worked by full-time employees in main job, selected EU countries, 2014

Country	Hours worked (full-time employees)
Greece	44.2
Austria	43.0
UK	42.9
Spain	41.6
Germany	41.5
EU average	41.5
Netherlands	40.9
Sweden	40.8
France	40.5
Lithuania	39.5

Source: Eurostat, http://ec.europa.eu/eurostat/web/gdp-and-beyond/quality-of-life/average-number-of-usual-weekly-hours-of-work-in-main-job

8.3.2 Who works excessive hours?

High levels of weekly working hours tend to be concentrated among certain types of workers, namely full-time male managers and professionals, and male workers in specific sectors of the economy (Walsh 2010; Blyton 2011; BIS 2014). This reflects the large amount of overtime working that has long characterized employment relations in Britain—work that is undertaken in excess of the 'normal' working day or week. But we need to bear in mind that for workers in general there are two distinct motivations for undertaking overtime. Manual workers, particularly in transport, manufacturing, and process industries, often depend on overtime arrangements—with any additional hours they do being paid at a higher, premium rate—to supplement regular wages which might be quite low, and thus maintain their livelihoods.

For managers and professionals, though, overtime working is largely unpaid, and arises because the demands of their jobs mean that their work duties cannot be completed within normal working hours. The TUC estimates that over 5 million people perform some unpaid overtime, worth some £31.5 billion to the economy. It runs a campaign challenging the culture of unpaid overtime which exists in many organizations (see Contesting employment relations 8.3). Managerial and professional staff often have little choice other than to undertake unpaid overtime, because without it they are unable to perform their jobs to their employer's satisfaction, or demonstrate the requisite commitment to their position, jeopardizing their employment prospects (Blyton 2011). Yet a large part of the decline in 'long hours' working among men is related to a diminution in the level of overtime working (ONS 2015).

 Contesting employment relations 8.3: The TUC's Work Your Proper Hours Day campaign

The Trades Union Congress (TUC) campaigns against excessive working hours, claiming that they undermine people's work–life balance and damage their health. It reckons that over 5 million workers in the UK undertake some unpaid overtime work each year, amounting to some £31.5 billion worth of 'free work' for employers. In order to raise awareness of excessive working hours and their adverse consequences, every year the TUC announces a 'Work Your Proper Hours Day'. In 2016, it was 26 February, chosen because it was the day of the year that the average worker undertaking unpaid overtime stops working for free, and actually starts earning for him or herself. The TUC says that on this day workers should at least make sure they take a proper lunch break, and leave work on time.

8.3.3 The consequences of excessive working hours

There is a view that we need not be concerned about the number of working hours people undertake, even if they appear to be excessive. This is because they are a function of the choices workers make about how to balance their paid work and non-paid work responsibilities. People who work for lots of hours seem to have greater job satisfaction; they may put in more working hours because they find their jobs interesting and gratifying (Green and Whitfield 2009; Walsh 2010), or because the prospect of additional overtime payments is seen as desirable. The UK government emphasizes the importance of workers being able to exercise choices about the working hours they supply (BIS 2014).

Yet an over-reliance on paid overtime working can cause employers problems. It is a potentially very inefficient way of organizing working time. Workers may work more slowly during their normal contractual working hours in order to ensure that overtime—paid at a premium rate—is needed to complete their tasks. The preponderance of overtime working has long been criticized. Flanders (1975) viewed the existence of 'systematic overtime' as a sign of managerial irresponsibility; it was an inefficient, albeit relatively easy, way of securing increases in output without hiring new staff or, more importantly, investing in capital machinery, and thus stifled innovation. Workers welcomed the opportunity to undertake overtime since it enabled them to supplement their low basic wages. Overtime working became 'institutionalized', particularly among male manual workers (Arrowsmith 2002). This refers to the way in which overtime came 'to be accepted as a habit—as a way of life in industry—for which all kinds of justifications are then invented'. It gained 'a self-perpetuating character' (Flanders 1975: 56).

More importantly, there is now a large body of evidence demonstrating a link between excessive hours of work and adverse health outcomes. The negative effects of night work and other unsocial hours of work on employees' physiological and psychological well-being have long been recognized (e.g. Bara and Arber 2009). Studies show a link between excessive working hours and increased risk of strokes and heart disease (e.g. Virtanen et al. 2010; Kivimäki et al. 2015). The TUC (2009) highlights the range of conditions, including increased risk of heart disease, mental ill health, diabetes, and bowel problems, which are associated with people who habitually work for more than forty-eight hours a week.

People who work 'long hours' are generally more satisfied with their jobs, perhaps a reflection of their willingness to 'supply' greater work effort (see Section 8.5.2). However, on other measures—the extent to which they are contented with, and enthused by, their jobs—the picture is less positive, with data showing that undertaking excessive working hours is associated with lower levels of well-being (van Wanrooy et al. 2013b). More hours spent at work mean that the time workers can spend with friends and family members is diminished, a major catalyst for work–life imbalance.

 International perspective 8.4:   Swedish experiments with short working days

Sweden is a country where innovations in employment relations have often been prominent. In 2015, Swedish experiments with shorter working days garnered a large amount of international attention. There is nothing new about the concept of short working days in Sweden; in some Toyota service centres, for example, employees have been working six-hour days since the mid-2000s. There were also attempts to operate shorter working days in some public sector organizations during the 1990s, before a change in the political climate meant that they lost support. More recently, though, there has been a revival of interest in the benefits of the six-hour working day, including from a number of start-up businesses in the Swedish capital city Stockholm. The most notable initiative, though, occurred at a care home for the elderly in Gothenburg. In early 2015, the length of the working day for nursing staff was reduced from eight to six hours. Although it resulted in an increase in the direct financial costs to the employer, a provisional evaluation found that the change had also led to improvements in employee well-being, with staff taking less sick leave, as well as a better standard of care.

Sources: Crouch (2015a); Maddy Savage (2015)

Indeed, it would seem that greater demand from workers for working time arrangements that enable them to balance the competing demands of their working and non-working lives means that the question of long hours working, while it has by no means gone away, has become less imperative—as evidenced by the falling proportion of employees who usually work more than forty-five hours per week. There are other reasons why the extent of long hours working has diminished. Structural changes in the economy have played a part; in particular, the growth in the proportion of employment which is located in services—retail, care, hotels and restaurants, etc. Most jobs in these sectors are organized on a part-time basis, depressing the overall working hours figure (ONS 2011). Perhaps also we are simply seeing a reversion to the broad historical trend of falling working hours, linked to greater levels of affluence, which was evident through most of the twentieth century, with the increases of the 1980s and 1990s being a deviation from the norm (Green 2011). Moreover, the economic crisis, in particular the distinctive way in which it affected the labour market, through the marked shift in favour of part-time work and underemployment (see Chapter 2), may also have contributed to the trend of declining working hours. However, the number of employees working excessive hours seems to be on the rise again (TUC 2015b). Despite the lessons to be taken from Swedish experiments with short working days (see International perspective 8.4), some governments have tried to extend working hours as short-term competitiveness imperatives take priority over workers' health and well-being (Lang, Clauwert, and Schömann 2013).

 Section summary and further reading

- During the 1990s increasing working hours prompted concerns about the adverse effects of a 'long hours culture', particularly among managers, professionals, and certain groups of manual workers.

- Much 'long hours' working is a product of paid, or often unpaid, overtime working, which can have a detrimental effect on workers' well-being.

- Overall working hours have resumed their historical downward trajectory after the increase evident during the 1990s, a function of changes in the economy and composition of employment, and of demands from workers for working time arrangements that enable them to balance the demands of their jobs with activities outside of work.

- In addition to their adverse consequences for productivity, excessive working hours damage workers' health and well-being and impair their work–life balance.

Good overviews of working time trends are provided by Grimshaw and Rubery (2010), Blyton (2011), and BIS (2014). Messenger (2011) and Eurofound (2012) offer a broader European perspective. See Bittman (2016) for the importance of working time.

8.4 Flexible working time arrangements

As well as the duration of working time, measured by the number of hours people work in their jobs, another key issue in employment relations concerns the increasing prevalence of flexible working time arrangements. There is greater diversity of working time patterns, distinct from the conventional 'standard' full-time working week of, say, seven or eight hours per day over a five-day week, usually from Monday to Friday.

8.4.1 The growth of flexible working time arrangements

The significance of working time flexibility is particularly evident when it comes to the notable growth in the proportion of the workforce working on a part-time basis—see Tables 8.1 and 8.2 in Section 8.3.1. In 1992, 23.6 per cent of employees worked for thirty hours per week or less; this figure rose to 25.6 per cent in 2008 and to 26.8 per cent in 2016. Table 8.2 also shows the marked gender pattern in relation to working hours. Some two-fifths (41.4 per cent) of female employees work on a part-time basis (up to and including thirty hours per week), whereas just 12.7 per cent of male employees do so.

Although most employees continue to work a standard working week, it is by no means as commonplace as it once was, as working time arrangements become more variable and irregular—part of the 'de-standardization' of working hours (Bittman 2016; Grimshaw and Rubery 2010; Walsh 2010; Eurofound 2012). More than one in ten female employees usually work fewer than fifteen hours a week; and employers in some parts of the economy, such as in retail and social care, make use of highly irregular patterns of working time, which can change from week to week, or even from day to day (e.g. Rubery et al. 2015). This means that the concept of 'standard' working time needs to be used with some care, given the extent to which many people's 'normal' working hours now depart from the conventional model, including work-ing evenings and weekends (Blyton 2011). Working hours have also become increasingly polarized. Some managers and professionals regularly work in excess of fifty hours a week, whereas the incidence of part-time working has been growing. In a context of high levels of 'underemployment' (see Chapter 2), for many workers the problem is not one of a 'long hours culture', but of having insufficient hours to maintain their standard of living (Warren 2015*a*).

There are three main reasons why flexible working time arrangements have become more common. The first concerns changes in the economic context. Shifts in the composition of employment, particularly the growing proportion of the workforce based in the service sec-tor—e.g. shops, hotels, restaurants—where part-time working is more common, have had a pronounced effect (ONS 2011; Bittman 2016).

The second reason for the growing prevalence of flexible working patterns is because it suits employers, enabling them to manage labour in a more efficient manner. Using flexible work schedules helps employers to operate services outside of the conventional 'standard' working day, including in the evenings and at weekends, without having to pay out for pre-mium overtime payments (Bittman 2016; Grimshaw and Rubery 2010). In the social care sector employers have developed a range of 'fragmented' working time practices, such as contracts which do not offer any guaranteed minimum hours of work ('zero-hours contracts') for efficiency reasons and to enhance managerial control over labour utilization. In such cir-cumstances, managers use 'strict work schedules to focus paid work hours at high demand ... and do not reward or recognize work-related time between periods of high or direct cus-tomer demand' (Rubery et al. 2015: 754).

Some firms have developed 'annualized hours' systems to better enable them to match the supply of labour with demand. While they vary in their detail, the main feature of annualized hours arrangements is the specification of a certain number of hours to be worked by an employee in any given year, in exchange for a guaranteed (usually monthly) wage. The major benefit of annualized hours for employers is that it enables them to manage peaks and slumps in demand for a product over a year without having to resort to the use of expensive overtime when demand is high, or having workers sitting around idle when it is low. See Insight into practice 8.5 for the details of a system of annualized hours introduced in a food factory.

⊙ Insight into practice 8.5:   Annualized hours at Premier Foods

In 2012, Premier Foods introduced a system of annualized hours at its plant at Knighton in England, which makes a range of food products including custard powder and hot chocolate. Demand for its products is highly seasonal, with a significant peak during the winter months. Before making the change to annualized hours, the company secured the flexibility to cope with variation in demand over the course of the year by taking on additional temporary agency labour when needed, or through offering staff overtime opportunities. However, following the loss of a major contract, Premier Foods needed to cut costs. Instead of instituting job losses, the company saved money by introducing a system of annualized hours for manufacturing staff alongside new shift patterns. The new arrangements, which were agreed with the recognized trade union, meant that employees either worked 1,896 hours or 1,833 hours on an annual basis (depending on which part of the plant they worked in). This enabled

(continued...)

the company to organize working time more flexibly, by varying the number of shifts required over the year, while the workforce received twelve equal monthly wage payments. The changes—which resulted in a substantial saving in expenditure on agency workers and premium overtime payments—helped the company to cut costs, avoiding some redundancies (IDS 2013).

Since annualized hours schemes offer employers some major benefits, including reduced overtime payments, enhanced flexibility, and greater control over how working time is used, why are they not more common? In 2011, fewer than one in ten (8 per cent) of workplaces used annual hours contracts, although this was higher than in 2004 (van Wanrooy et al. 2013a).

Arrowsmith (2007) posits two reasons why annualized hours arrangements have not become more widely used. First, employers are satisfied with the flexibility offered by other types of working time arrangement—part-time working in areas like retail, for example, or shift-working in manufacturing industry. Moreover, there remains a strong preference for using overtime as a source of working time flexibility in order to respond to fluctuations in demand for products and services, despite its expense and inefficiency. Second, instituting annualized working arrangements demands a high degree of strategic management commitment, not least because of the need to overcome potential resistance from employees—and this is often absent. It is no coincidence that most annualized hours schemes operate in workplaces where there is a formal union presence, enabling the employer to negotiate their introduction in a way that helps to satisfy the interests of the workforce (Arrowsmith 2007).

The third reason for the growth of flexible working time arrangements relates to the increased female participation in the workforce, and the rising number of dual-earner households (where both partners are in employment). Flexible working time arrangements are often seen as desirable because they enable workers—especially female workers—to combine paid employment with unpaid household labour more readily. Warren, Pascall, and Fox's (2010) study of low-waged women in heterosexual couples illustrates just how important flexible work schedules are when it comes to accommodating childcare and fitting it around paid work. Given that their partners largely undertook full-time jobs, the bulk of the responsibility for childcare rested on the shoulders of these women, meaning that part-time working arrangements, often in the evenings and weekends when their partners were at home and could look after the children, were the only viable option for them, even though many would have liked to increase their hours.

Employers have responded to the greater demand from workers for flexible working time arrangements. In addition to part-time work, the availability of other forms of working time flexibility (such as compressed working weeks, where a standard number of working hours is worked over fewer than five full days, or flexi-time arrangements, which give workers some element of discretion over starting and finishing times) have become more commonplace—see Table 8.4 for a list of specific practices. The most commonly used forms of flexible working arrangements are: flexi-time, working from home, and part-time working (Tipping et al. 2012).

Governments in the UK have encouraged employers to increase the availability of flexible working time arrangements, for example by establishing a legal right for employees to request them. This is predicated on the belief that such flexibility generates important business benefits, including lower absenteeism and better recruitment and retention.

Table 8.4 Glossary of major flexible working time practices

Practice	Definition
Part-time working	Work that is undertaken on a less than full-time basis; any job which requires 30 or fewer hours each week is generally considered to be of part-time status.
Flexi-time	A form of working time arrangement that gives staff some discretion over their working hours, in particular their starting and finishing times.
Compressed working week	A way of organizing working time such that a standard number of working hours is worked over fewer than five full days; sometimes organized on the basis of a fortnight (e.g. nine days).
Annual hours	A type of working time arrangement in which people's hours are calculated on the basis of a year, rather than say a week. This gives organizations more flexibility to adjust the working hours of their staff to cope with seasonal fluctuations in demand without the use of expensive overtime.
Term-time working	An arrangement that enables staff with school-age children to work only during periods when the children are attending school.
Job-sharing/splitting	This involves an arrangement whereby a job is shared, or particular functions associated with a job are split, between two or more workers.
Voluntary reductions in working time	This term is used to refer to instances where workers and their managers agree to cut back on the number of hours worked.

The right to request flexible working was introduced in 2003, and originally applied just to parents of young or disabled children. Since 2014, though, once they have been in a job for twenty-six weeks any employee has the statutory right to request flexible working arrangements, such as moving from full-time to part-time employment. Importantly, this is not a right to flexible working, merely a right to have any request to work flexibly taken seriously by an employer (Anderson 2003). However, care is needed not to exaggerate the impact of the right to request flexible working, given the importance of pressure for change from workers themselves. While perhaps playing a part in securing wider consensus about the desirability of flexible working, the change seems to have 'been swimming with the tide of opinion, rather than initiating change' (Green 2011: 118). However, flexible working time arrangements are generally more common in the public sector, and in organizations which have a high proportion of female staff (Dex and Forth 2009; Walsh 2010; van Wanrooy et al. 2013b).

8.4.2 Problems with flexible working time arrangements

Although there would appear to be a consensus that, since they benefit both workers and employers, the greater prevalence of flexible working time arrangements is something to be welcomed, there are a number of major problems which should not be overlooked. One problem with flexible working time arrangements concerns the adverse consequences for gender equality that arise from their use. Part-time jobs predominate in low-paid and low-skilled sectors of the economy, with the result that those who undertake them, the large majority of whom are women, often experience considerable employment disadvantage

(Grimshaw and Rubery 2010; Warren, Pascall, and Fox 2010; Gregory 2016). The question of social class is also relevant here. It is far easier for workers in relatively well-paid managerial and professional jobs to contemplate reducing their hours, and taking a cut in pay as a result, than it is for their less well-remunerated counterparts further down the organizational hierarchy. They are also more likely to be able to exercise a degree of control over their own working time arrangements, such as starting and finishing times (Blyton 2011). Efforts to promote better work–life balance through flexible working arrangements are very much a 'middle-class problem'; for members of the working class, in lower-paid jobs, the main concern is with securing more hours and thus a higher wage (Warren 2015b).

A second problem with flexible working time arrangements concerns their 'dual logic': to what extent are they capable of meeting both the needs of employers and those of employees (Messenger 2011)? There is often a mismatch between organizational demands for flexibility—based on an efficiency rationale—and workers' demands for flexibility—which are predicated on the desirability of combining paid employment with family life. Part-time jobs are 'often organized and designed to maximize employer flexibility, to meet fluctuations in customer demand or to provide cover for sickness and holidays. There is thus a strong potential for conflict between the flexibility requirements of employers and those of employees' (Grimshaw and Rubery 2010: 370). In call centres, for example, conflict arises because the flexibility demanded by managers, in particular the expectation that staff will work additional hours at short notice to cope with an unanticipated rise in calls, clashes with demands from workers for predictable working time arrangements, so that they can plan their family responsibilities effectively (Hyman and Marks 2008).

This is related to a third problem with flexible working time arrangements, which concerns the increasing variability of working hours in some parts of the economy, such as retail and social care, as employers try to manage labour as efficiently as possible by continually tweaking staff numbers to match varying patterns of demand (Grimshaw and Rubery 2010; Blyton 2011; Rubery et al. 2015; Bittman 2016). The difficulty for workers is that their working hours become increasingly unpredictable, making it difficult for them to plan activities—including childcare provision—around the demands of their paid jobs. Evidence from the care sector shows how the increasing use of 'fragmented' working time arrangements, such as contracts that do not guarantee workers regular minimum hours ('zero-hours contracts'), can have adverse consequences for people's private and family life outside work (Rubery et al. 2015). Blyton and Jenkins (2012) talked to workers in South Wales, who had been made redundant when the Burberry clothing factory closed in 2007, about the characteristics of their new jobs. Many 'were subject to working time patterns that not only varied from week to week but were also highly unpredictable, in terms of both timing and duration', creating serious difficulties (Blyton and Jenkins 2012: 35). For example, a worker who had found a job as a hotel receptionist observed that the worst thing about the position was the timing and unpredictability of the shifts, which varied from week to week:

> You can't plan anything. I've just had to cancel a dentist's appointment because they've called me in for a shift and I can't make another appointment because I won't know what I'm working next week.
>
> (Blyton and Jenkins 2012: 36)

8.4.3 **Zero-hours contracts**

The increasing degree to which working time has become more variable and irregular is exemplified by the rise to prominence of so-called 'zero-hours contracts'. These are contractual arrangements where the number of hours to be worked, and when they are to be worked, are not specified in the employment contract. Employees are only paid for the hours that they actually do work (Pyper and Dar 2015: 3). Zero-hours contracts are not a new phenomenon; however, employers are making greater use of them because of the flexibility they offer, enabling them to manage the working time of their staff, and adjust it in response to variations in demand, in a highly cost-effective manner (ACAS 2014c; CIPD 2013b; Pennycook, Cory, and Alakeson 2013; Adams and Deakin 2014; TUC 2015a). According to official data, in the last quarter of 2015 some 800,000 people in the UK were employed on a zero-hours contract (2.5 per cent of the workforce) (ONS 2016a), a figure which had more than tripled in three years. However, it is widely acknowledged that the real number is rather higher than this calculation, which is based on a survey of the workforce. The problem is that workers may not recognize themselves as being on a zero-hours arrangement, given that their contracts are unlikely to specify this, leading to a high level of under-reporting (Pennycook, Cory, and Alakeson 2013; TUC 2015a).

In some parts of the economy, zero-hours contracts have become pervasive. In the care sector, for example, over two-thirds (69 per cent) of the providers studied by Rubery et al. (2015) made use of them. And there are some high-profile examples of retailers which make extensive use of zero-hours contracts. Around 90 per cent of those employed by the retailer Sports Direct in its shops, for instance, are employed on zero-hours contracts (Neville 2013). However, their use seems to be more prevalent in public and voluntary sector organizations (CIPD 2015c).

Supporters of zero-hours contracts claim that not only do they give employers flexibility but that they are also good for workers, who benefit from the flexibility to work when it is convenient for them to do so, enabling them to accommodate family responsibilities more easily. Business organizations such as the Confederation of British Industry (CBI) contend that, by giving employers flexibility and helping them to manage staff in an efficient way, zero-hours contracts helped to keep people in employment during the economic recession and its aftermath (ACAS 2014c; Pyper and Dar 2015). The Chartered Institute of Personnel and Development (CIPD) highlights the important extent to which employers benefit from being able to respond quickly to fluctuations in demand when using zero-hours contracts (CIPD 2013b). From this perspective, zero-hours contracts exemplify the key contribution that flexible employment arrangements, in a liberalized labour market, make to boosting jobs and improving economic competitiveness. There is also some evidence that zero-hours contracts may be attractive to workers, particularly when they have a good relationship with their manager. Students, for example, often like zero-hours contracts because they enable them to fit part-time jobs around their studies more easily (Pennycook, Cory, and Alakeson 2013; CIPD 2015c).

However, there are some major problems concerning the way zero-hours contracts are used by employers, which can lead to greater exploitation of workers. For one thing, the flexibility offered by zero-hours contracts is generally highly one-sided, with the power resting firmly with the employer. Workers are often expected to be available for work even though they are not guaranteed any hours or pay (TUC 2015*a*). In theory, zero-hours contracts should enable workers to turn down offers of work from the employer. In practice, however, the allocation of work, and thus wages, rests in the hands of managers, who may be inclined to favour workers who more readily agree to hours when they are offered them. The threat of reduced hours can exacerbate feelings of powerlessness among workers on zero-hours contracts, something which employers can use to their advantage. A female care worker claimed that:

> In reality there is not much flexibility because if you ever turn down hours or complain to the supervisor you simply stop getting offered work. The worst I had was a period being offered eight hours a week after I refused to do seven night runs (a 5.40am start and a 10pm finish).

> Pennycook, Cory, and Alakeson (2013: 18).

This is consistent with the view expressed by a care manager, that 'people who are not flexible, they don't get so many hours' (Rubery et al. 2015: 716).Therefore, zero-hours contracts provide 'temporal flexibility for employers to a far greater extent than for employees—increasing employers' ability to adjust working time patterns but at a cost of greater irregularity and unpredictability for employees' (Blyton 2011: 300).

A further issue concerns the lack of employment security for many workers on zero-hours contracts and the unpredictability of their earnings as a consequence (Pennycook, Cory, and Alakeson 2013; Clark 2014; O'Hara 2014). It can be a difficult struggle to make ends meet. A hotel worker employed on a zero-hours contract confessed to having 'sleepless nights' not knowing how much he will 'be getting to pay for essentials like rent—as one week [I] may have 35 hours—next week have only 15 hours' (TUC 2015*a*: 25). Even though they might have little guarantee of a regular income, because they are required by their employer to be available for work, workers on zero-hours contracts often cannot take up alternative employment opportunities. They may also have difficulty claiming welfare benefits, given that they are in employment, even if their jobs are paying them very little (Pyper and Dar 2015).

Employment relations reflection 8.6:   Regulating zero-hours contracts

Because of their exploitative potential, there have been calls for legislation to restrict employers' use of zero-hours contracts. Following a trade union campaign, in 2016 New Zealand effectively prohibited zero-hours contracts, with the introduction of a new law which compels employers to give workers a minimum number of guaranteed hours each week. In the UK, the coalition government carried out a review of zero-hours contracts during 2013–14. It consulted on four main issues: exclusivity, transparency, uncertainty of earnings, and the balance of power (Pyper and Dar 2015). Following this exercise, in 2014 the government published a rather limited response, which was centred on the issue of exclusivity clauses in zero-hours contracts. The Small Business, Enterprise and Employment Act 2015 made any clause requiring exclusivity in a zero-hours contract unenforceable. In theory, it enables a worker who has not been offered work by their employer to use the time available to work for another employer, thus helping to even out the balance of power. But it is not clear that this change will have much of a practical effect (Adams and Deakin 2014). Some, including the Labour opposition, have called for tougher measures, including the right of workers on zero-hours contracts to fixed hours after a specified period of time (Alakeson and D'Arcy 2014; Pickavance 2014).

To an important extent, the growth of zero-hours contracts exemplifies the trend towards more precarious employment identified in Chapter 2 (TUC 2015*a*). Not only that: the extensive use of zero-hours contracts is itself an integral feature of the development of a casualized, low-wage labour market. Workers who are fearful about not receiving sufficient hours will be less ready to take up with their employers issues such as rights to holiday entitlement, or to be paid at least the National Minimum Wage (TUC 2015*a*). To this extent, then, the growth of zero-hours contracts has the potential to undermine employment rights and working conditions across the entire labour market. No wonder there have been calls for the use of zero-hours contracts to be subject to stricter legal regulation (see Employment relations reflection 8.6). Whether or not more employers follow the lead of the pub chain Wetherspoons, which in 2016 offered staff employed on zero-hours contracts the opportunity of guaranteed hours, remains to be seen.

 ### Section summary and further reading

- The growth of working time flexibility, particularly manifest in the increasing proportion of part-time jobs in the economy, is a key trend in employment relations. It has been propelled by changes in the composition of employment, employers' demands for efficiencies, and the expectations of workers.

- While in theory both employers and employees can benefit from temporal flexibility, in practice flexible working time arrangements can exacerbate labour market disadvantage, reinforce managerial control, and engender conflict.

- The increasing prevalence of zero-hours contracts symbolizes the growth of more variable, irregular, and unpredictable working time arrangements. Zero-hours contracts are often used in a way that increases worker exploitation, stimulating calls for them to be more tightly regulated.

For good overviews of developments with regard to flexible working time arrangements see Grimshaw and Rubery (2010), Walsh (2010), and Blyton (2011). Rubery et al.'s (2015) in-depth study of 'fragmented' working time practices in the social care sector offers some fascinating insights. There is a growing body of work devoted to zero-hours contracts; see in particular Pennycook, Cory, and Alakeson (2013), Pyper and Dar (2015), TUC (2015*a*), and CIPD (2013*b*, 2015*c*).

8.5 Work pressures and work intensification

Having discussed working time trends, developments in one further feature of the wage–work bargain needs to be assessed. This concerns how working time is actually utilized by employers. What do workers do when they are at work, and how intensively, or with how much effort, do they perform their jobs? This is an important area of analysis since the concept of 'effort' is critical to employment relations. Employers, when they hire workers, as we know, buy their potential labour power, or their capacity to engage in productive effort. How this latent effort is then used is subject to an ongoing process of negotiation and re-negotiation between managers and workers. Thus the questions of how working time is used, and also why heightened work pressures seem so prevalent in modern workplaces, are clearly worthy of scrutiny.

8.5.1 **Work intensification trends**

Problems of measurement render judgements of work effort difficult to calculate with any degree of certainty (Nichols 1986; Green 2001). While one can attempt to measure the speed at which a job is undertaken, its physical and mental intensity is personal to the individual performing it, and is thus an inherently subjective phenomenon (McGovern et al. 2007). Work effort, then, is an ambiguous concept (Green 2006). Nevertheless, studies of work effort demonstrate that during the 1980s and 1990s work in the UK became more intensive, and stabilized at a relatively high level during the early 2000s, before increasing in intensity again between 2006 and 2012 (Green 2006; Felstead et al. 2013; Gallie et al. 2014). Greater work pressures are also evident in other industrialized countries such as Ireland (Green, Huxley, and Whitfield 2010; Russell and McGinnity 2014).

In the 1980s, both survey and case study evidence highlighted the importance of work intensification linked to demands from employers for improved flexibility in the utilization of labour (Elger 1990). For much of the ensuing decade there was a 'palpable increase in work intensity, with workers being required to work harder during the hours they were at work' (Green, Huxley, and Whitfield 2010: 383), something which is evident from a number of relevant research studies (e.g. Gallie et al. 1998; Burchell et al. 1999; Burchell 2002; McGovern et al. 2007).

While the intensity of work may have stopped rising during the early 2000s, it nonetheless evened out at a high level indeed (Green and Whitfield 2009; Green 2011). Perhaps it is the case that, physically and mentally, workers simply are incapable of working any harder, with the trend of work intensification having reached its natural limits (Green 2011). To what extent did the economic crisis of the late 2000s and early 2010s make a difference to work intensity? There is some evidence that it sparked a further increase in work pressures, so that those 'in jobs are working harder, faster and to tighter deadlines than they did in the past' (Felstead et al. 2013: 6; Gallie et al. 2014). Evidence from Ireland shows how the economic crisis led to increased work pressures, because of staff reductions and employer reorganizations (Russell and McGinnity 2014). Set against this, however, data from the Workplace Employment Relations Study (WERS) in the UK are less conclusive. On the one hand, the proportion of employees agreeing that their job required them to work very hard rose from 76 per cent in 2004 to 84 per cent in 2011; on the other hand, however, there was no change in the proportion of employees who thought that they never had enough time to get their jobs done (van Wanrooy et al. 2013b).

8.5.2 **The causes of work intensification**

But what has caused greater work pressures? Perhaps jobs have become more intrinsically satisfying, with workers willing to exert additional effort as a result? Work intensification is linked to increasing skill levels (Gallie et al. 1998). Some employees now enjoy greater responsibility and discretion in their jobs, making them harder, yes, but also more challenging (see Beynon et al. 2002: 280–1). The importance of such 'supply-side' factors—that greater work pressures are the result of workers supplying more effort—should not be entirely discounted, especially where people enjoy a degree of control over their jobs. However, work intensification seems to have mainly been demand-driven (Gallie 2005; Russell and McGinnity 2014), with three interrelated sources of added work pressure being particularly evident (see Table 8.5).

Table 8.5 The potential sources of work intensification

Supply-side factors	Demand-side factors
Greater job satisfaction	Greater competitive pressures
More highly skilled jobs	More sophisticated information and communications technologies (ICT)
Greater discretion and responsibility	Rigorous performance management arrangements

First, increasing competitive pressures compel employers to pursue efficiency gains, and ruthlessly manage costs in such a way that the same number of employees, or fewer, is obliged to produce ever greater quantities of work (Burchell 2002). The process of financialization (see Chapter 5) has helped to intensify work, through reductions in staff, and increased workloads for those who remain (Thompson 2013). For example, in their study of seven private and public sector organizations, Beynon et al. (2002) noted the large extent to which demands for enhanced organizational competitiveness and efficiency savings drove managers to intensify the labour of their staff. For the private sector companies, the obligation to satisfy the expectations of financial institutions, and thus enhance shareholder value, resulted in pressure to prune staff numbers as a means of taking out costs.

Developments in the food processing sector illustrate particularly well how increased levels of work intensity arise from competitive pressures. Supermarkets constantly badger their suppliers for cheaper products, and also often demand faster, more flexible delivery arrangements, in order to reduce their own costs. Supply chain pressures result in factories trying to pass cost savings down the line, with the burden falling on their production workers, in order to maintain their own competiveness. One way of achieving this is to increase the speed of production lines, meaning that staff are obliged to work at a quicker pace (James and Lloyd 2008). Investments in new automated technological processes that speed up production also have a marked effect. In the fruit and vegetable processing factory studied by Newsome, Thompson, and Commander (2009: 153), the implications of automation for work intensity were particularly evident. The 'speed of the lines is often so intense that it causes motion sickness. One line operator reported that she took travel sickness tablets to try to deal with the effects of motion sickness from working for long periods on the line'.

In front-line service work, moreover, where people have responsibility for dealing with customers, managers may use this relationship as a means of extracting greater work effort from staff. The telecommunications company studied by Beynon et al. (2002), for example, had given greater priority to service quality considerations, and expected its workers to be more sensitive to customer needs—an added source of pressure. The way in which customer expectations contribute to raised work intensity is particularly evident in some sectors. In hotels, for example, working around guests and responding to their needs are added sources of pressure for housekeeping and room cleaning staff (Sherman 2011). Interviews with hotel room attendants reveal the intense pressure they come under to get through their allocation of rooms ever more quickly (Roberts 2015).

A second source of added work pressure emanates from the greater capacity for managers to exercise control over employees, linked to the decline in workplace power of the trade unions (Green 2011). This is manifest in the use of increasingly robust performance management systems (McGovern et al. 2007)—see Chapter 5. Poynter (2000) demonstrates how managers in the financial services sector use sophisticated performance management techniques to increase the work effort of their staff, and to enhance their own control. In their study of Her Majesty's Revenue and Customs (HMRC), Carter et al. (2013) highlight the significant extent to which new working methods, associated with the introduction of a 'lean' model of operation, markedly increased work pressures for staff. Standardized operating procedures, intrusive monitoring by supervisors, individual targets, and close checks on work (supposedly for 'quality' purposes) were among the 'battery of performance management measures contributing to pressure' (Carter et al. 2013: 761).

Third, greater scope for managerial control of this kind is enhanced by the use to which new forms of information and communications technology (ICT) are put, in particular by enabling managers to monitor and adjust work flows more effectively (Green 2011). What Green (2006) calls 'effort-biased technological change' has been a major source of increased work pressure. In other words, ICT helps managers to secure extra effort from their subordinates, because their activities are more easily monitored and recorded. Evidently, innovations 'like the mobile phone and the laptop computer—devices that enable work to be carried out at what, previously, had been idle times—are only the most tangible signs' of how technology can be used to increase work effort (Green 2006: 174). More importantly, the profusion of ICT-based monitoring systems, and the way they are used to inform performance management arrangements, allows managers to secure greater employee compliance with organizational norms, standards, values, and targets.

The effectiveness of performance management systems is often based on the use of information and communication technology to monitor workers—so-called ICT-based monitoring techniques. Electronic Point of Sale (EPOS) arrangements can be used to monitor the performance of checkout staff in retail stores, for example. In call centres and other office-based environments, ICT monitoring systems can be used to record the number and length of telephone calls, and even the keystrokes on a computer. Over a half of employees (52 per cent) in one survey reported that their work activities were recorded in some way by a computer system; nearly a quarter (23 per cent) indicated that information gathered in this way was used to monitor their performance (McGovern et al. 2007: 170). Call centres are environments where the use of ICT enables managers to control the pace of work and monitor staff with particular ease—a source of work intensification. According to one worker:

> The major pressure is ... the calls ... and that is understandable because we work in a call-centre environment, and you also get the pressure ... because you haven't got time to literally stand up and do what you need to do or take two minutes. You feel as though you're under pressure by taking the calls because it [the indicator] could be flashing 'there's eight minutes of calls waiting' which is quite regular in the evening.
>
> (Beynon et al. 2002: 289)

Clearly, the most obvious way in which technological change leads to increased work pressures is by enabling managers to monitor work flows and workers' activities more closely. Private care firms use sophisticated monitoring devices to track how long their staff spend visiting home-based clients (Ramesh 2013). But email and other forms of electronic communication also mean that in some cases employers can contact employees, and expect them to undertake work duties, outside of normal working hours, even when they are at home (Walsh 2010).

However, we should be careful not to exaggerate the capacity of managers to secure control over, and extract more effort from, their staff. Workers are capable of challenging the encroachment of managerial control initiatives in rather imaginative ways. Moreover, there is evidence that employers have had to pay a price for increases in work effort: in particular, the use of financial incentives, in the form of increased wages, to encourage higher effort. 'Additional earnings provide employees with the motive to increase effort, and employers have developed methods of monitoring and control to ensure that effort is increased' (McGovern et al. 2007: 186).

 Contesting employment relations 8.7:   The National Gallery dispute

In 2011, a dispute broke out at the National Gallery in London over its decision to increase the number of rooms gallery assistants are required to guard, from one to at least two. It argued that the change would enhance security, pointing out that the new arrangement was standard practice in other museums and art galleries. However, the gallery assistants were outraged by the change, claiming that it was prompted by the need for substantial reductions in staffing costs. What they called 'doubling-up' would—in their view—in fact compromise security, since it would be less easy to ensure that works of art were protected effectively, and reduce the amount of help they would be able to provide to visitors. As a result, during 2012 the PCS union organized a series of relatively short walk-outs by gallery assistants in protest against the change, resulting in the temporary closure of many of the National Gallery's rooms.

While the weakness of the trade unions means that workers are less well defended from work intensification, increases in work effort are nonetheless accompanied by higher earnings, suggesting that managers cannot simply impose higher workloads, but rather have to bargain over them with employees. In addition, as the case of the dispute at the National Gallery shows, under some circumstances workers challenge attempts by managers to increase their workloads (see Contesting employment relations 8.7).

8.5.3 The effects of work intensification

What, though, are the effects of work intensification? For organizations, it seems that the conditions for increases in the levels of trust and cooperation necessary to stimulate long-term, real improvements in economic performance are unlikely to exist. Employers often prefer to 'sweat' their staff, generating short-term improvements in output by intensifying workloads or using overtime. One of the main effects is the exhaustion of the workers concerned. This is particularly evident among hotel cleaning and room staff, who work to stringent quotas specifying the number of rooms that need to be serviced per shift. The resulting 'imperative of speed' creates an 'atmosphere of stress' as the staff labour to complete their duties as quickly as possible (Sherman 2011: 24). In order to realize efficiency savings, and thus improve their competitiveness, hotels operate onerous work schedules, and put a lot of pressure on their housekeeping staff to increase their efforts. In September 2012, for example, BBC Newsnight reported that contract cleaners at the prestigious London Hilton Waldorf hotel had their quota raised from two to three rooms per hour, with disciplinary action threatened if they did not comply. In the study of hotel cleaners by Guégnard and Mériot (2009: 106) a worker commented:

> We have to rush, and they tell us to work faster. The hotel should hire more staff. In eight hours, I am supposed to achieve my work, but whereas one hour is supposed to be enough to clean two rooms, each room generally takes at least 40 minutes.

The work is not easy; the physical effort required by their jobs, and the pace at which they have to be performed, ends up exhausting the workers concerned, as this comment indicates:

> After a single working day, I am already broken. I even got problems with my muscles that I have never had before. And that tires me even more. I would like to take another job. If only I could stop!

> (Guégnard and Mériot 2009: 107)

While pressure is an aspect of all work, and can have an important part in stimulating and maintaining motivation, excessive workloads not only undermine performance at work, but can also make people ill. In 2014–15, there were around 440,000 cases of work-related stress, depression, or anxiety in the UK, with nearly 10 million working days not being worked as a consequence. Pressure arising from workloads, including tight deadlines, excessive amounts of work, and too much responsibility, is by far the biggest cause of work-related stress (HSE 2015). It can have serious adverse consequences for mental and physical well-being, including putting workers at an increased risk of heart disease and depression. It is unsurprising that high levels of work-related stress persist, given the pressures under which many people work (Green and Whitfield 2009; Green 2011), especially among men in 'high strain' jobs (Gallie et al. 2014). In the food industry the burden of constant demands from supermarkets for lower costs and greater flexibility is passed by factory managers on to the production workers in the form of increases in the pace of work, to the marked detriment of their well-being (James and Lloyd 2008).

The evidence of a 'widespread intensification of work effort and its detrimental impact on well-being is unambiguous' (Green 2006: 174). This is something which is supported by studies of call centres, further education colleges, and the Child Support Agency (CSA)—the organization responsible for assessing and collecting child maintenance payments from non-resident parents (Beynon et al. 2002; Nolan 2002; Atkinson and McKay 2005). In their study of HMRC, Carter et al. (2013) found that increased work pressures arising from the introduction of a new system of 'lean' operation were associated with a higher prevalence of workers' ill health, encompassing a range of conditions including mental fatigue, tiredness, self-reported stress, and headaches, especially among women. Administrative staff reflected on how the adverse effects of the changes had affected them:

> Individuality [was] their mantra but this has been pushed aside by ... senior management to create a battery-hen environment which makes for a very unhappy and very, very stressed workforce.

> (Carter et al. 2013: 757).

> The lean process has led to more illness—especially more and more stress—and has encouraged bullying.

> (Carter et al. 2013: 757).

Section summary and further reading

- Although there are difficulties associated with measuring how much effort people expend in their jobs, there is nonetheless overwhelming evidence that employment relations in the 1980s and 1990s was marked by work intensification, after which effort levels stabilized at a high level during the 2000s before rising again as a result of the economic crisis.

- While an increase in their job responsibilities may in part have led some people to work harder, the principal causes of increased work pressures are the growing competitive pressures on organizations that have compelled them to increase staff workloads, and extensive use of new systems for managing performance, linked to developments in information technology.

- It is unlikely that the increases in work effort seen in the UK will generate long-term improvements in economic performance. There is also evidence of adverse consequences for workers' health and well-being.

For data on work effort, and explanations of why it has increased, see Green (2006: chapters 3 and 4) and McGovern et al. (2007: chapters 5 and 6). Green (2011) reviews trends in work intensification. For case studies, see Carter et al. (2013) on HMRC and James and Lloyd (2008) on food processing.

8.6 The legal regulation of working time

Unlike elsewhere in Europe, traditionally the law has played little role in regulating working time in the UK, with the exception of historical legislation restricting the working hours of women and children. In unionized sectors of the economy matters such as the length of the standard working week were regulated through collective bargaining; however, the diminishing reach of joint regulation since the 1980s has reduced the effectiveness of this approach (Grimshaw and Rubery 2010). Since the 1990s, though, EU legislation, particularly the 1993 Working Time Directive (WTD), and the Working Time Regulations (WTR) 1998 which enacted it in the UK, has come to play a prominent part in efforts to regulate working hours and associated matters.

During the 1980s, there was growing concern in the European Commission that the regulation of working time needed to be addressed across the EU as a health and safety measure (Bridgford and Stirling 1994; Cabrita 2015b). The principal outcome of this interest was agreement to enact a Directive on the Adaptation of Working Time (the 'Working Time Directive') in 1993. John Major's Conservative government tried to prevent its application, arguing that because the Directive was a 'social' measure it could only be enacted through the so-called 'Social Chapter', from which the UK, because of its Maastricht 'opt-out', was at that time exempt (see Chapter 3). Yet the European Court of Justice (ECJ) ruled that the Directive was, as the European Commission maintained, a 'health and safety' measure and thus fell outside the 'Social Chapter' and, having thus been enacted, had to be extended to the UK.

8.6.1 The 1998 Working Time Regulations

Nevertheless, Tony Blair's Labour government, which took office in 1997, was able to win some significant concessions when the WTR were eventually enacted in 1998, notably the so-called 'right' of workers to choose whether or not they want to work for more than forty-eight hours a week, a source of much controversy as shown in Section 8.6.2.

The WTR provide for:

- a limit of forty-eight hours on the weekly time that a worker is required to work (including overtime), normally averaged out over a seventeen-week reference period;

- workers to have at least eleven consecutive hours of rest in any twenty-four-hour period;

- workers to have a rest period of at least twenty-four consecutive hours in any seven-day period, or forty-eight hours in a fourteen-day period;

- workers to have at least a twenty-minute unpaid rest break if the working day is longer than six hours;

- night workers (defined as workers who normally work at least three hours between 11pm and 6am) to be limited to an average of eight hours of work in any twenty-four-hour period; and

- a minimum of four weeks' paid annual leave.

There are additional restrictions that apply to workers aged below 18: for example, they are limited to an eight-hour working day and a forty-hour working week.

Some groups of workers—junior doctors and workers in transport, for example—were originally excluded from the scope of the forty-eight-hour maximum working week, as were senior managers, and others whose working time is said to be 'unmeasured'. Employers can reach a collective agreement with a recognized trade union, or by means of a 'workforce agreement' with elected employee representatives in the absence of a recognized union, to benefit from certain flexibilities; for example, the seventeen-week reference period over which the forty-eight-hour maximum limit is calculated can be extended to up to a year. The most controversial aspect of the WTR—and something that the British government fought hard to include, and even harder to retain—is the provision that workers can, by virtue of an 'individual agreement' with their employer, 'opt out' from coverage of the forty-eight-hour average weekly limit (Cabrita 2015*b*).

Employers frequently use such individual agreements automatically, routinely asking new employees to sign opt-out clauses when they commence employment (Neathy and Arrowsmith 2001; Barnard, Deakin, and Hobbs 2003; Crail 2007). Nearly a third of all workplaces (32 per cent) contain at least one employee who has signed an opt-out clause; and all employees have opted out in 15 per cent of workplaces (van Wanrooy et al. 2013*a*). Many workers, it is argued, have very little real choice about whether or not their working week is limited to an average of forty-eight hours. The TUC (2009) claims that in many cases employers put pressure on employees to 'agree' to opt out.

Yet both workers and their employers have a vested interest in ensuring that the opt-out remains, and that excessive working hours continue (Barnard, Deakin, and Hobbs 2003). Workers either need the additional income provided by paid overtime or, where it is unpaid, to do the extra work in order to ensure that they keep their jobs, or are well regarded for promotion purposes. Employers, as we have seen, are reliant on overtime working as a key means of securing workplace flexibility. The widespread use of opt-outs is suggestive of a certain amount of 'pragmatic collusion' between workers and their employers (Goss and Adam-Smith 2001). In the food processing sector, for example, where extensive use is made of overtime to respond to fluctuating patterns of demand, there is evidence that workers willingly agree to sign opt-outs because of the extra income that working more hours brings (James and Lloyd 2008).

During the 2000s, the legal regulation of working time developed and evolved in some significant ways. The first thing to be aware of is that working time legislation was extended to cover groups of workers who had originally been excluded from the WTR, such as non-mobile workers in the transport industry. Junior doctors were also brought within the scope of the WTR, with their weekly hours capped at forty-eight since 2009 (see the end-of-chapter case study for more details). As a result of union pressure, the Labour government also made a change to the WTR—the exclusion of bank holidays from the four-week entitlement to paid annual leave. As a result, paid holiday entitlement increased to 4.8 weeks (twenty-four days for people working a five-day week) in 2007, and to 5.6 weeks (twenty-eight days) in 2009.

There have also been some important case law developments, with the provisions of the legislation being subject to close scrutiny by the courts. One issue which has caused particular difficulty concerns how periods when workers are not actually engaged in work duties, but are 'on call'—that is, available on the employer's premises to work if required—should be treated for the purpose of the Working Time Directive. ECJ judgments have specified that the period of time when workers are 'on call' should be counted as working time, even if the workers concerned use it to rest or sleep. This has caused considerable difficulties for employers across Europe which operate such 'on call' arrangements, particularly in the health sector where around-the-clock availability of medical staff is often essential.

Although you would be forgiven for thinking otherwise, given the fuss made by businesses, the actual impact of the WTR has been rather modest. The legislation appears to have had little effect on working time patterns. During the 2000s average weekly hours of work for full-time employees did fall. Yet there are a number of reasons why this decline was unlikely to be the result of the WTR. For one thing, it commenced before the legislation came into effect (Green 2011). Moreover, the presence of the individual opt-out means that the effect of the forty-eight-hour maximum working week provision was substantially diluted (Green 2011; Green and Whitfield 2009). This raises the important question of whether or not workers should be entitled to opt out of legal coverage designed to protect their health and safety at work. The continued existence of the opt-out also has potentially adverse consequences for productivity, since the quality of work performed by people working excessive hours often declines, as they tire, leading to reduced output per hour (TUC 2009).

There are other, more plausible explanations for the decline in working hours since the mid-1990s. One is that it marks a return to the long-term trend of falling working hours, evident for much of the twentieth century, which is a function of greater prosperity and more desire for leisure time (Green 2011). Similarly, the decline in working hours reflects the greater extent to which workers have been demanding, and employers instituting, more family-friendly working arrangements, and the growth of a broader concern with securing a better work–life balance. Economic factors seem to have played a part too, with the impact of the economic recession evident in fewer working hours being required by employers, and a notable rise in part-time working arrangements, since the late 2000s.

Yet, the forty-eight-hour week aside, the force of working time regulation is evident in other respects, particularly in the provision of statutory paid holiday entitlement. The enactment of the WTR meant that, for the first time ever in the UK, all workers became legally entitled to paid annual leave, a provision that benefited perhaps as many as one in ten workers

(Green 2003; Green and Whitfield 2009). However, there is some evidence that unscrupulous employers fail to give their staff the holiday leave to which they are legally entitled (Citizens Advice 2011).

8.6.2 The Working Time Directive: issues and prospects

As mentioned earlier, the 'individual agreement' provision, which allows workers to opt out from the forty-eight-hour upper limit placed on the average working week, is perhaps the most controversial feature of the WTR. During the 2000s there was extensive activity at EU level concerning whether or not the opt-out should be retained. The UK government and CBI lobbied vociferously in Europe for the opt-out to be kept on the grounds that, without it, employers would have reduced flexibility over working time arrangements, and thus be rendered less competitive. The TUC, though, wanted to see the opt-out scrapped. It contended that even without the opt-out the WTD gives employers plenty of flexibility; the seventeen-week reference period for calculating working time (which can be increased to fifty-two weeks if there is union agreement) enables them to cope with variations in demand.

> If a business genuinely cannot survive without its staff working excessive hours on a permanent basis, then management need to think again about how work is organised. However, in most cases managers would find that they could manage these working time limits quite easily if they had to. All too often the problem is that they do not want to bother to manage this issue.
>
> (TUC 2009)

Efforts to reach an agreement on the future of the individual opt-out at EU level failed to make much progress. On the one hand, the main employers' body at EU level, Business Europe, wants to see workers continue to have access to opt-outs, that when workers are on call this should not be treated as working time, and that business flexibility should be prioritized. On the other hand, the European Trade Union Confederation (ETUC) has argued for the opt-out to be scrapped, for ECJ rulings on on-call time to be respected by any new legislation, and for the existing arrangements when it comes to reference periods to be maintained (EIRO 2012).

The question of the WTD has intruded onto the UK domestic political arena. Prior to 2010, the Labour government fought to maintain the individual opt-out because it was viewed as so crucial to employers' flexibility. Rhetorically at least, the 2010–15 coalition government was even more hostile to the Directive. The May 2010 coalition agreement included an aspiration to 'work to limit the application of the WTD in the UK'; however little tangible progress was made, other than the commissioning of a review of the legislation as it applies to junior doctors. Yet there can be little doubt about the Conservative Party's antipathy towards the WTD, notwithstanding the evidence that its practical effects have been rather limited.

Many Conservatives see the WTD as a prime example of where powers over social and employment legislation could be repatriated from the EU. Conservative ministers unsuccessfully tried to use the efforts of other EU member states to respond to the global economic crisis by developing new economic and financial integration instruments as an opportunity to re-open negotiations over the repatriation of EU social and employment law, especially in respect of the Working Time Directive (Rogowski 2015). Hostility to this legislation not only exemplifies Conservative opposition to employment regulation, but also the deep hostility of many in the party towards the EU (Gall 2011c). Unsurprisingly, then, in 2014 the government used a review of the WTR as an opportunity to reaffirm its hostility to the principle of the legislation, based on the claim that there is 'no clear causal link between working long hours and detrimental effects on health and safety', and to make a robust argument for the individual opt-out to be retained (BIS 2014: 13).

Employment relations reflection 8.8:   Restricting 'out-of-office' working

The author of this book tries to avoid sending or replying to work-related emails on weekends or on public holidays as much as possible. But not all employees are able to 'switch off' from work in this manner. Their employers expect them to be available and responsive outside of 'normal' working hours, not just when they are at home, but sometimes even when they are on vacation. A London-based advertising consultant explained the pressure she is under to reply to emails, many of which arrive between 6pm and 10pm in the evening. She turns her phone off before going to bed, just to ensure she is not disturbed at night. Some people, like Paul Sellers of the TUC, argue that the use of mobile devices for work-related reasons means that too many workers are prevented from being able to stop work, relax, and enjoy their leisure time. He asks: 'Why are we expecting people to work at 8.30 at night?'

Should employers be restricted from contacting employees by phone or email outside of 'normal' working hours? The CIPD argues that such a ban might have adverse consequences for workers who might want to take advantage of the greater flexibility over working time permitted by mobile devices. However, in Germany some employers, including Volkswagen and BMW, have instituted their own restrictions; and in 2013 the German Labour Ministry prohibited its managers from contacting staff outside of work. The car firm Daimler has reportedly installed software on its servers that automatically deletes emails sent to staff outside of normal working hours. In 2016 the French government enacted a new law requiring companies with more than fifty staff to establish those periods of time—evenings and weekends—when staff are not supposed to be dealing with emails: the so-called 'right to disconnect'.

Sources: De Castella (2014); Stuart (2014); Schofield (2016)

One of the most profound issues relating to working time, particularly the difficulty of regulating it effectively, concerns the growing extent to which new mobile information and communication technologies enable people to work remotely—at home, or on the move—outside of normal 'office hours', blurring the distinction between working and non-working time, and eroding the 'traditional concept of the continuous working day' (BIS 2014: 26). Some workers are 'always on' (Grimshaw and Rubery 2010: 368), having to be available for, and often actually undertaking, work-related activities during ostensible periods of leisure. Management consultants, for example, find that working and non-working time becomes blurred because of the pressure they are under to satisfy their clients (Donnelly 2011). On the positive side, the widespread use of mobile personal communications technologies may give workers more scope to arrange work activities, particularly the times when they are undertaken, in a flexible manner which is suitable to them. However, the 'loosening' of the concept of standard working time also has some notable adverse consequences for working people, particularly increased work pressures (Rose 2014). This raises the question of whether or not an employer's access to its employees outside of 'normal' working hours should be restricted—see Employment relations reflection 8.8.

Section summary and further reading

- Due to concerns about the adverse consequences of excessive working hours for workers' health, in 1993 the EU enacted the Working Time Directive (WTD), which among other things provides for a maximum average working week of forty-eight hours, minimum rest periods and rest breaks, and a minimum of four weeks' paid leave. It was put into effect in the UK by the 1998 Working Time Regulations (WTR).

- One of the most controversial features of the WTR concerns the provision for opting out of the forty-eight-hour week, meaning that the legislation has done little to tackle the problem of excessive working hours.

- The future of the WTD is somewhat uncertain, with the European Commission engaged in a review of the legislation.

Studies of the impact of the WTR include Goss and Adam-Smith (2001) and Barnard, Deakin, and Hobbs (2003). For an overall evaluation, see Green (2011).

8.7 Conclusion

This chapter has demonstrated the importance of working time as an employment relations issue: its length, the way in which it is organized, how it is used, and how it is regulated. For much of the twentieth century the duration of working time was commonly regulated jointly through collective bargaining between employers and trade unions. The diminution of joint regulation, however, gave managers more scope to exercise unilateral control over working time, something that is particularly manifest in the greater incidence of flexible working hours, rising work pressures, and expectations that work duties should be undertaken outside of 'normal' working hours. Working time patterns are marked by an increasing amount of variation and unpredictability, as employers endeavour to manage labour as efficiently as possible by constantly adjusting staff numbers to match changes in demand for services. While it is important not to overlook the extent to which flexible working hours can be operated in ways that benefit workers, overall working time trends would appear to have had some major adverse consequences for employees, particularly the harm to their well-being caused by excessive working hours and high work pressures.

That said, though, some aspects of working time—including the maximum length of the working week, paid holiday entitlement, rest breaks, and rest periods—have come within the scope of legal regulation, mainly as a result of the EU's 1993 Working Time Directive (put into effect in the UK by the 1998 Working Time Regulations). However, given the scope for opt-outs enjoyed by employers, the legislation has evidently done little to challenge excessive working hours in Britain. This further demonstrates how statutory regulation of the employment relationship is, by itself, not an adequate replacement for joint regulation as a means of securing improvements in working conditions. Nevertheless, the law has had a more positive effect when it comes to guaranteeing most workers a minimum amount of paid holidays each year. Whether or not working time regulation can have a more profound impact on working hours depends on the extent to which trade unions in Europe can mobilize effectively to secure changes in the WTD which support workers' interests.

Assignment and discussion questions

1. Account for the main working time trends since the 1990s.

2. To what extent do you agree with the view that flexible working hours arrangements are generally beneficial for workers?

3. To what extent, and in what ways, should employers' use of zero-hours contracts be restricted?

4. Assess the main causes of work intensification.

5. Critically assess the arguments for and against using the law to regulate the duration of working time.

 Visit the Online Resource Centre that accompanies this book to develop your understanding of this chapter and keep up to date with the latest developments in this area.
www.oxfordtextbooks.co.uk/orc/williams4e/

 Chapter case study: Junior doctors and the Working Time Directive

The application of the Working Time Directive (WTD) in the health sector has provoked a considerable degree of controversy. During the 1990s, some junior doctors undertaking postgraduate training in clinical environments regularly worked for more than 100 hours each week. Amidst concerns about the need for patient safety and ensuring effective training, the implementation of the WTD was staged for junior doctors, with the forty-eight-hour limit finally coming into force in August 2009. This provoked a lot of opposition from some quarters, particularly doctors' organizations like the Royal Colleges, who claimed that the maximum working week would mean that there was insufficient time to provide training, and would hamper the response to medical emergencies. The president of the Royal College of Surgeons warned that the WTD would lead to a dramatic reduction in the level of contact between doctors and patients, with potentially damaging consequences for patient care. In September 2012, the Royal College of Physicians published a report—*Hospitals on the Edge*—which asserted that the forty-eight-hour working limit had adversely affected continuity of patient care, increased the hours of senior doctors (consultants), and reduced the effectiveness of the training offered to junior doctors by consultants (RCP 2012).

Conservative MP Charlotte Leslie campaigned to exempt junior doctors from the forty-eight-hour maximum working week. She claimed that doctors in acute medical and surgical units find it necessary to work for more than forty-eight hours. Moreover, the working time limit adversely affects the standard of patient care by eroding continuity of care, reducing the amount of training given to junior doctors, and limiting the availability of appropriate clinical expertise. In an April 2012 Westminster Hall debate, Leslie claimed that, while she was not advocating a return to the days when junior doctors worked an excessive number of hours, the WTD was 'compromising' care, 'devastating the NHS', and 'eroding that professional ethos which upholds the NHS and beginning to replace it by a clock on, clock off culture'. As a result, the safety of patients was 'being seriously jeopardized on a day-to-day basis'. However, others argue that the application of the WTD to junior doctors has been put into practice relatively smoothly, with few of the negative outcomes claimed by the Royal Colleges and Conservative politicians. The NHS Employers organization, for example, emphasizes the effective way in which hospitals and other organizations have adapted to the maximum working week, for example through revised shift patterns and the use of more sophisticated flexible working time

(continued...)

arrangements. The independent Temple Review of the implications of the WTD for junior doctors' training found that, with the exception of out-of-hours services, high-quality training could be delivered in forty-eight hours a week, as long as there was proper supervision. There is also evidence that reducing junior doctors' hours so that they are compliant with the WTD enhances patient safety by reducing the number of errors made. Following a House of Lords debate on the issue, in October 2012 the then chair of the British Medical Association's Junior Doctors Committee, Ben Molyneux, recognized that while there was a range of opinion on the matter, the maximum working week was beneficial overall. He said:

> Tired doctors make mistakes, and we must think of the welfare of doctors and the resultant impact fatigue can have on patient care ... There is a mounting body of evidence to support the move to reduced working hours in terms of patient safety. While flexibility may be appropriate, scrapping the [WTD] is not.

In 2016, the working time of junior doctors—all those below the level of consultant—became headline news when the doctors' union, the British Medical Association (BMA), organized a series of strikes in England over changes to employment contracts. As Chapter 1 describes, government plans to increase NHS capacity at weekends led to the threatened imposition of new contracts that would, among other things, abolish premium payments for Saturday daytime working. Disputes like these demonstrate the importance of working time issues in employment relations.

Sources: BBC News (2009*d*, 2011); BBC Democracy Live (2012); RCP (2012)

Questions

To what extent is it desirable to regulate the working hours of junior doctors by law? How can working time legislation be implemented in ways that do not jeopardize patient safety?

Part 4

Conflict and employment relations

9 Labour conflict and employment relations

⊙ Chapter objectives

The main objectives of this chapter are to:

- demonstrate the relevance of labour conflict in contemporary employment relations;
- examine the nature and purpose of strikes, and their significance as a form of labour conflict;
- account for recent strike trends, and discuss their implications for employment relations;
- examine the contribution made by mobilization theory to understanding the circumstances under which labour conflict arises; and
- assess the nature and significance of forms of labour conflict other than strikes.

9.1 Introduction

Chapter 1 observed that the employment relationship, given that it is a wage–work or effort bargain, is characterized by a basic antagonism; thus there is always the potential for conflict to arise in the relationship between employers and employees (Edwards 1986). Labour conflict, however, is often overlooked, particularly in texts on human resource management. This is justified with reference to the diminution of strike activity and other forms of industrial action (e.g. 'overtime bans'), particularly in the private sector. Yet there is strong evidence that labour conflict continues to be an integral feature of employment relations. See the series of 2014 strikes by care workers in Doncaster detailed in the introductory case study, for example.

In this chapter, the resurgence of strikes and labour conflict in the context of ongoing economic recession is highlighted. There is also an examination of the main influences on strike levels and the key features of the legal framework governing industrial action by trade unions. It is important to bear in mind that conflict in employment relations is about much more than strikes, manifesting itself in a number of forms. The concept of 'labour conflict' is used to refer to a variety of behaviours undertaken by workers and their allies, both inside and outside the workplace, which reflect the basic antagonism underlying the employment relationship and are designed to challenge the interests of employers and/or governments. Mobilization theory helps us to understand the circumstances under which workers' grievances translate into instances of actual labour conflict, and that this conflict, when it does arise, can take a variety of forms, and is not just restricted to strikes.

Introductory case study: 2014 strikes by care workers in Doncaster

One of the most prominent instances of labour conflict in recent years concerns the 2014 series of strikes by care workers in the Yorkshire town of Doncaster, organized by the trade union Unison. In 2013, the private firm Care UK took over responsibility for providing learning disability services to clients in their own homes. As an efficiency measure, the firm instituted substantial cuts to workers' pay and conditions. In response, during 2014 up to seventy workers, many of whom earned around £7.00 per hour, took some ninety days of strike action in total, with the aim of challenging the employer's changes, and in pursuit of a pay increase which would have given them a living wage (then £7.65 per hour). Care UK insisted that the union's pay demands were 'unaffordable', and that it was doing the best it could to safeguard carers' jobs in an increasingly tight financial environment. Unison, however, said that its members were simply unable to survive on the pay rates offered by Care UK, and that the company's actions symbolized the 'privatized greed' which it claimed was becoming more evident in the delivery of public services. The dispute ended in November 2014 when the workers accepted a deal which had been agreed between the company and the union. Although the agreement meant that the workforce would benefit from a modest pay increase, not just in 2014, but also in 2015 and 2016, it still left them substantially worse off as a result of the employer's earlier pay cuts. This case illustrates how strikes can occur when workers who are organized in a trade union have a collective grievance which, to them, is sufficiently serious to warrant taking action to withdraw their labour. In such circumstances strikes are used as a bargaining tool, undertaken to put pressure on employers to withdraw or amend decisions that have aggrieved workers.

Sources: BBC News (2014b); Boffey (2014); Marshall (2014)

9.2 The nature and purpose of strikes

Understandably, strikes—the withdrawal by workers of their labour—dominate analyses of conflict in employment relations (Kelly 2015). They are the 'most obvious manifestation' of labour conflict (Hyman 1975: 186), 'being relatively more open, visible and important, in turn, making them more worthy of measurement and more measurable' (Gall and Hebdon 2008: 597). A strike can be defined as 'a temporary stoppage of work by a group of employees in order to express a grievance or to enforce a demand' (Griffin 1939, cited in Hyman 1977: 17). There are five dimensions of strikes that warrant specific attention:

- First, strikes are a form of 'industrial action'. The term 'industrial action' refers to those manifestations of labour conflict that involve explicitly collective behaviour by workers.

- Second, strikes are generally organized by trade unions, on the basis that when workers mobilize on a collective basis they will enjoy greater bargaining leverage over employers and governments. Strike action is difficult to uphold without the presence of a union, which can mobilize workers, organize the action, and coordinate responses to the efforts of employers and governments to prevent, or counteract the effects of, strikes (Hyman 1989).

- Third, strikes are designed to be a temporary act; employees withdraw their labour based on the understanding that work will be resumed once the dispute that has caused the strike is resolved.

- Fourth, strikes involve a stoppage of work. As a manifestation of conflict in employment relations, they can therefore be distinguished from other forms of industrial action, such as the overtime ban, which we consider later on in this chapter.

- Fifth, strikes are a form of behaviour undertaken by workers with a specific purpose in mind: to get a dismissed colleague reinstated, for example, or to secure an increase in pay. Strikes, then, generally have a calculative, purposive character (Hyman 1977, 1989). They rarely arise without a reason, even if it is only implicit.

There are two broad types of strikes—'economic' strikes and 'political' strikes (Gall and Hebdon 2008). The former are directed mainly at employers and concern issues such as pay, benefits, and working conditions—matters which have economic consequences for the firms and workers involved. In 2015, nearly three-quarters (71 per cent) of all strikes in the UK, and 83 per cent of days not worked because of strikes, related to disputes over pay (ONS 2016b). The action by care workers in Doncaster (see the introductory case study) is an example of an 'economic' strike.

Political strikes, though, are generally targeted at governments, and concern broader policy issues. In the UK there is strict legislation in place which prevents unions from organizing strikes over political matters. Elsewhere in Europe, though, such action is commonplace; indeed there seems to be a trend towards using strikes to achieve political rather than economic goals, evident in the growing frequency of general strikes—those involving workers from more than one industry, who withdraw their labour on a mass scale in protest against government policies (Kelly 2011, 2015).

A distinction can also be made between official and unofficial strikes. Official strike activity is that which, once it has been approved by its appropriate decision-making machinery, has the formal, or official, backing of a trade union. Unofficial strikes, however, occur when employees withdraw their labour, perhaps by walking off the job, without receiving the formal support of their union.

Since unofficial strike action is often of rather a short duration, involving relatively few workers, it is sometimes portrayed as being largely spontaneous behaviour undertaken to redress an immediate grievance (Knowles 1952), hence the popularity of the term 'wildcat strike' to describe such activity (Gouldner 1955). However, unofficial strikes cannot be treated as if they are spontaneous; their occurrence reflects the ongoing efforts of employees to resist potentially damaging changes to their working conditions, or to improve their position and power, in the context of the wage–work bargain (Cronin 1979). Such activity demands organization, and hence calculation. During the 1960s and 1970s the overwhelming majority of strikes undertaken were of an unofficial kind (Lyddon 2015). Changes in the law mean that unofficial strikes have become much rarer (see Section 9.4). However, the organized basis of unofficial action was evident in January 2009 when union activists helped to coordinate the apparently spontaneous walk-outs around the country in support of workers at the Lindsey Oil Refinery in their dispute over the use of foreign labour (Gall 2012b)—see Contesting employment relations 9.1.

 ### Contesting employment relations 9.1: Unofficial strike action—Lindsey Oil Refinery

One of the most notable major examples of an unofficial strike occurred in early 2009, when a number of companies around the UK suffered disruption after thousands of workers walked off their jobs to demonstrate their support for striking workers at the Lindsey Oil Refinery in Lincolnshire, who were protesting about the use of foreign labour. Construction work on the expansion of the refinery, owned by the French oil company Total, was subcontracted to an Italian firm which had brought in its own workforce to do the job. Against a background of rising unemployment, many workers were angry that the work on the refinery was being undertaken by foreign staff, at lower rates of pay, instead of local workers. According to Stephen Briggs, one of the protesting workers, while they 'have got nothing against foreign workers, the fact is that there are a lot of people out of work and are looking for jobs' (BBC News 2009a; Gall 2012b).

Two implications arise from the purposeful and organized nature of strike activity. First, the notion sometimes advanced by governments and employers that strikes are abnormal, a deviation from the normal character of stable, ordered, and peaceful employment relations, cannot be upheld. In the context of an exploitative employment relationship, the withdrawal of their labour by workers is a rational form of behaviour designed to achieve a particular purpose: to alter the terms of the wage–work bargain in a way, or ways, favourable to them (Hyman 1977). It also reflects the capacity of workers to act collectively, to mobilize in pursuit of their interests through the vehicle of a trade union (Cronin 1979; Hyman 1989). This high-lights the second main implication of the strike being an activity that is both purposeful and organized: the importance of the collective organization of workers in trade unions. Without the presence of a strong union that is able to mobilize workers, organize the action, and co-ordinate resistance to employers' efforts to defeat it, effective strike activity is hard to uphold (Edwards 1983; Hyman 1989).

 Section summary and further reading

- Given the inherent potential for conflict that characterizes the employment relationship, it is understandable that strikes, the collective withdrawal by workers of their labour, are a feature of employment relations.

- Strikes are the most obvious and visible manifestation of labour conflict. They are purposive and calculative types of behaviour in employment relations, undertaken to pursue a demand or express a grievance.

- Strikes can occur for economic reasons, concerned with matters relating to pay, working conditions, and other workplace-related issues, or on political grounds, relating to matters of government policy (though political strikes are unlawful in the UK).

- Official strikes are those that have the formal, explicit backing of a trade union. Unofficial strikes, however, occur when employees withdraw their labour, perhaps by walking off the job, without receiving the formal support of their union.

The classic introduction to the topic is Hyman's book on *Strikes* (Hyman 1977, and other editions). Gall and Hebdon (2008) provide a good account of the nature and purpose of strike activity in their book chapter on conflict at work.

9.3 Strike trends

Having outlined what strikes are, and how they are to be understood as a feature of employ-ment relations, in this section the focus is on strike trends. The starting point is an outline of some issues relating to measuring the level of strike activity, before going on to consider the main strike trends in more detail and looking to account for them.

9.3.1 **Measuring strikes**

Strikes are often taken as a key measure of the level of labour conflict because the availability of relevant data means they are apparently easy to quantify (Kelly 2015). There are three main ways of ascertaining the level of strike activity in any given period, usually over the course of a year:

- The duration of strike activity is measured by calculating the number of working days not worked due to strike activity.

- The breadth of strike activity is calculated by measuring the number of workers involved.

- The frequency of strike activity is determined by totalling up the number of strikes, or stoppages, in any given year.

Unless the total number of days not worked amounts to 100 or more, strikes involving fewer than ten workers, or lasting less than one day, are excluded from official data (ONS 2016*b*). While official strike data can be used constructively to map trends in strike activity over time (Edwards 1995), they should nonetheless be treated with caution (Hyman 1977; Godard 2011). Managers sometimes do not record strikes, for example (Batstone, Boraston, and Frenkel 1978). Generally, government statistics understate levels of labour conflict, not least because they are only concerned with strikes, and disregard other types of industrial action by trade unions, such as overtime bans (Gall and Hebdon 2008). Moreover, an infrequent number of very large strikes can disproportionately affect how strike statistics are presented. This was evident in 2011 when a small number of major public sector strikes, especially the 'coordinated' one-day strike action of 30 November 2011 by thirty-two unions in protest over proposed changes to pensions, contributed to a nearly four-fold increase in the duration of strike activity compared to the previous year (Lyddon 2015).

9.3.2 **The declining level of strike activity**

That said, though, one of the most prominent features of employment relations has been the diminution in the level of strike activity since the 1970s. Table 9.1 shows that strike levels

Table 9.1 The level of strike activity in Britain, 1946–99

	Strikes	Workers involved (000s)	Days not worked (000s)
1946–52	1,698	444	1,888
1953–59	2,340	790	3,950
1960–68	2,372	1,323	3,189
1969–73	2,974	1,581	12,497
1974–79	2,412	1,653	12,178
1980–85	1,276	1,213	9,806
1986–89	893	781	3,324
1990–94	334	223	824
1995–99	193	180	495

Annual averages.

Sources: Edwards (1995); Office for National Statistics (http://www.statistics.gov.uk); licensed under the Open Government licence v.3.0

peaked during the 1970s, when on average each year there were well over 2,000 recorded strikes and over 12 million working days not worked as a consequence. While the 1980s were characterized by occasional large-scale strikes, in industries such as steel making and coal mining, as workers and their unions fought rationalization initiatives that threatened their jobs, livelihoods, and communities (Gilbert 1996)—the nine-month miners' strike in 1984–5 being the most famous example—the decade saw a marked diminution of strike activity, as measured by the frequency, breadth, and duration of strikes.

During the 1990s the decline in strike activity continued—a trend which persisted into the 2000s, when it reached historically low levels (Kelly 2015). Table 9.2 provides further details of strike levels between 2000 and 2015. The year 2005 saw the lowest recorded number of working days not worked due to strike activity—157,000—while the lowest number of strikes, just ninety-two, was recorded some five years later, in 2010. Yet, despite the overall historically low levels of strike activity during the 2000s, there were notable annual fluctuations. Some years saw a pronounced upsurge in strikes. In 2002, for example, over 1.3 million working days were not worked, largely as a result of two major public sector strikes involving local government workers and firefighters. The similarly high number of days not worked in 2011 reflected that year's incidence of large national public sector strikes, involving a large number of workers. While the decline in the level of strike activity is an international phenomenon (Gall 2013a; Vandaele 2011), it is especially marked in the UK. See Chapter 11 for a discussion of strikes and labour conflict in global perspective.

Why has the incidence of strike activity fallen to such low levels in contemporary employment relations? Clearly, the changing composition of employment has been an important factor. Levels of employment in traditionally strike-prone industries, such as coal mining and the docks, have fallen considerably. Job growth has been concentrated in private sector service industries where trade unionism is weaker and strike action less commonplace.

Table 9.2 The level of strike activity in Britain, 2000–15

	Strikes	Workers involved (000s)	Days not worked (000s)
2000	212	183	499
2001	194	180	525
2002	146	943	1,323
2003	133	151	499
2004	130	293	905
2005	116	93	157
2006	158	713	755
2007	142	745	1,041
2008	144	511	759
2009	98	209	455
2010	92	133	365
2011	149	1,530	1,390
2012	131	237	249
2013	114	395	444
2014	155	733	788
2015	106	81	170

Source: ONS (2016b), licensed under the Open Government Licence v.3.0

That said, though, the idea that workers in certain occupations and industries are particularly 'strike-prone' (e.g. Kerr and Siegel 1954) often fails to stand up to critical scrutiny (Edwards 1977). Strike levels may vary considerably from workplace to workplace even within the same industry.

The rise of service-based economies is sometimes associated with the diminution of labour conflict, since workers supposedly enjoy fewer opportunities to engage in collective solidarity (Wallace and O'Sullivan 2006). Strikes are more difficult to organize in the service sector, where the jobs are often precarious, workers are isolated, and a trade union presence scarce. But too great an emphasis on compositional change means that the capacity of service sector workers to mobilize and challenge the interests of their employers is under-appreciated. As Section 9.5 shows, effective collective action by service sector workers increasingly takes the form of protests and demonstrations, rather than conventional strikes.

Workers in the public services, where unions continue to enjoy major support, demonstrate a readiness to take strike action. During the 2000s, public sector disputes—among post office workers, college lecturers, local government workers, civil servants, and firefighters in particular—increasingly dominated the strike statistics (Kelly 2015; Lyddon 2015). Much of their action, moreover, was relatively short, or discontinuous, in nature, for example a series of one- or two-day strikes, something which increases the pressure on the employer while reducing the costs to the employee of striking, in particular loss of wages (Gall 2016b).

Another reason for the diminution of strike activity concerns changes in the economic climate. Chapter 11 shows how greater competitive pressures, associated with globalization, have undermined the bargaining power of labour. They also mean that employers have a greater incentive to avoid potentially disruptive strikes (Piazza 2005). Increasingly mobile global capital can use the threat of relocation to pacify labour, for example, helping to engender a more 'disciplined' and thus quiescent workforce (Vandaele 2011).

A further reason that can be posited for the decline of strike activity is that the rise of sophisticated forms of human resource management (HRM), manifest particularly in the use of high-commitment management practices, has generated a more cooperative climate at work, rendering strikes and other manifestations of labour conflict unnecessary. Workers, the assumption goes, are increasingly engaged at work, more committed to their employing organizations, and are thus less likely to have reason to challenge the interests of their employers (Emmott 2005; CBI 2011a). The main difficulty with this explanation for the decline in the level of strike activity is that, as was shown in Chapter 5, there is little evidence that a high-commitment approach to managing employment relations has become commonplace. Claims that the management of employment relations has been transformed along cooperative lines do not withstand critical scrutiny (e.g. Cushen and Thompson 2012).

Therefore it seems doubtful that the level of strike activity has diminished because workers are more contented. What does seem to have changed, though, is that many employers are managing employment relations more assertively. They concentrate on fostering a workplace climate in which it is made apparent to employees that, given greater competitive pressures, their cooperation is essential to prevent job losses and the erosion of pay and working conditions.

Perhaps the most important reason for the decline of strike activity, and one that is related to the compositional, economic, and managerial factors already mentioned, concerns the changing balance of power between trade unions and employers (see Godard 2011). The decline in their membership and organizational capacities has rendered the unions less capable of undertaking effective industrial action. Many union leaders have placed their faith in partnership and cooperative employment relations as the route to greater influence, largely because they are operating from a position of weakness (see Chapter 6). Moreover, the highly restrictive legal framework imposes substantial constraints on the ability of unions to organize effective strike action (see Section 9.4), though its precise effects are difficult to gauge.

A key question is whether or not the diminution of strike activity evident between the 1980s and the 2000s will continue in the future. One thing that is clear, however, is the increasing degree to which strike action is concentrated in the public services, and in industries that used to be in the public sector, such as the railways. This reflects the relatively strong degree of trade union membership and organization in these areas (Kelly 2015; Lyddon 2015). The majority of days not worked because of strike activity tend to be in the public sector (ONS 2016b). Since 2010 there has been a series of major strikes in the public sector among schoolteachers, civil servants, lecturers, doctors and others in response to government austerity measures resulting in pay cuts and/or freezes, the erosion of pension rights, and job losses. In November 2011, the National Association of Headteachers organized its first ever strike as part of the wider public sector action over pensions. Decisions by some local councils to impose pay cuts resulted in some notable disputes, highlighting the contribution made by neo-liberal austerity to generating labour conflict. In 2011, for example, workers and unions in Southampton reacted furiously to pay cuts imposed by the Conservative-led local authority, with refuse collectors, social workers, port staff, and parking wardens among others all taking part in strike action (BBC News 2012b; Milmo 2012b).

Contesting employment relations 9.2: Striking for the living wage: the Brixton Ritzy dispute

Although most strike activity is concentrated in the public sector, there are instances of low-paid workers in private sector companies striking in pursuit of better pay and conditions. One of the most prominent examples of this occurred during 2014 when workers employed by the Ritzy cinema in Brixton, London—part of the Picturehouse chain—undertook a number of strikes as part of their campaign for a pay rise from £7.24 per hour to the level of the London living wage (then £8.80 per hour). In addition to the strikes, the workers, supported by the BECTU trade union, organized a series of protests and related activities designed to draw attention to their cause. Their efforts were successful. In September 2014, the Ritzy workers ended their dispute after their union reached an agreement with the company which not only provided an immediate pay rise, but also involved a commitment to paying the London living wage by September 2015. That was not the end of the matter, however, as soon after settling the pay dispute the workforce was called upon to mobilize once again—this time to successfully fight management proposals to make a large number of staff redundant. The BECTU trade union subsequently initiated a campaign to get the living wage adopted across all the cinemas in the Picturehouse chain. During 2015 Ritzy workers also broadened their campaign, taking the fight for a living wage to arts venues around the UK.

However, care needs to be taken not to assume that strikes are solely a public sector phenomenon. While most days not worked because of strikes tend to be in the public sector—because strikes there tend to be larger, and often organized on a national basis—around half of actual stoppages occur in the private sector (ONS 2016b), over issues around pay, pensions, and jobs. Since the late 2000s strikes have affected a wide range of sectors, including transport, energy, local newspapers, and manufacturing, where workers are organized in unions and have the motivation and capacity to take action to challenge their employers' actions. In November 2014, for example, around 800 workers employed at the Jacobs Biscuits factory in Liverpool went on strike to protest against proposed changes to sick pay arrangements. Demands from workers to be paid a 'living wage' are also becoming a source of contention in employment relations, resulting in strike incidents of the kind seen at the Ritzy cinema in Brixton, London (see Contesting employment relations 9.2).

 ## Section summary and further reading

- There are a number of ways in which the level of strike activity can be measured, though the accuracy of the data should be treated with caution. Nevertheless, the amount of strike activity in Britain would seem to have fallen to historically very low levels indeed.

- A number of factors appear to be responsible for the diminution of strike levels, including compositional change and, in particular, changes in the balance of power at the workplace resulting in weaker unions who, given the more restrictive legal framework, are less capable of initiating or organizing effective strikes.

- The economic recession, and government austerity measures designed to tackle it, have contributed to a resurgence of strike activity, especially in the public sector, though the future trends are uncertain.

The government's Office for National Statistics publishes strike data on its website, and publishes an annual overview (ONS 2016b). For strike trends, see Kelly (2015) and Lyddon (2015). Godard (2011) provides a thoughtful analysis of the factors underlying the decline of strikes.

9.4 The legal regulation of strikes and industrial action

Unlike many other European countries, in Britain workers have never enjoyed a 'right' to go on strike (Lyddon 2015), although under the influence of the European Court of Human Rights (ECHR) this may be changing (Bogg and Ewing 2014; Ewing and Hendy 2010). Under the common law, based on the primacy of freedom of contract and the importance of property rights, workers who strike, or undertake any form of industrial action, generally act in breach of their employment contracts. Trade unions that organize industrial action potentially transgress the common law in a range of areas; most notably they are liable to commit the offence of inducing workers to breach their contracts.

During the late nineteenth and early twentieth centuries, legislation was enacted that gave unions and their officials immunities from criminal prosecution for organizing industrial action, and from civil proceedings for damages by employers, as long as the action was 'in contemplation or furtherance of a trade dispute' (Wedderburn 1986). The concept of 'immunities' gave the misleading impression that trade unions were above the law, and attracted much judicial hostility (Wedderburn 1991). In reality, all this did was to ensure that the common law of contract and property rights did not make the conduct of employment relations impossible to uphold in practice (Davies and Freedland 1993).

Without these immunities, trade unions would have been in no position to bargain effectively on behalf of their members. The only alternative was a system of positive rights for workers and their unions, something that was contrary to the preference for voluntarism and autonomous self-regulation that characterized employment relations in Britain. However, during the 1980s and 1990s the Conservative governments enacted six major pieces of legislation restricting the capacity of trade unions to undertake lawful industrial action. The main focus of their interventions was to reduce the scope of the immunities that enabled unions to organize industrial action within the boundaries of the law (Dunn and Metcalf 1996; Dickens and Hall 2003). Among other things, legislation was enacted that:

- obliged unions to win majority support for industrial action from the workers concerned in a properly constituted secret postal ballot, and give employers at least seven days' notice of the action (effectively prohibiting 'unofficial' action);

- prohibited any form of 'secondary' industrial action, meaning that a strike is only lawful when it involves a 'primary' dispute between workers and their own employer;

- enabled employers and other aggrieved parties to sue a union for damages arising out of unlawful industrial action; and

- gave employers greater scope to dismiss workers who take industrial action.

The legislation was a major element of the Conservatives' efforts to challenge the power of the unions in Britain. After 1997, Labour retained the bulk of the anti-strike legislation it inherited from its Conservative predecessors in government, and showed no inclination to repeal any of it, despite representations by union leaders (Davies and Freedland 2007).

The extent to which the restrictive legal framework weakened the capacity of trade unions to mount effective strikes was evident in a number of high-profile disputes, particularly in the newspaper publishing and transport sectors, during the 1980s and 1990s (Gennard 1984; McIlroy 1991). However, employers can sometimes be reluctant to invoke the law when facing industrial action by trade unions, on the basis that legal action would only inflame the dispute, making it harder to resolve. Nevertheless, the complex legislation governing industrial action ballots gives employers plenty of scope to challenge—and thus delay—any planned action, even if their substantive case turns out to be weak (McIlroy 1999). This has been evident in some high-profile industrial disputes when employers seized on minor discrepancies over how the ballot was conducted, or the notice required to be given to employers was arranged, to instigate court proceedings and win injunctions from sympathetic judges prohibiting the strike from going ahead (Lyddon 2015; Gall 2016b). A particularly egregious example of this occurred in December 2009 when British Airways cabin crew were prevented from holding a strike, despite a 92 per cent vote in favour, because of some relatively minor balloting irregularities which would not have affected the outcome in any way.

The impact of the restrictive legal framework on union behaviour is by no means straightforward though. Where workplace union organization is relatively strong, the obligation to hold a ballot before taking industrial action can work to a union's advantage. A large vote in favour, for example, can be used to exert pressure on employers to grant concessions. In situations where they are confident that they have the support of the workforce, canny union officials sometimes use ballots to strengthen their bargaining power in negotiations with employers (Undy et al. 1996). The overwhelming majority of ballots going in favour of industrial action do not actually result in any action occurring, but they nonetheless help to facilitate a settlement (Lyddon 2015). One of the most disruptive industrial disputes of recent years did not actually involve a strike taking place at all. Following votes in favour of strike action by tanker drivers across a number of companies, in a 2012 dispute over demands for more common industry working standards, there was panic buying at petrol stations across the UK, albeit exacerbated by some inept government advice that motorists should stockpile petrol.

It is difficult to quantify the contribution made by the restrictive legislative framework to the declining level of strike activity in the UK. Many other European countries have also seen falling strike levels, suggesting that broader economic and industrial trends, the changing composition of the workforce, and the reduction of the number of people employed in 'strike-prone' industries in particular, have exercised greater influence (Dunn and Metcalf 1996). Yet the indirect effects of the anti-strike laws, in particular the large degree to which they restrict the capacity of the unions to challenge employers' actions, have certainly contributed to the decline in the incidence of strikes and industrial action over recent decades.

The coming to power of a Conservative-dominated coalition government in 2010 provided a fillip to those—particularly employers' organizations—keen on imposing further legal restrictions on strikes and industrial action (see CBI 2010 for example). As time went on, and particularly in the context of a series of disruptive transport and public sector strikes, their ideas were seized on by senior Conservative politicians, including Prime Minister David Cameron, who were concerned with finding new ways of weakening the trade unions. No changes were enacted between 2010 and 2015, largely because of opposition from Liberal Democrat ministers, who saw little need for any further measures (Darlington and Dobson 2015; Smith 2015). During the 2015 general election campaign, the Conservatives pledged to introduce new legislation to impose additional restrictions on the ability of unions to engage in strikes and industrial action, should it be returned to office. Following their electoral success, in July 2015 the Conservatives pressed ahead with new legislative proposals accordingly (see Legislation and policy 9.3).

LEGISLATION AND POLICY 9.3:   The Conservative government's new strike law—the Trade Union Act 2016

In July 2015, the newly elected Conservative government published a parliamentary bill which proposed to impose additional new legal restrictions on the ability of unions to engage in strikes and industrial action. The Trade Union Act became law in May 2016. Among other things, it mandates strict new eligibility thresholds in industrial action ballots. Whereas previously only a simple majority of those voting in a ballot was required for industrial action to be lawful, the Trade Union Act 2016 introduces two additional conditions:

- at least 50 per cent of all union members entitled to vote must have participated in the ballot; and

- in 'important' public services (e.g. schools, the NHS, the fire service) at least 40 per cent of all the union members entitled to vote (including those who do not vote) must have voted in favour—any non-voters, therefore, are treated as if they are voting against.

(continued...)

The Trade Union Act also requires trade unions to give employers at least two weeks' written notice of industrial action in most circumstances, as opposed to one week previously. Opposition to the Conservative government's proposals, led by the TUC, meant that some particularly controversial measures—such as a plan to allow employers to hire agency staff to substitute for striking workers, and a proposed requirement for unions to provide details in advance of picketing and social media campaigns—were dropped as the legislation passed through Parliament (Gall 2016a). Nevertheless, the Trade Union Act 2016 will have profound implications for employment relations in general, and trade unions in particular. The legal framework already made it difficult enough for unions to organize a lawful strike, but the new law will make it even harder (Smith 2015). In particular, the 50 per cent balloting threshold is expected to 'dramatically reduce the number of legally protected strikes' (Darlington and Dobson 2015: 3).

What explains the Conservative 'government's attempt to rush into law the most sweeping and radical tightening of the rules on industrial action seen since the Thatcher era of the 1980s', the effect of which will be to put 'enormous obstacles' in the way of unions wanting to organize a strike (Darlington and Dobson 2015: 4)? Given that strike levels are at historically very low levels, one might be forgiven for thinking that enacting further restrictive legislation should hardly have been a priority for a government which—presumably—had plenty of other, more pressing matters to contend with. There were two reasons behind the government's enthusiasm for imposing additional legal restrictions on strikes and industrial action. One was that it stems from the Conservatives' ardent ideological belief in the desirability of weakening trade unions for its own sake. The second reason was that the Conservative government expected that its plans at the time to extend and intensify austerity measures would generate substantial opposition from public sector trade unions which, as a consequence of the new balloting thresholds, would have been less able to counter these plans (Darlington and Dobson 2015; Ford and Novitz 2015; Smith 2015).

Even before the measures contained in the Trade Union Act came into law, the ability of UK trade unions to organize strikes and industrial action was already circumscribed to an extreme degree—in ways that contravene recognized international labour standards. With regard to the provisions covering ballots and notice periods, for instance, the 'law appears to impose obligations that appear impossible in practice for trade unions to comply with' (Ewing and Hendy 2010: 21). International bodies, including International Labour Organization (ILO) committees, have expressed concerns that the existing legal framework negates workers' freedom of association, and undermines the ability of unions to organize workers and bargain effectively. The prohibition of all forms of secondary action is viewed as particularly objectionable; workers in the UK are also considered to have insufficient protection from dismissal when taking lawful industrial action. The ILO raised concerns about elements of the Trade Union Act as it passed through Parliament (Perraudin 2016b). In the past, successive governments ignored international criticism of the UK's strike laws; however, recent judgments from the ECHR, which articulate the right to bargain collectively essentially as a human right, with the freedom to take industrial action an essential component of that right, may provide unions with an opportunity to challenge aspects of the current legal framework (Bogg and Ewing 2014; Ewing and Hendy 2010).

Section summary and further reading

- Workers in the UK do not enjoy the 'right' to strike; rather they enjoy certain protections when taking industrial action, as do unions when organizing it, as long as the action is lawful and in furtherance of a trade dispute.

- Conservative governments of the 1980s and 1990s enacted some major changes to the law governing strikes and industrial action, making it much more restrictive, which Labour left largely unchanged after 1997. The laws are so strict that it is virtually impossible for a union to organize industrial action which is wholly lawful in every respect.

- In July 2015, the newly elected Conservative government proposed additional legal restrictions on the ability of unions to organize strikes and industrial action. These were introduced by the Trade Union Act 2016. The legal framework contravenes recognized international labour standards in some important ways.

For further information about the legal framework, see McIlroy (1991, 1999), Dickens and Hall (2003), and Davies and Freedland (2007: 110–14). Darlington and Dobson (2015) provide an analysis of the measures contained in the Trade Union Act and their potential consequences.

9.5 Understanding labour conflict: insights from mobilization theory

While broader industrial, economic, and political factors clearly affect the level of strike activity, it is important to recognize that the causes of strikes are rooted in the dynamics of the relationship between managers and workers in particular workplace environments. Strikes, then, are both social and political phenomena (Batstone, Boraston, and Frenkel 1978; Hyman 1989). They happen primarily because workers mobilize collectively in order to resist or influence decisions made by their employers. Thus their occurrence constitutes a political challenge to the established order of the organization.

To understand why strikes take place, then, attention must be directed at the way in which workers, organized in trade unions, perceive the need to undertake industrial action, and the effectiveness with which they are able to do so (Shorter and Tilly 1974). Broader structural factors clearly exercise an influence on strike levels in as much as they generate grievances, or a more general sense of disaffection; but whether or not such discontent produces a strike in a particular organization or workplace depends on the mobilizing capacity of the workers involved, as well as their willingness and opportunity to take action (Batstone, Boraston, and Frenkel 1978). Strikes are social and political phenomena, whose manifestation is contingent on the capacity of workers, organized in trade unions, to mobilize and defend their conditions or challenge their employer, albeit within particular contexts. This helps to explain variations in strike activity between different organizations and workplaces. For example, at times the further education sector in England and Wales has been greatly disrupted by industrial action, but the level of strike activity varies considerably between colleges, reflecting variations in the mobilizing capacities of the lecturers' union at different sites (Williams 2003).

A focus on the capacity of workers to organize themselves collectively in response to problems at work, and engage in some form of industrial action to redress them, is central to the contribution that mobilization theory makes to understanding changes in the level of strike activity. The fall in the incidence of strikes does not reflect greater contentment at work, and thus a diminution in the potential for labour conflict; rather, in the absence of trade unions, where discontent arises it is expressed in different forms, as exemplified by the sharp rise in the number of complaints made by aggrieved employees to employment tribunals during the 2000s, concerning matters such as unfair dismissal and discrimination (see Chapter 10).

In the largely non-unionized hotel industry, the unilateral exercise of managerial authority is the source of numerous grievances among employees concerning their perceived unfair treatment, many of which are submitted to tribunals (Head and Lucas 2004). Far from declining, the potential for conflict in employment relations has been increasing. Given evidence that people are willing to act collectively to pursue their interests in society (Kelly 1998), how, then, can the decline in the level of strike activity be explained?

Mobilization theory helps us to understand the social processes that enable, and constrain, the development of collective industrial action. It 'directs our attention to the social relations of the workplace and the processes by which employees perceive and respond to injustice and assert their rights' (Kelly 1998: 51). Mobilization theory holds that it is not enough for workers just to hold a grievance for industrial action such as a strike to arise. Rather, the workers concerned must hold a collective sense of injustice, recognize that their interests are different from those of their employer (agency), and attribute the source of their grievance to the actions of their employer. Moreover, a mechanism needs to exist, in the form of union activists, that channels the discontent into collective action (see Figure 9.1). Thus mobilization theory seeks to explain the circumstances under which individual grievances take on a collective dimension, inform the collective organization of workers, and result in collective industrial action (Kelly 1998, 2005b).

In the United States, efforts by low-paid workers in the service sector—in retailing and fast-food jobs especially—to improve their pay and conditions and combat perceived injustice demonstrate the relevance of mobilization theory to understanding developments in employment relations. The OUR Walmart campaign, for example, illustrates that workers' dissatisfaction with the pay and conditions provided by the giant retailer was insufficient, on its own, to prompt them to mobilize. Rather, mobilization was fostered by the development of a sense of injustice among workers at the way they were treated which, fostered by key activists

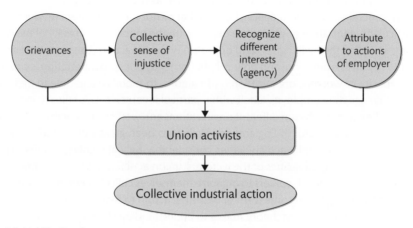

Figure 9.1 Mobilization theory

and the extensive use of social media to generate a sense of togetherness, was articulated collectively and attributed to the behaviour of the company (Wood 2015).

What, then, is the relevance of mobilization theory to understanding levels of labour conflict and strike activity in contemporary employment relations? It offers four key insights. First, mobilization theory suggests that the absence of strikes does not imply that industrial harmony prevails in workplaces. Mobilization theory shows that effective collective action by workers is a highly contingent process, something that takes root in particular circumstances, and often in the face of determined opposition from employers and government (Kelly 2011). There are a number of ways in which such counter-mobilization can manifest itself. Employers often draw on the highly restrictive legal framework in their efforts to prevent industrial action from occurring, or at least reduce its potency. Another response to strikes is to threaten, and in some cases actually impose, sanctions on striking workers. For example, in the 2009–11 British Airways cabin crew dispute the airline responded to the initial strike action by revoking staff travel concessions.

Second, mobilization theory highlights the importance of workers organizing and acting collectively when it comes to challenging employers successfully. Simms and Dean (2015), for example, demonstrate that where workers and unions are capable of 'building collective solidarities', effective mobilization can arise even in situations where it would otherwise be difficult, for example because of the presence of highly flexible employment arrangements. The case of OUR Walmart shows the potential that social media has to develop collective solidarity between workers in ways that promote mobilization. 'Through engaging in discussions over Facebook, workers were able to learn of situational similarities at each other's stores and provide each other with practical and emotional support and thus fostered identification with each other's situation' (Wood 2015: 265).

The third way in which mobilization theory enhances our understanding of labour conflict is through the importance it attaches to leadership: the role activists play in using the existence of grievances to mobilize workers, and to encourage them to challenge the interests of, or even contemplate collective action against, their employer. In France, for example, activists in some railway unions have played a prominent part in fostering mobilization among contract cleaners, in pursuit of better pay and conditions (Connolly 2010).

The fourth key contribution of mobilization theory concerns its emphasis on the fact that collective action by workers can take a variety of forms, and is thus not just restricted to strikes (Kelly 2011). The case of OUR Walmart again illustrates this well. Here, workers realized that, used on their own, traditional forms of action—especially strikes—might not be very effective since these workers are relatively easily substituted and lack economic bargaining power. Instead, successful mobilization involved using measures that enabled workers to secure a degree of 'symbolic power' over the company (Chun 2009), particularly through actions—such as protests, demonstrations, and internet campaigns, designed to damage its reputation (Wood 2015: 270). 'Living wage' campaigns are aimed at tackling the injustice of the extensive low-paid work undertaken by many workers in service sector jobs, such as cleaners. Instead of strikes, they rely on civic campaigns, street protests, petitions, and demonstrations, which are used to mobilize public opinion and put pressure on companies who use such workers, often through subcontracting arrangements, to change their practices (see Waldinger et al. 1998; Erickson et al. 2002; Silver 2003: 109–10; Kelly 2015: 726–7). Protests by living wage activists were a key feature of efforts to get HSBC Bank to enter into discussions over the implementation of a living wage (Holgate 2009; Wills 2008), which it conceded in London in 2005, and extended to the rest of the UK in 2012.

Also in 2012, the living wage campaign reached the department store chain John Lewis, whose flagship Oxford Street store was the target of a one-day strike by minimum wage contract cleaners demanding to be paid the living wage. (See Insight into practice 9.4 for an example of a successful living wage campaign.) Living wage campaigns demonstrate that effective mobilization by workers is not just limited to conventional strikes. In parts of the service sector, in particular, 'companies are vulnerable not only to the economic costs of labour withdrawal but to the political costs associated with reputation damage arising out of hostile public campaigns' (Kelly 2015: 726–7). The '3 Cosas' campaign, for example, featured in Chapter 6, involved a combination of workplace strikes, employment tribunal claims, social media activity, and street protests and demonstrations (Alberti 2016*b*).

 Insight into practice 9.4: The successful living wage campaign at the University of East London

Lopes and Hall (2015) examine the successful campaign to secure the living wage for a largely migrant contract cleaning workforce at the University of East London. The workers had numerous grievances over matters such as late or missing wage payments and increased workloads. However, they rapidly and effectively mobilized in a way that not only saw them secure a pay rise equivalent to the level of the London living wage, but also benefit from improved conditions and better treatment by managers. By generating a collective sense of injustice, and providing ideas about how they could act to change things for the better, meetings between the workers played an important part in the campaign. They were able to appreciate how their own individual problems translated into a collective injustice which could be attributed to the actions of the management of the cleaning company. With regard to missing payments, for example, the meetings meant that a worker could see that:

> it hadn't [just] happened to me, but I saw my colleagues complaining a lot; I realised that if it happened with them it could also happen with me. That's when I thought it was important to take part.
>
> (Lopes and Hall 2015: 216)

A particularly innovative mobilizing tactic was the formation of a 'complaints choir', which involved composing a song outlining the workers' grievances, the performance of which was filmed and posted on the internet. While tactics such as these helped the cleaners in their fight to secure the living wage, a crucial ingredient in the success of the campaign was the collective solidarity forged by their shared faith and community backgrounds.

The study of workers' responses to the closure of two South Wales garment factories—owned by Dewhirst and Burberry respectively—by Blyton and Jenkins (2013) provides two further insights about mobilization theory. First, their research demonstrates the dynamic and reflexive nature of mobilization. It is not something which is simply driven by union activists in a unilinear fashion; rather, mobilization is a process, one which is affected and strengthened by the activities of the workers themselves. Thus the 'process of engaging in collective action was itself transformative, increasing solidarity, cementing ideas of injustice and influencing its leaders as well as being under their apparent direction' (Blyton and Jenkins 2013: 750).

Their second insight is to demonstrate the importance to successful mobilization of external linkages and interactions. The mobilization of the Burberry workers was marked by the involvement of politicians and outside unions; it also grabbed the attention of the media—factors that were largely absent in the Dewhirst case.

Some aspects of mobilization theory as articulated by Kelly (1998, 2005b) have attracted critical scrutiny. Drawing on insights from a study of car factories in Argentina, Atzeni (2009), for example, questions the role attributed to workers' feelings of 'injustice', seeing this as a subjective concept which, since it varies from individual to individual, is not something capable of generating collective action. Rather, mobilization, where it occurs, is the product of the material social and economic conditions experienced by workers collectively, which generate solidarity. Atzeni (2009) also raises a question about the role of activists, suggesting that when it comes to labour conflict activism can emerge out of mobilization, rather than just initiating it.

These critical points notwithstanding, by highlighting the potential constraints on collective action in workplaces, as well as pointing to the features that make it possible, mobilization theory makes an important contribution to our understanding of employment relations and the nature of labour conflict. It recognizes that the potential for conflict exists in all employment relationships. Yet the extent to which this latent conflict is expressed, and also the means of its expression, is contingent on the pattern of relationships between workers and their managers in particular workplace settings, the nature and actions of the workforce itself, including the extent to which strong social relationships exist (see Blyton and Jenkins 2013), and the influence of external linkages and interactions.

 ### Section summary and further reading

- It is important to understand the causes of strikes with reference to the mobilizing capacity of workers and their unions. Mobilization theory can be used to understand the circumstances which generate labour conflict, with its focus on how individual grievances, which stem from a sense of injustice, become manifest in collective industrial action.

- Mobilization theory provides a number of important insights when it comes to understanding labour conflict. It shows us that collective action by workers is a highly contingent process, often constrained by the counter-mobilization efforts of employers and governments; that collective action by workers is not just confined to strike action; and that the leadership provided by activists plays a crucial part in translating grievances into instances of actual labour conflict.

For the relevance of mobilization theory as applied to employment relations, see Kelly's (1998) book *Rethinking Industrial Relations*, or his book chapter (Kelly 2005b). See Wood (2015) for details of the OUR Walmart campaign. Atzeni (2009) provides a sympathetic critical engagement with Kelly's version of mobilization theory.

9.6 Other forms of labour conflict

The application of mobilization theory demonstrates that although strikes are the most conspicuous form of labour conflict in employment relations, they are by no means the only one. In this section, then, the concept of labour conflict is broadened to encompass other manifestations. Following Scott et al.'s (1963) study of the coal mining industry, it is conventional to

Table 9.3 The main forms of 'organized' and 'unorganized' labour conflict

'Organized' conflict	'Unorganized' conflict
Strikes	Fiddles
Protests, demonstrations, and occupations	Sabotage
Lock-outs	Absence
'Cut-price' industrial action	Quitting
Working-to-rule	
Go-slows	
Overtime bans	

distinguish between 'organized' and 'unorganized' forms of conflict in the workplace. The latter is distinguished by its spontaneous, individualistic character, and sometimes goes under the label of 'organizational misbehaviour' (Ackroyd and Thompson 1999). Workers respond to the demands of the work environment through some form of resistance, by taking actions that allow them individually to express their frustration, by committing sabotage for example, or by distancing themselves from the causes of their problems, like going absent or quitting their jobs.

Organized forms of conflict, though, are imbued with a more formal, collective, and purposeful character, undertaken in order to challenge and change managerial decisions, not merely to enable workers to cope with them. Such conflict is 'far more likely to form part of a conscious strategy to change the situation which is identified as the source of discontent' (Hyman 1977: 53). Although a strike is the most obvious manifestation of organized conflict, other forms of collective industrial action short of a strike, including overtime bans and work-to-rules for example, are used by workers collectively, usually in trade unions, to influence organizational decision-making. See Table 9.3 for the main forms of 'organized' and 'unorganized' labour conflict.

9.6.1 Forms of organized labour conflict

Forms of organized labour conflict other than strikes are often referred to as 'action short of a strike', or as 'cut-price' (Flanders 1975) methods of industrial action. While they are types of behaviour designed to disrupt an employer's ability to produce goods and services, as a strike does, they do not involve a complete withdrawal of labour. These are forms of action in which workers mostly continue to undertake their duties. There are three main types of cut-price industrial action:

- The 'go-slow' occurs in situations where workers carry on performing their jobs, but do so at a much slower pace than normal. In 2003, for example, in a dispute over safety, London Underground train drivers threatened to limit their speeds to 25 miles per hour, well below normal.

- The 'work-to-rule' generally involves a refusal by workers to undertake some aspect, or aspects, of their job in order to disrupt the normal production of goods or delivery of a service. In September 2012, for example, the main teachers' unions launched action 'short of a strike' in their dispute over pay and conditions. Among other things, this included a boycott of meetings outside standard working hours, restrictions on involvement in performance management and classroom observation activities, and a refusal to provide cover for absent staff, invigilate exams, or supervise pupils during their lunch break.

- The 'overtime ban' is another example of industrial action short of a strike. Since many organizations rely on their workers undertaking overtime to maintain production levels or to ensure that services are maintained, overtime bans, where workers collectively refuse to participate in overtime working, can be extremely disruptive for them. In 2014, for example, the Public and Commercial Services (PCS) union instituted an overtime ban in the Civil Service in a dispute over pay, conditions, and job security. In addition, as mentioned in Chapter 8, rail unions frequently use bans on overtime working as a bargaining lever in disputes with employers.

Like strikes, these forms of industrial action are designed and undertaken with a purpose: to challenge managerial decisions, for example, or to put pressure on an employer to adjust the terms of the wage–work bargain in a way that benefits the workforce. Nevertheless, they are seen as less risky forms of action than strikes. Moreover, workers do not lose as much in wages as they would if they were to go on strike. Like strikes, though, go-slows, working-to-rule, and overtime bans require organization and coordination, generally through the activities of a trade union (Edwards 1995).

In rare circumstances it is employers, not the union, who initiate industrial action, by instituting a 'lock-out' of the workforce—in effect sending staff home and refusing to pay them—as a means of trying to bring about an end to a dispute. One of the most prominent examples of a lock-out occurred in October 2011 when the Australian airline Qantas shut down its operations for two days, grounding all domestic and international flights, until ordered to re-open by the Australian government agency responsible for regulating employment relations. The company's actions were designed to try and force an end to a long-running dispute with many of its staff, who had mounted a series of strikes in protest against restructuring proposals that threatened their jobs.

Cut-price industrial action can be an effective way for organized groups of workers to challenge managerial decision-making, express a grievance, or enforce a demand in contemporary employment relations. As we have seen, schoolteachers sometimes enforce effective work-to-rules by not providing cover for absent colleagues, or by refusing to help undertake tests, among other things. However, recorded action of this kind seems to be quite rare; there is no indication that strikes have been substituted by alternative forms of collective industrial action (Kelly 2015; van Wanrooy et al. 2013b). Nevertheless, while they may be relatively uncommon—not least because managers have taken a more assertive approach to dealing with cut-price industrial action, by deducting wages for 'partial performance' for example—instances like these demonstrate that organized labour conflict should not be equated simply with strike activity, even if the two seem to be complementary rather than used as alternatives (Dix, Sisson, and Forth 2009; Kelly 2015).

Simply focusing on established, conventional forms of collective industrial action would seem to indicate that labour conflict has markedly diminished in importance. However, there are some emerging signs that traditional forms of contention—namely the strike and other manifestations of collective industrial action, which are generally rooted in specific workplaces—are beginning to be supplanted by alternative forms of conflict, such as protests, demonstrations, and other types of direct action. When the Homeform Group, the owner of Moben Kitchens, went into administration in June 2011, with the loss of over 500 jobs, workers held protests outside its Manchester head office demanding unpaid wages. The Unite trade union has pioneered the use of innovative 'leverage' campaigns during industrial disputes (see Insight into practice 9.5). It has also developed wider campaigns against employers, often in conjunction with activist groups, aimed at pressurizing them to alter their practices. This is illustrated by the campaign against the use of zero-hours contracts by the retailer Sports Direct and the use of 'inflatable "protest rats" in a number of high profile industrial disputes such as the strike at St Mungo's Housing Association' (French and Hodder 2016: 174).

 Insight into practice 9.5: Unite's 'leverage' campaigns

The trade union Unite has developed an innovative form of industrial action—known as 'leverage'—which is designed to operate as a strategic, managed campaign against targeted employers. The nature of the campaign, and the type of 'leverage' tactics used, depend on the specific circumstances of each case. The aim is to identify specific techniques, actions, and arguments that will change the employer's position, identifying and exploiting areas where they are perceived to be weak, and then to 'tactically and deliberately' exert any necessary pressure or create uncertainty (French and Hodder 2016: 174). In so doing, Unite (no date) 'will ask those who object to the behaviour of an immoral employer to conduct in lawful protest against the actions of the employer'. Up to 2015, Unite had run seven leverage campaigns, all of which had been successful, including winning a supplementary bonus payment for London bus staff during the 2012 Summer Olympics.

However, Unite's leverage tactics have generated controversy. In 2013, Unite responded to the threatened closure of the Ineos refinery at Grangemouth in Scotland by organizing protests targeted at the Ineos Chairman, Jim Ratcliffe, businesses and properties associated with Ineos and Ratcliffe, and Ineos's suppliers. These events prompted the UK coalition government to commission a review led by Bruce Carr QC into the alleged use of 'intimidation tactics' in industrial disputes (French and Hodder 2016: 175). In the event, there was nothing in Carr's report to suggest that Unite's activities in relation to the Grangemouth dispute were anything other than peaceful, and it upheld that unions should be able to mount public protests against the actions of employers (Carr 2014). However, it is clear that events at Grangemouth were one of the factors that encouraged the Conservatives to impose tighter legal restrictions on industrial action in the Trade Union Act 2016 (French and Hodder 2016).

The economic crisis stimulated manifold instances of direct action by workers in an effort to forestall workplace closures and preserve their jobs, encompassing protests and occupations (Gall 2010a, 2011a). In the spring of 2009, for example, workers who had been employed by the car parts firm Visteon, which had gone into administration, secured an enhanced redundancy package after mounting an occupation of two of its sites, in Belfast and Enfield. While the workers would not get their jobs back, their willingness to challenge the terms on which they had been dismissed ensured that they at least got increased financial compensation for losing their employment. See Chapter 10 for additional examples of workers challenging redundancy decisions by engaging in conflict. In France, some workers have taken a particularly innovative form of collective industrial action in protest against proposed plant closures and job cuts by employers (see International perspective 9.6).

These examples point to the variety of ways in which 'organized' labour conflict can become manifest. It is not that conflict in general has become less relevant; rather that a particular type of labour conflict—collective action organized by unions in particular workplaces—has diminished in importance. There are signs that labour conflict may be becoming increasingly subsumed within broader political struggles, and located in new spaces of contention outside of workplaces, rather than occurring in organized, temporary withdrawals of labour in the form of strikes as has largely been the case in the past (Gall 2013*b*; Godard 2011).

 International perspective 9.6: The 'bossnapping' phenomenon

Since 2008, a series of incidents in France have involved workers holding their senior managers captive for a short time, with the aim of protecting their jobs or improving their redundancy settlements—actions which, despite being clearly illegal, not only attracted widespread popular support but also met with little opposition from the authorities. Senior managers of multinational companies including Sony and Caterpillar have been temporarily held captive following the announcement of plant closures or job losses (Gall 2011*b*). The French head of office equipment firm 3M, Luc Rousselet, was released following two days and nights of captivity after the company agreed to re-negotiate redundancy terms for its staff—to the disgust of many workers, who felt that more concessions could have been extracted. In January 2014 workers at the closed Goodyear tyre factory in Amiens, Northern France, held the plant's Production Director and its HR Director overnight as part of a campaign to improve redundancy payments.

One French trade union leader claimed that holding bosses captive in this way was often the 'only remaining bartering tool' workers have. 'Bossnapping' is a rational—albeit defensive—form of behaviour. Workers use direct action of this kind in an effort to prevent job losses or to improve their severance terms, not as part of a revolutionary challenge to the existing order. It can be viewed as a 'ritualized, symbolic form of protest aimed at securing publicity and public sympathy for the plight of those facing redundancy' (Parsons 2013: 305). The bossnapping phenomenon is not new to France. However, factory closures, exacerbated by the economic recession, prompted a spate of such incidents, behaviour which was widely seen as a legitimate response from workers fighting against the adverse effects of neo-liberal economic globalization (Parsons 2013).

9.6.2 **Forms of unorganized labour conflict**

Clearly, levels of strike activity and also other conventional forms of organized industrial action, compared to the past, have become less common. Yet we need to view labour conflict more broadly, encompassing forms of unorganized conflict and organizational misbehaviour. Here, fiddling, sabotage, absenteeism, and quitting are considered—four types of employee behaviour that are often held to exemplify unorganized conflict in employment relations in as much as they are ostensibly spontaneous or unconsidered acts undertaken by individual workers to enable them to cope with the frustrations and pressures of the working environment. Before considering these, however, some initial questions arise that will help to inform the reader's understanding of the nature and dimensions of unorganized labour conflict.

First, to what extent do the types of worker behaviour considered here conflict with managerial objectives? Can they really be interpreted as labour conflict, along with more purposeful and organized activities such as strikes and overtime bans for example?

Second, how far are the behaviours associated with so-called unorganized forms of conflict spontaneous, lacking in purpose, and thus distinct from organized activity? Is it wise, therefore, to make a rigid distinction between organized and unorganized forms of conflict?

Third, unorganized types of labour conflict are often portrayed as alternatives to strikes or other manifestations of organized action (Knowles 1952), the implication being that if conflict in the employment relationship is not expressed by means of, say, a strike, it will simply take another form. Are different manifestations of conflict to be regarded as alternatives? Or do they act in concert, complementing one another?

Fiddles

Fiddling can encompass a wide range of illicit activities, ranging from employee theft to actions that alter the terms of the wage–work bargain to the benefit of the workers. Much of the early interest in fiddles focused on the latter. Roy (1952) and Lupton (1963) examined the way in which workers, through the process of 'making-out', collectively manipulated piece-rates, that is the amount they were paid per item of production, by regulating their effort. In as much as they influence the wage–work bargain in a way that runs counter to the interests of the employer, such activities are unambiguously an expression of conflict at work (Edwards 1992).

The term 'fiddling' is also used to describe more illicit behaviours at work. McIntosh and Broderick (1996) examine the practice of 'totting' among refuse collectors, something that was commonplace before the increased work pressures created by contracting out the collection service rendered it more difficult to operate. It involved 'sifting through bags and bins in search of "valuables" or "sellables" which were then either kept or sold—many refuse collectors regularly took part in car boot sales' (cited in Noon, Blyton, and Morrell 2013: 237).

The most well-known account of employee fiddles is contained in Mars's book *Cheats at Work* (Mars 1982). He examines the way in which the characteristics of particular jobs encourage certain types of employee fiddle to emerge. Supermarket workers, for example, being closely supervised and monitored, tend to be opportunistic in their fiddling behaviour, making the most of opportunities such as the chance to secure a free bar of chocolate, as and when they arise. Other groups of workers, sales staff for instance, tend to have developed well-articulated and sophisticated fiddling techniques, often collectively, such as the manipulation of expenses claims.

Many fiddles, then, are underpinned by a collective ethos and cannot be seen simply as a spontaneous reaction on the part of an individual worker; they are often informed by collectively generated norms and assumptions that govern the limits of what is, and what is not, acceptable. This is evident from a Swedish hotel cleaner's experience of working life in a Finnish hotel. She describes the intense nature of the work and the pressures cleaners are under to service guest rooms in the limited time available. In order to cope, the cleaners resort to 'cheating', drawing on a repertoire of tricks designed to lighten their workloads without managers or guests noticing. For example:

> The best time-gaining trick is to refrain from changing the bed sheets when a new guest is arriving, although it is possible only if they still look fresh and are not too crumpled. The changing of sheets and the making of the bed is the most time-consuming and heavy work task and when I can get away with not doing that is a real victory.
>
> (Lundberg and Karlsson 2011: 146)

They also steal hotel equipment and supplies, food and drink from minibars, and occasionally items left behind by guests. It is not so much that the cleaners want these goods; rather, the action of stealing in its own right gives them a sense of satisfaction and helps to ease the pressures of work.

> The thefts become a positive trait of our working day as we get something else than the boring work tasks to think about. Stealing has become a game and through it we have found some meaning in work. Not once do [we] feel that we are doing something morally wrong—rather our bitterness at our working conditions justifies more thefts. Considering all the stress and hard work we think we actually deserve some free soap.
>
> (Lundberg and Karlsson 2011: 146)

Hence there is a difficulty with seeing fiddles as an unambiguously unorganized form of conflict; many of the most effective workplace fiddles are the product of collective effort by workers to secure for themselves a more favourable working environment, or to increase the rewards from their employment.

To what extent, though, can fiddling really be conceptualized as a form of labour conflict? Workers who participate in fiddles are engaged in activities that would appear to run counter to the interests of their employer, but 'making-out' sometimes operates in ways that support managerial objectives (Edwards 1986). Moreover, one of the most prominent features of studies of workplace fiddling is the often high level of managerial toleration of, or indulgence towards, such behaviour.

Why should managers tolerate such activities? For one thing, fiddles help to sustain employee morale in an otherwise mundane working environment, and thus help make the task of supervision less burdensome. In some industries, like hospitality for example, toleration of fiddles enables managers to keep wages low. They can also be extremely difficult to eradicate. As long as fiddling is kept within what managers consider to be appropriate limits, and does not overly damage the interests of the business, it is often tolerated on the basis that if challenged it would only reappear in another, perhaps more damaging, guise elsewhere (Edwards 1988).

Sabotage

One of the main difficulties presented by employee sabotage is defining what it is. Sabotage at work, which has been the subject of a number of academic studies (e.g. Taylor and Walton 1971; Brown 1977), is often portrayed rather narrowly as involving the deliberate vandalism or breaking of machinery. The term 'usually makes one think of people engaged in wilful acts of destruction, as retribution for some felt injustice ...' (Noon, Blyton, and Morrell 2013: 252). Some writers, however, prefer a broader, more inclusive definition, such that the term sabotage can be used to refer to any type of employee behaviour that does not comply with managerial objectives, such as the fiddles just discussed for example (see 'Fiddles'). By this reckoning, incidents of sabotage cannot just be seen as the product of individual frustration with the pressures of work, but may also, in some circumstances, have a collective dimension, being used by organized groups of workers to alter the terms of the wage–work bargain in their favour (Dubois 1979).

Rather than acting as an alternative to more conventional forms of industrial action, sabotage may complement them. During 1999, for example, incidents of sabotage were a feature of industrial disputes in Spain. They included 'the cutting of electric cables during a rail dispute, engine drivers destroying the safety mechanism in their cabs, and striking shipyard workers immobilizing the bridge giving access to the Bay of Cadiz' (Rigby and Marco Aledo 2001: 291).

Given its association with the breaking and destruction of machinery, sabotage is sometimes thought to be something that is specific to manufacturing industry and thus, given the diminution of manufacturing employment in countries like Britain and the United States, of little importance now. Nevertheless, reports of alleged sabotage still occur. In 2001, for example, the US Federal Bureau of Investigation (FBI) was called in to investigate a suspected incident of sabotage involving damaged wiring at Boeing's Renton plant in Washington state, which manufactures the 737 series aircraft. Workers at the plant faced an uncertain future since the company had announced its intention to relocate some production and other activities away from the state.

Incidents of sabotage, broadly defined, can be found in many parts of the service sector and, in so far as they cause the quality of service offered to customers to deteriorate, can potentially damage the interests of the business (see Insight into practice 9.7). In his study of employment relations in McDonalds, Royle (2000) discovered employees engaged in competitions to see which of them could perspire the most over the company's food products. Even the reluctance of customer-facing staff to relate to customers in the approved manner, for example by not smiling when they are supposed to (see Fuller and Smith 1991), can be interpreted as a form of sabotage.

 Insight into practice 9.7: Employee sabotage in the service sector

The most extensive analysis of sabotage in the service sector is Harris and Ogbonna's (2002) study of four firms in the hospitality industry. They use the term 'service sabotage' to refer to behaviours by workers and managers 'that are intentionally designed negatively to affect service', and report that over 85 per cent of the customer service employees they interviewed admitted to having committed 'some form of service sabotage behaviour' in the preceding week (Harris and Ogbonna 2002: 166, 168). One waiter explained how he might deal with a rude customer: 'There are lots of things that you do that no one but you will ever know—smaller portions, dodgy wine, a bad beer—all that and you serve it with a smile! Sweet revenge!' (quoted in Harris and Ogbonna 2002: 169). The researchers encountered examples of service sabotage behaviour involving hygiene issues: 'ranging from spitting in consumables to adding dirt to food to spoiling guest rooms in a discreet fashion (an unpleasant example including the wiping of a used tissue around the rim of a drinking glass)' (Harris and Ogbonna 2002: 171). While some of these activities were the product of an attempt on the part of the individual worker concerned to deal with the pressures of the working environment, such as the demands of rude customers for example, others were far from spontaneous affairs, with employees collectively complicit in such behaviours, sometimes with the tacit approval of their managers.

Absence

Dealing with absence appears to be a much greater challenge for managers in contemporary employment relations than confronting strikes. It has been claimed that the annual cost to UK business of sickness absence could be as high as £29bn (PwC 2013). The Confederation of British Industry (CBI) suggests that around one-sixth of sickness absence is not the result of genuine illness or injury, but rather attributable to skiving by workers (CBI 2011b). We have to take care with claims about the costs of sickness absence, not least because the research which underpins them is often lacking in rigour. Also, few of the costs to society of work-related injury and ill-health are borne by employers (Taylor et al. 2010). Nevertheless, there is a widely held assumption that much sickness absence is not the product of genuine illness or injury, but rather can be attributed to the laziness of many workers, who are therefore prone to 'absenteeism' (Ackroyd and Thompson 1999).

Rather than laziness, however, perhaps more accurately absenteeism often reflects workers' dissatisfaction with the conditions of their labour, and can thus constitute a form of withdrawal from work (Hill and Trist 1953, cited in Nichols 1997). The frustrations, pressures, and tensions that confront individuals in the working environment are relieved by taking an occasional spontaneous 'sickie'. In this way, absence from work may be viewed as the archetypal form of unorganized labour conflict.

Yet the observation that absence rates vary according to sector, organization, and department suggests that, as a form of conflict, absence from work cannot be understood purely in individualistic terms. Perspectives that treat absence as a means by which individuals withdraw themselves from work generally ignore the powerful influence of structural factors, such as the nature of the work environment, or the incidence of injuries and ill-health at work (Nichols 1997). Absence 'norms', tacitly accepted, perhaps even institutionalized, and collectively held assumptions concerning acceptable levels of attendance, are commonplace. This was traditionally the case in the docks, for example (Turnbull and Sapsford 1992). Levels of absence often vary according to the nature of managerial control. They can thus be understood as collective worker responses to efforts by managers to exercise control (Edwards and Scullion 1982). This was evident in the food factories studied by Hopkins (2014). Competitive pressures and demands for efficiencies meant that directly employed staff were subject to a strict and punitive attendance management regime. Fearful of the consequences of taking time off work, they felt under pressure to attend work even when they were sick. However, agency workers, whose attendance was not as closely monitored, enjoyed more leeway.

Absence may be used as a tactic by organized groups of workers to alter the terms of the wage–work bargain or to resist managerial challenges to jobs and working conditions (see Insight into practice 9.8). For example, in his study of a plant manufacturing agrochemicals and dyestuffs, Heyes (1997) demonstrates how the introduction of an annualized hours system undermined the practice of 'knocking'. In one of its manifestations, knocking would involve a worker reporting sick in order to generate lucrative overtime opportunities for a colleague. At a later date, the roles would be reversed and the joint proceeds shared.

There are, however, some problems with viewing absence as a manifestation of conflict at work. For one thing, in the majority of cases it is the product of ill-health and not a reaction to unpleasant working conditions or part of a protest against management decisions. Moreover, the extent to which absence can be conceptualized as a form of labour conflict often depends on the context in which it occurs. For the poorly organized women workers in the clothing factories studied by Edwards and Scullion (1982), for example, absence was an 'escape valve', giving them the opportunity to relieve the tensions associated with an authoritarian working environment and the tedium of their jobs, while posing little challenge to managerial control. In the engineering factories in the study, though, the well-organized male workforce enjoyed an important degree of collective control over the pace of their work, and thus had less of a need to use absence as a means of escaping their jobs.

 Insight into practice 9.8: Worker resistance and labour conflict in a call centre

The case of PhoneCo, a call centre located in Northern Ireland, indicates the degree to which workers are able to collectively resist managerial control, and the endemic state of conflict, even without the presence of a strong trade union. In a highly pressurized and demanding working environment, sales workers cheated the system by engaging in the activity of 'slammin'—that is, pretending to be involved in sales encounters: going absent while actually at work. Workers also challenged managerial control by avoiding work—'scammin': absenting themselves on smoking breaks, for example, regardless of whether or not they smoked. Efforts by managers to clamp down on unauthorized absence simply exacerbated the shared sense of grievance felt by the workers. Ostensibly unorganized forms of behaviour were in fact underpinned by a strong collective identity which enabled the workforce to challenge managerial control more effectively.

Source: Mulholland (2004)

Quitting

Perhaps the most unambiguously unorganized and individualistic expression of labour conflict, and the most explicit manifestation of withdrawal from work, is the practice of leaving, or quitting, one's job as a reaction against unpleasant working conditions. Thus high levels of labour turnover are often interpreted as evidence of a conflict-ridden working environment.

In one of the call centres studied by Beynon et al. (2002), managers reported that in the preceding three months 300 staff had resigned, suggesting an annual turnover rate of some 130 per cent. The causes were obvious. For one thing, working conditions were exceptionally onerous. 'Managers talked of "burn-out" and frequently expressed scepticism over whether anyone could effectively perform the job for an extended period' (Beynon et al. 2002: 152). Workers also found the unsocial working hours distinctly unappealing. A further factor was the organization's reliance on large numbers of agency-supplied temporary workers, many of whom left because it was unlikely that they would be offered a permanent contract.

For many workers, particularly those based in industries where unions are weak, and thus more organized forms of conflict are inappropriate, resigning from one's job is one of the few ways of expressing one's grievances. In the US fast-food industry, for example, young 'workers generally do not see fast-food work as a long-term career, so quitting is a more common response to dissatisfaction with wages, working conditions, or management than is a collective effort to improve the work' (Leidner 2002: 18).

But there are problems in equating quitting with conflict in an over-deterministic way. For one thing, many workers voluntarily resign from their jobs not out of dissatisfaction with the conditions of their labour, but because of better employment opportunities elsewhere (Edwards and Scullion 1982; Edwards 1995). A high turnover rate may operate to the benefit of management since it gives them greater flexibility to adjust staff numbers to meet fluctuations in demand, and thus secure control over costs, particularly in labour-intensive customer service industries like hospitality. Here, turnover levels are contingent on the characteristics of the workforce. Whereas turnover among the bar workers may be very high, as businesses compete to recruit a mainly young, student labour force, it is often much lower among hotel housekeeping staff. Workers in these positions are generally mature women whose employment is structured around childcare responsibilities. They enjoy fewer opportunities to find alternative jobs, have established relatively stable working arrangements, and are thus less likely to consider quitting, even though the conditions of their jobs are no better, and often somewhat worse, than those of the bar workers (Adam-Smith, Norris, and Williams 2003).

9.6.3 'Unorganized' labour conflict—an assessment

Having considered the main types of so-called unorganized labour conflict, what conclusions can be drawn about the nature of conflict at work? Five points are particularly worthy of note. First, in order to understand the significance of conflict in contemporary employment relations it is necessary to look beyond the level of strike activity, and even other cut-price forms of industrial action, and consider the implications of fiddles, sabotage, absenteeism, and quitting. The fall in the incidence of collective industrial action cannot therefore be equated with a decline in labour conflict. Declining trade unionism means that workers increasingly lack traditional routes to express their discontent at work; alternative manifestations of conflict, of the kind considered in this section, may provide non-unionized workers with an effective means of expressing their demands (Dundon and Rollinson 2004; van den Broek and Dundon 2012).

Second, the analytical distinction between so-called organized and unorganized forms of conflict is rarely so clear-cut in practice (Blyton and Turnbull 2004). Seemingly spontaneous and individualistic behaviour, such as absenteeism for example, is often underpinned by collectively established norms governing appropriate levels of absence.

Third, the types of behaviour we have considered as examples of unorganized conflict often appear to operate in ways that benefit managers. They may tolerate a certain amount of fiddling, for example, or some relatively minor sabotage, if it helps them to maintain control in the workplace. That such activities occur cannot be taken as evidence of conflict since the way in which they function may not hinder, and can even act to support, management objectives. Moreover, in so far as they enable people to cope more easily with the pressures, demands, and frustrations of their jobs, these activities help to reconcile workers with the exploitative nature of the system of wage labour. Thus a 'given form of behaviour can ... involve aspects of accommodation and adaptation to a system of work relations as well as being in conflict with or a form of resistance against it' (Edwards 1986: 76). Whether or not a particular type of behaviour can be labelled as conflict depends on the particular context in which it exists, and the meanings which workers and managers attach to it (Edwards and Scullion 1982).

Fourth, what is meant by the concept of labour conflict? Quitting one's job because the working environment is particularly unpleasant, for example, or behaving towards customers in a way that does not comply with managerial wishes because one is dissatisfied with one's working conditions both reflect the antagonism that characterizes the employment relationship. But in general these are expressions of frustration; they are not intended to challenge managerial decisions or to influence the terms of the wage–work bargain in the purposeful manner of a strike or an overtime ban.

Fifth, it is clear that, rather than acting as alternatives, different manifestations of labour conflict often complement one another (Turnbull and Sapsford 1992). This can be seen in the case of sabotage incidents, for example, which are sometimes used by groups of workers to supplement other forms of industrial action during the course of a dispute.

 Section summary and further reading

- Strikes are not the only manifestation of collective industrial action by workers. Labour conflict can take the form of so-called 'cut-price' industrial action, such as overtime bans, or the range of different behaviours that come under the label of 'unorganized' conflict, including fiddling and sabotage among other things.

- The conventional distinction made between 'organized' and 'unorganized' forms of conflict is hard to uphold in practice. Seemingly spontaneous and individual behaviour, such as sabotage, is often underpinned by collective norms and expectations. Furthermore, it frequently exists in conjunction with, rather than as a substitute for, more ostensibly collective and organized actions.

- One must be cautious about ascribing the label of 'conflict' to behaviours such as fiddling, sabotage, absenteeism, and quitting. They may operate to the advantage of managers. Whether or not such types of behaviour can be classified as conflict depends on the context in which they occur, and the meanings the participants attach to them.

For discussions of labour conflict, how it can be understood, and the various examples of behaviour that constitute it, see Edwards (1988, 1992). Mars's *Cheats at Work* (Mars 1982) is an engaging analysis of various types of fiddling behaviour. Good overviews of workplace conflict can also be found in Blyton and Turnbull (2004) and Noon, Blyton, and Morrell (2013).

9.7 Conclusion

Labour conflict is a major feature of contemporary employment relations. Since the employment relationship is characterized by a 'basic antagonism' between an employer and a worker there is always the potential for conflict to arise (Edwards 1986). The fall in the level of strike activity cannot be equated with a decline in the level of labour conflict. The low number of strikes in contemporary employment relations is the product of a number of factors: restrictive government legislation; changes in the composition of employment, and lower levels of employment in 'strike-prone' industries; a more assertive and interventionist managerialism; and the declining level of unionization. Some of these developments—compositional change for example—are an international phenomenon; others, like the highly restrictive legislative framework, are more specific to the UK. Thus the declining level of strike activity has not come about because the potential for conflict has diminished in importance, but rather it is the expression of a number of political, economic, and industrial developments.

Therefore the need to understand strikes, why they occur, and their significance remains of pressing importance in contemporary employment relations. Mobilization theory is an important tool for identifying the factors that contribute to, and also those that constrain, strikes. It also holds that labour conflict should not be equated with strikes. Other forms of collective action, such as protests and demonstrations for example, are perhaps more effective ways of redressing grievances for workers in sectors where there is little tradition of robust trade unionism or where proposed workplace closures mean that conventional strikes are not viable. Labour conflict can also be expressed in a range of so-called 'unorganized' behaviours, such as sabotage and quitting. Moreover, as is shown in Chapter 10, where the focus is on how labour disputes are resolved, complaints submitted to employment tribunals by aggrieved workers are a further sign of the prevalence of conflict at work.

 ### Assignment and discussion questions

1. Discuss the view that the decline in strike activity means that labour conflict is not an important feature of contemporary employment relations.

2. Why did the incidence of strike activity fall so precipitously between the 1980s and 2000s?

3. Critically assess the proposition that the legal framework governing strikes and industrial action in the UK is too restrictive, to the extent that it impedes the fundamental right of workers to associate freely in trade unions and bargain collectively.

4. How does mobilization theory explain why labour conflict occurs?

5. How far is it sensible to distinguish between 'organized' and 'unorganized' forms of labour conflict?

 Visit the Online Resource Centre that accompanies this book to develop your understanding of this chapter and keep up to date with the latest developments in this area.
www.oxfordtextbooks.co.uk/orc/williams4e/

 ### Chapter case study: The RMT dispute over 'driver-only operation' on Southern Rail

During 2016, rail services in the south of England operated by Southern Rail, part of the Govia Thameslink Railway group (GTR), suffered extensive disruption because of a dispute over the role of guards on its trains. Pressed by the government—which had awarded GTR a management contract to run Southern Rail services—to save money, GTR proposed changing the duties and responsibilities of its train guards. The most contentious proposal concerned moving towards 'driver-only operation', with the train driver on a service becoming responsible for opening and closing passenger doors at a station, rather than a guard. Although independent railway safety organizations claim that driver-only operation is safe, the Rail, Maritime, and Transport Union (RMT), which represents guards, opposed the change, citing concerns about passenger safety, especially on crowded platforms. It reckoned that the change would result in around 400 guards losing their jobs. The union also claimed that the government and rail operator were too focused on reducing costs, with staffing an obvious target. Moreover, there were suggestions that the government and senior rail industry figures had provoked the dispute as part of an attempt to weaken the position of the unions in the industry.

In April 2016, the RMT began a series of strikes, causing extensive disruption to Southern Rail services. Yet the standard of the company's services was already poor. The terms of Govia's contract with the government meant that it was paid to operate rail services, with no incentive to maintain, let alone improve, the quantity or quality of these services. Moreover, not running services did not attract much in the way of penalties. Even before the dispute commenced, service cancellations were a commonplace feature of daily life on Southern Rail. Matters came to a head in early July 2016 when GTR established an 'emergency timetable' on Southern Rail, involving the cancellation of 341 daily services and causing massive inconvenience to passengers, because of what it claimed were 'unprecedented' levels of staff sickness. The company suggested that much of this supposed sickness was not genuine; rather workers were claiming to be sick as a form of unofficial industrial action,

(continued...)

supplementing the regular strike days and thus exacerbating the disruption. However, there was no evidence presented for this claim. The RMT alleged that GTR was deliberately cancelling services and blaming them on staff sickness, even when staff were available. Even before the dispute started concerns had been raised about chronic levels of understaffing on Southern Rail's services, and the adverse impact on services. Part of the reason why the disruption was so marked was that fed-up and disgruntled staff were more reluctant to undertake voluntary overtime.

Following the imposition of driver-only operation, in September 2016, the dispute over the role of guards intensified. Although GTR was able to restore some of its cancelled services, the RMT announced a series of further strikes for the autumn. In response, the company specified its intention to dismiss all of its guards, and re-hire them on new contracts, as 'on-board supervisors'. However, its attempts to win over passengers backfired after a £500,000 advertising campaign to encourage them to send tweets to the RMT telling the union 'how they feel' resulted in many using social media to criticize the company and castigate it for its poor service instead.

Questions

What were the main factors that caused the extensive disruption to Southern Rail services in 2016? What insights does this case offer into the nature and dynamics of labour conflict?

10 Resolving labour conflict

◉ Chapter objectives

The main objectives of this chapter are to:

● examine the principal features of procedures designed to resolve labour conflict, including the role of negotiation in settling collective disputes;

● investigate the role of grievance and disciplinary procedures, and the nature and function of mediation;

● explore the nature of the redundancy process; and

● critically assess the role of the state in resolving employment disputes and enforcing rights at work, including the system of employment tribunals.

10.1 Introduction

Having looked at labour conflict in Chapter 9, the focus of this chapter is on employment relations procedures, particularly those used to resolve labour conflict and employment disputes. The starting point, in Section 10.2, is with arrangements for resolving collective disputes—those arising between trade unions and employers—encompassing the process of negotiation, and the part played by external, third-party arrangements for collective dispute resolution, including the role of the Advisory, Conciliation, and Arbitration Service (ACAS). In Section 10.3, attention switches to procedures for handling disputes that arise when individual employees have complaints about their treatment, or are alleged to have breached organizational rules in some way, or whose performance is deemed substandard—namely grievance and disciplinary procedures. The section which follows (Section 10.4) is concerned with the nature of redundancy as an employment relations process. While it is supposedly a fair and justifiable way of dismissing staff when fewer employees are required, redundancy has become a convenient way for employers to implement job cuts, prompting challenges by workers and unions. The focus of the final main section (Section 10.5) is on the role of the state in resolving employment disputes and enforcing rights at work. There is a particular emphasis on the system of employment tribunals: quasi-judicial bodies that adjudicate in employment disputes. Although successive governments have tried to reduce the number of tribunal cases, claiming that they constitute too much of a burden on employers, the main problem with the tribunal system is its failure to make sure that employment rights are effectively enforced.

Introductory case study: Redundancy compensation
for ex-Woolworths staff

In November 2008, the major high-street retail chain Woolworths went into administration. After
failing to find a buyer for the business, the administrator had closed all of the company's stores by
January 2009, with the loss of nearly 30,000 jobs. However, the shopworkers' union USDAW claimed
that the administrator had failed to comply with an EU-derived law relating to 'collective redundancy'
situations. This requires employers to consult in advance with representatives of recognized unions,
or with elected staff representatives where there is no union presence, when proposing to make large-
scale redundancies. USDAW litigated on behalf of the ex-Woolworths workers. In January 2012, an
employment tribunal ruled in USDAW's favour that the administrator of Woolworths had failed to meet
its legal obligation to consult with the unions in advance of the redundancies going ahead. It awarded
£67.8 million in compensation, to be shared between around 24,000 former Woolworths workers, who
would each receive up to eight weeks' worth of wages (capped at £400 per week), although workers
who had been employed in smaller stores were excluded. Because Woolworths no longer existed,
the compensation was paid by the government. This case shows the important role of the law in
employment relations, and how it influences processes like redundancy. It draws attention to the part
played by employment tribunals in adjudicating claims by workers that employment rights have been
breached.

Sources: USDAW (2012, 2013)

10.2 Resolving collective disputes

Collective disputes are those that occur between employers and a trade union as the collective representative of the workforce. They generally occur over matters relating to pay
and conditions and, as Chapter 9 demonstrated, have the potential to give rise to disruptive
instances of labour conflict, including strikes. The purpose of this section is to consider the
main ways in which employment relations actors try to resolve collective disputes. While
negotiation is a commonly used process, where this fails to produce a settlement collective
disputes procedures frequently provide for assistance from an external, independent source.
In the UK, for example, the Advisory, Conciliation, and Arbitration Service (ACAS) can intervene to settle disputes, including through the use of conciliation services.

10.2.1 Negotiating agreements in employment relations

When thinking about negotiation, perhaps the first thing that comes to mind is an image of
trade unions and employers sitting across a table from each other, bargaining over pay and
employment conditions. Such collective negotiation continues to be an important facet of
employment relations; however it is important to bear in mind that the concept of negotiation has a much broader meaning, in as much as it characterizes the relationship that
individuals have with their employers as well. The basis of the employment relationship as a
'negotiated order', marked by an ongoing process of 'dialogue, day-to-day consensus building, and "give and take"' (Sisson 2010: 150), is considered in Chapter 1. What this means
is that, given its indeterminate nature, employers do not enjoy complete control over the

workers they have hired to undertake a job; inevitably there is some discretion enjoyed by both parties over the nature and pace of work, how it is remunerated, and the conditions under which it is performed: matters which are thus open to negotiation (Brown 2010). Negotiation can be defined as 'a collection of processes that individuals as well as groups use to define and redefine the terms of their interdependence with other parties—it is especially important where this interdependency is characterized by uncertainty and incompleteness as in the case of the employment relationship' (Sisson 2010: 148). Attempts to resolve disputes in employment relations generally involve some form of negotiated settlement. By enabling disputes to be resolved, either individually or collectively, negotiation helps to ensure that differences of interest are contained, institutionalized, and thus prevented from creating too much disruption, particularly by causing instances of labour conflict.

For present purposes, this analysis of the process of negotiation will focus on its role in resolving collective disputes—those arising between employers and trade unions. Walton and McKersie (1965) distinguished between two broad types of negotiation—'distributive' and 'integrative' bargaining. Distributive bargaining 'deals with issues where one party's goals are in basic conflict with those of another' (Sisson 2010: 152): being concerned with resolving conflicts of interest about how resources should be divided up. The most obvious example concerns trade union pay claims; what the union is successful in winning in the form of higher pay for the workforce, the employer loses, because of their increased costs. Distributive bargaining, then, often has a rather confrontational dimension (Brown 2014).

'Integrative bargaining', though, embodies a more cooperative approach to negotiation. This often occurs where employers and unions negotiate over how to deal with workplace issues and problems, such as health and safety. This is viewed as a 'positive-sum' approach, because in theory both parties benefit from engaging in the negotiation exercise, in contrast to the 'zero-sum' nature of distributive bargaining, with its assumption that the outcome will produce a winner and a loser (Brown 2010: 264). Greater competitive pressures seem to have facilitated a shift from distributive to integrative bargaining, because of the onus placed on reducing costs and restructuring work and employment arrangements, and the weakened state of the trade unions (Sisson 2010); the rise to prominence of 'partnership agreements' (see Chapter 6) exemplifies this more cooperative dimension of relations between management and unions (Brown 2014).

What does negotiation actually entail? In essence, it is a means of resolving disputes by concluding a mutually acceptable agreement. It is a social process in which the parties argue with one another, try to convince each other of the merits of their respective cases, come to appreciate the virtues of their opponent's position, and thus draw closer together so that a settlement is made possible (Torrington 1991; Martin 1992). Without compromises, or 'trade-offs', in which a party will offer to back down in one area in return for a perhaps more important concession from their opponent, negotiation will not resolve a dispute. But each side will attempt to wrest more concessions from its opponents than it is obliged to concede in return. As a social process, then, the practice of negotiation exemplifies the struggle for control that characterizes relations between employers and unions. That said, though, a distinctive feature of employment relations is that almost always the mutual, interdependent relationship between the employees and their employer will endure once any negotiation event has concluded. As a consequence, no matter how 'bitter the dispute of the day, both sides know that, in the near future, they will have to pick up the bits and make amends' (Brown 2014: 140).

What determines the extent to which an employer or trade union emerges victorious from a negotiation event? Clearly, the expertise and skills of the participants exercise an influence on the outcome of negotiations, particularly their knowledge of relevant issues, how effectively they can process and handle information, and their ability to persuade their opponent of the strengths of their case. Preparation is also important. Not only do effective negotiators rigorously plan the issues on which they are prepared to trade, in exchange for something more worthwhile, and those they are not, but they also consider the likely arguments and negotiating position of their opponents. Another important influence over the outcomes of negotiation exercises concerns the nature of the relationship that exists between the negotiators (Brown 2010). Where it is strong, and levels of mutual trust are high, an agreement is more likely, because negotiators will feel more at ease when it comes to highlighting areas for possible compromise, thus making for a more effective bargaining relationship (Brown 2014). However, union representatives in particular have to be careful to make sure they keep their distance from managers, and refrain from agreeing with them too readily—the 'history of trade unionism is littered with negotiators who were considered to have 'sold out' by developing too close a relationship with management' (Brown 2010: 267).

Two other important features of negotiation in employment relations were identified by Walton and McKersie (1965). The first of these concerns what they called 'intra-organizational bargaining'. What this means is that both employers and unions have to manage the expectations of, and secure consensus from, their own sides. Managers representing the employer's side have to be concerned with what outcomes of the negotiation process are acceptable to their colleagues across the organization as a whole, and may take active steps to shape their expectations—particularly through effective communication. Trade unions often find trying to maintain intra-organizational consensus particularly challenging, because of the need to win the acceptance of the workforce to any deal. In situations where negotiators find themselves overly restricted by the demands of their respective sides, fewer compromises are likely to emerge, reducing the likelihood of a negotiated agreement (Brown 2010: 266).

The second other feature of negotiation considered by Walton and McKersie (1965) concerns what they termed 'attitudinal structuring'. This is best seen as a process whereby negotiators 'seek to influence the wider climate of opinion and expectation, not least of the opposing side' (Brown 2010: 264). Negotiation is thus a matter of 'influencing and shaping preferences' (Sisson 2010: 156). The negotiating event itself is characterized by the efforts of each party to influence the attitudes of the opposing sides; adjournments are often useful in helping a party to discuss and, if necessary, adjust its position, and can also help to maintain unity among the negotiating team (Walton and McKersie 1965). However, the process of attitudinal structuring can operate at a wider level. Managers may use communication and employee involvement arrangements (see Chapter 5) in an attempt to shape and influence the attitudes and expectations of the workforce—before, during, and after a negotiating event (Sisson 2010). By emphasizing the difficulty of the competitive environment, for example, managers can lower any expectations that a high pay award is in the offing, making this more difficult for the union to achieve when it comes to the actual negotiation event.

The presence of attitudinal structuring highlights the important extent to which the outcomes of negotiation are influenced by the prevailing balance of power between the parties.

The concept of bargaining power refers to the ability of a party to induce its opponent to make concessions it would otherwise not entertain. Clearly, the skills and expertise of a negotiating team, and the extent to which it is able to control a negotiation event, are important sources of power (Martin 1992). But the nature of the environment also influences negotiation outcomes. For example, if an employer is struggling to increase capacity to meet a rapid influx of orders, other things being equal, it will be less capable of resisting a union pay demand, given the importance of avoiding potentially disruptive industrial action. Thus environmental variables can provide employers and unions with latent bargaining power, influencing their capacity to secure negotiation outcomes. See Employment relations reflection 10.1 for some practical guidance on effective negotiating.

Employment relations reflection 10.1: Effective negotiating in employment relations

What can managers and union representatives do to improve their chances of success from a negotiating encounter? There are four key areas which prospective negotiators need to address.

1. **Preparation**. Negotiators need to prepare effectively, by making themselves aware of all the relevant issues. For example, if the negotiation is over pay, this should encompass data relating to the economic outlook, the organization's current and future prospects, local and sector-wide pay developments, and affordability. It is imperative that negotiators set out explicit objectives, ensuring they are clear about their ideal, realistic, and fall-back (bottom-line) positions. They should also establish the key arguments they intend to use during the negotiating encounter in order to secure these objectives, and anticipate the other side's objectives and how they are likely to respond.

2. **The negotiating encounter**. During the negotiating encounter itself, the aim is to arrive at a settlement which is as close as possible to your side's ideal position. Negotiators have to be prepared to compromise, otherwise an agreement is unlikely. However, the key thing is to make sure that, as far as possible, your side gives away less, in return for more from the other side. This involves periods of quite lengthy argument, which can nonetheless signal areas where there is potential opportunity for movement and thus the basis for a firm proposal from either side.

3. **Negotiation skills**. Effective negotiating demands the application of a number of relevant skills. Clearly negotiators need to be able to communicate effectively. They also need to have the kind of social and interpersonal skills essential for building and maintaining rapport during the negotiation encounter. Negotiation can involve handling considerable amounts of quite complex data—especially when it concerns pay and grading issues. Thus the ability to process information effectively is another key skill required of negotiators.

4. **Aftermath**. Ideally, but by no means always, a negotiating encounter will result in an agreement which management and union find mutually acceptable. It is important that the details of any agreement are absolutely clear, and that there are no unresolved issues or loose ends. Remember also that while the management side, representing the employer, should find implementing any agreement relatively straightforward, the union side faces the challenge of having to sell the deal to the workforce.

The extent to which one side's latent bargaining power is translated into their ability to wrest concessions from their opponents depends on how effectively they can use it: in other words their mobilizing capacity (Martin 1992). Unions which are in a position to make credible threats of strikes or industrial action in pursuit of their objectives, because of their ability to mobilize their members, will enjoy greater bargaining power. One of the reasons that the 2015–16 junior doctors dispute in England was so prolonged was because of the strong mandate provided by the large ballot in favour of taking industrial action against the government's new contract. In a study of a dispute over contracts of employment in the further education sector, Williams (2004) demonstrates the way in which environmental change—the removal of colleges from local authority control in particular—weakened the bargaining power of the main trade union relative to that enjoyed by the college employers. But the main cause of the union's difficulties, and a factor prolonging the dispute, was the superior mobilizing capacity of the employers' leaders, and the way they used the characteristics of the more commercial environment in which the colleges operated to resist union demands.

10.2.2 Collective disputes procedures and third-party intervention

Procedures for resolving collective disputes between unions and employers are a long-standing feature of employment relations (see Hyman 1972). Such procedures are best viewed as formal arrangements that set out the method for resolving disputes and, as such, 'provide a framework within which workplace industrial relations are conducted' (Brown 1981: 42). The 1970s saw a rise in the incidence of disputes procedures (Kessler 1993), a reflection of the pluralist character of reform in employment relations during that period. Although their prevalence has diminished, collective disputes procedures remain an important feature of employment relations. They are present in around a third (35 per cent) of all workplaces, and in three-quarters (75 per cent) of workplaces with a recognized union (van Wanrooy et al. 2013b: 159).

Collective disputes procedures set out the arrangements that exist to resolve disputes between employers and trade unions. For example, the procedure operated by Worcestershire Mental Health Partnership NHS Trust was agreed with the recognized unions in 2008. It stresses that invoking the procedure should be a last resort, only when 'all other means have failed'. There is an emphasis placed on trying to resolve disputes informally, or 'at the lowest level of the procedure as possible'. The procedure specifies that disputes should proceed through a series of stages, starting at the level of the manager of the employees concerned, and the means by which they should be raised. Where a dispute cannot be resolved at a lower level, the procedure provides that ultimately it will go to a sub-committee of the Trust Board. The procedure also sets out the arrangements for dispute hearings. The union representative is expected to present the case, and take questions from a management representative, who then has an opportunity to put forward a response and also to be questioned themselves (Worcestershire Mental Health Partnership NHS Trust 2008). In general, the mere fact of having a collective disputes procedure is not associated with a lower level of industrial action; however, their presence makes a dispute much easier to resolve when it does occur (Dix, Sisson, and Forth 2009).

The majority of collective disputes procedures provide for some sort of third-party intervention in circumstances where a dispute cannot be settled internally. UK governments have long recognized the advantages to be gained by facilitating machinery for resolving disputes.

State intervention in this area, which dates from the late nineteenth century, was predicated on the need to ensure that potentially harmful industrial action could be resolved without it causing the country too much economic disruption (Wood 1992). Such third-party intervention was primarily conceived of as a way of 'supporting and facilitating collective bargaining and assisting voluntary resolution of disputes' (Dickens 2012a: 31). Since the 1970s, the Advisory, Conciliation, and Arbitration Service (ACAS) has offered conciliation, mediation, and arbitration services in the UK.

The main purpose of conciliation is to 'facilitate independent collective bargaining' (Brown 2010: 268). It is concerned with helping an employer and union in dispute to reach their own agreement by intervening to draw them closer together (Wood 1992). This can involve just helping to improve the flow of information between the parties in a rather passive fashion, or it may take on a more active character, with the conciliator playing a prominent part in shaping the terms of any eventual settlement (Brown 2010). Importantly, conciliation is a voluntary process; ACAS cannot compel the parties to cooperate (Goodman 2000). ACAS conciliators often become involved in a dispute before the formal reference to conciliation is made. By 'running alongside' the dispute, they are able to understand its dimensions, and thus consider potential aspects of a settlement, more quickly (Dix and Oxenbridge 2004). Conciliators work to try and get the respective parties to focus on, and develop a more effective understanding of, the nature of their dispute and its causes. In so doing, this helps find room for compromise, in a way that potentially satisfies the interests of both parties, providing the basis for a settlement (Brown 2010, 2014).

The process of mediation is similar to conciliation, but the third-party actor plays a more directive role, with the scope to make recommendations in particular (Wood 1992; Brown 2014). There is growing interest in how mediation can be used to settle disputes between individual workers and employers (see Section 10.3.4). With arbitration, a dispute is submitted to a third party—an individual arbitrator or sometimes an arbitration board—who, after weighing up the arguments of the two sides and taking into account any other relevant information, decides the issue. It is often used where negotiation and conciliation have both failed to resolve a dispute, particularly in the area of pay. In general, arbitration awards are not legally binding; like collective agreements, they are binding in honour only. Disputes procedures that make reference to arbitration will specify whether it can be invoked unilaterally (that is, by just of one of the parties), or jointly (requiring the agreement of both).

Since the 1980s the extent of the collective conciliation work undertaken by ACAS involving efforts to resolve disputes between an employer and trade union has fallen markedly (Goodman 2000; Dix and Barber 2015), a function of the decline in the level of joint regulation. Nevertheless, collective conciliation continues to be an important priority for ACAS. In 2013–14, for example, it intervened in 858 disputes—in the overwhelming majority of cases helping to avoid industrial action (ACAS 2015c). ACAS has intervened to conciliate settlements in a number of prominent industrial disputes, including efforts to facilitate an agreement in the case of the dispute over junior doctors' contracts in England in 2016. Third-party arrangements for resolving disputes are commonplace in many countries (Brown 2010, 2014). See International perspective 10.2 for details of the development of arbitration arrangements in China.

International perspective 10.2: The development of labour arbitration in China

Employment relations in China is marked by extensive and rising levels of labour conflict as workers combine to challenge the adverse consequences of economic reforms for their jobs and livelihoods. As a result, the Chinese authorities have tried to develop new methods of resolving labour disputes, including arbitration arrangements, to keep labour unrest under control. Between 1993 and 2011 there was a substantial increase in the annual number of labour disputes which went to arbitration committees, from 12,358 to 589,244 (Liu 2014). Evidently, 'arbitration has become increasingly popular . . . as the preferred mechanism for resolving labour disputes in China' (Shen 2007: 536). The effectiveness of existing arbitration arrangements, however, is limited by their lack of independence from government control, something which reduces their legitimacy as employment relations institutions.

Over the years, the main priorities of ACAS have changed in important ways, from an early focus on the improvement of collective employment relations and a duty to promote collective bargaining, to a greater concern with resolving individual disputes, providing advice about workplace problems (see Section 10.5), and with working to prevent problems from arising in the first place (Hawes 2000; Purcell 2000; Dix and Oxenbridge 2004; Brown 2014). A growing aspect of ACAS's work involves supporting 'workplace effectiveness', by taking action to demonstrate that 'good' relations between employers and employees can boost business performance, for example through carefully designed attendance management policies that help to reduce employee absence levels (ACAS 2010). The purpose of ACAS has changed, from its original pluralist emphasis on promoting collective bargaining, towards a more unitary concern with supporting harmonious employment relations climates. Conciliation itself, moreover, has increasingly become less about resolving specific disputes between unions and employers, and more concerned with promoting greater cooperation in employment relations through a greater focus on advisory work designed to prevent disputes (Brown 2014; Dix and Barber 2015).

 ## Section summary and further reading

- Attempts to resolve disputes between employers and unions generally involve some kind of negotiated settlement. The nature of any settlement is strongly influenced by the extent of the respective parties' bargaining power. The characteristics of the environment give the parties a degree of latent power, but the outcome of negotiations is largely determined by how effectively they mobilize to make use of it.

- There is a long history of state support for third-party dispute-resolution machinery, aiming to ensure that potentially damaging disputes can be settled without causing too much disruption. An important function of ACAS is to provide collective conciliation in disputes between employers and trade unions.

For perspectives on negotiations and the skills needed for effective negotiation, see Torrington (1991). Sisson (2010: chapter 5), Brown (2010: 263–7), and Brown (2014: 140–4) provide good overviews of the process of negotiation in employment relations. Third-party arrangements for resolving disputes are covered by Wood (1992), Hawes (2000), and Brown (2014).

10.3 Workplace conflict: grievance and disciplinary procedures in employment relations

Trade union decline (see Chapter 6), and falling levels of collective industrial action, especially strikes (see Chapter 9), mean that a greater amount of attention has been directed at ostensibly more individualized forms of workplace conflict, and the resolution of disputes that arise between individual workers and their employers. This is in the context of the increasing scope of employment protection legislation, which provides workers with individual entitlements that may have to be asserted (Saundry and Dix 2014). Having considered procedures for resolving collective disputes in Section 10.2, the purpose of this section is to examine arrangements for handling instances of workplace conflict that ostensibly involve employees as individuals. Employers commonly operate formal procedures for dealing with employee grievances, and for disciplining and dismissing staff deemed to have breached organizational rules or whose performance is considered unsatisfactory. While the focus of such arrangements is on addressing issues ostensibly relating to individual employees, it is important to bear in mind that when such conflict at work arises it may not be something which is just related to a single person, but can have a more collective dimension. Moreover, the growing interest in mediation in employment relations highlights the increasing extent to which handling workplace conflict is not just limited to operating procedures designed to resolve disputes, but also concerns preventing disputes from arising in the first place (Saundry 2016).

10.3.1 The nature and purpose of grievance and disciplinary procedures

Procedures for handling employee grievances and for disciplining and dismissing staff ostensibly exist to provide a formal means for resolving individual disputes arising from alleged breaches of organizational rules or failures to maintain acceptable standards of conduct or performance. Disciplinary procedures set out the arrangements for dealing with employees who are suspected of contravening organizational rules in some way, for example by being persistently late for work, or whose performance is poor. Employees may also have cause to complain about the managerial interpretation of organizational rules, particularly if they feel they have been treated unfairly in some way, by being denied access to promotion opportunities for example. Therefore, grievance procedures are designed to offer a formal means of resolving a dispute that arises when an individual employee has a complaint regarding their treatment at work.

Before the 1960s, few organizations had their own written procedures for dealing with grievances and disciplinary issues (Edwards 2005). Since then, though, there has been a remarkable increase in the growth of formal arrangements for handling such matters. By 2011, 89 per cent of workplaces were covered by formal procedures for dealing with individual employee grievances and for disciplining and dismissing staff. Such procedures are practically ubiquitous in large workplaces; because of this, some 97 per cent of all employees are in workplaces covered by a formal procedure (van Wanrooy et al. 2013b).

There are three reasons why formal grievance and disciplinary procedures have become so commonplace. First, they operate as mechanisms for handling the inevitable disputes between workers and employers that arise from time to time because of the inherent potential for conflict that exists in all work and employment relationships. Procedures thus help to contain and accommodate otherwise potentially disruptive workplace conflict. There is a good deal of evidence that workplace conflict between individual workers and employers is widespread. It reflects the belief of many workers that managers put them under too much pressure, ignore their views, treat them unfairly, fail to follow organizational procedures, and are too prone to dismissing staff for no good reason (Fevre et al. 2012; Gallie et al. 2012). The economic recession, by increasing performance pressures on employees, prompted the greater use of disciplinary sanctions by employers (Saundry et al. 2014). Workplace conflict has some profound adverse consequences for both workers and employers, being associated with lower levels of motivation, productivity, and attendance (ACAS 2014*a*; Saundry et al. 2016).

There is a belief that increasingly 'conflict at work is manifested through individual rather than collective disputes' (van Wanrooy et al. 2013*b*: 152). However, as Chapter 9 shows, ostensibly individual manifestations of conflict are often rooted in broader collective issues and problems, flowing from the nature of the relationship that exists between employer and employees in general, which necessarily affect more than one worker (Saundry and Dix 2014; Saundry 2016). It is not that workplace conflict has become more individualized; it is generally an expression of collective perceptions of injustice. However, declining levels of union representation (see Chapter 6), and the obstacles that prevent workers from taking collective industrial action (see Chapter 9), mean that when disputes arise, they tend to operate through more individual channels (Saundry et al. 2014).

The second reason is that formal procedures for handling grievances and disciplinary cases help to define the authority of managers, and thus enhance managerial control (Saundry 2016). Grievance machinery, for example, enables employee complaints to be dealt with in a seemingly fair and consistent manner. This can help to enhance perceptions of procedural justice among employees, improving their attachment to an employer (Klass 2010). Formal disciplinary procedures have a number of managerial benefits. Their presence demonstrates that punishing an employee, by dismissing them for example, is a fair outcome, the result of following due process, and not just an arbitrary decision. They also enable managers to establish appropriate standards of performance and conduct expected of employees (Klass 2010). Thus it is important to see grievance and disciplinary procedures less as arrangements for resolving disputes, and more as methods of maintaining managerial control in organizations. This is especially important when we consider that such procedures generally come under the unilateral control of management (Saundry and Dix 2014).

The third reason for the growth of formal procedures for handling grievances and disciplinary issues is that they can provide employers with a defence in cases of litigation by current and former employees (Klass 2010; Saundry and Dix 2014). The use of an appropriate formal procedure to discipline or dismiss employees, and a formal grievance procedure to enable staff to raise complaints and then have them resolved, either helps employers to avoid litigation, or enables them to defend employment tribunal claims more effectively (see Section 10.5).

10.3.2 Handling grievances

Grievances raised by employees typically concern issues such as alleged unfair treatment by managers, pay and grading matters, allegations of bullying and harassment, and complaints about discrimination (Wood, Saundry, and Latreille 2014). As already mentioned, while griev-ance procedures are concerned with handling complaints from employees about how they have been treated as an individual, it is often the case that the substantive issue in question has a more collective dimension.

How, then, are grievances typically handled in organizations? The most important thing to bear in mind is that grievance procedures establish a process which aggrieved employees can use to express their complaint. They usually specify that an effort must be made to resolve the matter in question informally with the relevant line manager first of all, without recourse to triggering the formal procedure. Should the informal route not prove appropriate or effec-tive, the first stage of the formal procedure normally involves the employee submitting a writ-ten statement outlining their grievance. Grievance procedures usually then make provision for a meeting between the complainant and one or more relevant managers to discuss the issue in question, and to try and resolve it. ACAS (2015b) provides some very useful guidance about preparing and handling grievance meetings. An employee is legally entitled to be ac-companied by a fellow worker or a union representative. If the outcome of the meeting fails to satisfy the aggrieved employee, then there is generally a right to appeal, which is usually heard by a more senior manager who has hitherto not been involved in the case.

Frequently grievance procedures make provision for external assistance where a dispute cannot be resolved internally to the complainant's satisfaction, or make reference to the op-portunity for mediation (see Section 10.3.4), something which is becoming increasingly pop-ular. The provisions of the ACAS Code of Practice exercise a strong influence over the content of organizational grievance procedures—see Legislation and policy 10.3. Employers are under no obligation to follow the Code. However if an issue proceeds to litigation, then not only can an employment tribunal (see Section 10.5) take the Code into account when making a judgment, but it can also vary any financial award by up to 25 per cent if it feels that either the worker or the employer has unreasonably failed to follow the Code's guidance.

LEGISLATION AND POLICY 10.3: The ACAS Code of Practice on grievance procedures

The ACAS Code of Practice makes the following recommendations:

- Where it is not possible to resolve a grievance informally, an employee should raise the grievance in writing with a manager who is not the subject of the grievance, specifying what it is about, and without unreasonable delay.

- When an employer has received notice of a grievance, they should convene a meeting to discuss the grievance, again without unreasonable delay.

- At the meeting, the employee should be given the opportunity to explain their grievance and explain how they think it should be resolved. The employee is entitled to be accompanied by a fellow worker or union representative. If further investigation is required, then the meeting should be adjourned as appropriate.

- The decision of the meeting, and details of any action arising from the meeting, especially what the employer intends to do to resolve the grievance, should be communicated to the employee without unreasonable delay.

(continued...)

- If the employee feels that the grievance has not been resolved to their satisfaction then they should communicate their grounds for appeal in writing and without unreasonable delay. An appeal hearing should be convened, again without unreasonable delay, and, where possible, with the involvement of a manager who has previously not been involved in the case. Employees have the right to be accompanied in appeal hearings by a fellow worker or a trade union representative.

Source: ACAS (2015*a*); licensed under Open Government v. 3.0

It is important to bear in mind that organizational grievance procedures are managerial procedures designed to serve managerial ends. They rarely seem to lead to issues being handled in a way that satisfies the aggrieved employees. A study of workers who had left their employer as a result of a dispute suggests that both informal attempts to resolve problems and the formal machinery of the grievance procedure had been of little use in dealing with their complaints. Either the procedure was not followed, or managers had made up their minds not to uphold the complaint beforehand (Abbott 2007).

10.3.3 Handling discipline

When it comes to handling disciplinary matters in organizations, employers are encouraged to ensure that rules and standards of performance are clear, so that employees are aware of what is expected of them (ACAS 2015*b*). Typically, formal procedures set the appropriate standards of conduct expected from employees and delineate areas of unsatisfactory activity. They generally list the kind of behaviours classified as misconduct, that would lead to disciplinary procedure being invoked. Instances of misconduct, such as unwarranted absence from work, tend to be distinguished from gross misconduct, which could, among other things, encompass cases of theft or violence at work. In cases of minor misconduct procedures usually encourage efforts to resolve the matter informally, by means of a conversation between the relevant manager and the employee, before invoking the formal procedure (ACAS 2015*b*).

Disciplinary procedures also provide guidance as to the process that managers should use to investigate allegations of offending behaviour. It is important that any investigation is undertaken fairly and reasonably, with a level of thoroughness appropriate to the matter in hand (ACAS 2015*b*). Typically, disciplinary procedures outline the constitution of any disciplinary hearing, including the right of employees to voice their response to any allegations made against them. As with grievance procedures, employees have the right to be accompanied by a fellow worker or trade union representative. Disciplinary procedures also set out the relevant sanctions to be used in the event of a confirmed breach of discipline. For minor offences, such as a small number of illegitimate absences, the penalty might be a verbal warning by an employee's immediate supervisor, or a written warning. Where the offence is repeated, or in instances of gross misconduct, which can include matters such as sexual harassment for example, the disciplinary procedure might provide for dismissal. Finally, disciplinary procedures almost always make provision for the right of an employee to appeal against the outcome of a disciplinary meeting, commonly to a senior manager who has had no previous involvement in the case. As with grievance procedures, the prospect of litigation, and its potential consequences, means that the provisions of the ACAS Code of Practice strongly influence the content of organizational disciplinary procedures—see Legislation and policy 10.4 for details. Often, employers will use separate capability procedures for dealing with performance issues.

LEGISLATION AND POLICY 10.4: The ACAS Code of Practice on disciplinary procedures

The ACAS Code of Practice recommends that employers take the following actions:

- Establish the facts of the case, by carrying out a proper investigation, without unreasonable delay. Where practicable, the person undertaking the investigation should be different from the person involved in the meeting.

- Inform the employee concerned, in writing, of the problem, and if a disciplinary hearing is deemed appropriate; also provide sufficient information about the alleged misconduct or poor performance to enable the employee to prepare their case.

- Arrange a disciplinary meeting with the employee concerned to discuss the alleged misconduct or poor performance, without unreasonable delay, but giving the employee a reasonable amount of time to prepare their case.

- Hold a disciplinary meeting at which the details of the alleged misconduct or poor performance are communicated to the employee, and at which the employee is allowed the opportunity to present their case, respond to any allegations, put forward appropriate evidence, and call relevant witnesses. The employee is entitled to be accompanied by a fellow worker or trade union representative.

- Decide whether or not any disciplinary or other action is required following the conclusion of the meeting; and if disciplinary action is required, determine the sanctions (e.g. written warning) to be applied.

- Provide employees with the opportunity to appeal against any disciplinary action taken against them, which should be submitted in writing and without unreasonable delay. Where practicable, the appeal should be heard by a manager who has not been involved in the case, and employees have the right to be accompanied in appeal hearings by a fellow worker or a trade union representative.

Source: ACAS (2015a); licensed under Open Government v. 3.0

One of the most notable features of the application of discipline in organizations concerns the increasing extent to which sanctions are being applied for reasons of alleged poor performance, particularly in the context of the recession and its aftermath. Greater performance pressures, as employers look to cut costs and manage labour more efficiently, have evidently made managers less tolerant of perceived under-performance by their staff—a key source of workplace conflict (Saundry et al. 2014; Saundry 2016; Saundry et al. 2016). This is particularly apparent when it comes to the management of absence. This has become a greater priority for employers, given the imperative to improve performance standards and realize efficiency savings. As a result, absence is often managed in a highly punitive way, with many staff 'dragging themselves into work when sick, fearful of disciplinary action or even of losing their job' (Taylor et al. 2010: 282). Increasing performance pressures mean that employee absence is often treated as a disciplinary issue, something that can have negative consequences for workers who are disabled or genuinely sick, including perceptions of bullying and harassment (Foster and Scott 2015).

It is important not to see procedures in general, and disciplinary procedures in particular, as impartial devices, designed to reconcile the interests of employees and employers by effectively resolving instances of workplace conflict for the good of all in the organization. As an explicitly managerial tool designed to serve managerial purposes, discipline, especially, is concerned with maintaining order and control in the workplace (Saundry 2016). By giving legitimacy to decisions to impose sanctions on employees, disciplinary procedures are designed to buttress managerial authority (Fenley 1986). They reflect managerial aspirations and, by formalizing the application of workplace discipline, help persuade employees that the rules elaborated within them should be obeyed. In his study of a British-based Japanese television plant, Nippon CTV, Delbridge (1998) demonstrates the effectiveness of disciplinary rules in regulating workplace order. During induction, new recruits were instilled with the need to comply with the firm's rules, particularly those concerning absenteeism and punctuality.

With this in mind, it would be wrong to assume that the formalization of disciplinary practice has provided workers with added protection against arbitrary discipline. Managers generally evince a preference for flexible, pragmatic approaches (Jones and Saundry 2012), and frequently fail to follow their own procedures, or use them simply to cover their actions, having determined the outcome beforehand anyway (Saundry, Jones, and Wibberley 2015). Workers who have been subject to disciplinary proceedings tend to feel that managers had assumed their guilt beforehand and paid little attention to anything they might say in mitigation (Rollinson et al. 1997). A study of workplace discipline among nurses identified numerous procedural irregularities, including reports that managers were prepared to lie during disciplinary cases in order to get their desired outcome (Cooke 2006). Line managers often find it frustrating having to follow formal procedures because of the constraints they are perceived to impose on their ability to manage staff flexibly. Yet there is some evidence that, under the influence of specialist human resource practitioners, who view procedures as advantageous because of the extent to which they are seen to promote consistency and inculcate a sense of fairness, thus enhancing managerial authority, line managers may actually be becoming too dependent on procedures and less willing to use their own judgement on matters (Saundry et al. 2014; Saundry, Jones, and Wibberley 2015).

The 'consensus' approach holds that there has been a shift over time away from a generally punitive style of discipline towards a greater emphasis on using disciplinary procedures to correct and improve workers' behaviour (Henry 1982). However, the exercise of discipline continues to be marked by a 'punitive' rather than a 'corrective' ethos. In other words, the emphasis is on getting workers to obey managerial rules for fear of the punishment, such as dismissal, that would result from any failure to comply (Fenley 1998), rather than helping them to identify any failings and thus improve their behaviour. Investigations into the experience of workers tend to bear this out (e.g. Rollinson et al. 1997). Cooke's (2006) study of nursing demonstrates not only that disciplinary action against staff was commonplace, but also that it was undertaken largely for punitive reasons, whatever managers said about the need to improve performance or protect patient care. The 'six strikes and you're out' rule which operates in Sports Direct warehouses, and which can see workers facing sanctions for sickness absence (House of Commons Business, Skills, and Innovation Committee 2016: 8), is a prime example of punitive discipline in action. See Insight into practice 10.5 for examples of workers being punished for alleged misuse of social media.

 Insight into practice 10.5: Discipline and social media

The prevalence of a punitive approach to workplace discipline is evident when it comes to responses by some employers to comments made by their employees on social media sites such as Facebook and Twitter. Somewhat controversially, employees have been subject to disciplinary action, and even dismissal, for posting online comments which their employer claims have caused it reputational damage. In one notable case, Apple Store worker Samuel Crisp made negative comments about his employer and its products on his 'private' Facebook page; however, one of his Facebook 'friends' saw the comments and alerted Crisp's manager. Crisp was sacked for gross misconduct as a result. His 2011 claim for unfair dismissal was rejected by an employment tribunal on the grounds that, while it might seem harsh, Apple does have a clear social media policy prohibiting its employees from making critical comments about the brand and its products—something that is particularly important for a company whose image is a key feature of its success. Writing anything that could be interpreted as negative about an employer or its products can result in dismissal. In 2011, David Rowat was sacked by his retail employer Argos after returning from work and posting these comments on his Facebook page: 'Had a great day back at work after my hols who am I kidding!!' and 'Back to the shambles that is work'.

Sources: Barnett (2011); Smith (2011)

A further critical point to make about discipline concerns the care that needs to be taken not to overlook the importance of informal expectations and understandings, given the nature of work and employment relationships as a wage–work bargain (Edwards 2005). Formal procedures for disciplining staff suspected of transgressing organizational rules, and the application of formal sanctions like warnings as a result, are commonplace features of workplace life. In practice, however, workplace rules, whether or not they are obeyed, and how far managers choose to enforce them, are contingent on the relationship that exists between managers and workers in specific settings. Discipline, then, 'means more than the application of sanctions by management' (Edwards and Whitston 1994: 320). Workplace rules are not laid down by managers and then obeyed by workers, in an totally clear-cut manner. Rather, they are interpreted, and then adjusted, by managers and workers as part of the continuing process of negotiation and re-negotiation that characterizes the employment relationship as a wage–work bargain.

Andrew Scott (1994) offers a good example of this in his account of employment relations in a non-union chocolate factory. On coming across evidence that workers were leaving to go home before the end of a shift, and without tidying the changing room first, managers instituted a 'first and last hour' rule. Anyone leaving the production line during the first and last hours of their shift without their manager's approval would receive a written warning. During the first few weeks of the new rule's existence, a number of workers received warnings as a result of breaching it. Having to ask permission to go to the toilet, for example, was, for the workers, a distasteful experience, and most considered the rule to be 'silly' and 'unfair' (Scott 1994: 113). Nor did the rule find favour among all the managers, who 'found it inconvenient and tiresome to spend two hours of each day making sure their staff did not slip away without permission' (Scott 1994: 113). Not all managers, then, enforced the rule, though its continued existence in the rule-book meant that it could always be re-imposed should they wish to enforce their authority more rigorously at any time.

10.3.4 Mediation

There is growing interest in how mediation can be used both to settle employment disputes and also tackle workplace conflict in general (Latreille and Saundry 2014). Mediation sometimes plays a part in settling collective disputes between employers and unions. Along with conciliation and arbitration, it is generally viewed as a form of 'alternative' dispute resolution, in the sense that it provides for a non-legalistic settlement of conflict (Dickens 2012a). It has some features in common with conciliation, particularly the emphasis on helping the disputing parties to reach their own agreement, but with the mediator playing a more prominent part in promoting a settlement (Brown 2014). Mediation has become an increasingly important part of organizational efforts to manage more ostensibly individual workplace conflict. Over three-fifths (62 per cent) of grievance and disciplinary procedures make some kind of provision for mediation (Saundry and Dix 2014; Wood, Saundry, and Latreille 2014). As part of its efforts to facilitate the earlier resolution of workplace disputes, and thus reduce the amount of litigation arising from them (see Section 10.5), the UK government has been particularly keen to encourage the greater use of mediation (Gibbons 2007; Saundry et al. 2014).

What, then, does mediation involve? Essentially it is a non-judgemental approach to tackling conflict whereby an 'impartial third party, the mediator, helps two or more people in dispute to attempt to reach an agreement. Any agreement comes from those in dispute, not from the mediator' (CIPD/ACAS 2008: 8). In addition to providing a mechanism for resolving disputes, there is an emphasis placed on trying to influence future behaviour by tackling potential sources of conflict (Ridley-Duff and Bennett 2011). In this respect, then, mediation may offer an alternative to using conventional, formal grievance and disciplinary procedures, the use of which often generates conflict in its own right, in as much as it offers greater scope to promote a more positive, less confrontational organizational culture (Latreille and Saundry 2014; Saundry et al. 2014; Saundry, Bennett, and Wibberley 2016).

Critical to the effectiveness of mediation is that it should operate on a confidential and voluntary basis. Participants should feel able to contribute fully, without having to be suspicious about how their interventions will be used or interpreted. Moreover, mediation will not work if the parties to a dispute are compelled to participate (Latreille and Saundry 2014). Maintaining impartiality and being non-judgemental are key features of the mediator's role (Latreille 2011). The mediator tends to operate as a facilitator, helping to prompt 'a constructive discussion of the issues so that the parties can themselves find a mutually acceptable resolution' (IDS 2009: 26). Mediation is considered to be particularly suitable for resolving grievances, especially those arising from difficult working relationships. However, it is not thought to be quite so appropriate when it comes to disciplinary matters or issues relating to pay and conditions.

For employers, mediation has the potential benefit of reducing litigation by aggrieved employees. It is also viewed as being more likely to promote a long-term, non-adversarial climate than is the case with relying on formal grievance and disciplinary procedures (Latreille and Saundry 2014). There is some evidence for the positive benefits of mediation when it comes to reducing levels of workplace conflict (Saundry et al. 2014). One study of the development of in-house mediation in an NHS hospital trust showed how the new scheme improved the way in which individual disputes were handled. Moreover, by lessening the reliance on formal procedures, mediation helped to initiate a shift away from an adversarial, confrontational employment relations climate, promoted greater trust in the employment relationship, and led to improved relations between management and unions (Saundry, Mc-Cardle, and Thomas 2013). There is also some evidence that workers view mediation in positive terms, and that it can provide them with an opportunity to express some voice over what goes on in their workplaces and challenge poor treatment by managers (Saundry, Bennett, and Wibberley 2016).

That said, although there is widespread provision for mediation, its actual use is not very common (Latreille and Saundry 2014; Saundry and Dix 2014). Mediation is only used in 7 per cent of workplaces (Wood, Saundry, and Latreille 2014). It is often invoked only when all other attempts to resolve a dispute have proved unsuccessful, and because the formal procedure stipulates it (Saundry et al. 2016). Managers are often wary of becoming involved in mediation, or only participate reluctantly, because of a belief that it challenges their authority (Saundry, Bennett, and Wibberley 2016). And when managers do promote mediation, this is often done for the purpose of promoting organizational efficiency, not because they are concerned with providing workers with justice or ensuring that they are treated fairly (Saundry, Bennett, and Wibberley 2016).

Mediation is important because of the extent to which its use is suggestive of a broader approach to tackling workplace conflict, one which is concerned with reducing the scope for conflict in work and employment relationships and preventing disputes from arising in the first place, rather than just a narrow focus on using procedures to resolve them when they do (Gibbons 2007). However, there seems little prospect that mediation by itself can do much, if anything, to mitigate conflict (Saundry et al. 2014). A key problem concerns the unwillingness or inability of front-line managers in organizations to deal with workplace conflict effectively, because they lack the requisite knowledge, skills, and self-confidence. Conflict is viewed as too difficult, and thus to be avoided unless absolutely necessary (Saundry, Jones, and Wibberley 2015; Saundry et al. 2016).

Along with the diminished role of workplace trade unionism and the increasing extent to which specialist human resources (HR) practitioners eschew any direct role in managing employees themselves, this has contributed to the rise of a 'resolution gap' in many workplaces (Saundry and Dix 2014; Saundry et al. 2014). This refers to the lack of any robust capacity to handle workplace conflict, despite its clear importance and the problems it can cause. The consequence of all this is that managers become too risk averse, and rely too much on following formal procedures in an overly prescriptive way, rather than exercising their own judgement (Saundry and Dix 2014; Saundry et al. 2014). Calls for a greater emphasis on using more informal approaches for dealing with workplace conflict are all very well, but it is not altogether clear that front-line managers have the wherewithal to do so effectively (Saundry, Jones, and Wibberley 2015; Saundry et al. 2016).

Section summary and further reading

- Formal procedures for handling employee grievances and for dealing with alleged breaches of workplace discipline help employers to manage employment relations more effectively: by providing a seemingly non-arbitrary method of resolving workplace conflict, defining the authority of managers, and providing a defence against litigation.

- Grievance and disciplinary procedures help to maintain managerial control, rather than act as impartial methods of resolving workplace disputes. The practice of discipline at work often has a marked punitive and arbitrary character. It is important to recognize the role played by informal expectations and understandings in producing workplace discipline.

- There is growing interest in the extent to which mediation can be used to mitigate levels of workplace conflict. However, its use is by no means common. The presence of a 'resolution gap' in many workplaces, caused by a number of factors, including a lack of managerial competence and confidence, has resulted in a prescriptive approach to dealing with conflict, one which is dominated by procedural compliance.

The best overview of workplace conflict and conflict management is provided by Saundry and Dix (2014). Klass (2010) is good on grievance and discipline in organizations. ACAS (2015b) publishes advice and guidance about handling grievance and disciplinary issues. For a critical approach to workplace discipline see Edwards (2005). Latreille and Saundry (2014) offer an overview of workplace mediation.

10.4 Redundancy and employment relations

Losing one's job, or the threat of losing one's job, is perhaps the most unsettling of experiences for workers in employment relations. It also demonstrates in a stark fashion the difference of interest that marks the employment relationship: between an employer, whose decision it is to terminate someone's employment, and the employee, who has to bear the consequences of losing their job. This section considers the nature of redundancy as an employment relations process, particularly how procedures enable employers to dismiss staff in a supposedly fair and justifiable way, and thus help to accommodate and contain conflict. However, efforts by working people to challenge redundancy decisions illustrate the contested basis of work and employment relationships.

10.4.1 The nature and causes of redundancy

'Redundancy' in employment relations refers to situations where an employer plans to dismiss employees, because fewer employees are needed to undertake a specific set of work activities in a particular area, in return for financial compensation. In law, it is potentially a fair reason for dismissing staff, and employers only have to demonstrate that changing business circumstances mean that fewer employees are required, not that there has been a reduction in the amount of actual work. A redundancy situation can arise when there is no change, or even an increase, in the amount of work required, if the needs of the business mean that job losses are desired to produce efficiency savings.

During the 1960s, legislation was introduced to make it easier for employers to institute redundancies. It recognized that workers hold property rights in their jobs, stipulating that cash compensation, in the form of severance payments based on age and length of service, be awarded to those made redundant by their employer (Anderman 1986). But the main aim was to promote economic efficiency by enabling the more rational use of labour in a climate of full employment (Mukherjee 1973). Although redundancy legislation appeared to satisfy the twin rationales of stimulating greater economic efficiency, while at the same time providing displaced workers with cash compensation for the loss of their jobs, it was none-theless infused by 'a clear managerial agenda' (Turnbull and Wass 1997: 30). The legislation was underpinned by a desire to make it easier for employers to dismiss employees, in that it was designed to reduce both union opposition to dismissals, and the workplace disputes that they often provoked, thus strengthening managerial prerogative (Fryer 1973, 1981).

Having outlined what redundancy means, and examined some key elements of the policy background, what are the principal causes of redundancies in employment relations? A num-ber of specific reasons for redundancies can be identified:

- Industrial decline (e.g. during the 1980s and 1990s hundreds of thousands of jobs were eliminated as the importance of traditional industries like coal mining dwindled).

- Declining demand for an organization's products or services (e.g. in 2016 Bombardier, which makes trains and planes, announced plans for 7,000 job losses worldwide, and 1,350 in the UK, because of a deterioration in market conditions).

- New technology is often introduced in a way that displaces jobs (e.g. during the 1960s and 1970s the process of containerization caused the decline of many jobs in the docks).

- Organizational restructuring (e.g. in 2011 the multinational drugs company Pfizer announced it was to close its research and development facility in Sandwich, south-east England, with the loss of some 2,400 jobs).

- Business insolvency: unless a new buyer is found quickly, job losses ensue when a firm goes out of business (e.g. in 2016, the retailer BHS collapsed, with some 11,000 redundancies).

Generally, though, redundancies are instituted in order to maintain or improve organizational competitiveness, helping employers benefit from the cost savings associated with any result-ing efficiency gains (Cascio 2010). In the public sector, since 2010 austerity measures have resulted in widespread redundancies, particularly across local government. Following the private equity takeover of the AA (see Chapter 5), the new management team made around 3,000 redundancies as part of its efforts to rationalize the company and extract greater value from it (Clark 2010). This last point highlights an increasingly important aspect of how redun-dancies are used as a cost-cutting measure, not as a way of responding to poor performance, or because there has been a diminution in what workers are expected to do, but rather as a means of enhancing performance by improving competitiveness. Redundancy has therefore become a popular means of instituting efficiency savings through cuts in labour costs, be-coming far removed from its original stated purpose of improving the economy-wide supply of labour (Blyton and Turnbull 2004).

10.4.2 Handling redundancies

When it comes to handling redundancies, ACAS (2014b) recommends that employers oper-ate formal redundancy procedures, which should be agreed with trade union or employee representatives. Nevertheless, it is important to recognize that managers enjoy a considerable amount of discretion over the decision to shed labour, who should be dismissed, and how and when they should go. Redundancy has become a convenient way for managers to dismiss staff. Judicial interpretations of the relevant legislation largely support the supremacy of managerial prerogative over redundancy decisions (Turnbull 1988; Turnbull and Wass 1997). The concept of redundancy, moreover, has been treated increasingly loosely, to such an extent that it is taken to apply to an employer's decision that fewer employees are required to undertake particular work, without any obligation to demonstrate that the amount of work has in fact diminished (Lewis 1993: 72). It is important to recognize that redundancy is essentially a managerial process, something that is used by an organization to secure greater flexibility, performance, and competitiveness, and also to maintain control over the attitudes and behaviour of staff (Turnbull 1988).

Generally, redundancy procedures cover five key issues. First, ACAS (2014b) advocates that redundancy procedures should include a commitment to measures designed to avoid having to make employees compulsorily redundant and, where redundancies cannot be avoided, to moderate the number of dismissals. For employers looking to improve competitiveness, there are a number of ways of realizing efficiency savings without having to resort to redundancies. These include instituting reductions in overtime, for example, or operating temporary wage freezes. Other alternatives to redundancies include operating a policy of attrition (by not replacing staff who leave the organization) or encouraging older employees to take early retirement—though this is often viewed as a form of 'disguised redundancy'. The problem with attrition and early retirement as alternatives to redundancy is that they can be rather slow ways of reducing costs, when managers may be under pressure to secure efficiency savings more quickly. ACAS (2014b) also encourages employers to consider the extent to which staff at risk of redundancy could be moved—redeployed—to positions in other parts of the organization. Often, though, an absence of appropriate alternative job roles means that redeployment is not a genuine alternative to redundancy.

One of the ways in which management can intensify their control over redundancy exercises is to encourage workers to depart voluntarily, with the promise of an enhanced cash payment if they agree to go supposedly of their own volition. This must seem odd. One would assume that voluntary redundancy, as opposed to being made compulsorily redundant, at least gives workers a large element of discretion. In reality, however, it is not as simple as that; voluntary redundancy is marked by a combination of managerial control and employee choice, that varies from situation to situation (Clarke 2007)—see Insight into practice 10.6. If the redundancy decision is genuinely voluntary, then employees with more up-to-date and marketable skills—those who may feel more optimistic about securing a position with an alternative employer—are the ones who are most likely to be lost to the organization (Cascio 2010). Ostensibly voluntary redundancy programmes are subject to extensive managerial influence over the selection of who will leave (Wass 1996). Managers may reserve the right to refuse applications for voluntary redundancy from people they would prefer to keep, particularly if they have 'certain skills, knowledge or capabilities deemed essential to the firm' (Turnbull and Wass 1997: 33). On the other hand, they may actively encourage—and indeed impose—take-up of voluntary redundancy by people they do want gone. Thus the term 'voluntary redundancy' may be 'something of a misnomer' (Turnbull 1988; Turnbull and Wass 1997), in so far as it communicates the misleading impression that workers can exercise much choice over whether they go or not.

 Insight into practice 10.6: Voluntary redundancy—managerial control or employee choice?

Clarke (2007) identifies two features of voluntary redundancy that distinguish it from a compulsory approach: employees supposedly exercise choice over whether or not they leave the organization; and enhanced severance payments are used as an incentive to encourage people to volunteer. Her study of the voluntary redundancy experiences of Australian workers found that the extent of genuine employee choice varied considerably. Some workers resented the way in which they were effectively forced out, with little alternative but to leave. Others, however, offered a more positive assessment of the voluntary redundancy process. This was particularly the case among workers who, realizing that alternative positions were unavailable, welcomed the opportunity to 'escape' demanding jobs with an enhanced severance payment.

The second key issue generally covered by redundancy procedures concerns the nature of the selection criteria to be used when employees have to be made compulsorily redundant (ACAS 2014b). Traditionally, under the principle of 'last in, first out' (LIFO), staff with the least experience in the organization were the ones chosen to go first. But this is a very crude method of selecting for redundancy, and has become much rarer. As well as being potentially discriminatory on grounds of age, from a managerial perspective LIFO makes very little sense. It values the most recently hired staff the least, when it is likely that these are the ones whose capabilities are more closely matched to those needed by the organization. ACAS (2014b) recommends that organizations devise scoring systems based on supposedly objective criteria such as attendance and disciplinary records, performance standards, and skills or experience when selecting for redundancy. Certain selection criteria (e.g. on the grounds of union membership) are unlawful.

Importantly, the selection criteria used to pick people for redundancy can be used to communicate and reinforce managerial priorities (Cascio 2010). The use of attendance records as a selection criterion during a redundancy programme, for example, whereby staff with high absence rates are selected for dismissal first, sends out a message that absence is being taken seriously and that less tolerance is to be shown to staff who have poor attendance records. Thus the process of redundancy enables managers to restructure their workforces in ways that benefit the employer's interests. It is 'a time when new standards can be laid down as the organization gears up to operating in a changed environment' (Lewis 1993: 39).

The third feature of redundancy procedures concerns severance payments, the financial compensation due to employees made compulsorily redundant. The up-front financial costs of making severance payments are rarely onerous for employers (Turnbull 1988). In the UK employees with at least two years of continuous service with an employer are entitled to minimum redundancy payments, depending on the length of time they have been employed, and also which of three age bands they come under. Redundancy payments are calculated thus:

- 0.5 week's pay for each full year of service for workers aged under 22;
- 1 week's pay for each full year of service for workers aged from 22 to 40;
- 1.5 weeks' pay for each full year of service for workers aged 41 and over.

There are caps on the number of years' service that count towards redundancy payments (twenty) and on the amount of a week's pay that can be taken into account (£479 in 2016). Thus the maximum redundancy payment to which a redundant employee is legally entitled is £14,370 (twenty years' service × 1.5 weeks' pay × £479–2016 figures).

Fourth, in handling redundancies effectively ACAS (2014b) emphasizes the importance of engaging in meaningful consultation with the affected workforce. Consultation enables unions and employee representatives to put forward practical alternative proposals, mitigating the need for redundancies and helping to maintain staff engagement. Where an employer proposes to dismiss twenty or more employees, within a ninety-day period (or a forty-five-day period if they propose to dismiss 100 or more employees) they are obliged to consult with union representatives if there is a recognized trade union present, or with elected employee representatives if there is not. In theory, this consultation should be meaningful and be undertaken with a view to reaching an agreement over matters such as ways of avoiding the need for dismissals, reducing the number of people to be dismissed, and alleviating the consequences of dismissal for affected staff (ACAS 2014b). Failure to undertake appropriate consultation can lead to employees being awarded compensation, as in the case of Woolworths (see the introductory case study).

There is some evidence that appropriate consultation, especially where union representatives are involved, may encourage managers to reform their proposals, for example by getting an employer to substitute voluntary redundancy for compulsory measures (Hall and Edwards 1999). However, just two-fifths (40 per cent) of consultation initiatives actually result in changes to management proposals (van Wanrooy et al. 2013a). The decision to make redundancies is generally taken before any consultation commences (Turnbull and Wass 2000). In only a minority of cases does consultation actually result in fewer redundancies occurring (van Wanrooy et al. 2013a). Moreover, firms often avoid their obligation to consult and 'operate outside the law by using voluntary severance arrangements and offering enhanced severance payments' (Turnbull and Wass 1997: 32) to encourage staff to depart, in lieu of consultation.

 Contesting employment relations 10.7:   Challenging redundancies

Redundancy can be a major source of labour conflict. Workers and unions often challenge and contest management proposals to instigate redundancies. In 2006, for example, the car parts manufacturer Dura Automotive Systems announced that its plant in Llanelli, South Wales would close by the end of that year. The company claimed that rising costs, competitive pressures, and overcapacity had combined to make the plant uneconomic. The workforce, unhappy about the low level of proposed redundancy payments, took strike action, which resulted in management having to increase the compensation on offer by some £4 million. Other groups of workers, including BBC journalists, have also gone on strike in protest against redundancies. Economic recession provoked some notable instances of workers contesting proposed job losses, including protests and direct action. In France, for example, some workers and trade unionists occupied their workplaces and organized 'bossnapping' events (see Chapter 9). Workplace occupations have also occurred in the

UK. In the summer of 2009, for example, Vestas, a company which made wind turbines at its plant on the Isle of Wight, announced the closure of the factory with the loss of over 500 jobs. Before the shutdown was completed, however, some of its workers took control of the factory and blockaded themselves inside for over a fortnight.

Fifth, ACAS (2014*b*) also recommends that redundancy procedures contain provisions designed to mitigate the effects of redundancies on the affected staff, encompassing measures that help people find alternative jobs outside the organization. Employees who are under notice of redundancy, and have two years' continuous employment with the organization, are entitled to a reasonable amount of time away from work to search for other jobs, or to arrange training. Yet people who have been made redundant often face a period of unemployment, or are forced to accept jobs that offer worse pay and conditions than their previous jobs (Harris 1987; Donnelly and Scholarios 1998; Turnbull and Wass 1997, 2000). In 2005, the MG Rover car plant at Longbridge near Birmingham closed, with the loss of around 6,000 jobs. While most of those made redundant found alternative employment or took up self-employment, their pay and conditions were generally markedly inferior, with many ending up facing financial difficulties (De Ruyter, Bailey, and Mahdon 2010). Understandably, decisions by employers to make redundancies, and also the terms on which those redundancies are then put into effect, do not go unchallenged by workers—see Contesting employment relations 10.7.

 Section summary and further reading

- Redundancy is a way in which employers can dismiss employees in circumstances where fewer employees are required to undertake work in a particular area. It is a salient feature of employment relations, given the extent to which organizations use it as a means of shedding jobs to realize efficiency savings.

- Managers have considerable scope to exercise their prerogative during redundancy programmes. Not only do they enjoy discretion over the decision to shed labour, who should be dismissed, and how and when they should go, but they are also rarely hindered by the obligation to consult with trade union or employee representatives.

- For people who have been made redundant, the aftermath is often characterized by periods of unemployment, or employment in jobs that offer worse pay and conditions than in their previous jobs. Understandably, then, workers and unions often keenly contest redundancy proposals.

Cascio (2010) provides a good up-to-date overview of the issues relating to redundancy. For a managerial perspective on redundancy, see Lewis (1993). Turnbull and Wass (1997) offer a more critical interpretation of management's control of the redundancy process, situating it within an assessment of the public policy framework. ACAS (2014*b*) provides practical guidance on handling redundancy matters.

10.5 The system of employment tribunals and arrangements for enforcing rights at work

Many countries operate specialist arrangements for dealing with cases arising out of disputes between workers and employers. In the UK, employment tribunals (ETs)—independent quasi-judicial bodies comprising a legally qualified chair and two lay representatives—adjudicate on claims brought by workers against their current or former employers. The purpose of this section is to examine the nature and development of the ET system, and to assess the motivations behind, and the key implications of, efforts by successive governments to reform it, largely by aiming to reduce the number of claims. Whereas in the past workers generally tried to settle employment cases collectively, through trade union negotiation, the growth in the number of ET claims reflects the increased importance of individual rights at work (see Chapter 3), and the greater role of the law in resolving disputes (Renton 2012). However, the failure of ETs to provide adequate redress to workers has prompted growing interest in alternative arrangements for enforcing employment rights.

10.5.1 The employment tribunal system

Since the 1960s, employment tribunals, which were called industrial tribunals until 1998, have dealt with individual disputes between an employee and his or her employer, with the number of their jurisdictions having increased markedly over time. They are the main mechanism available to workers who wish to pursue redress for breaches of their legal employment rights. Tribunals were originally conceived as relatively informal forums within which employers and employees could resolve disputes cheaply and quickly without the formalities associated with traditional courts of law (Dickens et al. 1985; Hepple 1992; Corby 2015).

A key imperative for the system of ETs was the importance attached to reducing the incidence of conflict arising from employment disputes, especially those relating to the dismissal of employees (Renton 2012). Reflecting the growth in the scope of employment legislation, over the years tribunals have accumulated an increasing number of jurisdictions: claims relating to sex, race, and disability discrimination; non-payment of, or unauthorized deductions from, wages; and complaints about the failure of employers to pay the National Minimum Wage. One of the most common types of complaint, though, still concerns unfair dismissal. Redress is generally in the form of compensation; it is extremely rare for workers judged to have been unfairly dismissed to get their job back (Morris 2012; Renton 2012).

During the 1990s and 2000s the number of claims submitted to tribunals rose substantially. In 1980 there were 41,000 tribunal claims; by 2000–1 the number had risen to over 100,000, and to 236,000 by 2009–10. Table 10.1 provides details of the number of ET claims submitted for the

Table 10.1 Number of employment tribunal claims, 2008–9 to 2015–16

	Total number of claims	Single claims	Multiple claims
2008–9	151,028	62,370	88,658
2009–10	236,103	71,280	164,823
2010–11	218,096	60,591	157,505
2011–12	186,331	59,247	127,084
2012–13	191,541	54,704	136,837
2013–14	105,803	34,219	71,584
2014–15	61,308	16,420	44,888
2015–16	83,032	16,986	66,046

Source: Ministry of Justice, https://www.gov.uk/government/statistics/tribunals-and-gender-recognition-certificate-statistics-quarterly-january-to-march-2016, licensed under Open Government Licence v.3.0

period 2008–9 to 2015–16. The table shows that the majority of claims submitted are of a 'multiple' kind. In the UK, it is not possible for workers to engage in 'class actions', where a single case is taken through the system in a way that is representative of many other workers in the same position. Instead, individual workers need to put in their own claims, although ETs can then deal with them together. Such multiple claims are particularly common in disputes around equal pay and sex discrimination (Morris 2012; Renton 2012). During the 2000s, there was a marked increase in the number of sex discrimination and equal pay claims, largely as a result of actions initiated by women in local government and the health service looking for financial restitution after years of unequal treatment (see Chapter 4). The high number of claims relating to the Working Time Directive is largely the product of multiple claims, especially relating to airline pilots.

Table 10.1 shows a fall in the number of ET claims submitted since 2009–10. The particularly steep decline evident after 2013–14 was the result of coalition government changes designed to reduce the number of claims, including the introduction of a new fees regime (see Section 10.5.3). Table 10.2 highlights the most common jurisdictions within which claims fall—including unfair dismissal, unauthorized deductions from wages, and breaches of contract. ET claims can cover more than one jurisdiction; a worker claiming unfair dismissal, for example, might contend that sex discrimination was also present.

10.5.2 Reforming employment tribunals

Employers' bodies and business lobbyists often claim that an excessive number of unwarranted ET claims impose a heavy burden. Employers incur substantial costs, not just in potentially having to engage lawyers, but also in the amount of management time and resources

Table 10.2 Employment tribunal claims by jurisdiction; selected jurisdictions, 2015–16

Jurisdiction	Number of claims*
Total ET claims	83,032
Working Time Directive	36,648
Unauthorized deductions from wages	36,178
Equal pay	17,035
Unfair dismissal	13,294
Age discrimination	12,629#
Breach of contract	9,253
Sex discrimination	5,359
Redundancy—failure to inform and consult	4,073
Redundancy pay	3,830
Disability discrimination	3,449
Race discrimination	1,997
Discrimination—religion or belief	336
National Minimum Wage	238
Discrimination—sexual orientation	187

* Claims can be registered under more than one jurisdiction; # figure for 2015–16 boosted by a notable increase in multiple claims—just 1,087 age discrimination claims were submitted in 2014–15.

Source: Ministry of Justice, https://www.gov.uk/government/statistics/tribunals-and-gender-recognition-certificate-statistics-quarterly-january-to-march-2016, licensed under Open Government Licence v.3.0

expended in having to respond to an unwarranted number of supposedly weak and unmeritorious claims (Emmott 2001; CBI 2011c; Saundry et al. 2014). The technical complexity of multi-jurisdictional cases involving equal pay and discrimination issues means that tribunals have had to become more legalistic, at the expense of the original emphasis on informality. This has made them more like conventional courts of law—including the greater reliance of parties on formal legal representation (Corby and Latreille 2012; Corby 2015). There is some evidence that ETs may not sufficiently take into account the preference of small firms for managing staff in flexible and informal ways (Earnshaw, Marchington, and Goodman 2000). Right-wing critics of tribunals, and especially of the growth in the number of jurisdictions and claims, contend that the regulatory burden they impose on businesses makes employers reluctant to hire staff and damages economic competitiveness (Shackleton 2002).

During the 2000s, Labour took steps to try to reduce the number of claims made against employers, by introducing measures designed to encourage workers and employers to resolve disputes at an earlier stage, in the workplace, and to weed out supposedly weak or 'misconceived' cases before a tribunal hearing is convened (Colling 2004, 2010; Pollert 2007; Corby 2015). Tribunals gained the power to adjust the amount of compensation due to successful claimants by up to 25 per cent depending on the extent to which they were judged to have behaved 'unreasonably' in relation to the relevant ACAS code of practice. Yet a major problem with encouraging the internal resolution of complaints is that it potentially restricts employees' access to justice, and their rights to be treated justly and fairly, by giving managers too much control over the resolution of legitimate employment disputes (Colling 2004; Dickens 2012a).

While the claim of pro-business lobbyists and employers' bodies that workers have become more keen to 'take a punt' in order to pursue unmerited compensation at the expense of virtuous and over-burdened employers is superficially attractive (see Employment relations reflection 10.8), it is far from the truth, and conceals a more complex set of contributory factors which led to the growth in the number of ET claims. One, no doubt, is simply the marked growth in the number of jurisdictions for which tribunals enjoy responsibility (Pollert 2007). Much of the increase in the number of tribunal claims occurred because of a growth in the coverage of individual legal employment rights, particularly in respect of equality and discrimination issues, where the law tends to be rather complex. As already mentioned, claims relating to equal pay are often submitted on a multiple basis, further increasing the number of registered claims (Dix, Sisson, and Forth 2009; Morris 2012).

Employment relations reflection 10.8: Employment tribunal claims—a 'compensation culture'?

Claims made by pro-business lobbyists and employers' bodies about the supposed burden of the ET system generally rest on rather weak grounds; views and assertions often masquerade as evidence (Renton 2012). One particular difficulty concerns complaints that the growth in the number of claims to tribunals during the 2000s was the product of a 'compensation culture' in which employees are increasingly prone to make spurious and vexatious claims against their employers in the hope of gaining unjustified financial recompense. Yet the number of weak and unmerited claims is actually very small; and there is no evidence that workers make speculative claims with the expectation of receiving an unwarranted payout, as proponents of the 'compensation culture' argument have maintained (Morris 2012; Dickens 2014; Kirk, McDermont, and Busby 2015).

A second reason for the growth in the number of tribunal claims is that it reflected persistently high levels of discontent at work. Just because strikes and other forms of organized labour conflict have declined in significance (see Chapter 9) does not mean that the potential for conflict in general in the employment relationship has diminished. It remains important but, due to the reduced salience of trade unions and collective bargaining, has become more commonly expressed in different ways. In this sense, then, the high level of tribunal claims reflects the 'strong sense of many employees that work itself is a hostile environment characterised by unequal power relationships which require the intervention of an outside force to prevent unfair treatment', and which are an inevitable source of disputes (Renton 2012: 100). The rise in tribunal claims therefore signals a climate of growing discontent at work, with conflict on the increase, rather than the somewhat nebulous notion of a 'compensation culture' (Tailby et al. 2011).

Linked to this, the rise in the number of tribunal claims by individual workers also reflects the decline in the level of unionization and the increasing proportion of employment in sectors of the economy where unions are weak (Dickens 2000c; Hawes 2000; Dickens 2012a; Kirk, McDermont, and Busby 2015). Most tribunal claims relate to the treatment of workers in workplaces with no union recognition (Dickens 2012a). Where a union is present, it is more likely that any grievances can be resolved internally through negotiation and agreement, making resort to an ET unnecessary (Knight and Latreille 2000).

10.5.3 The 2010–15 coalition government's reforms

As Chapter 3 shows, the 2010–15 coalition government in the UK was highly sympathetic to employers' concerns that employees have too many rights, and that employers need more confidence to hire staff. Despite the weight of evidence saying otherwise, it sided with employers' bodies and business lobbyists in contending that further, more radical measures were needed to reduce the supposedly excessive number of weak and vexatious claims being taken by workers against employers. This was predicated on the unwarranted belief that employers faced too big a burden in having to respond to unmeritorious claims from employees (Renton 2012; Dickens 2014). The costs of doing so, the coalition believed, held back employers and rendered them uncompetitive (Dickens 2014; Mangan 2013). Therefore additional measures were needed to encourage the earlier resolution of disputes, in the workplace, and thus also reduce the ET caseload, helping to generate efficiency savings (Tailby et al. 2011; Pyper and McGuinness 2016).

In 2012 an increase in the qualifying period before a worker can claim they have been unfairly dismissed, from one year in a job, to two years, was implemented. The coalition government's Enterprise and Regulatory Reform Act 2013 contained a number of provisions designed to reduce the ET caseload, including the introduction of a new 'rapid resolution scheme' for resolving supposedly straightforward disputes and measures to streamline tribunal procedure. The government also took steps to encourage greater use of alternative methods of resolving disputes, including the encouragement to use mediation (see Section 10.3.4), and the introduction of a new mandatory process of 'early conciliation' involving ACAS.

Much of the work of ACAS now involves trying to resolve disputes between individual employees and their employers, or prevent them from arising in the first place (Dix and Oxenbridge 2004; Sisson and Taylor 2006). Employment relations reflection 10.9 provides details of its helpline service; by giving workers and employers effective advice and guidance it has helped to reduce the number of tribunal applications (Dickens 2012a).

Employment relations reflection 10.9:   The ACAS helpline service

The provision of information and advice about employment matters has become one of ACAS's most important activities. Much of the information is available in publications, many of which can be accessed by going to the ACAS website. However, a growing amount of advice and information is being disseminated through its telephone helpline service. The helpline is open to, and used by, both workers and employers. There has been a growing demand for the impartial and confidential information and advice offered by the service—in 2014–15 it received over 900,000 calls. The topics on which advice and information are most frequently sought are grievances, discipline, and dismissals—38 per cent of calls (ACAS 2015c). The complex nature of the helpline adviser role has come in for praise. 'The skill of the help-line advisers is key in disentangling the various problems, identifying the key point, providing the relevant information and, where appropriate, pointing them towards other sources of help and advice' (Sisson and Taylor 2006: 29).

ACAS has long had a statutory duty to offer conciliation on a voluntary basis when an employee makes a complaint against his or her employer to an employment tribunal. Its intervention operates as a 'very cost-effective filter', reducing the number of cases reaching tribunal hearings (Dickens 2012a: 36). Among other things, ACAS conciliators discuss the features of the case with both parties, point out how tribunals have dealt with similar cases in the past, and act as an intermediary between the sides in trying to promote a settlement. The purpose of conciliation is partly to 'explain the way tribunals operate and what they take into account in deciding claims', helping the parties to make a realistic judgement of the likely outcome (Dickens 2012a: 39). As with collective conciliation (see Section 10.2), its purpose is to help workers and employers reach their own compromise settlement without recourse to a tribunal.

The skill, sensitivity, and competence of ACAS conciliators tend to be highly regarded (Latreille, Latreille, and Knight 2007). Nevertheless, one criticism of conciliation is that, by encouraging the parties to reach their own settlement before a dispute gets as far as a tribunal, or by inducing workers to withdraw their complaint, it militates against effective justice (Dickens 2012a). The new system of mandatory early conciliation seems likely to encourage aggrieved workers to settle their dispute even in situations where they have strong claims and could expect a more generous financial award from a successful tribunal outcome (Welch 2016).

Perhaps the most controversial measure enacted by the coalition government was the 2013 introduction of a charging system under which most workers have to pay an up-front fee (£160 for supposedly more straightforward 'Type A' claims, such as those relating to unpaid wages; and £250 for 'Type B' claims, relating to matters such as unfair dismissal, equal pay, and discrimination) before they can make a tribunal claim, and an additional, higher fee (£230 Type A or £950 Type B) if the claim reaches a hearing (Dickens 2014; Welch 2016).

Workers already faced substantial obstacles to bringing tribunal claims, let alone winning them, even when they have legitimate cause for dispute. Only around one in twenty workers with a genuine grievance actually submits an ET claim, and most of those who do so don't get as far as a tribunal hearing (Renton 2012). Aggrieved workers whose employment rights have been breached mostly eschew litigation, because they lack awareness of their rights, are insufficiently confident about asserting them, or are discouraged by the costs of taking action and its potential consequences (Pollert 2005; TUC 2008; Pollert 2009). Problems with costs, delays, and excessive legalism are generally of greater concern for workers, who are often put off from making a claim, or pursuing it to a hearing, because of what Renton (2012) calls the 'tribunal obstacle race'. Given the magnitude of workplace conflict, perhaps the most surprising thing is not that there are so many tribunal claims, but so few.

Even before the coalition's reforms only around a quarter of tribunal claims actually got as far as a hearing anyway, with most being either withdrawn or settled beforehand, sometimes as a result of ACAS intervention (Tailby et al. 2011). For the relatively small proportion of claimants who actually win their case at a tribunal—fewer than one in ten—restitution is often limited. Even when complainants win their claim for unfair dismissal, the tribunals' power to order their re-employment is rarely used (Morris 2012); financial compensation is the most common form of restitution. Contrary to the impression one might have gained from accounts of isolated, but high-profile, sex discrimination cases which have resulted in professional women receiving large financial settlements, most awards are relatively modest (Morris 2012; Renton 2012). The median compensation award for a worker found to have been unfairly dismissed is between £4,000 and £5,000 (Dickens 2014). Moreover, the unwillingness of some employers to pay compensation awards appears to be a growing problem (Renton 2012). Only a half of successful claimants actually end up getting the full award they are due; and around a third receive nothing at all (House of Commons Justice Committee 2016).

The coalition's reforms, especially the July 2013 introduction of the fees regime, had an immediate, major impact on the amount of employment tribunal claims (Pyper and McGuinness 2016). Table 10.1 in Section 10.5.1 shows that the number of single claims fell from 54,704 in 2012–13 (the last full year before the fees regime came into effect) to 16,420 in 2014–15 (the first full year in which the fees regime operated)—a 70 per cent decline. This was welcomed by many employers, who felt that the introduction of fees had brought a 'fairer balance' to the process of resolving disputes, and had led to fewer weak claims (CIPD 2015a: 5). Others, however, have emphasized the adverse consequences of the fees regime, particularly the extent to which it has discouraged genuinely aggrieved workers from presenting valid, meritorious claims, especially where they concern alleged unlawful discrimination (House of Commons Justice Committee 2016). To this extent, the introduction of fees has dramatically undermined the capacity of workers to enforce their rights, effectively pricing many out of justice, and allowing unscrupulous employers to defy employment protection laws (Dickens 2014; TUC 2014c; Corby 2015; Kirk, McDermont, and Busby 2015).

Initial research on the impact of the introduction of tribunal fees shows that they have not encouraged an immediate increase in the use of a more arbitrary approach to workplace discipline by managers in organizations (Saundry et al. 2016). Yet the coalition government's tribunal reforms in general, and the fees regime in particular, will inevitably reduce still further the ability of many workers to assert their statutory rights. The main problem with the system of employment tribunals is not that it places too much of a burden on employers, but that it does not deliver effective justice for workers who have been treated in a harsh and arbitrary manner by their employers, and whose rights have been breached. Workers are rarely in a position to assert their legal employment rights effectively, and their chances of success are low even if they do embark on litigation (Colling 2010). We should be sceptical about the exaggerated claims made by employers and business lobbyists about the supposed burden of the employment tribunal system. Rather than complain about the time and energy that has to be expended in defending a claim, employers might be better off ensuring that their staff have as few grounds as possible for complaint in the first place, by taking a less punitive approach to discipline for example, or by handling equality and diversity issues more effectively.

10.5.4 Enforcing employment rights

One of the most important current issues in work and employment relations concerns the difficulties many workers face when it comes to ensuring that employers uphold their legal employment rights. The UK operates a 'light touch' system for enforcing employment rights (MAC 2014: 179). With employment tribunals the onus is on individual workers themselves being in a position to pursue redress for breaches of their rights by making a complaint. However, they may lack knowledge and awareness of their rights, or be fearful of employer intimidation and of losing their job if they do submit a tribunal claim (Citizens Advice 2011; Dickens 2014). Low-skilled migrant workers are particularly prone to exploitation arising from the existence of a weak regime for enforcing employment rights (MAC 2014). Clearly, moreover, the introduction of the fees regime in 2013 has put a further, even more substantial obstacle in the way of workers wanting to assert their employment rights and secure justice, as evidenced by the 70 per cent drop in the number of claims since fees came into effect.

There have been growing calls for more effective enforcement of individual employment rights, moving away from an approach where the onus is on aggrieved individuals to make a complaint themselves, towards a system marked by greater proactive enforcement by state agencies (TUC 2008; Citizens Advice 2011; Dickens 2012b; MAC 2014; Corby 2015; Barnard and Ludlow 2016).

In some areas, state-supported enforcement arrangements already exist in the UK. HM Revenue and Customs (HMRC) has a role in enforcing payment of the National Minimum Wage, for example (see Chapter 7). The Health and Safety Executive (HSE) is responsible for ensuring that the maximum forty-eight-hour working week and night work limits under the Working Time Regulations (see Chapter 8) are enforced. The Gangmasters Licensing Authority (GLA) operates a licensing regime for labour providers and employment agencies which aims to ensure that people working in the agriculture, horticulture, and related industries receive the pay, benefits, and conditions to which they are legally entitled—see the end-of-chapter case study for more details. Yet actual enforcement of employment rights remains problematic (MAC 2014). In addition, the austerity policies pursued by the 2010–15 coalition government compromised the capacity of state bodies, such as the Equality and Human Rights Commission (EHRC—see Chapter 4), to enforce and improve employment standards.

The last Labour government took some limited measures to improve workers' awareness of their rights (Dickens 2012b), including the establishment of a new Pay and Work Rights Helpline in 2009 (this became part of ACAS in 2015). Enforcement of rights at work would be made more effective, however, if an overarching agency existed, responsible for making sure that employers complied with employment law, and perhaps supplemented by a state-supported, proactive system of inspection (Dickens 2012b; Corby 2015). The charity Citizens Advice, for example, has called for the establishment of a single Fair Employment Agency, in order to 'simplify the enforcement framework and enhance the protection of vulnerable workers', whose employers often flout the law (Citizens Advice 2011: 3).

However, there seems little prospect of such an agency being established in the UK any time soon. Although problems with the current system for enforcing employment rights were acknowledged by the coalition, the broader deregulatory agenda favoured by government (see Chapter 3) means that the prospect of any radical change is remote (Dickens 2012b). One reform that has occurred, though, has been a move to improve governmental coordination of enforcement activity and enhance information sharing, linked to the introduction of a new Director of Labour Market Enforcement role (BIS/Home Office 2016). A much more powerful move would be to encourage stronger arrangements for providing workers with voice in the workplace, particularly trade union representation. This would do much to ensure not only that people's employment rights are better respected, but also that any disputes arising from alleged breaches get resolved at an early stage, obviating the need for litigation (Dickens 2014).

 ## Section summary and further reading

- Employment tribunals were conceived as relatively quick, informal, inexpensive, and accessible forums for resolving disputes between an individual employee and his or her employer, and for giving workers redress for breaches of their employment rights.

- The increase in the number of tribunal claims prompted complaints from employers' bodies and business lobbyists that the tribunal system imposes an excessive burden on employers, particularly in relation to the costs associated with defending cases. However, there is little evidence to support the view that many tribunal claims lack merit, and thus need to be discouraged.

- Successive governments have attempted to reform the system of employment tribunals, with the focus mainly on reducing the number of claims. The role of ACAS in conciliating settlements has been extended. The 2010–15 coalition government's measures, particularly the introduction of a fees regime, resulted in a large fall in the number of meritorious tribunal claims, further curtailing workers' access to justice.

- The main problem with tribunals is their failure to provide justly aggrieved employees with adequate redress. There is a growing interest in the desirability of developing stronger, more proactive arrangements for enforcing employment rights.

David Renton provides a highly readable and well-informed critique of the employment tribunal system in his 2012 book *Struck Out* (Renton 2012). Both Colling (2010) and Morris (2012) cover employment tribunals in their respective book chapters. Corby (2015) provides an overview of the development of the tribunal system. See Dickens (2012b) for issues around the proactive enforcement of employment rights.

10.6 Conclusion

One of the key features of work and employment relationships is the presence of an inherent potential conflict of interest between a worker and an employer. The form which this conflict takes when it appears, and the factors that influence it, were the focus of Chapter 9. In this chapter, the concern has been with examining the role of processes in employment relations designed to prevent conflict from becoming manifest in disputes, either collectively or individually, or with resolving disputes when it does. As has been evident, a key purpose of these processes is to contain, accommodate, and institutionalize conflict in a pluralist fashion. Negotiation is designed to reconcile differences of interest in employment relations, with the involvement of third parties providing help through arrangements like conciliation where necessary. Yet procedures for dealing with grievances, disciplinary cases, and redundancy largely come under the control of management, and are used primarily for managerial purposes—by making it easier to realize efficiency gains through job cuts, for example.

Of course, managerial prerogative is limited by the existence of legal employment standards, such as the right not to be unfairly dismissed, or the right not to be discriminated against for reasons of sex, race, disability, and so on. Workers who believe that their rights have been contravened are—in theory at least—able to pursue redress by taking a case to an employment tribunal. However, there are a number of major obstacles preventing workers from properly exercising their rights. Many lack knowledge and awareness of their statutory entitlements, or are fearful of the consequences of pursuing a claim. The introduction of a fees regime has prevented many justifiably aggrieved workers from pursuing meritorious claims. Moreover, the financial compensation awarded in successful cases is rather modest, giving the lie to suggestions by employers' bodies and business lobbyists that a supposed 'compensation culture' was responsible for the growth in tribunal claims during the 2000s. While the quantity of legal employment rights may have increased, much more needs to be done to ensure that they are enforced effectively.

 ## Assignment and discussion questions

1. What are the main factors that influence the outcomes of negotiation exercises in employment relations?

2. What is the purpose of grievance and disciplinary procedures? To what extent does their presence protect workers from arbitrary managerial actions?

3. To what extent, and in what ways, do redundancy exercises help to strengthen managerial control in workplaces?

4. Critically assess the effectiveness of the system of employment tribunals as a means of enforcing the employment rights of workers.

5. What are the main advantages and disadvantages of the UK's 'light touch' system for enforcing employment rights?

 Visit the Online Resource Centre that accompanies this book to develop your understanding of this chapter and keep up to date with the latest developments in this area. **www.oxfordtextbooks.co.uk/orc/williams4e/**

 Chapter case study: The role of the Gangmasters Licensing Authority

The work of the Gangmasters Licensing Authority (GLA) provides an example of proactive enforcement of employment rights. Established in 2005 in response to the Morecambe Bay tragedy, when twenty-three Chinese cockle pickers drowned, the GLA's mission is to 'protect vulnerable and exploited workers' based in the agriculture, horticulture, shellfish gathering, and food processing and packaging sectors. It runs a licensing and inspection regime covering the supply of labour in these sectors. Employment agencies, labour providers, and gangmasters operating in these areas of work must by law hold a GLA licence; the GLA is also empowered to inspect licensed businesses where evidence of worker exploitation or other illegal activity arises. The GLA asserts that its licensing regime has advantages for: workers, who benefit from fair treatment; labour providers, who can operate legitimately, without fear of being undercut by unscrupulous competitors who do not pay the minimum wage or avoid tax; labour users, such as major food processing companies, who can be assured that the workers they use are employed lawfully; and consumers, who can be satisfied that their food purchases have been ethically sourced. Operating as a gangmaster without a licence and using an unlicensed gangmaster are both criminal offences.

The GLA's licensing and inspection regime has been praised for the contribution it has made to tackling labour rights abuses in sectors dominated by low-skilled migrant workers, and which are particularly at risk of forced labour (see Chapter 2). The TUC's Sally Brett, for example, claims that 'inspections have been key to driving up labour standards and uncovering and preventing the exploitation of workers ... and they have ensured a level playing field for legitimate businesses and created confidence in supply chains for retailers, manufacturers and consumers' (Brett 2016). For Robinson (2014: 3), the success of the 'GLA in preventing and identifying trafficking for labour exploitation in the UK demonstrates the effectiveness of pro-active, intelligence led, labour inspections as a core prevention measure'. Between 2010 and 2015, however, there were concerns that the emphasis placed by the coalition government on reducing the burden of employment regulation on employers had undermined the effectiveness of the GLA's enforcement activities. The policy of austerity, moreover, also damaged the GLA's capacity to enforce labour rights as its inspection budget came under strain. Between 2010–11 and 2015–16 the number of front-line inspectors fell by 25 per cent. Another problem concerned the 2014 switch in responsibility for the GLA, from the Department for Environment, Farming and Rural Affairs (DEFRA) to the Home Office. This was undertaken as part of a wider effort to strengthen law enforcement activity around matters relating to undocumented migrants. However, there are concerns that this undermined the GLA's work in enforcing labour standards, not least because it makes vulnerable migrant workers less likely to come forward to report abuses.

Under the Conservative government's 2016 Immigration Act the name and scope of the GLA will change. As the Gangmasters and Labour Abuse Authority (GLAA) its remit—to investigate labour rights abuses—will be extended across the economy as a whole. However, the TUC and others have raised concerns about the proposed more 'flexible' inspection regime and the potential dilution of the GLA's licensing regime. There are also doubts about whether the new GLAA will be sufficiently well funded to be able to undertake its remit effectively.

Sources: GLA website; Lawrence (2012); MAC (2014); Robinson (2014); BIS/Home Office (2016); Brett (2016).

Question

To what extent do you agree with the view that a properly funded, comprehensive, and proactive system of inspecting and enforcing employment rights is desirable?

Part 5

Employment
relations:
perspectives
and prospects

Globalization and employment relations

⊙ Chapter objectives

The main objectives of this chapter are to:

- explore the main features of the process of globalization in relation to employment relations;

- examine the extent to which globalization, as a neo-liberal project, has been responsible for promoting greater convergence in employment relations;

- examine the role and activities of multinational companies in employment relations, particularly the extent to which they have been responsible for producing a 'race to the bottom' in labour standards;

- assess the main approaches to regulating international labour standards; and

- explore international trade union responses to globalization.

11.1 Introduction

The purpose of this chapter is to offer an international focus on contemporary employment relations, which is delivered through an examination of globalization and its implications. Historically, there have been important cross-national differences in employment relations. However, the growth in worldwide interconnectedness—which is what is meant by the concept of globalization—implies that these differences may be diminishing in importance. This final main chapter, then, adopts an explicitly global perspective on employment relations.

It does this in four main ways. First, in Section 11.2, there is a concern with understanding globalization both as a process—involving greater internationalization of economic activity and international labour mobility—and as a neo-liberal project designed to open up markets and promote free trade. The question of how far neo-liberal globalization has promoted greater uniformity—or 'convergence'—in employment relations is a matter of serious debate. Multinational companies (MNCs) are often viewed as powerful agents of convergence. The second main part of the chapter—Section 11.3—examines the influences on employment relations in MNC subsidiaries and considers the part played by MNCs in undermining employment conditions and workers' rights and protections around the world. Concerns about a 'race to the bottom' in labour standards have prompted a growing interest in how regulation can be effected on an international basis. This is the focus of the third main part of the chapter—Section 11.4. The final substantive part of the chapter—Section 11.5—examines international trade union responses to globalization. Although globalization has caused unions some major difficulties, their efforts to organize workers and improve labour standards, often by engaging in conflict, are integral features of employment relations in a globalized world.

Introductory case study: The Accord for Fire and Building Safety in Bangladesh

One of the main features of this chapter is a concern with critically assessing efforts to improve labour standards in the global supply chains of multinational companies. This is in the context of concerns that demands for cheap goods put pressure on supplier firms to cut the labour costs of production in a way that degrades working conditions and jeopardizes workers' health and safety. In April 2013, the eight-storey Rana Plaza building, based in the outskirts of the Bangladeshi capital Dhaka, collapsed. Resulting in the deaths of 1,129 garment workers, and injuries to many more, who were employed by a number of garment factories supplying international brands and retailers such as Primark and Walmart, the tragedy was a terrible consequence of demands from Western consumers for cheap clothes.

In the aftermath of the disaster, multinational companies, governments, and international agencies responded by developing new regulatory initiatives aimed at improving labour protections, particularly workplace health and safety standards, in the Bangladeshi garment industry. One of these, the Alliance for Bangladesh Worker Safety, was supported by a group of mainly US brands and retailers, including Gap and Walmart. However, although it advocated a five-year programme of safety improvements, this Alliance was criticized by labour rights campaigners both for its voluntary approach and for the absence of any role for trade unions and workers' rights groups. An alternative legally binding agreement—the Accord on Fire and Factory Safety in Bangladesh—was struck between the unions (global union federations and local, Bangladeshi unions) and 190 retailers and brands from twenty countries, including Next and Marks & Spencer. This covers health and safety standards in Bangladeshi garment factories, committing the parties to funding a five-year fire and building safety programme in Bangladesh. It also involves a number of transnational workers' rights organizations, provides for the implementation of rigorous safety inspections, and specifies the involvement of trade unions and the International Labour Organization (ILO). The response to the Rana Plaza disaster points to the increasingly important efforts being made to regulate labour standards on an international basis, particularly the influence of unions and activist campaigning organizations.

Sources: Butler (2013); Reinecke and Donaghey (2015)

11.2 Employment relations in a global economy

The growing degree of global economic interconnectedness, or 'globalization' as it is generally called, has had a major influence over work and employment relations. What, then, do we mean by the concept of globalization? Although economic activity has long spread across national borders, it is suggested that there has been a major increase in the extent of economic interconnectedness on a worldwide scale, facilitated by innovations in information technology and communication networks (Held and McGrew 2007). This section is concerned with exploring the main implications of globalization for employment relations, particularly in so far as it can be viewed not just as a process, but also as a neo-liberal project designed to undermine national-level employment regulation and weaken trade unions.

11.2.1 **Globalization and employment relations**

There is a growing interest in the concept of globalization in general (see Dicken 2015), and also in what it means for employment relations in particular (Wailes et al. 2016). In essence, the term globalization is used as shorthand to describe the increasing extent to which economic, social, and cultural activities around the world are becoming 'interconnected' (Frenkel 2006; Held and McGrew 2007; Kuruvilla and Lakhani 2013; Dicken 2015; Wailes et al. 2016). Globalization has been associated with major changes that have occurred in employment relations since the 1980s, including the decline of manufacturing employment in Western countries such as the UK (see Chapter 2), the rise of new management techniques under the label of 'human resource management' (Chapter 5), pressures to relax employment laws (Chapter 3), the decline of union membership (Chapter 6), and the growth of inequality (Chapter 7) (Kelly and Frege 2013; Farnham 2015; Wailes et al. 2016).

As a process, globalization is manifest in four main ways, each of which has important implications for employment relations. First, it involves the growing interconnectedness of financial markets on a worldwide basis, and the development of a globally integrated international financial system. This is evident in the role played by international bond markets and the like which are involved with, and help to facilitate, an ever-increasing amount of cross-border financial transactions. The growing importance of globally integrated and interconnected financial markets has helped to drive the process of 'financialization', whereby there is an increasing emphasis on creating value through various forms of financial manipulation and speculation, rather than from producing goods.

Chapter 5 demonstrates how the process of financialization influences the management of employment relations. There is an increasing focus on generating short-term value, through asset sales for example, or reductions in employment, to sate the demands of bond markets and other financial intermediaries. The result is a kind of 'disconnected capitalism', characterized by the inability of employers to develop long-term relationships with their staff (Thompson 2003, 2011). Moreover, 'as the events of the post-2007 global financial crisis demonstrated, the increasing importance and interconnectedness of global financial markets have placed new and common pressures on governments and firms across countries' (Wailes et al. 2016: 2). Austerity measures and action taken to weaken employment protections and allow employers greater flexibility in employment relations were predicated on the belief that without them, global financial markets would lose confidence in the capacity of national governments to effect reform, and restrict the supply of credit (Prosser 2014).

The second way in which globalization can be viewed as a process concerns the growing, and increasingly interconnected, system of world trade in goods and services. There has been a marked growth in international trade, especially since the establishment of the World Trade Organization in 1995, which has a mandate to facilitate the process of trade liberalization. Emerging economies, such as China, have also become more integrated into the international trading system (Dicken 2015).

Workers and trade unions in Europe and North America are often sceptical about globalization because of the perceived adverse consequences of international trade for jobs and labour standards in their countries. For example, some 600 manufacturing workers lost their jobs when Dyson moved production of its vacuum cleaners from Wiltshire in England to Malaysia in 2002. And in 2007, the clothing company Burberry closed its plant in Treorchy, South Wales, which made polo shirts, with the loss of some 300 jobs. It claimed that the factory had become commercially unviable, and that it was more cost-effective to switch production to sites in Asia and Southern and Eastern Europe where wages and employment costs were lower (Jenkins and Turnbull 2011). More recently, global competition in the steel industry, particularly the threat posed by cheap steel imports from China, has resulted in plant closures and large-scale job losses in the UK—see Employment relations reflection 11.1.

Employment relations reflection 11.1: The impact of global competition on the UK steel industry

In March 2016, the Indian multinational Tata Steel announced plans to offload its entire UK steel business, putting some 15,000 jobs directly at risk, 4,000 of them at the UK's largest steel plant in Port Talbot, South Wales. Tata claimed that energy costs, and an influx of cheap steel from China, had made its UK operations increasingly untenable, with reported losses of some £1 million per day. The UK steel industry, though, has been shedding jobs for years, largely because a growing amount of cheap imported steel has rendered it increasingly uncompetitive. In 2015, the Thai firm SSI closed its Redcar plant, on the east coast of England, with the loss of over 2,000 jobs. Tata Steel itself had previously cut hundreds of jobs at the Port Talbot site in 2014. The UK government was clearly caught unawares by the Tata Steel announcement, but quickly looked to facilitate a search for prospective buyers of parts of the company's operations, with some success. However, the European Steel Association alleged that the UK government was complicit in allowing the increase of cheap steel imports into the EU from China by obstructing efforts to restrict them.

Sources: Farrell (2016); Perraudin (2016a)

Some, however, are unconvinced by claims that globalization has been directly responsible for job losses in industrialized countries. In the US, for example, job losses in manufacturing have been caused more by domestic policy decisions than by greater exposure to international competition (Doogan 2009). However, firms may use threats of possibly relocating production to cheaper sites elsewhere to gain leverage over workers, getting them to moderate their wage demands and make other concessions as a consequence.

A third dimension of globalization as a process concerns the increasing amount of foreign direct investment (FDI) evident around the world—where firms invest in overseas production sites, acquire foreign subsidiaries, or engage in international mergers (Dicken 2015). Multinationals are a key source of greater levels of FDI. Their activities can often be controversial, not least because of the potentially adverse consequences for jobs. In 2010, for example, the US firm Kraft acquired the British confectionery company Cadbury. During the acquisition process, Kraft pledged that it would maintain production at all of Cadbury's UK sites. Once it owned the business, however, it backtracked on this pledge, and closed a factory near Bristol, with the loss of around 400 jobs, claiming it now realized that the site was not viable.

MNCs exercise an increasingly important influence over employment relations, not just in their capacity as sources of FDI, but also to the extent that they endeavour to operate arrangements for managing employment relations which transcend national borders (Wailes et al. 2016). The term MNC is used to refer to companies that invest in, and are thus directly responsible for, foreign subsidiaries beyond the boundaries of their national territorial base. By the late 2000s, there were some 82,000 multinationals in existence, responsible for hundreds of thousands of affiliates around the world (UNCTAD 2009). Importantly, they enjoy 'the power to coordinate and control operations in more than one country, even if they do not own them' (Dicken 2015: 58).

While MNCs have long been a feature of the international business environment, since the 1980s the scale and scope of their activities have grown markedly. As a result, MNCs have contributed substantially to the process of economic globalization (Edwards and Ferner 2002). Investment flows from multinationals, rather than through patterns of trade between different countries, increasingly dominate international economic activity (Hirst, Thompson, and Bromley 2009). The activities of MNCs are one of the clearest manifestations of economic globalization in action (Jones 2005). Companies such as Walmart, Microsoft, and Apple have been able to develop a massive worldwide presence, not just benefiting from the growing interconnectedness of the global economy, but also, through their activities, helping to stimulate it still further. The UK economy, in particular, is dominated by the activities of multinationals since it is a particularly open and attractive venue for investment by overseas companies (Marginson and Meardi 2010). Car production, for example, is dominated by the likes of Honda, Nissan, Toyota, and BMW, all of which are foreign firms. How far this will continue, should the UK eventually leave the European Union's single market, is open to question.

Perhaps the most notable feature of globalization in practice concerns the cross-border arrangements MNCs operate for designing, sourcing, manufacturing, distributing, and retailing goods in a way that maximizes efficiency, particularly in sectors such as electronics, clothing, and footwear (Dicken 2015). They often do not own, or even directly control, the sites where goods are made; instead, factories are owned and managed through a complex network of contractor and sub-contractor firms in a way designed to minimize costs (Dicken 2015; Hale and Wills 2005). The manufacture of popular consumer electronics devices, like Apple iPods, iPhones, and iPads, is outsourced to a wide range of factories in the emerging economies of Asia, particularly in China (Chan, Pun, and Selden 2013).

Processes of financialization, global trade, and FDI are all examples of capital mobility. They represent the important extent to which globalization has been driven by, and operates to the benefit of, business and employers. However, a fourth globalization process involves the mobility of labour. Migration, the movement of people across regions, national borders, or even continents, is a phenomenon of long-standing historical significance. As Chapter 3 shows, EU enlargement has been responsible for greater levels of cross-border migration in Europe. There may be as many as 12 million undocumented migrant workers, originally from Mexico and other parts of Latin America, in the US. It is clear that globalization has facilitated an increase in the extent to which people are willing and able to migrate, particularly across national borders (Williams et al. 2013). The Philippines, for example, is a major provider of female nurses and carers to the healthcare systems of Europe and North America (Kingma 2006). Growing levels of investment in Africa by Chinese firms has been accompanied by an influx of Chinese migrant construction workers (Cooke 2014). The construction boom seen in parts of the Middle East has depended on the labour of migrant workers from countries such as Pakistan, Bangladesh, and Nepal. See the end-of-chapter case study for the controversy that has arisen as a result of the treatment of migrant construction workers on building sites for the 2022 Football World Cup in Qatar.

Unlike capital, which can move across national borders relatively smoothly, labour is generally less mobile, especially at an international level. There are two main reasons for this. First, workers are human beings: they have friends, families, and community ties; these attachments are an understandable constraint on people's willingness to move in search of jobs.

Second, labour mobility is much more heavily restricted than capital mobility. The case of the EU, where workers have long enjoyed the right to freedom of movement (see Chapter 3), is rather exceptional. The impact of migration on 'receiving' countries is a source of particular political controversy. Most rich countries operate tight, and often increasingly strict, controls over immigrant labour, mostly to the detriment of migrant workers, who are rendered more vulnerable (Anderson 2010). Yet they frequently fill jobs that indigenous workers are unwilling to take. They have an extensive presence in the agriculture and food-processing industries, for example, where they constitute a cheap source of labour for employers, enabling the major supermarket chains to keep prices low while at the same time improving their profitability. Undocumented migrant workers are particularly vulnerable, and thus prone to harsher treatment from managers than others (Bank Muñoz 2008).

11.2.2 Globalization as a neo-liberal project—towards convergence?

Globalization is more than just a process of greater global interconnectedness—it also operates to a large degree as a neo-liberal project fostered by, and operated for the benefit of, multinationals and corporate elites (Frenkel 2006). Enthusiasts for greater globalization emphasize the economic benefits—in terms of growth and prosperity—that derive from efforts to boost international trade and open up markets around the world (Kuruvilla and Lakhani 2013; Williams et al. 2013). Central to neo-liberal ideology is the primacy accorded to free markets (Harvey 2005)—see Chapters 1 and 3. The regulation of work and employment relationships by states and trade unions is viewed as highly undesirable: by constraining the freedom of individuals and companies to contract freely with one another, it impedes business competitiveness. Seen as a neo-liberal project, then, globalization not only involves efforts to liberalize trade and open up markets around the world, but is also associated with attempts to weaken employment protections and undermine the role of the unions, given the extent to which these are seen as obstacles to growth and prosperity (Kalleberg 2009; Farnham 2015).

From this perspective, globalization is a project designed to weaken the bargaining power of workers and unions relative to employers. In order to compete more effectively in a globalized environment, the neo-liberal agenda determines that countries should seek to deregulate their labour markets and promote greater employment flexibility; although, as Stiglitz (2002: 84) points out, by 'flexibility' globalization enthusiasts generally mean 'lower wages and less job protection'. The process of greater 'financialization' exemplifies how globalization operates as a neo-liberal project in a way that undermines rights and protections for workers. This is because countries come under increasing pressure to secure the continued 'confidence' of international financial institutions, such as the global bond markets, which demand that governments institute deficit-reduction measures and weaken social and employment protections as integral elements of market-friendly reforms (Prosser 2014; Streeck 2014).

Employment relations reflection 11.2: The Transatlantic Trade and Investment Partnership (TTIP) and employment relations

In 2013, the EU and US started negotiations on a new agreement for the purpose of radically liberalizing trade between them. The Transatlantic Trade and Investment Partnership (TTIP) initiative was designed to give companies in the EU and US much better access to each other's markets through reduced trade barriers and lower tariffs. Supporters of the TTIP initiative contended that by facilitating increased trade in goods and services it would have had massively beneficial economic effects. However, the TTIP negotiations attracted a lot of hostility from campaigners who contended that the process was driven by the needs of big business and that an agreement would have allowed powerful US multinationals to undermine EU social, environmental, and labour laws. Firms could potentially have used the courts to challenge regulatory arrangements that threatened to reduce their profits. The TUC expressed a concern that TTIP could dilute labour standards, because of the potential scope for US firms to exploit the weaker employment protections that apply in their home territories. There was also a worry that TTIP would have allowed US corporations greater access to providing public services in the UK, accelerating the privatization of the National Health Service. Trade unions in the UK, such as Unite, campaigned vigorously against TTIP on this basis. During 2015 and 2016 opposition to TTIP grew, with demonstrations occurring in some European countries and challenges coming from the European Parliament.

Sources: TUC (2015e); Quinn (2016)

One of the most profound effects of neo-liberal globalization is the impact of deregulatory policies on work and employment relations. In order to remain competitive, and thus make their countries 'employer-friendly' locations, governments repress independent trade unions and weaken systems of employment regulation, such as legislation on pay and working conditions, or fail to enforce laws effectively (Kuruvilla and Lakhani 2013; Williams et al. 2013). The controversy generated by the proposed Transatlantic Trade and Investment Partnership (TTIP), including its potential implications for employment relations, highlights the anxieties many people feel about the role of globalization in undermining social and employment standards—see Employment relations reflection 11.2.

The EU's response to the financial and economic crisis (see Chapter 3) was predicated on the neo-liberal belief that deficit reduction, austerity, and employment deregulation are the most effective tools for promoting economic growth and increasing employment levels in a more globally interconnected world (Williams and Scott 2016c). Even in a country like France, which has traditionally maintained a strong degree of legal protection for workers, a neo-liberal belief in the virtues of deregulation and weakened employment rights has taken a firm hold amongst policy-makers. In 2016, the French socialist government proposed a series of controversial labour law changes, designed to give employers greater flexibility over pay and working time arrangements and to make it easier for them to dismiss staff.

Neo-liberal globalization often has some highly adverse consequences for workers, however. It is associated with greater job insecurity, higher levels of inequality, and the rise of more precarious work and employment relationships (see Chapter 2), particularly among young workers, migrant workers, and black and minority ethnic workers (Webster, Lambert, and Bezuidenhout 2008; Kalleberg 2011; Standing 2011). The importance accorded to deregulatory measures in the aftermath of the 2007–8 financial and economic crisis seems to have accentuated the shift towards more insecure and precarious employment (ILO 2012).

Thinking about globalization as a neo-liberal project, then, associated with the weakening of employment protections and unions for the purpose of enhancing employers' flexibility and thus increasing business competitiveness and economic growth, raises the important question of how far it has generated 'convergence', in the sense of a greater degree of uniformity, in global employment relations. The concept of convergence is not new. It was originally developed in the early 1960s to capture the way in which the process of industrialism, with its associated technical and institutional arrangements (such as collective bargaining, for example), seemed to be generating greater uniformity in employment relations systems around the world (Kerr et al. 1962), diminishing national-level diversity (Katz and Wailes 2014). The idea of convergence implies 'a universal tendency for technological and market forces associated with industrialism to push national employment systems towards uniformity' (Wailes et al. 2016: 9–10).

Convergence theory in employment relations has attracted much criticism. For one thing, it places too much of an emphasis on the role of technological change, it is overly dominated by the experience of one country—the US—and too wedded to the notion that change in employment relations should be designed to facilitate order and stability. Much of the work done in the following decades highlighted the resilience of national diversity in employment relations (Frege and Kelly 2013). However, the concept of convergence resurfaced during the 1980s and 1990s in the context of debates relating to the concept of 'Japanization'. A considerable amount of interest was evinced in the extent to which certain employment and working practices identified with leading Japanese companies such as Toyota—including teamworking and so-called 'lean production' arrangements, for example—were becoming diffused as global best practice (e.g. Elger and Smith 1994).

Since the 1990s, globalization has stimulated renewed interest in the question of convergence, particularly the extent to which employment relations around the world has become dominated by a neo-liberal emphasis on deregulation and privileging employers' flexibility (Barry and Wilkinson 2011; Wailes et al. 2016). Globalization is held to be responsible for producing growing uniformity around a new employment relations 'paradigm' based on deregulated labour markets, employment flexibility, weak or decentralized collective bargaining arrangements, and increasingly powerless trade unions (Katz and Wailes 2014). Competitive pressures mean that firms are expected to operate a common set of 'best practice' arrangements, so-called because they are seen as the most economically efficient for managing work and employment relations, irrespective of the national context (Rubery and Grimshaw 2003; Frenkel 2006).

Moreover, since these policies are viewed as essential to attracting multinational investment and competing effectively in the global economy, it is thought that countries have little option other than to implement them (Williams et al. 2013). As a neo-liberal project, then, globalization implies that individual countries have limited scope to operate national-level regulatory arrangements in employment relations (Frege and Kelly 2013). The power of multinational corporations over national governments is perhaps best illustrated by an example from the film industry. In order to ensure that the Hobbit films were made in New Zealand rather than elsewhere, the New Zealand government complied with a demand from the films' maker, the Hollywood studio Warner Bros, that it change its employment laws so that actors were classified as self-employed contractors, rather than as employees, with fewer rights and protections as a consequence (A. Clark 2010). All this would seem to imply that neo-liberal convergence pressures, in a more globalized economy, make national diversity in employment relations increasingly less important (Katz and Wailes 2014; Wailes et al. 2016).

11.2.3 The limits of neo-liberal convergence in employment relations

Clearly there are important convergence pressures in employment relations around the world, reflecting the influence of globalization as a neo-liberal project. However, there is plenty of evidence that national governments and national-level systems of employment relations continue to have an important role in employment relations. Although they face similar global economic pressures, national governments nonetheless have a great deal of leeway when it comes to developing and operating employment relations policies (Wailes et al. 2016). Not only does this suggest that there is no straightforward, unambiguous trend towards convergence in employment relations, but also that national systems of employment relations continue to demonstrate resilience, indicating that a substantial degree of national-level diversity (or 'divergence') continues to prevail. The concept of globalization is often used rhetorically by national governments as a means of persuading working people that, given the enhanced mobility of employers and the supposed pressures of global competition, deregulated labour markets and weakened trade unions are essential attributes of a competitive economy (Hirst, Thompson, and Bromley 2009).

Efforts to understand cross-national diversity in employment relations tend to be influenced by perspectives from the field of comparative political economy. There is a particular concern with understanding the contribution of distinctive national-level institutions—political and legal structures, business systems, employment relations arrangements—when it comes to mediating global pressures for convergence; the implication is that an important degree of cross-national diversity continues to prevail (Wailes et al. 2016).

The most prominent institutional approach is the 'Varieties of Capitalism' (VoC) model developed by Hall and Soskice (2001). With a focus on the role of firms, it highlights the 'embeddedness' and durability of established employment relations structures and institutions. Change in employment relations is gradual, incremental, and largely path-dependent, in the sense that it is conditioned by the historical circumstances and institutional characteristics of the territory in question. The VoC approach distinguishes between 'liberal market economies', including Britain and the US, and 'coordinated market economies', such as Germany. The former are characterized by the predominance of a neo-liberal policy agenda such that the 'result should be some weakening of organized labour and a substantial amount of deregulation, much as conventional views predict' (Hall and Soskice 2001: 57). However, among the 'coordinated market economies', deregulatory pressures are more likely to be constrained, or at least moderated, by the presence of robust national-level employment relations systems. Here, trade unions and centralized systems of collective bargaining are less brittle in the face of pressures for enhanced flexibility (see Frege and Kelly 2013: 14–15; Williams et al. 2013: 22–4; Wailes et al. 2016: 12–18).

The main benefit of the VoC approach is that it helps us to understand cross-national variations in employment relations in the face of common neo-liberal pressures for convergence (Wailes et al. 2016). However, it has been criticized for not being sufficiently sensitive to the sheer range of policy approaches evident around the world, a trait it shares with other methods of conceptualizing cross-national diversity, and for being too static (Crouch 2005; Frege and Kelly 2013; Wailes et al. 2016). The VoC approach also pays insufficient heed to the efforts of working people and trade unions to challenge national systems and bring about change in work and employment relations arrangements (Hamann and Kelly 2008).

All that said, though, the VoC approach is useful in that it captures the extent to which, despite the existence of global convergence pressures, cross-national diversity remains an important feature of employment relations. Moreover, increasing efforts have been made to accommodate the emphasis on 'embeddedness' and 'path-dependency' characteristic of the VoC approach within an overall perspective which recognizes the importance of change in employment relations, and how change can be explained, especially its political dynamics (Thelen 2004; Crouch 2005; Streeck and Thelen 2005).

Neo-liberal convergence pressures exist, to be sure, but their speed, scale, and scope vary from country to country, and are themselves path-dependent (Baccaro and Howell 2011; Thelen 2014; Wright et al. 2016). For example, while there have been quite strong moves to enact deregulatory, neo-liberal measures in coordinated market economies like Germany and Sweden, they have been moderated by the presence of robust institutional structures and political climates which remain broadly supportive of trade unions and collective bargaining. Convergence pressures, then, are by no means incompatible with the persistence of national diversity (Marginson and Sisson 2004).

Clearly, there is a complex relationship between the convergence pressures associated with globalization and divergence imperatives based on national differences (Katz and Wailes 2014). The 'converging divergences' approach, for example, recognizes that there is evidence of convergence across countries, manifest in trade union decline among other things. However, convergence is more prevalent in sectors of the economy which are more open to international competition, and marked by the presence of multinationals (Katz and Darbishire 2000). Thus there is evidence of growing divergence within nation states. Convergence pressures associated with the project of neo-liberal globalization clearly exist; however, their impact is by no means straightforward, being shaped and mediated by a variety of national-level influences.

While much of the debate around globalization and employment relations concerns the relationship between convergence pressures and national-level imperatives for divergence, there is a growing appreciation that globalization has some potentially more far-reaching implications. Although MNCs often act as important vehicles of convergence, with their activities playing an important part in facilitating a 'race to the bottom' in labour standards (see Section 11.3), the process of globalization has the potential to transform employment relations in some quite fundamental ways. This is evident when it comes to the material in Section 11.4 which concerns the development of new transnational regulatory arrangements and processes. Furthermore, unions and campaigning organizations are making increased efforts themselves to shape employment relations in a more globalized world, in ways that challenge the interests of powerful corporations (see Section 11.5). With these things in mind, then, viewing globalization purely as a neo-liberal project is perhaps rather unhelpful.

 ## Section summary and further reading

- Globalization has some profound implications for employment relations. As a process of greater worldwide interconnectedness, it is marked by an increase in the amount of cross-border financial transactions, the growth of world trade, a rise in the activities of multinationals, often as sources of FDI, and greater levels of international labour mobility.

- Globalization is often viewed as a neo-liberal project. The emphasis on freeing up trade and opening up markets comes at the expense of weakened employment protections, labour rights, and trade unions.

- Globalization has not been responsible for a straightforward process of convergence in employment relations. There are certainly important convergence pressures, promoting greater liberalization. But their influence is mediated by country-specific, national-level influences that foster divergence.

Dicken (2015) is the leading work on economic globalization. For overviews of globalization and employment relations, including the debate around 'convergence', see Frege and Kelly (2013), Wailes et al. (2016), and Williams et al. (2013: chapter 1).

11.3 Globalization, multinational companies, and the 'race to the bottom' in labour standards

As mentioned in Section 11.2.1, the increasing activity of multinationals has been an integral feature of the development of globalization. There are two main ways in which the growing prominence of MNCs has affected employment relations. The first concerns the nature of employment relations, and particularly how it is managed, in their subsidiaries around the world. Second, the power of multinationals, particularly the extent to which they have developed complex global supply chains as a flexible and relatively cheap means of organizing production, has raised concerns about the adverse impact on employment conditions and workers' rights and protections, in a way that drives a 'race to the bottom' in labour standards.

11.3.1 Managing employment relations in MNC subsidiaries

One of the most important ways in which MNCs influence employment relations in a global context is the extent to which they endeavour to operate as transnational actors by diffusing management practices across national borders to their network of subsidiaries in different countries. MNCs thus operate as potentially powerful agents of convergence (Grimshaw and Rubery 2003), contributing to a more globalized system of employment relations, and eroding the influence of national-level regulatory arrangements.

Multinationals often attempt to replicate employment relations techniques that prevail in their home countries in their foreign subsidiaries, through a process of 'forward diffusion'. The 'home country' or 'country-of-origin' effect can exercise an important influence over employment relations arrangements in the foreign subsidiaries of MNCs (Ferner 1997), particularly in multinationals that originate from those countries, like the US, that are dominant in the global economy. A good example of this is the way in which firms from the US attempt to operate union-free workplaces in their foreign operations, reflecting the practice which prevails in their home-country base (Almond and Ferner 2006). In some cases, the MNC itself is so dominant that it wields a profound influence over employment relations in the sector in which it operates. In Italy, for example, the robust anti-union policy favoured by the US fast-food giant McDonalds was copied by its local competitors (Royle 2006).

Yet the characteristics of the host country environment in which a subsidiary is located often exercise a profound influence over the way employment relations is managed within them, obliging multinationals to adapt their practices rather than diffuse them in a straight-forward manner (Edwards 2011). For example, in their study of an American multinational company, ITCO, Almond et al. (2005) discovered that it was able to implement its preferred non-union system of employment relations relatively easily in the UK and Ireland. Elsewhere in Europe, however, the presence of stronger national-level employment regulations meant that it was obliged to establish relationships with trade unions.

This highlights the important extent to which some host country environments are more amenable to diffusion than others. In the UK, for example, where employers enjoy a rela-tively large degree of flexibility over employment relations matters, US multinationals gener-ally find it not too difficult to remain union-free (Edwards and Ferner 2002; Marginson and Meardi 2010; Gunnigle et al. 2015). There is evidence that some German MNCs have taken advantage of more lightly regulated environments in Eastern Europe to develop more flex-ible employment relations practices than would be possible in the more regulated context of their home country (Meardi et al. 2009).

In addition to the respective influences of the MNC's country of origin and the nature of the host country environment where its subsidiaries are based, there is also an increasing recognition of the extent to which structural and organizational factors influence the man-agement of employment relations in multinationals (Gunnigle et al. 2015). An MNC's overall strategic orientation, for example, can have an important effect on the policies and practices in its subsidiaries (Delbridge, Hauptmeier, and Sengupta 2011).

Moreover, the more globally integrated a firm is, and the extent to which it is responsible for standardized products and services on a global basis, the easier it is to undertake detailed scrutiny of, and thus be able to compare, the respective performance of each of its subsidi-aries (Marginson and Sisson 1994). Firms in this position enjoy the ability to make 'coercive comparisons' between different plants, whether operating in the same or in different coun-tries (Mueller and Purcell 1992). The concept of 'coercive comparisons' is used to refer to the way multinationals use intricate financial, productivity, and output data to make detailed comparisons of the performance of their respective plants. These can then be used to exert pressure on workers and unions in plants that are found to be under-performing to increase their work effort or accept more flexible working arrangements as a means of catching up, with threats to relocate production acting to enforce compliance (Rubery and Grimshaw 2003; Marginson and Meardi 2009). Coercive comparisons seem to be used extensively in East European car factories owned by major US and German multinationals (Meardi et al. 2009). Managers can take advantage of greater global interconnectedness to stimulate com-petition between sites across different countries in ways that enable them to drive through desired reforms (Greer and Hauptmeier 2016).

However, it should not be assumed that MNCs are supremely rational entities that are always capable of acting in a calculated and predictable manner. Just like any other firm, the activities of MNCs are marked by the presence of power relations and the interplay of organi-zational politics, matters which inevitably constrain their ability to secure the compliance of foreign subsidiaries with corporate objectives (Ferner and Edwards 1995; Ferner, Edwards, and Tempel 2012; Gunnigle et al. 2015). Managers of subsidiaries often draw on aspects of work and employment relations in the country where they are based in order to challenge, or seek to change, policies emanating from corporate headquarters in the MNC's home country that are not viewed as appropriate (Edwards, Colling, and Ferner 2007; Ferner 2010). See Insight into practice 11.3 for details of an example of this in practice.

 Insight into practice 11.3: Managing diversity in US multinationals

A study of the management of equality and diversity issues in the UK subsidiaries of US multinationals provides a good illustration of how managers of subsidiaries can use and develop power resources to alter, and even subvert, inappropriate or undesirable corporate policies. The MNCs concerned had all made the global diffusion of international diversity policies a priority. But subsidiary managers considered them to be much too focused on the experience of the US, and not really very appropriate for adoption in non-US environments, which often have different priorities. The managers were able to negotiate changes in the implementation of corporate diversity policies by drawing on the specific legal framework of their own 'host' country environment. This rendered the practices more appropriate to the specific context of UK society. The case highlights the important extent to which multinationals operate as fundamentally social entities whose objectives and activities are the product of dynamic and relational processes of interaction between different actors within and around them.

Source: Ferner, Almond, and Colling (2005)

A focus on organizational power and politics highlights the important extent to which the management of employment relations in MNC subsidiaries is the product of relationships between different groups of managers, and between managers and workers, in specific work-places (Elger and Smith 2005). This is particularly well illustrated by the case of a UK retailer which operates sites in China. On the face of it the company was able to diffuse a set of corporate management practices from its UK-based headquarters to its Chinese operations relatively easily. However, once these practices were established, workers and managers in China understood and responded to them in ways that altered how they functioned—in a manner that diverged from corporate expectations. Thus management practices diffused across national borders by multinationals do not 'enter a void. The way host country employees respond to them is coloured by unique configurations of experiences, norms and expectations' (Gamble 2011: 79). To be sure, MNCs are increasingly powerful actors in a more globalized system of employment relations. However, their capacity to act as agents of convergence is limited by a number of factors, not least the important extent to which workers and managers in specific subsidiaries influence and shape policies and practices themselves (McKenna et al. 2010).

11.3.2 A 'race to the bottom' in labour standards?

The growing power of multinational firms in a more globalized world has raised concerns about their ability to avoid, or subvert, national-level employment relations arrangements that obstruct their interests. In the fast-food industry, for example, companies like McDonald's often enjoy a level of power sufficient to enable them to avoid employment regulations—especially those governing collective bargaining and employee rights to information and consultation—that do not suit them (Royle and Towers 2002). Countries frequently offer

MNCs incentives, including the relaxation of employment regulations, as a means of attract-ing investment, or of preventing it from going elsewhere. Multinationals can shrewdly use the threat of withdrawal, of disinvestment, to secure government favour or to control their employees' behaviour.

This highlights the potential for MNCs to engage in 'regime competition' (Streeck 1997), a term which refers to the way multinationals base decisions about investment, or disin-vestment, on the relative attractiveness of a country's employment 'regime'—that is, its set of employment laws and regulations. The multinational white goods manufacturer (fridges etc.) Electrolux, for example, has operated a policy of 'regime shopping': actively seeking out locations which offer supportive regulatory environments, in the form of permissive labour laws and weak unions, as areas for investment (Webster, Lambert, and Bezuidenhout 2008). To attract investment in a globalized economy, then, governments come under pressure to relax the supposed regulatory burden for fear that if they do not do so, MNCs will transfer their activities to countries that will. This provokes competition between countries to attract multinational investment, based on which of them can offer the most desirable regulatory environment. During the 2000s, for example, major auto firms such as Toyota and Hyundai engaged in such a process when selecting locations for new manufacturing plants in Central and Eastern Europe (Meardi 2012). There is even a kind of 'race to the bottom' evident in the airline industry, given the extent to which the low labour costs of the highly successful Gulf carriers gives them a competitive advantage (see Insight into practice 11.4).

 Insight into practice 11.4: A 'race to the bottom' in the global airline industry?

Increasing competitive pressures are eroding labour standards in the global airline industry. The growth of low-cost competitors such as Ryanair, and the rising market share of the Gulf carriers— Etihad, Emirates, and Qatar Airways—have had adverse consequences for the more established airlines in Europe and North America (e.g. Air France, Lufthansa, British Airways), whose labour costs have become increasingly uncompetitive. They have been obliged to undertake major restructuring initiatives, which have resulted in a substantial number of job losses, reductions in pay, and poorer employment conditions. Some US airlines have complained that because they are able to operate with such low labour costs, the Gulf carriers enjoy an unfair competitive advantage. The chief executive of Emirates has acknowledged that his airline is free from the 'legacy issues' that affect the established carriers, namely staff on traditional contracts. None of the Gulf carriers respect the right of workers to join trade unions. Indeed, the chief executive of Qatar Airways has described unions as a 'pain in the ass'. In 2015, the International Labour Organization (ILO) highlighted the widespread violations of labour rights evident in Qatar Airways, particularly the extensive discrimination against its female employees.

Sources: ILO (2013a); Topham (2014, 2015); Harvey and Turnbull (2015)

The practice of regime 'shopping' or 'competition', then, can have adverse consequences for labour standards as governments use the prospect of a relaxed regulatory environment to attract multinational investment (Tsogas 2001). This can often entail efforts to suppress trade unions (McKay 2006). Many emerging economies—such as China, Sri Lanka, and the Philip-pines—have established dedicated locations, known as 'export processing zones' (EPZs) or 'special economic zones', which are characterized by the presence of fewer tax, planning, and labour regulations, in order to attract foreign investment (Cantin 2008; Gunawardana 2014; Henning 2015). According to one estimate, there are some 3,500 EPZs in operation around the world, across 130 countries (Barrientos et al. 2011).

In her well-known book, *No Logo*, the Canadian writer Naomi Klein investigated EPZs in the Philippines, where workers making goods for the export market endure low pay and poor working conditions. She visited the Cavite free-trade zone, which covers nearly 700 acres to the south of the capital Manila. Here, Klein discovered over 200 factories employing some 50,000 workers engaged in producing goods for IBM, Nike, and Gap, among others. She found that the 'management is military-style, the supervisors often abusive, the wages below subsistence and the work low-skill and tedious' (Klein 2000: 205). Abuses of labour rights were commonplace. Perhaps most telling, however, was the prevailing climate of insecurity that characterized the zone. The government, factory owners, and workers were all aware of the inherently precarious nature of the jobs that multinational investment delivered, and realized how easily they could be transferred elsewhere if the multinationals discovered alternative, cheaper sources of production.

Multinationals have increasingly developed intricate global supply chains and global production networks that enable them to source goods efficiently and flexibly (see Section 11.2.1), in a way that has generated a complex division of international labour (Williams et al. 2013). Mass-produced consumer goods, such as clothing, footwear, toys, and electronic products, are made largely by workers in factory-based, emerging economies, particularly in Asia, including China, Cambodia, Vietnam, and Bangladesh. The factories are rarely, if ever, owned directly by multinational companies and brands. The Taiwanese company Yue Yuen is a major supplier of products to global sports-shoe brands such as Nike and Reebok (Merk 2008). For MNCs, outsourcing manufacturing processes in this way is highly advantageous. Not only does it help to drive down manufacturing costs—with workers in global factories in Asia paid only a small proportion of what they could expect if they were based in Europe or North America, but it is also a highly flexible model of production, one which gives MNCs and global brands a considerable degree of power (Chan, Pun, and Selden 2013).

Violations of labour standards in the supply chains of multinationals, including very low wages, excessive hours of work, poor health and safety standards, child labour, harsh discipline, manifold employment discrimination, and trade union repression, have been extensively documented (e.g. Mosley 2011). Firms such as Monsoon, Primark, and WalMart are among the many retailers who have faced allegations about unsafe and highly exploitative working conditions in some of their supplier factories in countries such as Bangladesh and China. One 2015 investigation of a factory in China which produces toys for global firms, including Hasbro, Disney, and Mattel, discovered an extensive range of labour standard violations, for instance excessive working hours, mandatory overtime, union suppression, and grossly inadequate health and safety provisions, including instances of locked fire exits and a lack of any heating or air conditioning (Institute for Global Labour and Human Rights 2015). Concerns have also been expressed about the prevalence of child labour in the global economy; the ILO estimates that in 2008 some 306 million children around the world aged between 5 and 17 were in employment of some kind (Diallo et al. 2010). The appalling consequences of the drive for cheap labour and the neglect of basic employment standards were highlighted by the April 2013 collapse of the eight-storey Rana Plaza building, on the outskirts of the Bangladeshi capital Dhaka. It resulted in the deaths of over a thousand work-ers who were employed by a number of garment factories supplying Western multinationals (see the introductory case study).

The global brand that has attracted the most controversy about working conditions in the factories that make its products is Apple. In the first quarter of 2016 its total revenue was $50.6 billion. One of the reasons why the firm has been so hugely successful is down to the outsourced production model it operates, which provides it with a highly profitable degree of flexibility and responsiveness. Fundamentally, it is based around a model of managing em-ployment relations which relies on the widespread application of harsh working conditions, in highly authoritarian environments, in order to drive down labour costs—which comprise less than 2 per cent of the price of an iPhone (Chan, Pun, and Selden 2013).

Investigative reports have documented the extensive labour rights violations throughout Apple's network of supplier factories in China, including illegally high working hours, the use of child labour, unsafe and dangerous working conditions, extreme work pressures, and low pay (China Labor Watch 2012; Duhigg and Barboza 2012; Chan, Pun, and Selden 2013; BBC Panorama 2014). According to Chan, Pun, and Selden (2013: 106), the:

> ineluctable drive to reduce costs and maximise profits is the source of the pressure placed on Chinese workers employed by Foxconn, many of them producing signature Apple products. While Apple and Foxconn together squeeze Chinese workers and demand 12-hour working days to meet demand, the costs of Chinese labour in processing and assembly are virtually invisible in the larger success of Apple's balance sheets.

In 2010, a series of suicides among Chinese workers employed in factories owned by the Taiwanese company Foxconn, which makes iPads and iPhones, drew attention to the highly alienating nature of work in such environments. The story of Tian Yu, a 17 year old worker who had moved from a rural part of China to Shenzhen, in the south of the country, to take up a job in a Foxconn factory, reveals the overwhelming pressures that can lead someone to contemplate taking their own lives. She threw herself off the fourth floor of her dormitory building, sustaining serious injuries which left her paralysed:

> The accumulated effects of endless assembly line toil, punishing work schedules, harsh fac-tory discipline, a friendless dormitory and, rejection from managers and administrators, compounded by the company's failure to provide her with income, and then her inability to make contact with friends and family, were the immediate circumstances of her attempted suicide. Her testimony reveals how she was overwhelmed, 'I was so desperate that my mind went blank'.
>
> (Chan 2013: 91)

Yet care needs to be taken not to assume that multinationals are supremely powerful entities helping to drive, and being the prime beneficiaries of, globalization. To be sure, they often use their power as dominant actors in the global economy in ways that damage the interests of working people, being responsible for manifold incidents of labour repression and viola-tions of workers' rights around the world on a large scale. However, their activity is often vulnerable to challenges from activist groups and trade unions which campaign on behalf of working people around the world to protect and improve labour standards on an interna-tional basis (Seidman 2007, 2011)—see Section 11.5.

Section summary and further reading

- There are a range of different factors that influence the management of employment relations in MNC subsidiaries. The importance of organizational power and politics, and the capacity of workers and managers to interpret and negotiate how corporate practices operate in specific workplaces, must be recognized.

- Because of the extent to which MNCs can switch, or threaten to switch, the location of production to cheaper sites with lower labour costs, their activities have helped to drive a 'race to the bottom' in labour standards as supplier factories and governments look to offer more lightly regulated environments in order to attract investment.

- Violations of labour standards in factories supplying multinationals have been extensively documented. They include low wages, excessive working hours, mandatory overtime, union repression, alleged child labour, poor health and safety, and abusive management approaches.

See Marginson and Meardi (2010) for the role of multinationals in employment relations. Both Ferner (2010) and Edwards (2011) provide good overviews of the influences on the management of employment relations in MNC subsidiaries. For an in-depth account of the Apple outsourced production model and its implications for employment relations, see Chan, Pun, and Selden (2013).

11.4 Regulating international labour standards

Efforts to regulate labour standards on an international basis have a long history, dating back to the early twentieth century (Brown 2001). Since the 1990s, however, the rise of globalization has generated much interest in how the greater mobility of employers across national borders can be reconciled with the effective protection of employment rights and working conditions of workers around the world (Hepple 2005; Royle 2011).

11.4.1 The debate on international labour standards

Evidence of a 'race to the bottom' in labour standards has prompted trade unions, non-governmental organizations (NGOs), and labour rights activists to mount high-profile campaigns against leading multinationals such as Nike, Apple, and Reebok, which have reportedly sourced some of their products from factories which operate exploitative practices, such as the use of child labour (Seidman 2007; Tsogas 2009; Garside 2013).

Traditionally, labour rights and protections have been derived and enforced at a national level. However, the growth of increasingly complex cross-border global supply chains has created a regulatory 'gap' or 'void' at transnational level (Fichter 2013; Locke 2013). Moreover, national governments often fail to enforce the labour laws that apply within their own territories (Kuruvilla and Verma 2006). This is evident in China, for example, which in theory has a tough system of labour protections, including the right of workers to be paid a minimum wage. However, regional and local administrations are often unwilling to enforce compliance with minimum wage and other labour laws because of a concern that doing so would drive away investment (Yu 2008).

Globalization enthusiasts criticize attempts to regulate labour standards globally, on the grounds that they hinder efforts by developing countries wishing to use one of their key competitive advantages, low labour costs, to attract investment and pursue economic growth.

They contend that workers in poor countries benefit from the prosperity generated by free trade and MNC investment. Rather than viewing it as a threat to labour standards, globalization should be welcomed, and indeed accelerated, since a globalizing economy offers the best hope of more jobs and increased prosperity (Flanagan 2006). While the jobs created are poorly paid by the standards of developed countries, the opportunities globalization gives to people, especially women, who would otherwise be entrenched in poverty, means that it should be welcomed. Moreover, MNCs and their suppliers tend to offer higher wages and better working conditions than do indigenous firms. In this interpretation, then, the proposition that globalization results in a 'race to the bottom' in respect of labour standards is misplaced; rather, the investment it generates creates jobs, economic opportunities, and the potential for prosperity in places where they would otherwise be absent. Setting minimum employment rights, which developing countries are less likely to be able to meet, hinders free trade and unfairly protects companies and workers in the developed world from the rigours of global competition, leading to fewer job opportunities and reduced prosperity in poorer countries (Bhagwati 2004; Wolf 2004; Flanagan 2006).

However, this view has been challenged by studies which demonstrate that the presence of rigorous labour standards may contribute to economic growth rather than hinder it. The absence of standards encourages countries to follow a 'low road' route to economic development, based on promoting export-led growth with competitive advantage gained through low pay and weak employment protections. But such an approach is inimical to the long-term prosperity of emerging economies. Instead, a more sustainable economic model is desirable, one that is contingent on wage levels that are sufficient to boost demand-led growth and strong labour laws that encourage effective independent trade unions who can use their bargaining endeavours to raise wages (Palley 2004). Improvements in labour standards can complement productivity. Effective health and safety provision, for example, reduces the likelihood of workplace injuries, reducing welfare and absence costs for firms and raising employee morale (ILO 2009).

Nevertheless, the case for international labour standards does not rest on economic grounds alone. Rather, they are often advanced as a means of stimulating social justice, including dignity at work, something that has informed the perspective of the ILO in particular (Leisink 1999). There are some interventions, such as the abolition of child labour, which might be seen as basic—and thus universally applicable—human rights, regardless of context. There is an argument that while child labour may be undesirable, it is nonetheless an indispensable feature of economic and social development in some societies because the additional wages are a vital contribution to family incomes. However, it is doubtful that economic development is contingent on the practice of widespread child labour. Rather, its existence helps to keep wages low, to the advantage of unscrupulous employers (Tsogas 2001).

The assumption that a system of international labour standards is inimical to globalization, free trade, and increased prosperity is far too simplistic. Indeed, properly organized, it could be used not just to resist the pressure towards a 'race to the bottom' in labour standards, but also to stimulate 'a race to the top' (Hepple 2005: 24), by promoting positive economic freedoms for workers (Warnecke and De Ruyter 2010). Moreover, in so far as it has the potential to raise living standards in poorer nations, and to give the internationalization of economic activity greater support and legitimacy in richer ones, an effective system of minimum international labour standards could help to produce a fairer and more socially just process of globalization (Elliott and Freeman 2003).

Table 11.1 The main approaches to promoting international labour standards

Type of approach	Main features
Multilateral efforts through the ILO or other international agencies (e.g. UN, OECD)	Quasi-legal, non-company-specific approaches to setting labour standards, based mainly on encouraging and supporting countries in their efforts to ratify and comply with ILO conventions or adopt certain guidelines
Social clauses in trade agreements	A non-company-specific approach which involves inserting binding clauses dealing with labour standards into unilateral, bilateral, or multilateral trade agreements between different countries
Corporate codes of conduct	Unilateral, company-specific, and non-legally binding arrangements established by multinational companies, designed to promote minimum labour standards in their supply chains
Multi-stakeholder codes of conduct	Non-company-specific and non-legally binding arrangements designed to promote minimum labour standards in multinational supply chains, which involve unions, labour activist organizations, and NGOs, as well as firms themselves
International framework agreements	Negotiated, company-specific, non-binding arrangements concluded between global union federations and leading multinational companies (see Section 11.5.1)

11.4.2 Approaches to regulating international labour standards

The main approaches to regulating international labour standards are specified in Table 11.1: multilateral action by more than one country; the inclusion of so-called 'social clauses' that deal with labour rights issues in trade agreements; the efforts of MNCs to develop voluntary codes of conduct, either by themselves or on a multi-stakeholder basis; and efforts made by global union federations (GUFs) to conclude international framework agreements with MNCs (see Section 11.5.1).

With regard to multilateral arrangements, both the United Nations, in its 1999 Global Compact, and the Organisation for Economic Co-operation and Development (OECD), in its 2000 Guidelines for Multinational Enterprises (updated in 2011), have published non-binding recommendations for good practice in international labour standards. Since they are largely exhortative in character, though, such interventions are generally rather ineffective when it comes to securing substantive improvements in labour rights and protections (Hepple 2005; Kuruvilla and Verma 2006). However, there is some evidence from the UK which suggests that the OECD guidelines have helped trade unions to secure agreements over employment relations matters with leading MNCs, such as British American Tobacco and Unilever (Ewing 2013: 436).

However, the main body responsible for promoting labour standards on a multilateral basis is the International Labour Organization (ILO). Founded in 1919, the ILO holds that economic growth should be reconciled with the 'creation of decent work', so that the benefits of globalization can be more equitably shared and not be achieved at the expense of workers' freedom, welfare, or dignity (ILO 2009: 10). An agency of the United Nations, the ILO comprises representatives of governments, trade unions, and employers' organizations from among its 187 member states.

The main instruments it uses to promote labour standards are conventions, which its member countries are invited to ratify. By 2016, 189 conventions had been agreed. Among other things, they provide for the eradication of child labour (Convention 138, 1973), and the right of workers to enjoy freedom of association by being able to organize in trade unions and bargain collectively with employers (Conventions 87, 1948, and 98, 1949). The most recent convention, no. 189, which aims to provide domestic workers with new rights and protections, was enacted in 2011 (Albin and Mantouvalou 2012). Once a country has ratified a convention, it is supposed to uphold its provisions. However, countries are not obliged to ratify any of the conventions, and many do not do so (Kuruvilla and Verma 2006; Ewing 2013). The US, for example, has only ratified fourteen ILO conventions, compared to the UK's figure of eighty-seven.

LEGISLATION AND POLICY 11.5:   The ILO's Declaration of Fundamental Principles and Rights at Work

The ILO's Declaration of Fundamental Principles and Rights at Work consists of eight 'core' conventions covering freedom of association and the right to collective bargaining, the elimination of forced or compulsory labour, the elimination of workplace discrimination, and the abolition of child labour. All member states are required to comply with the obligations imposed by these conventions even if they have not ratified them.

- Freedom of Association and Protection of the Right to Organize Convention (Convention 87), 1948.
- Right to Organize and Collective Bargaining Convention (98), 1949.
- Forced Labour Convention (29), 1930.
- Abolition of Forced Labour Convention (105), 1957.
- Equal Remuneration Convention (100), 1951.
- Discrimination (Employment and Occupation) Convention (111), 1958.
- Minimum Age Convention (138), 1973.
- Worst Forms of Child Labour Convention (182), 1999.

Since the 1990s, the ILO has more actively propagated the need for effective international labour standards as a means of regulating employment relations at a global level (Elliott and Freeman 2003). In 1998, it published a Declaration of Fundamental Principles and Rights at Work, containing a number of 'core' conventions (see Legislation and policy 11.5). For the ILO, these core standards embody certain basic principles and rights that all countries should aspire to respecting (ILO 2009). Unlike conventions in general, which have to be ratified before they impose any duty to comply, there is an obligation on all ILO members to work towards upholding the core labour standards. Yet the ILO possesses no sanctions to enforce compliance with its conventions (O'Brien 2002) apart from expulsion, and that is only ever used in extreme circumstances as a last resort. The main problem with a more rigorous enforcement regime is that it would discourage countries from ratifying ILO conventions, or even cause them to quit the organization entirely (Hepple 2005).

The ILO has increasingly focused on promoting the use of core labour standards—by influencing the policies of multinationals (explained later in this section—see Ewing 2013), or through technical assistance work—rather than on standard-setting through conventions (Alston 2004). The Declaration of Fundamental Principles and Rights at Work has played an important part in this shift, by setting in 'train a process of more regular scrutiny of Member States on their compliance with the principles and the offer of greater support ... to help them meet their obligations' (Ewing 2013: 429).

There is some evidence that interventions by the ILO can help to improve labour standards. In the Middle East, for example, ILO technical assistance has helped to promote the independent representation of workers' interests even in countries where trade unions are banned (Kuruvilla and Verma 2006). However, critics assert that this shift in emphasis has diminished the effectiveness of the ILO when it comes to protecting and advancing the interests of workers around the world (Alston 2004; Standing 2008, 2010). Some think that the problem with an approach which is concerned with encouraging the adoption of core labour standards is that as a result the work of the ILO has become too focused on upholding certain broad principles rather than with enforcing substantive labour rights through standard-setting and conventions (Royle 2011). Others, however, contend that a focus on gaining support for the eight core conventions, accompanied by rigorous promotional activity, has helped to enhance the importance of the ILO, and to ensure that it continues to play a significant part in improving labour standards in a more globalized world, not least to the extent that it is able to influence practices within the global supply chains of MNCs (Ewing 2013).

An alternative approach to regulating international labour standards involves the inclusion of what are known as 'social clauses' in trade deals between individual countries or groups of countries (Ewing 2013). Both the European Union (EU) and the United States, for example, operate Generalized System of Preferences (GSP) regimes whereby developing countries are given favourable trading rights in exchange for agreeing to abide by minimum labour standards. However, the GSP process is extremely susceptible to political interference, with foreign policy considerations often playing an influential part in the selection of countries for inclusion (Tsogas 2009).

A further problem is that although social clauses in trade agreements often mandate that signatory countries commit to upholding ILO labour standards, 'there is a certain unreality about them, an unreality reinforced by the lack of any ILO involvement in their supervision and enforcement' (Ewing 2013: 437). Despite pushing for social clauses in trade agreements, which make reference to upholding 'internationally recognized labour rights', the US itself is a serial offender when it comes to failing to ratify, let alone enforce, ILO conventions (Ewing 2013). Thus it would be unwise to expect that an approach to promoting international labour standards through social clauses in trade agreements will do much to improve employment conditions worldwide.

LEGISLATION AND POLICY 11.6:   The Ethical Trading Initiative's 'Base Code'

The ETI Base Code is an internationally recognized voluntary code of labour practice which is founded on the conventions of the ILO. It contains nine clauses:

- Employment is freely chosen (e.g. there is no forced labour).
- Freedom of association and the right to collective bargaining are respected.
- Working conditions are safe and hygienic.

(continued...)

- Child labour should not be used.

- Living wages are paid (enough to meet basic needs and to provide some discretionary income).

- Working hours are not excessive (working hours comply with national laws and benchmark industry standards, whichever affords greater protection).

- No discrimination is practised (on a number of grounds, including race, nationality, gender, and trade union membership).

- Regular employment is provided.

- No harsh or inhumane treatment is allowed (e.g. no physical abuse or sexual harassment).

Source: http://www.ethicaltrade.org/eti-base-code

A further approach to regulating labour standards concerns the efforts of multinationals themselves to establish, and get their suppliers to abide by, voluntary codes of conduct governing employment practices and working conditions. For Locke (2013: 11), such 'private voluntary regulation has emerged as the dominant approach' used by global corporations to promote improvements in international labour standards. Private regulatory interventions— 'private' in the sense that they largely fall outside the public authority of states and governments—became increasingly common in the 1990s and 2000s. In the sportswear, garment, and fashion industries, for example, global brands developed labour codes of conduct, specifying minimum labour standards to be observed in their supply chains, in response to activist campaigns that publicized manifold labour rights abuses, and to demonstrate their corporate social responsibility (CSR) credentials (Hepple 2005; Royle 2011; Fichter 2013; Locke 2013).

A code of conduct is a 'formal statement specifying the ethical standards that a [multinational] company holds and applies to the factories of its suppliers or to its trade partners' (Pun 2005: 102). In 1992, Levi-Strauss and Nike were the first major US corporations to establish their own corporate codes covering labour issues in their respective supply chains. The content of such corporate codes is often heavily influenced by the ILO core conventions (Ewing 2013). Apple's Supplier Code of Conduct specifies that its suppliers should treat workers in a fair and non-discriminatory manner, not use forced or child labour, and respect workers' rights to associate in trade unions and bargain collectively.

In addition to corporate codes of conduct, designed and operated by individual firms, there are also multi-stakeholder codes involving MNCs, unions, and NGOs (Fichter 2013). Nike, for example, is a member of the Fair Labor Association (FLA), a US body that also includes Puma and Adidas among its membership. As a multi-stakeholder organization, the FLA comprises companies, universities, and NGOs, and has its own code of conduct requiring that, among other things, member firms ensure that their suppliers comply with local labour laws and respect workers' rights to organize in trade unions and use collective bargaining. In the UK, the Ethical Trading Initiative (ETI), which includes Tesco, Marks & Spencer, and W H Smith among its members, as well as the Trades Union Congress (TUC) and leading non-governmental organizations like Oxfam, fulfils a similar function. It operates a voluntary 'Base Code', under which companies agree to source their products from suppliers who, among other things, respect workers' rights to form trade unions and pay 'living wages', defined as 'enough to meet basic needs and to provide discretionary income' (see Legislation and policy 11.6 for further details).

11.4.3 **The effectiveness of codes**

There is some evidence that voluntary codes of conduct can lead to improvements in labour standards. Egels-Zandén (2014), for example, studied toy factories in China, and found that the presence of a code had helped to mitigate health and safety problems and the practice of excessive working hours. Codes can be useful tools for raising labour standards, especially when they are rigorously enforced, ideally through some kind of independent verification arrangement (Barrientos and Smith 2006). In general, though, the effectiveness of private, voluntary regulatory interventions is rather limited, despite all the efforts MNCs make to promote them, with improvements in labour standards confined to certain areas, particularly workplace health and safety (Locke 2013).

Codes have made little progress in advancing the rights of workers to associate freely in trade unions; any improvements tend to involve 'visible superficial working conditions' such as health and safety signs (Egels-Zandén and Merk 2014: 467). A large part of the difficulty, undoubtedly, concerns the questionable motivations behind the codes. Many US retailers have instituted codes of conduct only because of consumer and activist pressure, not from a genuine commitment to improving working conditions in their supply chains (Compa 2001); they are sometimes established primarily with the aim of improving a company's public relations image (O'Brien 2002).

A key reason for the development of voluntary codes is the importance attached by corporations to protecting their reputation and safeguarding the image of their brands, in response to pressure from campaigns by labour rights activists and growing consumer awareness of the poor working conditions and exploitation experienced by many developing country workers producing goods for major global brands (Frenkel 2001; Frenkel and Scott 2002: Locke 2013). Workers and unions generally have little influence over the content of corporate codes—which, given that they come under the control of managers, is often highly selective (Esbenshade 2004; Merk 2009). Perhaps understandably, trade unions often doubt the value of corporate codes, viewing them as a weak approach to promoting improvements in labour standards, particularly where there are no independent verification arrangements (Kuruvilla and Verma 2006).

In response to activist campaigns that have criticized codes of conduct for their ineffectiveness, some multinationals have made improvements in monitoring arrangements, including opening them up to greater independent, external scrutiny (e.g. Frenkel and Kim 2004; Locke et al. 2007). That said, however, auditing and monitoring arrangements are often highly flawed (Royle 2011). In particular, suppliers have become adept at misleading auditors, giving the false impression that the code is being properly enforced, when the reality is rather different.

Workers and managers in supplier factories report that codes are frequently violated in practice (Pun 2005; Egels-Zendén 2007). In advance of inspection visits, workers are often coached by their employers to give positive answers to the auditors. Both workers and employers have a vested interest in asserting that the codes are being complied with; otherwise a multinational might change to another supplier, threatening the viability of the firm and putting jobs at risk. A Chinese worker was clearly aware of the danger:

> You know we are afraid of losing production orders. We also don't want to give wrong answers and get into trouble.
>
> (Pun 2005: 107)

A large part of the problem with many codes concerns the way in which they tend to be enforced. There is an emphasis on using auditors to visit factories, collect data, and meet managers to ascertain how far suppliers are meeting their provisions (Locke 2013). However, this gives rise to a 'compliance' ethos, whereby factories are penalized for failing to meet the specifications of the code. This encourages factories to concentrate on showing that they do conform to codes, in a 'ritual of compliance', rather than focusing on actually promoting substantive improvements in labour standards (Locke, Amengual, and Mangla 2009: 328).

A further difficulty with codes is that while they might promote improvements in labour standards, this often comes at a price. Take the case of a Chinese factory that makes sports shoes for Reebok, for example. The only way that the firm could afford to comply with the specifications of Reebok's code and still remain profitable was by intensifying work and implementing a payment scheme that disadvantaged the workforce (Yu 2008). Demands from multinationals for lower prices make it difficult for suppliers to keep to the provisions of codes, given the potential increase in labour costs associated with compliance (Bulut and Lane 2011; Robinson 2010). MNCs expect suppliers in developing countries to abide by the terms of their codes, but they rarely give them any money to do so. Poor labour standards are not necessarily the fault of local factory managers in emerging economies like China; the demands of powerful multinational brands for low-cost, flexible production strategies often leave suppliers with little option other than non-compliance with codes if they are to retain their contracts (Locke 2013).

 Insight into practice 11.7:   Alleged violations of the ETI's Base Code

There are frequent allegations that practices in factories around the world which produce goods sold by major UK retailers violate elements of the Ethical Trading Initiative's (ETI) Base Code. In 2010, for example, there were claims that the self-styled 'ethical fashion chain' Monsoon—a founder member of the ETI—had sourced some of its products from suppliers in India that use child labour and pay illegally low wages. In responding to the allegations, Monsoon emphasized the efforts it makes to tackle violations of labour standards in its supply chain.

A series of investigations by the charity War on Want has unearthed numerous examples of labour practices that do not comply with the ETI Base Code. The charity has investigated the experiences of garment and textile workers in India who make products for ETI members such as Marks & Spencer, Debenhams, and Next. It alleges that insufficient progress has been made when it comes to ensuring that workers receive a living wage, and that they are often prevented from joining unions. War on Want claims that pressure from retailers to keep the costs of production low, and thus ensure that the prices of items in their shops, such as jeans, t-shirts, and dresses, are cheap, means that factories have no alternative but to violate the terms of the ETI Base Code. It criticizes the efforts made by corporations to improve labour standards, claiming that they are strong on rhetoric but weak on substance. Retailers have responded by denying that pressure to cut production costs results in exploitation, emphasizing that their suppliers must comply with the appropriate ethical standards, and stressing that any violations of labour standards are investigated.

Sources: War on Want (2006, 2008, 2010)

Since they are private voluntary arrangements, there is a high level of variation in respect of both the content of codes (Hepple 2005), and also their effectiveness. The presence of an independent trade union can help to ensure that codes operate to the benefit of workers in a more sustained way (Frenkel and Kim 2004). However, it needs to be recognized that corporate codes of conduct, in particular, are essentially managerial interventions, designed with managerial aims in mind; they are not put in place to foster the better representation of workers' interests (Pun 2005). There is generally little knowledge and awareness of codes among the workers they are intended to help (Kuruvilla and Verma 2006; Egels-Zandén and Merk 2014). Even multi-stakeholder codes, like the one operated by the ETI, have been criticized for being ineffective (see Insight into practice 11.7).

The most effective way of improving labour standards would be to encourage independent worker representation, particularly by allowing workers to organize in trade unions and engage in collective bargaining. However, when it comes to regulating labour standards, codes are sometimes preferred as an employer-friendly alternative to having a union presence (Egels-Zandén and Merk 2014). If labour codes of conduct are to play an effective role in raising international labour standards, more needs to be done to involve workers and unions in their design, development, and implementation; this would help to eschew a compliance-based approach in favour of one oriented more towards promoting empowerment and collaboration (Locke 2013).

 ## Section summary and further reading

- There has been growing interest in the desirability of regulating labour standards on an international basis. Though open to criticism that they hinder economic growth in a way that unfairly protects jobs in developing countries, international labour standards can help to stimulate improved social and economic well-being.

- A number of approaches to regulating labour standards on an international basis are evident, including multilateral efforts by the ILO, voluntary codes of conduct often put in place by multinationals themselves, and international framework agreements (IFAs) negotiated between global union federations (GUFs) and leading MNCs—see Section 11.5.1 for more details.

- Codes of conduct are somewhat ineffective tools for raising labour standards. The greater involvement of workers and unions, and a less compliance-oriented approach, could enable codes to play a more important part in improving working conditions around the world.

The website of the International Labour Organization (ILO) is a key source of information on international labour standards. The chapter-length overviews provided by Royle (2011) and Williams et al. (2013: chapter 4) are highly recommended. See Ewing (2013) for the role of the ILO. The best in-depth study of voluntary labour codes is Locke (2013).

11.5 Globalization and labour

The material in the previous section on regulating international labour standards points to a problem with viewing globalization either straightforwardly as a process of greater worldwide interconnectedness, or as a corporate neo-liberal project. It shows the extent to which employment relations is in fact being transformed in a more globalized world. This transformationalist approach to globalization is particularly apparent from the way in which labour unions and social movement organizations are attempting to respond to, and challenge, the power of multinationals, manifest in new forms of trade union internationalism and the prevalence of labour conflict.

11.5.1 **Global unions and international framework agreements**

Globalization has posed some major challenges to union movements around the world. In particular, the increased power enjoyed by multinationals, arising from their greater capacity for mobility, has eroded the capacity of unions to affect the joint regulation of employment relations (Anner et al. 2006). Since unions are primarily national actors, whose power and capacity to influence employment relations stems from their ability to organize and mobilize workers in a specific country, and whose operations are to a large extent concerned with national-level employment regulation, the internationalization of economic activity has undoubtedly weakened them (Lillie and Martinez Lucio 2004; Bieler, Lindberg, and Pillay 2008). This has been evident in the European airline industry. The rise to prominence of low-cost carriers such as Ryanair has to a large extent been predicated on their capacity to transcend national borders as a means of reducing labour costs. This includes being able to subvert national-level employment regulation over matters including union recognition and collective bargaining. However, despite the efforts of the airline industry unions to develop transnational strategies to counteract the power of companies like Ryanair, their activities remain largely informed by a national-level focus (Harvey and Turnbull 2015).

There is a growing recognition that unions need to operate more effectively on a transnational basis in order to advance the interests of workers around the world in a more globalized economy (Frege 2006). However, there are some notable difficulties. For one thing, national-level union movements in rich countries face accusations that by campaigning for more rigorous labour standards around the world they are acting in their own self-interest. By making it more difficult for emerging economies to compete, this would help to protect the jobs and wage levels of their members from foreign competition (Rubery and Grimshaw 2003). Moreover, while there is a long history of efforts by trade unions to organize and operate at international level, their effectiveness has often been diminished by a range of significant practical, political, and ideological obstacles (Gumbrell-McCormick 2013).

Yet international solidarity action is also a prominent feature of union responses to globalization. Workers and unions from around the world often take action to demonstrate their support for, and sympathy with, workers in a different country who are engaged in a dispute over their terms and conditions of employment. Such activity has a particularly long history in the port transport industry, for example (Lillie and Martinez Lucio 2004; Turnbull 2006). In Turkey, workers employed by Novamed, a subsidiary of a German multinational, won their dispute over union recognition partly because of the strong support provided by workers and unions from other countries, particularly solidarity action pursued by foreign trade unions (Fougner and Kurtoğlu 2011).

Moreover, the establishment of the new International Trade Union Confederation (ITUC) in 2006, which replaced a number of pre-existing organizations, portends the development of a more strategic and effective union response to globalization. Calling itself the 'global voice of the world's working people', the ITUC has over 300 affiliates—including the UK's Trades Union Congress (TUC)—across 162 countries and territories. Whereas the work of its predecessor organizations had been dominated by political and ideological quarrels, bureaucratic wrangling, and a pronounced lack of concern with the interests of workers in emerging economies, the formation of the ITUC was predicated on the basis that a stronger, international union response to neo-liberal globalization was required, one that involved a greater emphasis on campaigning and advocating on behalf of working people (Gumbrell-McCormick 2013).

Unions themselves have given more attention to regulating labour standards on an international basis, particularly through the development of 'international framework agreements' (IFAs), or 'global framework agreements' (GFAs) as they are sometimes now called. These are negotiated arrangements struck between global union federations and individual MNCs which establish a set of non-binding rules designed to govern work and employment relationships on an international basis, in particular by establishing a set of minimum employment standards which often extend to the supply chains (Wills 2002; Riisgaard 2005; Stevis and Boswell 2007; Papadakis 2011; Fichter 2013; Ford and Gillan 2015).

While the first IFA, covering the French multinational Danone, was instituted during the 1980s, it was only in the 2000s that their number really grew, with around eighty-five of them now in existence (Fichter 2013). They are to be found mainly in European-headquartered multinationals such as the French retailer Carrefour, the German motor vehicle manufacturer Volkswagen, and the Spanish firm Indetix, which owns the Zara chain (Croucher and Cotton 2009; Niforou 2014).

The development of IFAs symbolizes efforts by union movements to fashion a strategic response to the challenges of globalization (Croucher and Cotton 2009). IFAs are important because they represent a new and innovative approach by the international trade union movement to regulating employment relationships above and beyond national borders (Hammer 2005). Their growth during the 2000s was stimulated by some important changes in the structure and orientation of the international trade union movement. In particular, in 2002 the long-standing industry-based international union organizations—the International Trade Secretariats—became known as Global Union Federations (GUFs).

There are nine GUFs in total, including the International Transport Workers Federation (ITF) and IndustriALL, which represents workers in mining, energy, and manufacturing industries. The GUFs have put a considerable amount of effort into IFAs, viewing them as a means of enabling unions to play a larger part in regulating international labour standards, in a way that does more for working people, by improving employment conditions and worker protections, than corporate codes (see Section 11.4.3) (Ford and Gillan 2015). There are good business reasons why some multinationals—particularly those based in Europe—have been apt to sign IFAs. They are useful public relations devices, in as much as they help to convey a concern that the business is keen to operate in a socially responsible manner. However, for the GUFs, the agreements 'represent a means of globalizing labour-management relations and creating space for building and strengthening unions' (Fichter 2013: 397). See Insight into practice 11.8 for details of the agreement between IndustriALL and Swedish-based retailer H&M.

 Insight into practice 11.8: The H&M global framework agreement

In 2015, the IndustriALL global union federation, together with the Swedish trade union IF Metall, signed a new global framework agreement with H&M, covering up to 1.6 million garment workers, in some 1,900 factories around the world, who make products for the Swedish-based retailer. The agreement requires factories in H&M's supply chain to respect a range of appropriate international

(continued...)

labour standards, with reference to the respective ILO conventions. Among other things, it prohibits the use of child labour, forced labour, and employment discrimination (on grounds including sex, race, and age), mandates that workers should be paid a 'fair living wage', and requires workplaces to be safe, healthy, and hygienic. Importantly, the agreement not only specifies H&M's commitment to respecting human and trade union rights in the workplace, including the 'rights of unions to organize and negotiate collective agreements', but also includes a promise that the company will use 'all its leverage' to establish union rights among its suppliers. Moreover, there is an explicit commitment made to 'increasing trade union capacity', as a means of ensuring that the agreement functions effectively as a tool for improving the conduct of employment relations throughout the factories in H&M's global supply chain. Workers and unions are to be part of monitoring arrangements at factory, national, and international levels. According to Jyrki Raina, the general secretary of IndustriALL, the agreement 'opens an exciting new chapter in the relationship between IndustriALL Global Union and H&M. It cements the path towards a sustainable garment industry with unionized workforces, constructive labour-management relations, living wages through industry level collective agreements, and safe workplaces'.

Sources: Clean Clothes Campaign (2015); IndustriALL (2015)

Like the codes of conduct covered in Section 11.4.3, IFAs are private, voluntary arrangements. However, the involvement of the unions means that there are some notable differences in their purpose and content. Whereas codes, by operating as corporate management tools, act to disempower workers, IFAs often embody a concern with promoting the interests of working people and their capacity to associate and organize in unions (Williams, Davies, and Chinguno 2015). Like corporate codes, the content of IFAs is often heavily influenced by ILO core labour standards. However, IFAs generally have a much stronger focus on workers' freedom to associate in, and organize, trade unions, and to engage in collective bargaining (Fichter 2013; Williams, Davies, and Chinguno 2015; Ford and Gillan 2015). Moreover, they can also enable local unions to develop their organizing potential, not least by providing them with a means of taking action over alleged violations of labour standards (Fichter 2013).

There is some evidence that IFAs can help to promote stronger trade union activity. The agreement between Indetix and IndustriALL, for example, includes provisions designed to strengthen independent union representation in countries such as China, Bangladesh, and Cambodia—all places where the company has factories in its supply chain. Having stronger local union representation in place makes for better compliance with the terms of the IFA, thus protecting labour standards (Ford and Gillan 2015). Set against this, however, where knowledge and awareness of the IFA is lacking, then its potential to deliver positive change is much reduced (Riisgaard 2005). A further problem concerns the tendency for IFAs to focus on getting employers to comply with national labour laws, which in some parts of the world are often weak or poorly enforced (Croucher and Cotton 2009; Niforou 2012; Williams, Davies, and Chinguno 2015). There can also be difficulties in identifying where the responsibility for tackling violations of IFAs lies (Niforou 2014). All this suggests that the nature of the local context is crucial to the effectiveness of IFAs when it comes to improving labour standards (Ford and Gillan 2015).

IFAs are still relatively few in number (Niforou 2012). Yet, while their direct impact on work and employment relations has so far been somewhat limited, they are still just about the only directly negotiated international agreements between unions and multinationals in existence. In this respect, the potential they have to 'imagine, trigger, and coordinate transnational labour action' (Ford and Gillan 2015: 469) should not be disregarded. As agreements, IFAs are 'only the starting point, not ends in themselves' (Williams, Davies, and Chinguno 2015: 198)—their effectiveness depends on how far they enable unions in supply chain factories around the world to organize effectively, and thus bargain with managers from a position of greater strength.

The activities of the GUFs, particularly their propagation of IFAs, are by no means the only manifestations of the renewed emphasis on trade union internationalism evident during the 2000s. In some cases union representatives within individual multinationals themselves have developed transnational, 'corporate-centred' union networks (Helfen and Fichter 2013). This has been a particularly prominent feature of the motor vehicle manufacturing sector, which is dominated by multinationals such as General Motors, Toyota, and Volkswagen. Union representatives have tried to challenge the practice of 'regime competition' (see Section 11.3.2) by using formal transnational structures within firms, such as European Works Councils (see Chapter 6), to promote cross-border collaboration and mobilization (Greer and Hauptmeier 2008).

Clearly, the unions have attempted to respond to the challenges posed by neo-liberal globalization by increasing the extent of their cross-border activities and through their efforts to develop transnational responses to the increased power of multinationals. Some critics, however, claim that the unions' efforts, while welcome, do not go far enough in promoting the kind of labour internationalism that is needed to counteract the power of multinationals and advance the interests of working people in a more globalized world. For example, there is too much of an emphasis placed on workers in the supply chains of MNCs. What about the growing number of workers operating in precarious employment, particularly in the informal economy? The activities of the ITUC and the GUFs are too distant from, and thus do not engage with, the experiences of working people. Unions should also be doing more to collaborate with sympathetic organizations around the world as a means of advancing the interests of workers which might otherwise go neglected. A greater emphasis on 'social movement unionism' posits a new kind of labour internationalism, one that goes beyond operating within, and trying to strike agreements with, multinationals, to encompass a broader concern with securing progressive political and social change through building alliances and coalitions (Munck 2011).

11.5.2 Globalization, labour conflict, and transnational activism

From a global perspective, labour conflict remains a central feature of contemporary employment relations. Strike activity has not vanished. In fact it is increasingly evident in emerging economies, such as China. Moreover, there is evidence that economic globalization is a major source of labour unrest around the world. The decline in the level of recorded strike activity between the 1970s and the 2000s was not just restricted to the UK—see Chapter 9; internationally, there was also a marked fall in the incidence of strikes (Wallace and O'Sullivan 2006; Vandaele 2011; Gall 2013a). Particularly where unions are relatively weak, globalization seems to have been a major cause of the diminution in strike levels, given its tendency to erode the power of organized labour (Piazza 2005).

Yet care must be taken not to write off strikes and labour unrest. A number of major disputes have occurred in South Africa, for example. In 2010 there was a massive three-week public sector strike which involved nearly a million and a half workers taking action in pursuit of higher pay. And during 2012–13 there was widespread disruption in the country's mining sector as a result of strikes by miners in pursuit of improved pay and conditions, some of which were violently suppressed (Chinguno 2013). In some countries, such as Egypt, South Korea, and Indonesia, strikes have been a major feature of efforts by workers' movements to challenge authoritarian employers and governments and thus help to instigate political change (Koo 2001; La Botz 2001; Alexander 2013). Even where the odds seem heavily stacked against it, action by workers wanting to improve the conditions under which they labour, and the reward for that labour, is always possible. This is evident from the experience of Dubai (see International perspective 11.9).

 International perspective 11.9:   Strikes and labour unrest in Dubai

During the 2000s, the emirate of Dubai in the Middle East was one of the fastest growing places in the world, with scores of new hotel complexes, luxury apartments, and shopping centres springing up to service a growing tourism and leisure industry. The construction industry boomed. However, conditions for the workforce, overwhelmingly made up of migrant labourers from countries such as India, Pakistan, and Bangladesh, are highly oppressive. Low and unpaid wages often leave many of the workers, who share rooms in concrete barrack compounds, heavily in debt. They are often required to surrender their passports, so are not free to leave. Although any form of industrial action by workers is illegal in Dubai, and there is no right to join a trade union, the period between 2004 and 2008 saw some notable instances of labour conflict reported as construction workers took strike action and protested over low pay, inadequate accommodation, and poor working conditions (Buckley 2013).

The global economic recession of the late 2000s, and the austerity policies devised by many governments as a response to it, generated increases in strike activity, particularly in emerging Latin American economies such as Argentina, Brazil, and Chile, which subsequently declined (ILO 2011, 2013b). In some parts of Europe, particularly where the effects of neo-liberal austerity measures were felt most keenly, there has been an upsurge of labour unrest, including mass general strikes by workers in protest against government policies (Gall 2013a; Kelly 2015). The economic crisis in Greece, for example, produced numerous general strikes between 2010 and 2016 as workers protested against cuts to pay and pensions and tax increases that slashed their standard of living. This illustrates the important extent to which worker discontent informs, and is subsumed within, broader social and political struggles, with a focus on challenging governments rather than employers (Godard 2011).

Moreover, the development of export-oriented manufacturing industries in countries such as China, and the concomitant need for cheap labour on a massive scale, has produced a highly propitious environment for labour conflict (Silver 2003). Economic reforms, in particular the development of capitalist market relations, have generated widespread incidents of labour conflict, including strikes, over matters such as unpaid wages and employer violations of labour regulations (see Lee 2007; Friedman and Lee 2010; Cooke 2013; Friedman 2014). In April 2014, for example, tens of thousands of shoe factory workers employed at the Yue Yuen factory complex in Dongguan, who make products for retailers such as Nike and Reebok, undertook a series of strikes and protests relating to unpaid social welfare payments. In some more advanced parts of the economy, rising expectations have encouraged workers to contemplate strike action in pursuit of higher wages. For example, in 2010 a wave of strikes affected car and electronics plants over demands for substantial pay rises. Striking workers in Honda won pay rises of 20–30 per cent as a result of their action (Chan and Hui 2012).

Importantly, labour conflict and contention in a more globalized world are not just limited to strikes by trade unions. Multinationals can be distinctly vulnerable to activist campaigns that draw attention to violations of labour standards in their supply chains. Private, voluntary codes, of the kind covered in Section 11.4, are often established, or strengthened, in response to the activities of transnational labour rights activists (Bartley 2007; Seidman 2007; Fransen 2012; Donaghey et al. 2014). In the garment sector, for example, social movement organizations such as the Clean Clothes Campaign have been at the forefront of efforts to induce multinationals to improve labour standards in their global supply chains (Ross 2012; Balsiger 2014). There is often a particular emphasis placed on promoting consumer activism as a means of securing improvements in labour standards. This is based on the rationale that multinational brands are particularly vulnerable to the potential adverse reputational consequences of negative publicity about labour abuses in their supply chains (Micheletti and Stolle 2007; Donaghey et al. 2014; Reinecke and Donaghey 2015).

The introductory case study of the 'Accord' in Bangladesh, which was established in response to the 2013 Rana Plaza tragedy, illustrates how labour unions and organizations concerned with mobilizing consumers can collaborate in ways that help to leverage improvements in labour standards (Reinecke and Donaghey 2015). There are two lessons to be taken from both this particular example, and also the broader ways in which unions and social movement organizations, by engaging in activist campaigns, have endeavoured to advance the interests of working people around the world. One is that multinationals are far from being all-powerful organizations; neo-liberal globalization has provoked considerable opposition, to the extent that it would be mistaken to view it as omnipotent.

Related to this, a second lesson concerns how we should understand employment relations in a more globalized world. The cross-border mobilization efforts of unions, labour conflict, and transnational activism by social movement organizations are all integral features of globalization. Their presence demonstrates the important extent to which globalization is not simply something that working people are affected by; workers, unions, and activists around the world are actively engaged in shaping how globalization operates, not least through their efforts to challenge the way that multinational employers behave (Williams et al. 2013).

 ## Section summary and further reading

- Unions have responded to the challenges of neo-liberal globalization by making renewed efforts to operate effectively at a transnational level. The most prominent feature of the emergent trade union internationalism is the growing number of international (and global) framework agreements concluded with multinationals.

- Globalization has been responsible for some notable changes in the location and dimensions of labour conflict. This includes the development of transnational labour activism. In this respect, globalization can be viewed as having a transformative effect on employment relations—something which involves workers, unions, and activists as well as multinational employers and their supply chains.

Croucher and Cotton (2009) offer an excellent assessment of issues relating to trade union internationalism. For the global unions and IFAs, see the overview by Ford and Gillan (2015). See Friedman's (2014) book *The Insurgency Trap* for a detailed analysis of labour unrest in China. Cooke (2013) offers a good, shorter overview.

11.6 Conclusion

On a global scale, the efforts of powerful multinational companies to undermine national systems of employment relations, and to shift production to locations where it is cheaper to employ staff, are major consequences of the process of globalization. Moreover, the erosion of labour standards in many emerging economies is evidence of how the neo-liberal process of globalization, as an intensification of capitalist relations, often undermines workers' interests. For many workers in emerging economies like China, who produce clothes, shoes, and other consumer items for Western markets, conditions are often extremely poor, and their jobs precarious. However, one would be mistaken in assuming that the convergence pressures associated with globalization have made national systems of employment relations and organized labour impotent. For one thing, it has been established that national-level diversity remains an important feature of contemporary employment relations, with global convergence pressures being moderated by the institutions and policies characteristic of different countries. Furthermore, evidence of a 'race to the bottom' in labour standards has stimulated pressure for more effective regulation on an international basis. It has also fostered mobilization by workers, often organized in trade unions. The potential for conflict of interest that lies at the heart of the employment relationship is perhaps most readily apparent in the export processing zones and their like, which are dotted around the world. As long as the exploitative capitalist employment relationship endures, workers will endeavour to combine and look to secure improvements by means of collective action.

 Assignment and discussion questions

1. What are the main ways in which globalization has affected employment relations?

2. What is meant by the concept of 'convergence' in employment relations? To what extent has globalization been responsible for a straightforward process of convergence?

3. 'Investment in developing countries by multinational companies leads to improvements in living standards by providing opportunities for paid employment that would otherwise not be available. Such investment should therefore be encouraged.' Discuss.

4. Critically assess the main strengths and weaknesses of corporate codes of conduct as arrangements for delivering improvements in international labour standards.

5. To what extent, and in what ways, have the trade unions been able to forge an effective international response to the challenges of globalization?

 Visit the Online Resource Centre that accompanies this book to develop your understanding of this chapter and keep up to date with the latest developments in this area. **www.oxfordtextbooks.co.uk/orc/williams4e/**

 Chapter case study: The Qatar 2022 Football World Cup—built on forced labour?

In 2010, the right to hold the 2022 Football World Cup was controversially awarded to Qatar in the Middle East. This activated around £100 billion of planned infrastructure projects, including new hotels, transport infrastructure projects, and nine new stadia for the matches themselves. There are about 1.7

million migrant workers in Qatar—some 90 per cent of the workforce—with many, who often originate from countries like Nepal, employed on massive construction sites. Since 2013, however, evidence of sustained and widespread labour and human rights abuses in Qatar has come to light, particularly in the construction sector. They include the non-payment, or irregular payment of wages; in some cases workers have to wait months before they are paid. Living conditions are often poor, with workers having to share squalid, cramped, and unhygienic accommodation in labour camps. Moreover, working conditions can be appalling, particularly during the summer, given the oppressively hot temperatures. In 2013, it was reported that dozens of mainly Nepalese workers had died as a result of work-related conditions. The International Trade Union Confederation (ITUC) reckons that before the World Cup commences in 2022, at least 7,000 migrant workers will have died, mainly from injuries or illnesses connected with their work.

A particularly egregious feature of the situation facing migrant workers in Qatar is that under the *Kafala* system which operates there, in order to work they have to be sponsored by an employer. Without the explicit permission of their sponsor, a worker cannot change jobs or leave the country. There is plenty of evidence that employers confiscate the passports of migrant workers, effectively making it impossible for them to leave their jobs, even in the most intolerable of conditions. An additional constraint is that many workers owe large amounts of money to pay the fees due to the recruitment agents who provide them with employment. As a result, the 2022 World Cup is being built on a wide-ranging and highly institutionalized system of forced labour, in blatant breach of ILO conventions. The ITUC calls *Kafala* a system of 'slave-like sponsorship'.

In response to the international outrage generated by stories of labour rights abuses, the Qatari authorities pledged to take remedial action to improve the situation of migrant workers. Qatar has invested in the development of new, improved accommodation facilities, for example, although only a rather small proportion of migrant workers have benefited from them. The Qatari government has promised to improve welfare standards for migrant workers. It has also made changes to the *Kafala* system which, once they come into effect, may give some workers greater scope to leave their employer, or the country, once their employment contracts expire. However, critics such as Amnesty International and the ITUC have castigated the slow pace of change. They also question how far the labour reforms will have any effect: the Qatari authorities fail to enforce existing worker protections, meaning that construction companies are at liberty to engage in gross labour rights abuses. The ITUC believes that the *Kafala* system needs to be abolished, rather than amended, otherwise Qatar will remain a 'slave state'.

Perhaps the organization with the greatest culpability is the international football association, FIFA, which was responsible for awarding the World Cup to Qatar, and could signal its distaste for the situation there by threatening to take it away unless there is evidence of sustained improvements in labour standards. Yet FIFA's response to the stories of human rights and labour rights abuses emanating from Qatar has been pitiful, being mainly limited to promising to establish a panel which will meet to ensure 'decent working conditions' for workers on construction sites. It also commissioned a report which, while acknowledging that problems existed in Qatar, blandly called for improved respect for human rights issues, and for risks to human rights to be better identified and addressed.

Sources: Pattison (2013); ITUC (2015*b*); Amnesty International (2016); Booth (2016); Gibson (2016*a*, 2016*b*); ILO (2016); Ruggie (2016)

Questions

To what extent should the football authorities take greater responsibility for tackling labour rights abuses in Qatar? What should they do, and why?

12 Conclusion: understanding employment relations

To a large extent, employment relations as a field of study is concerned with how work and employment relationships are regulated. In the past, it was dominated by a focus on joint regulation, particularly by collective bargaining between employers or employers' associations, and trade unions. However, one of the most prominent trends since the 1980s has been the diminution of joint regulation, as evidenced by the contraction of collective bargaining coverage (see Chapter 7), particularly in the private sector. This is associated with declining levels of unionization (see Chapter 6) and the fall in the incidence of union recognition (see Chapter 5)—trends which have been driven by the greater reluctance of employers to contemplate joint regulation, along with the changing composition of employment, such that employment growth has been concentrated in sectors where joint regulation is relatively scarce. Nevertheless, the continuing importance of collective bargaining as a means of regulating work and employment relationships should not be overlooked. It is still a commonplace feature of public sector employment relations, for example. Moreover, many major private sector employers maintain joint regulatory arrangements. Where it remains, however, collective bargaining has become less influential, its coverage has narrowed, and it has taken on a more consensual dimension, as is evident from the prevalence of partnership agreements (see Chapter 6).

Three other major regulatory trends can be identified. The first is that there is now much more of a concern with the efforts of employers to regulate work and employment relationships unilaterally, through relevant managerial policies and practices. For example, Chapter 7 showed how greater managerial attempts to exercise control over pay is a prominent feature of contemporary employment relations, particularly through the use of variable payment systems. There has been much interest in the potential of the 'sophisticated human resource management (HRM)' approach to transform employment relations by generating greater organizational commitment and engagement from employees (see Chapter 5).

However, insights drawn from a 'political economy' perspective on HRM highlight the fragile basis of commitment-based approaches (Thompson 2011). Most importantly, 'they demonstrate' the difficulties and obstacles managers face in trying to enhance the commitment and engagement of employees, given the demands placed on organizations for short-term financial success. Managers might emphasize the importance of commitment and engagement, but in a more financialized environment often come under pressure to ensure that labour is cheaper, more flexible, and disposable.

It is important to recognize how managers have *attempted* to regulate work and employment relationships unilaterally, not that they have necessarily been successful in doing so. The nature of the employment relationship as a wage–work bargain implies that their efforts are invariably influenced by the need to respond to their employees' interests, or to secure their consent and cooperation. Custom and practice expectations remain an important feature of employment relations. The exercise of managerial prerogative is always an aspiration and, given that the employment relationship *is* a relationship in which managers must, to some degree, gain workers' cooperation, can never be fully realized in practice.

The second trend concerns the growing influence of the law on work and employment relationships, which increased especially under Labour between 1997 and 2010. Employment protection and the rights of working people have become much more dependent on the law, as opposed to the situation in the past, when joint regulation was more influential (Dickens and Hall 2010). The growth in statutory employment rights has not just been the product of national-level legislation, like the National Minimum Wage (NMW) (see Chapter 7) and the statutory union recognition procedure (see Chapter 5). Following the Labour government's agreement to sign up to the 'Social Chapter' in 1997, European Union (EU) legislation increasingly came to affect work and employment relations. The work of the trade unions is increasingly concerned with campaigning for better legal rights for workers, with ensuring that existing statutory protections are upheld, and with using them as a base from which to bargain for improvements, such as over work–life balance arrangements (see Chapter 4).

Employer bodies and business lobbyists frequently complain that the legal framework relating to employment matters has become too onerous and burdensome; in particular, the system of employment tribunals has attracted a large amount of criticism for the costs it imposes on employers (see Chapter 10). Yet the framework of law is in fact highly favourable to employers. It does little in practice to limit employers' flexibility or constrain managerial prerogative. By international standards, the UK labour market is very lightly regulated. Nevertheless, the 2010–15 Conservative–Liberal Democrat coalition government thought that employment protection laws hindered the UK's economic recovery, despite the lack of supporting evidence for such an assertion (e.g. Jordan et al. 2013). Under the influence of a 'reasserted neo-liberalism', the coalition took various measures to weaken employment protections (Grimshaw and Rubery 2012; Welch 2016). The majority Conservative government, which took office in 2016, picked up where its 1980s and 1990s predecessors left off, by enacting a further set of unnecessary restrictions on trade unions by means of the 2016 Trade Union Act (see Chapters 3 and 9).

Moreover, arrangements for enforcing employment rights remain weak. They depend too much on the preparedness of the worker concerned to exercise his or her rights, with all the risks that entails. Take the issue of pregnancy discrimination, for example (see Chapter 4). Evidently unlawful behaviour by employers seems to be widespread. Yet they are able to get away with it because the onus is on aggrieved workers not only being aware of their rights and entitlements, but also being prepared to instigate proceedings against their employer. Bogus self-employment arrangements (see Chapter 2), scams that enable employers to avoid paying the minimum wage (see Chapter 7), and the exploitation of vulnerable migrant workers (see Chapters 2 and 10) are contingent on the presence of a weak regime for enforcing employment rights and protections.

For all their talk about advancing the interests of workers, neither David Cameron's nor–yet–Theresa May's governments showed any interest in making it easier for people to assert their statutory employment rights. Indeed, by establishing a system of employment tribunal fees, Cameron's administration made it far more difficult for aggrieved workers to gain access to justice (see Chapter 10). A government that was genuinely interested in upholding workers' rights and protections would encourage the expansion of trade unionism and joint regulation, especially in sectors of the economy characterized by poor working practices. Not only would a union presence help to uphold workers' rights and protections, but it would also promote and advance their interests. Yet the Conservatives' Trade Union Act was designed to weaken the capacity of unions to mobilize effectively, and thus hinder the work they do in representing workers. The government is prepared to extend workers' rights itself—as evidenced by the introduction of the 2016 National Living Wage (see Chapter 7); but allowing workers themselves to assert and improve their rights, by organizing and mobilizing collectively in unions, is clearly viewed as undesirable. Evidently, giving low-paid workers a pay rise by government is good; workers taking action themselves to pursue a living wage—by means of strikes and other forms of labour conflict—is bad.

The third trend concerns the increasing extent to which many employers are attempting to commodify work and employment relationships, manifest in the rise of bogus self-employment arrangements for example, and in the practice of companies operating in the 'gig economy', like Deliveroo, who do not recognize people as workers or employees (see Chapters 1 and 2). The effect of this is to promote a more market-oriented form of work and employment relationship, in which the employing organization eschews any obligations or responsibilities towards its workforce. Greater commodification is associated with the development of a more 'financialized' capitalism (see Chapter 5), marked by the primacy of short-term financial objectives and the consequent imperative to manage labour as efficiently as possible. Moreover, globalization is associated with a 'race to the bottom' in labour standards, as powerful multinationals such as Apple use global supply chains to source their products as cheaply as possible, often with highly adverse consequences for workers (see Chapter 11).

Yet, as Chapter 5 shows, there are important limits to commodification; labour is not a commodity, even if employers try to operate on that basis. Chapter 11 shows the extent to which concerns about labour rights abuses have generated new, albeit often inadequate, regulatory arrangements at transnational level. The activities of companies like Sports Direct (see Chapter 2) have not only generated a considerable amount of controversy, but also contributed to pressures for re-regulation. In this context, there is growing interest in developing mechanisms, such as the greater use of proactive inspection arrangements, to ensure that employers abide by their legal obligations when it comes to how they treat their staff; this is part of a concern with making statutory employment rights more effective (Dickens 2012b). The establishment of the Gangmasters and Labour Abuse Authority reflects a concern that more action is needed to uphold employment protections in sectors of the economy populated by vulnerable workers (see Chapter 10). Furthermore, the 2016 establishment of the National Living Wage—a rise in the minimum wage for people aged 25 and over—was in part predicated on the belief that the government needed to be seen to be doing something about tackling low pay.

The initial approach taken by Theresa May's Conservative government would seem to signal a departure from a neo-liberal policy emphasis which encourages labour commodification. There was talk of doing more to reduce inequality, putting workers' representatives on company boards, and tackling abusive and coercive working practices. It remains to be seen whether or not such talk is converted into actual substance. The opposition Labour Party, under the leadership of veteran left-winger Jeremy Corbyn, has explicitly repudiated the neo-liberal emphasis on the desirability of deregulated labour markets which characterized the Party's approach when it was in government, under Tony Blair and Gordon Brown, from 1997 to 2010. Labour has advanced a set of concrete proposals designed to improve workers' rights. They include scrapping anti-union legislation, such as the 2016 Trade Union Act, and radically extending the rights of unions to be recognized for collective bargaining purposes.

There are two other important aspects of the regulatory environment in employment relations. One concerns the extent to which devolution in the UK has given the governments of Scotland, Wales, and Northern Ireland more powers in some areas, particularly when it comes to the public sector (Williams and Scott 2016c)—see Chapter 3. The junior doctors' dispute (see Chapter 1), for example, was confined to England. The second concerns the causes and implications of the June 2016 referendum vote which went narrowly in favour of the UK leaving the European Union (EU)—see Chapter 3. To a large extent the outcome of the referendum reflected discontent about stagnant living standards, poor employment opportunities, and the adverse consequences of austerity, which many people, influenced by a partisan media, blamed on EU migration. As this book shows, however, it is employers, given the extent to which they have promoted greater labour commodification, and governments, which have tended to favour a light touch regulatory environment which privileges employers' flexibility and advocated austerity, who should bear the culpability for such problems, not migrant workers.

At the time of writing it was expected that Article 50, which the UK government must invoke to begin the two-year process of EU withdrawal, would be triggered some time early in 2017. What happens to the body of EU employment law, covering such matters as working time, and information and consultation rights for workers, remains to be seen; although the expectation is that existing rights and protections would, initially anyway, be maintained. Yet this is a rather odd position for the government to take, given the Conservatives' previous hostility to EU social and employment legislation, and their claims about its damaging effects on the UK's economic competitiveness (see Chapter 3). Freedom of movement for workers, though, seems destined to perish, at least as it applies to the UK. What will replace it, however (a system of work permits?), is unclear.

Employment relations cannot simply be understood as the study of how work and employment relationships are regulated, since such an approach does not adequately capture the dynamic nature of the subject matter. This book is informed by the view that studying employment relations must involve a concern with not only how workers experience their employment relationships, but also how they contest and challenge their terms. This gives us a better, and more rounded, perspective on employment relations. For one thing, it is important to recognize that workers' experiences influence the regulation of work and employment relationships. The growth of pay inequality, for example, and related concerns about the prevalence of low pay in the economy, helped to stimulate efforts to secure the minimum wage and living wage campaigns (see Chapter 7). Moreover, governments have improved statutory provisions relating to family-friendly working arrangements partly in response to pressure from workers experiencing difficulties in combining paid employment with family responsibilities (see Chapter 4).

What, then, is to be said when it comes to making an overall assessment of workers' experiences in employment relations? On a positive note, it would seem that investment by employers in voice arrangements (see Chapter 5) means that workers are better informed about workplace and organizational decisions than in the past. They also seem to be more at-tached to their employing organizations: three-quarters of employees agree or strongly agree that they feel some loyalty to their organization (van Wanrooy et al. 2013b). More negatively, however, it seems that genuine employee involvement and participation is rather limited in practice; workers have few opportunities actually to influence workplace or organizational decision-making. On a more profound note, there is little evidence that the sophisticated HRM agenda has had a positive effect on the experience of workers. Persistently poor levels of employee engagement have been attributed to the low-trust climate that pervades many or-ganizations (Sanders 2012), in part reflecting a growing perception that senior managers are increasingly distant from, and uninterested in, the well-being of the majority of their staff (see Chapter 5). Excessive and unjustifiable pay rises for senior executives, at a time when most workers are seeing a real-terms decline in wages, has not only increased the gap between the pay of those at the top and those further down the earnings hierarchy (see Chapter 7), but has also contributed to the diminution of trust in employment relations (CIPD 2015b).

The economic recession of the late 2000s and its aftermath had a marked adverse effect on the experiences of working people. Chapter 2 highlights the slump in real wages that oc-curred. While the number of people in employment has reached a record high, many workers suffer from 'underemployment', and would like to be offered more hours. Employment has often become more insecure and precarious, particularly for those, frequently young workers and migrant workers, confined to irregular working arrangements such as zero-hours con-tracts (see Chapters 2 and 8). Moreover, workers often come under pressure to forego their statutory employment rights and protections in order to secure a job, for example by being falsely categorized as 'self-employed'. Financialization pressures have stimulated a process of greater commodification of labour, marked by the reluctance of employers to accept any ob-ligations and responsibilities towards workers who are treated as disposable (see Chapters 2 and 5). One of the main contributions of this book, then, is to offer a perspective on work and employment relations that differs from conventional human resource management (HRM) texts. These rarely, if at all, consider the experiences of workers, and as a result often present a rather anodyne and insufficiently complex understanding of what happens in workplaces.

This concern with exploring the experiences of workers demonstrates that, whatever their other characteristics, work and employment relationships are marked by a basic antagonism between a generally powerful employer, who is driven by the need to manage staff in as ef-ficient a way as possible, and a relatively powerless individual worker, who, in addition to having an interest in the success of their organization, is also concerned with being treated fairly and having some say over workplace and organizational decisions (Budd 2004). This difference of interests means that there is always the potential for conflict to arise in employ-ment relations (Edwards 1986). This is made evident at a number of points in the book. The case of Deliveroo (see Chapter 1), for example, illustrates the increasing propensity for ag-grieved workers in the 'gig economy' to challenge the interests of employers by engaging in contention. The discussion of organizing unionism in Chapter 6 demonstrates the potential for unionization among groups of workers who often have considerable and well-justified grievances about the way they are treated at work but have traditionally not been attracted to trade unions. Even in small, non-union firms, where one might expect managerial author-ity to be absolute, managers must accommodate the demands of workers. They are obliged to negotiate informally with workers over such matters as the organization and pace of work (Ram 1994; Dundon and Rollinson 2004)—see Chapter 5. Workers, then, are never entirely passive actors; they always enjoy some—however limited—capacity to challenge and contest the terms of their employment relationships.

The topic of labour conflict was given a substantial amount of attention in Chapter 9. Clearly, the strike is the most visible manifestation of such conflict (Hyman 1975). Among the reasons for the decline of strike activity are: the diminishing proportion of employment in 'strike-prone' industries; the contraction of trade union organization; the articulation of a more assertive management style that aims to make strikes superfluous; and, in particular, the enactment of a whole raft of restrictive legislation. The legal framework places numerous obstacles in the way of trade unions hoping to undertake industrial action, including opportunities for employers to apply to the courts for injunctions to prevent it. However, just because there has been a decline in the level of strike activity it does not follow that conflict is no longer an important feature of employment relations. Mobilization theory, by focusing on how employees acquire a sense of disaffection and the way resulting grievances are translated into collective action, suggests that the capacity of unions to organize workers and mobilize around their discontents is a crucial determinant of whether or not industrial action occurs (Kelly 1998). There are a variety of behaviours at work that can come under the umbrella of labour conflict, including sabotage and absenteeism for example. The growth in the number of employment tribunal claims during the 2000s reflected high levels of discontent among workers—further evidence of the potential for conflict at work (see Chapter 10).

While the decline of joint regulation has given employers more opportunities to attempt to regulate work and employment relationships on a unilateral basis, the inherent potential for conflict within them means that workers will always need, and demand, independent means of expressing their interests. In the expanding 'gig economy', for example, some workers seem increasingly prepared to act collectively in defending their interests, and challenging those of employers, often using social media to facilitate mobilization (Osborne and Butler 2016). The potential for conflict lies at the heart of employment relations. The legal regulation of employment relationships (e.g. anti-strike laws, minimum wages, etc.), joint regulation (union recognition agreements), and efforts at unilateral regulation by employers (e.g. voice mechanisms like company councils) can all help to contain it. They prevent the basic antagonism that marks the employment relationship from manifesting itself in the form of disputes, industrial action, or other kinds of conflictual behaviour. Ultimately, though, the imbalance of power that exists between a relatively powerful employer and a relatively powerless individual employee, and the different interests that they have, means that employment relations has to be concerned with the ways in which employment relationships are contested, as well as how they are experienced and regulated.

Key terms and concepts

Agenda for Change: a national pay and grading scheme that covers employees in the National Health Service.

Annualized hours: arrangements that specify the number of hours to be worked by employees over a year, in return for a guaranteed wage.

Arbitration: a process of resolving disputes in which an independent third party proposes a settlement based on information supplied by, and the arguments of, the respective parties.

Coercive comparisons: a process used by multinational companies to compare the performance data of plants in different countries, in order to exert pressure on under-performing plants to improve.

Collective agreements: agreements that are the outcomes of collective bargaining exercises.

Collective bargaining: this term is used to refer to the process by which pay and other conditions of employment are regulated jointly by an employer, or employers' association, and one or more trade unions.

Conciliation: a process of resolving disputes in which an independent third party helps the parties to reach their own settlement.

Convergence: an approach to understanding the impact of globalization which emphasizes the growing degree of uniformity in employment relations arrangements around the world.

Custom and practice: tacit and informal expectations and understandings that govern behaviour at work.

Divergence: an approach to understanding the impact of globalization which emphasizes the persistence of national-level diversity in the employment relations arrangements of different countries.

Employee involvement and participation: arrangements that enable workers to exercise influence over organizational or workplace decisions, or that allow managers to communicate with their staff.

Employers' association: a body that represents the employment and employment relations interests of a collective group of employers, often on an industry-wide basis.

Employment tribunal: a quasi-judicial body that deals with complaints from workers that employers have failed to uphold their employment rights.

Equality bargaining: trade union initiatives that are designed to reduce disadvantage at work through interventions targeted at employers.

Equal opportunity: an approach to reducing employment disadvantage, which focuses on the use of formal procedures to ensure that people are treated the same regardless of their social and personal characteristics.

European Employment Strategy: an EU-level initiative designed to tackle unemployment, social exclusion, and labour market disadvantage by promoting employability and better quality jobs.

European works councils: arrangements that exist in multinational companies for informing and consulting with employee and trade union representatives at a European level.

Gangmaster: a person or organization responsible for supplying firms with labour on a casual, irregular basis, especially in sectors such as agriculture and food processing.

Gig economy: refers to arrangements whereby workers undertake irregular, one-off assignments ('gigs') for clients, often by means of online labour platforms.

Globalization: refers to the growing interconnectedness of economic activities across and beyond national borders.

Hard regulation: the use of legally binding methods to secure policy objectives.

Harmonization: a process whereby any differences in non-wage terms and conditions of employment between different groups of staff in the same organization are reduced and eradicated.

Horizontal segregation: the over-representation of a specific category of workers in some occupations, and their under-representation in others.

Industrial action: a term that is generally used to refer to more 'organized' manifestations of labour conflict, such as working to rule, and the strike.

International labour standards: arrangements for regulating the terms and conditions of employment relationships above and beyond individual nation states.

Joint consultation: a form of workplace and organizational decision-making under which managers submit their proposals to employees (or their representatives) to gauge their views, but retain the right to make the final decision.

Joint regulation: a term used to refer to the process by which terms and conditions of employment are determined jointly, as a result of bargaining between employers, or employers' associations, and one or more trade unions.

Juridification: a term used to refer to the way in which aspects of economic and social policy are regulated by the law.

Labour codes of conduct: voluntary arrangements under which multinational companies agree to uphold certain specified labour standards across their supply chains.

Labour conflict: a term that is generally used to refer to the broad range of behaviours that express the antagonistic basis of the employment relationship.

Living wage: a voluntary, minimum level of pay deemed necessary to enable workers to maintain an adequate standard of living.

Management style: the set of underlying principles that govern how employees are managed in particular organizations.

Managerial prerogative: managers' belief that they should exercise unilateral control over workplace relations.

Managing diversity: an approach to reducing employment disadvantage which is concerned with recognizing and celebrating individual differences between employees.

Mediation: a non-judgemental approach to resolving disputes, where the mediator helps the parties to reach an agreement.

Mobilization theory: a theoretical perspective used to explain why individual grievances are translated into collective action against employers.

Multi-employer bargaining: this term applies to situations where collective bargaining takes place between a collective group of employers, usually in the form of an employers' association, and one or more trade unions.

Multinational company: a firm that invests in, and is responsible for, subsidiaries located in territories beyond its home country base.

Negotiation: a process of resolving employment disputes through the presentation of arguments and compromise.

Neo-liberalism: a political and economic perspective which holds that economic prosperity is best achieved through deregulated markets, privatization, and weak trade unions.

Neo-unitary: a variant of the unitary perspective in which the emphasis is placed on the use of sophisticated human resource management practices to elicit employees' commitment.

Open Method of Coordination: a means of realizing the social and employment objectives of the European Union through voluntary, non-legally binding methods.

Overtime ban: a form of labour conflict which involves workers collectively refusing to undertake paid or unpaid overtime arrangements.

Partnership agreement: a term used to describe a formal relationship between an employer and a union that is based on the importance of cooperation and shared interests, rather than conflict.

Pay review body: independent bodies whose purpose is to make non-binding recommendations to government concerning the pay of particular groups of public sector workers.

Performance-related pay: an arrangement for determining pay that links an element of a worker's reward to some measure of their performance at work.

Pluralist: a perspective on employment relations that recognizes that employers and employees may have conflicting interests, but that these can be resolved to the mutual benefit of both by means of formal procedures, particularly bargaining relationships with trade unions.

Positive action: measures designed to correct the under-representation of certain groups of workers through interventions which help their employment prospects.

Positive discrimination: measures designed to correct the under-representation of certain groups of workers by giving them preferential treatment—this is unlawful in the UK.

Precariat: a category of workers, often comprising young people engaged in insecure, low-paid, and irregular jobs which offer few, if any, prospects for career progression.

Procedural agreement: a type of agreement that sets out the rules, or procedure, governing the relationship between the parties to it (such as the issues to be determined by collective bargaining, for example).

Protectionism: a political and economic perspective which holds that jobs in one's own country should be given priority over those in other countries.

Race to the bottom: an escalating process of weakened labour protections, caused by the tendency for multinationals to prefer investing in locations with low employment costs.

Radical: a perspective on employment relations that recognizes that employers and employees have potentially conflicting interests, which are so deep-rooted that when disputes arise they are incapable of being resolved to the mutual satisfaction of both parties.

Redundancy: a term used to refer to the dismissal of workers on the grounds that the number of workers required in a particular area has diminished.

Regime competition: the process by which multinational companies use investment and disinvestment decisions to encourage countries to dilute their labour regulations.

Secondary industrial action: sometimes referred to as 'sympathy' action, this term is used to describe action undertaken by a group of workers, who are not involved in a dispute with their own employer, to support another group of workers who are engaged in a dispute with their employer.

Self-employment: a form of employment under which an individual worker works for him or herself, and not under the control of another employer.

Shop steward: a term that is often used in the UK to refer to unpaid union representatives in the workplace.

Social class: hierarchical divisions in society which reflect differences in people's access to material resources and that influence their life chances.

Social clause: the part of a trade agreement that deals with non-economic matters, such as employment standards.

Social dialogue: a term that is used particularly by the European Union to refer to discussions, consultations, exchanges of information, and negotiations between the social partners.

Social dumping: a term that is used to refer to situations where multinational corporations redirect investment, and therefore jobs, to locations where the costs of employment are lower.

Social partners: a term that is commonly applied by the European Union to the representative bodies of employees, trade unions, and employers.

Soft regulation: the use of non-legally binding methods to secure policy objectives (e.g. guidelines, targets).

Sophisticated human resource management: an approach to managing people at work based on engaging employees and winning their commitment to the organization, as a means of driving improvements in business performance.

Status divide: refers to the differential treatment, in respect of non-wage terms and conditions of employment, accorded to different groups of workers in the same organization.

Statutory union recognition procedure: a legislative basis for establishing union recognition under certain defined circumstances.

Strike: the temporary withdrawal of labour by a group of workers, undertaken in order to express a grievance or to enforce a demand.

Substantive agreement: a type of agreement that covers the substance, or the outcomes, of a collective bargaining encounter.

Team briefing: a form of employee involvement and participation which involves front-line managers or supervisors sharing information with, and sometimes responding to queries from, their immediate staff.

Teamworking: a form of employee involvement and participation under which workers are organized collectively into specific groups for the purposes of making a product or delivering a service, sometimes with a degree of autonomy and self-management.

Trade union: a collective organization of working people which works to improve their terms and conditions of employment.

Tripartism: a term used to refer to arrangements that facilitate the involvement of three parties—the government, unions, employers—in economic and social policy-making.

Union derecognition: the act of an employer who decides not to maintain union recognition.

Union recognition: the act of an employer who agrees to enter into a formal relationship, usually involving collective bargaining, with a trade union.

Unitary: a perspective on employment relations that emphasizes the harmony of interests that exist between employers and their employees.

Vertical segregation: the over-representation of a specific category of workers in low-paid and poorly skilled jobs, and their under-representation in managerial roles.

Voluntarism: a term that is used to describe the absence of state intervention in relations between employers and their employees, and between employers and trade unions.

Voluntary redundancy: a form of redundancy whereby workers supposedly put themselves forward for dismissal, in return for an enhanced severance payment.

Work intensification: a term that is used to describe the process of greater work effort.

Work-to-rule: a form of industrial action where the workers involved refuse to carry out a part, or parts, of their normal duties while continuing to attend work.

Zero-hours contract: a contract of employment that does not guarantee, or specify, the number of hours to be worked, or when they are to be worked.

Bibliography

Abbott, B. (2004). 'Worker representation through the Citizens' Advice Bureaux', in G. Healy, E. Heery, P. Taylor, and W. Brown (eds.), *The Future of Worker Representation*. London: Routledge, 245–63.

Abbott, B. (2007). 'Workplace and employment characteristics of the Citizens Advice Bureau clients'. *Employee Relations*, 29/3: 262–79.

Ackers, P. (2011). 'Finding the future in the past? The social philosophy of Oxford industrial relations pluralism', in K. Townsend and A. Wilkinson (eds.), *The Edward Elgar Research Handbook on Work and Employment Relations*. Cheltenham: Edward Elgar, 45–66.

Ackers, P. (2015). 'Trade unions as professional associations', in S. Johnstone and P. Ackers (eds.), *Finding a Voice at Work? New Perspectives on Employment Relations*. Oxford: Oxford University Press, 95–126.

Ackers, P. and Wilkinson, A. (2003). 'Introduction: the British industrial relations tradition—formation, breakdown and salvage', in P. Ackers and A. Wilkinson (eds.), *Understanding Work and Employment: Industrial Relations in Transition*. Oxford: Oxford University Press, 1–27.

Ackers, P. and Wilkinson, A. (2005). 'British industrial relations paradigm: a critical outline history and prognosis'. *Journal of Industrial Relations*, 47/4: 443–56.

Ackroyd, S. and Proctor, S. (1998). 'British manufacturing organization and workplace industrial relations: some attributes of the new flexible firm'. *British Journal of Industrial Relations*, 36/2: 163–83.

Ackroyd, S. and Thompson, P. (1999). *Organizational Misbehaviour*. London: Sage.

Adam-Smith, D., Norris, G., and Williams, S. (2003). 'Continuity or change? The implications of the National Minimum Wage for work and employment in the hospitality industry'. *Work, Employment and Society*, 17/1: 29–45.

Adams, A., Hood, A., and Levell, P. (2014). 'The squeeze on incomes', in C. Emmerson, P. Johnson, and H. Miller (eds.), *The IFS Green Budget 2014*. London: IFS, 126–40.

Adams, Z. and Deakin, S. (2014). *Re-regulating Zero-hours Contracts*. Liverpool: Institute of Employment Rights.

Adnett, N. and Hardy, S. (2005). *The European Social Model: Modernisation or Evolution?* Cheltenham: Edward Elgar.

Advisory, Conciliation, and Arbitration Service (ACAS) (2010). *Managing Attendance and Employee Turnover*. London: ACAS.

Advisory, Conciliation, and Arbitration Service (ACAS) (2014a). *Managing Conflict at Work*. London: ACAS.

Advisory, Conciliation, and Arbitration Service (ACAS) (2014b). *Handling Large Scale Redundancies*. London: ACAS.

Advisory, Conciliation, and Arbitration Service (ACAS) (2014c). *Give and Take? Unravelling the True Nature of Zero-hours Contracts*. London: ACAS.

Advisory, Conciliation, and Arbitration Service (ACAS) (2015a). *Code of Practice on Disciplinary and Grievance Procedures*. London: ACAS.

Advisory, Conciliation, and Arbitration Service (ACAS) (2015b). *Discipline and Grievances at Work: The ACAS Guide*. London: ACAS.

Advisory, Conciliation, and Arbitration Service (ACAS) (2015c). *Advisory, Conciliation, and Arbitration Service Annual Report and Accounts 2014/15*. HC 282. London: ACAS.

Ahlstrand, B. (1990). *The Quest for Productivity: A Case Study of Fawley after Flanders*. Cambridge: Cambridge University Press.

Aitkenhead, M. and Liff, S. (1991). 'The effectiveness of equal opportunities policies', in J. Firth-Cozens and M. West (eds.), *Women at Work*. Buckingham: Open University Press, 26–41.

Alakeson, V. and D'Arcy, C. (2014). *Zeroing In: Balancing Flexibility and Protection in the Reform of Zero-Hours Contracts*. London: Resolution Foundation.

Alberti, G. (2016a). 'Moving beyond the dichotomy of workplace and community unionism: the challenges of organising migrant workers in London's hotels'. *Economic and Industrial Democracy*, 37/1: 73–94.

Alberti, G. (2016b). 'Mobilizing and bargaining at the edge of informality: the "3 Cosas Campaign" by outsourced migrant workers at the University of London'. *Working USA*, 19: 81–103.

Albin, E. and Mantouvalou, V. (2012). 'The ILO Convention on Domestic Workers: from the shadows to the light'. *Industrial Law Journal*, 41/1: 67–78.

Alexander, A. (2013). 'Egyptian workers rediscover the strike', in G. Gall (ed.), *New Forms and Expressions of Conflict at Work*. Basingstoke: Palgrave Macmillan, 130–51.

Alfes, K., Truss, C., Soane, E., Rees, C., and Gatenby, M. (2013). 'The relationship between line manager behavior, perceived HRM practices, and individual performance: examining the mediating role of engagement'. *Human Resource Management*, 52/6: 839–59.

Almond, P., Edwards, T., Colling, T., Ferner, A., Gunnigle, P., Müller-Camen, M., Quintanilla, J., and Wächter, H. (2005). 'Unravelling home and host country effects: an investigation of the HR policies of an American multinational in four European countries'. *Industrial Relations*, 44/2: 276–306.

Almond, P. and Ferner, A. (eds.) (2006). *American Multinationals in Europe*. Oxford: Oxford University Press.

Alston, P. (2004). '"Core labour standards" and the transformation of the international labour rights regime'. *European Journal of International Law*, 15/3: 457–521.

Amnesty International (2016). *The Ugly Side of the Beautiful Game: Exploitation of Migrant Workers in a Qatar 2022 World Cup Site*. London: Amnesty International.

Anderman, S. (1986). 'Unfair dismissals and redundancy', in R. Lewis (ed.), *Labour Law in Britain*. Oxford: Basil Blackwell, 415–47.

Anderson, B. (2010). 'Migration, immigration controls and the fashioning of precarious workers'. *Work, Employment and Society*, 24/2: 300–17.

Anderson, L. (2003). 'Sound bite legislation: the Employment Act 2002 and the new flexible working "rights" for parents'. *Industrial Law Journal*, 32/1: 37–42.

Anderson, P. (2009). 'Intermediate occupations and the conceptual and empirical limitations of the hourglass economy thesis'. *Work, Employment, and Society*, 23/1: 169–80.

Anderson, P. (2011). *The New Old World* (paperback edn). London: Verso.

Anner, M., Greer, I., Hauptmeier, M., Lillie, N., and Winchester, N. (2006). 'The industrial determinants of transnational solidarity: global interunion politics in three sectors'. *European Journal of Industrial Relations*, 12/7: 7–27.

Applebaum, E. and Batt, R. (2014). *Private Equity at Work: When Wall Street Manages Main Street*. New York: Russell Sage Foundation.

Arrowsmith, J. (2002). 'The struggle over working time in nineteenth and twentieth century Britain'. *Historical Studies in Industrial Relations*, 13: 83–117.

Arrowsmith, J. (2007). 'Why is there not more "annualised hours" working in Britain?' *Industrial Relations Journal*, 38/5: 423–38.

Arrowsmith, J. (2009). 'Regulating pay: the UK's national minimum wage', in S. Corby, S. Palmer, and E. Lindop (eds.), *Rethinking Reward*. Basingstoke: Palgrave Macmillan, 120–38.

Arrowsmith, J. and Marginson, P. (2010). 'The decline of incentive pay in British manufacturing'. *Industrial Relations Journal*, 41/4: 289–311.

Arrowsmith, J. and Marginson, P. (2011). 'Variable pay and collective bargaining in British retail banking'. *British Journal of Industrial Relations*, 49/1: 54–79.

Arrowsmith, J., Nicholaisen, H., Bechter, B., and Nonell, R. (2010). 'The management of variable pay in European banking'. *The International Journal of Human Resource Management*, 21/15: 2716–40.

Arrowsmith, J. and Sisson, K. (1999). 'Pay and working time: towards organization-based systems?' *British Journal of Industrial Relations*, 37/1: 57–75.

Arrowsmith, J. and Sisson, K. (2000). 'Managing working time', in S. Bach and K. Sisson (eds.), *Personnel Management* (3rd edn). Oxford: Blackwell, 287–313.

Ashley, L. (2010). 'Making a difference? The use (and abuse) of diversity management at the UK's elite law firms'. *Work, Employment, and Society*, 24/4: 711–27.

Ashley, L. and Empson, L. (2016). 'Understanding social exclusion in elite professional service firms: field level dynamics and the "professional project"'. *Work, Employment, and Society*, DOI: 10.1177/0950017015621480

Aston, J., Hill, D., and Tackey, N. (2006). *The Experience of Claimants in Race Discrimination Employment Tribunals*. DTI Employment Research Series No. 55. London: DTI.

Atkinson, A. and McKay, S. (2005). *Child Support Reform: The Views and Experiences of CSA Staff and New Clients*. Department for Work and Pensions Research Report No. 232. London: Department for Work and Pensions.

Atkinson, C., Mallet, O., and Wapshott, R. (2016). '"You try to be a fair employer": regulation and employment relationships in medium-sized firms'. *International Small Business Journal*, 34/1: 16–33.

Atzeni, M. (2009). 'Searching for injustice and finding solidarity? A contribution to the mobilization theory debate'. *Industrial Relations Journal*, 40/1: 5–16.

Auerbach, S. (1990). *Legislating for Conflict*. Oxford: Clarendon.

Baccaro, L. and Howell, C. (2011). 'A common neoliberal trajectory: the transformation of industrial relations in advanced capitalism'. *Politics and Society*, 39/4: 521–63.

Bach, S. (2010). 'Public sector industrial relations: the challenge of modernisation', in T. Colling and M. Terry (eds.), *Industrial Relations: Theory and Practice* (3rd edn). Chichester: John Wiley, 151–77.

Bach, S. (2011). 'Assistant roles in a modernised public service: towards a new professionalism?', in S. Corby and G. Symon (eds.), *Working for the State*. Basingstoke: Palgrave Macmillan, 129–46.

Bach, S. (2012). 'Shrinking the state or the Big Society? Public service employment relations in an era of austerity'. *Industrial Relations Journal*, 43/5: 399–415.

Bach, S. (2016). 'Britain: contracting the state. Public service employment relations in a period of crisis', in S. Bach and L. Bordogna (eds.), *Public Service Management and Employment Relations in Europe: Emerging from the Crisis*. New York and Abingdon: Routledge, 136–63.

Bach, S. and Kessler, I. (2012). *The Modernisation of the Public Sector and Employee Relations: Targeted Change*. Basingstoke: Palgrave Macmillan.

Bach, S., Kessler, I., and Heron, P. (2006). 'Changing job boundaries and workforce reform: the case of teaching assistants'. *Industrial Relations Journal*, 37/1: 2–21.

Bach, S., Kolins Givan, R., and Forth, J. (2009). 'The public sector in transition', in W. Brown, A. Bryson, J. Forth, and K. Whitfield (eds.), *The Evolution of the Modern Workplace*. Cambridge: Cambridge University Press, 307–31.

Bacon, N. (1999). 'Union derecognition and the new human relations: a steel industry case study'. *Work, Employment and Society*, 13/1: 1–17.

Bacon, N. and Hoque, K. (2012). 'The role and impact of trade union equality representatives in Britain'. *British Journal of Industrial Relations*, 50/2: 239–62.

Bacon, N. and Hoque, K. (2015). 'The influence of trade union disability champions on employer disability policy and practice'. *Human Resource Management Journal*, 25/2: 233–49.

Bacon, N. and Samuel, P. (2009). 'Partnership agreement adoption and survival in the British private and public sectors'. *Work, Employment and Society*, 23/2: 231–48.

Bacon, N. and Wright, M. (2008). 'Private equity: friend or foe? The case for'. *People Management*, 21 August: 21–2.

Bacon, N., Wright, M., Scholes, L., and Meuleman, M. (2010). 'Assessing the impact of private equity on industrial relations in Europe'. *Human Relations*, 63/9: 1343–70.

Badigannavar, V. and Kelly, J. (2004). 'Labour-management partnership in the UK public sector', in J. Kelly and P. Willman (eds.), *Union Organization and Activity*. London: Routledge, 110–28.

Badigannavar, V. and Kelly, J. (2005). 'Why are some union organizing campaigns more successful than others?' *British Journal of Industrial Relations*, 43/3: 515–35.

Badigannavar, V. and Kelly, J. (2011). 'Partnership and organizing: an empirical assessment of two contrasting approaches to union revitalization in the UK'. *Economic and Industrial Democracy*, 32/1: 5–27.

Bailey, C., Madden, A., Alfes, K., and Fletcher, L. (2015). 'The meaning, antecedents and outcomes of employee engagement: a narrative synthesis'. *International Journal of Management Reviews*, DOI: 10.1111/ijmr.12077

Bain, G. and Price, R. (1983). 'Union growth: dimensions, determinants and destiny', in G. Bain (ed.), *Industrial Relations in Britain*. Oxford: Basil Blackwell, 3–33.

Balch, A. (2015). 'Understanding and evaluating UK efforts to tackle forced labour', in G. Craig, L. Waite, H. Lewis, and H. Skrivankova (eds.), *Vulnerability, Exploitation, and Migrants: Insecure Work in a Globalised Economy*. Basingstoke: Palgrave Macmillan, 86–98.

Balch, A. (2016). 'Tightening the grip: the coalition government and migrant workers', in S. Williams and P. Scott (eds.), *Employment Relations under Coalition Government: The UK Experience, 2010-2015*. Abingdon: Routledge, 144–64.

Baldamus, W. (1961). *Efficiency and Effort*. London: Tavistock.

Baldry, C., Bain, P., Taylor, P., Hyman, J., Scholarios, D., Marks, A., Watson, A., Gilbert, K., Gall, G., and Bunzel, D. (2007). *The Meaning of Work in the New Economy*. Basingstoke: Palgrave Macmillan.

Balsiger, P. (2014). *The Fight for Ethical Fashion: The Origins and Interactions of the Clean Clothes Movement*. Farnham: Ashgate.

Bandasz, K. (2014). 'A framework agreement in the hairdressing sector: the European social dialogue at a crossroads'. *Transfer*, 20/4: 505–20.

Bank Muñoz, C. (2008). *Transnational Tortillas: Race, Gender, and Shop-Floor Politics in Mexico and the United States*. Ithaca NY: ILR Press.

Bara, A. and Arber, S. (2009). 'Working shifts and mental health—findings from the British Household Panel Survey (1995-2005)'. *Scandinavian Journal of Work, Environment, and Health*, 35/5: 361–7.

Barley, S. and Kunda, G. (2004). *Gurus, Hired Guns, and Warm Bodies*. Princeton NJ: Princeton University Press.

Barnard, C. (2009). '"British jobs for British workers": the Lindsey Oil Refinery dispute and the future of local labour clauses in an integrated EU market'. *Industrial Law Journal*, 38/3: 245–77.

Barnard, C. (2012). 'The financial crisis and the Euro Plus Pact: a labour lawyer's perspective'. *Industrial Law Journal*, 41/1: 98–114.

Barnard, C., Deakin, S., and Hobbs, R. (2003). 'Opting out of the 48-hour week: employer necessity or individual choice? An empirical study of the operation of article 18(1)(b) of the Working Time Directive in the UK'. *Industrial Law Journal*, 32/4: 223–52.

Barnard, C. and Ludlow, A. (2016). 'Enforcement of employment rights by EU-8 migrant workers in employment tribunals'. *Industrial Law Journal*, 45/1: 1–28.

Barnard, C., Ludlow, A., and Fraser Butlin, S. (2016). 'Why Minimum Wage? Why Enforcement of EU Migrants' Employment Rights Matters', LSE BrexitVote blog: http://blogs.lse.ac.uk/brexitvote/2016/05/11/why-the-failure-to-enforce-eu-workers-employment-rights-matters/

Barnes, C. (1992). 'Disability and employment'. *Personnel Review*, 21/6: 55–73.

Barnett, E. (2011). 'Employers warned about snooping on staff via social networks'. *The Telegraph*, 1 September, http://www.telegraph.co.uk/technology/news/8734904/Employers-warned-about-snooping-on-staff-via-social-networks.html

Barrientos, S., Mayer, F., Pickles, J., and Posthuma, A. (2011). 'Decent work in global production networks: framing the policy debate'. *International Labour Review*, 150/3–4: 299–317.

Barrientos, S. and Smith, S. (2006). *The ETI Code of Labour Practice: Do Workers Really Benefit?* University of Sussex: Institute of Development Studies.

Barry, M. and Wilkinson, A. (2011). 'Re-examining comparative employment relations', in M. Barry and A. Wilkinson (eds.), *Research Handbook of Comparative Employment Relations*. Cheltenham: Edward Elgar, 3–21.

Barry, M. and Wilkinson, A. (2016). 'Pro-social or pro-management? A critique of the conception of employee voice as a pro-social behaviour within organizational behaviour'. *British Journal of Industrial Relations*, 54/2: 261–84.

Bartley, T. (2007). 'Institutional emergence in an era of globalization: the rise of transnational private regulation of labor and environmental conditions'. *American Journal of Sociology*, 113/2: 297–351.

Bassett, P. (1987). *Strike Free*. London: Papermac.

Batstone, E., Boraston, I., and Frenkel, S. (1978). *The Social Organization of Strikes*. Oxford: Basil Blackwell.

BBC Democracy Live (2012). 'Westminster Hall Debate', 26 April, http://news.bbc.co.uk/democracylive/hi/house_of_commons/newsid_9715000/9715541.stm

BBC News (2009a). 'Striking workers stand firm on British jobs', 4 February, http://news.bbc.co.uk/1/hi/england/humber/7869873.stm

BBC News (2009b). 'Job cuts at Mini spark angry rows', 16 February, http://news.bbc.co.uk/1/hi/business/7891913.stm

BBC News (2009c). 'Sacked Mini workers express anger', 16 February, http://news.bbc.co.uk/1/hi/business/7892174.stm

BBC News (2009d). 'Cap on junior doctor hours starts', 1 August, http://news.bbc.co.uk/1/hi/health/8177878.stm

BBC News (2011). 'MP Charlotte Leslie wants to scrap doctors hours rule', 13 May, http://www.bbc.co.uk/news/uk-england-bristol-13386320

BBC News (2012a). 'Five million paid less than living wages, says KPMG', 29 October, http://www.bbc.co.uk/news/business-20104177

BBC News (2012b). 'Southampton council pay cuts will be reversed', 16 August, http://www.bbc.co.uk/news/uk-england-hampshire-19288806

BBC News (2013a). 'GMB union holds protests at Amazon sites', 13 February, http://www.bbc.co.uk/news/uk-21444710

BBC News (2013b). 'Back-to-work scheme breached laws, says Court of Appeal', 12 February, http://www.bbc.co.uk/news/business-21426928

BBC News (2014a) 'City Link parcel delivery company goes into administration', 25 December, http://www.bbc.co.uk/news/business-30602326

BBC News (2014b). 'Doncaster care workers start 21-day strike over pay', 25 August http://www.bbc.co.uk/news/uk-england-south-yorkshire-28925893

BBC News (2016). 'Relax Sunday trading laws to help shops, MPs say', 21 February, http://www.bbc.co.uk/news/uk-35623976

BBC Online (2013). 'The Great British Class Survey', http://www.bbc.co.uk/labuk/experiments/the-great-british-class-survey

BBC Panorama (2011). *All Work and Low Pay*, BBC One, 3 October.

BBC Panorama (2013a). *Amazon: the Truth Behind the Click*, BBC One, 25 November.

BBC Panorama (2013b). *Blacklist Britain*, BBC One, 10 June.

BBC Panorama (2014). *Apple's Broken Promises*, BBC One, 18 December.

Beaumont, P. (1981). 'Trade union recognition: the British experience 1976–1980'. *Employee Relations*, 3/6: 2–39.

Beaumont, P. and Harris, R. (1990). 'Union recruitment and organising attempts in Britain in the 1980s'. *Industrial Relations Journal*, 21/4: 274–86.

Beauregard, T. and Henry, L. (2009). 'Making the link between work–life balance practices and organizational performance'. *Human Resource Management Review*, 19/1: 9–22.

BECTU (2015a). 'Royal Albert Hall staff vote for BECTU recognition'. BECTU Press Release, 5 August, https://www.bectu.org.uk/news/2454

BECTU (2015b). 'Royal Albert Hall rejects staff vote for BECTU recognition'. BECTU Press Release, 21 September, https://www.bectu.org.uk/news/2466

Beech, M. (2015). 'The ideology of the Coalition: More liberal than conservative', in M. Beech and S. Lee (eds.), *The Conservative–Liberal Coalition: Examining the Cameron-Clegg Government*. Basingstoke: Palgrave Macmillan, 1–15.

Behling, F. and Harvey, M. (2015). 'The evolution of false self-employment in the British construction industry: a neo-Polanyian account of labour market formation'. *Work, Employment, and Society*, 29/6: 969–88.

Behrend, H. (1957). 'The effort bargain'. *Industrial and Labor Relations Review*, 10/4: 503–15.

Belfield, C., Cribb, J., Hood, A., and Joyce, R. (2016). *Living Standards, Poverty, and Inequality in the UK: 2016*. London: Institute for Fiscal Studies.

Bennett, F. and Lister, R. (2010). *The 'Living Wage': The Right Answer to Low Pay?* London: Fabian Society.

Berry, C. (2014). 'Quantity over quality: a political economy of "active labour market policy" in the UK'. *Policy Studies*, 35/6: 592–614.

Bewley, H. (2006). 'Raising the standard? The regulation of employment, and public sector employment policy'. *British Journal of Industrial Relations*, 44/2: 351–72.

Bewley, H. and Fernie, S. (2003). 'What do unions do for women?', in H. Gospel and S. Wood (eds.), *Representing Workers*. London: Routledge, 92–118.

Beynon, H. (1973). *Working for Ford*. Harmondsworth: Penguin.

Beynon, H. (ed.) (1985). *Digging Deeper: Issues in the Miners' Strike*. London: Verso.

Beynon, H., Grimshaw, D., Rubery, J., and Ward, K. (2002). *Managing Employment Change*. Oxford: Oxford University Press.

Bhagwati, J. (2004). *In Defense of Globalization*. Oxford: Oxford University Press.

Bieler, A., Lindberg, I., and Pillay, D. (eds.) (2008). *Labour and the Challenges of Globalization*. London: Pluto.

Bieling, H.-J. (2012). 'EU facing the crisis: social and employment policies in times of tight budgets'. *Transfer: European Review of Labour and Research*, 18/3: 255–71.

Birkwood, S. (2015). 'Royal Albert Hall refuses recognition to trade union Bectu'. *Third Sector Digital*, 20 October, http://www.thirdsector.co.uk/royal-albert-hall-refuses-recognition-trade-union-bectu/management/article/1369127

Bittman, M. (2016). 'Working time', in S. Edgell, H. Gottfried, and E. Granter (eds.), *The SAGE Handbook of the Sociology of Work and Employment*. London: SAGE, 520–40.

Blackburn, D. and Puerto, M. (2013). 'Colombia: the most dangerous place to be a union member', in G. Gall and T. Dundon (eds.), *Global Anti-Unionism: Nature, Dynamics, Trajectories and Outcomes*. Basingstoke: Palgrave Macmillan, 184–206.

Blakemore, K. and Drake, R. (1996). *Understanding Equal Opportunity Policies*. Hemel Hempstead: Harvester-Wheatsheaf.

Blanchflower, D. (2015). 'As good as it gets? The UK labour market in recession and recovery'. *National Institute Economic Review*, 231: F76–80.

Blanchflower, D. and Bryson, A. (2009). 'Trade union decline and the economics of the workplace', in W. Brown, A. Bryson, J. Forth, and K. Whitfield (eds.), *The Evolution of the Modern Workplace*. Cambridge: Cambridge University Press, 48–73.

Blanden, J., Machin, S., and Van Reenen, J. (2006). 'Have unions turned the corner? New evidence on recent trends in union recognition in UK firms'. *British Journal of Industrial Relations*, 44/2: 169–90.

Blyton, P. (2011). 'Working time, work–life balance and inequality', in P. Blyton, E. Heery, and P. Turnbull (eds.), *Reassessing the Employment Relationship*. Basingstoke: Palgrave Macmillan, 299–317.

Blyton, P., Heery, E., and Turnbull, P. (2011). 'Reassessing the employment relationship: an introduction', in P. Blyton, E. Heery, and P. Turnbull (eds.), *Reassessing the Employment Relationship*. Basingstoke: Palgrave Macmillan, 1–17.

Blyton, P. and Jenkins, J. (2012). 'Life after Burberry: shifting experiences of work and non-work life following redundancy', *Work, Employment and Society*, 26/1: 26–41.

Blyton, P. and Jenkins, J. (2013). 'Mobilizing protest: insights from two factory closures'. *British Journal of Industrial Relations*, 51/4: 733–53.

Blyton, P. and Turnbull, P. (2004). *The Dynamics of Employee Relations* (3rd edn). Basingstoke: Palgrave Macmillan.

Boffey, D. (2014). 'Care UK workers celebrate pay offer to end 90 days of strikes', *The Guardian*, 8 November, http://www.theguardian.com/society/2014/nov/08/care-uk-workers-celebrate-pay-offer-strikes

Bogg, A. (2012). 'The death of statutory union recognition in the United Kingdom'. *Journal of Industrial Relations*, 54/3: 409–25.

Bogg, A. and Ewing, K. (2014). 'The implications of the RMT case'. *Industrial Law Journal*, 43/3: 221–52.

Bolton, S. (2004). *Emotion Management in the Workplace*. Basingstoke: Palgrave Macmillan.

Bonner, C. and Gollan, P. (2005). 'A bridge over troubled water: a decade of representation at South West Water'. *Employee Relations*, 27/3: 238–58.

Booth, R. (2016). 'UN gives Qatar a year to end forced labour of migrant workers'. *The Guardian*, 24 March, http://www.theguardian.com/world/2016/mar/24/un-gives-qatar-year-end-forced-labour-migrant-workers

Booth, R., Evans, T., and Osborne, H. (2016). 'Revealed: delivery giant Hermes pays some couriers less than living wage'. *The Guardian*, 18 July, https://www.theguardian.com/society/2016/jul/18/hermes-couriers-paying-staff-less-than-living-wage

Bowers, S. (2015). 'Amazon's UK business paid just £11.9m in tax last year'. *The Guardian*, 24 June, https://www.theguardian.com/technology/2015/jun/24/amazons-uk-business-paid-119m-tax-last-year

Boxall, P. and Purcell, J. (2011). *Strategy and Human Resource Management* (3rd edn). Basingstoke: Palgrave Macmillan.

Boyd, S. (2012). 'Amazon is a tax avoider because Amazon is a predatory, anti-union employer'. *Union-News.co.uk*, 13 April, http://union-news.co.uk/2012/04/amazon-is-a-tax-avoider-because-amazon-is-a-predatory-anti-union-employer/

Bradley, H. (1989). *Men's Work, Women's Work*. Cambridge: Polity.

Bradley, H. (1999). *Gender and Power in the Workplace*. Basingstoke: Macmillan.

Bradley, H. (2014). 'Class descriptors or class relations? Thoughts towards a critique of Savage et al'. *Sociology*, 48/3: 429–36.

Bradley, H., Erickson, M., Stephenson, C., and Williams, S. (2000). *Myths at Work*. Cambridge: Polity.

Bradley, H. and Healy, G. (2008). *Ethnicity and Gender at Work*. Basingstoke: Palgrave Macmillan.

Bradley, H., Healy, G., and Mukherjee, N. (2002). *Inclusion, Exclusion and Separate Organisation—Black Women Activists in Trade Unions*. ESRC Future of Work Programme, Working Paper No. 25. Swindon: ESRC.

Brannen, P. (1983). *Authority and Participation in Industry*. London: Batsford.

Breman, J. (2013). 'A bogus concept'. *New Left Review*, 84: 130–8.

Brett, S. (2016). 'Behind the government's tough talk on tackling worker exploitation'. *Touchstone*, 15 January, http://touchstoneblog.org.uk/2016/01/behind-the-governments-tough-talk-on-tackling-worker-exploitation/

Brewer, M., Muriel, A., Phillips, D., and Sibieta, L. (2008). *Poverty and Inequality in the UK: 2008*. IFS Commentary No. 105. London: Institute for Fiscal Studies.

Bridgford, J. and Stirling, J. (1994). *Employee Relations in Europe*. Oxford: Blackwell.

Brinkley, I. (2012). 'Technology is stretching the working day, but it doesn't have to be bad news'. *The Guardian*, 27 June, http://www.guardian.co.uk/commentisfree/2012/jun/27/technology-stretching-working-day-bad-news?INTCMP=SRCH

Brinkley, I. (2016). *In Search of the Gig Economy*. London: The Work Foundation.

Briskin, L. (2014). 'Austerity, union policy, and gender equality bargaining'. *Transfer*, 20/1: 115–33.

British Universities Industrial Relations Association (BUIRA) (2009). 'What's the point of industrial relations?', in R. Darlington (ed.), *What's the Point of Industrial Relations? In Defence of Critical Social Science*. London: BUIRA, 46–59.

Brodtkorb, T. (2012). 'Statutory union recognition in the UK: a work in progress'. *Industrial Relations Journal*, 43/1: 70–84.

Bronfenbrenner, K. and Juravich, T. (1998). 'It takes more than house calls: organizing to win with a comprehensive union-building strategy', in K. Bronfenbrenner, S. Friedman, R. Hurd, R. Oswald, and R. Seeber (eds.), *Organizing to Win: New Research on Union Strategies*. Ithaca NY: ILR Press, 19–36.

Brown, D. (2001). 'Labor standards: where do they belong on the international trade agenda?'. *Journal of Economic Perspectives*, 15/3: 89–112.

Brown, D. and Crossman, A. (2000). 'Employer strategies in the face of a national minimum wage: an analysis of the hotel sector'. *Industrial Relations Journal*, 31/3: 206–19.

Brown, G. (1977). *Sabotage*. Nottingham: Spokesman.

Brown, W. (1973). *Piecework Bargaining*. London: Heinemann.

Brown, W. (ed.) (1981). *The Changing Contours of British Industrial Relations*. Oxford: Basil Blackwell.

Brown, W. (2000). 'Putting partnership into practice in Britain'. *British Journal of Industrial Relations*, 38/2: 299–316.

Brown, W. (2009). 'The process of fixing the British National Minimum Wage, 1997–2007'. *British Journal of Industrial Relations*, 47/2: 429–43.

Brown, W. (2010). 'Negotiation and collective bargaining', in T. Colling and M. Terry (eds.), *Industrial Relations: Theory and Practice* (3rd edn). Chichester: John Wiley, 255–74.

Brown, W. (2011). 'Industrial relations under New Labour, 1997–2010: a post mortem'. *Journal of Industrial Relations*, 47/2: 402–13.

Brown, W. (2014). 'Third-party processes in employment relations', in W. Roche, P. Teague, and A. Colvin (eds.), *The Oxford Handbook of Conflict Management in Organizations*. Oxford: Oxford University Press, 135–49.

Brown, W., Bryson, A., and Forth, J. (2009). 'Competition and the retreat from collective bargaining', in W. Brown, A. Bryson, J. Forth, and K. Whitfield (eds.), *The Evolution of the Modern Workplace*. Cambridge: Cambridge University Press, 22–47.

Brown, W., Deakin, S., Hudson, M., and Pratten, C. (2001). 'The limits of statutory union recognition'. *Industrial Relations Journal*, 32/3: 180–94.

Brown, W., Marginson, P., and Walsh, J. (1995). 'Management: pay determination and collective bargaining', in P. Edwards (ed.), *Industrial Relations: Theory and Practice in Britain*. Oxford: Blackwell, 123–50.

Brown, W., Marginson, P., and Walsh, J. (2003). 'The management of pay as the influence of collective bargaining declines', in P. Edwards (ed.), *Industrial Relations* (2nd edn). Oxford: Blackwell, 189–213.

Brown, W. and Marsden, D. (2011). 'Individualization and growing diversity of employment relationships', in D. Marsden (ed.), *Employment in the Lean Years: Policy and Prospects for the Next Decade*. Oxford: Oxford University Press, 73–86.

Brown, W. and Nash, D. (2008). 'What has been happening to collective bargaining under New Labour?' *Industrial Relations Journal*, 39/2: 91–103.

Brown, W. and Nolan, P. (1988). 'Wages and labour productivity: the contribution of industrial relations research to the understanding of pay determination'. *British Journal of Industrial Relations*, 26/3: 339–61.

Brown, W. and Walsh, J. (1991). 'Pay determination in Britain in the 1980s; the anatomy of decentralization'. *Oxford Review of Economic Policy*, 7/1: 44–59.

Brown, W. and Walsh, J. (1994). 'Managing pay in Britain', in K. Sisson (ed.), *Personnel Management* (2nd edn). Oxford: Blackwell, 437–64.

Buckley, M. (2013). 'Locating neoliberalism in Dubai: migrant workers and class struggle in the autocratic city'. *Antipode*, 45/2: 256–74.

Budd, J. (2004). *Employment with a Human Face: Balancing Efficiency, Equity, and Voice*. Ithaca NY: Cornell University Press.

Budd, J. (2011). *The Thought of Work*. Ithaca NY: Cornell University Press.

Budd, J. and Bhave, D. (2008). 'Values, ideologies and frames of reference in industrial relations', in P. Blyton, N. Bacon, J. Fiorito, and E. Heery (eds.), *The SAGE Handbook of Industrial Relations*. London: Sage, 92–112.

Budd, J., Gollan, P., and Wilkinson, A. (2010). 'New approaches to employee voice and participation'. *Human Relations*, 63/3: 1–8.

Bulut, T. and Lane, C. (2011). 'The private regulation of labour standards and rights in the global clothing industry: an evaluation of its effectiveness in two developing countries'. *New Political Economy*, 16/1: 41–71.

Burchell, B. (2002). 'The prevalence and redistribution of job insecurity and work intensification', in B. Burchell, D. Ladipo, and F. Wilkinson (eds.), *Job Insecurity and Work Intensification*. London: Routledge, 61–76.

Burchell, B., Day, D., Hudson, M., Ladipo, D., Mankelow, R., Nolan, J., Reed, H., Wichert, I., and Wilkinson, F. (1999). *Job Insecurity and Work Intensification*. York: Joseph Rowntree Foundation.

Burchill, F. (2000). 'The pay review body system: a comment and a consequence'. *Historical Studies in Industrial Relations*, 10/3: 141–57.

Burton, B. (2014). 'Neoliberalism and the Equality Act 2010: a missed opportunity for gender justice?' *Industrial Law Journal*, 43/2: 122–48.

Business in the Community (BITC) (2015). *Race at Work 2015*. London: BITC.

Butcher, T. (2012). 'Still evidence-based? The role of policy evaluation in recession and beyond: the case of the National Minimum Wage'. *National Institute Economic Review*, 219/1: R26–R40.

Butler, P. (2009). 'Non-union employee representation: exploring the riddle of managerial strategy'. *Industrial Relations Journal*, 40/3: 198–214.

Butler, P., Lavelle, J., Gunnigle, P., and O'Sullivan, M. (2015). 'Skating on thin ICE? A critical evaluation of a decade of research on the British Information and Consultation regulations'. *Economic and Industrial Democracy*, DOI:10.1177/0143831X15610205

Butler, S. (2013). 'Three factory safety deals in Bangladesh aim to improve conditions'. *The Guardian*, 23 October, http://www.theguardian.com/world/2013/oct/23/factory-safety-bangladesh-rana-plaza

Butler, S. (2016a). 'Amazon says "business as usual" with plans to hire 1,000 extra staff'. *The Guardian*, 6 July, https://www.theguardian.com/technology/2016/jul/06/amazon-hire-1000-extra-staff-one-hour-delivery-service-prime-now

Butler, S. (2016b). 'Employers claw back living wage in cuts to perks, hours, and pay'. *The Guardian*, 16 April, https://www.theguardian.com/uk-news/2016/apr/16/employers-claw-back-national-living-wage-cuts-pay-perks

Byford, I. (2009). 'Union renewal and young people: some positive indications from British supermarkets', in G. Gall (ed.), *Union Organising: Current Practice, Future Prospects*. London, Palgrave Macmillan, 223–38.

Byford, I. (2011). 'The effectiveness of the organising model in higher education'. *Employee Relations*, 33/3: 289–303.

Cabrita, J. (2015a). 'Doors opening for more Sunday working in the EU'. *Eurofound*, 1 September, http://www.eurofound.europa.eu/observatories/eurwork/articles/working-conditions-law-and-regulation/doors-opening-for-more-sunday-work-in-the-eu

Cabrita, J. (2015b). *Opting out of the European Working Time Directive*. Dublin: Eurofound.

Cam, S. (2012). 'Involuntary part-time workers in Britain: evidence from the Labour Force Survey'. *Industrial Relations Journal*, 43/3: 242–59.

Cantin, É. (2008). 'Making the "workshop of the world": China and the international division of labour', in M. Taylor (ed.), *Global Economy Contested: Power and Conflict Across the International Division of Labour*. Abingdon: Routledge, 51–76.

Carley, M. (1993). 'Social dialogue', in M. Gold (ed.), *The Social Dimension: Employment Policy in the European Community*. Basingstoke: Macmillan, 105–34.

Carley, M. and Hall, M. (2000). 'The implementation of the European Works Councils Directive'. *Industrial Law Journal*, 29/2: 103–24.

Carr, B. (2014). *The Carr Report: The Report of the Independent Review of the Law Governing Industrial Disputes*. London: HMSO.

Carr, F. (1999). 'Local bargaining in the National Health Service: new approaches to employee relations'. *Industrial Relations Journal*, 30/3: 197–211.

Carter, B. (2000). 'Adoption of the organising model in British trade unions: some evidence from Manufacturing, Science and Finance (MSF)'. *Work, Employment and Society*, 14/1: 117–36.

Carter, B., Danford, A., Howcroft, D., Richardson, H., Smith, A., and Taylor, P. (2011). '"All they lack is a chain": lean and the new performance management in the British civil service'. *New Technology, Work, and Employment*, 26/2: 83–97.

Carter, B., Danford, A., Howcroft, D., Richardson, H., Smith, A., and Taylor, P. (2013). '"Stressed out of my box": employee experience of lean working and occupational ill-health in clerical work in the UK public sector'. *Work, Employment and Society*, 27/5: 747–67.

Carter, B. and Fairbrother, P. (1999). 'The transformation of British public-sector industrial relations: from "model employer" to marketised relations'. *Historical Studies in Industrial Relations*, 7: 119–46.

Cascio, W. (2010). 'Downsizing and redundancy', in A. Wilkinson, N. Bacon, T. Redman, and S. Snell (eds.), *The SAGE Handbook of Human Resource Management*. London: Sage, 337–48.

Cassell, C. and Lee, B. (2009). 'Trade unions learning representatives: progressing partnership?' *Work, Employment, and Society*, 23/2: 213–30.

Castells, M. (2001). *The Internet Galaxy*. Oxford: Oxford University Press.

Central Arbitration Committee (CAC) (2016). *Annual Report 2015–16*. London: CAC.

Certification Officer (2016). *Annual Report of the Certification Officer, 2015–16*. London: Certification Officer.

Chakrabortty, A. (2014). 'The true cost of private contracts in Universities'. *The Guardian*, 24 March, https://www.theguardian.com/education/2014/mar/24/cost-private-contracts-universities-documents-services-workers

Chakrabortty, A. (2016a). 'Being self-employed means freedom. Freedom to be abused and underpaid'. *The Guardian*, 5 April, http://www.theguardian.com/commentisfree/2016/apr/05/self-employed-freedom-underpaid-contractors

Chakrabortty, A. (2016b). 'How Boots went rogue'. *The Guardian*, 13 April, https://www.theguardian.com/news/2016/apr/13/how-boots-went-rogue

Chan, C. K.-C. and Hui, E. S.-l. (2012). 'The dynamics and dilemma of workplace trade union reform in China: the case of the Honda workers' strike'. *Journal of Industrial Relations*, 54/5: 653–68.

Chan, J. (2013). 'A suicide survivor: the life of a Chinese worker'. *New Technology, Work, and Employment*, 28/2: 84–99.

Chan, J., Pun, N., and Selden, M. (2013). 'The politics of global production: Apple, Foxconn, and China's new working class'. *New Technology, Work, and Employment*, 28/2: 100–15.

Channel Four (2015a). 'Dispatches: the Secrets of Sport Direct', 27 April.

Channel Four (2015b). 'Dispatches: Low Pay Britain', 18 January.

Charles, N. (1986). 'Women and trade unions', in Feminist Review (ed.), *Waged Work: A Reader*. London: Virago, 160–85.

Charlwood, A. (2007). 'The de-collectivisation of pay setting in Britain 1990–98: incidence, determinants and impact'. *Industrial Relations Journal*, 38/1: 33–50.

Charlwood, A. and Forth, J. (2009). 'Employee representation', in W. Brown, A. Bryson, J. Forth, and K. Whitfield (eds.), *The Evolution of the Modern Workplace*. Cambridge: Cambridge University Press, 74–96.

Charlwood, A. and Terry, M. (2007). '21st-century models of employee representation: structures, processes, and outcomes'. *Industrial Relations Journal*, 38/4: 320–37.

Chartered Institute of Personnel and Development (CIPD) (2010). *Creating an Engaged Workforce*. London: CIPD.

Chartered Institute of Personnel and Development (CIPD) (2012). *The Rise in Self-Employment*. London: CIPD.

Chartered Institute of Personnel and Development (CIPD) (2013*a*). *Labour Market Outlook: Winter 2012–13*. London: CIPD.

Chartered Institute of Personnel and Development (CIPD) (2013*b*). *Zero-hours Contracts: Myth and Reality*. London: CIPD.

Chartered Institute of Personnel and Development (CIPD) (2014). *Employee Outlook, Autumn 2014*. London: CIPD.

Chartered Institute of Personnel and Development (CIPD) (2015*a*). *Conflict Management: A Shift in Direction?* London: CIPD.

Chartered Institute of Personnel and Development (CIPD) (2015*b*). *The View from Below: What Employees Really Think about their CEO's Pay Packet*. London: CIPD.

Chartered Institute of Personnel and Development (CIPD) (2015*c*). *Zero-hours and Short-hours Contracts in the UK: Employer and Employee Perspectives*. London: CIPD.

Chartered Institute of Personnel and Development/ Advisory, Conciliation and Arbitration Service (CIPD/ ACAS) (2008). *Mediation: An Employer's Guide*. London: CIPD.

China Labor Watch (2012). 'Beyond Foxconn: Deplorable Working Conditions Characterize Apple's Entire Supply Chain', http://www.chinalaborwatch. org/pdf/2012627-5.pdf

Chinguno, C. (2013). 'Marikana massacre and strike violence post-apartheid'. *Global Labour Journal*, 4/2: 160–6.

Chrisafis, A. (2016). 'France hit by day of protest as security forces fire teargas at taxi strike'. *The Guardian*, 26 January, http:// www.theguardian.com/world/2016/jan/26/ french-taxi-drivers-block-paris-roads-in-uber-protest

Chun, J. (2009). *Organising at the Margins*. Ithaca NY: Cornell University Press.

Citizens Advice (2011). *Give us a Break! The CAB Service's Case for a Fair Employment Agency*. London: Citizens Advice.

Citizens Advice (2015). *Neither One Thing nor the Other: How Reducing Bogus Self-employment could Benefit Workers, Business, and the Exchequer*. London: Citizens Advice.

Clark, A. (2010). 'New Zealand changes labour laws to save filming of the Hobbit series'. *The Guardian*, 31 October, https://www. theguardian.com/business/2010/oct/31/ warner-bros-new-zealand-hobbit-film

Clark, I. (2008). 'Private equity: friend or foe? The case against'. *People Management*, 21 August: 18–20.

Clark, I. (2009). 'Owners and managers: disconnecting managerial capitalism? Understanding the private-equity business model'. *Work, Employment and Society*, 23/4: 775–86.

Clark, I. (2010). 'Private equity, "union recognition" and value extraction at the Automobile Association: the GMB as an emergency service?' *Industrial Relations Journal*, 42/1: 36–50.

Clark, I. (2016). 'Financialisation, ownership and employee interests under private equity at the AA, part two'. *Industrial Relations Journal*, 47/3: 238–52.

Clark, N. (2011). 'Migration and work: discrimination obligatory', in T. Wright and H. Conley (eds.), *The Gower Handbook of Discrimination at Work*. Farnham: Gower, 139–54.

Clark, T. (2014). *Hard Times: The Divisive Toll of the Economic Slump*. New Haven and London: Yale University Press.

Clarke, M. (2007). 'Choices and constraints: individual perceptions of the voluntary redundancy experience'. *Human Resource Management Journal*, 17/1: 76–93.

Claydon, T. (1996). 'Union de-recognition: a re-examination', in I. Beardwell (ed.), *Contemporary Industrial Relations: A Critical Analysis*. Oxford: Oxford University Press, 151–74.

Clean Clothes Campaign (2015). 'Clean Clothes Campaign response to agreement between H&M and IndustriALL'. Clean Clothes Campaign Press Release, 11 November, http://www.cleanclothes.org/ news/2015/11/11/clean-clothes-campiagn-response- to-agreement-between-h-m-and-industriall

Clegg, H. (1975). 'Pluralism in industrial relations'. *British Journal of Industrial Relations*, 13/3: 309–16.

Clegg, H. (1979). *The Changing System of Industrial Relations in Great Britain*. Oxford: Basil Blackwell.

Clegg, H., Fox, A., and Thompson, A. (1964). *A History of British Trade Unions since 1889. Volume I, 1889–1910*. Oxford: Clarendon.

Coates, D. (2000). 'New Labour's industrial and employment policy', in D. Coates and P. Lawler (eds.), *New Labour in Power*. Manchester: Manchester University Press, 122–35.

Coates, K. and Topham, T. (1980). *Trade Unions in Britain*. Nottingham: Spokesman.

Coats, D. (2007). *The National Minimum Wage: Retrospect and Prospect*. London: Work Foundation.

Coats, D. (2010). *Time to cut the Gordian Knot—the Case for Consensus and Reform of the UK's Employment Relations System*. London: Smith Institute.

Cockburn, C. (1989). 'Equal opportunities: the short and long agenda'. *Industrial Relations Journal*, 20/3: 213–25.

Cockburn, C. (1991). *In the Way of Women*. Basingstoke: Macmillan.

Colgan, F. (1999). 'Recognising the lesbian and gay constituency in UK trade unions: moving forward in UNISON'. *Industrial Relations Journal*, 30/5: 444–63.

Colgan, F., Creegan, C., McKearney, A., and Wright, T. (2007). 'Equality and diversity policies and practices at work: lesbian, gay, and bisexual workers'. *Equal Opportunities International*, 26/3: 590–609.

Colgan, F. and Ledwith, S. (2000). 'Diversity, identities and strategies of women trade union activists'. *Gender, Work and Organization*, 7/4: 242–57.

Colgan, F. and Ledwith, S. (2002). 'Gender and diversity: reshaping union democracy'. *Employee Relations*, 24/2: 167–89.

Colgan, F. and McKearney, A. (2012). 'Visibility and voice in organisations: lesbian, gay, bisexual, and transgendered employee networks'. *Equality, Diversity, and Inclusion: An International Journal*, 31/4: 359–78.

Colgan, F. and Wright, T. (2011). 'Lesbian, gay, and bisexual equality in a modernizing public sector 1997–2010: opportunities and threats'. *Gender, Work, and Organization*, 18/5: 548–70.

Colling, T. (2004). 'No claim, no pain? The privatization of dispute resolution in Britain'. *Economic and Industrial Democracy*, 25/4: 555–79.

Colling, T. (2010). 'Legal institutions and the regulation of workplaces', in T. Colling and M. Terry (eds.), *Industrial Relations: Theory and Practice*. Chichester: John Wiley, 323–46.

Colling, T. and Dickens, L. (1989). *Equality Bargaining—Why Not?* London: HMSO.

Colling, T. and Dickens, L. (1998). 'Selling the case for gender equality: deregulation and equality bargaining'. *British Journal of Industrial Relations*, 36/3: 389–411.

Colling, T. and Dickens, L. (2001). 'Gender equality and trade unions: a new basis for mobilisation?', in M. Noon and E. Ogbonna (eds.), *Equality, Diversity and Disadvantage in Employment*. Basingstoke: Palgrave Macmillan, 136–55.

Colling, T. and Terry, M. (2010). 'Work, the employment relationship and the field of industrial relations', in T. Colling and M. Terry (eds.), *Industrial Relations: Theory and Practice* (3rd edn). Chichester: John Wiley, 3–25.

Commons, J. (1924). *Legal Foundations of Capitalism*. New York: Macmillan.

Compa, L. (2001). 'Free trade, fair trade and the battle for labor rights', in L. Turner, H. Katz, and R. Hurd (eds.), *Rekindling the Movement: Labor's Quest for Relevance in the Twenty-first Century*. Ithaca NY: Cornell University Press, 314–38.

Confederation of British Industry (CBI) (2010). *Keeping the Wheels Turning: Modernising the Legal Framework of Industrial Relations*. London: CBI.

Confederation of British Industry (CBI) (2011*a*). *Thinking Positive: The 21st Century Employment Relationship*. London: CBI.

Confederation of British Industry (CBI) (2011*b*). *Healthy Returns? Absence and Workplace Health Survey 2011*. London: CBI.

Confederation of British Industry (CBI) (2011*c*). *Settling the Matter: Building a More Effective and Efficient Tribunal System*. London: CBI.

Confederation of British Industry (CBI) (2014). *Making Britain Work for Everyone*. London: CBI.

Conley, H. (2011). 'The road to equality: legislating for change?', in T. Wright and H. Conley (eds.), *The Gower Handbook of Discrimination at Work*. Farnham: Gower, 23–31.

Conley, H. (2012*a*). 'Book review symposium. Guy Standing—The Precariat: the New Dangerous Class'. *Work, Employment, and Society*, 26/4: 686–8.

Conley, H. (2012*b*). 'Using equality to challenge austerity: new actors, old problems'. *Work, Employment and Society*, 26/2: 34–59.

Conley, H. (2014). 'Trade unions, equal pay, and the law in the UK'. *Economic and Industrial Democracy*, 35/2: 309–23.

Conley, H. and Page, M. (2016). 'Revisiting Jewson and Mason: the politics of gender equality in UK local government in a cold climate'. *Gender, Work, and Organization*, DOI: 10.1111/gwao.12135

Connolly, H. (2010). 'Organizing and mobilizing precarious workers in France: the case of cleaners in the railways', in C. Thornley, S. Jeffreys, and B. Appay (eds.), *Globalization and Precarious Forms of Production and Employment: Challenges for Workers and Unions*. Cheltenham: Edward Elgar, 182–98.

Cooke, F. L. (2013). 'New dynamics of industrial conflicts in China: causes, expressions and resolution alternatives', in G. Gall (ed.), *New Forms and Expressions of Conflict at Work*. Basingstoke: Palgrave Macmillan, 108–29.

Cooke. F. L. (2014). 'Chinese multinational firms in Asia and Africa: relationships with institutional actors and patterns of HRM practices'. *Human Resource Management*, 53/6: 877–96.

Cooke, H. (2006). 'Examining the disciplinary process in nursing: a case study approach'. *Work, Employment and Society*, 20/4: 687–707.

Corby, S. (2000). 'Employee relations in the public services: a paradigm shift?' *Public Policy and Administration*, 15/3: 60–74.

Corby, S. (2015). 'British employment tribunals: from the side-lines to centre stage'. *Labor History*, 56/2: 161–79.

Corby, S. and Latreille, P. (2012). 'Employment tribunals and the civil courts: isomorphism exemplified'. *Industrial Law Journal*, 41/4: 387–406.

Corby, S., Palmer, S., and Lindop, E. (2009). 'Trends and tensions: an overview', in S. Corby, S. Palmer, and E. Lindop (eds.), *Rethinking Reward*. Basingstoke: Palgrave Macmillan, 3–20.

Corlett, A., Finch, D., and Whittaker, M. (2016). *Living Standards 2016: The Experiences of Low to Middle Income Households in Downturn and Recovery*. London: Resolution Foundation.

Corlett, A. and Gardiner, L. (2015). *Low Pay Britain 2015*. London: Resolution Foundation.

Coulson, A. and Bonner, J. (2014). *Living Wage Employers: Evidence of UK Business Cases*. London: Living Wage Foundation.

Crail, M. (2007). 'Employers make liberal use of working time regulations opt-out'. *Personnel Today*, 26 November, http://www.personneltoday.com/ articles/2007/11/26/43407/employers-make-liberal-use-of-working-time-regulations-opt-out.html

Creegan, C. and Robinson, C. (2008). 'Prejudice and the workplace', in A. Park, J. Curtice, K. Thomson, M. Phillips, M. Johnson, and E. Clery (eds.), *British Social Attitudes: The 24th Report*. London: Sage, 127–38.

Cremers, J. (2010). 'Rules on working conditions in Europe: subordinated to freedom of services?' *European Journal of Industrial Relations*, 16/3: 293–306.

Cremers, J., Erik Dølvik, J., and Bosch, G. (2007). 'Posting of workers in the single market: attempts to prevent social dumping and regime competition in the EU'. *Industrial Relations Journal*, 38/6: 524–41.

Crespy, A. and Menz, G. (2015). 'Introduction: the pursuit of Social Europe in the face of crisis', in A. Crespy and G. Menz (eds.), *Social Policy and the Euro Crisis*. Basingstoke: Palgrave Macmillan, 1–23.

Crompton, R. and Sanderson, K. (1990). *Gendered Jobs and Social Change*. London: Unwin Hyman.

Cronin, J. (1979). *Industrial Conflict in Modern Britain*. London: Croom Helm.

Crouch, C. (1995). 'The state: economic management and incomes policy', in P. Edwards (ed.), *Industrial Relations: Theory and Practice in Britain*. Oxford: Blackwell, 229–54.

Crouch, C. (1996). 'Review essay. Atavism and innovation: labour legislation and public policy since 1979 in historical perspective'. *Historical Studies in Industrial Relations*, 2: 111–24.

Crouch, C. (2005). *Capitalist Diversity and Change*. Oxford: Oxford University Press.

Crouch, D. (2015*a*). 'Efficiency up, turnover down: Sweden experiments with six-hour working day'. *The Guardian*, 17 September, http://www. theguardian.com/world/2015/sep/17/ efficiency-up-turnover-down-sweden-experiments-with-six-hour-working-day

Crouch, D. (2015*b*). 'Ryanair closes Denmark operation to head off union row'. *The Guardian*, 17 July, https:// www.theguardian.com/business/2015/jul/17/ryanair-closes-denmark-operation-temporarily-to-sidestep-union-dispute

Croucher, R. and Cotton, E. (2009). *Global Unions, Global Business*. Hendon: Middlesex University Press.

Croucher, R. and White, G. (2007). 'Enforcing a National Minimum Wage'. *Policy Studies*, 28/2: 145–61.

Cullinane, N., Donaghey, J., Dundon, T., and Dobbins, T. (2012). 'Different rooms, different voices: double-breasting, multi-channel representation and the managerial agenda'. *International Journal of Human Resource Management*, 23/2: 368–84.

Cullinane, N. and Dundon, T. (2014). 'Unitarism and employer resistance to trade unionism'. *The International Journal of Human Resource Management*, 25/18: 2573–90.

Cullinane, N., Hickland, E., Dundon, T., Dobbins, T., and Donaghey, J. (2015). 'Triggering employee voice under the European Information and Consultation Directive: a non-union case study'. *Economic and Industrial Democracy*, DOI:10.1177/0143831X15584085

Cully, M., Woodland, S., O'Reilly, A., and Dix, G. (1999). *Britain at Work*. London: Routledge.

Cunningham, R., Lord, A., and Delaney, L. (1999). '"Next Steps" for equality? The impact of organizational change on opportunities for women in the civil service'. *Gender, Work and Organization*, 6/2: 67–78.

Cunnison, S. and Stageman, J. (1993). *Feminizing the Unions*. Aldershot: Avebury.

Curtice, J. (2016). 'How Deeply Does Britain's Euroscepticism Run?', http://www.bsa.natcen.ac.uk/ media/39024/euroscepticism.pdf

Cushen, J. and Thompson, P. (2012). 'Doing the right thing? HRM and the angry knowledge worker'. *New Technology, Work, and Employment*, 27/2: 79–92.

Daly, M. (2012). 'Paradigms in EU social policy: a critical account of Europe 2020'. *Transfer: European Review of Labour and Research*, 18/3: 273–84.

Danford, A. (1998). 'Teamworking and labour regulation in the autocomponents industry'. *Work, Employment and Society*, 12/3: 409–31.

Danford, A., Durbin, S., Richardson, M., Stewart, P., and Tailby, S. (2014). 'Workplace partnership and professional workers: "about as useful as a chocolate teapot?"' *The International Journal of Human Resource Management*, 25/6: 879–94.

Danford, A. and Richardson, M. (2016). 'Why partnership cannot work and why militant alternatives can: historical and contemporary evidence', in S. Johnstone and A. Wilkinson (eds.), *Developing Positive Employment Relations: International Experiences of Labour Management Partnership*. London: Palgrave Macmillan, 49–73.

Danford, A., Richardson, M., Stewart, P., Tailby, S., and Upchurch, M. (2005). *Partnership and the High Performance Workplace*. Basingstoke: Palgrave Macmillan.

Daniel, W. and Millward, N. (1983). *Workplace Industrial Relations in Britain*. London: Heinemann.

Daniels, G. (2009). 'In the field: a decade of organizing', in G. Daniels and J. McIlroy (eds.), *Trade Unions in a Neo Liberal World: British Trade Unions under New Labour*. Abingdon: Routledge, 254–82.

Daniels, G. and McIlroy, J. (eds.) (2009). *Trade Unions in a Neo Liberal World: British Trade Unions under New Labour*. Abingdon: Routledge.

D'Arcy, C. and Davies, G. (2016). *Weighing up the Wage Floor: Employer Responses to the National Living Wage*. London: Resolution Foundation.

D'Arcy, C. and Finch, D. (2016). *Making the Living Wage: The Resolution Foundation Review of the Living Wage*. London: Resolution Foundation.

D'Arcy, C. and Gardiner, L. (2014). *Just the Job or a Working Compromise? The Changing Nature of Self-employment in the UK*. London: Resolution Foundation.

Darlington, R. (2009). 'Leadership and union militancy: the case of the RMT'. *Capital and Class*, 33/3: 3–32.

Darlington, R. (2012). 'The interplay of structure and agency dynamics in strike activity'. *Employee Relations*, 45/5: 518–33.

Darlington, R. and Dobson, J. (2015). *The Conservative Government's Proposed Strike Ballot Thresholds: The Challenge to the Trade Unions*. Salford Business School Research Working Paper, August. Salford: Salford Business School.

Davies, A. and Thomas, R. (2000). 'Gender and human resource management: a critical review'. *International Journal of Human Resource Management*, 11/6: 1125–36.

Davies, Lord (2015). *Women on Boards: Five Year Summary*. London: Department of Business, Innovation, and Skills.

Davies, P. and Freedland, M. (1993). *Labour Legislation and Public Policy*. Oxford: Clarendon.

Davies, P. and Freedland, M. (2007). *Towards a Flexible Labour Market*. Oxford: Oxford University Press.

De Castella, T. (2014). 'Could work emails be banned after 6pm?' *BBC News Magazine*, 10 April, http://www.bbc.co.uk/news/magazine-26958079

De Linde Leonard, M., Stanley, T., and Doucouliagos, H. (2014). 'Does the UK minimum wage reduce employment? A meta-regression analysis'. *British Journal of Industrial Relations*, 52/3: 499–520.

De Menezes, L. and Kelliher, C. (2011). 'Flexible working and performance: a systematic review of the evidence for a business case'. *International Journal of Management Reviews*, 13/4: 452–74.

De Ruyter, A., Bailey. D., and Mahdon, M. (2010). 'Changing lanes or stuck in the slow lane? Employment precariousness and labour market status of MG Rover workers four years after closure', in C. Thornley, S. Jeffreys, and B. Appay (eds.), *Globalization and Precarious Forms of Production and Employment: Challenges for Workers and Unions*. Cheltenham: Edward Elgar, 214–29.

Dean, D. and Liff, S. (2010). 'Equality and diversity: the ultimate industrial relations concern', in T. Colling and M. Terry (eds.), *Industrial Relations: Theory and Practice* (3rd edn). Chichester: John Wiley, 422–46.

Deery, S., Iverson, R., and Walsh, J. (2010). 'Coping strategies in call centres: work intensity and the role of co-workers and supervisors'. *British Journal of Industrial Relations*, 48/1: 181–200.

Degryse, C. (2015). *The European Sectoral Social Dialogue: An Uneven Record of Achievement?* ETUI Working Paper, 2015: 02. Brussels: European Trade Union Institute.

Degryse, C. (2016). *Digitalisation of the Economy and its Impact on Labour Markets*. ETUI Working Paper, 2016:02. Brussels: European Trade Union Institute.

Delbridge, R. (1998). *Life on the Line in Contemporary Manufacturing*. Oxford: Oxford University Press.

Delbridge, R., Hauptmeier, M., and Sengupta, S. (2011). 'Beyond the enterprise: broadening the horizons of international HRM'. *Human Relations*, 64/4: 483–505.

Dellot, B. and Reed, H. (2015). *Boosting the Living Standards of the Self-employed*. London: Royal Society of Arts.

Demos (2015). *Rising to the Top*. London: Demos.

Department for Business, Innovation and Skills (BIS) (2011). *Flexible, Effective, Fair: Promoting Economic Growth Through a Strong and Efficient Labour Market*. London: BIS.

Department for Business, Innovation and Skills (BIS) (2012a). *Employment Law Review: Annual Update 2012*. London: BIS.

Department for Business, Innovation and Skills (BIS) (2012b). *Dealing with Dismissal and 'Compensated No Fault Dismissal' for Micro Businesses: Call for Evidence*. London: BIS.

Department for Business, Innovation and Skills (BIS) (2012c). *Executive Pay: Shareholder Voting Rights Consultation*. London: BIS.

Department of Business, Innovation, and Skills (BIS) (2013). *National Minimum Wage: Work Experience and Internships*. London: BIS.

Department of Business, Innovation and Skills (BIS) (2014). *The Impact of the Working Time Regulations on the UK Labour Market: A Review of Evidence*. BIS Analysis Paper Number 5. London: BIS.

Department of Business, Innovation and Skills (BIS) (2016a). *Pregnancy and Maternity-related Discrimination and Disadvantage: Government Response*. London: BIS.

Department of Business, Innovation and Skills (BIS) (2016b). *Trade Union Membership 2015: Statistical Bulletin*. London: BIS.

Department of Business, Innovation and Skills (BIS) (2016c). 'Extended Sunday trading due in the autumn'. BIS Press Release, 9 February, https://www.gov.uk/government/news/extended-sunday-trading-due-in-the-autumn

Department for Business, Innovation and Skills/Her Majesty's Revenue and Customs (BIS/HMRC) (2013). *National Minimum Wage Compliance and Enforcement: Report for 18 Months to 30 September 2012*. London: BIS/HMRC.

Department of Business, Innovation and Skills (BIS)/Home Office (2016). *Tackling Exploitation in the Labour Market: Government Response*. London: BIS.

Department of Trade and Industry (DTI) (1998). *Fairness at Work*. London: HMSO.

Department of Trade and Industry (DTI) (2005). *Code of Practice: Access and Unfair Practices during Recognition Ballots*. London: DTI.

Department of Trade and Industry (DTI) (2006). *Success at Work*. London: DTI.

Dex, S. and Forth, J. (2009). 'Equality and diversity at work', in W. Brown, A. Bryson, J. Forth, and K. Whitfield (eds.), *The Evolution of the Modern Workplace*. Cambridge: Cambridge University Press, 230–55.

Diallo, Y., Hagemann, F., Etienne, A., Garbuzer, Y., and Mehran, F. (2010). *Global Child Labour Developments: Measuring Trends from 2004 to 2008*. Geneva: ILO.

Dicken, P. (2015). *Global Shift: Mapping the Changing Contours of the World Economy* (7th edn). London: Sage.

Dickens, L. (1992). 'Anti-discrimination legislation: exploring and explaining the impact on women's employment', in W. McCarthy (ed.), *Legal Intervention in Industrial Relations: Gains and Losses*. Oxford: Basil Blackwell, 103–46.

Dickens, L. (1994). 'The business case for women's equality: is the carrot better than the stick?' *Employee Relations*, 16/8: 5–18.

Dickens, L. (1997). 'Gender, race and employment equality in Britain: inadequate strategies and the role of industrial relations actors'. *Industrial Relations Journal*, 28/4: 282–91.

Dickens, L. (1999). 'Beyond the business case: a three-pronged approach to equality action'. *Human Resource Management Journal*, 9/1: 9–19.

Dickens, L. (2000a). 'Still wasting resources? Equality in employment', in S. Bach and K. Sisson (eds.), *Personnel Management* (3rd edn). Oxford: Blackwell, 137–69.

Dickens, L. (2000b). 'Collective bargaining and the promotion of gender equality at work: opportunities and challenges for trade unions'. *Transfer*, 6/2: 193–208.

Dickens, L. (2000c). 'Doing more with less: ACAS and individual conciliation', in B. Towers and W. Brown (eds.), *Employment Relations in Britain: 25 Years of the Advisory, Conciliation and Arbitration Service*. Oxford: Blackwell, 67–91.

Dickens, L. (2007). 'The road is long: thirty years of equality legislation in Britain'. *British Journal of Industrial Relations*, 45/3: 463–94.

Dickens, L. (2012a). 'Employment tribunals and alternative dispute resolution', in L. Dickens (ed.), *Making Employment Rights Effective: Issues of Enforcement and Compliance*. Oxford: Hart Publishing, 29–47.

Dickens, L. (2012b). 'Fairer workplaces: making employment rights effective', in L. Dickens (ed.), *Making Employment Rights Effective: Issues of Enforcement and Compliance*. Oxford: Hart Publishing, 205–28.

Dickens, L. (2014). 'The coalition government's reforms to employment tribunals and statutory employment rights—echoes of the past'. *Industrial Relations Journal*, 45/3: 234–49.

Dickens, L. and Hall, M. (2003). 'Labour law and industrial relations: a new settlement?', in P. Edwards (ed.), *Industrial Relations* (2nd edn). Oxford: Blackwell, 124–56.

Dickens, L. and Hall, M. (2006). 'Fairness—up to a point. Assessing the impact of New Labour's employment legislation'. *Human Resource Management Journal*, 16/4: 338–56.

Dickens, L. and Hall, M. (2009). 'Legal regulation and the changing workplace', in W. Brown, A. Bryson, J. Forth, and K. Whitfield (eds.), *The Evolution of the Modern Workplace*. Cambridge: Cambridge University Press, 332–52.

Dickens, L. and Hall, M. (2010). 'The changing legal framework of employment relations', in T. Colling and M. Terry (eds.), *Industrial Relations: Theory and Practice* (3rd edn). Chichester: John Wiley, 298–322.

Dickens, L., Jones, M., Weekes, B., and Hunt, M. (1985). *Dismissed: A Study of Unfair Dismissal and the Industrial Tribunal System*. Oxford: Basil Blackwell.

Dickens, R. and Manning, A. (2003). 'Minimum wage, minimum impact', in R. Dickens, P. Gregg, and J. Wadsworth (eds.), *The Labour Market under New Labour*. Basingstoke: Palgrave Macmillan, 201–13.

Dix, G. and Barber, B. (2015). 'The changing face of work: insights from ACAS'. *Employee Relations*, 37/6: 670–82.

Dix, G. and Oxenbridge, S. (2004). 'Coming to the table with ACAS: from conflict to co-operation'. *Employee Relations*, 26/5: 510–30.

Dix, G., Sisson, K., and Forth, J. (2009). 'Conflict at work: the changing pattern of disputes', in W. Brown, A. Bryson, J. Forth, and K. Whitfield (eds.), *The Evolution of the Modern Workplace*. Cambridge: Cambridge University Press, 176–200.

Dobbins, T. and Dundon, T. (2014). 'Non-union employee representation', in A. Wilkinson, J. Donaghey, T. Dundon, and R. Freeman (eds.), *Handbook of Research on Employee Voice*. Cheltenham, Edward Elgar, 342–60.

Dobbins, T. and Dundon, T. (2015a). 'The chimera of sustainable labour-management partnership'. *British Journal of Management*, DOI: 10.1111/1467-8551.12128

Dobbins, T. and Dundon, T. (2015b). 'The EU information and consultative directive in liberal market economies', in S. Johnstone and P. Ackers (eds.), *Finding a Voice at Work? New Perspectives on Employment Relations*. Oxford: Oxford University Press, 239–62.

Doherty, L. (2004). 'Work–life balance initiatives: implications for women'. *Employee Relations*, 26/4: 433–52.

Dølvik, J. E. and Visser, J. (2009). 'Free movement, equal treatment and workers' rights: can the European Union solve its trilemma of fundamental principles?' *Industrial Relations Journal*, 40/6: 491–509.

Donaghey, J. (2016). 'Trojan horse or tactic? The case for partnership', in S. Johnstone and A. Wilkinson (eds.), *Developing Positive Employment Relations: International Experiences of Labour Management Partnership*. London: Palgrave Macmillan, 25–47.

Donaghey, J., Cullinane, N., and Dundon, T. (2015). 'Legislating for NER? NER and the ICE Regulations at Manufacture Co', in P. Gollan, B. Kaufman, D. Taras, and A. Wilkinson (eds.), *Voice and Involvement at Work: Experience with Non-Union Representation*. New York and Abingdon: Routledge, 127–45.

Donaghey, J., Cullinane, N., Dundon, T., and Dobbins, T. (2012). 'Non-union employee representation, union avoidance and the managerial agenda'. *Economic and Industrial Democracy*, 33/2: 163–83.

Donaghey, J., Reinecke, J., Niforou, C., and Lawson, B. (2014). 'From employment relations to consumption relations: balancing labor governance in global supply chains'. *Human Resource Management*, 53/2: 229–52.

Donaghey, J. and Teague, P. (2006). 'The free movement of workers and social Europe: maintaining the European ideal'. *Industrial Relations Journal*, 37/6: 652–66.

Donnelly, M. and Scholarios, D. (1998). 'Workers' experiences of redundancy: evidence from Scottish defence-dependent companies'. *Personnel Review*, 27/4: 325–42.

Donnelly, R. (2011). 'The organization of working time in the knowledge economy: an insight into the working time patterns of consultants in the UK and the USA'. *British Journal of Industrial Relations*, 49/S1: s93–s114.

Doogan, K. (2009). *New Capitalism?* Cambridge: Polity.

Dromey, J. (2014). *Meeting the Challenge: Successful Employee Engagement in the NHS*. London: IPA.

Druker, J. (2016). 'Blacklisting and its legacy in the UK construction industry: employment relations in the aftermath of the exposure of the Consulting Association'. *Industrial Relations Journal*, 47/3: 220–37.

Druker, J. and White, G. (2009). 'Introduction', in G. White and J. Druker (eds.), *Reward Management: A Critical Text* (2nd edn). Abingdon: Routledge, 1–22.

Dubois, P. (1979). *Sabotage in Industry*. Penguin: Harmondsworth.

Dugan, E. (2015). 'British Muslim women 71% more likely to be unemployed due to workplace discrimination'. *The Independent*, 15 April, http://www.independent.co.uk/news/uk/home-news/british-muslim-women-71-more-likely-to-be-unemployed-due-to-workplace-discrimination-10179033.html

Duhigg, C. and Barboza, D. (2012). 'In China, human costs are built into an iPad'. *The New York Times*, 25 January, http://www.nytimes.com/2012/01/26/business/ieconomy-apples-ipad-and-the-human-costs-for-workers-in-china.html

Dundon, T., Cullinane, N., Donaghey, J., Dobbins, T., Wilkinson, A., and Hickland, E. (2015). 'Double-breasting employee voice: An assessment of motives, arrangements and durability'. *Human Relations*, 68/3: 489–513.

Dundon, T. and Rollinson, D. (2004). *Employment Relations in Non-Union Firms*. London: Routledge.

Dundon, T., Wilkinson, A., Marchington, M., and Ackers, P. (2005). 'The management of voice in non-union organisations: managers' perspectives'. *Employee Relations*, 27/3: 307–19.

Dunlop, J. (1958). *Industrial Relations Systems*. New York: Holt.

Dunn, S. and Gennard, J. (1984). *The Closed Shop in British Industry*. London: Macmillan.

Dunn, S. and Metcalf, D. (1996). 'Trade union law since 1979', in I. Beardwell (ed.), *Contemporary Industrial Relations: A Critical Analysis*. Oxford: Oxford University Press, 66–98.

Dwyer, P. (2008). 'The conditional welfare state', in M. Powell (ed.), *Modernising the Welfare State: The Blair Legacy*. Bristol: Policy Press, 199–208.

Earnshaw, J., Marchington, M., and Goodman, J. (2000). 'Unfair to whom? Discipline and dismissal in small establishments'. *Industrial Relations Journal*, 31/1: 62–73.

The Economist (2015). 'There's an app for that'. 3 January, http://www.economist.com/news/briefing/21637355-freelance-workers-available-moments-notice-will-reshape-nature-companies-and

The Economist (2016). 'From zero to seventy (billion)'. 3 September, http://www.economist.com/news/briefing/21706249-accelerated-life-and-times-worlds-most-valuable-startup-zero-seventy

Edwards, P. (1977). 'The Kerr-Siegel hypothesis of strikes and the isolated mass: a study of the falsification of sociological knowledge'. *Sociological Review*, 25/3: 551–74.

Edwards, P. (1983). 'The pattern of collective industrial action', in G. Bain (ed.), *Industrial Relations in Britain*. Oxford: Basil Blackwell, 209–34.

Edwards, P. (1986). *Conflict at Work*. Oxford: Basil Blackwell.

Edwards, P. (1988). 'Patterns of conflict and accommodation', in D. Gallie (ed.), *Employment in Britain*. Oxford: Basil Blackwell, 187–217.

Edwards, P. (1992). 'Industrial conflict'. *British Journal of Industrial Relations*, 30/3: 361–404.

Edwards, P. (1995). 'Strikes and industrial conflict', in P. Edwards (ed.), *Industrial Relations: Theory and Practice in Britain*. Oxford: Blackwell, 434–60.

Edwards, P. (2003). 'The employment relationship and the field of industrial relations', in P. Edwards (ed.), *Industrial Relations* (2nd edn). Oxford: Blackwell, 1–36.

Edwards, P. (2005). 'Discipline and attendance: a murky aspect of people management', in S. Bach (ed.), *Managing Human Resources* (4th edn). Oxford: Blackwell, 375–97.

Edwards, P. and Ram, M. (2006). 'Surviving on the margins of the economy: working relationships in small, low-wage firms'. *Journal of Management Studies*, 43/4: 895–916.

Edwards, P., Ram, M., Sen Gupta, S., and Tsai, C.-J. (2006). 'The structuring of working relationships in small firms: towards a formal framework'. *Organization*, 13/5: 701–24.

Edwards, P. and Scullion, H. (1982). *The Social Organisation of Industrial Conflict*. Oxford: Basil Blackwell.

Edwards, P. and Whitston, C. (1994). 'Disciplinary practice: a study of railways in Britain, 1860–1988'. *Work, Employment and Society*, 8/3: 317–37.

Edwards, R. (1979). *Contested Terrain: The Transformation of the Workplace in the Twentieth Century*. London: Heinemann.

Edwards, T. (2011). 'The transfer of employment practices across borders in multinational companies', in A.-W. Harzing and A. Pinnington (eds.), *International Human Resource Management* (3rd edn). London: Sage, 267–90.

Edwards, T., Colling, T., and Ferner, A. (2007). 'Conceptual approaches to the transfer of employment practices in multinational companies: an integrated approach'. *Human Resource Management Journal*, 17/3: 201–17.

Edwards, T. and Ferner, A. (2002). 'The renewed "American challenge": a review of employment practice in US multinationals'. *Industrial Relations Journal*, 33/2: 94–111.

Egels-Zandén, N. (2007). 'Suppliers' compliance with MNCs' codes of conduct: behind the scenes at Chinese toy suppliers'. *Journal of Business Ethics*, 75: 45–62.

Egels-Zandén, N. (2014). 'Revisiting supplier compliance with MNC codes of conduct: recoupling policy and practice at Chinese toy suppliers'. *Journal of Business Ethics*, 119: 59–75.

Egels-Zandén, N. and Merk, J. (2014). 'Private regulation and trade union rights: why codes of conduct have limited impact on trade union rights'. *Journal of Business Ethics*, 123: 461–73.

Einarsdóttir, A., Hoel, H., and Lewis, D. (2015). '"It's nothing personal": anti-homosexuality in the British workplace'. *Sociology*, 49/6: 1183–99.

Elger, T. (1990). 'Technical innovation and work reorganisation in British manufacturing in the 1980s: continuity, intensification or transformation?' *Work, Employment and Society*, special issue: 67–101.

Elger, T. and Smith, C. (eds.) (1994). *Global Japanization? The Transnational Transformation of the Labour Process*. London: Routledge.

Elger, T. and Smith, C. (2005). *Assembling Work*. Oxford: Oxford University Press.

Elliott, K. and Freeman, R. (2003). *Can Labor Standards Improve under Globalization?* Washington DC: Institute for International Economics.

Emmott, M. (2001). 'Tribunals are judged wanting'. *The Guardian*, 12 March.

Emmott, M. (2005). *What is Employee Relations?* London: CIPD.

Emmott, M. (2015). 'Employment relations over the last 50 years: confrontation, consensus, or neglect?' *Employee Relations*, 37/6: 658–69.

Equality and Human Rights Commission (EHRC) (2009). *Working Better: Phase 1 Report*. London: EHRC.

Equality and Human Rights Commission (EHRC) (2010). *Triennial Review 2010: How Fair is Britain?* London: EHRC.

Equality and Human Rights Commission (EHRC) (2014). *The Invisible Workforce: Employment Practices in the Cleaning Sector*. London: EHRC.

Equality and Human Rights Commission (EHRC) (2016a). *Healing a Divided Britain: The Need for a Comprehensive Race Equality Strategy*. London: EHRC.

Equality and Human Rights Commission (EHRC) (2016b). *Pregnancy and Maternity Discrimination in the Workplace: Recommendations for Change*. London: EHRC.

Erickson, C., Fisk, C., Milkman, R., Mitchell, D., and Wong, K. (2002). 'Justice for Janitors in Los Angeles: lessons from three rounds of negotiation'. *British Journal of Industrial Relations*, 40/3: 543–67.

Erickson, M., Bradley, H., Stephenson, C., and Williams, S. (2009). *Business in Society*. Cambridge: Polity.

Esbenshade, J. (2004). *Monitoring Sweatshops: Workers, Consumers and the Global Apparel Industry*. Philadelphia PA: Temple University Press.

Eurofound (2010). *Extending Flexicurity—the Potential of Short-Time Working Schemes*. Dublin: European Foundation for the Improvement of Living and Working Conditions.

Eurofound (2012). *Working Time in the EU*. Dublin: European Foundation for the Improvement of Living and Working Conditions.

European Commission (2012). 'Women on boards: Commission proposes 40 per cent objective'. European Commission press release, 14 November, http://europa.eu/rapid/press-release_IP-12-1205_en.htm

European Commission (2013). 'Europe 2020 in a nutshell'. 13 May, http://ec.europa.eu/europe2020/europe-2020-in-a-nutshell/

European Industrial Relations Observatory (EIRO) (2002). 'Diageo Concludes Innovative EWC Agreement'. *EIRO online*, http://www.eurofound.europa.eu/eiro/2002/11/feature/ie0211204f.htm

European Industrial Relations Observatory (EIRO) (2012). 'Social partners launch review of Working Time Directive'. *EIRO online*, http://www.eurofound.europa.eu/eiro/2011/11/articles/eu1111051i.htm

European Trade Union Confederation (ETUC) (2014). *The Functioning of the Troika: An ETUC Report*. Brussels: ETUC.

European Trade Union Confederation (ETUC) (2015). *ETUC Resolution on Rebalancing the EU Approach to Fundamental Rights*. Brussels: ETUC.

Evans, C., Harvey, G., and Turnbull, P. (2012). 'When partnerships don't "match-up": an evaluation of labour-management partnerships in the automotive components and civil aviation industries'. *Human Resource Management Journal*, 22/1: 60–75.

Ewing, K. (2009). *Ruined Lives: Blacklisting in the UK Construction Industry*. London: UCATT.

Ewing, K. (2010). 'Labour leaves blacklisted high and dry'. *The Guardian*, 10 March, http://www.guardian.co.uk/commentisfree/2010/mar/10/labour-leaves-blacklisted-high-dry

Ewing, K. (2013). 'International regulation: the ILO and other agencies', in C. Frege and J. Kelly (eds.), *Comparative Employment Relations in the Global Economy*. Abingdon: Routledge, 425–43.

Ewing, K. and Hendy, J. (2010). 'The dramatic implications of *Demir* and *Baykara*'. *Industrial Law Journal*, 39/1: 2–51.

Ewing, L. (2011). 'Anti-blacklist campaigner Steve Acheson's picket pledge'. *BBC News Online*, http://www.bbc.co.uk/news/uk-england-14080162

Fair Pay Network (2012). *Face the Difference: The Impact of Low Pay in National Supermarket Chains*. London: Fair Pay Network.

Fairhurst, D. (2008). 'Am I "bovvered?" Driving a performance culture through to the front line'. *Human Resource Management Journal*, 18/4: 321–6.

Farnham, D. (2015). *The Changing Face of Employment Relations: Global, Comparative, and Theoretical Perspectives*. Basingstoke: Palgrave Macmillan.

Farnham, D. and Pimlott, J. (1995). *Understanding Industrial Relations* (4th edn). London: Cassell.

Farrell, C. and Morris, J. (2004). 'Resigned compliance: teacher attitudes towards performance-related pay in schools'. *Educational Management Administration and Leadership*, 32/1: 81–104.

Farrell, C. and Morris, J. (2009). 'Still searching for the evidence? Evidence-based policy, performance pay, and teachers'. *Journal of Industrial Relations*, 51/1: 75–94.

Farrell, S. (2016). 'How the UK steel crisis unfolded'. *The Guardian*, 20 April, https://www.theguardian.com/business/2016/apr/20/how-the-uk-steel-crisis-unfolded

Fawcett Society (2012). *The Impact of Austerity on Women*. London: Fawcett Society.

Felstead, A., Gallie, D., Green, F., and Inanc, H. (2013). *Work Intensification in Britain: First Findings from the Skills and Employment Survey 2012*. Cardiff: ESRC Centre for Learning and Life Chances in Knowledge Economies and Societies.

Felstead, A. and Jewson, N. (1999). 'Flexible labour and non-standard employment: an agenda of issues', in A. Felstead and N. Jewson (eds.), *Global Trends in Flexible Labour*. Basingstoke: Macmillan, 1–20.

Felsted, A. (2015). 'Big UK supermarkets adopt different living wage strategies'. *Financial Times*, 28 October, https://www.ft.com/content/1b3abf2a-7c08-11e5-98fb-5a6d4728f74e

Fenley, A. (1986). 'Industrial discipline: a suitable case for treatment'. *Employee Relations*, 8/3: 1–30.

Fenley, A. (1998). 'Models, styles and metaphors: understanding the management of discipline'. *Employee Relations*, 20/4: 349–64.

Ferner, A. (1997). 'Country of origin effects and HRM in multinational companies'. *Human Resource Management Journal*, 7/1: 19–37.

Ferner, A. (2010). 'HRM in multinational companies', in A. Wilkinson, N. Bacon, T. Redman, and S. Snell (eds.), *The SAGE Handbook of Human Resource Management*. London: Sage, 541–60.

Ferner, A., Almond, P., and Colling, T. (2005). 'Institutional theory and the cross-national transfer of employment policy: the case of "workforce diversity" in US multinationals'. *Journal of International Business Studies*, 36: 304–21.

Ferner, A. and Edwards, P. (1995). 'Power and the diffusion of organizational change within multinational corporations'. *European Journal of Industrial Relations*, 1/2: 229–57.

Ferner, A., Edwards, T., and Tempel, A. (2012). 'Power, institutions and the cross-national transfer of employment practices in multinationals'. *Human Relations*, 65/2: 163–87.

Fernie, S. (2005). 'The future of British unions: introduction and conclusions', in S. Fernie and D. Metcalf (eds.), *Trade Unions: Resurgence or Demise?* London: Routledge, 1–18.

Fevre, R., Lewis, D., Robinson, A, and Jones, T. (2012). *Trouble at Work*. London: Bloomsbury Academic. https://www.bloomsburycollections.com/book/trouble-at-work/

Fichter, M. (2013). 'Voluntary regulation: codes of practice and framework agreements', in C. Frege and J. Kelly (eds.), *Comparative Employment Relations in the Global Economy*. Abingdon: Routledge, 390–406.

Fine, J. (2006). *Worker Centers: Organizing Communities at the Edge of the Dream*. Ithaca NY: ILR Press.

Fitzgerald, I. (2009). 'Polish migrant workers in the North—new communities, new opportunities?', in J. McBride and I. Greenwood (eds.), *Community Unionism: A Comparative Analysis of Concepts and Contexts*. Basingstoke: Palgrave Macmillan, 93–118.

Fitzgerald, I. and Hardy, J. (2010). '"Thinking outside the box"? Trade union organizing strategies and Polish migrant workers in the United Kingdom'. *British Journal of Industrial Relations*, 48/1: 131–50.

Flanagan, R. (2006). *Globalization and Labor Conditions: Working Conditions and Worker Rights in a Global Economy*. New York: Oxford University Press.

Flanders, A. (1964). *The Fawley Productivity Agreements*. London: Faber and Faber.

Flanders, A. (1974). 'The tradition of voluntarism'. *British Journal of Industrial Relations*, 12/3: 352–70.

Flanders, A. (1975). *Management and Unions*. London: Faber and Faber.

Flanders, A. and Clegg, H. (eds.) (1964). *The System of Industrial Relations in Great Britain*. Oxford: Basil Blackwell.

Fleming, P., Harley, B., and Sewell, G. (2004). 'A little knowledge is a dangerous thing: getting below the surface of the growth of "knowledge work" in Australia'. *Work, Employment and Society*, 18/4: 725–47.

Ford, M. and Gillan, M. (2015). 'The Global Union Federations in international industrial relations: a critical review'. *Journal of Industrial Relations*, 57/3: 456–75.

Ford, M. and Novitz, T. (2015). 'An absence of fairness … restrictions on industrial action and protest in the Trade Union Bill 2015'. *Industrial Law Journal*, 44/4: 522–50.

Forde, C. (2001). 'Temporary arrangements: the activities of employment agencies in the UK'. *Work, Employment and Society*, 15/3: 631–44.

Forde, C., MacKenzie, R., and Robinson, A. (2008). '"Help wanted". Employers' use of temporary agencies in the UK construction industry'. *Employee Relations*, 30/6: 679–98.

Forde, C. and Slater, G. (2014). *The Effects of Agency Workers Regulations on Agency and Employer Practice*. London: ACAS.

Foster, D. (2007). 'Legal obligation or personal lottery? Employee experiences of disability and the negotiation of adjustments in the public sector workplace'. *Work, Employment and Society*, 21/1: 67–84.

Foster, D. (2011). 'Understanding workplace adjustments for disabled employees', in T. Wright and H. Conley (eds.), *The Gower Handbook of Discrimination at Work*. Farnham: Gower, 173–84.

Foster, D. and Scott, P. (2015). 'Nobody's responsibility: the precarious position of disabled employees in the UK workplace'. *Industrial Relations Journal*, 46/4: 328–43.

Foster, J. and Woolfson, C. (1986). *The Politics of the UCS Work-in*. London: Lawrence and Wishart.

Fougner, T. and Kurtoğlu, A. (2011). 'Transnational labour solidarity and social movement unionism: insights from and beyond a women workers' strike in Turkey'. *British Journal of Industrial Relations*, 49/S2: s353–75.

Fox, A. (1966). *Industrial Sociology and Industrial Relations*. Research Paper No. 3, Royal Commission on Trade Unions and Employers' Associations. London: HMSO.

Fox, A. (1974). *Beyond Contract: Work, Power and Trust Relations*. London: Faber and Faber.

Fox, A. (1985a). *History and Heritage: The Social Origins of the British Industrial Relations System*. London: Allen and Unwin.

Fox, A. (1985b). *Man Mismanagement* (2nd edn). London: Hutchinson.

Fransen, L. (2012). *Corporate Social Responsibility and Global Labor Standards: Firms and Activists in the Making of Private Regulation*. Abingdon: Routledge.

Fraser, J. and Gold, M. (2001). '"Portfolio workers": autonomy and control among freelance translators'. *Work, Employment and Society*, 15/4: 679–97.

Freedland, M. and Prassl, J. (eds.) (2015). *EU Law in the Member States: Viking, Laval and Beyond*. Oxford: Hart Publishing.

Freeman, R. and Diamond, W. (2003). 'Young workers and trade unions', in H. Gospel and S. Wood (eds.), *Representing Workers: Union Recognition and Membership in Britain*. London: Routledge, 29–50.

Frege, C. (2006). 'International trends in unionization', in M. Morley, P. Gunnigle, and D. Collins (eds.), *Global Industrial Relations*. London: Routledge, 221–38.

Frege, C. (2008). 'The history of industrial relations as a field of study', in P. Blyton, N. Bacon, J. Fiorito, and E. Heery (eds.), *The SAGE Handbook of Industrial Relations*. London: Sage, 92–112.

Frege, C. and Kelly, J. (2013). 'Theoretical perspectives on comparative employment relations', in C. Frege and J. Kelly (eds.), *Comparative Employment Relations in the Global Economy*. Abingdon: Routledge, 8–26.

French, S. and Hodder, A. (2016). '*Plus ça change*: the coalition government and the trade unions', in S. Williams and P. Scott (eds.), *Employment Relations under Coalition Government: The UK Experience, 2010–15*. Abingdon: Routledge, 165–83.

Frenkel, S. (2001). 'Globalization, athletic footwear commodity chains and employment relations in China'. *Organization Studies*, 22/4: 531–62.

Frenkel, S. (2006). 'Towards a theory of dominant interests, globalization, and work', in M. Korczynski, R. Hodson, and P. Edwards (eds.), *Social Theory at Work*. Oxford: Oxford University Press, 388–423.

Frenkel, S. and Kim, S. (2004). 'Corporate codes of labour practice and employment relations in sports shoe contractor factories in South Korea'. *Asia Pacific Journal of Human Resources*, 42/1: 6–31.

Frenkel, S. and Scott, D. (2002). 'Compliance, collaboration, and codes of labor practice: the Adidas connection'. *California Management Review*, 45/1: 29–49.

Friedman, A. (1977). *Industry and Labour: Class Struggle at Work and Monopoly Capitalism*. London: Macmillan.

Friedman, E. (2014). *The Insurgency Trap: Labor Politics in Postsocialist China*. Ithaca and London: ILR Press.

Friedman, E. and Lee, C. K. (2010). 'Remaking the world of Chinese labour: a 30-year retrospective'. *British Journal of Industrial Relations*, 48/3: 507–33.

Fryer, R. (1973). 'Redundancy, values and public policy'. *Industrial Relations Journal*, 4/2: 2–19.

Fryer, R. (1981). 'State, redundancy and the law', in R. Fryer, A. Hunt, D. McBarnet, and B. Moorhouse (eds.), *Law, State, and Society*. London: Croom Helm, 136–59.

Fuller, L. and Smith, V. (1991). 'Consumers' reports: management by customers in a changing economy'. *Work, Employment and Society*, 5/1: 1–16.

Gall, G. (2003). 'Marxism and industrial relations', in P. Ackers and A. Wilkinson (eds.), *Understanding Work and Employment: Industrial Relations in Transition*. Oxford: Oxford University Press, 316–24.

Gall, G. (2007). 'Trade union recognition in Britain: an emerging crisis for trade unions?' *Economic and Industrial Democracy*, 28/1: 78–109.

Gall. G. (2010a). 'Resisting recession and redundancy: contemporary worker occupations in Britain'. *Working USA*, 13/1: 107–32.

Gall, G. (2010*b*). 'The first ten years of the third statutory union recognition procedure in Britain'. *Industrial Law Journal*, 39/4: 444–8.

Gall, G. (2010*c*). 'Statutory union recognition provisions as stimulants to employer anti-unionism in three Anglo-Saxon countries'. *Economic and Industrial Democracy*, 31/1: 7–33.

Gall, G. (2011*a*). 'Contemporary workplace occupations in Britain: motivations, stimuli, dynamics and outcomes'. *Employee Relations*, 33/6: 607–23.

Gall, G. (2011*b*). 'Worker resistance and responses to the crisis of neo-liberal capitalism'. *Employee Relations*, 33/6: 588–91.

Gall, G. (2011*c*). 'Why revisit the Working Time Directive?' *The Guardian*, 21 November, http://www.guardian.co.uk/commentisfree/2011/nov/21/working-time-directive-lisbon-treaty?INTCMP=SRCH

Gall, G. (2012*a*). 'Union recognition in Britain: the end of legally induced voluntarism?' *Industrial Law Journal*, 41/4: 407–38.

Gall, G. (2012*b*). 'The engineering construction strikes in Britain, 2009'. *Capital and Class*, 36/3: 411–31.

Gall, G. (2013*a*). 'Quiescence continued? Recent strike activity in nine Western European economies'. *Economic and Industrial Democracy*, 34/4: 667–91.

Gall, G. (ed.) (2013*b*). *New Forms and Expressions of Conflict at Work*. Basingstoke: Palgrave Macmillan.

Gall, G. (2016*a*). 'The Trade Union Bill is now law—assessing the campaign to stop it'. *Huffington Post*, 5 May, http://www.huffingtonpost.co.uk/gregor-gall/trade-union-bill_b_9845574.html

Gall, G. (2016*b*). 'Injunctions as a legal weapon in collective industrial disputes in Britain, 2005–2014'. *British Journal of Industrial Relations*, DOI: 10.1111/bjir.12187

Gall, G. and Fiorito, J. (2011). 'The backward march of labour halted? Or, what is to be done with "union organising"? The cases of Britain and the USA'. *Capital and Class*, 35/2: 233–51.

Gall, G. and Hebdon, R. (2008). 'Conflict at work', in P. Blyton, N. Bacon, J. Fiorito, and E. Heery (eds.), *The SAGE Handbook of Industrial Relations*. London: Sage, 588–605.

Gall, G. and McKay, S. (2001). 'Facing "fairness at work": union perception of employer opposition and response to union recognition'. *Industrial Relations Journal*, 32/2: 94–113.

Gallie, D. (2005). 'Work pressure in Europe 1996–2001: trends and determinants'. *British Journal of Industrial Relations*, 43/4: 351–75.

Gallie, D., Felstead, A., Green, F., and Inanc, H. (2012). *Fear at Work in Britain: First Findings from the Skills and Employment Survey, 2012*. London: Centre for Learning and Life Chances in Knowledge Economies and Societies, Institute of Education, http://www.cardiff.ac.uk/research/explore/find-a-project/view/117804-skills-and-employment-survey-2012

Gallie, D., Felstead, A., Green, F., and Inanc, H. (2014). 'The quality of work in Britain over the economic crisis'. *International Review of Sociology*, 24/2: 207–24.

Gallie, D., White, M., Cheng, Y., and Tomlinson, M. (1998). *Restructuring the Employment Relationship*. Oxford: Clarendon.

Gamble, A. (2015). 'Austerity as statecraft'. *Parliamentary Affairs*, 68/1: 42–57.

Gamble, J. (2011). *Multinational Retailers and Consumers in China: Transferring Organizational Practices from the United Kingdom and Japan*. Basingstoke: Palgrave Macmillan.

Gardiner, L. (2015). *The Scale of Minimum Wage Underpayment in Social Care*. London: Resolution Foundation.

Garrahan, P. and Stewart, P. (1992). *The Nissan Enigma*. London: Mansell.

Garside, J. (2013). 'Child labour uncovered in Apple's supply chain'. *The Guardian*, 25 January, https://www.theguardian.com/technology/2013/jan/25/apple-child-labour-supply

Gatrell, C. (2005). *Hard Labour: The Sociology of Parenthood*. Maidenhead: Open University Press.

Gayle, D. and Butler, S. (2016). '"A potentially oppressive model": key points of Sports Direct Review'. *The Guardian*, 6 September, https://www.theguardian.com/business/2016/sep/06/sports-direct-inquiry-key-points-working-practices

Geary, D. (1985). *Policing Industrial Disputes, 1893 to 1985*. Cambridge: Cambridge University Press.

Geary, J. and Trif, A. (2011). 'Workplace partnership and the balance of advantage: a critical case analysis'. *British Journal of Industrial Relations*, 49/S1: s44–s69.

Geddes, A., Craig, G., Scott, S., Ackers, L., Robinson, O., and Scullion, D. (2013). *Forced Labour in the UK*. Joseph Rowntree Foundation.

Gennard, J. (1984). 'The implications of the Messenger Newspaper Group dispute'. *Industrial Relations Journal*, 15/3: 7–20.

Gentleman, A. (2014). 'Wisbech: the end of the road for migrant workers'. *The Guardian*, 8 October, https://www.theguardian.com/uk-news/2014/oct/08/wisbech-migrant-workers-exploited-gangmasters-eastern-europe

Gibbons, M. (2007). *Review of Employment Dispute Resolution in Great Britain*. London: DTI.

Gibson, O. (2016a). 'Fifa faces "tough decision" over Qatar World Cup if human rights abuses continue'. *The Guardian*, 14 April, https://www.theguardian.com/football/2016/apr/14/fifa-qatar-world-cup-report-human-rights

Gibson, O. (2016b). 'Fifa promises panel to ensure decent conditions for 2022 World Cup'. *The Guardian*, 22 April, https://www.theguardian.com/football/2016/apr/22/fifa-2022-qatar-world-cup-workers-conditions-gianni-infantino

Gilbert, D. (1996). 'Strikes in postwar Britain', in C. Wrigley (ed.), *A History of British Industrial Relations 1939–1979*. Cheltenham: Edward Elgar, 128–61.

Glover, J. and Kirton, G. (2006). *Women, Employment, and Organizations*. London: Routledge.

Glover, L., Tregaskis, O., and Butler, P. (2014). 'Mutual gains? The workers' verdict: a longitudinal study'. *The International Journal of Human Resource Management*, 25/6: 895–914.

Godard, J. (2004). 'A critical assessment of the high-performance paradigm'. *British Journal of Industrial Relations*, 42/2: 349–78.

Godard, J. (2011). 'What has happened to strikes?' *British Journal of Industrial Relations*, 49/2: 282–305.

Godard, J. (2014). 'The psychologisation of employment relations'. *Human Resource Management Journal*, 24/1: 1–18.

Gold, M. and Artus, A. (2015). 'Employee participation in Germany: tensions and challenges', in S. Johnstone and P. Ackers (eds.), *Finding a Voice at Work? New Perspectives on Employment Relations*. Oxford: Oxford University Press, 177–92.

Goldthorpe, J. (1977). 'Industrial Relations in Great Britain: a critique of reformism', in T. Clarke and L. Clements (eds.), *Trade Unions under Capitalism*. Glasgow: Fontana, 184–224.

Goldthorpe, J. (1980). *Social Mobility and Class Structure in Modern Britain*. Oxford: Clarendon Press.

Goldthorpe, J. (2016). 'Decades of investment in education have not improved social mobility'. *The Guardian*, 13 March, https://www.theguardian.com/commentisfree/2016/mar/13/decades-of-educational-reform-no-social-mobility

Goldthorpe, J. and Jackson, M. (2007). 'Intergenerational class mobility in contemporary Britain: political concerns and empirical findings'. *British Journal of Sociology*, 58/4: 525–46.

Gollan, P. (2003). 'All talk but no voice: employee voice at the Eurotunnel call centre'. *Economic and Industrial Democracy*, 24/4: 509–41.

Gollan, P. (2007). *Employee Representation in Non-union Firms*. London: Sage.

Gollan, P. (2010). 'Employer strategies towards non-union collective voice', in A. Wilkinson, P. Gollan, M. Marchington, and D. Lewin (eds.), *The Oxford Handbook of Participation in Organizations*. Oxford: Oxford University Press, 212–35.

Gollan, P. and Kalfa, S. (2015). 'Partnership at Eurotunnel. Challenges for NER and union representation', in P. Gollan, B. Kaufman, D. Taras, and A. Wilkinson (eds.), *Voice and Involvement at Work: Experience with Non-Union Representation*. New York and Abingdon: Routledge, 166–93.

Gollan, P., Kaufman, B., Taras, D., and Wilkinson, A. (2015). 'Voice and involvement at work: introduction', in P. Gollan, B. Kaufman, D. Taras, and A. Wilkinson (eds.), *Voice and Involvement at Work: Experience with Non-Union Representation*. New York and Abingdon: Routledge, 1–41.

Gollan, P. and Lewin, D. (2013). 'Employee representation in non-union firms: an overview'. *Industrial Relations*, 52/S1: 173–93.

Gollan, P. and Wilkinson, A. (2007). 'Implications of the EU Information and Consultation Directive and the Regulations in the UK—prospects for the future of employee representation'. *International Journal of Human Resource Management*, 18/7: 1145–58.

Goodley, S. and Ashby, J. (2015a). 'Revealed: how Sports Direct effectively pays below minimum wage'. *The Guardian*, 9 December, http://www.theguardian.com/business/2015/dec/09/how-sports-direct-effectively-pays-below-minimum-wage-pay

Goodley, S. and Ashby, J. (2015b). 'A day at "the gulag": what it's like to work at Sports Direct's warehouse'. *The Guardian*, 9 December, http://www.theguardian.com/business/2015/dec/09/sports-direct-warehouse-work-conditions

Goodman, J. (2000). 'Building bridges and settling differences: collective conciliation and arbitration under ACAS', in B. Towers and W. Brown (eds.), *Employment Relations in Britain: 25 Years of the Advisory, Conciliation and Arbitration Service*. Oxford: Blackwell, 31–65.

Goos, M. and Manning, A. (2007). 'Lousy and lovely jobs: the rising polarization of work in Britain'. *The Review of Economics and Statistics*, 89/1: 118–37.

Gospel, H. (1992). *Markets, Firms and the Management of Labour in Modern Britain*. Cambridge: Cambridge University Press.

Gospel, H. and Druker, J. (1998). 'The survival of national bargaining in the electrical contracting industry: a deviant case?' *British Journal of Industrial Relations*, 36/2: 249–67.

Gospel, H. and Willman, P. (2003). 'Dilemmas in worker representation: information, consultation and negotiation', in H. Gospel and S. Wood (eds.), *Representing Workers*. London: Routledge, 144–63.

Goss, D. (1991). *Small Business and Society*. London: Routledge.

Goss, D. and Adam-Smith, D. (2001). 'Pragmatism and compliance: employer responses to the Working Time Regulations'. *Industrial Relations Journal*, 32/3: 195–208.

Gouldner, A. (1955). *Wildcat Strike*. London: Routledge and Kegan Paul.

Grahl, J. (2015). 'Social Europe and the crisis of the European Union', in J. Jäger and E. Springler (eds.), *Aysmmetric Crisis in Europe and Possible Futures: Critical Political Economy and Post-Keynesian Perspectives*. Abingdon: Routledge, 168–85.

Gratton, L., Hope-Hailey, V., Stiles, P., and Truss, C. (1999). *Strategic Human Resource Management: Corporate Rhetoric and Employee Reality*. Oxford: Oxford University Press.

Gray, J. (2010). 'Progressive, like the 1980s'. *London Review of Books*, 21 October: 3–7.

Grayson, R. (2010). *The Liberal Democrat Journey to a Lib-Con Coalition—and Where Next?* London: Compass.

Green, F. (2001). 'It's been a hard day's night: the concentration and intensification of work in late twentieth century Britain'. *British Journal of Industrial Relations*, 39/1: 53–80.

Green, F. (2003). 'The demands of work', in R. Dickens, P. Gregg, and J. Wadsworth (eds.), *The Labour Market under New Labour*. Basingstoke: Palgrave Macmillan, 137–49.

Green, F. (2006). *Demanding Work*. Princeton NJ: Princeton University Press.

Green, F. (2011). 'Job quality in Britain under the Labour Government', in P. Gregg and J. Wadsworth (eds.), *The Labour Market in Winter: The State of Working Britain*. Oxford: Oxford University Press, 111–28.

Green, F., Huxley, K., and Whitfield, K. (2010). 'The employee experience of work', in A. Wilkinson, N. Bacon, T. Redman, and S. Snell (eds.), *The SAGE Handbook of Human Resource Management*. London: Sage, 377–92.

Green, F. and Whitfield, K. (2009). 'Employees' experience of work', in W. Brown, A. Bryson, J. Forth, and K. Whitfield (eds.), *The Evolution of the Modern Workplace*. Cambridge: Cambridge University Press, 201–29.

Greene, A.-M. (2003). 'Women and industrial relations', in P. Ackers and A. Wilkinson (eds.), *Understanding Work and Employment*. Oxford: Oxford University Press, 305–15.

Greene, A.-M. and Kirton, G. (2009). *Diversity Management in the UK: Organizational and Stakeholder Experiences*. Abingdon: Routledge.

Greene, A.-M. and Kirton, G. (2011). 'Diversity management meets downsizing: the case of a government department'. *Employee Relations*, 33/1: 22–39.

Greenhouse, S. (2008). *The Big Squeeze: Tough Times for the American Worker*. New York: Alfred Knopf.

Greer, I. and Hauptmeier, M. (2008). 'Political entrepreneurs and co-managers: labour transnationalism at four multinational auto companies'. *British Journal of Industrial Relations*, 46/1: 76–97.

Greer, I. and Hauptmeier, M. (2016). 'Management whipsawing: the staging of labor competition under globalization'. *ILR Review*, 69/1, 29–52.

Gregg, P. and Gardiner, L. (2015). *A Steady Job? The UK's Record on Labour Market Security and Stability since the Millennium*. London: Resolution Foundation.

Gregory, A. (2016). 'Work–life balance', in S. Edgell, H. Gottfried, and E. Granter (eds.), *The SAGE Handbook of the Sociology of Work and Employment*. London: Sage, 502–19.

Griffin, J. (1939). *Strikes: A Study in Quantitative Economics*. New York: Colombia University Press.

Grimshaw, D. (2015). 'Britain's social model: rapid descent from "liberal collectivism" to a "market society"', in D. Vaughan-Whitehead (ed.), *The European Social Model in Crisis: Is Europe Losing its Soul?* Cheltenham: Edward Elgar, 553–613.

Grimshaw, D. and Rubery, J. (2010). 'Pay and working time: shifting contours of the employment relationship', in T. Colling and M. Terry (eds.), *Industrial Relations: Theory and Practice* (3rd edn). Chichester: John Wiley, 349–77.

Grimshaw, D. and Rubery, J. (2012). 'The end of the UK's liberal collectivist social model? The implications of the coalition government's policy during the austerity crisis'. *Cambridge Journal of Economics*, 36/1: 105–26.

Guégnard, C. and Mériot, S.-A. (2009). 'Housekeepers and the siren call of hotel chains', in S. Bolton and M. Houlihan (eds.), *Work Matters: Critical Reflections on Contemporary Work*. Basingstoke: Palgrave Macmillan, 97–113.

Guest, D. (2011). 'Human resource management and performance: still searching for some answers'. *Human Resource Management Journal*, 21/1: 3–13.

Guest, D. (2014). 'Employee engagement: fashionable fad or long-term fixture?', in C. Truss, R. Delbridge, K. Alfes, A. Shantz, and E. Soane (eds.), *Employee Engagement in Theory and Practice*. Abingdon and New York: Routledge, 221–35.

Guest, D., Brown, W., Peccei, R., and Huxley, K. (2008). 'Does partnership at work increase trust? An analysis based on the 2004 Workplace Employment Relations Survey'. *Industrial Relations Journal*, 39/2: 124–52.

Guest, D. and Peccei, R. (2001). 'Partnership at work: mutuality and the balance of advantage'. *British Journal of Industrial Relations*, 39/2: 207–36.

Gumbrell-McCormick, R. (2013). 'The International Trade Union Confederation: from two (or more?) identities to one'. *British Journal of Industrial Relations*, 51/2: 240–63.

Gumbrell-McCormick, R. and Hyman, R. (2010). 'Works councils: the European model of industrial democracy?', in A. Wilkinson, P. Gollan, M. Marchington, and D. Lewin (eds.), *The Oxford Handbook of Participation in Organizations*. Oxford: Oxford University Press, 286–314.

Gunawardana, S. (2014). 'Reframing effective voice: a case study of Sri Lanka's export processing zones'. *Work, Employment, and Society*, 28/3: 452–68.

Gunnigle, P., Pulignano, V., Edwards, T., Belizón, M., Navrbjerg, S., Olsen, K., and Susaeta, L. (2015). 'Advancing understanding on industrial relations in multinational companies: key research challenges and the INTREPID contribution'. *Journal of Industrial Relations*, 57/2: 146–65.

Gunnigle, P., Turner, T., and D'Art, D. (1998). 'Counterposing collectivism: performance-related pay and industrial relations in greenfield sites'. *British Journal of Industrial Relations*, 36/4: 565–79.

Hale, A. and Wills, J. (eds.) (2005). *Threads of Labour: Garment Industry Supply Chains from the Workers' Perspective*. Oxford: Blackwell.

Hall, M. (1994). 'Industrial relations and the social dimension of European integration: before and after Maastricht', in R. Hyman and A. Ferner (eds.), *New Frontiers in European Industrial Relations*. Oxford: Blackwell, 281–311.

Hall, M. (2005). 'Using a multi-level consultation framework: the case of B&Q', in J. Storey (ed.), *Adding Value through Information and Consultation*. Basingstoke: Palgrave Macmillan, 240–53.

Hall, M. (2006). 'A cool response to the ICE Regulations? Employer and trade union approaches to the new legal framework for information and consultation'. *Industrial Relations Journal*, 37/5: 456–72.

Hall, M. and Edwards, P. (1999). 'Reforming the statutory redundancy consultation procedure'. *Industrial Law Journal*, 28/4: 299–318.

Hall, M., Hutchinson, S., Purcell, J., Terry, M., and Parker, J. (2013). 'Promoting effective consultation? Assessing the impact of the ICE Regulations'. *British Journal of Industrial Relations*, 51/2: 355–81.

Hall, M. and Marginson, P. (2005). 'Trojan horses or paper tigers? Assessing the significance of European Works Councils', in B. Harley, J. Hyman, and P. Thompson (eds.), *Participation and Democracy at Work*. Basingstoke: Palgrave Macmillan, 204–21.

Hall, M. and Purcell, J. (2012). *Consultation at Work: Regulation and Practice*. Oxford: Oxford University Press.

Hall, M., Purcell, J., and Adam, D. (2015). *Reforming the ICE Regulations—what chance now?* Warwick Papers in Industrial Relations, 102. Warwick: University of Warwick, Industrial Relations Research Unit.

Hall, M., Purcell, J., Terry, M., Hutchinson, S., and Parker, J. (2015). 'Trade union approaches to the ICE Regulations: defensive realism or missed opportunity?' *British Journal of Industrial Relations*, 53/2: 350–75.

Hall, M. and Terry, M. (2004). 'The emerging system of statutory worker representation', in G. Healy, E. Heery, P. Taylor, and W. Brown (eds.), *The Future of Worker Representation*. Basingstoke: Palgrave Macmillan, 207–28.

Hall, P. and Soskice, D. (2001). 'An introduction to varieties of capitalism', in P. Hall and D. Soskice (eds.), *Varieties of Capitalism: The Institutional Foundations of Comparative Advantage*. Oxford: Oxford University Press, 1–68.

Hamann, K. and Kelly, J. (2008). 'Varieties of capitalism and industrial relations', in P. Blyton, N. Bacon, J. Fiorito, and E. Heery (eds.), *The SAGE Handbook of Industrial Relations*. London: Sage, 129–48.

Hammer, N. (2005). 'International framework agreements: global industrial relations between rights and bargaining'. *Transfer*, 4/5: 511–30.

Handy, C. (1994). *The Empty Raincoat*. London: Hutchinson.

Hannon, E. (2016). 'Economic policy and employment under the coalition government', in S. Williams and P. Scott (eds.), *Work and Employment Relations under Coalition Government: The UK Experience, 2010–15*. Abingdon: Routledge, 29–48.

Harari, D. (2010). *Welfare to Work Programmes: An Overview*. Standard Note SN/EP/5627. London: House of Commons Library.

Harley, B. (2015). 'The one best way? "Scientific" research on HRM and the threat to critical scholarship'. *Human Resource Management Journal*, 25/4: 399–407.

Harris, C. (1987). *Redundancy and Recession*. Oxford: Basil Blackwell.

Harris, L. and Ogbonna, E. (2002). 'Exploring service sabotage: the antecedents, types and consequences of frontline, deviant, antiservice behaviors'. *Journal of Service Research*, 4/3: 163–83.

Harris, M. (2015). 'Uber: why the world's biggest ride-sharing company has no drivers'. *The Guardian*, 16 November, https://www.theguardian.com/technology/2015/nov/16/uber-worlds-biggest-ride-sharing-company-no-drivers

Harvey, D. (2005). *A Brief History of Neoliberalism*. Oxford: Oxford University Press.

Harvey, G. and Turnbull, P. (2015). 'Can labor arrest the "sky pirates"? Transnational trade unionism in the European civil aviation industry'. *Labor History*, 56/3: 308–26.

Harwood, R. (2015). 'The Impact of the Coalition Government on Disabled Workers: Workplace Experiences and Job Quality', http://dpac.uk.net/2015/04/new-study-finds-workplace-hell-for-disabled-workers/

Hatfield, I. (2015). *Self-Employment in Europe*. London: Institute for Public Policy Research.

Hawes, W. (2000). 'Setting the pace or running alongside? ACAS and the changing employment relationship', in B. Towers and W. Brown (eds.), *Employment Relations in Britain: 25 Years of the Advisory, Conciliation and Arbitration Service*. Oxford: Blackwell, 1–30.

Hay, C. (2015). 'What do Low-paid Workers Think Would Improve their Working Lives?' Joseph Rowntree Foundation Report, https://www.jrf.org.uk/report/what-do-low-paid-workers-think-would-improve-their-working-lives

Hayter, S. and Weinberg, B. (2011). 'Mind the gap: collective bargaining and wage inequality', in S. Hayter (ed.), *The Role of Collective Bargaining in the Global Economy: Negotiating for Social Justice*. Cheltenham: Edward Elgar, 136–86.

Head, J. and Lucas, R. (2004). 'Employee relations in the non-union hotel industry: a case of "determined opportunism"?'. *Personnel Review*, 33/6: 693–710.

Health and Safety Executive (HSE) (2015). 'Work Related Stress, Anxiety, and Depression Statistics in Great Britain 2015', http://www.hse.gov.uk/statistics/causdis/stress/stress.pdf

Healy, G., Bradley, H., and Mukherjee, N. (2004). 'Individualism and collectivism revisited: a study of black and minority ethnic women'. *Industrial Relations Journal*, 35/5: 451–66.

Healy, G. and Kirton, G. (2000). 'Women, power and trade union government in the UK'. *British Journal of Industrial Relations*, 38/3: 343–60.

Healy, G., Kirton, G., and Noon, M. (2010). 'Inequalities, intersectionality and equality and diversity initiatives: the conundrums and challenges of researching equality, inequalities, and diversity', in G. Healy, G. Kirton, and M. Noon (eds.), *Equality, Inequalities, and Diversity: Contemporary Challenges and Strategies*. Basingstoke: Palgrave Macmillan, 1–17.

Healy, G. and Oikelome, F. (2007). 'Equality and diversity actors: a challenge to traditional industrial relations?' *Equal Opportunities International*, 26/1: 44–65.

Heery, E. (1997). 'Performance-related pay and trade union de-recognition'. *Employee Relations*, 19/3: 208–21.

Heery, E. (1998*a*). 'A return to contract? Performance related pay in a public service'. *Work, Employment and Society*, 12/1: 73–95.

Heery, E. (1998*b*). 'Campaigning for part-time workers'. *Work, Employment and Society*, 12/2: 351–66.

Heery, E. (1998*c*). 'The relaunch of the Trades Union Congress'. *British Journal of Industrial Relations*, 36/3: 339–60.

Heery, E. (2006). 'Equality bargaining: where, who, why?' *Gender, Work, and Organization*, 13/6: 522–42.

Heery, E. (2009*a*). 'The representation gap and the future of worker representation'. *Industrial Relations Journal*, 40/4: 324–36.

Heery, E. (2009*b*). 'Worker voice and reward management', in G. White and J. Druker (eds.), *Reward Management: A Critical Text* (2nd edn). Abingdon: Routledge, 100–19.

Heery, E. (2015). 'Unions and the organising turn: reflections after 20 years of Organising Works'. *The Economic and Labour Relations Review*, 26/4: 545–60.

Heery, E. (2016). 'British industrial relations pluralism in the era of neoliberalism'. *Journal of Industrial Relations*, 58/1: 3–24.

Heery, E., Bacon, N., Blyton, P., and Fiorito, J. (2008). 'Introduction: the field of industrial relations', in P. Blyton, N. Bacon, J. Fiorito, and E. Heery (eds.), *The SAGE Handbook of Industrial Relations*. London: Sage, 1–32.

Heery, E. and Frege, C. (2006). 'New actors in industrial relations'. *British Journal of Industrial Relations*, 44/4: 601–4.

Heery, E. and Simms, M. (2008). 'Constraints on union organising in the United Kingdom'. *Industrial Relations Journal*, 39/1: 24–42.

Heery, E. and Simms, M. (2010). 'Employer responses to union organising: patterns and effects'. *Human Resource Management Journal*, 20/1: 3–22.

Heery, E. and Simms, M. (2011). 'Seizing an opportunity? Union organizing campaigns in Britain, 1998–2004'. *Labor History*, 52/1: 23–47.

Heery, E., Simms, M., Simpson, D., Delbridge, R., and Salmon, J. (2000*a*). 'Organizing unionism comes to the UK'. *Employee Relations*, 22/1: 38–57.

Heery, E., Simms, M., Delbridge, R., Salmon, J., and Simpson, D. (2000*b*). 'The TUC's Organising Academy: an assessment'. *Industrial Relations Journal*, 31/5: 400–15.

Heery, E., Simms, M., Delbridge, R., Salmon, J., and Simpson, D. (2000*c*). 'Union organizing in Britain: a survey of policy and practice'. *International Journal of Human Resource Management*, 11/5: 986–1007.

Heery, E., Simms, M., Delbridge, R., Salmon, J., and Simpson, D. (2003). 'Trade union recruitment policy in Britain: form and effects', in G. Gall (ed.), *Union Organizing: Campaigning for Union Recognition*. London: Routledge, 56–78.

Held, D. and McGrew, A. (2007). *Globalization/Anti-Globalization*. Cambridge: Polity.

Helfen, M. and Fichter, M. (2013). 'Building transnational union networks across global production networks: conceptualising a new arena of labour–management relations'. *British Journal of Industrial Relations*, 51/3: 553–76.

Helier, D. (2015). 'Uber drivers protest over fee rise in first London demo'. *The Guardian*, 12 November, http://www.theguardian.com/business/2015/nov/12/uber-drivers-protest-at-fee-hike-in-first-london-demo

Hemley, M. (2015). 'Royal Albert Hall and BECTU in dispute over staff ballot'. *The Stage*, 23 September, https://www.thestage.co.uk/news/2015/royal-albert-hall-bectu-dispute-staff-ballot/

Henning, C. (2015). 'Free trade zones/export processing zones', in D. Thomas Cook and J. Michael Ryan (eds.), *The Wiley Blackwell Encyclopedia of Consumption and Consumer Studies*. Chichester: Wiley-Blackwell, 310–12.

Henry, S. (1982). 'Factory law: the changing disciplinary technology of industrial social control'. *International Journal of the Sociology of Law*, 10/8: 365–83.

Hepple, B. (1992). 'The fall and rise of unfair dismissal', in W. McCarthy (ed.), *Legal Intervention in Industrial Relations: Gains and Losses*. Oxford: Blackwell, 79–102.

Hepple, B. (2005). *Labour Laws and Global Trade*. Oxford: Hart Publishing.

Hermann, C. (2014). 'Crisis, structural reform and the dismantling of the European Social Model(s)'. *Economic and Industrial Democracy*, DOI:10.1177/0143831X14555708

Hewison, K. (2016). 'Precarious work', in S. Edgell, H. Gottfried, and E. Granter (eds.), *The SAGE Handbook of the Sociology of Work and Employment*. London: SAGE, 428–43.

Heyes, J. (1997). 'Annualised hours and the "knock": the organisation of working time in a chemicals plant'. *Work, Employment and Society*, 11/1: 65–81.

Heyes, J. and Gray, A. (2001). 'The impact of the National Minimum Wage on the textiles and clothing industry'. *Policy Studies*, 22/2: 83–98.

Heyes, J. and Lewis, P. (2015). 'Relied upon for the heavy lifting: can employment protection legislation reforms lead the EU out of the jobs crisis?' *Industrial Relations Journal*, 46/2: 81–99.

Heyes, J., Lewis, P., and Clark, I. (2014). 'Varieties of capitalism reconsidered: learning from the Great Recession and its aftermath', in M. Hauptmeier and M. Vidal (eds.), *Comparative Political Economy of Work*. Basingstoke: Palgrave Macmillan, 33–51.

High Pay Centre (2014). *Reform Agenda: How to Make Top Pay Fairer*. London: High Pay Centre.

High Pay Centre (2016). *The State of Pay: High Pay Centre Briefing on Executive Pay*. London: High Pay Centre.

Hill, J. and Trist, E. (1953). 'A consideration of industrial accidents as a means of withdrawal from the work situation'. *Human Relations*, 6/4: 357–80.

Hinton, J. (1973). *The First Shop Stewards' Movement*. London: Allen and Unwin.

Hirst, P., Thompson, G., and Bromley, S. (2009). *Globalization in Question* (3rd edn). Cambridge: Polity.

HM Government (2010). *The Coalition: Our Programme for Government*. London: Cabinet Office.

HM Government/EHRC (2016). *Pregnancy and Maternity-related Discrimination and Disadvantage: Experiences of Mothers*. London: EHRC.

HM Treasury and Department of Trade and Industry (DTI) (2003). *Balancing Work and Family Life: Enhancing Choice and Support for Parents*. London: HM Treasury/DTI.

Hochschild, A. (1983). *The Managed Heart*. London: University of California Press.

Hodder, A. (2015). 'Young workers and unions: context and overview', in A. Hodder and L. Kretsos (eds.), *Young Workers and Trade Unions: A Global View*. Basingstoke: Palgrave Macmillan, 1–15.

Hodder, A., Williams, M., Kelly, J., and McCarthy, N. (2016). 'Does strike action stimulate trade union membership growth?' *British Journal of Industrial Relations*, DOI: 10.1111/bjir.12188

Holgate, J. (2009). 'Contested terrain: London's living wage campaign and the tensions between community and union organising', in J. McBride and I. Greenwood (eds.), *Community Unionism: A Comparative Analysis of Concepts and Contexts*. Basingstoke: Palgrave Macmillan, 49–74.

Holgate, J. (2015a). 'An international study of trade union involvement in community organizing: same model, different outcomes'. *British Journal of Industrial Relations*, 53/3: 460–83.

Holgate, J. (2015b). 'Community organising in the UK: a "new" approach for trade unions?' *Economic and Industrial Democracy*, 36/3: 431–55.

Holgate, J., Hebson, G., and McBride, A. (2006). 'Why gender and "difference" matters: a critical appraisal of industrial relations research'. *Industrial Relations Journal*, 37/4: 310–28.

Holloway, L. (2012). 'The Equality and Human Rights Commission is being destroyed'. *The Guardian*, 24 August, http://www.guardian.co.uk/commentisfree/2012/aug/24/coalition-destroy-equality-human-rights-commission

Holmes, C. and Mayhew, K. (2012). *The Changing Shape of the UK Job Market and its Implications for the Bottom Half of Earners*. London: Resolution Foundation.

Holmes, E. and Oakley, M. (2012). *Local Pay, Local Growth: Reforming Pay Setting in the Public Sector*. London: Policy Exchange.

Hook, L. (2016). 'Uber drivers' class action lawsuit proceeds to trial', *Financial Times*, 28 January, http://www.ft.com/cms/s/0/bf0a302a-c557-11e5-b3b1-7b2481276e45.html#axzz46SP0zjOU

Hopkins, B. (2014). 'Explaining variations in absence rates: temporary and agency workers in the food manufacturing sector'. *Human Resource Management Journal*, 24/2: 227–40.

Hoque, K. and Bacon, N. (2011). 'Assessing the impact of Union Learning Representatives on training: evidence from a matched sample of ULRs and managers'. *Work, Employment and Society*, 25/2: 218–33.

Hoque, K. and Bacon, N. (2014). 'Unions, joint regulation, and workplace equality policy and practice in Britain: evidence from the 2004 Workplace Employment Relations Survey'. *Work, Employment, and Society*, 28/2: 265–84.

Hoque, K. and Noon, M. (2004). 'Equal opportunities policy and practice in Britain: evaluating the "empty shell" hypothesis'. *Work, Employment and Society*, 18/3: 481–506.

House of Commons (2015). *Impact of the Closure of City Link on Employment*. Business, Innovation, and Skills and Scottish Affairs First Joint Report, HC 928. London: The Stationery Office Limited.

House of Commons Business, Innovation, and Skills Committee (2016). *Employment Practices at Sports Direct*. Third Report of Session 2016–17, HC 219.

House of Commons Employment Committee (1994). *The Future of the Unions*. Third Report Volume II, *Minutes of Evidence*. London: HMSO.

House of Commons Justice Committee (2016). *Courts and Tribunals Fees*. Second Report of Session 2016–17, HC 167.

House of Commons Women and Equalities Select Committee (2016a). 'Employment Opportunities for Muslims in the UK', http://www.parliament.uk/business/committees/committees-a-z/commons-select/women-and-equalities-committee/news-parliament-2015/employment-opportunities-muslims-in-uk-launch-15-16/

House of Commons Women and Equalities Select Committee (2016b). *Pregnancy and Maternity Discrimination*. First Report of Session 2016–17, HC 90.

Howell, C. (2004). 'Is there a third way for industrial relations?' *British Journal of Industrial Relations*, 42/1: 1–22.

Howell, C. (2005). *Trade Unions and the State*. Princeton NJ: Princeton University Press.

Howell, C. and Kolins Givan, R. (2011). 'Rethinking institutions and institutional change in European industrial relations'. *British Journal of Industrial Relations*, 49/2: 231–55.

Huselid, M. (1995). 'The impact of human resource management practices on turnover, productivity, and corporate financial performance'. *Academy of Management Journal*, 38/3: 635–72.

Huws, U. and Joyce, S. (2016). *Size of the UK's 'Gig Economy' Revealed for the First Time*. Brussels: Foundation for European Progressive Studies.

Huzzard, T. and Docherty, P. (2005). 'Between global and local: eight European Works Councils in retrospect and prospect'. *Economic and Industrial Democracy*, 26/4: 541–68.

Hyman, J. and Marks, A. (2008). 'Frustrated ambitions: the reality of balancing work and life for call centre employees', in C. Warhurst, D. Eikhof, and A. Haunschild (eds.), *Work Less, Live More: Critical Analysis of the Work–Life Boundary*. Basingstoke: Palgrave Macmillan, 191–209.

Hyman, J. and Mason, B. (1995). *Managing Employee Involvement and Participation*. London: Sage.

Hyman, J. and Summers, J. (2004). 'Lacking balance? Work–life employment practices in the modern economy'. *Personnel Review*, 33/4: 418–29.

Hyman, R. (1971). *The Workers' Union*. Oxford: Clarendon Press.

Hyman, R. (1972). *Disputes Procedure in Action*. London: Heinemann.

Hyman, R. (1975). *Industrial Relations: A Marxist Introduction*. London: Macmillan.

Hyman, R. (1977). *Strikes* (2nd edn). Glasgow: Fontana/Collins.

Hyman, R. (1987). 'Strategy or structure? Capital, labour and control'. *Work, Employment and Society*, 1/1: 25–55.

Hyman, R. (1989). *The Political Economy of Industrial Relations*. Basingstoke: Macmillan.

Hyman, R. (2001). *Understanding European Trade Unionism: Between Market, Class and Society*. London: Sage.

Hyman, R. (2003). 'The historical evolution of British industrial relations', in P. Edwards (ed.), *Industrial Relations* (2nd edn). Oxford: Blackwell, 37–57.

Hyman, R. (2005). 'Trade unions and the politics of the European Social Model'. *Economic and Industrial Democracy*, 26/1: 9–40.

Hyman, R. (2010). 'British industrial relations: the European Dimension', in T. Colling and M. Terry (eds.), *Industrial Relations: Theory and Practice* (3rd edn). Chichester: John Wiley, 54–79.

Hyman, R. (2011). *Trade Unions, Lisbon and Europe 2020: From Dream to Nightmare*, LSE 'Europe in Question' Discussion Paper Series, No. 45. London: LSE.

Incomes Data Services (IDS) (2009). 'Discipline, Grievance, and Mediation'. *IDS HR Studies*, 906.

Incomes Data Services (IDS) (2011a). 'Employee consultation'. *IDS HR Studies*, 949, September.

Incomes Data Services (IDS) (2011b). *The Impact of the National Minimum Wage on Pay Setting since 1994: A Report for the Low Pay Commission*. London: IDS.

Incomes Data Services (IDS) (2012). *Crowding Out: Fact or Fiction?* London: IDS.

Incomes Data Services (IDS) (2013). 'Annual hours at Knighton plant saves Premier Foods almost £1m a year'. *IDS Case Study*, 17 June, https://ids.thomsonreuters.com/taxonomy/term/35/all?page=9

Independent Commission on Social Mobility (2009). *Report of the Independent Commission on Social Mobility*. London: Independent Commission on Social Mobility.

IndustriALL (2015). 'IndustriALL Global Union and H&M sign Global Framework Agreement'. 3 November, http://www.industriall-union.org/industriall-global-union-and-hm-sign-global-framework-agreement

Institute for Global Labour and Human Rights (2015). *Dirty Toys Made in China: The Zhenyang Wanju Sweatshop Factory*. Pittsburgh: Institute for Global Labour and Human Rights.

International Labour Organization (ILO) (2009). *Rules of the Game: A Brief Introduction to International Labour Standards* (revised edn). Geneva: ILO.

International Labour Organization (ILO) (2011). *World of Work Report 2011: Making Markets Work for Jobs*. Geneva: International Institute for Labour Studies.

International Labour Organization (ILO) (2012). *World of Work Report 2012: Better Jobs for a Better Economy*. Geneva: ILO, International Institute for Labour Studies.

International Labour Organization (ILO) (2013a). *Civil Aviation and its Changing World of Work*. Geneva: ILO.

International Labour Organization (ILO) (2013b). *World of Work Report 2013: Repairing the Economic and Social Fabric*. Geneva: ILO.

International Labour Organization (ILO) (2016). 'Complaint Concerning Non-observance by Qatar of the Forced Labour Convention, 1930 (No. 29), and the Labour Inspection Convention, 1947 (No. 81), made by Delegates to the 103rd Session (2014) of the International Labour Conference under Article 26 of the ILO Constitution'. International Labour Office Governing Body, 326th Session, Geneva, 10–24 March, http://www.ilo.org/wcmsp5/groups/public/---ed_norm/---relconf/documents/meetingdocument/wcms_459148.pdf

International Trade Union Confederation (ITUC) (2012). *Annual Survey of Violations of Trade Union Rights 2012*. Brussels: ITUC.

International Trade Union Confederation (ITUC) (2015a). *ITUC Global Rights Index: The World's Worst Countries for Workers*. Brussels: ITUC.

International Trade Union Confederation (ITUC) (2015b). *Qatar: Profit and Loss. Counting the Cost of Modern Day Slavery in Qatar: What Price is Freedom?* Brussels: ITUC.

Jagodzinski, R. (2011). 'EWCs after 15 years—success or failure?' *Transfer*, 17/2: 203–16.

James, G. (2011). 'The law relating to pregnancy and maternity leave', in T. Wright and H. Conley (eds.), *The Gower Handbook of Discrimination at Work*. Farnham: Gower, 47–56.

James, P. (2016). 'Protecting life and death under the coalition', in S. Williams and P. Scott (eds.), *Employment Relations under Coalition Government: The UK Experience, 2010–2015*. Abingdon: Routledge, 127–43.

James, P. and Karmowska, J. (2016). 'British union renewal: does salvation really lie beyond the workplace?' *Industrial Relations Journal*, 47/2: 102–16.

James, P., Tombs, S., and Whyte, D. (2013). 'An independent review of British health and safety regulation? From common sense to non-sense'. *Policy Studies*, 34/1: 36–52.

James, S. and Lloyd, C. (2008). 'Too much pressure? Retailer power and occupational health and safety in the food processing industry'. *Work, Employment and Society*, 22/4: 713–30.

Jefferys, S. (2000). 'A "Copernican Revolution" in French industrial relations: are the times a' changing?' *British Journal of Industrial Relations*, 38/2: 241–60.

Jefferys, S. (2003). *Liberté, Égalité and Fraternité at Work: Changing French Employment Relations*. Basingstoke: Palgrave Macmillan.

Jenkins, S. and Delbridge, R. (2007). 'Disconnected workplaces: interests and identities in the "high performance" factory', in S. Bolton and M. Houlihan (eds.), *Searching for the Human in Human Resource Management*. Basingstoke: Palgrave Macmillan, 195–218.

Jenkins, J. and Turnbull, P. (2011). 'Can workers of the world unite? Globalization and the employment relationship', in P. Blyton, E. Heery, and P. Turnbull (eds.), *Reassessing the Employment Relationship*. Basingstoke: Palgrave Macmillan, 195–224.

Jewson, N. and Mason, D. (1986). 'The theory and practice of equal opportunities policies: liberal and radical approaches'. *Sociological Review*, 34/2: 307–34.

Johnston, C. (2016). 'National Trust criticised for using unpaid interns to do admin jobs'. *The Guardian*, 11 June, https://www.theguardian.com/uk-news/2016/jun/11/national-trust-criticised-for-using-unpaid-interns-to-do-admin-jobs

Johnstone, S. (2015). 'The case for workplace partnership', in S. Johnstone and P. Ackers (eds.), *Finding a Voice at Work? New Perspectives on Employment Relations*. Oxford: Oxford University Press, 153–74.

Johnstone, S. (2016). 'Participation and partnership in the UK: progress and prospects', in S. Johnstone and A. Wilkinson (eds.), *Developing Positive Employment Relations: International Experiences of Labour Management Partnership*. London: Palgrave Macmillan, 77–99.

Johnstone, S., Ackers, P., and Wilkinson, A. (2009). 'The British partnership phenomenon: a ten year review'. *Human Resource Management Journal*, 19/3: 260–79.

Johnstone, S. and Wilkinson, A. (2015). 'Employee voice in a dot com. The rise and demise of the employee forum at Web Bank', in P. Gollan, B. Kaufman, D. Taras, and A. Wilkinson (eds.), *Voice and Involvement at Work: Experience with Non-Union Representation*. New York and Abingdon: Routledge, 146–68.

Johnstone, S. and Wilkinson, A. (2016). 'Developing positive employment relations: international experiences of labour-management partnership', in S. Johnstone and A. Wilkinson (eds.), *Developing Positive Employment Relations: International Experiences of Labour Management Partnership*. London: Palgrave Macmillan, 3–24.

Johnstone, S., Wilkinson, A., and Ackers, P. (2010). 'Critical incidents of partnership: five years' experience at NatBank'. *Industrial Relations Journal*, 41/4: 382–98.

Jones, C. and Saundry, R. (2012). 'The practice of discipline: evaluating the roles and relationship between managers and HR professionals'. *Human Resource Management Journal*, 22/3: 252–66.

Jones, G. (2005). *Multinationals and Global Capitalism: From the Nineteenth to the Twenty-First Century*. Oxford: Oxford University Press.

Jones, O. (2012). *Chavs: The Demonization of the Working Class*. London: Verso.

Jones, T. and Ram, M. (2010). 'Review article: ethnic variations on the small firm labour process'. *International Small Business Journal*, 28/2: 163–73.

Jordan, E., Thomas, A., Kitching, J., and Blackburn, R. (2013). *Employment Regulation. Part A: Employer Perceptions and the Impact of Employment Regulation*. Employment Relations Research Series No. 123. London: Department of Business, Innovation, and Skills.

Kahn-Freund, O. (1964). 'Legal framework', in A. Flanders and H. Clegg (eds.), *The System of Industrial Relations in Great Britain*. Oxford: Basil Blackwell, 42–127.

Kahn-Freund, O. (1977). *Labour and the Law* (2nd edn). London: Stevens.

Kalaayan (2015). 'For the Modern Slavery Bill to protect migrant domestic workers it must ensure basic rights'. *Kalaayan Briefing*, http://www.kalayaan.org.uk/wp-content/uploads/2014/09/Kalayaan-Briefing-for-Commons-MSB-17.3.15.pdf

Kalleberg, A. (2009). 'Precarious work, insecure workers: employment relations in transition'. *American Sociological Review*, 74/1: 1–22.

Kalleberg, A. (2011). *Good Jobs, Bad Jobs: The Rise of Polarized and Precarious Employment Systems in the United States, 1970s to 2000s*. New York: Russell Sage Foundation.

Kalleberg, A. (2012). 'Book review symposium. Guy Standing—*The Precariat: the New Dangerous Class*'. *Work, Employment, and Society*, 26/4: 685–6.

Kalleberg, A. (2016). 'Good jobs, bad jobs', in S. Edgell, H. Gottfried, and E. Granter (eds.), *The SAGE Handbook of the Sociology of Work and Employment*. London: SAGE, 111–28.

Kalman, D. (1999). 'Collective wisdom'. *People Management*, 25 February: 37–43.

Kamenou, N., Netto, G., and Fearfull, A. (2013). 'Ethnic minority women in the Scottish labour market: employers' perceptions'. *British Journal of Management*, 24/3: 398–413.

Kandola, B. and Fullerton, J. (1994). *Managing the Mosaic: Diversity in Action*. London: IPD.

Kantor, J. and Streitfeld, D. (2015). 'Inside Amazon: wrestling ideas in a bruising workplace'. *New York Times*, 15 August, http://www.nytimes.com/2015/08/16/technology/inside-amazon-wrestling-big-ideas-in-a-bruising-workplace.html?_r=4

Karamessini, M. (2015). 'Greece as an international test-case: economic adjustment through a Troika/state-induced depression and social catastrophe', in S. Lehndorff (ed.), *Divisive Integration: The Triumph of Failed Ideas in Europe—Revisited*. Brussels: ETUI, 95–126.

Katz, H. and Darbishire, O. (2000). *Converging Divergences: Worldwide Changes in Employment Systems*. Ithaca NY: ILR Cornell University Press.

Katz, H. and Wailes, N. (2014). 'Convergence and divergence in employment relations', in A. Wilkinson, G. Wood, and R. Deeg (eds.), *The Oxford Handbook of Employment Relations: Comparative Employment Systems*. Oxford: Oxford University Press, 42–61.

Kaufman, B. (2004). *The Global Evolution of Industrial Relations*. Geneva: ILO.

Kaufman, B. (2010a). 'The theoretical foundation of industrial relations and its implications'. *Industrial and Labor Relations Review*, 64/1: 74–108.

Kaufman, B. (2010b). 'SHRM theory in the post-Huselid era: why it is fundamentally misspecified'. *Industrial Relations*, 49/2: 286–313.

Kaufman, B. (2011). 'The future of employment relations: insights from theory', in K. Townsend and A. Wilkinson (eds.), *The Edward Elgar Research Handbook on Work and Employment Relations*. Cheltenham: Edward Elgar, 13–44.

Kaufman, B. (2013). 'Keeping the commitment model in the air during turbulent times: employee involvement at Delta Airlines'. *Industrial Relations*, 52/S1: 343–77.

Kaufman, B. (2014). 'History of the British Industrial Relations field reconsidered: getting from the Webbs to the new employment relations paradigm'. *British Journal of Industrial Relations*, 52/1: 1–31.

Kaufman, B. and Taras, D. (2010). 'Employee participation through non-union forms of employee representation', in A. Wilkinson, P. Gollan, M. Marchington, and D. Lewin (eds.), *The Oxford Handbook of Participation in Organizations*. Oxford: Oxford University Press, 258–85.

Keller, B. (2003). 'The European social partners: projects and future perspectives', in D. Foster and P. Scott (eds.), *Trade Unions in Europe: Meeting the Challenge*. Brussels: Peter Lang, 115–43.

Keller, B. and Sörries, B. (1999). 'The new European social dialogue: old wine in new bottles?' *Journal of European Social Policy*, 9/2: 111–25.

Keller, B. and Weber, S. (2011). 'Sectoral social dialogue at EU level: problems and prospects of implementation'. *European Journal of Industrial Relations*, 17/3: 227–43.

Kelly, J. (1998). *Rethinking Industrial Relations*. London: Routledge.

Kelly, J. (2005a). 'Social partnership agreements in Britain', in M. Stuart and M. Martinez Lucio (eds.), *Partnership and Modernisation in Employment Relations*. London: Routledge, 188–209.

Kelly, J. (2005b). 'Social movement theory and union revitalization in Britain', in S. Fernie and D. Metcalf (eds.), *Trade Unions: Resurgence or Demise?* London: Routledge, 62–82.

Kelly, J. (2011). 'Theories of collective action and union power', in G. Gall, A. Wilkinson, and R. Hurd (eds.), *The International Handbook of Labour Unions: Responses to Neo-Liberalism*. Cheltenham: Edward Elgar, 13–28.

Kelly, J. (2015). 'Conflict: trends and forms of collective action'. *Employee Relations*, 37/6: 720–32.

Kelly, J. and Badigannavar, V. (2004). 'Union organizing', in J. Kelly and P. Willman (eds.), *Union Organization and Activity*. London: Routledge, 32–50.

Kelly, J. and Frege, C. (2013). 'Introduction: global challenges at work', in C. Frege and J. Kelly (eds.), *Comparative Employment Relations in the Global Economy*. Abingdon: Routledge, 3–7.

Kerr, C., Dunlop, J., Harbison, F., and Myers, C. (1962). *Industrialism and Industrial Man*. London: Heinemann.

Kerr, C. and Siegel, A. (1954). 'The inter-industry propensity to strike', in A. Kornhauser, R. Dubin, and A. Ross (eds.), *Industrial Conflict*. New York: McGraw-Hill, 189–212.

Kersley, B., Alpin, C., Forth, J., Bryson, A., Bewley, H., Dix, G., and Oxenbridge, S. (2006). *Inside the Workplace: Findings from the 2004 Workplace Employment Relations Survey*. London: Routledge.

Kessler, I. (2000). 'Remuneration systems', in S. Bach and K. Sisson (eds.), *Personnel Management* (3rd edn). Oxford: Blackwell, 264–86.

Kessler, I. and Purcell, J. (1995). 'Individualism and collectivism in theory and practice: management style and the design of pay systems', in P. Edwards (ed.), *Industrial Relations: Theory and Practice in Britain*. Oxford: Blackwell, 337–67.

Kessler, S. (1993). 'Procedures and third parties'. *British Journal of Industrial Relations*, 31/2: 211–25.

Kessler, S. (1994). 'Incomes policy'. *British Journal of Industrial Relations*, 32/2: 181–99.

Kingma, M. (2006). *Nurses on the Move: Migration and the Global Health Care Economy*. Ithaca NY: Cornell University Press.

Kingsmill, D. (2014). *Taking Care: An Independent Report into Working Conditions in the Care Sector*. London: Labour Party.

Kirby, P. (2016). *Leading People 2016: The Educational Backgrounds of the UK Professional Elite*. London: Sutton Trust.

Kirk, E., McDermont, M., and Busby, N. (2015). *Employment Tribunal Claims: Debunking the Myths*. Policy Bristol, Policy Report 1. Bristol: University of Bristol.

Kirkpatrick, I. and Hoque, K. (2006). 'A retreat from permanent employment? Accounting for the rise of professional agency work in UK public services'. *Work, Employment and Society*, 20/4: 649–66.

Kirton, G. (1999). 'Sustaining and developing women's trade union activism: a gendered project?' *Gender, Work and Organization*, 6/4: 213–23.

Kirton, G. and Greene, A.-M. (2002). 'The dynamics of positive action in UK trade unions: the case of women and black members'. *Industrial Relations Journal*, 33/2: 157–72.

Kirton, G. and Greene, A.-M. (2009). 'The costs and opportunities of doing diversity work in mainstream organisations'. *Human Resource Management Journal*, 19/2: 159–75.

Kirton, G. and Greene, A.-M. (2015). *The Dynamics of Managing Diversity: A Critical Approach* (4th edn). London and New York: Routledge.

Kirton, G. and Healy, G. (1999). 'Transforming union women: the role of women trade union officials in union renewal'. *Industrial Relations Journal*, 30/1: 31–45.

Kirton, G. and Healy, G. (2013). 'Commitment and collective identity of long-term union participation: the case of women union leaders in the UK and USA'. *Work, Employment and Society*, 27/2: 195–212.

Kivimäki, M. et al. (2015). 'Long working hours and risk of coronary heart disease and stroke: a systematic review and meta-analysis of published and unpublished data for 603 838 individuals'. *The Lancet*, 386: 1739–46.

Klass, B. (2010). 'Discipline and grievances', in A. Wilkinson, N. Bacon, T. Redman, and S. Snell (eds.), *The SAGE Handbook of Human Resource Management*. London: Sage, 322–35.

Klein, N. (2000). *No Logo*. London: Flamingo.

Knight, K. and Latreille, P. (2000). 'Discipline, dismissals and complaints to employment tribunals'. *British Journal of Industrial Relations*, 38/4: 533–55.

Knight, S. (2016). 'How Uber conquered London'. *The Guardian*, 27 April, https://www.theguardian.com/technology/2016/apr/27/how-uber-conquered-london

Knowles, K. (1952). *Strikes—a Study in Industrial Conflict*. Oxford: Basil Blackwell.

Knox, A. (2010). '"Lost in translation": an analysis of temporary work agency employment in hotels'. *Work, Employment and Society*, 24/3: 449–67.

Kochan, T., Eaton, A., McKersie, R., and Adler, P. (2009). *Healing Together: The Labor–Management Partnership at Kaiser Permanente*. Ithaca NY: Cornell University Press.

Kochan, T. A. and Osterman, P. (1994). *The Mutual Gains Enterprise*. Boston: Harvard University Press.

Koo, H. (2001). *Korean Workers: The Culture and Politics of Class Formation*. Ithaca NY: Cornell University Press.

Korczynski, M. (2002). *Human Resource Management in Service Work*. Basingstoke: Palgrave.

Koukiadiki, A. and Kretsos, L. (2012). 'Opening Pandora's Box: the sovereign debt crisis and labour market regulation in Greece'. *Industrial Law Journal*, 41/3: 276–304.

KPMG (2015). 'Six Million Brits are Earning Less than a Living Wage'. KPMG Press Release, 1 November, https://home.kpmg.com/uk/en/home/media/press-releases/2015/11/six-million-brits-are-earning-less-than-a-living-wage.html

Krugman, P. (2012). *End this Depression Now!* New York: W. W. Norton.

Kumar, K. (1986). *Prophecy and Progress: The Sociology of Industrial and Post-industrial Society*. Harmondsworth: Penguin.

Kuruvilla, S. and Lakhani, T. (2013). 'Globalization', in C. Frege and J. Kelly (eds.), *Comparative Employment Relations in the Global Economy*. Abingdon: Routledge, 369–89.

Kuruvilla, S. and Verma, A. (2006). 'International labor standards, soft regulation, and national government roles'. *Journal of Industrial Relations*, 48/1: 41–58.

La Botz, D. (2001). *Made in Indonesia: Indonesian Workers since Suharto*. Cambridge MA: South End Press.

Labour Research (2016). 'Are workers getting a fair share of this gig?' *Labour Research*, August: 13–15.

Lamont, T. (2016). 'The big gamble. The dangerous world of British betting shops'. *The Guardian*, 31 May, https://www.theguardian.com/business/2016/may/31/big-gamble-dangerous-british-betting-shops

Lang, C., Clauwert, S., and Schömann, I. (2013). *Working Time Reforms in Times of Crisis*. Working Paper 2013.04. Brussels: European Trade Union Institute.

Langlois, M. and Lucas, R. (2005). 'The adaptation of hospitality and retail firms to the NMW: a focus on the impact of age-related clauses'. *Industrial Relations Journal*, 36/1: 77–92.

Lansley, S. (2011). *Britain's Livelihood Crisis*. London: TUC.

Lansley, S. (2012). *All in this Together? An Audit of the Impact of the Downturn on the Workforce*. London: TUC.

Lansley, S. and Mack, J. (2015). *Breadline Britain: The Rise of Mass Poverty*. London: Oneworld.

Lapavitsas, C. (2011). 'Theorizing financialization'. *Work, Employment and Society*, 25/4: 611–26.

Latreille, P. (2011). *Mediation: A Thematic Review of the ACAS/CIPD Evidence*. ACAS Research Paper, 13/11. London: ACAS.

Latreille, P., Latreille, J., and Knight, K. (2007). 'Employment tribunals and ACAS: evidence from a survey of representatives'. *Industrial Relations Journal*, 38/2: 136–54.

Latreille, P. and Saundry, R. (2014). 'Workplace mediation', in W. Roche, P. Teague, and A. Colvin (eds.), *The Oxford Handbook of Conflict Management in Organizations*. Oxford: Oxford University Press, 190–209.

Lawrence, F. (2012). 'How gangmasters exploit Britain's "on tap" flexible workforce'. *The Guardian*, 31 October, https://www.theguardian.com/commentisfree/2012/oct/31/gangmasters-exploit-flexible-workforce

Lawrence, F. (2016a). 'HMRC cleaners in Merseyside to strike in battle over pay'. *The Guardian*, 25 July, https://www.theguardian.com/uk-news/2016/jul/25/hmrc-cleaners-merseyside-strike-pay-national-living-wage

Lawrence, F. (2016b). 'HMRC cleaners striking over pay: "they've treated us appallingly"'. *The Guardian*, 28 July, https://www.theguardian.com/uk-news/2016/jul/28/hmrc-cleaners-striking-over-pay-national-living-wage

Lawrence, F. (2016c). 'HMRC cleaners call off industrial action after hours are reinstated'. *The Guardian*, 6 September, https://www.theguardian.com/uk-news/2016/sep/06/hmrc-cleaners-call-off-industrial-action-hours-reinstated

Leadbeater, C. (1999). *Living on Thin Air*. London: Viking.

Lee, C.-K. (2007). *Against the Law: Labor Protests in China's Rustbelt and Sunbelt*. Berkeley CA: University of California Press.

Lee, S. (2011). '"We are all in this together": the coalition agenda for British modernization', in S. Lee and M. Beech (eds.), *The Cameron-Clegg Government: Coalition Politics in an Age of Austerity*. Basingstoke: Palgrave Macmillan, 3–23.

Lee, S. (2015). 'Indebted and unbalanced: the political economy of the Coalition', in M. Beech and S. Lee (eds.), *The Conservative–Liberal Coalition: Examining the Cameron-Clegg Government*. Basingstoke: Palgrave Macmillan, 16–35.

Legge, K. (2005). *Human Resource Management: Rhetoric and Realities* (2nd edn). Basingstoke: Palgrave Macmillan.

Lehndorff, S. (2015). 'Europe's divisive integration—an overview', in S. Lehndorff (ed.), *Divisive Integration: The Triumph of Failed Ideas in Europe—Revisited*. Brussels: ETUI, 7–37.

Leidner, R. (2002). 'Fast-food work in the United States', in T. Royle and B. Towers (eds.), *Labour Relations in the Global Fast-Food Industry*. London: Routledge, 8–29.

Leighton, P. and Wynn, M. (2011). 'Classifying employment relationships—more sliding doors of a better regulatory framework?' *Industrial Law Journal*, 40/1: 5–44.

Leisink, P. (1999). 'Introduction', in P. Leisink (ed.), *Globalization and Labour Relations*. Cheltenham: Edward Elgar, 1–24.

Leopold, J. (1997). 'Trade unions, political fund ballots and the Labour party'. *British Journal of Industrial Relations*, 35/1: 23–38.

Leopold, J. (2006). 'Trade unions and the third round of political fund balloting'. *Industrial Relations Journal*, 37/3: 190–208.

Leschke, J., Theodoropoulou, S., and Watt, A. (2015). 'Towards "Europe 2020"? Austerity and new economic governance in the EU', in S. Lehndorff (ed.), *Divisive Integration: The Triumph of Failed Ideas in Europe—Revisited*. Brussels: ETUI, 295–329.

Lewis, P. (1993). *The Successful Management of Redundancy*. Oxford: Blackwell.

Lewis, S. (1997). '"Family friendly" employment policies: a route to changing organizational culture or playing about at the margins?' *Gender, Work and Organization*, 4/1: 13–23.

Liff, S. (1997). 'Two routes to managing diversity: individual differences or social group characteristics?' *Employee Relations*, 19/1: 11–26.

Liff, S. (1999). 'Diversity and equal opportunities: room for a constructive compromise?' *Human Resource Management Journal*, 9/1: 65–75.

Liff, S. (2003). 'The industrial relations of a diverse workforce', in P. Edwards (ed.), *Industrial Relations* (2nd edn). Oxford: Blackwell, 420–46.

Liff, S. and Wacjman, J. (1996). '"Sameness" and "difference" revisited: which way forward for equal opportunity initiatives?' *Journal of Management Studies*, 33/1: 79–94.

Liff, S. and Ward, K. (2001). 'Distorted views through the glass ceiling: the construction of women's understandings of promotion and senior management positions'. *Gender, Work and Organization*, 8/1: 19–36.

Lillie, N. and Martinez Lucio, M. (2004). 'International trade union revitalization: the role of national union approaches', in C. Frege and J. Kelly (eds.), *Varieties of Unionism*. Oxford: Oxford University Press, 159–80.

Lindley, J. and Machin, S. (2013). 'Wage inequality in the Labour years'. *Oxford Review of Economic Policy*, 29/1: 165–77.

Lindstrom, N. (2010). 'Service liberalization in the enlarged EU: a race to the bottom or the emergence of transnational political conflict?' *Journal of Common Market Studies*, 48/5: 1307–27.

Linneker, B. and Wills, J. (2015). 'The London living wage and in-work poverty reduction: impacts on employers and workers'. *Environment and Planning C: Government and Policy*, 34/5: 759–76.

Liu, M. (2014). 'Conflict resolution in China', in W. Roche, P. Teague, and A. Colvin (eds.), *The Oxford Handbook of Conflict Management in Organizations*. Oxford: Oxford University Press, 494–519.

Lloyd, C. (2001). 'What do employee councils do? The impact of non-union forms of representation on trade union organisation'. *Industrial Relations Journal*, 32/4: 313–27.

Lloyd, C. and Mayhew, K. (2010). 'Skill: the solution to low wage work?' *Industrial Relations Journal*, 41/5: 429–45.

Lloyd, C. and Payne, J. (2011). 'Flat whites: who gets progression in the UK café sector?' *Industrial Relations Journal*, 43/1: 38–52.

Locke, R. (2013). *The Promise and Limits of Private Power: Promoting Labor Standards in a Global Economy*. Cambridge: Cambridge University Press.

Locke, R., Amengual, M., and Mangla, A. (2009). 'Virtue out of necessity? Compliance, commitment, and the improvement of labor conditions in global supply chains'. *Politics and Society*, 37/3: 319–51.

Locke, R., Kochan, T., Romis, M., and Qin, F. (2007). 'Beyond corporate codes of conduct: work organization and labour standards at Nike's suppliers'. *International Labour Review*, 146/1–2: 21–40.

Logan, J. (2006). 'The union avoidance industry in the United States'. *British Journal of Industrial Relations*, 44/4: 651–75.

Loopstra, R., Reeves, A., Taylor-Robinson, D., Barr, B., McKee, M., and Stuckler, D. (2015). 'Austerity, sanctions and the rise of food banks in the UK', *British Medical Journal*, 350, DOI: http://dx.doi.org/10.1136/bmj.h1775

Lopes, A. and Hall, T. (2015). 'Organising migrant workers: the living wage campaign at the University of East London'. *Industrial Relations Journal*, 46/3: 208–21.

Loveday, B., Williams, S., and Scott, P. (2008). 'Workforce modernization in the police service: prospects for reform?' *Personnel Review*, 37/4: 361–74.

Low Pay Commission (LPC) (2004). *The National Minimum Wage: Protecting Young Workers*. Fifth report of the Low Pay Commission. London: HMSO.

Low Pay Commission (LPC) (2010). *National Minimum Wage: Low Pay Commission Report 2010*. Cm 7823. London: The Stationery Office.

Low Pay Commission (LPC) (2011). *National Minimum Wage: Low Pay Commission Report 2011*. Cm 8023. London: The Stationery Office.

Low Pay Commission (LPC) (2012). *National Minimum Wage: Low Pay Commission Report 2012*. Cm 8302. London: The Stationery Office.

Low Pay Commission (LPC) (2013). *National Minimum Wage: Low Pay Commission Report 2013*. Cm 8565. London: The Stationery Office.

Low Pay Commission (LPC) (2016). *National Minimum Wage: Low Pay Commission Report Spring 2016*. Cm 9207. London: The Stationery Office.

Luce, S. (2004). *Fighting for a Living Wage*. New York: Cornell University Press.

Lundberg, H. and Karlsson, J. (2011). 'Under the clean surface: working as a hotel attendant'. *Work, Employment and Society*, 25/1, 141–8.

Lupton, T. (1963). *On the Shop Floor*. Oxford: Pergamon.

Lyddon. D. (2015). 'The changing pattern of UK strikes, 1964–2014'. *Employee Relations*, 37/6: 733–45.

Lynch, P. (2015). 'The coalition and the European Union', in M. Beech and S. Lee (eds.), *The Conservative–Liberal Coalition: Examining the Cameron–Clegg Government*. Basingstoke: Palgrave Macmillan, 243–58.

Macalister, T. (2016). 'Blacklisted workers win £10m payout from construction firms'. *The Guardian*, 9 May, https://www.theguardian.com/business/2016/may/09/blacklisted-workers-win-10m-payout-from-construction-firms

Macalister, T. and Pidd, H. (2009). 'Uproar in Cowley as BMW confirms 850 job cuts at Mini factory'. *The Guardian*, 16 February, http://www.theguardian.com/business/2009/feb/16/bmw-mini-job-cuts

McBride, A. (2000). 'Promoting representation of women within UNISON', in M. Terry (ed.), *Redefining Public Sector Unionism: UNISON and the Future of Trade Unions*. London: Routledge, 100–18.

McBride, A. (2001). *Gender Democracy in Trade Unions*. Aldershot: Ashgate.

McBride, J. and Greenwood, I. (eds.) (2009). *Community Unionism: A Comparative Analysis of Concepts and Contexts*. Basingstoke: Palgrave Macmillan.

McCarthy, W. (1964). *The Closed Shop in Britain*. Oxford: Basil Blackwell.

McColgan, A. (2000). 'Missing the point? The Part-time Workers (Prevention of Less Favourable Treatment) Regulations 2000 (SI 2000, No 1551)'. *Industrial Law Journal*, 29/3: 260–7.

McDowell, L., Batnitzky, A. and Dyer, S. (2008). 'Internationalization and the spaces of temporary labour: the global assembly of a local workforce'. *British Journal of Industrial Relations*, 46/4: 750–70.

McDowell, L., Batvitzky, A. and Dyer, S. (2012). 'Global flows and local labour markets: precarious employment and migrant workers in the UK', in J. Scott, S. Dex, and A. Pagnol (eds.), *Gendered Lives: Gender Inequalities in Production and Reproduction*. Cheltenham: Edward Elgar, 123–51.

MacDuffie, J.-P. (1995). 'Human resource bundles and manufacturing performance: organizational logic and flexible production systems in the world auto industry'. *Industrial and Labor Relations Review*, 48/2: 195–221.

McGovern, P., Hill, S., Mills, C., and White, M. (2007). *Market, Class, and Employment*. Oxford: Oxford University Press.

Machin, S. (1999). 'Wage inequality in the 1970s, 1980s and 1990s', in P. Gregg and J. Wadsworth (eds.), *The State of Working Britain*. Manchester: Manchester University Press, 185–205.

Machin, S. (2000). 'Union decline in Britain'. *British Journal of Industrial Relations*, 38/4: 631–45.

Machin, S. (2011). 'Changing wage structures: trends and explanations', in D. Marsden (ed.), *Employment in the Lean Years*. Oxford: Oxford University Press, 151–67.

McIlroy, J. (1991). *The Permanent Revolution? Conservative Law and the Trade Unions*. Nottingham: Spokesman.

McIlroy, J. (1999). 'Unfinished business—the reform of strike legislation in Britain'. *Employee Relations*, 21/6: 521–39.

McIlroy, J. (2009). 'Under stress but still enduring: the contentious alliance in the age of Tony Blair and Gordon Brown', in G. Daniels and J. McIlroy (eds.), *Trade Unions in a Neo Liberal World: British Trade Unions under New Labour*. Abingdon: Routledge, 165–201.

McIlroy, J. and Daniels, G. (2009). 'An anatomy of British trade unionism since 1997: organization, structure and factionalism', in G. Daniels and J. McIlroy (eds.), *Trade Unions in a Neo Liberal World: British Trade Unions under New Labour*. Abingdon: Routledge, 127–64.

McIntosh, I. and Broderick, J. (1996). 'Neither one thing nor the other: compulsory competitive tendering and Southburg Cleansing services'. *Work, Employment and Society*, 10/3: 413–30.

McIntosh, S. (2013). *Hollowing Out and the Future of the Labour Market*. BIS Research Paper 134. London: Department of Business, Innovation, and Skills.

McIvor, A. (1996). *Organised Capital*. Cambridge: Cambridge University Press.

McKay, S. (2001). 'Annual review article 2000. Between flexibility and regulation: rights, equality and protection at work'. *British Journal of Industrial Relations*, 39/2: 285–303.

McKay, S. (2006). *Satanic Mills or Silicon Islands? The Politics of High-Tech Production in the Philippines*. Ithaca NY: Cornell University Press.

McKay, S. and Markova, E. (2010). 'The operation and management of agency workers in conditions of vulnerability'. *Industrial Relations Journal*, 41/5: 446–60.

McKenna, S., Richardson, J., Singh, P., and Xu, J. J. (2010). 'Negotiating, accepting and resisting HRM: a Chinese case study'. *The International Journal of Human Resource Management*, 21/6: 851–72.

McKinlay, A. and McNulty, D. (1992). 'At the cutting edge of new realism: the engineers' 35 hour week campaign'. *Industrial Relations Journal*, 23/3: 205–13.

McKnight, A. (2015). *The Coalition's Record on Employment: Policy, Spending and Outcomes 2010–2015*. Social Policy in a Cold Climate Working Paper 15. London School of Economics: Centre for Analysis of Social Exclusion.

MacLeod, D. and Clarke, N. (2009). *Engaging for Success: Enhancing Performance through Employee Engagement*. London: BIS.

McLoughlin, I. and Gourlay, S. (1994). *Enterprise without Unions*. Buckingham: Open University Press.

Macmillan, L., Tyler, C., and Vignoles, A. (2015). 'Who gets the top jobs? The role of family background and networks in recent graduates' access to high-status professions'. *Journal of Social Policy*, 44/3: 487–509.

Malik, S. (2012). 'Unemployed bussed in to steward river pageant'. *The Guardian*, 4 June, http://www.guardian.co.uk/uk/2012/jun/04/jubilee-pageant-unemployed

Malik, S., Ball, J., and Davies, L. (2012). 'Jobseekers forced to clean private homes and offices for nothing'. *The Guardian*, 29 February, http://www.guardian.co.uk/politics/2012/feb/24/jobseekers-unpaid-work-placements

Manfredi, S. (2016). 'Equality and diversity at work under the coalition', in S. Williams and P. Scott (eds.), *Employment Relations under Coalition Government: the UK Experience, 2010–2015*. Abingdon: Routledge, 108–26.

Mangan, D. (2013). 'Employment tribunal reforms to boost the economy'. *Industrial Law Journal*, 42/4: 409–21.

Manning, A. (2011). 'Minimum wages and wage inequality', in D. Marsden (ed.), *Employment in the Lean Years*. Oxford: Oxford University Press, 134–50.

Manning, A. (2012). *Minimum Wage: Maximum Impact*. London: Resolution Foundation.

Marchington, M. (1989). 'Joint consultation in practice', in K. Sisson (ed.), *Personnel Management*. Oxford: Basil Blackwell, 378–402.

Marchington, M. (1994). 'The dynamics of joint consultation', in K. Sisson (ed.), *Personnel Management* (2nd edn). Oxford: Blackwell, 662–93.

Marchington, M. (2001). 'Employee involvement at work', in J. Storey (ed.), *Human Resource Management: A Critical Text* (2nd edn). London: Thomson Learning, 232–52.

Marchington, M. (2008). 'Employee voice systems', in P. Boxall, J. Purcell, and P. Wright (eds.), *The Oxford Handbook of Human Resource Management*. Oxford: Oxford University Press, 231–50.

Marchington, M. and Parker, P. (1990). *Changing Patterns of Employee Relations*. Hemel Hempstead: Harvester Wheatsheaf.

Marginson, P. (2009). 'Performance pay and collective bargaining: a complex relationship', in S. Corby, S. Palmer, and E. Lindop (eds.), *Rethinking Reward*. Basingstoke: Palgrave Macmillan, 102–19.

Marginson, P. (2012). '(Re)assessing the shifting contours of Britain's collective industrial relations'. *Industrial Relations Journal*, 43/4: 332–47.

Marginson, P. (2015). 'The changing nature of collective employment relations'. *Employee Relations*, 37/6: 645–57.

Marginson, P., Gilman, M., Jacobi, O., and Krieger, H. (1998). *Negotiating European Works Councils: An Analysis of Agreements under Article 13*. Luxembourg: Office of Official Publications of the European Community.

Marginson, P. and Meardi, G. (2009). *Multinational Companies and Collective Bargaining*. Dublin: European Foundation for the Improvement of Living and Working Conditions.

Marginson, P. and Meardi, G. (2010). 'Multinational companies: transforming national industrial relations?', in T. Colling and M. Terry (eds.), *Industrial Relations: Theory and Practice* (3rd edn). Chichester: John Wiley, 207–30.

Marginson, P. and Sisson, K. (1994). 'The structure of transnational capital in Europe: the emerging Euro-company and its implications for industrial relations', in R. Hyman and A. Ferner (eds.), *New Frontiers in European Industrial Relations*. Oxford: Blackwell, 15–51.

Marginson, P. and Sisson, K. (2004). *European Integration and Industrial Relations: Multi-Level Governance in the Making*. Basingstoke: Palgrave Macmillan.

Marks, A., Findlay, P., Hine, J., McKinlay, A., and Thompson, P. (1998). 'The politics of partnership? Innovation in employment relations in the Scottish spirits industry'. *British Journal of Industrial Relations*, 36/2: 209–26.

Marlow, S. (2002). 'Regulating labour management in small firms'. *Human Resource Management Journal*, 12/3: 25–43.

Mars, G. (1982). *Cheats at Work*. London: Allen and Unwin.

Mars, G. and Mitchell, P. (1976). *Room for Reform? A Case Study of Industrial Relations in the Hotel Industry*. Milton Keynes: Open University Press.

Marsden, D. (1999). *A Theory of Employment Systems*. Oxford: Oxford University Press.

Marsden, D. (2009). *The Paradox of Performance Related Pay Systems: Why do we Keep Adopting them in the Face of Evidence that they Fail to Motivate?* Centre for Economic Performance, Discussion Paper No. 946. London: Centre for Economic Performance.

Marsden, D. and French, S. (1998). *What a Performance: Performance Related Pay in the Public Services*. London: London School of Economics, Centre for Economic Performance.

Marshall, D. and Laws, D. (2004). *The Orange Book: Reclaiming Liberalism*. London: Profile Books.

Marshall, S. (2014). 'Doncaster Care UK workers accept strike deal'. *The Star*, 26 November, http://www.thestar.co.uk/news/doncaster-care-uk-workers-accept-strike-deal-1-6973285

Martin, A. and Ross, G. (1999). 'In the line of fire: the Europeanization of Labor representation', in A. Martin and G. Ross (eds.), *The Brave New World of European Labor*. Oxford: Berghahn, 312–67.

Martin, R. (1992). *Bargaining Power*. Oxford: Clarendon.

Martin, R., Smith, P., Fosh, P., Morris, H., and Undy, R. (1995). 'The legislative reform of union government 1979–94'. *Industrial Relations Journal*, 26/2: 146–55.

Mason, P. (2009). *Meltdown: The End of the Age of Greed*. London: Verso.

Mason, P. (2016). 'George Osborne's recovery is in danger: the only option now is to steal Jeremy Corbyn's clothes'. *The Guardian*, 15 March, https://www.theguardian.com/commentisfree/2016/mar/14/george-osborne-recovery-danger-jeremy-corbyn-britain-cheap-imports-zero-hours-contracts-budget

Mason, R. (2016). 'Government revives plans to amend Sunday trading laws'. *The Guardian*, 2 February, http://www.theguardian.com/business/2016/feb/02/government-plans-amend-sunday-trading-laws

Maternity Action (2013). *Overdue: A Plan of Action to Address Pregnancy Discrimination Now*. London: Maternity Action.

Mather, K. and Seifert, R. (2014). 'The close supervision of further education lecturers: "You have been weighed, measured and found wanting"'. *Work, Employment and Society*, 28/1: 95–11.

Mather, K. and Seifert, R. (2016). 'Police pay—contested and contestable'. *Industrial Relations Journal*, 47/3: 204–19.

Meadway, J. (2015). 'Taxpayers spend £11 billion to top up low wages paid by UK companies'. *The Guardian*, 20 April, https://www.theguardian.com/sustainable-business/2015/apr/20/taxpayers-spend-11bn-to-top-up-low-wages-paid-by-uk-companies

Meardi, G. (2012). *Social Failures of EU Enlargement: A Case of Workers Voting with their Feet*. Abingdon: Routledge.

Meardi, G. (2014*a*). 'The (claimed) growing irrelevance of employment relations'. *Journal of Industrial Relations*, 56/4, 594–605.

Meardi, G. (2014*b*). 'Employment relations under external pressure: Italian and Spanish reforms during the Great Recession', in M. Hauptmeier and M. Vidal (eds.), *Comparative Political Economy of Work*. Basingstoke: Palgrave Macmillan, 332–50.

Meardi, G., Donaghey, J., and Dean, D. (2016). 'The strange non-retreat of the state: implications for the sociology of work'. *Work, Employment, and Society*, 30/4: 559–72.

Meardi, G., Marginson, P., Fichter, M., Frybes, M., Stanojević, M., and Tóth, A. (2009). 'Varieties of multinationals: adapting employment practices in Central Eastern Europe'. *Industrial Relations*, 48/3: 489–511.

Merk, J. (2008). 'Restructuring and conflict in the global athletic footwear industry: Nike, Yue Yuen and labour codes of conduct', in M. Taylor (ed.), *Global Economy Contested: Power and Conflict Across the International Division of Labour*. Abingdon: Routledge, 79–97.

Merk, J. (2009). 'Jumping scale and bridging space in the era of corporate social responsibility: cross-border labour struggles in the global garment industry'. *Third World Quarterly*, 30/3: 599–615.

Messenger, J. (2011). 'Working time trends and developments in Europe'. *Cambridge Journal of Economics*, 35/2: 295–316.

Metcalf, D. (1999). 'The British National Minimum Wage'. *British Journal of Industrial Relations*, 37/2: 171–201.

Metcalf, D. (2005). 'Trade unions: resurgence or perdition? An economic analysis?', in S. Fernie and D. Metcalf (eds.), *Trade Unions: Resurgence or Demise?* London: Routledge, 83–117.

Metcalf, D. (2008). 'Why has the British National Minimum Wage had little or no impact on employment?' *Journal of Industrial Relations*, 50/3: 489–512.

Micheletti, M. and Stolle, D. (2007). 'Motivating consumers to take responsibility for global justice'. *Annals of the American Academy of Political and Social Science*, 611/1: 157–75.

Migration Advisory Committee (MAC) (2014). *Migrants in Low-Skilled Work*. London: Migration Advisory Committee.

Milburn, A. (2012). *Fair Access to Professional Careers: A Progress Report by the Independent Reviewer on Social Mobility and Child Poverty*. London: Cabinet Office.

Milkman, R. (ed.) (2000). *Organizing Immigrants: The Challenge for Unions in Contemporary California*. Ithaca NY: Cornell University Press.

Millward, N., Bryson, A., and Forth, J. (2000). *All Change at Work*. London: Routledge.

Millward, N., Stevens, D., Smart, N., and Hawes, W. (1992). *Workplace Industrial Relations in Transition*. Aldershot: Dartmouth.

Milmo, D. (2012*a*). 'UK's largest union redefines Cameron's "big society"'. *The Guardian*, 1 May, https://www.theguardian.com/society/2012/may/01/unite-union-redefines-big-society

Milmo, D. (2012*b*). 'Unions and Southampton council go head to head over cuts'. *The Guardian*, 24 January, http://www.guardian.co.uk/society/2012/jan/24/southampton-council-strikes-royston-smith

Milne, S. (2004). *The Enemy Within: Thatcher's Secret War against the Miners* (2nd edn). London: Verso.

Milne, S. (2012). 'Blacklisting is the scandal that now demands action'. *The Guardian*, 4 December, http://www.guardian.co.uk/commentisfree/2012/dec/04/blacklisting-scandal-corporate-spying

Milner, S. and Gregory, A. (2014). 'Gender equality bargaining in France and the UK: an uphill struggle?' *Journal of Industrial Relations*, 56/2: 246–63.

Monaghan, A. and Nardelli, A. (2014). 'British workers suffer biggest real-wage fall of major G20 countries', *The Guardian*, 5 December, http://www.theguardian.com/business/2014/dec/04/british-workers-suffered-biggest-real-wage-fall-major-g20-countries

Moody, K. (2013). 'Beating the union: union avoidance in the US', in G. Gall and T. Dundon (eds.), *Global Anti-unionism: Nature, Dynamics, Trajectories, and Outcomes*. Basingstoke: Palgrave Macmillan, 143–62.

Moore, S. (2004). 'Union mobilization and employer counter-mobilization in the statutory recognition process', in J. Kelly and P. Willman (eds.), *Union Organization and Activity*. London: Routledge, 7–31.

Moore, S. (2011). *New Trade Union Activism: Class Consciousness or Social Identity?* Basingstoke: Palgrave Macmillan.

Moore, S., McKay, S., and Veale, S. (2013). *Statutory Regulation and Employment Relations: The Impact of Statutory Trade Union Recognition*. Basingstoke: Palgrave Macmillan.

Morris, G. (2012). 'The development of statutory employment rights in Britain and enforcement mechanisms', in L. Dickens (ed.), *Making Employment Rights Effective: Issues of Enforcement and Compliance*. Oxford: Hart Publishing, 7–28.

Mosley, L. (2011). *Labor Rights and Multinational Corporations*. New York: Cambridge University Press.

Mueller, F. and Purcell, J. (1992). 'The Europeanization of manufacturing and the decentralization of bargaining: multinational management strategies in the European automobile industry'. *International Journal of Human Resource Management*, 3/1: 15–24.

Mukherjee, S. (1973). *Through No Fault of Their Own: Systems for Handling Redundancies in Britain, France and Germany*. London: PEP.

Mulholland, K. (2004). 'Workplace resistance in an Irish call centre: slammin', scammin' smokin' an' leavin' '. *Work, Employment and Society*, 18/4: 709–24.

Munck, R. (2011). 'Unions, globalisation and internationalism: results and prospects', in G. Gall, A. Wilkinson, and R. Hurd (eds.), *The International Handbook of Labour Unions: Responses to Neo-Liberalism*. Cheltenham: Edward Elgar, 291–310.

Munro, A. (1999). *Women, Work and Trade Unions*. London: Mansell.

Munro, A. and Rainbird, H. (2000). 'The new unionism and the new bargaining agenda: UNISON–employer partnerships on workplace learning in Britain'. *British Journal of Industrial Relations*, 38/2: 223–40.

Myerscough, P. (2013). 'Short cuts'. *London Review of Books*, 3 January: 25.

Nash, D. (2006). 'Recent industrial relations developments in the United Kingdom: continuity and change under New Labour 1997–2005'. *Journal of Industrial Relations*, 48/3: 401–14.

National Audit Office (NAO) (2016). *Ensuring Employers Comply with National Minimum Wage Regulations*, HC 889. London: National Audit Office.

National Union of Journalists (NUJ) (2015). 'Newspaper group charges students £120 for chance of a by-line'. 10 February, https://www.nuj.org.uk/news/newspaper-groups-charges-students-120-for-chance-of-a-by-line/

Neathy, F. and Arrowsmith, J. (2001). *The Implementation of the Working Time Regulations*. Employment Relations Research Series No. 11. London: DTI.

Neumark, D. and Wascher, W. (2008). *Minimum Wages*. Cambridge MA: MIT Press.

Neville, S. (2013). 'Sports Direct: 90% of staff on zero-hours contracts'. *The Guardian*, 28 July, http://www.theguardian.com/business/2013/jul/28/sports-direct-staff-zero-hour-contracts

Newsome, K., Thompson, P., and Commander, J. (2009). 'The forgotten factories: supermarket suppliers and dignity at work in the contemporary economy', in S. Bolton and M. Houlihan (eds.), *Work Matters: Critical Reflections on Contemporary Work*. Basingstoke: Palgrave Macmillan, 145–61.

Newsome, K., Thompson, P., and Commander, J. (2013). '"You monitor performance at every hour": labour and the management of performance in the supermarket supply chain'. *New Technology, Work, and Employment*, 28/1: 1–15.

Nichols, T. (1986). *The British Worker Question*. London: Routledge and Kegan Paul.

Nichols, T. (1997). *The Sociology of Industrial Injury*. London: Mansell.

Niforou, C. (2012). 'International framework agreements and industrial relations governance: global rhetoric versus local realities'. *British Journal of Industrial Relations*, 50/2: 352–73.

Niforou, C. (2014). 'International framework agreements and the democratic deficit of global labour governance'. *Economic and Industrial Democracy*, 35/2: 367–86.

Nolan, J. (2002). 'The intensification of everyday life', in B. Burchell, D. Ladipo, and F. Wilkinson (eds.), *Job Insecurity and Work Intensification*. London: Routledge, 112–36.

Nolan, P. and Slater, G. (2003). 'The labour market: history, structure and prospects', in P. Edwards (ed.), *Industrial Relations* (2nd edn). Oxford: Blackwell, 58–80.

Nolan, P. and Wood, S. (2003). 'Mapping the future of work'. *British Journal of Industrial Relations*, 41/2: 165–74.

Noon, M. (2007). 'The fatal flaws of diversity and the business case for ethnic minorities'. *Work, Employment and Society*, 21/4: 773–84.

Noon, M., Blyton, P., and Morrell, K. (2013). *The Realities of Work* (4th edn). Basingstoke: Palgrave Macmillan.

O'Brien, R. (2002). 'The varied paths to minimum global labour standards', in J. Harrod and R. O'Brien (eds.), *Global Unions? Theory and Strategies of Organized Labour in a Global Political Economy*. London: Routledge, 221–34.

O'Brien-Smith, F. and Rigby, M. (2010). 'The work–life balance strategies of USDAW: mobilising collective voice'. *Industrial Relations Journal*, 41/3, 206–17.

O'Connor, S. (2013). 'Amazon unpacked'. *FT Magazine*, 8 February, https://www.ft.com/content/ed6a985c-70bd-11e2-85d0-00144feab49a

O'Connor, S. and Barrett, C. (2015). 'Online delivery model relies on low-paid drivers'. *Financial Times*, 2 January, https://www.ft.com/content/13ce0668-927d-11e4-b213-00144feabdc0

Oesch, D. (2013). *Occupational Change in Europe: How Technology and Education Transform the Job Structure*. Oxford: Oxford University Press.

Office for National Statistics (ONS) (2011). *Hours Worked in the Labour Market–2011*. Newport: Office for National Statistics.

Office for National Statistics (ONS) (2013). 'Full Report–Women in the Labour Market', http://webarchive. nationalarchives.gov.uk/20160105160709/http:// www.ons.gov.uk/ons/dcp171776_328352.pdf

Office for National Statistics (ONS) (2014*a*). 'Self-employed workers in the UK–2014', http://webarchive.nationalarchives.gov. uk/20160105160709/http://www.ons.gov.uk/ons/ dcp171776_374941.pdf

Office for National Statistics (ONS) (2014*b*). 'Underemployment and Overemployment in the UK', http://webarchive.nationalarchives.gov. uk/20160105160709/http://www.ons.gov.uk/ons/ rel/lmac/underemployed-workers-in-the-uk/2014/ rpt-underemployment-and-overemployment-2014.html

Office for National Statistics (ONS) (2015). 'Annual Survey of Hours and Earnings: 2015 Provisional Results', http://www.ons.gov.uk/ employmentandlabourmarket/peopleinwork/ earningsandworkinghours/bulletins/annualsurveyofh oursandearnings/2015provisionalresults

Office for National Statistics (ONS) (2016*a*). 'Contracts that do not guarantee a minimum number of hours: March 2016', https://www. ons.gov.uk/employmentandlabourmarket/ peopleinwork/earningsandworkinghours/ articles/contractsthatdonotguaranteeamini mumnumberofhours/march2016

Office for National Statistics (ONS) (2016*b*). *Labour Disputes in the UK: 2015*. London: ONS.

Office for National Statistics (ONS) (2016*c*). *Trends in Self-employment in the UK: 2001 to 2015*. London: ONS.

Ogbonna, E. and Harris, L. (2002). 'Institutionalization of tipping as a source of managerial control'. *British Journal of Industrial Relations*, 40/4: 725–52.

O'Hara, M. (2014). *Austerity Bites*. Bristol: Policy Press.

Oliver, L., Stuart, M., and Tomlinson, J. (2014). 'Equal pay bargaining in the UK local government sector'. *Journal of Industrial Relations*, 56/2: 228–45.

Osborne, H. and Butler, S. (2016). 'Collective action via social media brings hope to gig economy workers'. *The Guardian*, 19 August, https://www.theguardian. com/money/2016/aug/19/collective-action-via-social-media-brings-hope-to-gig-economy-workers

O'Sullivan, M. and Gunnigle, P. (2009). 'Bearing all the hallmarks of oppression–union avoidance in Europe's largest low-cost airline'. *Labor Studies Journal*, 34/2: 252–70.

Oswick, C. and Noon, M. (2014). 'Discourses of diversity, equality, and inclusion: trenchant formulations or transient fashions?' *British Journal of Management*, 25/1: 23–39.

Oxenbridge, S. and Brown, W. (2002). 'The two faces of partnership? An assessment of partnership and co-operative employer/trade union relationships'. *Employee Relations*, 24/3: 262–7.

Oxenbridge, S. and Brown, W. (2004). 'A poisoned chalice? Trade union representatives in partnership and co-operative employer–union relationships', in G. Healy, E. Heery, P. Taylor, and W. Brown (eds.), *The Future of Worker Representation*. Basingstoke: Palgrave Macmillan, 187–206.

Oxenbridge, S. and Brown, W. (2005). 'Developing partnership relationships: a case of leveraging power', in M. Stuart and M. Martinez Lucio (eds.), *Partnership and Modernisation in Employment Relations*. London: Routledge, 83–100.

Oxenbridge, S., Brown, W., Deakin, S., and Pratten, C. (2003). 'Initial responses to the Employment Relations Act 1999'. *British Journal of Industrial Relations*, 41/2: 315–34.

Paauwe, J., Wright, P., and Guest, D. (2013). 'HRM and performance: what do we know and where should we go?', in J. Paauwe, D. Guest, and P. Wright (eds.), *HRM and Performance: Achievements and Challenges*. Chichester: John Wiley, 1–13.

Page, L. (2014). 'Internships: pressure mounts on employers to pay young workers'. *The Guardian*, 25 July, https://www.theguardian.com/education/2014/ jul/25/unpaid-internships-quarter-employers-unpaid

Pakulski, J. and Waters, M. (1996). *The Death of Class*. London: Sage.

Palley, T. (2004). 'The economic case for international labour standards'. *Cambridge Journal of Economics*, 28/1: 21–36.

Papadakis, K. (ed.) (2011). *Shaping Global Industrial Relations: The Impact of International Framework Agreements*. Basingstoke: Palgrave Macmillan.

Parker, J. (2002). 'Women's groups in British unions'. *British Journal of Industrial Relations*, 40/1: 23–48.

Parsons, N. (2013). 'Legitimizing illegal protest: the permissive ideational environment and "bossnappings" in France'. *British Journal of Industrial Relations*, 51/2: 288–309.

Pass, S. (2005). 'On the line'. *People Management*, 15 September: 38–40.

Patel, S. (2011). *Research into Employers' Attitudes and Behaviour Towards Compliance with the UK National Minimum Wage (NMW) Legislation*. Employment Relations Research Series, No. 121. London: Department for Business, Innovation and Skills.

Pattison, P. (2013). 'Revealed: Qatar's World Cup "slaves"'. *The Guardian*, 25 September, http://www.theguardian.com/world/2013/sep/25/revealed-qatars-world-cup-slaves

Pendleton, A., Whitfield, K., and Bryson, A. (2009). 'The changing use of contingent pay at the modern British workplace', in W. Brown, A. Bryson, J. Forth, and K. Whitfield (eds.), *The Evolution of the Modern Workplace*. Cambridge: Cambridge University Press, 256–84.

Pennycook, M. (2012). *What Price a Living Wage? Understanding the Impact of a Living Wage on Firm-Level Wage Bills*. London: Institute of Public Policy Research and Resolution Foundation.

Pennycook, M., Cory, G., and Alakeson, V. (2013). *A Matter of Time: The Rise of Zero-Hours Contracts*. London: Resolution Foundation.

Perkins, S. and White, G. (2010). 'Modernising pay in the UK public services: trends and implications'. *Human Resource Management Journal*, 20/3: 244–57.

Perlin, R. (2011). *Intern Nation*. London: Verso.

Perraudin, F. (2016a). 'UK accused of leading efforts to block limits to Chinese steel dumping'. *The Guardian*, 1 April, http://www.theguardian.com/politics/2016/apr/01/steel-crisis-uk-accused-blocking-eu-attempts-regulate-chinese-dumping

Perraudin, F. (2016b). 'UN labour body calls on government to review parts of trade union bill'. *The Guardian*, 14 February, http://www.theguardian.com/politics/2016/feb/14/international-labour-organization-trade-union-bill-uk-government

Pfeffer, J. (1998). *The Human Equation*. Boston MA: Harvard Business School Press.

Piazza, J. (2005). 'Globalizing quiescence: globalization, union density and strikes in 15 industrialized countries'. *Economic and Industrial Democracy*, 26/2: 289–314.

Pickavance, N. (2014). 'Zeroed Out: The Place of Zero-Hours Contracts in a Fair and Productive Economy', http://www.policyforum.labour.org.uk/uploads/editor/files/ZHCs_report_final_FINAL_240414.pdf

Platman, K. (2004). '"Portfolio careers" and the search for flexibility in later life'. *Work, Employment and Society*, 18/3: 573–99.

Plunkett, J., Hurrell, A., and Whittaker, M. (2014). *The State of Living Standards*. London: Resolution Foundation.

Pochet, P. and Degryse, C. (2010). 'Social policies of the European Union'. *Global Social Policy*, 10/2: 248–57.

Polanyi, K. (1957). *The Great Transformation*. Boston: Beacon Press.

Pollert, A. (1981). *Girls, Wives, Factory Lives*. Basingstoke: Macmillan.

Pollert, A. (2005). 'The unorganised worker: the decline in collectivism and new hurdles to individual employment rights'. *Industrial Law Journal*, 34/3: 217–38.

Pollert, A. (2007). 'Individual employment rights: paper tigers—fierce in appearance but missing in tooth and claw'. *Economic and Industrial Democracy*, 28/1: 110–39.

Pollert, A. (2009). 'The reality of vulnerability amongst Britain's non-unionised workers with problems at work', in S. Bolton and M. Houlihan (eds.), *Work Matters: Critical Reflections on Contemporary Work*. Basingstoke: Palgrave Macmillan, 60–80.

Pollert, A. and Charlwood, A. (2009). 'The vulnerable worker in Britain and problems at work'. *Work, Employment and Society*, 23/2: 343–62.

Poole, M. (1986). *Towards a New Industrial Democracy: Workers' Participation in Industry*. London: Routledge and Kegan Paul.

Poole, M. and Mansfield, R. (1993). 'Patterns of continuity and change in managerial attitudes and behaviour in industrial relations, 1980–1990'. *British Journal of Industrial Relations*, 31/1: 11–35.

Portes, J. (2016). 'Immigration, free movement and the EU referendum'. *National Institute Economic Review*, 236: 14–22.

Potter, M. and Hamilton, J. (2014). 'Picking on vulnerable migrants: precarity and the mushroom industry in Northern Ireland'. *Work, Employment, and Society*, 28/3: 390–406.

Poynter, G. (2000). *Restructuring in the Service Industries: Management Reform and Workplace Relations in the UK Service Sector*. London: Mansell.

Price, R. (1983). 'White-collar unions: growth, character and attitudes in the 1970s', in R. Hyman and R. Price (eds.), *The New Working Class? White Collar Workers and their Unions*. London: Macmillan, 147–83.

Price, R. (1989). 'The decline and fall of the status divide?', in K. Sisson (ed.), *Personnel Management in Britain*. Oxford: Blackwell, 271–95.

Proctor, S. (2008). 'New forms of work and the high performance paradigm', in P. Blyton, N. Bacon, J. Fiorito, and E. Heery (eds.), *The SAGE Handbook of Industrial Relations*. London: Sage, 149–69.

Proctor, S. and Benders, J. (2014). 'Task-based voice: teamworking, autonomy and performance', in A. Wilkinson, J. Donaghey, T. Dundon, and R. Freeman (eds.), *Handbook of Research on Employee Voice*. Cheltenham: Edward Elgar, 298–309.

Prosser, T. (2011). 'The implementation of the Telework and Work-related Stress agreements: European social dialogue through "soft" law?' *European Journal of Industrial Relations*, 17/3: 245–60.

Prosser, T. (2014). 'Financialization and the reform of European industrial relations systems'. *European Journal of Industrial Relations*, 20/4: 351–65.

Pun, N. (2005). 'Global production, company codes of conduct, and labor conditions in China: a case study of two factories'. *The China Journal*, 54: 101–13.

Purcell, J. (2000). 'After collective bargaining? ACAS in the age of human resource management', in B. Towers and W. Brown (eds.), *Employment Relations in Britain: 25 Years of the Advisory, Conciliation and Arbitration Service*. Oxford: Blackwell, 163–80.

Purcell, J. (2012). *The Limits and Possibilities of Employee Engagement*. Warwick Papers in Industrial Relations, 96. Warwick: Industrial Relations Research Unit, University of Warwick.

Purcell, J. (2014). 'Disengaging from engagement'. *Human Resource Management Journal*, 24/3: 241–54.

Purcell, J. and Hall, M. (2012). *Voice and Participation in the Modern Workplace: Challenges and Prospects*. ACAS Future of Workplace Relations discussion paper series. London: ACAS.

Purcell, J. and Hutchinson, S. (2007). 'Front-line managers as agents in the HRM-performance causal chain: theory, analysis, and evidence'. *Human Resource Management Journal*, 17/1: 3–20.

Purcell, J. and Kinnie, N. (2007). 'HRM and business performance', in P. Boxall, J. Purcell, and P. Wright (eds.), *The Oxford Handbook of Human Resource Management*. Oxford: Oxford University Press, 533–51.

Purcell, J., Kinnie, N., Hutchinson, S., Rayton, B., and Swart, J. (2003). *Understanding the People and Performance Link: Unlocking the Black Box*. London: CIPD.

Purcell, J., Kinnie, N., Swart, J., Rayton, B., and Hutchinson, S. (2009). *People Management and Performance*. Abingdon: Routledge.

Purcell, J., Purcell, K., and Tailby, S. (2004). 'Temporary work agencies: here today, gone tomorrow?' *British Journal of Industrial Relations*, 42/4: 705–25.

PwC (2013). 'Rising sick bills cost UK businesses £29bn a year', http://www.pwc.co.uk/services/human-resource-services/insights/the-rising-cost-of-absence-sick-bills-cost-uk-businesses-29bn-a-year.html

Pyper, D. and Dar, A. (2015). *Zero-hours Contracts*. House of Commons Library Standard Note, SN/BT/6553.

Pyper, D. and McGuinness, F. (2016). *Employment Tribunal Fees*. House of Commons Library Breifing Paper, No. 7081.

Quinn, B. (2016). 'Unite says government is reluctant to exempt NHS from TTIP'. *The Guardian*, 13 March, https://www.theguardian.com/business/2016/mar/13/unite-says-government-is-reluctant-to-exempt-nhs-from-ttip

Rainnie, A. (1989). *Industrial Relations in Small Firms*. London: Routledge.

Ram, M. (1994). *Managing to Survive*. Oxford: Blackwell.

Ram, M. and Edwards, P. (2003). 'Praising Caesar not burying him: what we know about employment relations in small firms'. *Work, Employment and Society*, 17/4: 719–30.

Ram, M. and Edwards, P. (2010). 'Industrial relations in small firms', in T. Colling and M. Terry (eds.), *Industrial Relations: Theory and Practice* (3rd edn). Chichester: John Wiley, 231–52.

Ram, M., Edwards, P., Gilman, M., and Arrowsmith, J. (2001). 'The dynamics of informality: employment relations in small firms and the effects of regulatory change'. *Work, Employment and Society*, 15/4: 845–61.

Ram, M., Edwards, P., and Jones, T. (2007). 'Staying underground: informal work, small firms, and employment regulation in the United Kingdom'. *Work and Occupations*, 34/3: 318–44.

Ramesh, R. (2013). 'How private care firms have got away with breaking the law on pay'. *The Guardian*, 14 June, https://www.theguardian.com/society/2013/jun/13/care-firms-law-on-pay

Rankin, J. and Butler, S. (2015). 'City Link's army of self-employed workers count cost of business failure'. *The Guardian*, 1 January, http://www.theguardian.com/business/2015/jan/01/city-link-army-self-employed-count-cost-failure

Ray, K., Foley, B., and Hughes, C. (2014). *Rising to the Challenge: A Policy Agenda to Tackle Low Pay*. London: The Work Foundation.

Rayton, B., Dodge, T., and D'Analeze, G. (2012). *The Evidence: Employee Engagement Task Force 'Nailing the Evidence' Workgroup*. London: Engage for Success.

Redfern, D. (2007). 'An analysis of the role of European Works Councils in British workplaces'. *Employee Relations*, 29/3: 292–305.

Reed, H. and Latorre, M. (2009). *The Economic Impacts of Migration on the UK Labour Market*. Economics of Migration Working Paper 3. London: Institute for Public Policy Research.

Rees, T. (1992). *Women and the Labour Market*. London: Routledge.

Reinecke, J. and Donaghey, J. (2015). 'After Rana Plaza: building coalitional power for labour rights between unions and (consumption-based) social movement organisations'. *Organization*, 22/5: 720–40.

Renton, D. (2012). *Struck Out: Why Employment Tribunals Fail Workers and What can be Done*. London: Pluto Press.

Resolution Foundation (2012). *Who Gains from Growth? Living Standards to 2020*. London: Resolution Foundation.

Resolution Foundation (2013). *Squeezed Britain 2013*. London: Resolution Foundation.

Richards, W. (2001). 'Evaluating equal opportunities initiatives: the case for a "transformative" agenda', in M. Noon and E. Ogbonna (eds.), *Equality, Diversity and Disadvantage in Employment*. Basingstoke: Palgrave Macmillan, 15–31.

Ridley-Duff, R. and Bennett, A. (2011). 'Towards mediation: developing a theoretical framework to understand alternative dispute resolution'. *Industrial Relations Journal*, 42/2: 106–23.

Rigby, M. and Marco Aledo, M. (2001). 'The worst record in Europe? A comparative analysis of industrial conflict in Spain'. *European Journal of Industrial Relations*, 7/3: 287–305.

Rigby, M. and O'Brien-Smith, F. (2010). 'Trade union interventions in work–life balance'. *Work, Employment and Society*, 24/2: 203–20.

Riisgaard, L. (2005). 'International framework agreements: a new model for securing workers rights?' *Industrial Relations*, 44/4: 707–37.

Riley, R., Metcalf, H., and Forth, J. (2013). 'The business case for equal opportunities'. *Industrial Relations Journal*, 44/3: 216–39.

Roberts, Y. (2015). 'Britain's hotel workers—bullied, underpaid and with few rights'. *The Guardian*, 30 May, http://www.theguardian.com/business/2015/may/30/hotel-workers-bullied-underpaid-few-rights-uk

Robinson, C. (2014). *Preventing Trafficking for Labour Exploitation*. Focus on Labour Exploitation, Working Paper 01:2014. London: Focus on Labour Exploitation.

Robinson, P. (2010). 'Do voluntary labour initiatives make a difference for the conditions of workers in global supply chains?' *Journal of Industrial Relations*, 52/5: 561–73.

Roche, W. and Teague, P. (2012). 'Business partners and working the pumps: human resource managers in the recession'. *Human Relations*, 65/10: 1333–58.

Rogowski, R. (2015). 'Implementation of the Working Time Directive in the United Kingdom', in J.-C. Barbier, R. Rogowski, and F. Colomb (eds.), *The Sustainability of the European Social Model: Governance, Social Protection and Employment Protections in Europe*. Cheltenham: Edward Elgar, 231–52.

Rolfe, H. and Hudson-Sharp, N. (2016). *The Impact of Free Movement on the Labour Market: Case Studies of Hospitality, Food Processing and Construction*. London: National Institute of Economic and Social Research.

Rollinson, D., Handley, J., Hook, C., and Foot, M. (1997). 'The disciplinary experience and its effects on behaviour'. *Work, Employment and Society*, 11/2: 281–311.

Roper, I., Cunningham, I., and James, P. (2003). 'Promoting family-friendly policies: is the basis of the government's ethical standpoint viable?' *Personnel Review*, 32/2: 211–30.

Rose, E. (2014). 'Who's controlling who? Personal communication devices and work'. *Sociology Compass*, 8/8: 1004–17.

Ross, R. (2012). 'Clean Clothes Campaign', in G. Ritzer (ed.), *The Wiley-Blackwell Encyclopaedia of Globalization*. Chichester: Wiley-Blackwell.

Ross, R. and Schneider, R. (1992). *From Equality to Diversity*. London: Pitman.

Roy, D. (1952). 'Quota restriction and goldbricking in a machine shop'. *American Journal of Sociology*, 5/5: 427–42.

Royal College of Physicians (RCP) (2012). *Hospitals on the Edge*. London: RCP.

Royal Commission (1968). *Report of the Royal Commission on Trade Unions and Employers' Associations*. London: HMSO.

Royle, T. (2000). *Working for McDonalds in Europe: The Unequal Struggle?* London: Routledge.

Royle, T. (2006). 'The dominance effect? Multinational corporations in the Italian quick-food service sector'. *British Journal of Industrial Relations*, 44/4: 757–79.

Royle, T. (2011). 'Regulating global capital through public and private codes: an analysis of international labour standards and corporate voluntary initiatives', in M. Barry and A. Wilkinson (eds.), *Research Handbook of Comparative Employment Relations*. Cheltenham: Edward Elgar, 421–40.

Royle, T. and Towers, B. (eds.) (2002). *Labour Relations in the Global Fast-Food Industry*. London: Routledge.

Rubery, J. and Edwards, P. (2003). 'Low pay and the National Minimum Wage', in P. Edwards (ed.), *Industrial Relations* (2nd edn). Oxford: Blackwell, 447–69.

Rubery, J. and Grimshaw, D. (2003). *The Organization of Employment: An International Perspective*. Basingstoke: Palgrave Macmillan.

Rubery, J., Grimshaw, D., Hebson, G., and Ugarte, S. (2015). '"It's all about time": time as contested terrain in the management and experience of domiciliary care work in England'. *Human Resource Management*, 54/4: 753–72.

Ruggie, J. (2016). *'For the Game. For the World': FIFA and Human Rights*. Cambridge MA: Harvard University Kennedy School.

Russell, H. and McGinnity, F. (2014). 'Under pressure: the impact of recession on employees in Ireland'. *British Journal of Industrial Relations*, 52/2: 286–307.

Rutherford, S. (1999). 'Equal opportunities policies—making a difference'. *Women in Management Review*, 14/6: 212–9.

Samuel, P. (2005). 'Partnership working and the cultivated activist'. *Industrial Relations Journal*, 36/1: 59–76.

Samuel, P. (2007). 'Partnership consultation and employer domination in two British life and pensions firms'. *Work, Employment and Society*, 21/3: 459–77.

Samuel, P. and Bacon, N. (2010). 'The contents of partnership agreements in Britain 1990–2007'. *Work, Employment and Society*, 24/3: 430–48.

Sanders, D. (2012). *Placing Trust in Employee Engagement*. Employment Relations Comment. London: ACAS.

Sargeant, M. (2010). 'The UK national minimum wage and age discrimination'. *Policy Studies*, 31/3: 351–64.

Saundry, R. (2016). 'Contemporary workplace conflict and conflict management', in R. Saundry, R. Latreille, and I. Ashman (eds.), *Reframing Resolution: Innovation and Change in the Management of Workplace Conflict*. London: Palgrave Macmillan, 13–33.

Saundry, R., Adam, D., Ashman, I., Forde, C., Wibberley, G., and Wright, S. (2016). *Managing Individual Conflict in the Contemporary British Workplace*. ACAS Research Paper, 02/16. London: ACAS.

Saundry, R., Antcliff, V., and Hollinrake, A. (2016). 'Union learning representatives in the UK: activity, impact, and organization'. *Work, Employment, and Society*, DOI:10.1177/0950017016630247

Saundry, R., Bennett, T., and Wibberley, G. (2016). 'Inside the mediation room—efficiency, voice and equity in workplace mediation'. *The International Journal of Human Resource Management*, http://dx.doi.org/10.1080/09585192.2016.1180314

Saundry, R. and Dix, G. (2014). 'Conflict resolution in the United Kingdom', in W. Roche, P. Teague, and A. Colvin (eds.), *The Oxford Handbook of Conflict Management in Organizations*. Oxford: Oxford University Press, 475–93.

Saundry, R., Jones, C., and Wibberley, G. (2015). 'The challenge of managing informally'. *Employee Relations*, 37/4: 428–41.

Saundry, R., Latreille, P., Dickens, L., Irvine, C., Teague, P., Urwin, P., and Wibberley, G. (2014). *Reframing Resolution—Managing Conflict and Resolving Individual Disputes in the Contemporary Workplace*. ACAS Policy Discussion Paper. London: ACAS.

Saundry, R., McArdle, L., and Thomas, P. (2013). 'Reframing workplace relations? Conflict resolution and mediation in a Primary Care Trust'. *Work, Employment, and Society*, 27/2: 213–31.

Savage, Maddy. (2015). 'The truth about Sweden's short working hours'. *BBC News Online*, 2 November, http://www.bbc.co.uk/news/business-34677949

Savage, Mike. (2015). *Social Class in the 21st Century*. London: Pelican.

Savage, M., Devine, F., Cunningham, N., Taylor, M., Li, Y., Hjellbrekke, J., Le Roux, B., Friedman, S., and Miles, A. (2013). 'A new model of social class? Findings from the BBC's Great British Class Survey experiment'. *Sociology*, 47/2: 219–50.

Schofield, H. (2016). 'The plan to ban work emails out of hours'. *BBC News Online*, 11 May, http://www.bbc.co.uk/news/magazine-36249647

Scholarios, D. and Marks, A. (2004). 'Work–life balance and the software worker'. *Human Resource Management Journal*, 14/2: 54–74.

Schulten, T. and Müller, T. (2015). 'European economic governance and its intervention in national wage development and collective bargaining', in S. Lehndorff (ed.), *Divisive Integration: The Triumph of Failed Ideas in Europe—Revisited*. Brussels: ETUI, 331–63.

Scott, A. (1994). *Willing Slaves? British Workers under Human Resource Management*. Cambridge: Cambridge University Press.

Scott, P. and Williams, S. (2016). 'The coalition government and employment relations in the public services', in S. Williams and P. Scott (eds.), *Employment Relations under Coalition Government: The UK Experience 2010–15*. New York and Abingdon: Routledge, 187–206.

Scott, W., Mumford, E., McGivering, I., and Kirkby, J. (1963). *Coal and Conflict*. Liverpool: Liverpool University Press.

Seely, A. (2015). *Self-employment in the Construction Industry*. House of Commons Library Briefing Paper 000196. London: House of Commons.

Ségol, B. (2015). 'Lowry Lecture. Social Europe, Yesterday, Today and Tomorrow', https://www.etuc.org/speeches/lowry-lecture-social-europe-yesterday-today-and-tomorrow#.VztLMtQrKt8

Seidman, G. (2007). *Beyond the Boycott: Labor Rights, Human Rights and Transnational Activism*. New York: Russell Sage Foundation.

Seidman, G. (2011). 'Workers' rights, union rights and solidarity across borders'. *International Labor and Working-Class History*, 80/1: 169–75.

Seierstad, C. (2011). 'Strategies for equality: the Norwegian experience of the use of gender quotas in the private sector', in T. Wright and H. Conley (eds.), *The Gower Handbook of Discrimination at Work*. Farnham: Gower, 279–92.

Seymour, R. (2013). 'After Boots' defeat, time to challenge the use of "meek" unions'. *The Guardian*, 18 February, https://www.theguardian.com/commentisfree/2013/feb/18/boots-defeat-meek-unions

Shackleton, J. (2002). *Employment Tribunals: Their Growth and the Case for Radical Reform*. Hobart Paper No. 145. London: Institute of Economic Affairs.

Shen, J. (2007). *Labour Disputes and their Resolution in China*. Oxford: Chandos Publishing.

Sherman, R. (2011). 'Beyond interaction: customer influence on housekeeping and room service work in hotels'. *Work, Employment and Society*, 25/1: 19–33.

Shorter, E. and Tilly, C. (1974). *Strikes in France*. Cambridge: Cambridge University Press.

Silver, B. (2003). *Forces of Labor: Workers' Movements and Globalization since 1870*. Cambridge: Cambridge University Press.

Simms, M. (2003). 'Union organizing in a not-for-profit organization', in G. Gall (ed.), *Union Organizing: Campaigning for Union Recognition*. London: Routledge, 97–113.

Simms, M. (2007). 'Interest formation in greenfield union organising campaigns'. *Industrial Relations Journal*, 38/5: 439–54.

Simms, M. (2015). 'Union organizing as an alternative to partnership. Or what to do when employers can't keep their side of the bargain', in S. Johnstone and P. Ackers (eds.), *Finding a Voice at Work? New Perspectives on Employment Relations*. Oxford: Oxford University Press, 127–52.

Simms, M. and Charlwood, A. (2010). 'Trade unions: power and influence in a changed context', in T. Colling and M. Terry (eds.), *Industrial Relations: Theory and Practice* (3rd edn). Chichester: John Wiley, 125–48.

Simms, M. and Dean, D. (2015). 'Mobilising contingent workers: an analysis of two successful cases'. *Economic and Industrial Democracy*, 36/1: 173–90.

Simms, M. and Holgate, J. (2010a). 'TUC Organizing Academy 10 years on: what has been the impact on British unions?' *The International Journal of Human Resource Management*, 21/3: 355–70.

Simms, M. and Holgate, J. (2010b). 'Organising for what? Where is the debate on the politics of union organising?' *Work, Employment, and Society*, 24/1: 157–68.

Simms, M., Holgate, J., and Heery, E. (2013). *Union Voices: Tactics and Tensions in UK Organizing*. Ithaca NY: Cornell University Press.

Sisson, K. (1987). *The Management of Collective Bargaining*. Oxford: Basil Blackwell.

Sisson, K. (2008). *Putting the Record Straight: Industrial Relations and the Employment Relationship*. Warwick Papers in Industrial Relations, No. 88. Warwick: University of Warwick, Industrial Relations Research Unit.

Sisson, K. (2009). *Why Employment Relations Matter*. Warwick Papers in Industrial Relations, No. 92. Warwick: University of Warwick, Industrial Relations Research Unit.

Sisson, K. (2010). 'Employment Relations Matters', https://www2.warwick.ac.uk/fac/soc/wbs/research/irru/erm/

Sisson, K. and Brown, W. (1983). 'Industrial relations in the private sector: Donovan re-visited', in G. Bain (ed.), *Industrial Relations in Britain*. Oxford: Basil Blackwell, 137–54.

Sisson, K. and Purcell, J. (2010). 'Management: caught between competing views of the organization', in T. Colling and M. Terry (eds.), *Industrial Relations: Theory and Practice* (3rd edn). Chichester: John Wiley, 83–105.

Sisson, K. and Storey, J. (2000). *The Realities of Human Resource Management*. Buckingham: Open University Press.

Sisson, K. and Taylor, J. (2006). 'The Advisory, Conciliation, and Arbitration Service', in L. Dickens and A. Neal (eds.), *The Changing Institutional Face of British Employment Relations*. Alphen aan den Rign: Kluwer Law International, 25–36.

Smith, C., Child, J., and Rowlinson, M. (1990). *Reshaping Work: The Cadbury Experience*. Cambridge: Cambridge University Press.

Smith, D. and Chamberlain, P. (2015). *Blacklisted: The Secret War between Big Business and Union Activists*. Oxford: New Internationalist Publications.

Smith, H. (2011). 'Apple sacks worker for ranting about iPhone on Facebook'. *Metro*, 29 November, http://metro.co.uk/2011/11/29/apple-sacks-worker-samuel-crisp-over-iphone-facebook-rants-237567/

Smith, P. (2001). *Unionization and Union Leadership: The Road Haulage Industry*. London: Continuum.

Smith, P. (2015). 'Labour under the law: a new law of combination, and master and servant, in 21st-century Britain?' *Industrial Relations Journal*, 46/5–6: 345–64.

Smith, P. and Morton, G. (1994). 'Union exclusion—next steps'. *Industrial Relations Journal*, 25/1: 3–14.

Smith, P. and Morton, G. (2006). 'Nine years of New Labour: neo-liberalism and workers' rights'. *British Journal of Industrial Relations*, 44/3: 401–20.

Smith, P. and Morton, G. (2009). 'Employment legislation: New Labour's neoliberal legal project to subordinate trade unions', in G. Daniels and J. McIlroy (eds.), *Trade Unions in a Neo Liberal World: British Trade Unions under New Labour*. Abingdon: Routledge, 205–29.

Social Mobility and Child Poverty Commission (SMCPC) (2015a). *State of the Nation 2015: Social Mobility and Child Poverty in Great Britain.* London: Social Mobility and Child Poverty Commission.

Social Mobility and Child Poverty Commission (SMCPC) (2015b). *A Qualitative Evaluation of Non-educational Barriers to the Elite Professions.* London: Social Mobility and Child Poverty Commission.

Sporton, D. (2013). '"They control my life": the role of local recruitment agencies in East European migration to the UK'. *Population, Space, and Place,* 19: 443–58.

Spours, K. (2015). 'The Osborne Supremacy: observing the new Conservative political hegemony'. *Juncture,* 22/2: 90–8.

Standing, G. (2008). 'The ILO: an agency for globalization?' *Development and Change,* 39/3: 355–84.

Standing, G. (2010). 'The International Labour Organization'. *New Political Economy,* 15/2: 307–18.

Standing, G. (2011). *The Precariat: The New Dangerous Class.* London: Bloomsbury.

Standing, G. (2014). *A Precariat Charter: From Denizens to Citzens.* London: Bloomsbury.

Stanworth, C. and Stanworth, J. (1995). 'The self-employed without employees—autonomous or atypical?' *Industrial Relations Journal,* 26/3: 221–9.

Stern, S. (2015). 'Deliveroo and its ilk are serving up low wages, insecurity and social division'. *The Guardian,* 17 December, http://www.theguardian.com/commentisfree/2015/dec/17/deliveroo-gig-economy-human-cost

Stevis, D. and Boswell, T. (2007). 'International framework agreements: opportunities and challenges for global unionism', in K. Bronfenbrenner (ed.), *Global Unions: Challenging Transnational Capital through Cross-border Campaigns.* Ithaca NY: Cornell University Press, 174–94.

Stewart, M. (2011). 'The National Minimum Wage after a decade', in D. Marsden (ed.), *Employment in the Lean Years.* Oxford: Oxford University Press, 121–33.

Stiglitz, J. (2002). *Globalization and its Discontents.* London: Allen Lane.

Stiglitz, J. (2010). *Freefall: Free Markets and the Sinking of the Global Economy.* London: Allen Lane.

Stopes, H. (2013). 'Not a recognised union'. *London Review of Books Blog,* 3 December, http://www.lrb.co.uk/blog/2013/12/03/harry-stopes/not-a-recognised-union/

Storey, J. (1983). *Managerial Prerogative and the Question of Control.* London: Routledge and Kegan Paul.

Storey, J. (1985). 'The means of management control'. *Sociology,* 19/2: 193–211.

Strauss, K. (2014). 'Unfree labour and the regulation of temporary agency work in the UK', in J. Fudge and K. Strauss (eds.), *Temporary Work, Agencies, and Unfree Labour: Insecurity in the New World of Work.* Abingdon: Routledge, 164–83.

Strauss, K. and Fudge, J. (2014). 'Temporary work, agencies, and unfree labour: insecurity in the new world of work', in J. Fudge and K. Strauss (eds.), *Temporary Work, Agencies, and Unfree Labour: Insecurity in the New World of Work.* Abingdon: Routledge, 1–25.

Streeck, W. (1997). 'Industrial citizenship under regime competition: the case of the European Works Councils'. *Journal of European Public Policy,* 4/4: 643–64.

Streeck, W. (2014). *Buying Time: The Delayed Crisis of Democratic Capitalism.* London: Verso.

Streeck, W. and Thelen, K. (2005). 'Introduction: institutional change in advanced political economies', in W. Streeck and K. Thelen (eds.), *Beyond Continuity: Institutional Change in Advanced Political Economies.* Oxford: Oxford University Press, 1–39.

Stuart, K. (2014). 'German minister calls for anti-stress law ban on emails out of office hours'. *The Guardian,* 29 August, http://www.theguardian.com/technology/2014/aug/29/germany-anti-stress-law-ban-on-emails-out-of-office-hours

Stuart, M. and Martinez Lucio, M. (2005). 'Partnership and modernisation in employment relations: an introduction', in M. Stuart and M. Martinez Lucio (eds.), *Partnership and Modernisation in Employment Relations.* London: Routledge, 1–22.

Suff, R. and Williams, S. (2004). 'The myth of mutuality? Employee perceptions of partnership at Borg Warner'. *Employee Relations,* 26/1: 30–43.

Sullivan, W. (2011). 'The role of trade unions in fighting racial discrimination', in T. Wright and H. Conley (eds.), *The Gower Handbook of Discrimination at Work.* Farnham: Gower, 129–38.

Sumption, M. and Somerville, W. (2010). *The UK's New Europeans: Progress and Challenges Five Years After Accession.* London: Equality and Human Rights Commission/Migration Policy Institute.

Sweiry, D. and Willitts, M. (2012). *Attitudes to Age in Britain 2010/11.* Sheffield: Department of Work and Pensions.

Tailby, S. and Pollert, A. (2011). 'Non-unionized young workers and organizing the unorganized'. *Economic and Industrial Democracy,* 32/3: 499–522.

Tailby, S., Pollert, A., Warren, S., Danford, A., and Wilton, N. (2011). 'Under-funded and overwhelmed: the voluntary sector as worker representation in Britain's individualised industrial relations system'. *Industrial Relations Journal,* 42/3: 273–92.

Tapia, M. (2013). 'Marching to different tunes: commitment and culture as mobilizing mechanisms of trade unions and community organizations'. *British Journal of Industrial Relations*, 51/4: 666–88.

Tapia, M. and Turner, L. (2013). 'Union campaigns as countermovements: mobilizing immigrant workers in France and the United Kingdom'. *British Journal of Industrial Relations*, 51/3: 601–22.

Tattersall, A. (2009). 'Using their sword of justice: the NSW Teachers Federation and its campaigns for public education between 2001 and 2004', in J. McBride and I. Greenwood (eds.), *Community Unionism: A Comparative Analysis of Concepts and Contexts*. Basingstoke: Palgrave Macmillan, 161–86.

Tattersall, A. (2010). *Power in Coalition: Strategies for Strong Unions and Social Change*. Ithaca NY: ILR Press.

Taylor, L. and Walton, P. (1971). 'Industrial sabotage: motives and meanings', in S. Cohen (ed.), *Images of Deviance*. Harmondsworth: Penguin, 219–45.

Taylor, M. (2012). 'Campaigners hold protest to highlight "low pay" at Sainsbury's'. *The Guardian*, 29 May, http://www.guardian.co.uk/society/2012/may/29/sainsburys-low-pay-protest-paralympics

Taylor, P. (2013). 'Performance Management: the New Workplace Tyranny?', http://www.stuc.org.uk/files/Document%20download/Workplace%20tyranny/STUC%20Performance%20Management%20Final%20Edit.pdf

Taylor, P., Cunningham, I., Newsome, K., and Scholarios, D. (2010). '"Too scared to go sick"—reformulating the research agenda on sickness absence'. *Industrial Relations Journal*, 41/4: 270–88.

Taylor, P. and Ramsay, H. (1998). 'Unions, partnership and HRM: sleeping with the enemy?' *International Journal of Employment Studies*, 6/1: 115–43.

Taylor, S. (1998). 'Emotional labour and the new workplace', in P. Thompson and C. Warhurst (eds.), *Workplaces of the Future*. Basingstoke: Macmillan, 84–103.

Teague, P. (1999). *Economic Citizenship in the European Union*. London: Routledge.

Teigen, M. (2012). 'Gender quotas for corporate boards in Norway: innovative gender equality policy', in C. Fagan, M. González Menéndez, and S. Gómez Ansón (eds.), *Women on Corporate Boards and in Top Management: European Trends and Policy*. Basingstoke: Palgrave Macmillan, 70–90.

Terry, M. (1983). 'Shop steward development and managerial strategies', in G. Bain (ed.), *Industrial Relations in Britain*. Oxford: Basil Blackwell, 67–91.

Terry, M. (1996). 'Negotiating the government of UNISON: union democracy in theory and practice'. *British Journal of Industrial Relations*, 34/1: 87–110.

Terry, M. (1999). 'Systems of collective representation in non-union firms in the UK'. *Industrial Relations Journal*, 30/1: 16–30.

Terry, M. (2004). '"Partnership": a serious strategy for the UK trade unions?', in A. Verma and T. Kochan (eds.), *Unions in the 21st Century: An International Perspective*. Basingstoke: Palgrave Macmillan, 205–19.

Terry, M. (2010). 'Employee representation', in T. Colling and M. Terry (eds.), *Industrial Relations: Theory and Practice* (3rd edn). Chichester: John Wiley, 275–97.

Thelen, K. (2004). *How Institutions Evolve: The Political Economy of Skills in Germany, Britain, the United States and Japan*. Cambridge: Cambridge University Press.

Thelen, K. (2014). *Varieties of Liberalization and the New Politics of Social Solidarity*. Cambridge: Cambridge University Press.

Theodore, N. and Peck, J. (2014). 'Selling flexibility: temporary staffing in a volatile economy', in J. Fudge and K. Strauss (eds.), *Temporary Work, Agencies, and Unfree Labour: Insecurity in the New World of Work*. Abingdon: Routledge, 26–47.

Thompson, P. (2003). 'Disconnected capitalism: or why employers can't keep their side of the bargain'. *Work, Employment and Society*, 17/2: 359–78.

Thompson, P. (2011). 'The trouble with HRM'. *Human Resource Management Journal*, 21/4: 355–67.

Thompson, P. (2013). 'Financialization and the workplace: extending and applying the disconnected capitalism thesis'. *Work, Employment, and Society*, 27/3: 472–88.

Thompson, P., Newsome, K., and Commander, J. (2013). '"Good when they want to be": migrant workers in the supermarket supply chain'. *Human Resource Management Journal*, 23/2: 129–43.

Thompson, P. and Warhurst, C. (1998). 'Hands, hearts and minds: changing work and workers at the end of the century', in P. Thompson and C. Warhurst (eds.), *Workplaces of the Future*. Basingstoke: Macmillan, 1–24.

Thornley, C. (1998). 'Contesting local pay: the decentralisation of collective bargaining in the NHS'. *British Journal of Industrial Relations*, 36/3: 413–34.

Timming, A. (2007). 'European Works Councils and the dark side of managing worker voice'. *Human Resource Management Journal*, 17/3: 248–64.

Timming, A. and Whittall, M. (2015). 'The promise of European works councils: twenty years of statutory employee voice', in S. Johnstone and P. Ackers (eds.), *Finding a Voice at Work? New Perspectives on Employment Relations*. Oxford: Oxford University Press, 218–38.

Tipping, S., Chanfreau, J., Perry, J., and Tait, C. (2012). *The Fourth Work–Life Balance Employee Survey*. Employment Relations Research Series No. 122. London: BIS.

Tolliday, S. and Zeitlin, J. (eds.) (1991). *The Power to Manage? Employers and Industrial Relations in Comparative-Historical Perspective*. London: Routledge.

Topham, G. (2014). 'Big 3 Gulf airlines brush aside obstacles in pursuit of dominance'. *The Guardian*, 8 June, https://www.theguardian.com/business/2014/jun/08/gulf-airlines-brush-aside-obstacles-qatar-doha

Topham, G. (2015). 'Gulf airlines success prompts hostility from US and European carriers'. *The Guardian*, 20 April, https://www.theguardian.com/business/2015/apr/20/gulf-airlines-emirates-etihad-qatar-success-hostility-us-european-carriers

Torrington, D. (1991). *Management Face to Face*. Hemel Hempstead: Prentice Hall.

Towers, B. (1997). *The Representation Gap: Change and Reform in the British and American Workplace*. Oxford: Oxford University Press.

Trades Union Congress (TUC) (1997). *General Council Report*. London: TUC.

Trades Union Congress (TUC) (2007). *Migrant Agency Workers in the UK*. London: TUC.

Trades Union Congress (TUC) (2008). *Hard Work, Hidden Lives: Report of the Commission on Vulnerable Employment*. London: TUC.

Trades Union Congress (TUC) (2009). *Slaying the Working Time Myths*. London: TUC.

Trades Union Congress (TUC) (2012a). *German Lessons: Developing Industrial Policy in the UK*. London: TUC.

Trades Union Congress (TUC) (2012b). *TUC Equality Audit 2012*. London: TUC.

Trades Union Congress (TUC) (2013). *Workers on Board: The Case for Workers' Voice in Corporate Governance*. London: TUC.

Trades Union Congress (TUC) (2014a). 'More than two in five jobs created since mid-2010 have been self-employed'. TUC Press Release, 14 April, https://www.tuc.org.uk/economic-issues/economic-analysis/labour-market/labour-market-and-economic-reports/more-two-five-new

Trades Union Congress (TUC) (2014b). *TUC Equality Audit 2014: Improving Representation and Participation in Trade Unions*. London: TUC.

Trades Union Congress (TUC) (2014c). *At What Price Justice?* London: TUC.

Trades Union Congress (TUC) (2015a). *The Decent Jobs Deficit: The Human Cost of Zero-Hours Working in the UK*. London: TUC.

Trades Union Congress (TUC) (2015b). '15 per cent increase in people working more than 48 hours a week risks a return to "Burnout Britain", warns TUC'. TUC Press Release, 9 September, https://www.tuc.org.uk/international-issues/europe/workplace-issues/work-life-balance/15-cent-increase-people-working-more

Trades Union Congress (TUC) (2015c). *Productivity—no Puzzle About it*. London: TUC.

Trades Union Congress (TUC) (2015d). *Enforcing the National Minimum Wage—Keeping up the Pressure*. London: TUC.

Trades Union Congress (TUC) (2015e). 'TUC Briefing on the Transatlantic Trade and Investment Partnership', https://www.tuc.org.uk/international-issues/tuc-briefing-transatlantic-trade-and-investment-partnership-ttip

Trades Union Congress (TUC) (2016a). 'UK workers experienced sharpest wage fall of any leading economy, TUC analysis finds'. TUC Press Release, 27 July, https://www.tuc.org.uk/economic-issues/labour-market/uk-workers-experienced-sharpest-wage-fall-any-leading-economy-tuc

Trades Union Congress (TUC) (2016b). *Black, Qualified, and Unemployed*. London: TUC.

Tremblay, D.-G. and Genin, E. (2010). 'IT self-employed workers between constraint and flexibility'. *New Technology, Work, and Employment*, 25/1: 34–48.

Trevor, J. and Brown, W. (2014). 'The limits on pay as a strategic tool: obstacles to alignment in non-union environments'. *British Journal of Industrial Relations*, 52/3: 553–78.

Truss, C. (2001). 'Complexities and controversies in linking HRM with organizational outcomes'. *Journal of Management Studies*, 38/8: 1121–49.

Truss, C., Delbridge, R., Alfes, K., Shantz, A., and Soane, E. (eds.) (2014). *Employee Engagement in Theory and Practice*. Abingdon and New York: Routledge.

Tsai, C.-J., Sengupta, S., and Edwards, P. (2007). 'When and why is small beautiful? The experience of work in the small firm'. *Human Relations*, 60/12: 1779–1807.

Tsogas, G. (2001). *Labor Regulation in a Global Economy*. New York: M. E. Sharpe.

Tsogas, G. (2009). 'International labour regulation: what have we really learnt so far?' *Relations Industrielles/Industrial Relations*, 64/1: 75–94.

Tuckman, A. and Snook, J. (2014). 'Between consultation and collective bargaining? The changing role of non-union employee representatives: a case study from the finance sector'. *Industrial Relations Journal*, 45/1: 77–97.

Turnbull, P. (1988). 'Leaner and possibly fitter: the management of redundancy in Britain'. *Industrial Relations Journal*, 19/3: 201–13.

Turnbull, P. (2006). 'The war on Europe's waterfront—repertoires of power in the port transport industry'. *British Journal of Industrial Relations*, 44/2: 305–26.

Turnbull, P. and Sapsford, D. (1992). 'A sea of discontent: the tides of organised and "unorganized" conflict on the docks'. *Sociology*, 26/2: 291–309.

Turnbull, P. and Wass, V. (1997). 'Job insecurity and labour market lemons: the (mis)management of redundancy in steel making, coal mining and port transport'. *Journal of Management Studies*, 34/1: 27–51.

Turnbull, P. and Wass, V. (2000). 'Redundancy and the paradox of job insecurity', in E. Heery and J. Salmon (eds.), *The Insecure Workforce*. London: Routledge, 57–77.

Turnbull, P. and Wass, V. (2011). 'Earnings inequality and employment', in P. Blyton, E. Heery, and P. Turnbull (eds.), *Reassessing the Employment Relationship*. Basingstoke: Palgrave Macmillan, 273–98.

Undy, R. (2008). *Trade Union Merger Strategies: Purpose, Process, and Performance*. Oxford: Oxford University Press.

Undy, R., Fosh, P., Morris, H., Smith, P., and Martin, R. (1996). *Managing the Unions*. Oxford: Clarendon.

Union of Construction, Allied Trades, and Technicians (UCATT) (no date). *False Self Employment*. London: UCATT, https://www.ucatt.org.uk/false-self-employment

Union of Shop, Distributive, and Allied Workers (USDAW) (2012). 'USDAW wins £67 million compensation for former Woolworths workers'. USDAW News Release, 20 January, https://www.usdaw.org.uk/About-Us/News/2012/January/Usdaw-wins-%C2%A367-million-compensation-for-former-Woo

Union of Shop, Distributive, and Allied Workers (USDAW) (2013). 'USDAW wins more than £5 million for ex-Woolies and Ethel Austin staff in landmark legal case'. USDAW News Release, 31 May, http://www.usdaw.org.uk/newsevents/news/2013/may/usdawwinsmorethan5million.aspx

Unite (2015). 'Unite Launches Campaign to Tackle 'Victorian' Work Practices in Sports Direct'. Unite News Release, 28 April, http://www.unitetheunion.org/news/unite-launches-campaign-to-tackle-victorian-work-practices-in-sports-direct/

Unite (no date). 'What is Leverage and How Does it Work?', http://www.unitetheunion.org/growing-our-union/organising-toolbox/leverage/

United Nations Conference on Trade and Development (UNCTAD) (2009). *World Investment Report: Transnational Corporations, Agricultural Production and Development*. New York and Geneva: United Nations.

University and College Union (UCU) (2016). *Transparency at the Top? The Second Report of Senior Pay and Perks in UK Universities*. London: UCU. https://www.ucu.org.uk/article/8096/Report-reveals-university-heads-pay-rises-and-perks

Upchurch, M. (2009). 'Some conclusions from a survey of BUIRA members on the teaching of industrial relations in British universities', in R. Darlington (ed.), *What's the Point of Industrial Relations? In Defence of Critical Social Science*. London: British Universities Industrial Relations Association, 77–83.

van den Broek, D. and Dundon, T. (2012). '(Still) up to no good: reconfiguring worker resistance and misbehaviour in an increasingly unorganized world'. *Relations Industrielles/Industrial Relations*, 67/1: 97–121.

van Wanrooy, B., Bewley, H., Bryson, A., Forth, J., Freeth, S., Stokes, L., and Wood, S. (2013*a*). *The 2011 Workplace Employment Relations Study: First Findings*. London: Department for Business, Innovation and Skills.

van Wanrooy. B., Bewley, H., Bryson, A., Forth, J., Freeth, S., Stokes, L., and Wood, S. (2013*b*). *Employment Relations in the Shadow of Recession*. Basingstoke: Palgrave.

Vandaele, K. (2011). *Sustaining or Abandoning 'Social Peace'?: Strike Developments and Trends in Europe since the 1990s*. European Trade Union Institute Working Paper 2011.05. Brussels: ETUI.

Vaughan-Whitehead, D. (2015). 'The European Social Model in times of crisis: an overview', in D. Vaughan-Whitehead (ed.), *The European Social Model in Crisis: Is Europe Losing its Soul?* Cheltenham: Edward Elgar, 1–65.

Virdee, S. and Grint, K. (1994). 'Black self-organization in trade unions'. *Sociological Review*, 42/2: 202–26.

Virtanen, M., Ferrie, J., Singh-Manoux, A., Shipley, M., Vahtera, J., Marmot, M., and Kivmäki, M. (2010). 'Overtime work and incident coronary heart disease: the Whitehall II participative cohort study'. *European Heart Journal*, 31/14: 1737–44.

Wacjman, J. (2000). 'Feminism facing industrial relations in Britain'. *British Journal of Industrial Relations*, 38/2: 183–201.

Waddington, J. (2003). 'Trade union organization', in P. Edwards (ed.), *Industrial Relations* (2nd edn). Oxford: Blackwell, 214–56.

Waddington, J. (2006). 'The performance of European Works Councils in engineering: perspectives of the employee representatives'. *Industrial Relations*, 45/4: 681–708.

Waddington, J. (2011*a*). *European Works Councils: A Transnational Industrial Relations Institution in the Making*. Abingdon: Routledge.

Waddington, J. (2011b). 'European works councils: the challenge for labour'. *Industrial Relations Journal*, 42/6: 508–29.

Waddington, J. and Hoffman, R. (2003). 'Trade unions in Europe: reform, organisation and restructuring', in D. Foster and P. Scott (eds.), *Trade Unions in Europe: Meeting the Challenge*. Brussels: Peter Lang, 33–63.

Waddington, J. and Kerr, A. (2002). 'Unions fit for young workers?' *Industrial Relations Journal*, 33/4: 298–315.

Waddington, J. and Whitston, C. (1997). 'Why do people join unions in a period of membership decline?' *British Journal of Industrial Relations*, 35/4: 515–46.

Wadsworth, J., Dhingra, S., Ottaviano, G., and Van Reenan, J. (2016). *Brexit and the Impact of Immigration on the UK*. LSE: Centre for Economic Performance.

Wailes, N., Wright, C., Bamber, G., and Lansbury, R. (2016). 'Introduction: an internationally comparative approach to employment relations', in G. Bamber, R. Lansbury, N. Wailes, and C. Wright (eds.), *International and Comparative Employment Relations: National Regulation, Global Changes* (6th edn). London: Sage, 1–19.

Walby, S. (1997). *Gender Transformations*. London: Routledge.

Waldfogel, J. (2010). *Britain's War on Poverty*. New York: Russell Sage Foundation.

Waldinger, R., Erickson, C., Milkman, R., Mitchell, D., Valenzuela, A., Wong, K., and Zeitlin, M. (1998). 'Helots no more: a case study of the Justice for Janitors campaign in Los Angeles', in K. Bronfenbrenner, S. Friedman, R. Hurd, R. Oswald, and R. Seeber (eds.), *Organizing to Win: New Research on Union Strategies*. Ithaca NY: ILR Press, 102–19.

Wall, T. and Wood, S. (2005). 'The romance of human resource management and business performance, and the case for big science'. *Human Relations*, 58/4: 429–62.

Wallace, J. and O'Sullivan, M. (2006). 'Contemporary strike trends since 1980: peering through the wrong end of a telescope', in M. Morley, P. Gunnigle, and D. Collings (eds.), *Global Industrial Relations*. London: Routledge, 273–91.

Wallis, E., Stuart, M., and Greenwood, I. (2005). '"Learners of the workplace unite!": an empirical examination of the UK trade union learning representative initiative'. *Work, Employment and Society*, 19/2: 283–304.

Walsh, J. (2007). 'Equality and diversity in British workplaces: the 2004 Workplace Employment Relations Survey'. *Industrial Relations Journal*, 38/4: 303–19.

Walsh, J. (2010). 'Working time and work–life balance', in A. Wilkinson, N. Bacon, T. Redman, and S. Snell (eds.), *The SAGE Handbook of Human Resource Management*. London: Sage, 491–506.

Walton, R. and McKersie, R. (1965). *A Behavioral Theory of Labor Negotiations*. New York: McGraw-Hill.

Wang, M. and Kelan, E. (2013). 'The gender quota and female leadership: effects of the Norwegian gender quota on board chairs and CEOs'. *Journal of Business Ethics*, 117/3: 449–66.

War on Want (2006). *Fashion Victims: The True Cost of Cheap Clothes at Primark, Asda, and Tesco*. London: War on Want.

War on Want (2008). *Fashion Victims II: How UK Clothing Retailers are Keeping Workers in Poverty*. London: War on Want.

War on Want (2010). *Taking Liberties: The Story Behind the UK High Street*. London: War on Want/Labour Behind the Label.

Warhurst, C. (2008). 'The knowledge economy, skills and government labour market intervention'. *Policy Studies*, 29/1: 71–86.

Warhurst, C., Eikhof, D., and Haunschild, A. (2008). 'Out of balance or just out of bounds? Analysing the relationship between work and life', in C. Warhurst, D. Eikhof, and A. Haunschild (eds.), *Work Less, Live More: Critical Analysis of the Work–Life Boundary*. Basingstoke: Palgrave Macmillan, 1–21.

Warhurst, C. and Thompson, P. (2006). 'Mapping knowledge in work: proxies or practices?' *Work, Employment and Society*, 20/4: 787–800.

Warnecke, T. and De Ruyter, A. (2010). 'Positive economic freedom: an enabling role for international labor standards in developing countries?' *Journal of Economic Issues*, 44/2: 385–92.

Warren, T. (2015a). 'Work-time underemployment and financial hardship: class inequalities and recession in the UK'. *Work, Employment, and Society*, 29/2: 191–212.

Warren, T. (2015b). 'Work–life balance/imbalance: the dominance of the middle class and the neglect of the working class'. *The British Journal of Sociology*, 66/4: 691–717.

Warren, T., Pascall, G., and Fox, E. (2010). 'Gender equality in time: low-paid mothers' paid and unpaid work in the UK'. *Feminist Economics*, 16/3: 193–219.

Wass, V. (1996). 'Who controls selection under "voluntary" redundancy? The case of the Redundant Mineworkers Payments Scheme'. *British Journal of Industrial Relations*, 34/2: 249–65.

Webb, J. (1997). 'The politics of equal opportunity'. *Gender, Work and Organization*, 4/3: 159–69.

Webb, J. and Liff, S. (1988). 'Play the white man: the social construction of fairness and competition in equal opportunity policies'. *Sociological Review*, 36/3: 532–51.

Webb, S. and Webb, B. (1920*a*). *Industrial Democracy*. London: Longmans, Green and Co.

Webb, S. and Webb, B. (1920*b*). *The History of Trade Unionism* (revised edn). London: Longmans, Green and Co.

Webster, E., Lambert, R., and Bezuidenhout, A. (2008). *Grounding Globalization: Labour in the Age of Insecurity*. Oxford: Blackwell Publishing.

Wedderburn, D. and Craig, C. (1974). 'Relative deprivation in work', in D. Wedderburn (ed.), *Poverty, Inequality and Class Structure*. Cambridge: Cambridge University Press, 141–64.

Wedderburn, Lord (1986). *The Worker and the Law* (3rd edn). Harmondsworth: Penguin.

Wedderburn, Lord (1989). 'Freedom of association and philosophies of labour law'. *Industrial Law Journal*, 18: 1–38.

Wedderburn, Lord (1991). *Employment Rights in Britain and Europe*. London: Lawrence and Wishart.

Wedderburn, Lord (1995). *Labour Law and Freedom*. London: Lawrence and Wishart.

Welch, R. (2016). 'The coalition government and the lifting of the floor of individual employment rights', in S. Williams and P. Scott (eds.), *Employment Relations under Coalition Government: the UK Experience, 2010–2015*. Abingdon: Routledge, 89–107.

Weldon, D. (2016). 'Stunted growth: the mystery of the UK's productivity crisis'. *The Guardian*, 25 April, http://www.theguardian.com/commentisfree/2016/apr/25/growth-uk-productivity-crisis

White, G. (2000). 'The pay review body system: its development and impact'. *Historical Studies in Industrial Relations*, 9: 71–100.

White, M., Hill, S., Mills, C., and Smeaton, D. (2004). *Managing to Change?* Basingstoke: Palgrave Macmillan.

Whiteley, P., Clarke, H., Sanders, D., and Stewart, M. (2015). 'The economic and electoral consequences of austerity policies in Britain'. *Parliamentary Affairs*, 68: 4–24.

Wilkinson, A. and Dundon, T. (2010). 'Direct employee participation', in A. Wilkinson, P. Gollan, M. Marchington, and D. Lewin (eds.), *The Oxford Handbook of Participation in Organizations*. Oxford: Oxford University Press, 167–85.

Wilkinson, A., Dundon, T., Donaghey, J., and Freeman, R. (2014*a*). 'Employee voice: charting new terrain', in A. Wilkinson, J. Donaghey, T. Dundon, and R. Freeman (eds.), *Handbook of Research on Employee Voice*. Cheltenham: Edward Elgar, 3–16.

Wilkinson, A., Dundon, T., Donaghey, J., and Townsend, K. (2014*b*). 'Partnership, collaboration and mutual gains: evaluating context, interests and legitimacy'. *The International Journal of Human Resource Management*, 25/6: 737–47.

Wilkinson, A., Dundon, T., and Marchington, M. (2013). 'Employee involvement and voice', in S. Bach and M. Edwards (eds.), *Managing Human Resources* (5th edn). Chichester: John Wiley, 268–88.

Wilkinson, A. and Fay, C. (2011). 'New times for employee voice?' *Human Resource Management*, 50/1: 65–74.

Wilkinson, M. (2012). 'Out of sight, out of mind: the exploitation of migrant workers in 21st century Britain'. *Journal of Poverty and Social Justice*, 20/1: 13–21.

Wilkinson, R. and Pickett, K. (2009). *The Spirit Level: Why More Equal Societies Almost Always do Better*. London: Allen Lane.

Williams, G., Davies, S., and Chinguno, C. (2015). 'Subcontracting and labour standards: reassessing the potential of international framework agreements'. *British Journal of Industrial Relations*, 53/2: 181–203.

Williams, S. (1997). 'The nature of some recent trade union modernization policies'. *British Journal of Industrial Relations*, 35/4: 495–514.

Williams, S. (2003). 'Conflict in the colleges: industrial relations in further education since incorporation'. *Journal of Further and Higher Education*, 27/3: 307–16.

Williams, S. (2004). 'Accounting for change in public sector industrial relations: the erosion of national bargaining in further education in England and Wales'. *Industrial Relations Journal*, 35/3: 233–48.

Williams, S., Abbott, B., and Heery, E. (2011*a*). 'New and emerging actors in work and employment relations: the case of civil society organisations', in K. Townsend and A. Wilkinson (eds.), *The Edward Elgar Research Handbook on Work and Employment Relations*. Cheltenham: Edward Elgar, 130–49.

Williams, S., Abbott, B., and Heery, E. (2011*b*). 'Non-union worker representation through civil society organisations: evidence from the UK'. *Industrial Relations Journal*, 42/1: 69–85.

Williams, S., Adam-Smith, D., and Norris, G. (2004). 'Remuneration practices in the UK hospitality industry in the age of the National Minimum Wage'. *Service Industries Journal*, 24/1: 171–86.

Williams, S., Bradley, H., Devadason, R., and Erickson, M. (2013). *Globalization and Work*. Cambridge: Polity.

Williams, S. and Scott, P. (2010). 'Shooting the past? The modernisation of Conservative Party employment relations policy under David Cameron'. *Industrial Relations Journal*, 41/1: 4–16.

Williams, S. and Scott, P. (2011). 'The contingent basis of Conservative Party modernisation under David Cameron: the trajectory of employment relations policy'. *Parliamentary Affairs*, 54/3: 513–29.

Williams, S. and Scott, P. (2016a). 'The coalition government 2010–15: an overview', in S. Williams and P. Scott (eds.), *Employment Relations under Coalition Government: The UK Experience, 2010–2015*. Abingdon: Routledge, 3–25.

Williams, S. and Scott, P. (2016b). 'Welfare-to-work policy under the coalition', in S. Williams and P. Scott (eds.), *Employment Relations under Coalition Government: The UK Experience, 2010–2015*. Abingdon: Routledge, 66–85.

Williams, S. and Scott, P. (2016c). 'Employment relations under coalition in perspective', in S. Williams and P. Scott (eds.), *Employment Relations under Coalition Government: The UK Experience, 2010–2015*. Abingdon: Routledge, 229–52.

Williams, S. and Scott, P. (eds.) (2016d). *Employment Relations under Coalition Government: The UK Experience, 2010–2015*. Abingdon: Routledge.

Williams, S., Scott, P., and Welch, R. (2016). 'Employment relations under coalition government: reflections, legacy, and prospects', in S. Williams and P. Scott (eds.), *Employment Relations under Coalition Government: The UK Experience, 2010–2015*. Routledge, Abingdon, 253–68.

Willman, P. (1989). 'The logic of "market share" trade unionism: is membership decline inevitable?' *Industrial Relations Journal*, 20/4: 260–70.

Willman, P., Gomez, R., and Bryson, A. (2009). 'Voice at the workplace: where do we find it, why is it there and where is it going?', in W. Brown, A. Bryson, J. Forth, and K. Whitfield (eds.), *The Evolution of the Modern Workplace*. Cambridge: Cambridge University Press, 97–119.

Willmott, H. (1993). 'Strength is ignorance; slavery is freedom: managing culture in modern organizations'. *Journal of Management Studies*, 30/4: 515–52.

Wills, J. (2000). 'Great Expectations: three years in the life of a European Works Council'. *European Journal of Industrial Relations*, 6/1: 85–107.

Wills, J. (2002). 'Bargaining for the space to organize in the global economy: a review of the Accor-IUF trade union rights agreement'. *Review of International Political Economy*, 9/4: 675–700.

Wills, J. (2004). 'Trade unionism and partnership in practice: evidence from the Barclays-Unifi agreement'. *Industrial Relations Journal*, 35/4: 329–43.

Wills, J. (2008). 'Making class politics possible: organising contract cleaners in London'. *International Journal of Urban and Regional Research*, 32/2: 305–23.

Wills, J. and Simms, M. (2004). 'Building reciprocal community unionism in the UK'. *Capital and Class*, 82: 59–84.

Wilson, R., Beaven, R., May-Gillings, M., Hay, G., and Stevens, J. (2014). *Working Futures 2012-2022*. London: UK Commission for Employment and Skills.

Winchester, D. and Bach, S. (1995). 'The state: the public sector', in P. Edwards (ed.), *Industrial Relations: Theory and Practice in Britain*. Oxford: Blackwell, 304–34.

Winchester, D. and Bach, S. (1999). 'Britain: the transformation of public service employment relations', in S. Bach, L. Bordogna, G. DellaRocca, and D. Winchester (eds.), *Public Service Employment Relations in Europe: Transformation, Modernisation or Inertia?* London: Routledge, 22–55.

Winsor, T. (2011). *Independent Review of Police Officer and Staff Remuneration and Conditions, Part 1 Report*. Cm 8024. London: HMSO.

Winsor, T. (2012). *Independent Review of Police Officer and Staff Remuneration and Conditions, Final Report—Volume 2*. Cm 8325-II. London: HMSO.

Wolf, A. (2010). *More than we Bargained for: The Social and Economic Costs of National Wage Bargaining*. London: CentreForum.

Wolf, M. (2004). *Why Globalization Works*. New Haven CT: Yale University Press.

Wolf, M. (2014). *The Shifts and the Shocks: What We've Learned and Have Still to Learn from the Financial Crisis*. London: Allen Lane.

Women and Work Commission (2006). *Shaping a Fairer Future: Final Report of the Women and Work Commission*. London: Women and Equality Unit.

Wood, A. (2015). 'Networks of injustice and worker mobilisation at Walmart'. *Industrial Relations Journal*, 46/4: 259–74.

Wood, J. (1992). 'Dispute resolution—conciliation, mediation and arbitration', in W. McCarthy (ed.), *Legal Intervention in Industrial Relations: Gains and Losses*. Oxford: Blackwell, 241–73.

Wood, S. (2013). 'HRM, organizational performance and employee involvement', in C. Frege and J. Kelly (eds.), *Comparative Employment Relations in the Global Economy*. Abingdon: Routledge, 89–107.

Wood, S. and Bryson, A. (2009). 'High involvement management', in W. Brown, A. Bryson, J. Forth, and K. Whitfield (eds.), *The Evolution of the Modern Workplace*. Cambridge: Cambridge University Press, 151–75.

Wood, S. and de Menezes, L. (1998). 'High commitment management in the UK: evidence from the Workplace Industrial Relations Survey, and Employers' Manpower and Skills Practices Survey'. *Human Relations*, 51/4: 485–515.

Wood, S. and Goddard, J. (1999). 'The statutory union recognition procedure in the Employment Relations Bill: a comparative analysis'. *British Journal of Industrial Relations*, 37/2: 203–45.

Wood, S., Moore, S., and Ewing, K. (2003). 'The impact of the trade union recognition procedure under the Employment Relations Act 2000–2', in H. Gospel and S. Wood (eds.), *Representing Workers*. London: Routledge, 119–43.

Wood, S., Saundry, R., and Latreille, P. (2014). *Analysis of the Nature, Extent, and Impact of Grievance and Disciplinary Procedures and Workplace Mediation using WERS 2011*. London: ACAS.

Woolfson, C. and Sommers, J. (2016). 'Austerity and the demise of Social Europe: the Baltic Model versus the European Social Model'. *Globalizations*, 13/1: 78–93.

Woolfson, C., Thörnqvist, C., and Sommers, J. (2010). 'The Swedish model and the future of labour standards after Laval'. *Industrial Relations Journal*, 41/4: 333–50.

Worcestershire Mental Health Partnership NHS Trust (2008). 'Disputes Procedure', www.hacw.nhs.uk/EasySiteWeb/GatewayLink.aspx?alId=8363

Wren-Lewis, S. (2015). 'The macroeconomic record of the coalition government'. *National Institute Economic Review*, 231: R5–16.

Wright, A. (2011). '"Modernizing" away gender pay inequality? Some evidence from the local government sector on using job evaluation'. *Employee Relations*, 33/2: 159–78.

Wright, C., Wailes, N., Lansbury, R., and Bamber, G. (2016). 'Conclusions: beyond varieties of capitalism, towards convergence and internationalisation?', in G. Bamber, R. Lansbury, N. Wailes, and C. Wright (eds.), *International and Comparative Employment Relations: National Regulation, Global Changes* (6th edn). London: Sage, 341–61.

Yannakourou, M. and Tsimpoukis, C. (2014). 'Flexibility without security and deconstruction of collective bargaining: the new paradigm of labor law in Greece'. *Comparative Labor Law and Policy Journal*, 35/3: 331–69.

Yu, X. (2008). 'Impacts of corporate code of conduct on labor standards: a case study of Reebok's athletic footwear supplier factory in China'. *Journal of Business Ethics*, 81/3: 513–29.

Index